This book was produced
with the assistance
of a grant from

Gold Fever

THE BEGINNING OF THE CALIFORNIA GOLD RUSH

Allan W. Eckert

January 30, 1931 - July 7, 2011

To all of us who love American history and love any master teacher-writer who can sharply illuminate and clarify the specific details of our short but dramatic and complex story, Allan has been a national treasure. I personally owe far more to him for my humble knowledge of the 18th- and 19th-century settling of the American wilderness than I do to any other historian, and I suspect that legions and legions of my fellow citizens are similarly indebted to him.

We will miss Allan and always be in his debt.

—Thayle Anderson
Professor Emeritus
Murray State University

Gold Fever

THE BEGINNING OF THE CALIFORNIA GOLD RUSH

by
Allan W. Eckert

Edited with an Introduction by
Thayle Anderson

JSF
JESSE STUART
FOUNDATION
Ashland, Kentucky
2014

FIRST EDITION

ISBN: 978-1-938471-33-9

Published by
Jesse Stuart Foundation
P.O. Box 669
Ashland, Kentucky 41105
(606) 326-1667
jsfbooks.com

To

Allan Eckert's

devoted editor and true friend

Thayle Anderson

Introduction

Allan Eckert's death in 2011 left many students of American history with a sobering sense of loss. The author of over thirty books covering myriad U. S. history topics, including his best-selling six-volume The Winning of America series, Mr. Eckert's presentations of his subjects within the context of highly detailed and accurate historical narratives have charmed and enlightened legions of loyal readers. During the last decade of his life, Mr. Eckert turned his attention to the mid-nineteenth century American colonization of the West, a national movement which began in the mid-1830s and reached its zenith with the California Gold Rush during the mid-century years, and his final four volumes, his The Winning of the West series, focus on this era. The first two volumes, *The Infinite Dream* (2011) and *Dark Journey* (2009), discuss the first fifteen years of this westward migration. This third series volume, *Gold Fever* develops the movement's greatest stimulus, beginning with the discovery of California gold early in 1848 and concluding in September of 1849 during the most intense period of the gold-rush madness. As always, Mr. Eckert has carefully organized the thousands of complex events and developments of this remarkable period into a clear and accurate chronological context, and he thereby enlightens his readers in prolific, highly absorbing detail on what was surely the most profoundly influential non-war-related American economic development of the nineteenth century. Readers of *Gold Fever* will finish the book thoroughly briefed on the most important and intriguing elements of this mid-century national tempest, a few of which are merely summarized below and on the following pages:

John Sutter's trusted assistant, James Marshall, initially found a gold nugget on January 24, 1848 on a site 45 miles upstream on the South Fork of the American River from Sutter's Fort (a farming and trading empire which would eventually evolve into the present-day Sacramento, California). Marshall was supervising a small crew in the construction of a sawmill, which was to provide much-needed building material for Sutter's far-flung operations. Immediately after this fateful discovery, Marshall, his workers, and Sutter, himself, spent ten days covertly trying to determine if they were dealing with mere pyrite or with the real thing, before finally concluding that the original nugget, along with the additional ones the construction crew members were now discovering, were, indeed, genuine. Still only dimly aware of the explosive events this discovery might trigger, Sutter and Marshall resolved to keep it secret, at least long enough for Sutter to ponder how this development might affect his vast holdings. Meanwhile the sawmill's crew members began quietly spending their spare time eagerly mining for more of the newfound minerals.

Sutter's and Marshall's cover-up attempts were inevitably futile, but the gradually spreading remarkable news generated very little excitement. The vast majority of the inhabitants living throughout the central California region (including those in the small port town of San Francisco) — citizens, small newspaper journalists, and U. S. military territorial governing officials alike — greeted the spreading rumors with disdainful skepticism and resolutely ignored them. The news did, however, attract small numbers of the local, most gullible, easily-distracted men to Fort Sutter, and then on to the saw-mill site. A few local speculators intrigued by the possibility of mining also appeared on the scene, including Sam Brannon, a ruthless, unscrupulous businessman whom the gold rush would later make the most wealthy man in California. Brannon rapidly established a large well supplied store at Sutter's Fort and then did everything he could (including purchasing a San Francisco newspaper a few months later) to trumpet the gold discovery news as loudly as he could in order to maximize his commercial traffic.

By late spring of 1848, the rapidly spreading stories of spectacular gold-strikes by those relatively few men who had taken the initial rumors seriously were beginning to attract a growing number of area residents to the early saw-mill discovery site, and many of these men, in turn, returned home with specific accounts of the fortunes they had made. Such stories then began multiplying at warp speed, and, aided by Sam Brannon's high-profile efforts to publicize them, reached a critical mass locally by mid-May, 1848. By this time, consequently, immediately after arriving ships would anchor in the San Francisco Bay, their entire crews would desert their responsibilities to seek their fortunes in the new gold fields, and the adult male populations of entire area towns — Monterey, Sonora, San Jose, and San Francisco — began abandoning their homes for the same purpose. At this stage of events, however, the social turmoil was strictly confined to the region. It took California Territory news nearly five months to reach the East, and any serious response to such extremely distant rumors would have been prohibitively expensive and labor-intensive. Easterners dismissed such tales even more resolutely than their California regional counterparts had done several months earlier in the year.

The California Territory U.S. Military governing officials, however, proceeded to investigate the now rampant gold-discovery rumors by making numerous visits to the rapidly expanding sites where such claims were being made. In the course of these inquiries, these dignitaries were confronted with widespread, compelling evidence: Many of the gold-seekers were, indeed, growing wealthy from their gold-panning efforts. The reports of specific individual gold strikes (many of which Mr. Eckert relates in detail) continued to pile up virtually on a daily basis, and consequently, the Fort Sutter area was being overwhelmed with huge, boisterous crowds of local fortune hunters and a riotous cacophony of construction noises. And of course, in this crowded locale demand far exceeded supply for the food, the camping provisions, and the mining equipment provided by Sam Brannon and other enterprising merchants, all of whom sold their products at outrageously marked up prices. A similar inflation hysteria gripped San Francisco, where property speculation and construction were radically transforming this once tiny, sleepy town. Now, too, the very volume of the gold-strike rumors were beginning to draw men outside the region — from Oregon Territory and from approaching emigrant wagon trains originally bound for Oregon. Californios, native Mexicans living in towns far to the south of the gold sites, also began flocking northwards. James Marshall, whose discovery had provided the original spark for this growing conflagration, was so besieged by mobs of gold-seekers that he fled the area in disgust and in fear for his life. John Sutter, too, was rapidly losing control of his vast properties and of the large legions of workers he had for many years employed to farm his vast acreage.

In mid-August of 1848, the California Territorial Military Governor, Richard Mason, entrusted a young officer with the voluminous reports confirming the frequent and widespread gold discoveries which his staff members and the American Territorial Consul had written, supplemented with fourteen pounds of gold samples, and dispatched this courier to Washington D.C. in order to present these findings to officials of the James Polk Administration. After the courier finally arrived in the nation's capital in early December, President Polk carefully perused the reports and them summarized them in detail days later in his final annual address to Congress. The President prefaced his dramatic news with a provocative declaration: "The accounts of the abundance of gold in California Territory are of such extraordinary character as would scarcely command belief were they not corroborated by authentic reports of officers in the public service, who have visited the mineral district and derived the facts which they detail from personal observation."

Throughout the winter and early-spring months of 1849, as President Polk's emphatic and enthusiastic confirmation of the

California gold discoveries spread throughout the nation and far beyond, doubt and skepticism evaporated. Tens of thousands of men, world-wide, became obsessed by dreams of emigrating to the Pacific Coast and of finding sufficient gold there to create immense personal wealth. After making extensive preparations, a minority of the more affluent American gold-fever victims on the east coast chose to travel by sea. Some of these seafarers secured accommodations on ships which sailed down the Atlantic coasts of North and South America, around Cape Horn, and then north on the Pacific Ocean to the California coast. The Cape Horn storms provided the greatest peril for these emigrants. Most of the seafarers, however, secured passage on ships which veered westward from the Atlantic, across the Gulf of Mexico to the Panama Isthmus. The travelers then had to make the difficult journey on foot, following hired guides, across the Isthmus, to the Pacific Coast, and then board ships bound for San Francisco. For these emigrants the Isthmus crossing was fraught with dangers. Mr. Eckert describes these long, harrowing sea route expeditions using numerous diary excerpts of several hardy but apprehensive passengers. Those who could afford this mode of transportation to the west coast could make the trip in somewhat less time than those who chose to emigrate by wagon westward across the entire continent to California, and travel by sea was not as arduous and exhausting on a daily basis as was overland travel. The vast majority of the excited gold-seekers, however, simply couldn't afford travel by sea, and the option wasn't practical for the tens of thousands of gold-seekers who lived in the interior states far from the east coast.

Parties of emigrants from the Eastern United States, of course, had been crossing the American continent in wagon trains — on a relatively limited basis — for nearly twenty years, and Mr. Eckert has previously described the daily routine of these pilgrimages in vivid, convincing detail in both *The Infinite Dream* and *Dark Journey*. The fact that this long journey had been made numerous times in previous years, however, didn't make the five-odd month ordeal — one fraught with uncertainties and mortal dangers — any less frightening to those who now faced the arduous enterprise. And as these travelers were soon to learn, they would not be struggling to follow the long, winding, difficult trails to the west alone; they would sometimes have to cope with literal traffic congestion created by many scores of other wagon companies, all departing from St. Louis during the spring months of 1849 — traffic congestion which resulted in three-day in-line waiting periods at several fording or ferry sites on the Platte and other sizeable rivers on the Oregon Trail. While Mr. Eckert relies on the diaries and accounts of several emigrants directly involved in this migration, his primary source is Alonzo Delano, a successful general store owner in Ottawa, Illinois, a family man in his mid-thirties convinced that his health was failing precipitously, that he could not live much longer. Restless and intensely intrigued by the prospect of seeking gold in distant California, he decided to leave his family behind and follow his dream, promising that he would send for his loved ones if and when he could survive the trip and accomplish some degree of gold-prospecting success. Delano was a remarkably literate, highly skilled writer who not only made frequent, copious entries in his diary, but also served as a traveling correspondent who wrote columns both for his hometown *Ottawa Free Trader* and for the *New Orleans Daily True Delta*. Delano's Ottawa Company, like the myriad other companies, departed from St. Louis in mid-April, 1849. Everyone — all of the thousands of wagon company members on the trail in 1849 felt a sense of urgency: They felt compelled to complete their continental crossing by early Fall. They were all acutely aware of the grim details of the Donner Party's tragic plight, trapped in the Sierras during an early 1845 winter because they had experienced numerous midsummer delays on the long cross-continent trek. Delano and his company would finally reach their long-term destination, the Sutter's Fort area, in late September (the point at which this volume concludes). Using frequent, carefully edited excerpts from Delano's writings, Mr. Eckert treats the reader to what is surely one of the most eloquent, good-humored, and exhaustive accounts available of the formidably perilous, extremely fatiguing, enormously difficult mid-nineteenth century odysseys across the vast prairies, deserts, and mountain ranges of western America.

Delano and his Ottawa Company, like the other tens of thousands of other traveling company members lured by California gold, endured cold, violent early spring rainstorms. They had anxiety-filled encounters with Sioux, Crow, and Snake Indians — and later, near the Sierras, with what the emigrants called the Digger Indians, who tried constantly to rustle their cattle. They encountered and traveled through alien, other-worldly topographies, and encountered boiling, poisonous, alkaline- or sodium-carbonate-filled springs. They struggled daily to find areas which provided both sufficient forage to feed their livestock and adequate drinking water for the entire company. At one point they wandered a full, anxiety-filled nineteen-days, after foolishly haven taken what they assumed to be a shortcut, trying desperately to rediscover and reconnect with the Oregon Trail. They experienced outbreaks of cholera, a disease which often crippled Delano during the long trek. Later in the trek they encountered individual families who because of wagon breakdowns or other serious setbacks, were isolated from their companies and helplessly stranded — families whom the hard pressed Ottawa Company members could offer little more than sympathy as they passed by. They endured and pulled off the exhausting ordeal of crossing the Sierras. Indeed, throughout the earlier months of the journey, Delano was haunted by the words of an experienced continent-crossing veteran who told him and other company members back in late April, "The first half of your wandrin' west is gonna be th' easy part. Things don't start t' gettin' really rough 'till you git past th' continental dee-vide. Up to then it's passable difficult. After that, though — after that, it's just plain damn god-awful hell!"

And finally, during the nineteen-odd months which expired between Marshall's discovery of California gold in early 1848 and the Ottawa Company's arrival on the scene in late September, 1849, San Francisco's population grew from approximately

12,000 to approximately 300,000 inhabitants — 95% of them men. (Percentage-wise, moreover, the growth of Sacramento, which had literally first sprung into existence during the local rush of mid-1848, was even more startling.) Mr. Eckert details the inevitable growing pains of such a dramatic, chaotic population explosion: The mind-boggling price-inflation of all goods and services (often reaching 1000% of early 1848 retail prices); the breathtaking speed with which construction projects were thrown together; the first two (of four eventual) fires which severely damaged San Francisco; the economic speculators' frenetic efforts to supply the overwhelming demands of tens of thousands of miners wintering in the city when the gold fields were too flooded and frigid to exploit — demands for living accommodations (satisfied primarily with primitive framed-canvas structures), for eateries, and for entertainment diversions such as gambling casinos, theaters, and brothels. And finally, Mr. Eckert devotes significant attention to the evolution of the gold fields' crime rates, which remained surprisingly low during this period but increased dramatically as gold became increasingly difficult to find.

Gold Fever most certainly won't disappoint either loyal reading fans of Allan Eckert or virtually all enthusiastic students of U. S. nineteenth-century history.

Thayle Anderson
Murray, Kentucky
August 2014

Gold Fever

THE BEGINNING OF THE CALIFORNIA GOLD RUSH

Prologue

The year 1848 has just begun and the war between Mexico and the United States is reaching its conclusion, with the latter emerging as victor. In the village called Guadalupe Hidalgo, west of Mexico City, treaty commissioners from the U.S. and Mexico are engaged in final negotiations to end the war and settle matters regarding the territories in dispute.

In the Northwest, with the 49th Parallel fixed as the boundary between British Canada and the Oregon Territory, American settlers are no longer fearing land confiscation by the British. As a result, the Oregon Trail has become dotted with scores of wagon trains bringing more pioneers from the East. Ever increasing numbers, however, hearing tales of California's better climate and its remarkable potential for agriculture and stock-raising, are detouring off the main Oregon Trail onto several new trails that cross the Sierras into the great Sacramento River Valley. At this stage, where population is concerned, California's non-Indian Mexicans — calling themselves Californios —form the far greater majority.

Yerba Buena village, the only port for sea-going vessels in San Francisco Bay, is growing rapidly and becoming a recognized trading center. The most important stream emptying into the bay offers excellent potential for settlement upstream — the great Sacramento River flowing from the east and north, carrying a vast volume of water from its principal tributaries: the American River (with three major branches), the Feather River (augmented by the Yuba), and the Pit River. They and their many tributaries, carrying the clear, cold, run-off from the Sierras, teem with salmon and sturgeon.

While there are several widely separated ranches on various land grants, the principal inland settlement in California as 1848 begins is

Sutter's Fort, situated on the left bank of the Sacramento River, close below the point where it is joined by the powerful American River. Just as Samuel Brannan, the acquisitive Mormon leader, has become the most influential and wealthy settler in the San Francisco Bay area, so, too, has John Sutter's power and influence grown in California's interior. Owner of some 300,000 head of cattle, 10,000 sheep, plus great herds of horses and mules, Sutter also has thousands of acres planted in various grain and fruit crops, and he operates wineries, distilleries, breweries, fisheries, flour mills, and tanneries, as well as employing hundreds of workers, primarily Indians. Yet, he is deeply in debt and only gradually paying off those who have backed his enterprises.

Far to the East, President James Knox Polk is beginning his fourth year in office under a dark cloud of distrust. Several opposition legislators in the U.S. House of Representatives, including Abraham Lincoln and Jefferson Davis, have openly accused him of deliberately, unnecessarily, and unconstitutionally beginning the War with Mexico simply to gain territory. Of equal seriousness, they are accusing him of collaborating with, even bribing, an enemy of the state — former exiled Mexican General Santa Ana, of Alamo infamy, who is now again in exile. They also accuse Polk of having brought the United States to the brink of war with Great Britain, in order to obtain the Oregon Territory. The President is clearly guilty of all these acts, and the nation is angered at his usurpation of powers entirely beyond those constitutionally authorized for his executive position..

At the same time, the court-martial instituted in Washington, D.C. during the autumn of 1847 by Brigadier General Stephen Kearny against Lt. Col. John C. Frémont on charges of mutiny, disobedience of orders, and insubordination while under Kearny's command in California, reaches its climax and the verdict is guilty. Frémont is to be cashiered and though Polk — still winnowing the favor of Frémont's father-in-law, powerful U.S. Senator Thomas Hart Benton of Missouri — offers Frémont a Presidential pardon, Frémont refuses to accept the boon and, instead, resigns his commission before his cashiering can take effect, reenters civilian life, and returns to his massive Mariposa Grant land purchase in central California.

Meanwhile, one of John Sutter's more important projects to lift himself out of debt is just now nearing fruition: construction of a sawmill (after years of searching for a feasible site) to provide much-needed lumber for central California and Yerba Buena on San Francisco Bay, as well as for export. In this enterprise he has entered into a partnership with his employee, James Wilson Marshall. The prospective mill-site found was initially located by Marshall 45 miles upstream on the South Fork of the American River and on January 24th, 1848, while inspecting improvements made to the saw-mill's tailrace, preparatory to going into full lumber production, Marshall (who is also an amateur geologist) discovers what he thinks is gold. When he excitedly blurts to his Mormon employees, "Boys, by God, I believe I have found a gold mine!," he opens a whole new era in the history of California, the United States of America, and, ultimately, the entire world.

This is how it all unfolded.

Chapter 1

[January 24th, 1848 • Monday]

As soon as the sun cleared the mountains to the east, James Marshall left his quarters at the lumber mill site and sauntered down to the tail-race near its fore-bay gate. He was pleased to see that the swift, all-night water flow which he had directed be commenced, had already, in accordance with his prior instructions, been turned off at daybreak by the closing of the main intake gate to the tail-race. This assigned task had been accomplished shortly after daybreak by two of his employees who were former Mormon Battalion members, 35-year-old Henry Bigler and 19-year-old Azariah Smith.

In the tail-race, the broadly-flanged water-wheel had at first been set too low. During his inspection yesterday, Marshall had become convinced that allowing a strong, swift, overnight current to flow through the race would effectively sweep away any smaller debris — sand, pebbles, whatever — while anything larger could, if necessary, then be blasted out by his crew or dug out and removed by the Indian laborers.

The water in the tailrace had largely drained away by now, and Marshall was pleased to see that the drainage was not only more complete than previously, but that the current created throughout the night, abetted by a heavy rainfall for an hour or so, had eroded the sides and bottom of the race and had swept away a substantial portion of the sand and small pebbles that had been accumulating. A number of large, newly exposed rocks remained in the principal channel, and these, he knew, would be cleared away today by the Indian crews working under supervision of their foreman, Peter Wimmer. By day's end, he thought, with another fresh flow of water passing through the race, the mill's large water-wheel would be turning freely, steadily, and with the power requisite for maintaining a consistent revolution of the giant saw blade. The final major chore was nearly completed.

As he walked down the race now, Marshall followed the newly opened and more clearly defined downward sloping of the channel as improvised by the work crews yesterday. He was some two hundred feet below the head-gate and mill, still passing the decomposing granite base rock that had been newly broken up to allow greater freedom of water passage, when he began to notice, in cracks of the granite bedrock below the surface of the water, sand and granules of material, as well as tiny pebbles that had been caught in them.

Marshall had previously entertained the idea that there might be some unusual minerals present, this probability perhaps bolstered by the recent, rather exciting discovery of an uncommonly rich deposit of mercury — which most were calling quicksilver — in an extensive deposit presently being mined not many miles northeast of Monterey Bay near Santa Clara, at a place called New Almaden. He had, in fact, only a week or so ago mentioned in an offhanded way to John Sutter that there might be "interesting" minerals to be found in the excavations they were making here in the mill-race, but Sutter at that time, as Marshall had written in his journal, "... had only laughed at such an idea and dismissed the notion."

Now, however, on closer inspection, Marshall's breath suddenly caught as he noted that the debris trapped in those granite cracks some six inches beneath the surface of the clear water included a glittering, golden-colored pebble about the size and shape of a garden pea. He stooped and carefully picked it up on his knife-point, then transferred it into the palm of his free hand. He examined it closely and noted that it seemed uncommonly heavy for its size.

"Pyrite," he muttered to himself, initially concluding that this was merely a larger piece of the residue of fine, sand-size or smaller iron pyrite deposits that were somewhat common in the stream beds in this area, deposits which the diggers had been encountering ever since excavation of the race had begun. Because of its size, however, this single piece was somewhat unusual, and when he brought it closer to his eye, his breath suddenly caught. Pyrite — Fool's Gold — was entirely familiar to him in his own rudimentary studies, and he had always been amused by those unfamiliar with mineral deposits who mistook that glittery substance for a precious material. But this — this piece — did not exhibit the characteristics he normally associated with pyrite: It had neither sharp nor broken edges; it was, on the contrary, quite smoothly rounded, evidently from the wear of being tumbled along the bottom by the current. The color, moreover, differed somewhat from the hues he had noted in the pyrite specimens he'd encountered and examined in the past, and the usual hard, bright brassiness was not evident here. This piece was exhibiting more of a warmer deep yellow, more of a truly golden hue.

Unwilling to allow himself to become unduly excited, he still felt his own heart beating a little faster as he removed his old white fedora hat and tilted his palm so the specimen rolled into the crown. Then he reached carefully and plucked up the piece between finger and thumb. He held it up and turned it about so the sunlight struck it from different directions. Though he now studied it more closely, it told him nothing more. He quickly decided it had to be one of four possible substances he'd been reading about in his geology book: Pyrite, mica, sulphuret of copper, or gold. Mica he ruled out at once because of the specimen's heaviness, and the color was clearly not right for it to be copper. Pyrite remained likely, but to test this, he leaned over one of the remaining larger emergent rocks and carefully set the specimen on top of it. With the tip of his hunting knife he put pressure on it, fully expecting it to flake or break as pyrite normally would.

It didn't break. Neither did it flake or crack. Instead, the knife tip scored the smooth surface, further ruling out, as nearly as he could recall, pyrite and sulphuret of copper. To be sure, he picked up a smooth, fist-size granite rock and banged it down on the piece. It clearly flattened and bent somewhat, exhibiting a malleability that suggested to him one thing only.

Gold!

The thought struck with an almost physical impact, and he sucked in a deep, shuddering breath. He touched his tongue to it but detected no bitter taste, nor was there any of the suspicious "smell" he associated with sulphuret of copper. Though he thought at first that the specimen was warm, he quickly chided himself for his overly active imagination. But the reality of the material was there, right before his eyes. Could it possibly be? What else might conceivably react like this? Nothing he knew of, unless this were some form of pyrite or copper he'd never before encountered, which he very much doubted; pyrite was iron and a knife blade could not score it so easily, if at all. But what, then? Copper? No! Definitely not; wrong color and no bitter, coppery taste, no vestige of a scent. He fumed at his own ignorance of what else it might possibly be.

Carefully, very carefully now, he picked up the piece — no, he corrected his own thought, the nugget — and dropped it onto the indented crown of his hat. His legs suddenly felt very weak, and he squinted his eyes for a moment against the sunlight and steadied himself. He then began moving along parallel to the newly opened channel, now scrutinizing intently every crack and behind every small projection, pausing now and again and using the tip of his knife-blade to gouge out other, similar pieces, some merely flakes, others as large as a grain of wheat. He placed these in his hat with his initial discovery. Before much longer he had a number of such pieces, totaling about an ounce, and he noted with wry amusement that his hands were trembling.

After another ten minutes of searching, he carefully climbed out of the race excavation and, his hat-crown clasped purse-like, made his way to the nearby small cabin where five of his Mormon workers were now quartering themselves. Hearing voices within, he tapped on the door with his free hand and stepped inside. All five men were sitting around a rough central table, drinking coffee and eating freshly-baked stick-bread.

Their voices fell away as he approached, and they noted on his face the oddest expression they had ever seen him exhibit. They watched, curious, as Marshall strode to the crude workbench table, cleared a spot in the center of it, and placed his hat directly beneath the lamplight. He opened the gap to the crown then and exposed a dozen rather small nuggets and a number of thin yellow flakes, the total amounting to about a teaspoonful. His voice was trembling and a little croaky as he spoke:

"Boys, by God, I believe I have found a gold mine!"

There was a scraping of chair legs as the men rose and crowded closer to see the material but, for the most part, they were skeptical. One of them flatly remarked, "Gold? There's no such good luck as that," and another agreed, saying, "I reckon not."

Azariah Smith brought out from his pocket a gold half-eagle coin, and they compared the color. The coin was a deep gold color, whereas the small nuggets and flakes were considerably lighter. None of the men had ever seen virgin gold before, but despite the difference in color between the coin and the particles Marshall had found, the consensus was that, indeed, the material that had been collected was native gold. They were considerably less convinced, however, that the pieces amounted to good evidence that more of the precious mineral might be found.

Of the five Mormons gathered around, only Bigler and Smith seemed to sense the enormity of the discovery, as evidenced by the fact that in a short while the novelty of the moment eroded and the majority drifted off to prepare themselves for the day's work. Bigler, however, lingered a while longer, looking at the small nuggets and flakes. Growing more convinced of Marshall's belief that they represented tracings from a more substantial gold deposit, he decided to do some prospecting of his own at the earliest opportunity.

As if to vindicate his own belief that this was gold, Marshall invited all five men to return to the race with him to see if more could be located. They did so and toward the tail end of the race, where the current had widened and it's swiftness diminished, they began finding more tiny particles of the yellow material beneath the water in crevices and small pockets.

Pleased that his men were now taking his discovery more seriously, Marshall returned to the cabin with them, then gathered up the nuggets in his hat and prepared to walk over to the adjacent cabin to show them to Peter and Jennie Wimmer and whoever else might be on hand there in the cookshed. He had already decided he would take some of the specimens back to Sutter's Fort to see if Sutter could help in accurately identifying them..

Bigler and his fellow workers were now exhibiting an eagerness to lay aside their tools and devote their time to goldseeking, but caution took precedence: No one had any idea whatsoever how extensive — or limited — the gold deposit might be. Further, all of them were keenly aware that they were making better than decent wages working here at constructing the lumber mill and that if they were to quit construction work for gold-seeking, the glittering stuff would very likely soon run out, and they would, themselves, turn out to be the losers. Marshall, fully agreeing with this line of reasoning, strongly exhorted them to continue their work. After he finished and saw that they were still undecided, he added his icing to the cake:

"I'll tell you what," he said, "you men continue at your jobs as usual, sunrise to sunset, six days out of the week until the work here is finished, and I'll give you the freedom, on Sundays, to hunt for gold as much as you want, and wherever you want — and — " he paused somewhat dramatically, "you'll be allowed to keep whatever gold you may find. And, when the construction work here on the mill is finished and a supply of lumber logs laid in, which will take about six weeks, we'll all devote a solid week or two to gold-hunting and see what we can make of it. Until then, however, I will ask that none of you to breathe a word of this discovery to anyone apart from ourselves. Agreed?"

Marshall's offer was more generous than they anticipated, and it didn't take the men long to reach a unanimous decision: "Agreed!"

Marshall left then, and as Bigler's four companions discussed briefly what had occurred before heading out to assume their tasks, Bigler quickly re-entered the cabin, rummaged in his locker-box, found his *diary* and made a hasty entry in it, correcting himself as he wrote:

> *~~Sun~~ [sic]Monday 24th this day some kind of mettle ~~was discover~~ [sic] was found in the tail race that looks like goald [sic], first discovered by James Martial [sic], the boss of the mill.*

Moments later he rejoined the others outside, where they had been joined by workers from other quarters, and then the group moved apart toward their individual tasks — Brown and Barger to do whip-sawing, Smith to hew timbers with his broad-axe, Scott to frame timbers at the mill, itself, Bigler with others from the camp to drill the larger boulders for blasting at the tailrace, and Wimmer with his Indian crew to clear the race of debris for better current flow.

All of the whites, however, had gold in mind, and throughout the day, whenever they spoke to one another, it remained the chief topic of their conversation.

[January 25th, 1848 • Tuesday]

Colonel Richard Mason, commander of the American forces in California and now temporary governor of the territory, was more than just a little concerned.

The War with Mexico was winding down, and treaty negotiations with Mexican officials were nearing their conclusion, but few were aware of just how militarily weak the U.S. Army had become here. No one was more acutely aware than Mason himself that the discharge of by far the greater majority of privates in the Mormon Battalion had created a significant deficit in the strength of the U.S. Army forces occupying the California Territory. An uprising of the Mexican population still residing in the territory could, he realized, easily swing the balance of power back into their hands, a possibility more than just a little unnerving.

At his headquarters in Monterey, Colonel Mason, confronted by the prospect of such a scenario, became apprehensive. He was not comforted by his awareness that, back East additional American troops were being assembled to be sent to California. After all, even those military detachments possibly already underway would not arrive within the next few months. It was clearly during that interval when the balance of power might easily shift.

The prospect of persuading the discharged Mormon men to reenlist was slight at best, as the commander of the Southern Military District, Col. S. D. Stevenson, had already discovered. Most of the men of the former Mormon Battalion, having been honorably discharged after their year of service and their exhausting march clear across the continent, wanted nothing so much as to return to their own people, now assembling in the Utah Territory close to the southeastern shore of the Great Salt Lake. Colonel Mason hoped, however, that if the incentives were significantly increased, a fair portion of those preparing to head back to their Zion might be swayed to remain here in military service for another six months or so, by which time regular army troops from the East would have arrived and the current potential crisis could be avoided.

With this in mind, the colonel had met with his young adjutant, 1st Lt. William Tecumseh Sherman, discussed with him what needed to be done, and directed him to prepare a letter to Colonel Stevenson to that effect. Lt. Sherman bent to the task, completing it with commendable skill, and now a copy of that letter had just been delivered to the colonel's desk. He read it closely, approving of how well organized it was and how clearly it explained the limitations, established by the War Department, of what the Army could do to induce enlistments and maintain troop strength. It was actually precious little, but Lt. Sherman had expressed it all so clearly, no one but an abject nincompoop could fail to understand.

The California commander chuckled as he finished reading the letter and set it aside. He was pleased, as usual, with Lt. Sherman, and made a mental note to commend him on the excellent job he had done.

Nevertheless, having had experience with Capt. Hunt before, he doubted that Mormon officer's ability re-enlist his discharged troops according to the agreements and requirements clearly explained by Sherman.

In that context, then, the colonel swiftly composed a personal letter of his own to Lansford W. Hastings, offering him a major's commission and command of the outfit that hopefully would be raised through Hunt's efforts. He did so not only because Hastings, he knew, was a go-getter and a strong promoter of whatever issue he tackled, but, as he mentioned in the letter now, the offer was "... based on your knowledge and extensive acquaintance with the immigrants in this country." Whether Hastings would rise to such bait, he had no idea, but it was worth a try.

Finishing that letter, he swiftly wrote another, this time to Samuel Brannan in San Francisco, who was still President of the Latter-day Saints in California. To Brannan he stressed that it was:

> *... all-important to raise a very strong force for the service in Mazatlan with all possible dispatch, since I doubt Commodore Shubrick will be able to hold it after the hurricane season in those seas sets in. I am working to raise one thousand men in Oregon, California, and from the settlement on the Great Salt Lake, and I urge you to use your influence in encouraging and supporting the effort of raising a battalion in California.*

Mason sealed the second letter and placed it with the first, both to be delivered quickly by special courier and, hopefully, with some positive results. "The last thing needed right now," he thought, "is something to cause any disruption of the present peace negotiations in progress."

[January 28th, 1848 • Friday]

After a long ride through drizzly rain, James Marshall finally reined up at Sutter's Fort at 9 o'clock this morning and uncharacteristically left his horse tied to a rail, exposed to the weather. He was intensely preoccupied with the stress of his recent discovery, a stress which had filled his chest like a great leaden weight ever since he departed yesterday from the lumber mill construction site on the South

Fork of the American River. He stepped up onto the porch, rapped on the door just once, and then, again quite uncharacteristically, opened it and stepped in without awaiting an invitation.

Seated at his desk and making an entry in one of his logbooks, John Sutter swiveled about, irked that anyone should enter his quarters unbidden. The irritation, however, faded away instantly when he recognized the dripping, slicker-clad figure of his partner and was replaced by concern when he saw the strange expression on Marshall's face, an expression he could not fathom. Setting his pen aside, he rose and, wordlessly, led his partner into an adjacent private sitting room, shutting the door behind them and wondering all the while what could have prompted this visit. Surely not lack of supplies, since he'd sent two wagonloads of fresh provisions to the mill site only yesterday; and why the arrival at this time of the morning, which suggested that he had probably ridden much of the night to get here.

The sitting room was dim, lighted only by a single low-flame lantern on a rough-hewn table, and Marshall glanced about, his gaze probing into the dimly lighted corners of the room. Sutter was about to ask what was wrong, when Marshall turned back to him and spoke first, his voice low and strained.

"Are you alone?"

"Yes. Or I was until you arrived." Sutter smiled, but the expression faded at the continued, almost animal-like wariness Marshall was exhibiting. "What's wrong?"

Marshall ignored the question and asked another of his own: "Did you lock the door?"

A small frown creased Sutter's brow as he shook his head. "No, but I will, if you wish it."

At his partner's brief nod, Sutter stepped back into the office and latched the main door, then returned to the sitting room. Marshall hadn't moved and again, before Sutter could demand an explanation, the visitor spoke.

"I want two bowls of water. And a stick of redwood. And some twine and sheet copper."

Sutter's patience was running thin. "What do you want with those things, Marshall?"

"To make a scale."

"I have scales enough in the apothecary's shop. Get hold of yourself while I go get one."

He left and was gone only a few minutes before returning with a fine brass balance which, after locking the office door again, he brought into the sitting room and placed on the table close to the lamp. By this time he'd had more than enough mystery, and he confronted Marshall directly, an edge in his voice when he spoke.

"Suppose you tell me what the hell this is all about, Jim."

Marshall gave a brief nod, reached into a pocket beneath his slicker, and withdrew a stained white cloth knotted about something. It was a knot which he now quickly untied.

"This," he said, emptying the several ounces of contents into the palm of his free hand, then stretched it toward his partner. "This is from the tailrace at the mill. I believe it's gold, but I don't know for sure. My men laughed at me and called me crazy when I showed them. I don't care. I still think it's gold, and I want you to tell me why you think I'm wrong."

Sutter pursed his lips and with an index finger, poked at the nuggets and flakes cupped in Marshall's palm, looking at them from different angles. He then picked up the largest piece, felt the heft of it in his own palm and then expelled a pent-up breath. "It certainly feels like it," he commented. "Heavy. Could be pyrite, though, but I'm no expert. Let's run some tests. We'll try it."

Sutter had Marshall dump the specimens into a clean saucer and then took a corked container from a closet shelf, opened it and poured the clear, faintly yellow liquid contents into a small glass. He grunted again, but this time followed it up with a comment.

This," he said, "is aquafortis. Fancy name for nitric acid. If it's gold, there'll be no effect."

He picked up one of the larger nuggets and gently, carefully dropped it into the fluid. Nothing happened. He did the same with several others as Marshall looked on, fascinated. There was still no change, and Sutter fished them out on an old wooden spoon, dropped them into a cupful of water, and nodded as he poured the acid back into its container, re-corked it and replaced it on the shelf. "So far so good," he muttered, more to himself than to Marshall.

He took one piece to an anvil and pounded it with a hammer, silently praying it wouldn't shatter as a chunk of pyrite undoubtedly would. It didn't; instead flattening, as he pounded it, to near tissue thinness. Further tests, biting hard on the specimens and dipping them into a cupful of boiling hot lye, were equally promising.

Next, Sutter removed from his pocket three silver dollars and placed them on one of the balance pans. The other he filled slowly with the nuggets and flakes until the pans balanced one another exactly. Both balance pans were then immersed in a large bowl of water as a check of their specific gravity. The pan holding the coins went up, while that holding the specimens went down.

"Still passing the test," he said, a broader smile quirking his lips. "No copper in it and no silver. Twenty-three karat, from what I can determine. That's about as close to pure gold as you can get. Now, let's see what the experts say about it."

He moved to a bookcase and brought down one of the volumes of his bedraggled set of the *American Encyclopedia* and opened it to the article on gold. Both men read it together, slowly, meticulously, and by the time they finished, any remaining doubts had vanished.

It was definitely gold.

The encyclopedia also made it clear that, considering the worn and rounded character of these nuggets, what they were finding was called placer gold — meaning gold that had eroded out of its original source and had been tossed and rolled downstream along the bottom by the current, gradually becoming worn but not broken. The question this raised sprang full-blown into Sutter's mind: What about the mother lode, the original source, where the gold had formed and from which it had been generated initially?

Sutter's own heart began beating faster, and abruptly he understood his partner's strain. The possibilities being opened seemed limitless, and a multitude of questions flooded his mind: How much was there? A small amount from a little pocket or a massive deposit? Where was the mother lode? On their own land? Didn't the Indians own that land? Could they lease it from them? Could it be mined? Could the claim be secured? How? What kind of equipment would they need? Who else knew about it? Could they keep the discovery muffled? What would happen if the word got out? How could their own interests be protected? The as yet unanswerable queries tumbled over one another in his mind.

The tests and talking had consumed the entire morning for the two men, and then stretched into the afternoon. Marshall became ever more agitated and anxious to get back to the mill. He wanted his partner to return with him at once, but Sutter shook his head. No, there were things he must do here before he could leave, chores to assign, orders to give in all his factories and shops. These were his responsibilities. Besides, it was still raining, even harder now than previously, and he recommended that Marshall stay; have a good hot meal and rest here overnight. Tomorrow, Sutter promised him; he'd return with Marshall tomorrow; then, hedging a little, he added, " -maybe even the next day, if everything can't be finished here tomorrow."

Marshall wouldn't wait, couldn't wait, not even for a meal.

Despite knowing that he couldn't possibly make it back to the mill before tomorrow, Sutter's partner nevertheless mounted up late in the afternoon and started back through the drenching rain, horse and man alike very weary. Marshall was relentlessly driven by a hopelessly jumbled conglomeration of thoughts, ideas, plans and concerns. John Sutter had given him his word he would follow, just as soon as it was possible for him to do so, but it might take a day or two, perhaps even three, before he could get away.

James Marshall understood, but he simply couldn't wait.

Now, only a short while after his partner's departure, John Sutter sat at his desk, preparing to begin writing his customary daily entry in his official logbook entitled *New Helvetia Diary*. For a long while he stared at the page he'd already dated January 28, 1848, considering best how to express such important news as Marshall's gold discovery four days ago, yet keep its content secret. Finally, exhaling a great sigh, he dipped his quill into the inkpot and wrote a ten-word sentence, quite likely the most significant understatement he had ever composed:

> *"Mr. Marshall arrived from the mountains on very important business."*

[January 31st, 1848 • Monday]

As yet wholly unaware of the discovery that had occurred a week ago today at the lumber mill site on the South Fork of the American River, the military governor of the California Territory, Colonel Richard Mason, had earlier today received a dispatch from Commodore William Shubrick, written aboard his warship moored in the bay within hailing distance of Mazatlan. Shubrick, not noted for being one to become overly excited at any turn of events, had written with an intense sense of urgency that Mason found disturbing, requesting more American troops be sent him without delay.

The dispatch revealed that Mexican Captain Manuel Pinéda,

whose men had earlier been turned back by Colonel Burton's New York Volunteers, had regrouped his force in Baja California and was now moving to attack the 72-man garrison of U.S. Marines under the command of Lt. Charles Heywood near the southern tip of the peninsula at San José del Cabo. Shubrick, insisting that he had no men of his own to spare, reported that his small force in Mazatlan had already been suffering guerilla attacks, and he requested a reinforcement of 500 to 1,000 men, in order to hold the port and to send aid to Lt. Heywood. Governor Mason had already forwarded the request to Commanding General Winfield Scott, alerting him that American forces in the West were presently being stretched to the danger point.

Now, only six days after his reply to Colonel Stevenson, regarding the latter's offer to command a new battalion of Mormons, Col. Mason found it necessary to order one of his own topographical engineers, Lt. Bill Warner, to contact Captain Hunt at Los Angeles. If necessary, Hunt should go with Warner to the Great Salt Lake area to raise, and return with, a new battalion of Mormon soldiers. Colonel Mason's own competent aide, Lt. Sherman, had now written out the instructions for Warner quite clearly, and nothing more could be done at this point but sit back and wait.

[February 1st, 1858 • Tuesday]

When James Marshall arrived back at the lumber mill site in mid-afternoon today, the sixth day since his departure, he was gratified to see all his employees hard at work. A vague fear had haunted him throughout his absence that without his steadying presence, and with their clear knowledge that what appeared to be gold was collecting nearby in the tailrace, just waiting to be picked up, they would have abandoned their tasks, seduced by the compelling lure the discovery had precipitated.

He needn't have worried. These were Mormons, and they had given their word to either remain on the job until the mill was satisfactorily operational or for six weeks, whichever came first; or, for that matter, until the boss himself excused them. They had done so, and as he rejoined them, Marshall felt a wash of pride within him for their steadfastness. They had earned a reward, and he meant to see they got it. Raising his voice over the almost continuous rasp of saw, bite of axe, and scrape of shovel, he called out loudly to catch their attention:

"All right, all right, everyone! Gather 'round. I've got something to tell you."

Within a few minutes he found himself surrounded by his keenly expectant workers. He nodded and held up a hand. They hushed and grew intensely attentive.

"As you know," he said, "I've been to the fort to confer with Captain Sutter. He wished me to stay longer, but I knew all of you would be eager to learn what occurred." As several of the men nodded, Marshall continued without pause. "The Captain was as much surprised as any of us over what had been found here, and just as eager to determine what it was, although his immediate reaction was that it couldn't possibly be gold. That reaction, however," he went on as a disappointed murmur arose from the men, "gradually diminished as together we put the stones — the nuggets — through every test his encyclopedia recommended. Without beating around the bush, I can tell you it passed them all — every one! It wasn't copper and it wasn't iron pyrite. Boys, by God, it was the pure stuff. Gold!"

After a momentary stunned silence and the men burst into cheers, thumped each other's backs, and shouted excitedly to one another. After finally restoring their attention minutes later, Marshall continued: "The old Cap and I locked ourselves up in a room and spent half a day trying every test we could. It agrees with all the encyclopedia says of gold. Aquafortis doesn't affect it. We balanced some of it with silver, and when we put the scale in water, the gold went down and the silver up." He paused and gestured graphically, raising one hand and lowering the other "And that told the story. It's the pure stuff!"

Again Bigler and the others grinned broadly, spontaneously shouting and chortling to one another. Marshall let their enthusiasm die down and then, becoming more serious, spoke again.

"There's no way of telling how big the deposit is," he said. "It may be pretty large, but chances are better it's only a small deposit, so don't get too excited about it. If you want to look for more, you're welcome to do so, but only on your own time, during your day off, not during our work week. Today, though, you've got the rest of the day off, and if you want to go into the race with me and look for some more, you're welcome to do so."

For a third time delighted cheers broke out, this time joined by the Indian workers, though understanding little English, they were merely bewildered by the excitement. Marshall smiled briefly before continuing.

"Mr. Sutter has promised to come here in a day or two, just as soon as he can break away from his responsibilities. When he does, he'll want to talk to you, and I want you, all of you, to listen very closely to what he'll have to say. In the meanwhile, let's go do some gold-hunting."

He led them off to the tailrace, and the entire group, seized by a jovial mood, scattered out behind him. Before nightfall ended their efforts, not a man among them had not found at least some small particles of gold.

[February 2nd, 1848 • Wednesday • 2:30 p.m.]

The sleepy little town of Guadalupe Hidalgo, not many miles northwest of Mexico City, had been selected by Mexican commissioners as the place where the peace treaty to end the war with the United States should be negotiated, and the American envoy who had been sent to negotiate that treaty was Nicholas Trist, a veteran diplomat with an excellent command of the Spanish tongue due to his previous years of foreign service in Cuba.

Trist had done all in his power to move the negotiations along ever since the Mexican capital had capitulated to the Americans last September 14, and a truce had been established allowing such discussions to occur, but the ensuing negotiations had involved a far more drawn-out process than he had anticipated. Trist had met for several days with the four foremost Mexican treaty commissioners — Miguel Atristan, Bernardo Couto, Ignacio Mora y Villamil, and José Herrera — and matters might have been settled then except for the obstinacy of the country's top military commander, General Antonio Lopez de Santa Ana, who was also President of Mexico. Santa Ana had at that time rejected the American proposals out of hand, and hostilities had resumed. But soon after General Winfield Scott's army defeated the enemy in the subsequent Battles of Contreras and Churubusco in August; and then following these victories, his troops prevailed in the Battle of Chapultepec and occupied Mexico City, forcing Santa Ana's political abdication and his eventual return to exile.

Peace negotiations since then had very nearly stalled until November, when a new Mexican government was formed at the city of Queretaro under the leadership of the country's former foreign minister, Manuel Pena y Pena, who was much more willing to consider the terms Trist proposed. Six months of negotiations, however, had tried the patience of the American supreme commander, President James Knox Polk, who, failing to understand the obstacles Trist had been forced to overcome, divested him of authority to make a treaty, and ordered him back to Washington in disgrace, just as those negotiations were finally being seriously considered.

Trist, fearful of losing such an opportunity, which he felt might collapse if not acted upon at once, and urged to persist not only by General Scott and the Mexicans but by the British legation in Mexico City as well, consequently chose to deliberately ignore President Polk's instructions in order to finish the job he'd been sent to do. The negotiations, which had been opened originally in Guadalupe Hidalgo, were resumed with two of the former Mexican negotiators, Atristan and Couto, plus foreign minister Luis Cuevas. Essentially, the terms of the treaty forced Mexico to cede to the United States the territories of New Mexico, Baja California (Lower California), and Alta California (Upper California) and to recognize the Rio Grande as the southern and partially western border of Texas. For these cessions, the U.S. was to pay Mexico $15 million in cash and assume another $3.25 million more in claims of American citizens on the Mexican government. Given the cold, hard reality that Alta California was virtually no longer under Mexican jurisdiction and could as easily be claimed by France, Russia or Great Britain as well as by the United States, and considering that New Mexico Territory was still virtually uninhabited except by Indian tribes, that the territory from the Nueces River to the Rio Grande was essentially desert terrain and that United States troops were already occupying Mexico City, the terms were extremely generous. Though Polk had been urged to annex the whole of Mexico to the United States, he refused to even consider such a proposal: His primary goal since inauguration had been acquisition of the entire west to the Pacific Ocean, and that goal had now, for all intents and purposes, been reached. Westward expansion, which had been Polk's watchword, indeed his obsession, since he had taken office, was now complete, so far as he was concerned.

The Mexicans had agreed to all the terms Trist proposed except for the cession of Baja California, which they steadfastly refused to give up, along with a strip of land that would permit them unrestricted passage from Sonora to Lower California. Trist at first refused to consider this, but eventually conceded it, after which the remainder of the negotiations had moved along well. Only one other point of cession remained: Whether or not San Diego was to be ceded to the Americans. After studying maps extensively, the Mexican commissioners finally agreed it should be ceded to the United States. Because Trist's original instructions had stated that the acquisition of Lower California was not as important to the administration as the cessions of Alta — Upper–California and New Mexico, he ceded the demand for that lower strip and pressured the Mexicans to complete the negotiations and agree to terms.

Today, then, Trist, Couto, Atristan, and Cuevas all put their signatures to the Treaty of Guadalupe Hidalgo, a treaty which also included a "secret" article allowing for eight months to elapse between the time of the treaty signing and the exchange of ratifications between the two governments. Immediately upon the signing, Trist dispatched a hand-carried copy to President Polk by special messenger James Freaner, who was a correspondent for the *New Orleans Delta* newspaper.

Despite the devastating — and well deserved — criticism already heaped upon the shoulders of President James Knox Polk for "inciting, instigating, and promoting an unconstitutional war" — criticism that continued unabated during the following years — an excerpt of the treaty epitomized its immense value to both countries:

> *There shall be firm and universal peace between the United States of America and the Mexican Republic, and between their respective countries, territories, cities, towns and people, without exception of places or persons.*

It was, in fact, a very good treaty: Good for the Mexicans, who had teetered on the brink of losing their entire nation to the United States; good for the United States which now had expanded to the dimensions James Knox Polk had envisioned at the time of his inauguration, fulfilling the "Manifest Destiny" he had felt was imperative to the country. Had Mexican governmental authorities known that gold had just been discovered in the territory they were presently ceding, the possibility was strong that they would not have ratified the treaty. But no one in the federal governments of either country was yet aware of that fact.

As of today, the United States had become an uninterrupted nation stretching from Canada to Mexico and from the Atlantic to the Pacific shore.

[February 2nd, Wednesday • 4:15 p.m.]

It was still daylight but the sun had set and shadows were deepening as James Marshall again visited Henry Bigler and his four fellow Mormons in their cabin. The saw-mill boss's face crinkled with a sort of conspiratorial amusement, and he seemed tickled with himself as he addressed them now.

"Well, the old Cap's got himself here even sooner than I expected. He's up at my place right now," he announced, tilting his head toward where his own small house perched on the hillside about a quarter-mile distant, "and pretty much worn out from the ride. He's lying down, and I told him I'd go out and see to his horse. 'Spect he's probably asleep by now, and I doubt he'll stir till morning. So I came here. I got an idea for a little prank we might pull on 'im that'd probably be a tickler for us all."

He reached into his pocket and carefully extracted one of his pipe tobacco tins and opened it. He had evidently cleaned the inside thoroughly, and it's only contents now were seven or eight of the nuggets that had been given into his keeping by these men, their total weight probably about three ounces or a bit more. "I expect he's going to want to take a walk down the race in the morning to see for himself what's there. Seems to me we picked up just about all the nuggets that were easy finding, and it'd be a good idea if he could come across some for himself without too much trouble. So I figured — an' I leave this up to you," he added quickly, " — that we could take some of these nuggets of ours and as soon as Mr. Bigler shuts off the water flow in the morning, he could scatter 'em here and there on the base rock in the race for ol' Cap to find on his own. Won't do it, though unless you're all in agreement. Might take us some searching, but I reckon we'll find some others to replace these pretty quick in the days ahead. Boys, the Cap'n always has his bottle with 'im and I figure he'll be so tickled with what he finds that he'll set it out and treat us all to a little drink."

There was somewhat of a hesitation and a bit of murmuring among them before the "boys" unanimously fell in with the plan. Bigler, caught up with the idea and grinning broadly, accepted the tin from Marshall and carefully put it into his own pocket.

"I'll do it," he said. "It'll be fun watching his expression when he finds 'em. And as you say, Boss, we'll probably have no trouble finding more when we get a chance to hunt for them again."

[February 3rd, 1848]

It was nearly 9 o'clock this morning before James Marshall and Peter Wimmer showed up at the workers' cabin with Captain Sutter walking slowly between them. All five of the employees, having finished their breakfast, were waiting inside, and they trooped out to greet the mill's co-owners. The head-gate to the race had been closed a bit more than a couple of hours ago, just after dawn, and the water flow had quickly dwindled to what it was now, little more than a trickle. Marshall and Bigler exchanged glances, and Bigler's small nod confirmed that he had done what was expected of him. Marshall's brief grin acknowledged Bigler's nod, but none of the men let on that this was anything but the ordinary scenario of workers trooping out after breakfast to begin their day's work.

The employees greeted the trio, and they all talked together for a short while, during which time Sutter distributed to each of them, from the small cloth bag he was carrying, the gift of a pocketknife. Pleased, the men thanked him and then shuffled about a bit, as if preparing to head out to do their appointed tasks, but Marshall stopped them. "Cap'n Sutter's come to see for himself the kind of pieces we've been finding in the tailrace. Suppose you boys come along and keep us company. Maybe one of us'll find a nugget to show him."

The five agreed, of course, and followed the two owners closely as they began walking toward the mill and race, a hundred yards or more distant. They had hardly gone a dozen steps, however, when 13-year-old Martin, the elder of the Wimmer boys, trotted past, tossed a wave at them and called, "I'm headin' down t'see if mebbe I kin find some more of them there nuggets like we found before."

They could hardly stop him without revealing their prank so they said nothing, except that a small groan issued from Will Johnson as the boy dashed on toward the race. A few moments later, a fair distance ahead of them, the boy disappeared from sight as he jumped down into the race. However, because Sutter suffered from gout and walked slowly, especially in the morning, it was the better part of ten minutes before the little group reached the point where Martin Wimmer had dropped from their view. Now, even before they could themselves carefully descend the bank into the race, Martin came running back, and stopped before them, panting, his face flushed.

"I found some, Cap'n Sutter," he cried, inordinately proud of himself. "I found some already. Look at 'em!" The boy held out his hand and in his palm were most of the nuggets Bigler had salted in bold view in the tailrace less than three hours previously.

Sutter leaned forward and looked at the nuggets closely, then nudged them with a forefinger to turn them over. They truly were a breathtaking sight in the morning sunlight, and he jabbed his cane into the ground and exclaimed, "By Jove, it is rich!"

The men looked on, not daring to say a word, their little prank having fallen through. They had no choice but to let the boy keep what he had found, and he raced off toward the Wimmer cabin chortling with glee. Bigler thought to himself that the lad had recovered somewhere between $20 and $50 worth of gold — easily the equivalent of many weeks worth of income for the average worker back east.

Swallowing their chagrin, they followed Sutter down into the race and engaged in some prospecting, finding a few of the pieces Martin Wimmer had missed, plus a few others not previously discovered. Most of the men, including the owners, found small nuggets, and several of the men gave pieces they had found to Sutter. Asariah Smith found the prize nugget on this outing, one that weighed just a bit over an ounce.

After an hour or so they returned to the cabin area and all, despite their joke having fallen through, had enjoyed themselves. Marshall and Sutter conferred quietly together for a time, and then Marshall sent several of the Indian workers out to invite to the camp any of the leading men of the nearby Coloma village and, even more importantly, the leading men of the Yalisumni village several miles downstream, who were said to be in control of this entire territory, even though the tribe's estimated total population at this time was only sixty-nine individuals. Several of them appeared, and the two partners spoke with them for a considerable while. The upshot of it all was that Sutter and Marshall leased for three years a rather large tract of land, some ten or twelve square miles up and down the river and flanking it on both sides for about a mile. For this they paid the natives partly in clothing, particularly shirts, pants, and hats, plus some handkerchiefs and some flour, vegetables and tobacco. The partners promised to pay them similar amounts once every year for so long as they were allowed to lease the land and guaranteed that the Indians would not be bothered by the workers here or elsewhere. Since Sutter was known to be the authorized Indian agent in this region and they addressed him as "Alcalde Granda," they considered his word as binding.

Immediately after the Indians departed with their goods, Sutter and Marshall discussed the situation and concluded that they should register their claim without delay with interim Governor Mason in Monterey for his legal confirmation of it in order to secure the claim for their own ultimate protection from possible encroachment or theft. Sutter promised to take care of this matter the moment he returned to the fort.

Nevertheless, despite such precautions and despite the fact that on a private walk which Sutter and Marshall took upstream, they found still more placer gold, although not its mother lode, both men remained reasonably convinced that the gold found thus far originated from nothing more than a pocket that was local and to some degree superficial. The mill hands evidently thought so, too, which was why they had readily agreed to continue as paid hands for at least another six weeks. The job was something they could count on; the gold, so far as anyone could determine, was not.

With his samples, carefully packed away, those he had found and those that had been given to him, Sutter addressed the mill hands before starting back to the fort. Already he was reasoning that the gold discovery could prove to be more of a curse than a blessing to him. He told them that he was counting on their promise of keeping the gold discovery secret for at least the next six weeks. "As you all know," he continued, "I have a crew building the large flour mill at Brighton, about five miles up the American from the fort. If even a whisper of this gold find were to reach them, I'm afraid they would desert their posts before the mill is finished and flock here to prospect and I would be entirely ruined. So I trust you'll honor your promises."

The nods and murmurs from the men were the confirmation he needed and, satisfied, John Sutter left for the fort.

[February 8th, 1848 • Tuesday]

Since arriving back at his fort, John Sutter had been considering who best might serve to carry the news of the gold discovery to Governor Mason in Monterey and lay before him the Sutter-Marshall Claim, as he was now thinking of it, to get confirmation and secure preemption and mining rights on the parcels he and his partner had paced off along both sides of the South Fork.

The choice of who would be a reliable messenger was not hard for Sutter to make. The name Charles Bennett immediately came to mind as a good choice to handle the mission, since Bennett was the one employee in particular at the Brighton gristmill whom Sutter had come to rely upon most to undertake a variety of chores and errands. Though he hadn't been employed by Sutter for terribly long, thus far he had proven to be steady in his work, dependable in performance and somewhat more intelligent than many of his companions. Sutter had sent for him shortly after sunrise this morning, with instructions to pack his bag for a somewhat lengthy trip. Bennett was then, bag in hand, to ride to the fort and present himself in Sutter's office by 10:00 a.m.

Bennett complied with the order immediately upon receiving it and arrived at Sutter's Fort a bit earlier than expected. This gave him a chance, after stabling his horse at the smithy's, to wander about inside the compound, marveling at the changes that had taken place in just the couple of months since he'd last been here. While Captain Sutter had not added anything actually new to the fort, there had been numerous improvements to the existing facilities. The twenty-foot-high adobe wall still enclosed a rectangular area of about two acres, with a pair of block-houses two stories tall located at diagonally opposing corners, each with an Indian lookout; all of those lookouts were relieved at regular four-hour intervals around the clock. To the east was a relatively new adobe building, which was the hospital Sutter had recently created. Inside this enclosure was one large shingle-roofed building that held Sutter's office and also served as a principal storehouse. All around the inside of the fort walls were houses, rooms and shops, each with the adobe wall forming the back wall of the smaller structure. These included a blacksmith, a carpenter's shop, a fruit-stand, a shoemaker's shop, a tiny tavern of sorts, and various dormitory-type quarters for workmen. Here and there Indian women were busy indoors and out, weaving coarse blankets, and a number of Indian men were similarly attending to a variety of chores. The main portal of the fort, through which Bennett had entered only a short time ago, consisted of a single large gate, open throughout the day, but always closed and barred at night, and two iron ship-guns were close at hand for protection, should the need arise.

An affable, gregarious sort, Bennett stopped and chatted here and there with little groups of men, and he was clearly delighted with how raptly they listened to the gossip he imparted about gold being found at the saw-mill site. While most did not believe the story for a moment, more often than not, Bennett left them talking excitedly when he walked away.

As the time neared 10:00 a.m., Bennett strode to Sutter's office structure, knocked on the door, and entered when bidden. Now he stood before his employer's big desk, shifting a bit uneasily from foot to foot, his packed bag on the floor beside him. He was obviously curious about why he had been summoned, and briefly wondered if he had done something wrong and was to be punished. It wasn't a very pleasant prospect, since he knew very well Cap'n Sutter was something of a dictator here in his own fort, his word constituting the law, and he with the power to punish any whom he found deserving of it, even unto death, if necessary. No, he shook his head slightly, unable to think of anything he might've done wrong and decided his own presence here most likely had something to do with the gold discovery up at the mill site. The fort's owner quickly confirmed Bennett's conclusion.

"I have an important errand I want to entrust to you," Sutter told him without preamble, and then briefly filled him in with a few more details in regard to what had actually been occurring at the saw-mill. Then he continued: "I've drawn up some papers in that respect that I want you to take to Governor Mason in Monterey. They're to be placed in his hands and no one else's. In private. Make sure of that. He'll no doubt have a reply for me, and I want you to bring it back to me as soon as he gives it to you."

The papers Sutter had hastily prepared during the night comprised a request to legally secure the land he and Marshall had staked out, though not specifically for gold mining. This was a formal request, seemingly for the purpose of expanding his current businesses of milling, lumbering, pasturing and agricultural purposes as the principal aim and mentioning mineral exploitation more as a casual afterthought than anything else. He was sure the governor would deduce rather quickly that the afterthought was actually the most important issue, but he did not want to emphasize the matter too expressly, nor give the governor himself cause to broadcast the news of the discovery.

"Since you're aware of the gold that's being found up at the saw-mill," the Captain continued to Bennett with calculated blandness, "and, while it actually doesn't amount to much, I'm afraid if word spreads about it we'll not only have an influx of people from elsewhere but also a loss of hands from their jobs here. Completion of the works in progress are the primary concerns at the moment, and I can't afford to have my employees abandon their jobs right now, not when the grist mill's just gone into production and the saw-mill's completion is so close."

He opened his desk drawer and removed a snugly closed drawstring pouch of buckskin containing some six ounces of native gold nuggets, which created a significant bulge in the little sack. He stretched across his desk and set the bag close to Bennett, then leaned back in his chair with a casualness that belied the tension he was experiencing.

"You're also to hand this bag of samplings from the tailrace at the saw-mill to the governor and ask him — and no one else — to inspect the contents carefully and give his opinion, preferably in writing. At the dock right now, the Sacramento is past due on her schedule to embark for San Francisco, but I asked her skipper, Cap'n Wilbur, to stand by until I could prepare a special passenger. That's you. He'll start downstream as soon as you've joined him. You are not to discuss your errand with anyone else; it's strictly confidential business, Mr. Marshall's and mine, and no one else's. Clear?"

Bennett's head bobbed, though a little uncertainly. "Yes sir."

"Then you can go to the launch immediately. I will trust you not to dally in any way on your journey, either on the way to Monterey or during the return."

"You can count on me, Mr. Sutter," Bennett replied, stuffing the leather drawstring pouch well into his pocket. He picked up his travel bag, hesitated and then turned to tell his employer he previously mentioned the gold discovery to others here, but Sutter had already dipped the quill pen and was entering a notation is his New Helvetia Logbook. Bennett waited a moment more, then shrugged and quickly left.

What Sutter was writing was a brief comment about what had just occurred, as he often did while it was still fresh in mind:

> *Tuesday, Febr'ry 8th 1848*
>
> *Despatched [sic] the Launch for San francisco [sic], Mr. Wilbur Master; Crew Yokmome, Ajeas, Guadalupe, Ensey, Yatchi, Uequele & Omise. Passenger Mr Charles Bennet [sic]*

Within another ten minutes the Sacramento was on her way downstream, carrying not only Bennett but a mailbag containing a letter Sutter had written to his old friend, Mariano Guadalupe Vallejo, former military commander of what used to be called the Northern Frontier District of California, which had encompassed practically the entire northern half of the territory. The letter was almost identical to three others he had written, all of them to be delivered today on horseback: The first to his friend and former chief clerk, John Bidwell, the second to his upstream neighbor who was also a grant holder, Bill Leidesdorf, and the third to one of his closer friends, Henry Leinhard, his Brighton grist mill supervisor.

Despite Sutter's strong pleas to his employees at the lumber mill site to maintain utter secrecy about the gold discovery, his own relatively brief letters to Vallejo, Leidesdorf, Bidwell and Leinhard indiscreetly revealed the essence of what was occurring at the saw-mill site. In the letter to Vallejo he asked his Mexican compadre to keep the matter secret for now, and then wrote in less-than-perfect Spanish, as he always attempted to write to every correspondent in that individual's own language:

> *"Y he hecho undescubrimiento do mina de oro qe sigun hemosesperimentado es extraordinarimente rica."*

He went on to explain in his letters the location of the discovery, exactly what had been found thus far, and the future prospects, certain that none of these friends would betray the confidence with which he was entrusting them. Sutter unfortunately at least partially misjudged the characters of the recipients of his confidences. He also erred in choosing Charles Bennett to be his messenger to the governor.

Too late, Sutter discovered that the now departed Bennett had left in his wake, here at the fort, little groups of men talking in wondering tones about Cap'n Sutter's newly discovered gold mine.

[February 11th, 1848 • Friday]

Dusk was just gathering this evening at Sutter's Fort when teamster Jacob Whitmer finished off-loading from his two wagons the first real cargo of pine planking brought from Sutter's saw-mill at Coloma. He'd seen to the horses, and now he was tired, thirsty, and very glad to be back again where his own comfortable bunk awaited him.

First, though, he headed for the shop where a reasonably well-executed sign with large red letters on a white background proclaimed the establishment to be Chas. Smith & Co., Mercantile. More a fairly well-stocked trading post than anything else, the store was a partnership business owned by Charley Smith and Sam Brannan, but this evening only Smith was on hand, for which Whitmer gave silent thanks, since Brannan was always much more tight-fisted than Smith in trading.

Whitmer knew exactly what he wanted, and he didn't dawdle in the slightest. He did not go to the beer barrel, from which he had often before been able to wheedle a drink on credit. This time he went directly to the shelves and quickly selected a pint bottle of quality brandy and then offered Smith as payment for it, a tiny solid yellow nugget.

"That's gold," he said. "Pure, solid gold. That little chunk there's worth about five or six dollars. The brandy sells for only half that much. Keep the nugget and we'll call it square."

Smith was very reluctant to accept the gold as payment at first, but when Whitmer boasted about what was occurring at the saw-mill site, he began having second thoughts. As Jake related it to him:

"With my wagonload of supplies from here — mostly food goods from Cap'n Sutter, such as a half-barrel of flour, a keg each of pickles in brine and salt salmon, plus a big bundle of venison jerky, an' sacks of dried peas an' wheat an' beans — I reckon I got to the saw-mill 'bout noon, day 'fore yesterday an' unloaded it all at the Wimmer cookhouse cabin. Pete Wimmer was overseein' the Injun boys over by the saw-house, an' Miz Jennie, she tol' me t'store the food supplies in that l'il larder she's got on the back wall. I done like she said an' here she's a-chatterin' away like she does. Gotta admit I warn't listenin' too close, but then I heard her sayin' her oldest boy, Martin, had found a bunch o'gold. 'Course, I laughed at that idea right off, but she said Martin was huntin' for more off an' on 'bout every other day since then."

Jake rambled on and on about it to Smith, telling him how Jennie Wimmer became so sharply nettled at his disbelief of the story and his ridicule of her son that she backed up her account by digging out a box from her trunk and showing him the fairly sizeable collection of small nuggets Martin had picked up since Captain Sutter left to return to his fort. Triumphantly gloating over how Whitmer's eyes widened when he saw them, and confident that her son could easily find more, as he was doing whenever he could find the time to search further, she gave Whitmer a few small pieces.

"An if that ain't pure gold," Jake concluded to Smith, "I'll sure 'nuff eat my hat! Hellfire, Cap'n Sutter's here an' he knows all about it. Dammit, ask him."

Smith knew Jake Whitmer was a braggart and was often careless with facts, but this had the ring of truth to it, and the small nugget the merchant was holding in his hand seemed to be the proof, but he still needed reassurance. His tone of voice was flat when he replied:

"Wait here while I go check with the Captain — and if you touch one drop of that beer or liquor while I'm gone, you'll never get another drop in this store!"

Smith hastened over to Sutter's office and showed him the little nugget and demanded to know if it was the real thing. Sutter became clearly exasperated at first, but he finally shook his head and admitted in a disgruntled tone, "Yes, it's gold, but I want you to keep quiet about it. You tell that to Jake, too, or there'll be hell to pay!"

Smith nodded and returned to his store where he grudgingly conceded that it was indeed gold but that its discovery and source were supposed to be held secret. "Take the brandy and get out of here," he warned, "and if you let the cat out of the bag, Captain Sutter'll skin you sure!"

With news so momentous, however, it was impossible for Whitmer to keep a lid on it. The more he drank, the looser his tongue became, and well before the bottle was emptied, he had rather broadly broadcast the news in increasingly explicit terms. Nor was he the only one; less than an hour later, Smith had given a trustworthy messenger private instructions and sent him on his way at once to San Francisco.

He was off to see Smith's partner, Sam Brannan.

[February 14th, 1848 • Monday]

The military service career of Lt. Col. John Charles Frémont, which he had intended to pursue for his active lifetime, was finished; the court-martial had found him guilty of insubordination and mutiny.

Deliberations, held in Washington, D.C., had not taken very long, once all the witnesses had been heard during December and January. There were many who had appeared to testify for him, including even his father-in-law, powerful U.S. Senator Thomas Hart Benton. All proclaimed him a fine and courageous leader, a fighter for his beliefs, a great explorer whose expeditions had opened the West for Americans, a champion of the people, a very great man. It was clear they spoke from their hearts and with great conviction. There was also a great outcry from the public that he be lauded, not castigated, for his remarkable achievements, and the great majority of major newspapers in the East reflected this general feeling in banner headlines, calling for his complete exoneration.

It wasn't enough.

There were equally those who testified against him and presented the Board of Courts-Martial with irrefutable evidence of his guilt, supporting the grave charges levied against him which had been brought by his erstwhile commander, Brigadier General Stephen W. Kearny. These were witnesses of high rank and unblemished character whose strong, unemotional testimony carried far greater legal weight.

Sentencing was postponed, but it was clear that the very best Frémont could hope for was to be cashiered from the United States Army under the black stigma of dishonorable discharge. The penalty could be worse. Much worse.

At that juncture, James Knox Polk, the President of the United States himself, evidently hoping this would instill friendlier relations with the opposition, personified in Senator Benton, stepped in and offered Frémont a full pardon from all charges and restoration of his rank in the Army. Tempting though the generous offer was, Frémont shook his head and flatly refused.

"I deeply appreciate your support, Mister President," he said, "but I cannot accept. To do so would constitute an admission of guilt and, irrespective of the findings of the court, I do not view myself as guilty of the charges brought against me. I will resign my commission before I allow that to occur."

And so he did.

Frémont's resignation was effective this day, his military career forever ended. Nevertheless, he and Jessie still owned his recently purchased massive Mariposa land grant, and so now he turned his vision to the West, feeling an unshakable conviction that his future would hereafter be intertwined with that of California.

[February 20th, 1848 • Sunday • 6:00 p.m.]

While Henry Bigler could not really understand the apparent apathy of his fellow workers at the lumber mill in regard to the gold discovery, he was pleased that this attitude was giving him the undisturbed time and opportunity to do some prospecting on his own.

For the first few days after Marshall had made his startling announcement to them about it, the workers had shown a certain amount of enthusiasm about searching the mill's tailrace for further nuggets, and a fair number of relatively small ones — rice-grain-size or smaller — had been found. However, as soon they had harvested all the nuggets which were exposed on the surface or wedged in cracks or crevices in the bedrock of the tailrace, their enthusiasm had sharply waned.

Six days later, on January 30th, the first Sunday after the discovery, Bigler had a difficult time finding anyone who would stir himself enough to go prospecting with him beyond the limits of the tailrace. All were evidently pleased with the bits they had recovered, but the prevailing feeling had grown that the gold already found had come from an isolated pocket that had now been worked out and that there was little, if any, remaining. As a result, no one else showed any inclination to expand the search into new areas.

On that Sunday, Bigler was determined to try a different location, and the most logical place seemed to be directly across the South Fork, opposite the saw-mill site. Going out alone, Bigler found the river at this point to be shallow enough that he could wade across, even though his clothing became soaked in the process. On the opposite side the terrain was slightly different, the river lapping at the very base of a steep hill, and Bigler could find few areas where sand or gravel bars had formed in eddies. He found a few very small nuggets, but was largely unrewarded and said nothing of his search to his companions when he returned. In his *journal* that evening he wrote:

> *Jan. 30th: Clear, and has been all the last week. Our mettal [sic] has been tried and proves to be gold. It is thought to be rich. We have picked up more than a hundred dollars' worth this week ...*

During the following week some of the workers continued their labors on improving the race, even while others, under James Marshall's direction, put the saw itself into operation at last and began turning out a quantity of excellent fir planking to the tune of the roar made by the big current-driven saw-blade. All worked very hard and were pleased when the next Sunday's respite came, so they could rest from such labors. All, that is, with the exception of Henry Bigler, who was eager to expand his prospecting more extensively into new areas.

Once again he sought a companion to accompany him, but the only one to show any real interest was 38-year-old Bill Barger, who waded across the river with Bigler, and the two spent the day searching upstream in the small creek that tumbled down the hill and entered the river there. Bigler, more attuned by now with what to look for and where to find it, was very pleased with his own good luck. As he wrote in his *diary* later in the evening:

> *Sunday; Feb. 6th. Today Barger and I visited the Creek opposite to the mill to look for gold. I found $6 [$172.80] worth.*

Barger, on the other hand, found nothing at all and decided he would go on no more of what he described as "foolish gold hunts."

Little of any significance had occurred during the ensuing week as more work was done in the tailrace and more lumber was sawn. On Saturday, February 12th, however, while all the others continued their work at the saw mill, Bigler decided to go off on his own again, avowedly to hunt for ducks, but actually to try prospecting in places he had not reached before. As he later that evening wrote in his *diary*:

> *Feb. 12th. — This afternoon I did not work, being tired and not very well. I took my pan and went down the creek pretending to hunt for ducks, but in reality to look for gold. About half a mile down the creek I discovered some rock on the opposite side that indicated Gold. I took off my shirt and pants, crossed over and soon picked up $21.50 [$619.20] worth lying in the seams of the rock. What is worst of all is that it is on Sutter and Marshall's claim, for after the gold was found in the mill tail, they leased a large scope of land from the Indians, and have sent to the Governor to have it secured. I cannot get a claim on the land.*

Pleased with his day's rewards, Bigler used his same duck hunting pretext the following day and collected another half-ounce in nuggets. He was all but giddy at his good fortune, and even though the work at the mill kept him very busy all week, he was finding it progressively harder keeping the news of his gold discoveries to himself. Finally, unable to contain himself any longer, he found time during the evening on Wednesday, February 15th, to write to three of his Mormon friends — mess-mates and former Mormon Battalion comrades — who were presently working at the Brighton grist mill, Jesse Martin, Israel Evans, and Ephraim Green. He told each that here at the lumber mill site they had found quite a bit of gold, and he elaborated about his own later finds away from the mill, but then added that this was all a secret and asked them not to reveal it to anyone else, or at least to "tell it to those only who could be trusted." Five days later he wrote virtually identical letters to three more of his former Mormon Battalion comrades who were now working at the Brighton grist mill — Levi Fifield, Wilford Hudson, and Sidney Willes.

The latter three replied that they would be coming to the lumber mill in a week or so to visit, which abruptly made Bigler fearful that he would be held at fault for revealing the secret of the gold find. Such fears were needless, since the news of it had already begun spreading, well before Bigler's indiscretion; not only had Sutter himself already announced it to several by mail, teamster Jake Whitmer had also drunkenly broadcast the secret to many at Sutter's Fort. Further, Charles Bennett, before leaving for Monterey, had told a good many others at the fort, and he was, at this very moment, boasting about it to any who would listen at his interim downriver stop at Benicia. He'd paused briefly in Pfister's Store, the principal emporium in that town, and there encountered a group of men who were enthusiastically discussing the recent discovery of coal near Mount Diablo and the possibility of establishing a coal mine near there, which could well become a very valuable asset. Bennett, unable to resist topping their remarks, interrupted loudly:

"Coal! Who cares about coal? I have something here that'll just beat hell out'a coal, an' it'll make this the greatest country in the whole dam' world!"

When the listeners demanded proof of such a claim, Bennett pulled out his pouch filled with gold and passed it around among the men, all the while boasting loudly about the gold discovery. He was more than a little disappointed when most of his listeners responded with persistent incredulity. Even those few who tended to believe him were lackadaisical in their reactions, most of them commenting that they would surely hesitate to invest the fair sum it would cost just to get to Sutter's Fort, much less to some obscure location along a river a considerable distance beyond the fort. Their general skepticism was exasperating to Bennett, but he consoled himself with the thought that before long he'd be arriving in the far more populous city of San Francisco, and he was convinced he'd find a more receptive audience there.

Back at the saw-mill, the edge of trepidation Bigler was experiencing about absenting himself from his job did not prevent him from continuing his own prospecting. And today, fully a mile downstream from the lumber mill, seeking gold once again by himself, he found a number of small nuggets comprising almost another ounce of the gleaming yellow metal. It brought the total weight of the gold he had found thus far in his solitary searches to a quarter-pound, with a value of no less than $32 [$920.60], which was well over half of what any of the privates of the former Mormon Battalion had been paid for their entire year of military service.

Henry Bigler was suddenly very pleased with himself.

[February 20th, 1848 • Sunday • 7:30 p.m.]

Jesse D. Hunter, former commanding officer of Company D in the Mormon Battalion, was one of the many Mormons who, when the Battalion was dissolved, had elected to remain in California. He had also, without notifying his superiors at Great Salt Lake, accepted Governor Mason's appointment of him to the position of Indian Agent at the San Luis Rey Mission and its outlying farm here in California.

Now, at Mason's urging, he was writing a letter to Brigham Young, asking permission to raise a new battalion of Saints here in California and hoping to tempt Young by pointing out that such a body would clearly give the theocratic Mormons military control over the territory. At the same time he could not refrain from expressing his own distinct leanings toward southern California as an ideal place to live, pointing out that this was a choice shared by many other members of the Church who had themselves settled in the San Bernardino region after having seen the Great Basin and experienced its harshness.

With the letter completed, Hunter now read it through a final time. It was immediately clear that the writer had not yet learned that the War with Mexico had ended fully a month ago and that the need for what was being requested was no longer a matter of urgency, as he thought. Hunter's grammar was distinctly faulty, but the letter's glaring lack of literary quality was well offset by its obvious sincerity: he reported to Mormon President Brigham Young and the Mormon hierarchy that he was offering himself and all others whom he could convince to join him, to remain in the U.S. Military Service in the position of occupying and patrolling the California interior — with, of course, Hunter himself as colonel in command.

[February 22nd, 1848 • Tuesday]

Henry Bigler was still strongly afflicted with gold fever, and he continued searching for more at every opportunity, even when the weather was not conducive for doing so. None of his companions were yet aware of the quantity of gold he had already recovered, and his intention was to keep it that way for as long as possible. The weather, however, changed all that today.

Yesterday it had been cloudy and rather cool; Bigler had spent the entire day working in the fields on Marshall's order, harrowing in three acres of peas. Despite the sudden drop in temperature, the fields were alive with wildflowers in bloom, and Bigler, always appreciative of nature, had marveled at their early beauty.

During the night, however, weather conditions had deteriorated considerably and when the Mormon crew arose this morning, they found the ground white with a light covering of snow. With the upper frame of the mill structure scheduled to be installed today, Marshall inspected the saw-mill just after dawn and was concerned with what he found. He strode to the Mormon workers' cabin and was invited in at just about the time they were sitting down to breakfast. At their invitation he joined them, but quickly turned the conversation to the day's work schedule.

"Boys," he said, "it's going to be pretty slippery today and sort'a nasty for trying to put up the frame. I'll leave it up to you — you can work if you see fit, or you can leave it alone."

Alexander Stephens, called Elie by all, was first to respond. "I do believe," he said, "I'll stay in and do some mending and patching on my ol' britches."

Jim Brown nodded. "It's going to be too disagreeable and dangerous to try raising that frame today," he said, "so I think I'll stay in and cook up a mess of peas, since we haven't had any for a good while."

Others, in turn, chimed in with their own reluctant reservations, and it was obvious no one was keen about working on the mill frame today. Bigler, being the only skilled hunter in the group, was last to reply, and he addressed Brown rather than Marshall:

"Brown, if you'll loan me your gun, I reckon I'll go hunting and maybe get us some fresh venison."

Brown shrugged and tilted his head toward the flintlock rifle standing in the corner. "There it is. Take it."

Within minutes Bigler had struck out up the nearby hill supposedly to look for deer, but when he reached the summit just a bit west and south of the mill, he changed his mind, turned, and headed directly for the river. When he reached it, he saw that the South Fork was running high from the rainfall and that it would be tricky to try crossing it, but the urge to hunt for more gold overcame his reluctance to enter the stream. He stripped, bundled his clothes and held them atop his head with one hand and lifted the rifle high with the other and started across.

"Faster than the tailrace," he muttered aloud, "and cold!"

Despite having a difficult time keeping from being swept off his feet, he continued the crossing, the water coming up chest-high with a bite that made him gasp. By the time he reached the opposite shore and put his clothes back on, he was trembling almost uncontrollably, and he decided to strike a fire to warm himself. He gathered up a little pile of tinder and kindling, but his fingers had become so benumbed that he couldn't properly hold the flint and steel. He decided he'd try to start the tinder aflame by snapping the gun's cap-lock close to it, but discovered that somehow, during the crossing, the load got wet, and despite all he tried, he could not set it off. With no choices remaining, he simply danced and stamped about, angry with himself for getting so cold, then even more irked at seeing a few small bits of gold on the windswept bare rock that his malfunctioning fingers could not pick up.

The air had begun warming somewhat, and he gradually danced his way toward the sand bar and adjacent rocks, which were already free of snow. The air grew somewhat warmer, and at times he was enveloped by rain-heavy mists, but his continued prancing finally warmed enough to commence his work. He felt and probed in every crevice without much luck until he neared the water's edge, where he began finding an abundance of specks and tiny nuggets of gold in the sand.

Here he sat hunched over in one position throughout the remainder of the day, uncovering and picking up the gold, grain by grain, nugget by nugget. Most of the pieces were very small, but he did find one bullet-shaped nugget that alone was worth more than $6 [$172.80], and his heart raced at the discovery. He continued his scraping and picking, oblivious to the passage of time. Finally, becoming suddenly aware at how difficult it was to see, he realized that dusk was creeping in and he must call it quits for the day. He had stayed in one position so long, however, that when he rose and straightened himself, he yelled aloud with pain. It felt to him as if his back were broken.

Grunting and groaning with each step, he made his way back upstream along the shoreline, and when he came to the mill dam he couldn't bear the thought of trying to wade the icy waters again. He called aloud for Brown to bring the camp raft across — a clumsy affair of four logs pinned together — and take him back over. By the time this was done, the other men had gathered at the shore, and they wanted to know the answers to their questions: Why hadn't Bigler used the raft to cross the river in the first place this morning? Why he had been gone so long? Where was the game he was supposed to have hunted? Where had he been until so late in the day? Bigler responded to the flood of questions with evasive answers at first, before finally admitting that he had been hunting gold, not game. Then, of course, they wanted to know how successful he'd been, and Bigler responded by leading them to his cabin and showing them the conglomeration of gold pieces that constituted the lump he'd tied into his shirt-tail.

This exhibit of new-found treasure prompted amazed explanations. Bigler called for the camp's scale and, as the home-made balance was brought out and set on the table, he gleefully remarked, "Now we'll weigh the game I actually was hunting."

Bigler's companions were deeply impressed, not only with the amount he had found but by the fact that none of it had come from the tailrace. Stephens volunteered to do the weighing, and they gathered around and watched closely as he carefully put every scrap of the gold on one side of the scale. Bigler recorded the moment in his diary, writing that the gold he had found:

> *...was weighed by Stevens [sic] and declared to be worth $22.50 [$648.00]. This was the first gold they had seen coming from any place outside of the mill-race, and my success in mining filled them with astonishment and pleasure. They were so happy that they repeatedly burst out into loud roars of laughter, and I laughed with them. ...*

The clearly overwhelming factor for them all was that Bigler had found such a quantity by himself in a single day using merely the blade of his pocket-knife. While everyone burbled with excitement, Bigler added another line to his diary entry:

All hands came very near leaving off work to turn our attention to hunting gold.

Despite the small traces of gold they'd all previously found in the tailrace here at the mill, the Mormon crew to this point — with the exception of Bigler — had looked upon that gold discovery as nothing more than an oddity that provided essentially an amusing pastime. Bigler's discoveries on this day, triggered the entire crew's staggering realization that there were fortunes to be made right here in their immediate surroundings. Gold-fever was now belatedly possessing them to the same powerful exent that it had gripped Bigler earlier.

These men had pledged their word to Marshall that they would continue at the job until the mill construction was finished, and they intended to abide by that promise. But the saw was now fully operational; well-cut planking was already being produced; and the remaining work to be done on the saw-mill structure itself was nearly completed. They were determined to finish that structural work as quickly as possible and, as soon as their promise was no longer binding, to begin their own serious searches for the beckoning treasure that they all were now wholly convinced could well transform their lives.

Though still merely in its formative infancy, the California gold rush had just begun.

[February 23rd, 1848 • Wednesday]

Charles Bennett had disembarked in San Francisco from the launch *Sacramento* just after sunrise this morning and had spent the ensuing few hours trying to locate the man who had been recommended to him during his brief stopover in Benicia. The man's name, he'd been told, was Isaac Humphrey, who was reputed to be a former gold miner from the state of Georgia. Bennett reasoned that such a man, could provide the first truly educated opinion about the gold being found at the lumber mill near Coloma.

After following several false leads to incorrect addresses in the city, Bennett finally found his man just before noon. He was a full-bearded individual sitting at a crowded lunch table in a boarding house close to San Francisco's wharf area. Bennett introduced himself to Humphrey and revealed that he was presently on a secret mission to see California's governor in Monterey. Humphrey's listened with flagging interest to Bennett's talk until the man from Sutter's Fort mentioned that gold had been discovered "in the hills," as Bennett put it, and that he wanted to learn more about its true value from an expert.

Bennett's revelation jolted Humphrey to sharp attention, and his gaze narrowed. "Who found gold?" he demanded. "How much and where and when?"

Another man sitting at the lunch table overheard Humphrey's words, glanced at the pair swiftly, and then looked away quickly again before they noted his interest, while remaining sharply attuned to their conversation. His name was Claude Chana, a Frenchman who had done a certain amount of gold-seeking in the past, and the overheard mention of gold had galvanized him, as well as Humphrey, to attention.

Chana had come west by ship, making landfall at San Francisco only a few months earlier, intent on doing some exploratory prospecting in the western mountains, where he had heard there were mercury deposits and possibly silver, as well. What little prospecting he had done here thus far, however, had been singularly unsuccessful. Over the past few weeks he had begun recruiting a small group of comrades who, like himself, were interested in finding mineral deposits, especially silver, that might be exploited. Because the other members of this group were relatively inexperienced with prospecting, Chana had quickly stepped into the leadership role and was beginning preparations to lead them, as soon as the rainy season ended, on a prospecting venture. Small wonder that he had become obsessively interested in the conversation he was now overhearing between the two men at the nearby table.

Chana overheard Bennett telling Humphrey about the saw-mill being constructed by James Marshall in partnership with Captain Sutter. Humphrey nodded and interjected that he'd met that latter gentleman briefly at Sutter's Fort which, he was well aware, was roughly a hundred miles up the Sacramento from San Francisco. Bennett nodded and cautiously responded:

"It was Mr. Marshall who found the gold first, so I've been told, and he found it in a saw-mill tailrace about forty miles farther upstream on the South Fork. I reckon everybody working at that mill's found some of it since, but I don't know how much. I don't know a whole lot about gold, and I just wondered how much the stuff is worth that they're finding."

"I can't answer that just from a description," Humphrey replied, shaking his head. "There's high-grade gold and there's low. I'd have to see it and test it to give an opinion."

Bennett nodded, looked around to make sure he wasn't being overheard, and then reached into his pocket, withdrawing the leather pouch. He continued, his voice lowered almost to the point where Chana could no longer hear it: "This is from there. Take a look and tell me what you think."

Humphrey picked up the bag, hefted its weight briefly, then untied it and poured some of the contents into his hand. His eyes widened and after a moment's study, he carefully poured it back into the pouch and returned it to Bennett. "Come with me," he said. "We'll test it privately in my room."

The pair climbed the stairs and walked down the hallway to the third door, which Humphrey opened with a large skeleton key and then locked it with a deadbolt from inside after they'd entered. Only a moment later, Chana, who had followed them upstairs, slipped quietly to the door and pressed his ear to it.

Inside, while Bennett sat down in a hardback chair and waited patiently, Humphrey dug into his traveling bag for various testing equipment, which he set up quickly on the small table. Then, taking the pouch from Bennett, he shook out a few small nuggets into his hand and began testing them, seeming even to forget Bennett's presence before he had finished his procedures. Finally, as if suddenly coming back into awareness from some distant place, Humphrey shook his head and took a deep breath.

"This is much finer gold than any I've ever seen from Georgia," he said. "Better, in fact, than any I've ever seen from anywhere else." Humphrey now realized that if the mill workers were finding gold like this and recovering it with no tools except a mere knife-blade, the prospects for gold discoveries using panning, sluicing, and rocking technology, procedures which he knew quite well, were nothing short of staggering.

"Worth how much?" Bennett asked eagerly.

Humphrey shrugged. "Back east, probably fifteen-sixteen bucks to the ounce. Here, I don't know. Probably something less than that, but still a good bit."

Bennett made a snap decision. "Will you come with me to Monterey to see the gov'nor and tell him exactly that? Right now, I mean?"

Humphrey, who had already decided not to let Bennett out of his sight until he'd learned everything he could from him about this gold, especially the precise location of the discovery, agreed to do so, adding, "I've got horses in the stable up the street. I presume you can ride?" At Bennett's nod, he grunted. "Good. We'll leave as soon as I pack up a few things."

In the outside hall, Claude Chana quickly drew away from the door where he'd been listening. He'd heard enough to know where he was going to lead his men as soon as their preparations were completed and the rainy season had ended enough for the swollen stream levels to drop and the ground to dry. Since the pair he'd been eavesdropping on were heading for Monterey, he figured he'd have plenty of leeway in time before they could return. He and his men could take their time with preparations, and then along about mid-April, with the ground by then probably travelable and the stream levels having by then subsided, he'd take his own group on what he considered a back trail instead of the principal route from here to the saw-mill at Coloma. With any luck at all, they'd stand a fair chance of finding the gold deposit and of staking out some claims, hopefully without much competition.

[February 25th, 1848 • Friday]

If there was one word in the English lexicon that could correctly describe Samuel Brannan, it surely had to be *opportunistic*. Those precious few who knew him well, could declare with remarkable accuracy that he was a man who had never in his lifetime let any kind of opportunity pass him by. Those equally precious few who felt kindly towards him praised his sharpness in whatever enterprise caught his interest. On the other hand, the virtual legions of those who disliked him, scathingly decried his acquisitiveness, sharply criticized what seemed to them to be his fundamental lack of ethics, and attributed his acuity in business deals to "plain dumb luck." In this vein, one of his acquaintances — some said he was a friend, others declared he was an enemy — at one point remarked, "Sam Brannan could trip and fall headfirst into a barrel of pig shit, and he'd come out with a smile on his face and a silver dollar in his hand that he'd found on the bottom."

Brannan already owned scores of business and residential lots in San Francisco and adjacent areas and was constantly acquiring more, much to the consternation and disapproval of his flock of Saints, many of whom were abjectly appalled by his repacious hunger for wealth and by what they disparagingly termed his "gentile popularity." When they had migrated to California from New York City aboard the ship *Brooklyn*, with young Brannan leading them as their regional elder in the Church of Jesus Christ of Latter Day Saints, he had forced them to sign a document binding themselves to the precept of holding all material things in common; a doctrine which he applied vigorously to them, but not to himself. When disgruntled members harshly criticized Brannon's tyrannical rule and his own growing affluence, he swiftly excommunicated them from the order and cast them out, destitute and friendless.

Brannon's relentless enthusiasm for investment opportunities received a seismic jolt when the messenger from Brannan's business partner, Charley Smith at Sutter's Fort, showed up at Brannan's pretentious mansion in San Francisco with news of the gold discovery at the Sutter-Marshall saw-mill site near Coloma on the American River's South Fork. The messenger had not brought Smith's evidence, a recently discovered nugget, with him, for fear of losing it. Immediately Brannan, with Smith's messenger in tow, took passage on the *Sacramento* on her return trip to the fort, where he conferred with Smith and inspected the small gold nugget his partner had accepted in payment for a drink. Satisfied that it was indeed pure gold, Brannan rented horse and saddle from Sutter and rode the remaining distance to the saw-mill.

Determined to establish a trading post close to that operation, Brannan turned on the charm for which he was noted and chatted affably, first with Marshall, then with the saw-mill's employees, especially Henry Bigler and the Wimmers, Jennie and Peter, and even their son, Martin. Bigler, like his fellow Mormon workers, had of course heard of Brannan previously, since this leader of the Mormon community had established the communal town of New Hope on the San Joaquin River, but he had never before met the man.

Charmed by Brannan's engaging personality, Bigler and his companions soon felt as if they'd known this dapper individual all their lives. Within a couple of hours he had, with unobtrusive skill, drawn from them, as well as from Marshall and the Wimmers, all the pertinent details regarding the discovery of the gold in the mill's tail-race. Indeed when Marshall showed him the crew's collection of gold nuggets, flakes and dust, Brannan's lavish but diplomatic praise inflated the egos of one and all.

It was Henry Bigler who attracted Brannan's special attention. He listened intently to Bigler's account of where and how he had found gold well beyond the confines of the mill-race, and he paid close attention to Bigler's growing conviction that the gold deposit was not just a local phenomenon, but extended in a natural belt far beyond what any of them had initially believed or could even yet imagine Recognizing the enormous economic potential of the discovery stories he had just heard, Brannan became obsessively determined to prosper from them.

On his return to Sutter's Fort, Brannan leased a newer, much larger building from Sutter in order to enlarge the presence of his and Smith's store and their retail goods inventory. He then left Smith to oversee this expansion of their enterprise and then immediately boarded another of Sutter's launches, the *Londressa* and returned to San Francisco. He arrived back home with a plan to call in all his agents, as well as hiring additional ones, to give them detailed instructions, and then to dispatch them to every credible purveyor of supplies and goods in every city and town in California, including distant Los Angeles. His instructions were to buy, without haggling over price, every pot and pan in their inventories, every shovel and spade, every pick and hoe and rake, every large hunting knife and pocketknife, every blanket and every implement that might conceivably be of benefit to a miner.

Brannan grew obsessively certain that when reliable word spread through the general populace about the discovery of gold, word which he was already considering plans to initiate, the news would trigger an unparalleled rush of men to the gold fields to tap what would surely be phenomenal wealth. He felt no real urge to dirty his own hands in a grubby search for gold, but he knew that hundreds, perhaps thousands, would flock to the scene, as soon as the word got out, to mine for their own gold.

No, Samuel Brannan had no intention of becoming a miner and engaging in the messy searching through water and earth for gold, but he had every intention of making his own grand fortune from the discovery through the much more genteel process of mining the miners.

[February 27th, 1848 • Sunday]

James Marshall was becoming more concerned about the future of the saw-mill he had worked so long and hard to establish if now, just when it was up and running in full operation, his crew should suddenly abandon him. With gold clearly beckoning, the likelihood of this occurring was strengthening daily, and Marshall had no plausible idea of how to combat it.

The mill's Mormon employees had lived up to their promise to remain on the job until the saw-mill was fully functioning, but now, with the saw running almost constantly during the daylight hours and excellent pine planking being turned out by the wagonload, what possible incentive could he offer to keep the men working here? Marshall had been reminded, once again, of the difficulty of this problem by what occurred early this morning when John Sutter's whip-sawyer, a Mormon Englishman named James Gregson, stopped by with two friends. Marshall knew him only slightly and his two comrades not at all. Gregson had been working for Sutter for close to half a year at this point, laboriously turning out rough-cut planking that Sutter had been selling at the fort for $30 [$864] a thousand feet. Sutter had, in fact, recommended that Gregson and his friends visit Marshall to see his new current-driven saw and to view the areas from which lumber was being harvested.

Marshall shook his head. "It's Sunday. The men aren't working today. We'll start sawing again first thing tomorrow morning. Still, if you want to see where we've been harvesting a little ways upstream from here, I'll be glad to show you."

Gregson gladly accepted this offer, and the four of them started walking upstream along the bank of the South Fork. Some three miles above the mill, after briefly inspecting two areas where some of the pines had already been harvested, the four encountered a fairly substantial sand and gravel bar with a single large live oak tree growing from its highest point, a foot or more above the high water mark. Almost immediately, as they began walking up the length of the bar, Marshall spied tiny bits and small nuggets of gold trapped in declivities of a projecting rock shelf, and he hoped the three hadn't noticed it. Unfortunately they had, and having already heard rumors at Sutter's Fort of gold having been discovered here, they happily invited Marshall to join them and enthusiastically began collecting the pieces. Giving in to the inevitable, Marshall did so, and the more they searched and the deeper they probed with their knives in the crevices, the more gold they found. Their excitement grew incrementally as the specimens being found became larger in the deeper recesses and along the edges of the live oak's gnarled projecting roots.

The four wound up spending most of this day there on the bar, dislodging the gold with their knife blades, picking it up by hand, and then putting it for safe-keeping into an empty pint-sized, screw-lid jar that Gregson had in his pack. By late afternoon all three visitors were worn out and ready to quit, their jar by this time filled all the way to its brim with what they gleefully estimated as "between two and three pounds" of gold, though none of the nuggets were larger than a small bean. Marshall was clearly not sharing their joy over the unexpected find, his concern having surfaced again as he envisioned what eould surely happen if word of this new find became widespread.

"I'd like the three of you," he said soberly. "right here, right now, to give me your promise that you'll not breathe a word of this find to anyone. You're here and you know where it is, and you can come back again to hunt for more, if you like, but," and now his tone became faintly menacing, "I don't want you breathing one word to anyone else about it. Understood?"

Taken somewhat aback but acknowledging that they understood, the three readily agreed to keep the location secret, but it was Gregson who added, "Maybe we ought'a fix a name t'this place."

Marshall nodded. "Not a bad idea."

"We could call it *Marshall's Bar*," one of Gregson's companions suggested.

The mill-owner shook his head. "No, that wouldn't be right. All of us found it together." His brow furrowed and he lifted his eyes as he thought for a moment. His gaze took in the outspread branches directly above them and he nodded. "All right, let's just call it *Live Oak Bar*."

So they did, but Marshall's concern that word would leak out about their find continued to haunt him. During their return he was mainly silent, lost in his own thoughts; he finally concluded that whatever was going to happen would simply happen, and there wasn't a thing he could do about it at this point; hence, worrying any further about it was useless. Consequently, on reaching the saw-mill again, just as dusk was gathering, Marshall was in a much better frame of mind, although he breathed a sigh of relief as the trio rode off almost immediately, determined to ride through the night in order to reach Sutter's Fort again as soon as possible.

His own workers having finished their labors for the day, Marshall strolled over to the Mormon cabin where he was welcomed heartily by Bigler and the others who had just finished their dinner and were relaxing. They sat and chatted for a while and then, just as nightfall was closing in, three more visitors showed up. These were Henry Bigler's friends from the former Mormon Battalion — Levi Fifield, Wilford Hudson and Sidney Willes. The three had arrived, supposedly, to go on a hunt, their guns in hand and blanket-rolls on their back. Yet, the first thing they did was to ask Marshall's permission to join Bigler in a search for gold in the saw-mill's tailrace tomorrow morning.

It was obvious to Marshall that Bigler had told them about the discovery some time before, a fact which previously would have angered him, but now he merely grinned and winked at Bigler who flushed deeply. Marshall nodded and granted permission and again issued his admonition that, regardless of whether or not they found anything, they tell no one what they had really come here for. The three readily agreed and invited Marshall to join them for their gold-hunt in the morning. He told them he would.

Later in the evening, after Marshall had gone to his own cabin and the others were settled in their bunks for the night, Bigler wrote by dimmed lantern-light in his diary of their own gold-hunting today.

> *Sunday, Feb. 27th. — I took the boys and five of us went to my gold mine, but the river had risen so that the part of it where I got the gold on the 22nd was under water. However, we spent the day hunting in the sand, frequently laying on our bellies, scratching and hunting for it. Five of us got nearly two ounces and of this I picked up more than a third. Barger said I could see gold where there wasn't any. We figured we got $33 [$950.40] worth. The day was warm and pleasant and tonight three men from below (Mormon boys), namely Sidney Willes, Wilford Hudson, and a Mr. Levi Fifield, came with their guns and blankets on their backs and arrived at our shanty to see for themselves about the gold discovery of which I had written to them and to Martin, Green, and Evans. [They said]They had let on to the mill hands below that they were going up to the saw-mill on a visit to see the boys and spend a few days hunting deer. Mr. Marshall happened to be in our house when they came, and as gold was all the talk, Marshall sat until a late hour before he left for his lodging and he was in a first rate good humor as he almost always was, and as usual, a very entertaining companion. Hudson asked him the privilege of prospecting the next morning in the tail-race, which was readily granted.*

[March 2nd, 1848 • Thursday]

Early this morning the main gate to the tailrace at the saw-mill was closed, and about half an hour later James Marshall came down to the now-drained waterway, leading his three Mormon guests. This was the same pattern they had followed for the past three days and, as on the previous mornings, they began following the tail-race again toward where it rejoined the South Fork. They'd located gold on each of the outings but, as Willes put it, "Nothin' to write home about." The largest specimens they found were, for the most part, not much bigger than a pinhead.

Today was different.

The four descended into the drained watercourse and had walked only a short distance when Wilford Hudson gave a loud shout and then crouched and used his long butcher knife to dig a fine nugget out of a crevice. Encouraged, the little group continued down to the end of the race, and they all found several nuggets, the largest only wheat-kernel size, before giving up the hunt and returning to the cabin. Hudson's nice nugget was weighed and found to be worth $6 [$172.80], a result which filled him with delight.

Having become more confident of finding gold on their own, the three guests now thanked Marshall, bade farewell to their friends and, accompanied by Henry Bigler, started back toward the grist mill at Brighton. Bigler had been chosen by Marshall to return with them in order to pick up a few saw supplies he needed that had finally reached Sutter's Fort. The four had hardly gotten out of sight of the mill, however, when they paused to hold a conference.

Still in excitement over the large nugget he had found yesterday, Hudson decided that rather than follow the trail back to the grist mill, he would follow the river, investigating its shores and bars as he went, in the hope of finding new deposits.

"I'm all for that!" Willes said with a laugh. "I'm going with you." He turned to the other pair and added, "How 'bout you fellows?"

Levi Fifield shook his head. "Not me," he said. "Not worth it. Remember, I'm nearly twice as old as you boys, and us old guys need our rest." He barked a short laugh. "I'm heading straight back so I can maybe get a good couple of days of nothing but sleep before starting in with the mill work again."

It was Bigler's turn and he gave a rueful shrug. "Nothing I'd like better than to prospect downstream with you," he said, "but Mr. Marshall needs his stuff for the saw, and I've got to pick it up and get it back to him as soon as possible. I'll have to tag along with Mr. Fifield on the more direct trail."

The four shook hands and separated, Fifield and Bigler striding purposefully down the beaten trail, Willes and Hudson already setting out cross-country on a direct line for the South Fork. It took the latter pair about a quarter-hour to get back to the river, where they turned and began following it downstream. It was a difficult job; often the hills rose abruptly from the water's edge, and in several places they had to detour around driftwood obstructions or large emergent rocks.

By late in the day they had followed the stream's course about halfway to the grist-mill at Brighton when they came to an exceptionally large bar, mostly sand, and separated from the shoreline by a divergent rill from the main riverbed which created a virtual elongated island of the bar. They walked on the bar for a little distance without finding any encouragement and then detoured up a small ravine that had formed in the shoreline about midway down the length of the bar. There they began finding bits of gold, and they concentrated their search in the area for about an hour longer, but found no more than a dozen such grains before continuing their trek toward the mill. With secrecy no longer a key issue, both men were looking forward to telling all their friends and fellow workers at the grist mill about their actually having struck gold, both at the saw mill and in smaller traces earlier today in this little ravine.

Willes admitted to being somewhat discouraged by the small amount they had just found, but Hudson was convinced they must have passed up plenty of areas where a bit more diligent searching might have turned up real pay-dirt. Both men were fairly exhausted when they reached the grist-mill and were met by Fifield and Bigler, the latter having decided to spend the night there and continue to Sutter's Fort in the morning.

The men listened closely to Willes' and Hudson's account of what they'd seen and found along the stream's course, studied their small trove of golden grains found in the small ravine entering the big bar, a location that piqued Bigler's interest considerably, and they tended to agree with Hudson that significantly more might be found in the ravine with a more dedicated search.

They chatted with some of the other men at the grist-mill as they ate an evening meal that had been prepared by Sidney Willes' brother, Ira, who also was very eager to explore further the big bar they had described as soon as possible. As he put it, "There's just got to be gold there, like you fellows found it upstream from there."

Both Sidney and Hudson were less enthusiastic now, and Sidney's response seemed to answer for both of them. "Me, I'm for sleep! You go check it out if you want to, Ira, but I think I've had enough of it for a while."

Later, after the others had turned in for the night, Bigler remained up long enough to note the day's activities in his diary:

> *March 2. Thrsdy. — The visitors remained with us until this morning, When Willis [sic] and Hudson concluded to return back to the flouring mill by following the river and prospect all the way down it. Fifield said he would not go that way but take the road. I accompanied Fifield back, and when all four of us met at the flouring mill the two boys reported that they had found a few particles at one place only. I saw the particles and passed my judgment that there was not to exceed fifty cents worth in very fine particles, so trifling a prospect in their estimation, that they had no notion of examining it any further. But Ephraim Green and Ira Willis [sic], a brother to Sidney, kept coaxing and urging them to go back, and they [said they] would go with them and examine close; it might be rich, said they.*

[March 4th, 1848 • Saturday]

In the former Presidential Palace in Monterey, U. S. Army Lieutenant William Tecumseh Sherman was preparing paperwork, along with his clerk, who was busy at a smaller desk nearby, when two men entered, one clean-shaven, the other heavily bearded, both wearing slickers dripping heavily from the rainfall which had enveloped the region for days. Sherman set aside his pen and the notes he'd been jotting for the governor and nodded his head slightly in greeting as the men stopped before his desk.

"Yes, gentlemen? How may I help you?"

The clean-shaven man nodded. "Name's Bennett. Charley Bennett. From Sutter's Fort. This here," he dipped his head at his companion, "is Mr. Isaac Humphrey, from San Francisco. We come to see the gov'nor."

Sherman's faint smile faded a little. "Governor Mason is presently rather busy," he replied. "May I inquire as to the nature of the business you wish to discuss?"

Bennett shook his head. "It's private. For the gov'nor only, from Captain Sutter hisself, who tol' me not to speak of it. Leastwise," he added hastily, shuffling his feet a bit nervously, "not to nobody else. Only to the gov'nor."

"I see." The lieutenant stood and turned toward a massive inner door decorated in bas relief; a door that was closed. "Please hang your rain gear on the rack there and take a seat. You'll have to excuse me a moment while I check."

He strode to the door, tapped on it twice, briskly, then entered, shutting it behind him. Less than a minute later he returned, leaving the ornate door open. He inclined his head toward the portal. "Colonel Mason—" he quickly corrected himself "— Governor Mason will see you, but requests that you be brief. Please follow me." He showed them in, took a step apart, standing rather stiffly at a quasi-attention until they passed him and then stepped back out and softly shut the door.

The American governor was a big man, but dwarfed by the expanse of the massive desk behind which he was sitting. He nodded and smiled pleasantly, noting that their hands and faces were scrubbed clean and that evidently some attempt had been made to straighten their rumpled clothing. "Gentlemen," he said, indicating a pair of high-backed, plush-covered chairs. "Please be seated. Now, then," he inquired as they sat down, "how may I help you?"

Bennett dug into an inner pocket of his suit and withdrew a disheveled envelope, on the front of which was written *for Gov. Mason only*, and placed it on the desk. Mason picked it up, silently studied it for a moment, and then slit open the sealed top flap and swiftly read the letter, his expression betraying nothing. Then he set it down to one side and returned his attention to the men.

"Captain Sutter states that you have brought with you some samples for my inspection. May I see them, please?"

Bennett dug into his suit's right outer pocket and withdrew the pouch containing the gold nuggets. He leaned across the desk and handed it to the colonel. Mason hefted the bag for a moment and then, untying the drawstring that was wrapped around the neck of the pouch, he spilled the half-dozen small paper packets onto his desktop; then one by one, he opened them and placed the nuggets they contained in a neat row. Their aggregate weight was just over half an ounce. He tipped a couple of them over gently with the tip of the letter-opener and then nodded. One moment, please," he said to the pair as he strode to the door and opened it.

"Lieutenant Sherman," he said, "please come in here."

Sherman did so and stood at respectful attention. "Sir?"

The commander indicated the stones aligned on the desk top.

"What is that?"

Sherman stepped forward and bent over to look at the small stones closely, then extended an index finger toward them. He glanced at his superior officer. "May I, Sir?" At Mason's nod he rolled a couple of them over and then picked up the largest, which he held close to his eyes and turned it over, inspecting it from several angles, then replaced it on the desktop.

"Is it gold?" he asked, then corrected himself quickly. "It's my opinion, governor, that these pebbles are native gold. A very high grade, I'd judge."

Bennett exhaled audibly and a small grin appeared at Humphrey's mouth, but neither of the officers appeared to notice. Mason, still expressionless, asked, "Have you ever actually seen native gold, Lieutenant?"

"Only once before, Sir. In 1844 I was in upper Georgia and there saw some native gold, but it was much finer — by that, I mean smaller — much smaller — than these. At that time it was in phials; some in transparent quills. Nothing of this size, however. If this is gold, it can easily be tested, first by its malleability, and next by acids."

The Colonel nodded. "Feel free to do so."

Sherman nodded and selected the larger piece again, put it between his teeth and bit it. "Density and metallic luster's perfect," he said, then raised his voice and called, "Baden!"

The man who had been at the other desk appeared in the doorway, and Bennett and Humphrey could see now his sergeant's chevrons. "Sir?"

"Please bring me an axe and hatchet from the back yard."

The peculiar request caused the sergeant to raise his eyebrows briefly, but he merely replied, "Yes Sir, right away."

Within three minutes he was back with the requested implements. Sherman took them and as the sergeant left the office, lay the axe flat on a carpet and the large nugget upon the broadest part of its blade. He gave the nugget two sharp raps with the blunt end of the hatchet and the pebble squashed flat without breaking.

Colonel Mason nodded, knowing this proved it to be a pure metal and undoubtedly gold, but he seemed to be unimpressed. Gold, after all, was known to exist to the south at San Fernando and yet was not considered of much value. He picked up Sutter's letter and extended it toward his junior officer. "Read, please."

Sherman read Sutter's comments stating that he was engaged in erecting a saw-mill at Coloma:

> *... some 40 miles up the American River above New Helvetia, for the general benefit of the settlers in that vicinity. I have incurred considerable expense and want a "preemption" to the quarter-section of land on which the mill is located, embracing the tail-race in which this particular gold had been found.*

When Lt. Sherman looked up from the letter, Colonel Mason then continued: "I'd like you to write a reply immediately, Lieutenant, for my signature, and to be entrusted to these two gentlemen, Mr. Bennett and Mr. Humphrey. Explain to Mr. Sutter that California is yet a Mexican province, simply held by us as a conquest; that no laws of the United States yet apply to it, much less the land laws or preemption laws, which can only apply after a public survey. The United States does not recognize the right of Indians to sell or lease their lands to private individuals before the Indian claim has been extinguished. Therefore it is impossible for the government to promise him a title to the land. Inform him that until a treaty of peace with Mexico has actually been concluded, the United States has no right to dispose of — or assign — rights or properties not yet belonging to them in California." He paused and then, with what seemed to be a decided twinkle in his eye, and looking intently at the visitors, he added: "Not for inclusion in the letter, Lieutenant, but Captain Sutter might do well to consider that ancient grim adage, 'He shall take who hath the power, and he shall keep, who can.' As there are no settlements within forty miles of his discovery, and none but his own for another hundred miles beyond that, I suspect he is quite unlikely to be disturbed by trespassers. All right, I guess that's it, then. As soon as you've finished, bring it here for my signature so I can hand it to these gentlemen who brought the gold samples, and they can depart."

Sherman did as instructed, and it was about forty minutes later when Bennett and Humphrey, once again clad in their rain gear and with Governor Mason's letter safely tucked away in Bennett's inner pocket, began preparing to return to Sutter's Fort.

[March 10th, 1848 • Friday]

In Washington, D.C., the United States Senate today ratified the Treaty of Guadalupe Hidalgo, finally and permanently ending all conflict with Mexico, whose dictatorial President Antonio Santa Ana had been permanently exiled to Jamaica.

The Treaty at last confirmed for the United States possession of Texas and California, as well as of the New Mexico Territory southward to the Gila River and then down that river to its merging into the Colorado River, the latter an ambiguous border and one that would have to be clarified at some later date. There were yet territorial and boundary questions of importance that needed to be settled, as well as still unresolved land acquisition matters: Determining whether or not the small, free state of Franklin, which had developed within the state of Ohio between 1843 and 1845, would actually be accorded federally recognized statehood; establishing actual governments for California and New Mexico, where the military governments established by General Stephen W. Kearny continued to function but with intrinsic instability; establishing a government for the Oregon Territory, where now there was none at all; and accepting or rejecting for statehood the vast area west of the Rocky Mountains that Brigham Young had designated as Deseret and for which he wished to see no federal governmental intervention whatsoever.

Young was experiencing his own deep-seated troubles in regard to the funds so many of the Saints in the Mormon Battalion had sent back to Mormon leaders, intended primarily for the support of their dependents. A large portion of these funds had allegedly somehow "disappeared" while in transit to Young in the care of his adopted son, John D. Lee. A number of the Battalion members' wives, now being housed at Winter Quarters, Iowa, grouped together, compared notes, and decided, with rising anger, that they had been bilked of what was rightfully theirs. Their complaint was lodged with Brigham Young himself — specifically alleging that Apostle Andrew Lytle refused to pay Young's adopted son, John D. Lee, $56.76 for the food and clothing Lee claimed to have provided for Lytle's family while the lieutenant was in service — but their expressed grievance had quite an opposite effect to what they had anticipated. Backed by some neighbors, Hannah Lytle denied she had ever received the items. When the matter was taken before a church court, Lee offered to "forgive the debt," but Young became violently incensed. Instead of standing up and coming to the women's defense with an investigation that could have shown how and where the funds had vanished, Young chose to interpret this as an accusation of his adopted son, and refused to let Lee settle.

"I know by the Spirit of God," Brigham Young thundered in court, "that the account was just. There has been no man in this Church that has done as much for the soldier wives and poor widows as Brother Lee has, but for myself. Brother Lee has run and exposed himself enough to wear him out. Those who choose to oppress and sacrifice John D. Lee will go down to Hell!"

Were that not enough, Young then wrote a letter to the Court that fiercely attacked not only the wives of the Mormon Battalion members, but the soldiers themselves, in an eruption of vitriol so intense and unjust that it made many of the dependants suspect Young himself had been behind the disappearance of their rightful funds. In that letter, Young wrote:

> *... I know that the lowest scrapings of Hell were in that Bat [Battalion], not withstanding there was some good men among them. The soldiers wives have lied & Tatled [tattled] about me & Bro. [Albert P.] Rockwood, and Said that we have cheated & wronged them out of their money & thereby Poisoned & soured the feelings of their Husband[s]; in so much that they give way to the Same spirit & commence finding Fault with their Brethren who has [sic] done all they could to Sustain the Soldiers Familys [sic] while their Husbands were gone.*
>
> *Great God! Could women Tramel [trammel] me in this manner? NO! All their council & wisdom (although there are many good women) don't weigh as much with me as the weight of a Fly Tird [turd]. Excuse me for my vulgarity. It is not common for me to use such Language, but I know of no Language to[o] mean to suit the case before us. It is not a woman's place to council her Husband & the moment a man follows a woman he is led astray & will go down to Hell unless he retracts his stepts [steps]. I could have a perfect Hell with my wives were I to listen to them, but when ever one begans [sic] to strut & lead out, I say go it & show your wisdom & soon she gets ashamed and curls [calms] down, but still my [wives] stick to me. I Treat them kindly acording*

> *[sic] to their delicate constitution, but, Elders in Israel, to stir up strife & contention & to try to destroy the influence of Each other and the Peace & Happiness of Families, it is a shame.*

Despite those issues so gravely affecting the Mormons, the United States was now, at last, the unbroken nation President James Knox Polk had striven for it to become; a tightly cemented union of states and territories that cohesively spanned the entire continent, north to south and east to west.

It was a dubiously grand achievement for which the eleventh President of the United States would ever after be blamed and castigated by the very people who benefited most directly from it.

[March 12th, 1848 • Sunday]

The Sutter-Marshall saw-mill on the South Fork of the American River was today, after stringent testing, finally and officially, declared by James Marshall to be complete and operational.

The first two wagonloads of well-cut pine planking had already been sent to Sutter's Fort, since the impressive saw had actually begun running yesterday afternoon after the rainy weather had subsided. In fact, as Henry Bigler wrote about it in his diary:

> *March 11th. — We started the saw-mill this afternoon, and it was a success, and a great surprise to the Indians, one of whom when previously told by Brown that the mill would saw of itself, said it was a lie. He had helped Brown at the whip-saw and knew a saw would not go unless there was a man at the end of it. Now he lay on his belly for two hours watching the saw cut boards much faster than any whip-saw, and finally got up, said it was bueno, and he wanted to learn to manage a saw-mill.*

Marshall, however, wasn't completely satisfied with the operation of the impressive new machine; certain adjustments had to be made, gears tightened, angles trued, axles and shafts greased. The fine-tuning had now been completed, and even though some further deepening of the tailrace would yet have to be completed, the giant saw was finally up and running, seven full months after its construction was first begun, and Marshall made his pronouncement immediately after his thorough inspection of it this morning.

The men who had labored on the mill's construction, primarily former members of the Mormon Battalion, cheered loudly at the announcement, as much with relief and pride at having finally completed a long and difficult job as for the fact that it set them free from their obligations to their employer and to one another. Even as Marshall congratulated them heartily on a job well done and pronounced them free to go or stay, as they chose, a few — Henry Bigler included — were actively planning to become full-time gold prospectors before the day was done. Most, however, had agreed to continue at the mill and work on a part-time basis, if given the unfettered opportunity to hunt for gold on the mill's property during their off-hours. Marshall readily agreed with this arrangement and gave them the entire afternoon off, though still holding them to their promise to maintain secrecy about the gold insofar as outsiders were concerned.

He was wise to do so. Early in the afternoon as a number of the men were just beginning to spread out in the tailrace to search for more nuggets, a stranger on horseback appeared in the distance. Immediately the men turned from their gold-hunting and began bustling busily about the saw-mill itself, giving the appearance, as the newcomer rode up, of being hard at work in clearing the tail-race of rocks, preparing timber to be fed through the big saw.

The rider turned out to be Edward Kemble, editor of Sam Brannan's newspaper, *The California Star*. Having heard what he considered to be wild rumors of a fabulous gold strike occurring at Sutters Saw-Mill, he had come to investigate for himself and to report to his readership. He saw at once that these workmen so busily engaged with their jobs were most certainly not prospecting for gold, as they undoubtedly would have been, had the rumors been even faintly true. After watching their activities for a while, Kemble was joined by Marshall, and the two of them laughed together over the wild goose chase Kemble admitted had brought him here. As he mounted up again to leave, he smiled down at the mill's co-owner.

"Never fear, Mr. Marshall," he chortled. "I will shoot holes in that absurd story of gold having been discovered at this saw-mill and will declare it to be humbug, just as I was sure from the beginning that it would turn out to be."

He touched his hat brim in farewell and cantered off in the direction from which he had arrived. No sooner had he disappeared from sight than the entire crew, laughing and joking, accepted Marshall's thanks and resumed their search for gold nuggets.

Henry Bigler was among the small number who chose to devote themselves, at least for some time to come, to the full-time pursuit of gold elsewhere, before striking out to attach themselves again to their lifetime Mormon obligations under Brigham Young at the order's new and permanent capital and Zion, Salt Lake City. Fundamental logic dictated to Bigler that he commence his prospecting where the gold was sure to be abundant — in the vicinity of the Sutter-Marshall lumber-mill and especially in its tail-race. Still, he reasoned, all that had been recovered thus far was placer gold; gold that had clearly been exposed by erosion from its native lode and gradually forced downstream by the river's current. So where might the mother lode itself be located — and just how rich might it be? Searching much farther upstream for the actual source of that gold, Bigler reasoned, might well be the smartest thing he could possibly do.

Despite being perplexed by conflicting theories as to where impressive of gold might be located, Bigler could not dispel the hunch that had been haunting him ever since he had been rejoined at the Brighton grist-mill by Wilford Hudson and Sidney Willes: His intuitive suspicion that the great sand bar they had discovered in the American River about halfway between the grist-mill and lumber-mill might well turn out to be a treasure trove of placer gold.

He decided that he would head for that spot at once, there to meet those two Mormon companions, along with the horde of other Mormon prospectors he fully expected that pair to have led there from the grist-mill. As Bigler made his way to the sandbar, however, his hopes and expectations for the site's potential began to flag. Perhaps all such enthusiastic speculation was simply illusory, far too rosy to ever be true.

Chapter 2

[March 13th, 1848 • Monday]

Charley Bennett's return to Sutter's Fort of from Monterey today, with a stranger named Isaac Humphrey at his side and a letter from Governor Mason in his pocket, betokened a bad day for John Sutter. He scowled as he read the governor's reasoning for not giving him priority to the land he'd requested along the South Fork on both sides of the river, and became certain that it would not be long, once word spread about the gold discovery, before the fort would be overwhelmed by a hoard of people poking around everywhere.

Now, too, he understood more clearly why Sam Brannan had shown up here so unexpectedly and why he and Smith had obtained a new lease from him and moved their little store into the much larger and more expansive quarters here at the fort. Brannan, the consummate opportunist, had undoubtedly concluded that there'd soon be hundreds of men running around in this area, and he was already taking aggressive steps to profit from it. Sutter believed that the two merchants' move was premature: Word that gold had been found at the mill on the South Fork was already circulating a bit in San Francisco, according to Bennett and Humphrey, but it was generally disbelieved or else, not taken seriously because so little was known about the nature or the extent of the deposits, too little, as Governor Mason had more or less intimated, to justify traveling at least one hundred forty miles just to get to there, propelled only by the vague hope of finding something worthwhile. It was, after all, not uncommon to hear rumors of gold being found here and there, not only in western America, but in Europe and Asia and Africa as well; the recovery of that gold, however, was so complex, and involved so much human labor that the likelihood of anything worthwhile developing from such sites — the South African deposits excepted — was remote at best.

Sutter remembered only too well the time, in 1843, when a French-Canadian named Jean Baptiste Ruelle, who preferred being addressed by his middle name, had come to him with grandiose plans for gold prospecting in the Sierras, because he was quite confident gold could be found there. Ruelle had a good background in gold prospecting, since in addition to having been a trapper and backwoodsman, he was mining in Mexico when gold had been discovered north and east of Los Angeles. He had gone there and studied closely the geologic features of the area where Chico Lopez had discovered gold and reasoned that the same topographic features were prevalent throughout much of the Sierras. At that time he had applied to Sutter to provide him with a grubstake — tools, food and mules, primarily — to prospect for gold, the profits from which, if he were successful, he would split evenly with his benefactor. Sutter had declined without hesitation, deeming Ruelle to be unreliable, but he did hire him as a whip-sawyer to work in the area where Sutter's men were harvesting by hand a relatively small plot of timber about a dozen miles east of Coloma along Weber Creek. Now Baptiste Ruelle had come back and was already approaching Humphrey about helping him to teach inexperienced prospectors the techniques of panning. Though Humphrey initially was quite as suspicious of the man as Sutter had been, he did warily agree to accept his help, at least for a time.

Yet, here was Sam Brannan, who was certainly no dunderhead when it came to exploiting possibilities that others let pass, obviously expecting a substantial influx of people and investing a lot of his time, energy and funds to prepare for their arrival. Sutter had already decided that Brannan was making a big mistake and would suffer for it, but that was his own business; if he wanted to throw away his money on preposterous schemes — and add some funds to Sutter's coffer in the process — then more power to him.

The newcomer, Humphrey, too, was very busy, though in a less public way. He was buying up some of the new planking from Sutter and constructing devices that, although entirely foreign to the fort's owner, Humphrey declared would be very useful in searching for gold in this area, just as they had been when he had searched for the mineral long ago in Georgia. The method called "panning," which he'd already explained to Sutter, seemed interesting and was certainly simple enough to employ, though the fort's owner doubted that he would himself have the time to spare to learn and become sufficiently skilled in the process to pan on his own. Two of the other devices Humphrey proposed to construct, however, seemed as if they'd be ideal for finding gold much more rapidly and efficiently than merely discovering it visually and gouging it out of rocky cracks and crevices with a knife blade, or even than panning for flakes and nuggets.

Assuming, of course, Sutter reflected, that there was sufficient gold to be found in the first place.

The first of Humphrey's projects was to construct what he was calling a "rocker" or "cradle." This, so he informed Sutter, was a device which at first seemed rather complex, but which turned out to be fairly simple. As Humphrey explained it, a wooden hopper was built and set over a sort of canvas apron which emptied into an open rectangular trough about four feet long.

"This trough," Humphrey told him, "is crossed by a series of small cleats that are called riffle bars or, more simply, just riffles, and its legs, so to speak, are rounded like the base of a cradle. When the combination of dirt, sand, and gravel, from an area where gold has been detected — or is at least suspected — is shoveled into the wooden hopper and water is then poured into it and sloshed back and forth, this causes the lighter materials to wash away and forces the heavier gold to settle to the very bottom at the riffle bars where it's easily recovered. And, one of the better things about it," he added, "is that it can be packed from one location to another without too much difficulty."

Sutter seemed on the verge of asking a question, but Humphrey moved quickly on, divining what it would be and answering it. "And yes, it's a little less awkward and tiresome than panning, where you're almost constantly squatting, and it doesn't require as much water, which is damned important in this country where water can be very scarce. Besides which, three or four men can work a rocker as a team and trade off at the various tasks, with the result that it's far less tiring and runs through a helluva lot more material in a day than any miner could possibly get through by panning. The one drawback is that a lot of fine gold gets lost through rocking, much more than occurs with panning, but the quantity you recover through rocking, especially with larger nuggets, more than makes up for it."

The other device which, to Sutter, was far more practical to use, even though much bulkier and heavier, was what the former Georgia miner called a sluice. As Humphrey explained it to him:

"This involves using a long sort of trough-like affair with similar riffles across the bottom, in which gold can be trapped because it's heavier than the other stuff, such as sand and gravel." Confronted by Sutter's blank look, Humphrey elaborated: "The sluice is carefully positioned with a downward tilt in a swift but shallow part of the current. Then the material from the stream's bottom and from likely-looking areas on shore is shoveled into it. If the sluice is properly positioned, the force of the water rushing through it, allows the current to wash away the lighter materials, but the gold, because it's heavier, settles on the bottom of the trough where it gets trapped at the riffles. Sometimes cloth — or, better yet, carpeting material — is laid on the bottom of the sluice, especially near the riffles, so the much smaller gold particles will become caught in the fibers and not get washed out with the other stuff."

Sutter was dubious. "So if that happens, how do you get it out of the carpeting?"

"Well," Humphrey explained, "you let the current carry the bottom stuff through the sluice for a while and then at intervals you pick out whatever nuggets have settled among the riffles. At that point you take out the carpeting and, holding it with the fabric side down, slosh it back and forth in a bucket or tub filled with water. This lets the heavier materials, including the gold, drop free and settle on the bottom. Then all that stuff that has collected this way can be panned for a more careful recovery."

Sutter snorted. "Sounds pretty involved," he said. "And time-consuming."

Humphrey shrugged. "I suppose it is, if you look at it that way, but if you're in a good diggins area, what you'll find makes it worthwhile. I found in north Georgia that it does work very well. I do believe it'll work quite well here, too."

"And if it doesn't?"

"Then that means there's no gold where you're looking and you just pull up stakes and go try it somewhere else."

Sutter shook his head. To him it all sounded very complicated and impractical. The majority of emigrants passing through this area and stopping off at the fort were, so far as he knew, more often farmers or gardeners who were much more interested in what they could grow and harvest than in digging in the ground or in stream bottoms for something that might be there. *Or might not.* He had casually mentioned gold prospecting to his physician friend , Bob Semple, when he'd stopped briefly at Benicia, and Semple had instantly scoffed at the idea.

"I would give more for a good coal mine," he'd said, "than for all the gold mines in the universe!"

Though he didn't actually say so, Sutter was inclined to agree; the whole idea of prospecting on a full-time basis seemed to be a colossal waste of time and energy. There were those, he knew, who would be convinced they could get rich quickly by hunting for gold, but the whole potential of the enterprise was, to him, far less likely to produce a dependable income than the cultivation of grain crops or fruits or, for that matter, raising cattle. Which, he reasoned, was why thus far there had been so little reaction from San Francisco residents to rumors presently being bandied about concerning the discovery of gold; they were less gullible by far than Sutter had believed would be the case, seeming to take to heart the old Spanish proverb, *"No es oro todo que reluce" — all is not gold that glitters*. Even though some of them were taking the account of the gold discovery quite literally, according to Humphrey and Bennett, they remained cagey, reasoning that even though it was gold that had been found, chances were that it was an isolated deposit that would probably never amount to much.

Notwithstanding Humphrey's keen interest and enthusiasm, Sutter was quite sure it would take a good bit more than mere rumors to spark any real sort of interest among the inhabitants to actually look for gold themselves.

No one was more keenly aware of that fact than Sam Brannan.

[March 15th, 1848 • Wednesday]

Today in his Monterey office, Col. Richard Mason received by special courier positive confirmation that the war with Mexico had ended and that the articles of peace, to which Mexico had agreed, were in the process of being ratified by the United States Congress. The gratifying news had taken six weeks to reach him, and it altered or obviated many of the plans or programs that he, as provisional governor of California Territory, had put into motion. Now Col. Mason no longer felt the urgent need to develop a new American defense system in California, and hence, he concluded that recruiting a new Battalion of Mormons to bolster the forces currently under command of Commodore William Shubrick at Mazatlan was no longer necessary.

Mason immediately dictated messages and orders to his subservient commanders gathering forces at different geographical locations, Capt. Jefferson Hunt and Lt. William Warner among them, that the former urgent need for strong military reinforcements in both Alta California and Baja California had now been eliminated and that the role of the occupational Army of the West was now reduced to little more than maintaining the peace. The eighty-one Mormon Battalion members currently under arms in Los Angeles in their new six-month enlistment and the remaining Mormon soldiers at San Diego were to be discharged from the service without delay. This also demolished Hunt's driving ambition to become commanding officer of a new Mormon Battalion, which was unfortunate, but couldn't be helped. The governor explained this to Hunt in a brief personal letter of thanks and regret.

The governor noted as well that Capt. Sutter's expressed hope to keep the gold discovery at the Coloma saw-mill a secret had obviously failed, despite the precautions he had put in effect to muzzle that news. The story broke today in a brief news item that appeared in the weekly *Monterey Californian* newspaper. It stated, in its entirety:

> *GOLD MINE FOUND — In the newly made raceway of the saw-mill recently erected by Captain Sutter on the American fork, gold has been found in considerable quantities. One person brought thirty dollars worth to New Helvetia, that was gathered there in a short time. California no doubt is rich in mineral wealth; great chances here for scientific capitalists. Gold has been found in every part of the country.*

Mason was pleased that this first account was not only inconspicuously buried at the bottom of the back page of the issue, but that the true impact of the discovery was supressed by the reporter's obvious editorializing in the final three lines of the item and by his wildly inaccurate concluding assertion that gold discoveries were widespread. He was convinced that few people who read the account would take the reports of gold discovery seriously, and he was hopeful that Captain Sutter would share his own similarly skeptical evaluation with all who would listen.

As much as Col. Mason was concerned about how the gold discovery might affect California's future, his interest was sparked far more by another more detailed piece in the same issue of the newspaper: A major editorial that dealt with the issue of slavery, which was far from a settled matter where California was concerned and was swiftly becoming, in the United States, an national issue so contentious and civilly divisive that it was clearly threatening to rend the nation in two. The *Californian* editorial was clearly not in favor of allowing slavery to take root in California, yet its bias against blacks was undeniable. It stated:

> *We entertain several reasons why slavery should not be introduced here. First, it is wrong for it to exist anywhere. Second, not a single instance of precedence exists at present in the shape of physical bondage of our fellow man. Third, there is no excuse whatever for its introduction into this country (by virtue of climate or physical conditions). Fourth, Negroes have equal rights to life, liberty, health and happiness with the whites. Fifth, it is every individual's duty, to self and to society, to be occupied in useful employment sufficient to gain self support. Sixth, it would be the greatest calamity that the power of the United States could inflict upon California. Seventh, we desire only a white population in California. Eighth, we left the slave states because we did not like to bring up a family in a miserable, can't-help-one's-self condition. Ninth, in conclusion, we dearly love the 'Union,' but declare our positive preference for an independent condition of California to the establishment of any degree of slavery, or even importation of free blacks.*

The ambiguous nature of the editorial was clear, but the author later took a stance that left little doubt as to California's fundamental feelings in regard to the issue:

> *The majority — four-fifths, we believe — of the inhabitants of California are opposed to slavery. They believe it to be an evil and a wrong . . . and while they would rigidly and faithfully protect the vested rights of the South, they deem it a high moral duty to prevent its extension and aid its extinction by every honorable means.*

Governor Mason, who had given the topic considerable thought previously, was not sure at all whether the issue of slavery, either in California or in the entire United States, could ever be resolved to the satisfaction of everyone.

He doubted it very much.

[March 16th, 1848 • Thursday]

Sidney Willes and Wilford Hudson were quite sure they'd have no trouble in gathering together a substantial number of their fellow Mormons working at the Brighton grist-mill to accompany them on a hunt for gold on the extensive sand and gravel bar they'd discovered a dozen miles up the American River from the mill. The potential, they thought, was sufficient to induce every Saint in the place to want to be included in the party.

They were wrong.

Even though the other workers had looked with mild interest at the specimens of gold the pair had collected, both adjacent to that big bar and another dozen miles or more upstream at the Sutter-Marshall lumber mill on the river's South Fork, they exhibited little enthusiasm for joining the pair in a hunt for more of the nuggets. Like the more distantly located San Franciscans, they, too, were skeptical and apathetic, doubting that the gold really existed in more than a small pocket which would quickly play itself out.

The forty Saints currently employed at the grist-mill were not inclined to leave their reasonably well-paying jobs to look for gold that might or might not be where this pair hoped to find it. Further, their very jobs would be seriously imperiled if they simply left without permission to do so, and there was little likelihood that Cap'n Sutter would condone such behavior. He was a good boss, more than fair in paying their wages, but he was tough as well. The prospect of discovering small quantities of gold was simply outweighed by the risk of losing their jobs. Consequently, only Sidney's younger brother, Ira, and four other men accepted Willes' and Hudson's invitation. After Henry Bigler, journeying from the lumber mill, joined the grist-mill party arriving at the big bar, the entire party numbered only nine.

With the Saints having only their blanket rolls and small quantities of food, plus sheath knives with which to do any digging, the little group was sorely ill-equipped for the kind of searching they were contemplating. They initially planned to spread out across the expansive surface of the big bar, select what each hoped might be a good spot and start digging. If anyone encountered pay-dirt, he was to shout out the news, and the others would immediately converge on the spot to help him dig further.

It didn't turn out quite that way.

Ira Willes was first to encounter gold, tiny nuggets showing up quickly, hardly more than a few inches beneath the surface, and he erupted in a delighted yelp. Almost simultaneously similar calls rose from two other Saints who, at separate locations, were making similar discoveries. Bigler was at the point of joining one of them when he encountered a gleaming nugget the size and shape of a sunflower seed, and he cried out as well and continued digging. Others joined the chorus and very soon everyone in the party was hooting and laughing aloud at what they were finding. The gold, it seemed, was everywhere, varying in size from tiny, barely visible particles that constituted gold dust to nuggets approaching fully an ounce in weight.

The day slipped away from them with lightning speed, so engrossed did they become in their hunting, and in the dusk of early evening they gathered together in a makeshift campsite, all nine of them so overwhelmed with delight over their good fortune that they virtually babbled to one another. They built a cozy little campfire out of the abundant driftwood lodged along the shoreline and munched away at their small, inadequate provisions. Then in the campfire light they again inventoried what each had found during the course of the day.

Although they had no scale to weigh their finds, it was obvious that none of the nine had found less than an ounce or two, and some had gleaned significantly more. Bigler estimated that the total weight of the nuggets he alone had found to be no less than six ounces. Sidney Willes guessed, rather accurately, that he had at least three-quarters of a pound, and his brother, Ira, had very nearly as much. Hudson had found the largest single nugget, a prize about the size and shape of an acorn and weighing, he guessed, well over an ounce.

The growing gold fever epidemic afflicted them all as they fondled their own nuggets and admired those found by the others. In the course of this single day, Wilford Hudson estimated that the individual members of the party, without the aid of even shovels or picks, had collected by hand an average of about five ounces apiece, an aggregate total of no less than 45 ounces — 2.8 pounds of top-quality gold! With the present value of gold in the nation's capital holding steadily at $16 per ounce, the value of this day's collecting alone amounted to a staggering $720 [$20,736].

Sidney Willes, who had a sharp mind for figures, did some quick calculations and then shook his head, amazed at his own deductions and aware of the impact they would have upon the others.

"Boys," he spoke up during a brief lull in the conversation, "figuring it on the basis of what today's wages are back East, which is roughly about five dollars a week, what we've found here during this one day would constitute an average family man's income, ten hours a day, six days a week, for the next twelve years!"

Little wonder these nine Saints babbled among themselves with almost hysterical glee until late into the night. Concluding that this expansive bar as yet had no name, they resolved to give it one.

And so they did. After rejecting numerous suggestions, they finally settled upon a title which from this time forward would surely bring them honor. They named it *Mormon Island*.

[March 25th, 1848 • Saturday]

A group of early Spring emigrants from the east had begun collecting again in western Missouri where its namesake river turned north, all preparing to strike out on the makeshift path that had now become widely known as the Oregon Trail. Aware that from this point on they would be traveling more to the west than to the north, they assembled in camps and towns along the Missouri's left bank, where that great river turned sharply to the north, forming the eastern boundary of the wild Nebraska country. Farther yet along, the river angled more northwestward through the bleak badlands of the region called the Dakotas before continuing westward through Montana country to its headwaters near the border of the barely explored region called the Idaho country. There the Missouri itself was formed by the convergence of several smaller and wilder streams, explored by Lewis and Clark, who named them as the *Gallatin*, the *Beaverhead*, the *Madison*, the *Jefferson*, and the *Big Hole*.

The early-spring emigrants assembled here planned to cross the river and begin the overland trek westward that would take them at least another thousand miles or more. They had arrived at this great northward bend of the Missouri in light canvas-covered wagons, conveyances that were often home-made, but which were far less cumbersome than those being purchased by many fellow emigrants at the large

Pennsylvania wagon-works southwest of Lancaster in the little town of Conestoga, conveyances which were quickly dubbed "Conestoga wagons." The conestogas, for the most part, proved to be much too large, too heavy, and too unwieldy for draft animals to pull on long treks without quickly wearing themselves out; the lighter wagons were much preferred by more experienced drivers.

The emigrants' journey thus far with only their lightly-loaded covered wagons had been reasonably easy; they had traveled westward across Pennsylvania on well established dirt roads to where the Monongahela River from the south and the Allegheny from the north merged at Pittsburgh to form the mighty Ohio River, and then stopped to purchase more supplies. From here the journey involved a paid passage by steamship, with their supply-crammed wagons aboard and their livestock crowded into tightly filled pens, down the thousand-mile stretch of the Ohio River to the Mississippi, and then up that great muddy stream another 250 miles to St. Louis — the final seat, so they'd been told, of genteel society. From that point they journeyed westward aboard another steamship up the turbulent Missouri to this great bend where finally they were forced to stop and camp, because it was still too early in the season to start their long trek across the vast prairie country. Ahead of them in those treeless plains were last year's buffalo grasses, withered, dry, and woefully unfit for livestock to graze upon, while this year's growth had not yet sprouted enough to sustain the horses, mules, oxen and other ruminating livestock accompanying the westward-bound emigrants.

The assembling horde gathered in camps at or near such western Missouri frontier towns as Independence and Westport and St. Joseph, and sometimes even farther north near Council Bluffs, Iowa; but it was bustling Independence that attracted most of the travelers, and now the emigrants had little choice but to wait for the weather to warm, the grasses to grow, and the mud from the winter's snows to dry enough to no longer impede them.

The camps and villages and communities where they waited on the weather became raucous frontier boomtowns, all of them vying strongly with one another to become the foremost gathering point for such a journey. The merchants, the trades-people, and those providing varieties of services could not help but profit significantly in selling, at outrageously elevated prices, whatever remaining supply of foods, clothing, tools, ammunition or other gear the travelers felt they still required to sustain them on the looming months-long journey. With the emigrants clearly dependent upon whatever last-minute supplies they could buy here, a fierce and often unscrupulous competition developed among the merchants to undermine one another, even to the point of hiring agents to ride east to meet westbound travelers and to bad-mouth in any way possible, not only such competitors but even the very communities in which they were established.

As emigrant William Rothwell of Chicago wrote, while still a day's journey away:

> *I have never in my entire life heard as many false statements as were told us in coming up here. We were frequently told that at least 15 to 20 cases of cholera were dying daily at St. Joseph.*

In reality, not one single fatality from cholera had been recorded thus far at St. Joseph.

Another traveler who camped at Independence and was eagerly awaiting the first opportunity to head out into the western unknown was a twenty-five-year-old writer from Boston, Massachusetts named Francis Parkman, who was determined to write an account of his western experiences. In his *journal* now he wrote:

> *A multitude of shops have sprung up to furnish emigrants with necessaries for the journey still ahead. The streets are thronged with men, horses and mules. There is an incessant hammering and banging from a dozen blacksmiths' sheds, where the heavy wagons are being repaired and the horses and oxen shod. While I was in the town, a train of emigrant wagons from Illinois passed through — a multitude of healthy children's faces were peeking out from under the covers of the wagons.*

The majority of the emigrants had reached this point by having traveled alone or in small groups of families or neighbors from their eastern points of origin. Now, however, they were gradually becoming aware of the need, for their own protection, to unite into large trains of wagons in which, when the need arose as surely it would, they could help others or themselves be helped. They truly believed, as they waited for conditions to become "right" beyond this point, that they were heading for a distant, freer place called Oregon Territory; a place where it was rumored their lives would be less controlled by the constraints of society and local governments; a place where they could have the opportunity to start their lives anew; a place where, they were assured, they could claim extensive acreage of their own merely by living upon it and improving it in some manner.

Assuming, of course, they survived the journey.

All were reasonably aware that there were numerous pitfalls ahead and that the great trek would become progressively more difficult the farther west they traveled. The closer they came to the Rocky Mountains, and then even beyond, the greater the peril would become, so they had been advised; but even their cautious awareness of it here scarcely prepared them for the actual dangers they would soon have to face. The unwritten code of a journey such as lay before them boiled down to essentially two alternatives: Either they would, through their own strength and tenacity and perseverance, overcome whatever difficulties lay ahead, or else they would fail, more often than not through misfortune generated by their own weaknesses — ignorance or outright stupidity, greed and bullheadedness — and their bones would be left to bleach unheralded in some unnamed prairie or canyon or desert beneath a merciless sun.

It seemed, however, that this year a significant portion of those who were poised to set off on the Oregon Trail would not make it to the far northwest. They were likely to be distracted from their original pursuit, though not necessarily because of accidents or injuries. While it hadn't yet occurred, word of California's gold discovery, once it began to spread more rapidly and more widely, surely could not be very long in reaching these emigrants bound for Oregon Territory, and wouldn't they be inclined to change their course and angle farther southward to central California Territory? After that, perhaps even the heavily populated cities of the East would eventually learn of the discovery of gold in California. How would they get the news? If word of it actually did reach them, why would they believe it, when even most of the Mormon workers only a few miles away at Sutter's grist-mill scoffed at the discovery, either not believing it at all or, if they did, convinced it could be nothing more than an isolated and very limited deposit?

Everything, it seemed, was balanced on a premise of *ifs*. If the news really did finally reach the East and *if* some unfathomable occurrence transpired to actually make them believe such accounts, and if not only the United States, but the rest of the world actually believed a major gold discovery was occurring in California, what might happen then?

Who could possibly predict for certain?

[March 31st, 1848 • Friday]

During the fortnight that had elapsed since the nine Mormons had made their discovery of placer gold in the extensive stretch of sand and gravel that they had named *Mormon Island*, much had occurred but, essentially, only on a peculiarly local level.

As soon as that little group returned downstream on the American River to the grist-mill at Brighton, word of their remarkable discovery of gold flashed through the mill's workforce with considerable impact. Virtually all the mill's workers, primarily Saints discharged from the former Mormon Battalion, had gathered about excitedly to view with considerable awe the significant amount of gold in nuggets and flakes and dust that their comrades had collected. They were utterly flabbergasted to learn that the nine had, in a single day, found $720 [$20,736] worth of the precious mineral, and now the less adventurous Mormons mentally scolded themselves for their earlier skepticism and caution. Before the day ended, clusters of men had turned their backs on their tasks at the grist-mill and hurried to *Mormon Island* to see if they, too, could reap such great fortune.

They did. They set up camps, and upwards of forty men spread themselves out over the big bar, gleefully claiming spots for themselves and set to work with their only tools — pocketknives, skinning and tanning knives, butcher knives, even ordinary table knives. They dug feverishly into the loose material of the bar and within mere minutes a veritable chorus of their exultant cries filled the air as they encountered the same sort of success their nine companions had enjoyed earlier. They yearned for more appropriate tools for the job, picks and shovels, to delve deeper, faster. The amount of gold they found was staggering, many times over what the original nine had recovered, though no accurate accounting of it all was made just then. Even when darkness closed in and forced them to quit for the day, their enthusiasm didn't flag; they laughed uproariously and talked excitedly far into the night, hardly able to believe their incredibly good fortune.

Within days each man began cutting stakes from the branches of trees and marking off the corners of an area he could reasonably work and then claiming it as his own. Some, leaving their "claims" in the guardianship of others, reluctantly left the bar and hastily returned to the grist-mill for better equipment, but the tools they needed and wanted were few, and soon parties of them were moving out and continuing downstream along the American to six-mile-distant Sutter's Fort to buy from Charles Smith & Co. the supplies so necessary.

They were available — for a price; an extraordinarily steep price.

Some of Sam Brannan's agents sent out earlier had already returned with full wagonloads of goods, and more were coming all the time. What they had themselves bought for a song from purveyors was now marked up to an exorbitant price. The novice Mormon miners grumbled, but, on the whole they didn't really care that much; gold was being accepted in lieu of cash money, and gold they now had in abundance. Sam Brannan's foresight in buying up existing tools, equipment and supplies, which his agents were still engaged in doing, made such goods unavailable anywhere else, thereby creating for Brannan a monopoly and leaving customers with no alternatives: They could either pay the grossly inflated prices demanded at the store owned by Smith and Brannan or do without, and the harsh truth was, they simply could not afford to do without. According to Brannan agents' preliminary accounting, thus far they had purchased 1,800 pans for fifteen cents [$4.32] apiece, for a total cost of $270 [$7,776], and Brannan had now re-priced them for sale at $20 [$576] each — an incredible profit-margin calculated bring $36,000 [$1,036,800] into his coffers — a profit he was quite confident he would earn. That was, moreover, only one item among a multitude of others Brannan's agents had gathered up for him to sell.

The California Star in San Francisco, under Edward Kemble's direction, continued resolutely to ignore the gradually increasing reports drifting in about the gold discovery, content instead to present statistics on the town's population growth: San Francisco's non-native population was now 812, including 575 males, 177 females and 60 children. The gold story continued to haunt, the Star's readers, however and when their clamor for information could no longer be ignored, Editor Kemble finally gave in and wrote a brief piece, to the effect that gold had indeed been found some forty miles above Sutter's Fort. Kemble's report troubled him, however, and in the next issue he could not restrain himself from superciliously proclaiming the gold discovery reports to be ". . .all sham — a supurb [sic] take-in, as was ever got up to guzzle the gullible ." Kemble added, with not-so-subtle sarcasm:

> *A good move it would be for all property holders in the place, who have no very settled purpose of improving the town, and distant idea of rare chances at speculation, to employ upon their unoccupied lands some few of our liquor-house idlers, and in the process of ploughing, harrowing, hoeing, and planting it is not idle to believe some hidden treasures would be brought out. Some silver mines are wanted in this vicinity, could they be had without experiencing the ill effects following in the train of their discovery. Monterey, our capital, rests on a bed of quicksilver, so say the cute and knowing. We say if we can discover ourselves upon a bed of silver we, for our single self, shall straightaway throw up the pen and cry aloud with Hood: "A pickaxe or a spade!" . . .So great is the quantity of gold taken from the mine recently found at [above] New Helvetia that it has become an article of traffic in that vicinity.*

Thus far the majority of San Francisco's population seemed to agree with the newspaper's editorial stance and remained highly skeptical of the sketchy reports of gold having been discovered. Nevertheless, it was becoming progressively difficult to slough off those gradually increasing reports, especially when, only three days after Kemble's sarcastic comments, a Mormon visitor from Sutter's Fort arrived in San Francisco and bought voluminous supplies from outlets other than Brannan's, paying for them in pure gold, which the merchants, uninformed, as was everyone else, of the exact current value of gold in the East, bargained for at the rate of $8 [$230.40] per ounce, only half its true value, an offer which the miners gladly accepted.

While other communities in California more distant from the gold discovery than Sutter's Fort almost universally believed the stance taken by Kemble that the entire discovery was all humbug, one San Franciscan most assuredly did not. That single exception was Sam Brannan who, through his own investigation, knew better and had swiftly acted upon that knowledge.

Meanwhile a significant controversy was developing among those few men actively pursuing gold near Sutter's sawmill and his grist-mill: Would the discovery sites in the area soon be exhausted or were the early finds here the first indications of a widespread deposit? Henry Bigler was convinced that there were vast amounts of gold yet to be found, as did a small scattering of others who began drifting in from Sutter's Fort and other areas in the Sacramento Valley, including Sutter's former chief clerk, John Bidwell, who had first come to California from Chautauqua, New York, in 1841. Since then, in addition to becoming Sutter's right hand man, he had been conspicuous as a soldier and landowner. Now he was dabbling in prospecting and, upon inspecting Mormon Island closely, he became convinced it differed very little from the bars that occurred abundantly in the Yuba and Feather River valleys where he had only recently relocated. He headed north and prospected for a short while on the Feather River at a location being referred to as Hamilton Bend, where he found a little "color." That was encouraging, but the deposit seemed too limited to satisfy him.

Continuing upstream Bidwell and his party had quickly explored along the Middle Fork Feather River near its convergence with the North Fork. There they found sand and gravel bars which, while not so extensive, were almost identical in composition to the gigantic Mormon Island. Close inspection of adjacent ravines and outcroppings turned up impressive specimens of gold, and when Bidwell dug in one of the larger bars, he encountered nuggets, flakes and dust in very nearly the same abundance as the Mormon party had encountered earlier on Mormon Island. He lost no time in staking out the site and claiming it under the name of *Bidwell Bar*.

Another new gold site discovered considerably farther north was located at about this same time by former Army Major Pierson B. Reading, who had some time before acquired a land grant, much as Sutter had, but some 200 miles up the Sacramento River from Sutter's Fort near a tributary called Clear Creek. Hearing rumors of the gold strike, Reading visited the Sutter-Marshall saw-mill, and after inspecting the tail-race and the gold that had been extracted from it, he was deeply impressed. Like Bidwell, he believed that the sand and gravel bars on his own grant did not differ discernibly from these on the South Fork. On his way back upstream, Reading paused to check out Clear Creek and quickly found placer gold in a bar which he immediately named *Readings Bar*. As with Bidwell Bar, its treasure was not so abundant as that of Mormon Island, but nevertheless yielded good quality gold. Equally important, it added credibility to the growing belief that the gold belt in California was far more extensive than anyone had previously imagined.

The conclusion was inescapable: The placer gold deposits were clearly not confined to one locality. Virtually every stream bed, in what was evidently still an undetermined (but greatly underestimated) range extending to the north was proving itself to be richly auriferous.

There was evidence of gold present far to the south as well. A party of four miners named Swain, Harris, Loveland and Curtis, along with four other men, were prospecting about March 18th in the low mountains some 15 miles south of the Merced River and discovered substantial gold in the vicinity of what was dubbed Burns Diggings. Before they were able to profit much from their discovery, however, they were attacked by a large number of Indians who drove them out, seriously wounding two of the miners in the process.

Henry Bigler had by no means been idle. As he recorded in his *diary*:

> *Sunday, March 19th — All hands hunted for gold. I was the luckiest one and found $31 [$892,80]. Last week we completed the tail-race and the saw did much better.*

Even John Sutter was not immune to the lure of gold. Succumbing to the temptation of mining for himself, he left Sutter's Fort and headed for the mines during the latter half of March with a procession of supply wagons well-filled with provisions, accompanied by 100 of his Indian workers and 50 of his Hawaiian Kanakas. They found little gold, however, and, disgruntled, he soon returned to his fort to tend to other matters. His departure, however, had set into motion a series of employee desertions which continued to escalate even after his return, leaving him sorely short of manpower for the work needing to be done. As he wrote of it in his *diary*:

> *The first party of Mormons employed by me left for washing and digging Gold and very soon all followed, and left me only the sick and lame behind. And at this time I could say that everybody left me, from the Clerk to the Cook; what for great Damages I am suffering in my tannery, which was just doing a profitable and extensive business, and the [tanning] Vatts was [sic] left filled and a quantity of half finished leather was spoiled, likewise a large quantity of raw*

> *hides collected by the farmers and of my own killing. The same thing is in every branch of business which I am carrying on at this time. I began to harvest my wheat, while others are digging and washing Gold, but even the Indians can not be kept longer at Work. They were impatient to run to the mines, and other Indians have informed them of the Gold and its Value; and so I have had to leave more as [than] ⅔ of my harvest in the fields. Looms are left with work begun but undone, crops and livestock are left unattended. Blacksmiths, carpenters, weavers, agriculturists, etc. head out and soon the fort is all but abandoned. Wages and prices for food and supplies reach absurd levels.*

The New York Volunteers presently stationed at Sutter's Fort were no more immune to gold fever than the Indians and Mormons, and now they, too, abandoned their duties and deserted to the mining areas. The steadfast few who remained at the fort were soon disbanded and discharged, and they quickly joined the hunt for gold. Captain Sutter darkly threatened to shoot them if they were rash enough to hunt gold on his property without permission, which he was increasingly less willing to grant, and so, since gold discoveries were being rumored in other areas, the men simply set off to do their own prospecting elsewhere.

When a team of three of Sutter's men — Perry McCoon, John Sheldon and William Daylor — prospected during the third week of March in the stream dubbed Weber Creek, several miles south of the lumber mill, they found good gold in quantity, but in bars significantly smaller than those near the mill site or at *Mormon Island*. An Indian in Sutter's employ searched farther upstream on Weber and, where the creek was formed by the convergence of the north and east branches, he followed the north branch upstream until he was about two miles above the Weber Creek diggings. There he found what was soon recognized as the third most important deposit, exceeded only by those at the Sutter-Marshall saw-mill site and at the Mormon Island diggings. Soon he was joined by a number of other Indians who collected remarkable amounts of the metallic yellow pebbles and traded them to the whites for insignificant quantities of food and clothing.

Impelled by curiosity over where the natives were finding such gold, a prospector named Patrick Kelsey followed them one day up the small branch and discovered amazingly abundant gold deposits. He quickly found a small fortune in gold in the bars, ravines and gulches of the area and, for some inexplicable reason, named the place *Old Dry Diggings*. The quantity of the gold found there and in several locations nearby , seemed limited only by the smaller size of the bars.

On March 22nd the first truly commercial shipment of nicely sawn planking from the lumber mill reached Sutter's Fort. It was an impressive load, and John Sutter would indeed have been very pleased with it, except for one drawback. The men whose job it would have been to unload and stack the lumber were all gone. There it remained in the wagon until later in the day when Sutter was finally able to browbeat several of his few remaining Indians to unload it. No sooner was the task completed than those Indians, too, disappeared. As Sutter looked about the anger that had risen in him drained away, and he slumped both physically and mentally. Piles of raw cow hides, his most precious product, were quickly becoming valueless, drawing swarms of flies and like those left in the tanning vats, would begin to rot if left unattended much longer.The defection of his workers, whites and Indians alike, seemed clearly to spell the doom of this enterprise and others, and there was simply no way he could stop it.

In the midst of all this, the issue of slavery, which was becoming so disruptive in the Eastern and Southern portions of the United States, was clearly making itself felt here in California. On March 25th Edward Kemble's editorial in the *California Star* made it clear in which direction he was encouraging the populace to lean. He wrote:

> *While we seriously entertain these views and value the union with the United States as highly as we should, the simple recognition of slavery here would be looked upon as a greater misfortune to the territory than though California had remained in its former state, or were at the present crisis, abandoned to its fate. We believe, though slavery could not be generally introduced, that its recognition would blast the prospects of the country. It would make it disreputable for the white man to labor for his bread, and it would thus drive off to other homes the only class of emigrants California wishes to see, the sober and industrious middle-class of society. We would, therefore, on the part of 90 per cent of the population of this country, most solemnly protest against the*

introducing of this blight upon the prosperity of the home of our adoption. We should look upon it as an unnecessary moral, intellectual and social curse to ourselves and posterity.

In California's interior, however, the men's dominant preoccupation was with gold, not slavery. On March 26, all remaining workers at the saw-mill hunted for gold and not surprisingly, Henry Bigler was the most successful. As he jotted in his *diary* for this date:

> *... All hands hunted for gold. I found six dollars [$172.80] worth.*

Rarely a day passed lately when Bigler didn't find at least an ounce or two of the gleaming yellow metal. His companions viewed Bigler's consistent good fortune with a mixture of approval and envy as they strove to emulate his success.

Goldseekers they were, and the farther they searched, the broader and longer this amazingly large gold field in California seemed to be. Just yesterday, March 30th, another group of the Saints who had abandoned Sutter's grist-mill and were extending their prospecting farther away from the early discovery sites, found a relatively rich placer more than 60 miles south, which they named *Mormon Gulch.* As delighted as the Saints were with the gold they were accumulating, there was one exasperating fly in the ointment.

It's name was Samuel Brannan.

Only the day before yesterday, Brannan had written a lengthy letter to Brigham Young, advising him of all that was occurring in California, subtly exalting himself and putting down others. He made no mention of his business partnership with Charles Smith, nor of his purchase of every container, tool or garment his agents could locate in the region, the sale of which, at phenomenally escalated prices, he was convinced would undoubtedly net him a considerable fortune. Nor did he mention the growing sense of apostasy that had been filling him of late. What he did write was a discourse predicated on his keen awareness that sooner or later his own rapacious graft and greed would be reported, and so he made a calculated, self-aggrandizing, and sanctimonious apology for whatever wrongs his detractors may have attributed to him. In part he wrote:

The wide distance that separates us at present and the peculiar circumstances under which I am at this time situated, occasions very peculiar feelings to rise in my heart, knowing fully the responsibility resting upon me, and my acts during my tarry here. That I am a man of errors, I most sincerely acknowledge; but with all my errors, I hope and trust they have not brought reproach upon the high and holy cause which I have had the pleasure to represent. . . .That I shall have many calumniators arising from jealousy and misrepresentation I am fully confident. But from my unbounded confidence in the known integrity and disposition to give justice to all men, especially to the household of faith, in yourself and council, I do not give myself any alarm — putting my trust in the "God of Israel" the great architect and director of His Kingdom on earth. . . . For myself, I note that I have labored under many disadvantages, from not having received my endowment; ambition on the part of those who have received it, disputing my Priesthood and joining their influence with the slanderer, in order to strengthen their own influence and exalt themselves. ...

Brannan went on at length to express his mistrust of such members of his flock as "Brother James Ferguson, formerly a sergeant-major of the Battalion," and of his own desire to erect a suitable "convention house" or meeting-place in order that all members of the region might hear the preached word. Yet at the same time he accused the Brethren under him of conducting a house-to-house "whispering campaign" against his initiative in the matter, stating that "they" were claiming his intention was to use such convention house facilities only to promote his own standing with the people of San Francisco. He concluded his diatribe by writing:

I long for the day when men will know their own place and keep it.

Heartily disinclined to wash gravels and sands or dig in the earth, Brannan was still very taken by the idea of acquiring gold and now, with that letter to his grand superior well out of the way, today he put into effect a little plan he'd worked out to bilk the prospecting Saints of a share of the gold they were finding.

Appearing at *Mormon Island* nattily clad in his crisp, clean black suit and derby hat, he assembled the men and announced to them with solemn demeanor:

"As President of the California Mormons, it is my bounden duty to collect tithes for the Church. Each Saint's share — at the risk of excommunication if he attempts to turn his back to this grave responsibility — is to be ten per cent of whatever gold he has already recovered or that he may recover in the future."

The Saints grumbled and groused about it, but they grudgingly accepted the edict, and Brannan scheduled weekly visits to the area to make such collections, rapaciously eager to do the same, if possible, with the Saints at the Sutter-Marshall saw-mill and other locations where they were working. He had brought along with him this day a wide-mouthed, pint-sized jar into which the tithes would be dropped. As each miner dutifully contributed his share, Brannan inwardly gloated at the mounting revenue he was collecting, which he had absolutely no intention of sharing with the Church.

In total for this first "offering," his jar became more than half-filled with gold — easily in excess of two pounds — which amounted to far more than any individual miner had yet accumulated. Without weighing it, at least not until he could do so in strict privacy, Brannan estimated he had collected just from the three dozen or more miners here at Mormon Island on this one day alone, gold valued at no less than $2,600 [$74,880].

As Brannan received the tithes from the prospecting brethren, he suppressed his jubilation, not only over this day's "take," but over the incredible wealth his future tithing collections from all of the area faithful promised to create for him. One factor stood out today with startling clarity: Whether he acknowledged it to himself or not, this day marked the true commencement of Samuel Brannan's apostasy.

[April 1st, 1848 • Saturday]

To date no adequate governmental installation had yet been established along the Platte River portion of the Oregon Trail to aid and protect the many Americans who had begun migrating to the West. Construction was begun today, however, on a substantial fortification that would provide those benefits. The site chosen was situated on the south side of the Platte River at the head of that stream's enormous Grand Island. A large construction crew for the task had been fitted out at Fort Kearny on the Missouri River at Table Creek, and plans were to abandon this fort soon, because it was now inadequately constructed and unsuitably located for most of the Oregon-bound travelers.

A construction crew of consisting of 175 men, recruited primarily from the Missouri Volunteers, left the fort today and soon would be employed in brick-making, molding adobe structures, harvesting the necessary timbers, and then cutting them at the on-site saw-mill that was to be erected. The men would also be involved in all the necessary carpentry work and the cutting and laying of sod both within and outside the fort's walls. The fort itself was to be laid out in a regular square, with the inside buildings, shaded by cottonwood trees, lining a parade ground fully four acres in area. A tall flagstaff set in stonework was to be placed in the exact center.

The entire operation was headed by Colonel L. E. Powell, but the construction work itself, scheduled to be completed before the year's end, was to be overseen by Lt. Daniel P. Woodbury of the U.S. Corps of Engineers. Woodbury immediately decided to name the new fort after his father-in-law, Col. Thomas Chiles, who had gained renown for his courage and sagacity during the War with Mexico. The name *Fort Chiles* did not, however, find favor at the U.S. War Department in Washington, which decided that the new fortification should have the same name as the inadequate, abandoned one on the Missouri that was being razed.

Therefore, the War Department order directed unequivocally that, in honor of Brigadier General Stephen W. Kearny, the new installation, too, should be known as *Fort Kearny*.

[April 7, 1848 • Friday]

Sam Brannan was visiting the gold-producing sites again, but this time with a new endeavor in mind which, he was sure, would in time fill his own coffers with markedly increased income.

A major project he had conceived during this past week was one he hoped would quickly encourage a new flood of emigrants in the east to head for California and its gold deposits. Numerous citizens of San Francisco, a town now growing prodigiously, were now beginning to take the news of gold discovery seriously, and a number of them were already heading for the gold fields or planning to do so. Skepticism was still pervasive, and the majority remained content to continue toiling in their jobs. Among these were two former Mormon Battalion members who had gone into partnership and formed a brick-making firm in the town. Zacheus Chaney and James Bailey built a substantial kiln and began turning out quality bricks in such numbers that they expected to have no less than 50,000 of them available for sale by June. In addition, their business was already expanding to include the production of roofing tiles, as well as ballast blocks for the increasing number of commercial sailing ships making dockage here.

Another of San Francisco's newer and more ambitious arrivals was a Yale University graduate named Thomas Douglas, who had arrived only recently from Honolulu, where he had been headmaster of the Young Chief's School. From the moment of his arrival in town, he was intent upon establishing the community's first public school, which he did without delay, determined not to be sidetracked by the growing rumors of gold having been discovered in the mountains to the east. A highly gifted and versatile man, described by some as "a one-man university," he quickly recruited an enrollment of 37 students for his classes and, being paid a salary of $1,000 [$28,800], personally gave instructions in reading, writing, spelling, geography, arithmetic, grammar, composition, history (both ancient and modern) astronomy, chemistry, geometry, trigonometry, algebra, navigation, surveying, mental and moral science, natural philosophy, and he topped it all off with both primary and advanced language classes in Greek and Latin.

Probably no individual in San Francisco, however, had more irons in the fire or was more successful in his dealings than Samuel Brannan. It was decidedly to his advantage that he had arrived here two years earlier as the leader of more than 200 Saints from the New York City vicinity and that he had forthwith established their New Hope community southeast of the bay along the San Joaquin River, but his success had to be attributed to far more than that. His all-consuming ambition and business acumen had already transformed him into one of San Francisco's leading businessmen, and he now owned or had major interests in a variety of enterprises that included real estate holdings, a hotel, the *California Star* newspaper and, of course, his very important partnership in the recently expanded mercantile firm of Charles Smith & Co. at Sutter's Fort. Gripped with a compulsive entrepreneur's obsession, the more he acquired, the more he wanted, and the more intensely determined he became to get his own fingers into every pot that might contain money.

Brannan was utterly convinced that once credible, detailed accounts of the discovery of gold reached the East, significant numbers of gold-seekers would begin arriving by late summer and that many more would follow next year. To this end he had conferred briefly last week with his employee Edward Kemble, editor of the *California Star*, and had suggested that it might be wise to devote and entire issue or two to praise eloquently and at great length the natural attributes that California had to offer to those who would come.

Though Brannan owned the newspaper, he rarely interfered in any way with its content. He had early last year hired Kemble as editor, and thus far had found the man to be very able, both in his command of the language and his innate story-sense, even though his editorials were sometimes a bit too rigid for Brannan's own personal tastes. Kemble had also evidenced a rather strong disinclination toward being told what to write, even by the paper's owner, but was usually accommodating if something was *suggested* that concurred with his own thinking, so Brannan had become very circumspect in how he presented any editorial idea. That was especially true with the present personal project.

"As you're already aware, sir," Brannan had remarked to Kemble, "I've been considering for some time organizing an overland mail service linking our thriving city here with Independence, Missouri. I've already hired some of the best riders I could find and believe — with the routing I've laid out for them — they can make the journey in sixty days or less, which is nothing less than phenomenal. They are all set to initiate this service next week. I would suggest that to commemorate this first run of the mail, a special edition of the *Star* be struck off the press and sent eastward with them, and I am prepared to underwrite the cost of expanding our circulation for that issue by two thousand copies."

Kemble's eyes widened at that, and Brannan was pleased that he had successfully snagged the editor's attention. He refrained, with difficulty, emphasizing the gold discovery too much, simply because he was sure he needn't do so; Kemble was aware of the prospecting occurring at both the Sutter-Marshall lumber mill-site and at what the gristmill Saints were referring to as *Mormon Island*. Brannan was planning to later instruct the writer to emphasize that point.

"It occurs to me," he said casually, "that the articles you commissioned Dr. Fourgeaud to do last October regarding California's attributes would probably form an excellent foundation." Dr. Victor J. Fourgeaud was a widely-known and highly respected San Francisco physician whom Kemble had commissioned to write a series of short pieces promoting what California had to offer for those who had taken up residence. "However, instead of the short pieces Dr. Fourgeaud is planning," Brannan went on, "you could perhaps group the information from two or three of them into a more expansive piece to run in next week's issue; a piece that might be revised to appeal more directly to Easterners who might be contemplating moving West."

At Kemble's momentary frown as he considered this, Brannan added hastily, "This could be a fine opportunity to promote California in a very positive way, don't you think?"

The editor nodded, slowly at first, but then with gathering enthusiasm. Dr. Fourgeaud's pieces were already finished, and it would take little added effort to rework his material to suit Brannan's proposals for the next issue. "I had been thinking along those very lines," he admitted, "and this appears to be an ideal opportunity. I'll schedule it."

Now a week had passed, and Brannan stopped by the newspaper's office this morning, his ten select riders behind him, each with a tethered mule trailing, and all but two with their saddlebags open and ready; the two exceptions had saddlebags already well stuffed with mail and tightly secured with rawhide thongs. The ten included six former members of the old Mormon Battalion, including William Hawk and his gangling twenty-year-old son, Nathan, plus Sanford Jacobs, Richard Slater, Silas Harris, and Daniel Rawson, plus four other riders recruited by the elder Hawk, non-Mormons whose names Brannan didn't know. Brannan had decided to ride with them as far as Sutter's Fort and then send them on their way at that point, after which he'd confer for a while with his partner, Charles Smith, at the new and much larger store site before continuing to the mines to collect tithes.

It pleased Brannan, as he entered the newspaper's print shop, to see that the printing of the numerically expanded issue of the Star was stacked in piles along one wall ready for loading by his riders. He nodded to Bill Hawk, who immediately instructed the other men to load their saddlebags to capacity and to secure them carefully. Brannan picked up a single copy of the issue and was gratified to see that the Fourgeaud article, entitled *The Prospects of California,* filled six entire columns in rather fine print, and he read the piece with keen anticipation. It was well done, but Brannan's spirits fell somewhat when he discovered that Fourgeaud's coverage of the gold discovery was nowhere near as accurate nor as enthusiastic as he had expected:

> *We saw, a few days ago, a beautiful specimen of gold from the mine newly discovered on the American fork. From all accounts the mine is immensely rich, and already we*

> *learn that gold from it, collected at random and without any trouble, has become an article of trade in the upper settlements. This precious [metal] abounds in this country. We have heard of several other newly discov-ered mines of gold, but as these reports are not yet authenticated, we shall pass over them. However, it is well known that there is a placero [sic] of gold a few miles from Ciudad de los Angeles and another on the San Joaquin. ... At the American diggings the gold is found at a depth of three feet below the surface, and in a strata of soft sand-rock. Explorations made recently southward to the distance of twelve miles, and to the north five miles, report the continuance of this strata and the mineral equally abundant. The vein has proven to be from twelve to eighteen feet in thickness. Most advantageously to this new mine, a stream of water flows in its immediate neighborhood, and the washing will surely be attended with comparative ease.*

Still, Brannan conceded, the information was presented well enough, and there was every reason to believe that Easterners reading about it might be impressed and perhaps even excited about it. He met at once with Kemble and was able to exact a promise from him to print another article about it, more detailed and more accurate than this one, in a near-future issue, possibly on June 3rd. He was sure it would stimulate even more of the Oregon-bound emigrants to detour instead to California.

As planned, Brannan accompanied the large procession of horses and men as far as Sutter's Fort and saw them on their way from there before visiting with his partner at their new, much larger quarters within the fort. Smith had worked hard moving the entire inventory from the former store to the numerous and expansive shelves of the new one. There was now, however, still ample room for three or four times as much stock as was currently on display, and Smith, while awaiting for more goods to arrive, had introduced a customer-friendly touch, a large open, pickle-barrel near the door accompanied by a sign inviting patrons to sample its contents.

Journeying on to the grist-mill at Brighton and then beyond, Brannan paused briefly at Mormon Island, impressed with the growing number of prospectors at the site and the industry of the men digging there. Since few had actual pans to use in separating the finer gold from other bottom debris in the manner Humphrey had instructed them, a fair number had taken to using the shallow, tightly-woven Indian baskets in the same manner and were enjoying remarkably good results with them. Some of the men were able to wash out as much as $7 [$201.60] worth of gold in a single load. Delighted to observe their continuing success, Brannan once again collected tithes from the Saints on hand, which this time amounted to nearly a full pint of nuggets. Such good fortune, with the evident promise of far more yet to come, caused Brannan to make a decision on the spot: Before heading on to the sawmill at Coloma, he selected a site on level ground adjacent to the big bar with the intention of erecting a store there within the next few weeks. The men were calling the site *Natoma,* after one of their Indian helpers.

Brannan then rode on to the lumber-mill, where he arrived today, efficiently collected another quarter-pound of gold as tithes from the workers there and then selected a site at Coloma for yet another store, the *Brannan Emporium,* which he hoped to have erected and operational within a fortnight. He was entirely confident both on-site stores would be big money-makers.

There were few things in life Samuel Brannan considered more delightful than making money.

[April 15th, 1848 • Saturday]

Henry Bigler was convinced that over these past several weeks he had worked harder than ever before in his life. He didn't add, although he could well have done so, that during this short time span he had amassed far more wealth than he had earned throughout all of his previous life.

More than any other individual among the growing number actively prospecting for gold, he had developed an ability to recognize the likely spots where gold would be found, and he concentrated his energies on such locales. So successful was he in recognizing where the placer gold would be found, and in recovering nuggets in those areas through utilizing the rocker techniques taught to him by Isaac Humphrey, that he now rarely resorted to the tedious and less rewarding effort of panning; indeed, he no longer concentrated on gathering the tinier particles — the gold dust and flakes. He now took great pride in his ability to discover newer, more distant areas which exhibited what he intuitively recognized to be tell-tale signs of imminent mineral deposits. His success, moreover, led him to realize that the placer gold was far more widespread than anyone else fully realized. He had already filled one quart-sized leather pouch to capacity with nothing but nuggets and buried it in a secret hiding place, and now he was rapidly filling a second similar pouch as well.

He continued to faithfully and accurately keep his daily *diary* in which he entered events of interest or importance apart from gold matters, but such entries became ever more brief and hurriedly written. In yesterday's entry, for example, he wrote:

> *April 14th. A sailor from the U.S. frigate Congress is baptized, probably the first baptism in California of a Mormon convert.*

Each day Bigler continued faithfully to accurately record his daily finds, but he was careful not ever to mention the location of his principal gold cache, and he intuitively recognized the wisdom of not returning to the cache until it became time for him to join his fellow Saints on their journey to Salt Lake City. In the meanwhile, he had every intention of continuing his dedicated gold-seeking.

More than any other tool, Bigler still used his sheath knife almost exclusively to expose and recover the nuggets from crevices in the bedrock, but at times he wished fervently that he had a pick and a good shovel or spade to aid him in the work. Such tools, unfortunately, if available at all, could be purchased only at Sam Brannan's stores and only at the extraordinarily high prices the merchant was charging. Just for a shovel, previously selling for only a dollar or two, Brannan was now charging upwards of $100 [$2,880], which was close to six months' wages back East, and his price was nearly twice as much for a good, sturdy pick. There were miners who, having no other choice, were reluctantly shelling out huge amounts in gold for such essential tools, but Bigler continued to balk at the charges he felt amounted to outright robbery and, unlike others who simply sighed and paid the asking price, he refused to give in to them.

Though he had mastered the rocker technique quite well and his own rocker had become an essential item in his equipment, he was not fond of the recovery device that had been fashioned by Alexander Stephens, which some were extolling as combining the advantages of both panning and rocking. It was a heavy wooden bowl, rounded on the bottom and so cumbersome to use that it had to be rocked rather than shaken. If the prospector slanted it at the proper angle while rocking it, the device became self-emptying, allowing Stephens and others to empty the heavier bottom residue periodically into a larger tub of water. At night the tub residue was carefully panned and the gold separated. Bigler considered the whole process far too exhausting to use for any length of time.

Among the first non-Mormons to join the prospectors at Mormon Island was William S. Clark, who had earlier settled in San Francisco at the place he named Clark's Point. He was one of a number of men who had come to Mormon Island as soon as word had filtered down that gold was being found there in quantity, and he was, thus far, quite as successful at the quality gold recovery as were the Saints themselves.

Bigler, more than normally busy these days, had little time or energy left by nightfall to write at any length in his *diary*. On April 2 he wrote: "Clear and warm. Found a new place for gold, and got thirty dollars [$864]," failing to specify whether he was prospecting in a new location on Mormon Island, or if he had made his discovery elsewhere. Five days later, "along with fellow Saints Alexander Stephens and John [James] S. Brown," Bigler had set out late in the day on horseback for the fort in order to settle accounts with John Sutter and to meet with the men of their Battalion who had assembled there to prepare for the forthcoming journey to Salt Lake City. The late start of the three, however, had allowed them to cover only a few miles before nightfall, and so they had camped in the mountains. John Bidwell, this same day, had reached San Francisco again and bragged of his discovery of new sources of placer gold well to the north of Sutter's Fort, but most of his listeners simply did not believe his boasts.

Continuing on to the grist-mill the next day, Bigler wrote in his diary just at twilight:

> *April 8th, Saturday — This evening we arrived at the lower camp or flouring mill. We found the mill not near completed. The frame was up, and whether it ever was started I never learned. Here we learned that Willis [Willes] and Hudson with several of the boys were up the river getting gold and had been for several days, but how they were making it no one seemed to know. I discovered, however, there*

> *was a fearfulness among the hands about leaving their work and go[ing] on uncertainty. Notwithstanding, some of the party had been down and reported they thought the digging was going to be good. I suppose in truth they were like Marshall was; they did not care about letting all the world know about it until they knew that there was a chance for all.*

The following day, having arrived at Sutter's Fort and conferred with a number of the Saints who had gathered there, Bigler wrote:

> *Sunday, April 9th — The members of our battalion held a meeting and we resolved to be ready to start for Salt Lake on the 1st of June, excepting those who are to leave next Saturday with an express for Salt Lake and perhaps for the Eastern States. It was further decided that we send out a few men as pioneers before that time to pioneer out a route across the Sierra Nevada and if possible find a much nearer way to go than to go the Truckee route and thus shun crossing the very deep and rapid Truckee River twenty-seven times. We were informed by Mr. Brannan that we would have to do so if we went that route.*

On April 10th Bigler and his two companions endeavored to have their discussion with Captain Sutter, but found him very busy with other matters. He told them his books were not yet posted, so a settlement with him was postponed for the time being. On the following day the three mounted their horses fairly late in the day and set out on their return to the saw-mill at Coloma, where they had decided to turn their attention to goldseeking for a while longer. They had already, before leaving Coloma, come to an understanding with Marshall that they be allowed to dig there on shares; Marshall to furnish all the food and tools so long as they worked on his claims there and turned over to him half of what they found. They camped that night on a creek some fifteen miles above the grist-mill. The three took their time, pausing here and there to prospect as they followed the American upstream. The next evening Bigler recorded full details of the day's activities in his diary:

> *April 12th. — This morning, while our horses were filling up on the grass, we concluded to prospect a little in the creek*

and we soon found it [the gold] and spent half the day having nothing but our knives and the two small basins we had with us to sip our coffee out of. We got about ten dollars [$288]. For supper and breakfast we baked our bread on flat stones. We straddled our horses and struck out to hunt the boys, who were not far from this place digging gold. We struck in close to the river, and following up its banks we soon found them.

We found seven of the boys at work, Willis [Willes], Hudson, and party. They had nicely taken out this day two hundred and fifty dollars [$7,200], or more than $41 [$1,180.80] to the man. This was the spot where the few parti- cles were found by the Messrs. Willis [Willes] and Hudson on the second of March while returning from the saw-mill and thought it not much account, and this is the place that afterwards went by the name of "Mormon Island." Here for the first time I saw an improvement for washing out gold. That was with Indian baskets. They had one or two old baskets and they would wash out from twenty-five cents [$7.20] to two dollars [$57.60] at a basket full of dirt. I suppose they [the baskets] were about the size of [an] eight- or ten-quart basin The names of the men who were here at work were Sidney Willis [Willes], Ira Willis, [Willes], Willford [sic] Hudson, Jesse B. Martin, and Ephraim Green [added later in Bigler's hand:] "The other two I disremember, but I think they were Israel Evans and James Sly." We camped with them. It was about this time that one or both of the Willises had business that called them from their mining to the Fort and they went to Yerba Buena; at all events they met with Sam Brannan and cautiously let him in to the secret. Mr. Brannan told them he could secure the mine as church property and advised for all the Battalion boys to go to work in the mine and pay one-tenth to him and he would turn it over to the church as their tithing, with the understanding, at the same time, that he was to come in with the Willises [Willeses] and Hudson, having a share with them in their claim. This they did.

Bigler and Brown finally arrived back at the Sutter-Marshall sawmill late in the afternoon and on the following day, April 14th, began searching for gold again with even greater determination now, in the realization they and the other Saints would be leaving the diggings permanently and heading for Salt Lake City in mid-June. Spending virtually every waking moment thereafter in gold-seeking, Bigler's *diary* entries became even more cryptically abbreviated than before, often accompanied by his expressed intent that he would later expand upon them at this leisure. On some days he simply failed to record his findings. As the days passed, however, each diary entry typically consisted merely of specifying the gold he had found on that day:

> *Friday, 14th. This morning we put out for hunting the "platter' [plata], as the Spaniards call it. I found $11.00 [$316.80.]*
>
> *Sat. 15th. I found 22 dollars [$633.60] worth.*
>
> *Sunday 16th. I picked up seven dollars [$201.60].*
>
> *Tuesday 18th. I carried dirt on my back five for six hundred yards to the River and washed it and got eleven dollars [$316.80] I used a wooden tray we use to knead dough in, to wash and gether [sic] my gold.*
>
> *Wed. 19th. I washed out 18 dollars [$518.40]; Brown and Steven [Steph-ens] found about the same each, we find it in small gulches leading to the River but have no water, and carry the dirt to the River to wash out the "Platter."*
>
> *Thursday 20th. Brown went to hunt our horses as they were Seen follow-ing off a mair [mare] and colt he had lately bought; today I hunted for gold and got 18 dollars [$518.40].*
>
> *Friday 21st. I found thirty dollars [$864] and Stevens [Stephens] 25 dollars [$720]. Brown returned without finding the horses, saw no sign of them leaving the Range.*
>
> *Sat. 22. Found 25 dollars [$720], Stevens [Stephens] 45 dollars [$1,296] and Brown 9 $ 20 cts. [$297.76].*

Sunday 23rd. Like Christians we kept the Sabbath day while a lot of Gen-tiles came into our camp to look for gold but found none.

In just the previous six days of gold-seeking, Bigler had gathered up 142 ounces of gold — almost nine pounds! — valued at $2,272 [$65,433.60], but despite his almost daily successes, he was becoming disgruntled at how long it was taking to separate the gold from the dirt, sand and other minerals. He had been entirely unsuccessful in his efforts to procure a basket from some of the Indians, and the only thing he had that he considered to be even partially suitable for the process was his wooden biscuit-dough tray.

Listening to others, Bigler learned that in recent days the transient population increase at Sutter's Fort had swelled significantly. A group of Saints Bigler recognized, but whom he did not know well, had arrived at the diggings here and exchanged their gossip, acquired at Sutter's Fort, for whatever information Bigler and others could impart about where and how to find gold. They told him that during the brief period they had stopped off at the fort, two men named Sidney Willis [Willes] and Jesse Martin had arrived from "a place they called Mormon Island" with what one of them described as "a great amount of raw gold" which they were in the process of exchanging for goods at the new and significantly expanded quarters of the Smith Mercantile store. When the group had queried the pair about where Mormon Island was located, the two had suddenly become very quiet and refused to talk about it further.

The men said they had also met "a doctor named Bates and an official named Sinclair" at the store who were excited about what they had seen during their own brief inspection of the Mormon Island site. The group of men, then having procured directions from Sutter, and still more gossip from John Sinclair, had left at once for the gold site and had very soon passed a large family group named Luther camped along the American River also heading slowly for Mormon Island " ... where we heard there was gold being found in a great big gravel bar"; and, shortly after that, the men had passed two wagons loaded with provisions that Sutter was sending "to his saw-mill at a place called Coloma, where the first gold had been discovered."

Bigler also learned that apparently a number of groups of settlers as well as "some folks from San Francisco" were beginning to spread out and, on their own initiative, were seeking gold in other ravines, gulches, and streambeds some distance away — some, such as Weber Creek, not terribly far distant to the south of the lumber mill-site but still part of the American River's drainage system; others well beyond in entirely different river systems thus far virtually unexplored.

A little later, with the events still fresh in his mind, Bigler expanded those earlier brief *diary* entries into more cogent explanations. After penning the amended accounts into his *diary*, he added:

> *April 14th. — This morning I set out with A. Stevens [Alexander Stephens] and J. S. Brown to hunt for plata, as the Spaniards call money, half a mile below the saw-mill on the north side of the river. ... I used a wooden trough, or tray, made by Stevens for kneading dough. Stevens, Brown and I worked to-gether under an agreement with Marshall that he should furnish us with tools, provisions, and Indians when we wanted them, and that we should give him half the gold. The richest dirt today was found 500 yards from the river, and we had to carry it so far in sacks to wash it. We had not sacks enough, and on one occasion, I filled my cap with dirt which yielded half an ounce of gold — $8 [$230.40].*

By mid-April the workers in the grist-mill began leaving their jobs in droves, even though it meant forfeiting their back-pay, and most of them joined those who were already digging at Mormon Island. A few wandered to stream systems far to the south and east, but others continued upstream to the lumber-mill, where Bigler, Brown and Stephens continued their own digging in the saw-mill's vicinity and where, on April 15th, Bigler dug out, mostly in large flakes and nuggets, $22 [$633.60] worth, followed on the next day by nuggets worth another $7 [$201.60].

One of the gold-seekers who showed up at their diggings was an elderly Spaniard from Sonora, who demonstrated for them his own method of separating the gold from other debris. The miner found a likely looking spot to dig near a water hole, and, as Bigler described it:

> *... He used a cotton sheet. He spread it down near a hole of water (a little slanting) put his pay dirt on it, then straddled the hole, and with his shovel he would throw water on to it,*

and thus wash away the dirt leaving the gold sticking to the cloth. Brown and myself saw that was quite an improvement by the side of our wooden dishes, and we adopted that plan for a while.

It was Brown, however, who described in his own *journal* how he and Bigler executed the process quite successfully in their own way. Brown wrote:

The next and last process that we used in gathering was to spread A sheet on the sand beach of the river, placing some big rocks on the corners and sides to keep it well stretched, then fill the rich dirt on the upper edge, then throw water on to wash the dirt down in the river, leaving the gold on the sheet, occasionally taking up the sheet and dipping it in a tub of water, thus washing the gold off the sheet into the tub, and at night clean up our day's work, averaging from $12 [$345.60] to $15 [$432] per hand — upwards of $30 [$864] per load — and our best paying dirt was carried on our shoulders from Dry Gulch all the way from fifteen to sixty rods, to where we could find water to wash it with.

On Wednesday, April 19th, Bigler, Stephens, and Brown, working together in small gulches leading to the river, carried dirt to the river from many rods distant and by the end of the day had collected a fine total of $54 [$1,555.20] worth, which they split equally among themselves, $18 [$518.40] per man, an amount that all three agreed, with gross understatement, was "a pretty good day."

The Indian workers, to whom the concept of money was still very difficult to grasp, were largely content being paid in food and clothing for the yellow pebbles they turned in to their white sponsors. By the end of April over a thousand Indians using shallow, tightly woven baskets and broad wooden bowls were recovering immense amounts of gold in the streams, gulches and ravines of Weber Creek, which seemed to have an abundance of rich deposits throughout its entire length. A branch of that waterway flowed in from the northeast; another branch, frequently in drier periods of weather, lost its water flow altogether. A great deal of gold was found in the dry creek bed, especially in the small ravines that fed it and behind large emergent rocks. Some four miles upstream from where the branch flowed into Weber Creek, an especially good deposit of placer gold was found, and very quickly numerous cabins were being erected there into a relatively stable little community already being referred to as Old Dry Diggings or, by some, Dry Diggings City. Nobody cared much for those names but, by the same token, no one offered a better suggestion.

In time, some of these earliest miners said, a big, important town would develop here and, with it, a name would evolve that would undoubtedly be much more appropriate and better. What most failed to realize was that "appropriate and better" were two designations that were not necessarily synonymous.

[May 2nd, 1848 • Tuesday]

It had taken Claude Chana somewhat longer than he had anticipated to get his party of prospectors selected, equipped, and prepared than he had initially anticipated, but they were on their way now. The sky was bright, almost cloudless, the so il underfoot dry once more, and the streams finally within their banks again with a normal clear flow. Each of the half dozen men, Chana included, was well mounted, each trailing a pack mule comfortably loaded with the supplies they'd need for the days and weeks ahead.

The route they were taking to check out the South Fork of the American River was somewhat more out of the way than the usually traveled route would have been, but it was a route Chana had traveled before; a route along which there were several areas he considered as possibly good prospecting sites they could check out en route. They would follow their present course northeastward from Sonora and strike the Sacramento, where fording the river would be somewhat easier than in the Sutter's Fort vicinity, close to where Feather River emptied into the mother stream. From there they would follow the Feather upstream to where the Bear River entered from the east and follow that tributary upstream as well for perhaps twenty miles or more, searching for any sign of silver deposits. Should they find nothing of value in that stretch, they'd leave that stream system entirely and turn southward to strike the North Fork of the American, which they'd cross and continue southeastward until they hit Coloma on the South Fork, where they planned to really begin prospecting in earnest.

Among Chana's party he, alone, had been through that country once before. During his previous trip the streams were flooding, and there'd been little opportunity for any kind of worthwhile prospecting. The conditions were obviously going to be much better along the way this time, but it was still the South Fork area, where the rumored gold strike had occurred, that Chana was most eager to reach.

If the gold Bennett had shown to Humphrey in Los Angeles had really come from the South Fork, then Chana was determined to find the source.

[May 11th, 1848 • Thursday]

During the nearly one month's span between mid-April and mid May, more and more people in such communities as San Francisco, San José, Monterey and a host of other, smaller coastal towns all the way south through Santa Barbara and Los Angeles, were beginning to take more seriously the continuing reports of gold being found in the Sierra Nevada, from its foothills up to its very peaks. No matter how much they heard, however, the consuming intensity of true gold fever had not yet gripped them with a voracious certainty that the stories must be true; nor were they even faintly convinced that whatever gold might have really been discovered constituted anything more than anomalies occurring in isolated locations, anomalies certainly not worthy of spending considerable time, energy, and funds to pursue.

True, an increasing number people were slipping away from their jobs and homes to investigate matters for themselves, but they were not numerous, and hardly any of these were broadcasting their intentions to family members, friends, neighbors or employers, for fear of being ridiculed as gullible fools. The vast majority of citizens still insisted that the entire gold-discovery report was nothing more than a gigantic hoax. As James H. Carson, erstwhile Sergeant in the New York Regiment, put it:

> *The months of April and May have carried off many of our inhabitants — not to their long homes, but to the gold mines. Many of the old fellows who had put the golden reports down as "dad drat humbug" had one after another gone to the mines. Some had left privately to prevent the remainder from laughing at them, while others, bordering on insanity, raved around crying for pick-axe, shovel and pan, had started off at speed.*

Even those determined to investigate the gold discovery rumors for themselves often concocted involved pretexts of "business elsewhere" or visits to sick relatives or friends or simply "vacations" taken to escape the heat already building in the valleys and enveloping the coastline. Seldom did anyone, Carson included, anywhere in "civilized" California, express even a tepid belief in the rumors of gold that were being bandied about. Some, in fact, even after actually seeing samples of the gold, utterly refused to believe it was anything more than pyrite.

A member of the latter group was former U.S. Army Captain Joseph L. Folsom, who was living at this time in San Francisco. Even when an exultant miner excitedly showed him a cigar box containing twenty ounces of gold — a pound and a quarter of spectacular nuggets valued at $720 [$20,736] — that he claimed to have accumulated during eight days of digging, Folsom simply dismissed the miner's account and his evidence as being fraudulent. Folsom thereupon wrote to Governor Mason on April 8th and flatly pronounced the nuggets to be " ... nothing but mica!"

C. L. Ross, who was visiting the mines, encountered men far less dogmatic in their views, and he wrote:

> *I found John M. Homer, of the Mission of San José, who told me he had left about 500 acres of splendid wheat for the cattle to roam over at will, he and his family having deserted the place entirely, and started off to the mines.*

Hearing rapidly increasing rumors of the gold discovery at the Sutter-Marshall Saw-mill, Edward Kemble, in his office at the *California Star*, was having second thoughts about his previously published accounts debunking the gold rumors and was finally overcome by a curiosity to see once again for himself if there was anything to it. He, therefore, on April 16th, blandly announced his intention to "ruralize among the rustics of the country for a few weeks," though he doubted he'd need that much time to "for once and all, get to the bottom of the matter."

On the following day, April 16th, Sutter was visited at his fort by William Gray of Virginia, who had just finished purchasing for himself and several associates a silver mine in the San José Valley. Because the visitor was returning immediately to the East, Sutter couldn't resist showing him some of the gold found at the saw-mill and even presented him with several specimens of it. Gray's eyes widened, and though he merely thanked Sutter briefly, he was determined to spread news of the discovery as soon as he was safely back East once again. In the evening Sutter wrote in his *diary*:

> *April 16th. Mr. Gray (from Virginia) who purchased Silver Mines in the San José Valley for a Compy [sic] and was interested himself [stopped here]. At the fort he learned the news of the Gold discovery. I presented him some Specimens of Gold. He left for the States across the Mountains. Some families are moving in the Mountains to camp and settle there.*

However few individuals were taking the gold discovery rumors seriously, it soon became obvious that these numerous accounts could no longer be entirely ignored. Before leaving for the mines again, Edward Kemble finally broke down and presented a brief piece in his *California Star*, much freer of the personal bias than had his previous accounts had been. He thereupon accompanied Pierson B. Reading aboard the launch *Rainbow* from San Francisco to Sutter's Fort and from there the three men, including Sutter, continued the 40-mile journey, now on muleback, to the saw-mill. Reading had by this time become the northernmost white settler in the valleys of tributaries of the Sacramento River, and he wanted one more good look at the bars occurring near Mormon Island that he thought were virtually identical to those to be found on the tract where he'd built his rancho along Cottonwood Creek, an icy cold stream fed by the run-off from the snow-capped summit of Mount Shasta.

What the trio found transformed their perspectives. When they returned on April 18th, Reading was intent on beginning to prospect for gold as soon as he could return to his own creek; Kemble's formerly skeptical opinions on the discovery rumors had been dramatically modified; Sutter, however, still remained extremely cautious about acknowledging the presence of gold at all. Kemble, by this time, far less concerned than Sutter about maintaining secrecy, wrote in his April 22nd issue of the *California Star*:

> *We have been informed, from unquestionable authority, that another still more extensive and valuable gold mine has*

> *been discovered toward the head of the American Fork, in the Sacramento Valley. We have seen several specimens taken from it, to the amount of eight or ten ounces of pure virgin gold.*

Abruptly the numerous sand and gravel bars downstream from both Coloma and Mormon Island that previously had been of little consequence, were, by April 23rd, suddenly important enough to attract gold-seekers from far and wide. Many of these bars now began bearing the names given to them by the prospectors: *Lacey Bar, Milkpunch, Deadman's, Granite,* and *Manhattan* — and each site became daily more crowded with prospectors. On some of the more gold-productive bars, crowding became so pervasive that the miners were staking claims only four feet square, and some were even sleeping in their claim holes to prevent others from usurping them. Between the lumber mill and Mormon Island, more bars were tested for gold, often with surprisingly good results, and even smaller bars there became known by the names with which they'd been casually dubbed: *Red Bar, Stony, Dutch, Missouri, Kanaka,* and *Michigan.*

On Friday, April 28th, Governor Mason wrote a cautious, carefully-worded letter to U.S. President James K. Polk, informing him that earlier rumors of gold having been discovered in the foothills of California's Sierra Nevada Mountains, which had at first broadly generated skepticism, were gaining in credulity almost on a daily basis. He said that there was sufficient evidence at this point to assume the stories were true, but that more information had to be gathered to verify irrefutably the discovery's validity. He promised that if it were indeed a genuine, significant gold strike, he would send proof of it as soon as such proof became available to him. He then concluded his note by writing:

> *It is my understanding, Mr. President, that well over half of the men who are alleged to be panning for gold at present here are Indians of various tribal affiliations, most of whom speak no English whatever. Verification from whites allegedly working these deposits is hopefully to be ascertained before much longer. Even if verified by them, however, I will not accept the full truth of it until I have personally gone to see the mines and witnessed what is transpiring.*

By late April James Marshall had not a single worker remaining on the job who had been part of his original crew at the saw-mill; all the others had departed to try their luck with prospecting or prepared to head for Salt Lake City without any further delay. Marshall's entire crew now consisted only of a teamster named Horace Loy, plus his blacksmith, Jim Gregson, and a handful of Indians. Even the Wimmers were gone, the holy terror, Jennie Wimmer, having been succeeded by Gregson's wife, Lucy.

Henry Bigler, still prospecting on a full time basis on the South Fork of the American River and making significant finds here and there, was saddened on this same day when his young companion, Azariah Smith, announced that he was heading home. He had already found over $500 [$14,400] worth of gold, but now he simply shook his head and said:

"That's enough. The gold's all well and good, but y'know, I'm just not that much interested in looking for more. I've got plenty." He kicked a little mound of earth with his shoe and reddened a bit as he admitted, "I'm homesick. I want to see my mother and I don't much care if there is still more gold to find. There's a group of us boys here who feel just like I do about it, and I'm heading for Salt Lake City with them."

Bigler nodded sympathetically, well aware of Smith's feelings in the matter and felt rather inclined to pack up and go along with him; but then he sighed, took Smith's hand, and shook it. "I'll wish you a safe journey, Azariah. I'll be heading for there, too, before the summer's out, but not yet. I'd like to make enough," he added, knowing full well he'd already made far more than he might normally have earned in his entire lifetime, "so I can contribute substantially to the Church and still have enough left over that I never really have to work again unless it's entirely my choice to do so."

The Mormon group including Azariah Smith started their long journey on the first day of May, but ran into difficulties at once. Former Sgt. Daniel Browett had been elected Captain to lead them and to pioneer, if possible, a new wagon road eastward over the Sierra Nevada. Included in the ten-man party were, in addition to Browett and Smith, Ira J. Willes, Israel Evans, Daniel Allen, Henderson Cox, Robert Pixton, J. R. Allred, Jacob G. Truman and James C. Sly. None were willing to risk a crossing over Donner Pass; the tragedy of the Donner Party being marooned there and half their number perishing was still too fresh in their minds to even consider doing so. They felt that crossing farther to the south and then passing around the south end of Lake Tahoe might give them a better chance.

Their chosen route actually *was* a better passage by far, especially for wagon travel, but as they quickly learned, nature still held all the trump cards. When they reached Iron Hill the snow was so deep they could travel no farther; so deep, in fact, one of the lead donkeys became buried to the point that only his large ears extended above the snow. Two of the men each grabbed an ear and pulled the animal back onto firmer footing; they then trampled the snow and made a camp while Brothers Sly, Evans and Willes ascended to the summit of the nearest mountain to check conditions and mark the route. Within a few hours they returned, filled with gloom.

"Nothing ahead," Evans reported, "except snow-covered peaks. We're not going to make it, boys. Might make a good wagon road later, but not now."

The group discussed the matter and wisely decided not to attempt progressing further, but to return to the warmer lowlands and wait for the weather at these upper elevations to warm as well. They turned about, and a single day's journey brought them back virtually to their starting point, during which they left the frigid elements of winter behind and emerged once again into a warm spring atmosphere, into a world of blooming flowers and thriving vegetation. The entire party decided to continue with their gold-seeking for a few weeks until the higher elevations warmed and thawed.

As May began, Sam Brannan set a crew to erecting his new trading post called *Natoma* on a stretch of flat ground close to Mormon Island. Hardly had construction even begun when the post was deluged by newcomers desperately needing tools with which to dig, regardless of the mind-boggling prices which confronted them. Farther downriver at Sutter's Fort, Captain Sutter jotted in his *New Helvetia Logbook*:

> *Monday May 1th [sic] 1848 Despatched a Wagon to the Mountains with provisions, etc, and send [sic] up there Horace Loy to be employed at the Saw-mill as a teamster. Several other men went up to the Gold Mines. Abeck returned from there, likewise Nash & Knight. A good many of the Mormons here. A very bussi [sic] day.*

At the same time, San Francisco, 100 miles farther downstream, the population of which now exceeded 1,000 inhabitants, virtually seethed with rumors of the gold discoveries, yet most residents still remained cautious, seeking further verification of the remarkable accounts they were hearing. Every day new arrivals were pouring into the town, and construction of new homes, in addition to the 200 erected within the last year or so, filled the air with the constant, cacophonous sounds of sawing and hammering.

A San Franciscan who was at this very moment some 2,000 miles to the east, Mountain Man Jim Clyman, had probably crossed America as many times as any man now alive. Having traveled with such widely known figures as Jim Bridger, Tom "Broken Hand" Fitzpatrick, and Jedediah Strong Smith, he was now, at age 54, poised to begin yet another cross-country trek to California. He had hired out his services as a guide to lead the small wagon train of the Mecomb family of Indiana across the Western vastness to a permanent new home in the burgeoning city on San Francisco Bay.

Clyman was doggedly determined to make this his last such journey. This time there would be nothing remaining to lure him back to the Midwest; he had sold his farm in Illinois and his woodland property in Wisconsin in order to reenter his beloved California for keeps. He intended to settle down on the acreage he had claimed in the Napa Valley north of San Francisco Bay, a sprawling ranch where he hoped to do nothing more exciting for the rest of his days than grow grapes, make very fine wines, and perhaps produce children. For the first time in his life he was in love, and he planned to marry the fine young woman who was the eldest daughter of the family he was now guiding, and who rode beside him at this moment, Hannah Mecomb.

In Monterey, Governor Mason was still trying to ascertain definitively whether the gold discovery stories, now rampant, were fact or fallacy. One aspect of the alleged discovery nagged him persistently: If the gold truly existed, and after viewing gold nuggets brought to him recently, he now believed it did, was it in small, confined, isolated deposits, or was it widespread throughout entire regions? Differing opinions — from those he felt should be more aware of the facts than he — had simply not been helpful. On May 2nd he was visited by one John Bradley, Captain Folsom's friend, and Mason posed that question to him.

Bradley at once snorted disdainfully and replied, "I have heard of it, and a few fools have hurried off to that place on the American where it was allegedly discovered, but Governor, you can count on this — there's nothing in those stories at all. There is no gold being found."

Still, Mason was not at all convinced. Of anything.

Pierson Reading, now back on his own property in far northwestern California, was not surprised when on the following day, May 3rd, in Clear Creek on the low approaches to Mount Shasta, he discovered extensive deposits of placer gold. He quickly summoned a crew of his Indian workers and instructed them to collect it in their tightly woven, shallow baskets. At least 500 miles or more to the south of Reading's property, moreover, a group of Mormons had also just discovered a rich deposit of placer gold on the land grant belonging to John C. Frémont, in a stream called Mariposa Creek. They named the deposit Mormon Bar, and its existence clearly confirmed the fact that the California gold belt was considerably more extensive than anyone had previously even dreamed.

In virtually the mid-point of that range, halfway up the main American River, Mormon Island had by this time become intensely crowded with gold-seekers, and a group of four miners, unable to find a claimable spot on the big bar itself, prospected on the hill opposite from it suddenly began encountering very noteworthy gold deposits. The four were black men, so the location was quickly named *Negro Hill,* and it grew prodigiously in population. Other mining camps seemed to pop up almost overnight and lined South Fork for miles. One such site was named *Marshall Gold Camp,* and it became a center for the numerous miners appearing on a pair of meandering streams called Shingle and Granite creeks. *Michigan Flat* bloomed almost overnight and generated further gold camps called *Coyote Diggings, Rich Gulch,* and *Red Hill,* which gave rise to tributary gold camps named *Green Springs, Jayhawk, Pinchemtight,* and *McDowell Hill.* Within a fortnight a group had formed, calling itself the Mormon Island Mining Association, which was already laying out plans to divert the course of the South Fork so that its bed could be mined.

John Sutter quickly grew exasperated by the number of men showing up eager to prospect. He abruptly ceased extending permission for them to hunt more extensively on his lands and simply ordered them away, more often than not in a peremptory manner, occasionally even at gunpoint. These ousted prospectors, outraged over Sutter's and Marshall's somewhat hostile treatment of them, vowed vengeance against the pair. Nevertheless, the trespassers had no real choice but to move away from the valley of the South Fork and try their luck in new areas. Their disappointment turned into exultation as many of them found excellent results on slopes and in streambeds both to the north and the south. One of the newcomers who had just arrived from the coast, Sam Dolan, remarked in his *journal*:

> *... the miners are running all over the country and picking gold out of the earth here and there just as a thousand hogs let loose in a forest would root up ground nuts.*

Their gold-seeking methods were improving, as well. Because pans were now available at Smith's and Brannan's large new store, Brannan's Emporium, at Sutter's Fort — still at phenomenally high prices, but somewhat less expensive now than previously — so now ever more miners were prospecting with the pan. This method was used primarily, however, to locate gold-bearing areas, after which the miners implemented the rocker process, which could separate gold from dross far more rapidly than could be done by hand manipulation of the pan.

Prospectors also still used long-bladed knives frequently, primarily to free nuggets located in crevices, although occasionally, in especially rich deposits, to dig with them when shovels were unavailable or when they balked at paying Brannan's high prices from $150 [$4,320] to almost $300 [$8,640] for spades that previously sold for around $1 [$28.80] to $5 [$144] apiece. Still, the returns for these prospectors were quite large, not only because there were fewer to share in the spoils, but because they had the choice of working through the surface of bars previously untouched by others; being unhampered by regulations or delays typically imposed by "officials," moreover, they could move quickly from placer to placer and skim off the easily accessible gold from each site.

If pans were unavailable or the miners couldn't bear parting with so much cash to purchase one, they often used pieces of stiff tin or even heavier sheet-iron to locate the gold. They would shape this metal into flat-bottomed trays from 10 to 14 inches across and with sides from four to six inches high, angling outward from the base, and their results with it remained so good that some of the miners did not "graduate" to a rocker at all, but systematically worked with the pan. Armed therewith, they separated the gold from earth, sand, and other materials by relying on the valuable metal's heavier specific gravity. They lowered the pan, partially filled with dirt from a deposit into the water and then swirled it with a sideways, rotary motion, causing the clays to dissolve and the sands and light gravel to be swept away by the current, while the heavier materials — larger pebbles and, of course the gold, could settle to the bottom. After they carefully raked out the gravel and stones by hand, hopefully all that remained at the bottom of the pan was the gold. Still, this was such a slow process that most miners used it only to initially locate a good gold source, before they took the trouble to set up a rocker in order to significantly accelerate their mining process.

The rocker itself had rounded supports resembling a child's cradle and was sloshed back and forth by means of an upright handle. The *cradle-box* was most often a wooden trough some 20 inches wide and twice that in length, with side pieces four inches high, except at the lower end of the device which was left open. Often the bottom of the rocker was lined with sheet tin or thin iron that had been pierced by a series of half-inch holes. A canvas chute was attached to the lower, open end of the rocker. The lighter, bulkier, unwanted material was quickly swept away by the current flowing through, but the heavier materials, if not entrapped by the inch-square riffle-bars nailed across the rocker's flat bottom, would work their way down the chute into another elongated box that could be more closely checked at intervals for golden nuggets, flakes and dust. If the diggings were relatively shallow and with plentiful gold near the surface, a pair of men — one to fill the hopper and the other to rock the device — could easily sift through the equivalent of 300 pans in a day, (based on a calculation that one-pan could sift a mere half-cubic foot of dirt). Obviously, if the gold was deeper and several feet of dross material had to be stripped off before reaching it, the process took longer. Often, if tough clays were involved, an hour or more were required to dissolve them to the point where the gold grains locked within could be set free.

The Mexican miners frequently favored a method called "dry-washing," by which a cloth was laid out and the dry dirt tossed by shovelsful into the air above it when a stiff breeze was blowing. The lighter materials could thus be blown away while the heavier materials, including the gold, fell back to the cloth for later panning and separation. A similar, more frequently employed method was called "coyoting," whereby the miner dug a square hole down to the bedrock and then burrowed coyote-like along that ledge by using an iron bar pointed at both ends. The material thus loosened — the pay-dirt — would be scraped up with a flat, paddle-like horn spoon, pounded into dust with great energy and shaken from a *batea* — a wooden bowl — over an extended cow hide during a brisk wind; the process was repeated until little remained to fall to the hide except the gold. This was, of course, hard, tedious work, but many of the men, having learned the process during their previous gold mining operations in Mexico — men often accused of being indolent — made small fortunes, especially during the hot, dry summer months when crowds of other miners were squandering their gold in the towns.

In Monterey, Lt. William Tecumseh Sherman, at last had an opportunity to meet the fabled mountain man he'd heard so much about, Kit Carson, who had finally arrived at Los Angeles, Sherman, who had fully expected a huge, full-bodied, bearded man, was ill prepared for the individual who showed up. As he wrote about it in his journal, the first overland mail

> *... was brought by Kit Carson in saddle bags from Taos in New Mexico. We heard of his arrival at Los Angeles, and waited patiently his arrival at headquarters. His fame was at its height, from publication of Frémont's books, and I was anxious to see a man who had achieved such feats of daring among the wild animals of the Rocky mountains, and still wilder Indians of the plains. At last his arrival was reported at the tavern at Monterey, and I hurried to hunt him up. I cannot express my surprise at beholding a small, stoop-shouldered man, with reddish hair, freckles, soft blue eyes, and nothing indicating extraordinary courage or daring. He spoke but little and answered questions in monosyllables. I asked for his mail, and he picked up his light saddle-bags containing the great overland mail, and we walked together to headquarters, where he delivered his parcel into Colonel Mason's own hands. ... We extracted with difficulty some items of his personal history. He was by commission a lieutenant in the Mounted Rifles Regiment serving in Mexico under Colonel Sumner, and, as he could not reach his regiment from California, Colonel Mason ordered that for a time he should be assigned to duty with A. J. Smith's company, First Dragoons, at Los Angeles. He will be sent back to the*

> *United States with dispatches, traveling two thousand miles almost alone, in preference to being encumbered by a large party.*

Carson, who was prepared to immediately carry mail and dispatches back to Saint Louis via Santa Fe, Taos, and Fort Leavenworth, mentioned to Lt. Sherman that he had heard rumors of a gold discovery, but having heard such tales before, he had shrugged it off. Sherman admitted that he, too, had heard such stories and that while he was now finally inclined to believe them, he had not yet had tried his hand with prospecting.

By this time editor Edward Kemble had returned to San Francisco from his recent trip to the Sutter-Marshall Saw-mill, but in his follow-up commentary in the May 6th issue of the *California Star*, his disjointed, flippant remarks on the gold discoveries merely confused his readers:

> *... great country, fine climate; visit this great valley, we would advise all who have not yet done so. See it now. Full-flowing streams, mighty timber, large crops, luxuriant clover, fragrant flowers, gold and silver.*

Meanwhile the Old Dry Diggings, a recently discovered site on the little northern tributary of Weber Creek, was already producing remarkable quantities of gold, especially considering the limited extent of its bars. Its discoverers — Daylor, McCoon and Sheldon of Captain Weber's group — were rapidly filling their leather drawstring bags with their finds. Bill Daylor and Perry McCoon, who worked shoulder to shoulder after they discovered the deposit, extracted during those first seven days $17,000 [$489,600], mainly in fair-sized nuggets.

Others of Captain Weber's party soon joined them and made similar discoveries — miners such as Dr. Isabell and the brothers John and Daniel Murphy, followed by strangers such as Murray and Phalen of San José and McKensey [McKinzie?] and Aram of Monterey. A man named Beamer had already established a tent-store of sorts near the site, and Mrs. Anna Cook, who dug as tirelessly as any of the men around her, was proudly boasting of being the first white woman on the spot.

Former General Mariano Guadalupe Vallejo noted in his *journal* on this same May 6th that a prospector, whom he did not identify, brought to him for weighing, a large quantity of gold also taken from

Weber Creek. He reported — truthfully, Vallejo was convinced — that he had collected the gold he brought in during a mere three days of work. The man's findings weighed a total of 25 pounds, mainly in larger nuggets, which Vallejo declared was worth a staggering $4,026 [$115,948.80]! Large numbers of the people in the California coastal areas were finally beginning to take the gold rumors seriously, but cautiously held back, still not inclined to join the prospecting mania. A small but increasing number, nevertheless, began falling victim to the now raging gold fever epidemic in the interior areas of California. One such victim, Sgt. James H. Carson, now living in Monterey and on extended leave, wrote on May 12:

> *The month of May, with all her flowers and balmy air had approached, and I an unbeliever still. This day I saw a form, bent and filthy, approaching me, and soon a cry of recognition was given between us. He was an old acquaintance and had been one of the first to visit the mines. Now he stood before me: his hair hung out of his hat — his chin with beard was black, and his buckskins reached to his knees; an old flannel shirt he wore, which many a bush had tore.*
>
> *Yes, Billy, I can see you yet, just as you stood before me earlier on this sunny tenth day of May, looking so much like the devil with that great bag of Tempter on your back. Then you told me that it was gold, and that you had made it in five weeks at Kelsey's and the dry diggings ... I could not believe it but told you the proof would be in your bag, which was soon opened, and out the metal tumbled; not in dust or scales, but in pieces ranging in size from that of a pea to hen's eggs; and, says you, "this is only what I picked out with a knife." There was before me proof positive that I had held too long to the wrong side of the question. I looked on for a moment; a frenzy seized my soul; unbidden my legs performed some entirely new movements of Polka steps — I took several — houses were too small for me to stay in; I was soon in the street in search of necessary outfits; piles of gold rose up before me at every step; castles of marble, dazzling the eye with their rich appliances; thousands of slaves, bowing to my beck and call; myriads of fair virgins contending with each other for my love, were among the fancies of my fevered imagina-*

> *tion. The Rothschilds, Girard and Astors appeared to me but poor people; in short, I had a very violent attack of the Gold Fever.*
>
> *One hour after I became thus affected, I was mounted on an old mule, armed with a wash-hand basin, fire shovel, a piece of square iron pointed at one end, a blanket, rifle, a few yards of jerked beef, and a bag of penola, and going at high-pressure mule speed for the 'diggin's.*

There were other men — San Francisco, Sonora, Monterey, San José were still full of them — who were still as skeptical as Carson had been, and yet who were at this moment teetering on the brink of succumbing to this same gold fever; men needing only a still more convincing, alluring account to send them over the edge — a plunge Carson had just made — into the maw of a frenzy which none of them had ever before experienced. All they needed was just that compelling impetus — and, in San Francisco, Samuel Brannan was finally prepared to provide it.

[May 12th, 1848 • Friday]

Samuel Brannan had set up his tableau and timed its beginning with the skill of an experienced showman. Last evening he had given his editor, Edward Kemble, specific instructions in regard to where he should station himself and at what time, with paper and pen in hand, to record every nuance of what would occur, and then write his impressions for Saturday's edition of the *California Star*.

"It will be, Mr. Kemble," he promised, his voice trembling with a fervor the editor had never heard from him before, "the most exciting and the most important news story you have ever in your life been present to witness and to write about. I predict that what you will write will intensely affect every soul in California Territory who has the ability to read, and probably a great many more who have not. Tomorrow, sir, there will be no one — no one! — in this entire region who is unaware of your words, and you have my absolute guarantee that we, you and I, will have created an indelible day in history."

If what Brannan had so enthusiastically told Kemble seemed to border on dramatic bombast, it assuredly did not. The impact was far more overwhelming than even Brannan himself had imagined would occur. At the height of the morning's hustle and bustle, when the streets of San Francisco were relatively crowded with resident shoppers and businessmen and transients, Edward Kemble, as directed, positioned himself on the town's busiest thoroughfare, Montgomery Street, adjacent to the central square. He had not long to wait.

The normally dapper and meticulously-clad Samuel Brannan appeared in the middle of the street, tieless, suit coat open and flaring, his characteristic derby hat missing and his hair in wild disarray. In one hand he was holding aloft a large, squat pickle jar crammed full of nothing but gleaming gold nuggets. In the other was a quinine bottle, equally filled with a combination of small nuggets, glistening flakes of gold and a large quantity of gold dust. He broke into a shambling run in the very middle of Montgomery Street and his bellowing cries stopped passers-by in their tracks.

"Gold!" he yelled. "Gold! Gold! They've found gold! It's everywhere! They're finding it by the bucketsful! Gold!"

At first the passers-by stared at him in amazement, and then, as his excited words began sinking in, clustered about him until he became the center of a seething crowd, everyone pressing in for a closer look. The glass containers he held had been tightly sealed with beeswax and so he let the closest onlookers hold them up, look at them from all angles, pass them from hand to hand and talk excitedly among themselves. For many, this was the first raw gold they had ever seen, and its very size and weight and color awed them, generating a bubbling excitement.

They fired questions at Brannan in rapid succession: Where did it come from? How much was it worth? Who found it? How was it located? How much more of it was there? Was this really a massive gold strike? Could others go there and find it as well? What kind of equipment was needed?

"From the South Fork of the American River," he replied. "Probably a thousand dollars worth or more in each jar. ... Prospectors found it; Mormons; farmers, ordinary people; even children! ... No skill required; it's lying right on the ground waiting to be picked up. Even more just under the surface. ... They're finding it visually and by digging and panning. ... No telling how much is there, but the supply seems endless. ... The deposits are stretching for miles and miles, covering perhaps half the Territory, and the end of it hasn't even been found yet. Yes! Yes! Anyone can go there and find it! It's everywhere! People are getting rich in a single day with what they find. They're using knives and shovels, spades and pans and baskets. The stores have plenty of the tools you'll need, at Sutter's Fort and beyond, right at the gold sites! Those who get there first will find the most. They'll be rich in a single day! There's never been a gold strike like this before. Never!"

On and on the questions came, and over and over Brannan answered them, generating within the crowd an intense, overwhelming lust for gold. Butchers, bakers, and shopkeepers, still in their aprons, locked their doors and headed for the diggings. Bankers, too, closed their offices and joined the wave of newly converted gold-seekers departing to pursue their fortunes. The mayhem closely resembled a scene in Monterey two days earlier, as described by James H. Carson. Blacksmiths, launderers, nurserymen, farmers, ranchers, mechanics, secretaries, saloonkeepers, cattlemen, vintners, derelicts, drunkards, drifters, sailors, and soldiers simply dropped what they were doing and, as if compelled by a powerful cosmic force, rushed to the gold sites on the South Fork of the American River. Homes and shops were abandoned. Ships at anchor lost their crews. Ranches emptied and their crops were left unharvested, their livestock loosed to feed on their own in garden plots and sown fields. Swarms of people crowded onto the docks and into the Sutter launches tied there, filling them to capacity. When no additional space was available on them, they launched their own sailing boats, rowboats, and canoes into San Francisco Bay, and the cost of such travel inevitably skyrocketed; tiny skiffs and rowboats that only a few days ago would have sold for much less than $50 [$1,440] were now suddenly priced at ten times that price and yet were quickly all sold. The frenetically excited hoards mounted horses and mules and set off leading strings of loaded pack animals; they pushed wheelbarrows crammed with supplies, rode in grossly overcrowded wagons and buggies pulled by oxen; and they even set out afoot shouldering tools along with nothing else but what they wore. All of them, in every imaginable conveyance or on foot, with or without equipment, were propelled by an overwhelming sense of excitement and a driving eagerness to get *there* as quickly as possible and to begin finding gold for themselves.

Fantasy-filled prosects of immense wealth filled their minds and overwhelming, compulsive sense of greed motivated their souls.

By noon today, May 12th, no less than 200 wagons, on their way to the reported gold sites sat motionless, awaiting their turn to be ferried across the swift expanse of the Sacramento River. In and around them crowded the men, women and children — whole families — who had closed up their homes and struck out overland until halted by the great stream. There was but one ferry, owned by Robert Semple, whose helpers, all but one, had already abandoned their ferrying jobs to head for the mines. The single exceptional worker offered to remain and help for two weeks at a pay of $25 [$720] per week, but Semple quickly sent him on his way and wrote that evening in his *logbook*, "... in three days there will not be two men left in Benicia." As the congestion at the river increased, Semple had established a system by which each wagon-owner was registered on his arrival and then each took his turn in crossing. The flat-bottomed ferry, pulled by ropes attached to teams of mules on each side, ran day and night, carrying at each crossing two wagons and the horses, people and equipment connected with them. Some of the later arrivals had to wait long hours to make the crossing. After half a day of this, someone brought in another boat, a flat-bottomed scow, and set up another ferry, dramatically shortening the waiting time, but not the cost. Semple and his competition alike each collected $20 [$576] in fares for a single individual's crossing, and often the ferries carried a dozen people or more, plus equipment and livestock, per trip.

Word of what was happening spread with phenomenal speed throughout the entire territory, taking on a word-of-mouth hyseria of its own, and generating virtually identical responses in Sonora, San José, and Monterey, as well as in more distant Santa Barbara and Los Angeles. Californians resembled lemmings, massing and rushing toward an unknown but totally irresistible destination.

The great California Gold Rush was now in progress — and it had only just begun.

[May 16th, 1848 • Tuesday]

With virtually nothing to show after two weeks of effort, Claude Chara's gold-seeking party had lost their initial enthusiasm. Thus far they had found nothing of any real value beyond a few traces of sulfurous outcroppings, along with glittering but worthless patches of mica, chunks of quartz lined red with oxidized iron, and small flakes and tiny cubes of pyrite. Shortly after they had reached Bear River, two of the men declared they'd had enough and turned back toward San Francisco. Chana and his remaining three men, however, had followed Bear River upstream some twenty miles from its mouth, but the only real luck they'd had was bagging a deer which had provided them with fresh venison for a few days, plus strips of jerky they had cut and smoke-dried.

Now, having turned south away from Bear River, they had finally neared the North Fork of the American River and carefully descended a steep ravine toward it, intending to ford it at a substantial bar skirting its northwestern shoreline. They were still in the ravine, however, when Chana suddenly gave a sharp cry, drawing up and dismounting. As his three companions still mounted, watched, Chana knelt and poked his hunting-knife blade at what had caught his eye. A coating of loose debris covering an emergent pebble had fallen away in one spot and revealed the brassy yellow glint he had seen. He turned the pebble over with the tip of his blade and caught his breath; its previously buried portion bore same solid warm brassy color.

"Gold, by God!" he murmured wonderingly as he picked it up, hefted it, then exclaimed louder, "It is! By God, boy's, we've found it! It's gold!"

His companions were off their horses in an instant, first taking a good close look at the nugget and then chortling gleefully as they hunched over and began inspecting the sides and bed of the ravine much more closely. In moments they found more, all four of them, wondering among themselves how they could possibly have missed seeing these deposits before. For a while they were like madmen as they spread out and scrambled about, stopping here and there to pry out or pick up more nuggets and bellowing gleefully each time one was found. Any thought of continuing the journey toward the saw-mill at Coloma, now still about 25 miles distant, was banished. They hurriedly set up a makeshift camp, used their coils of rope to make a corral of sorts over an area of good graze, then unsaddled, unloaded, settled the horses and mules within it, and spent the remainder of the day in an exhilarating and successful search for more gold until darkness curtailed their efforts. They had no balance on which to weigh their finds, but by nightfall the four had collected what they estimated to be close to a pound of nuggets apiece.

As they sat by their fire later, well after nightfall, and discussed their discoveries with wonder and joy, they selected an appropriate name for this place.

They called it *Rich Dry Diggings.*

[May 20th, 1848 • Saturday]

The second major step in Sam Brannan's grand plan — which not even he could clearly define beyond making a great deal of money —

was completed today, accompanied by the clamor and confusion of a huge crowd which had recently surged into Sutter's Fort. A great rush of people had begun arriving during the past week from points to the west, initially from San Francisco, and the growing turmoil did not diminish as the days progressed. The port city had become nearly a dead town, considering all who had left it, and throngs were now milling aimlessly about the fort. This congestion within and without the fort's walls increased noticeably with each passing hour. The din of voices trying to make themselves heard above the hammering of new construction and the banging of planking being moved about, horses whinnying and donkeys braying, was all but overwhelming. Everyone seemed to be asking everyone else questions for which, apparently, no one seemed to have satisfactory answers: Where should they go? What should they do? Where was the gold and how could they get at it?

As evening drew nigh, tents — manufactured and makeshift — were erected all around the outer walls of the fort, and everyone was hungry, with little food to be obtainable anywhere. John Sutter, who had run himself ragged throughout the day trying to help newcomers, was finally able to close himself away in his own quarters, bar his door, and spend a bit of time writing in his *diary*, his handwriting even less legible than usual:

> *May 19th. The great Rush from San Francisco arrived at the fort, all my friends and acquaintances filled up the houses and the whole fort, I had only a little Indian boy, to make them roasted Ripps etc. as my Cooks left me like every body else. The Merchants, Doctors, Lawyers, Sea Captains, Merchants etc. all came up and did not know what to do, all was in Confusion, all left their wives and families in San Francisco, and those which had none-locking Doors, abandoned their houses, even offered them for sale cheap, a few hundred dollars per House & Lot. ... some of these men were just like greasy [sic] Mexicans. My men all deserted me, which is not strange. Some of the Merchants has [sic] been the most purdentest [prudent?] of the Whole, visited the Mines and returned immediately and they began to do a very profitable business, and soon Vessels came from everywhere with all Kind of Merchandise, the whole old thrash [trash?] which was laying for Years unsold, on the Coasts of South*

> *& Central America, Mexico Sandwich Islands etc. All found a good Market here.*
>
> *Mr. Brannan is erecting a very large Warehouse, and have [sic] done an immense busines. ...*

After the Claude Chana party members discovered rich deposits along the North Fork of the American River, prospectors began finding new deposits farther to the north and not just in the American River and its tributaries. Jacob Leese, who was, in essence, the founder of San Francisco when it first came into being as a settlement called Yerba Buena, was decidedly one of the old-timers of the region. Now living in Sonoma, he, with some of his old cronies from the same period, including Dr. John Marsh, was wise enough not to head to the very same area where the whole California population now seemed to be flocking, in the basin of the American River. Instead, the pair formed a party and struck out northward on the Sacramento to the mouth of the Yuba River. They moved up the Yuba a short distance, and at the third bar they encountered they struck gold in a substantial deposit and immediately established what they called *Marsh Diggings*.

Farther eastward some 30 miles, in the location dubbed *Grass Valley*, three more Oregonians calling themselves the D. Stump Party found similarly abundant gold deposits during late May and named their prime deposit area *Boston Ravine*.

Today within the confines of Sutter's Fort, Charles Smith & Co., Mercantile, ceased to exist, at least by that name. The establishment was now officially S. Brannan Company. In a bold maneuver, Brannan had just bought sole interest in the store, eliminating Smith with a purchase offer of $50,000 [$1,440,000] that Smith simply could not resist. On instructions from Brannan, Sutter dispatched two wagons loaded with new supplies to the stores presently being built by Brannan's men at both Mormon Island and Coloma. The ghost town aspect of the larger towns was emphasized by the suspension — or at least temporary closing — of all major newspapers, including even the regionally prominent *California Star*, as their staffs left their jobs and hastened off to the gold sites.

The incoming traffic at the fort today surpassed even that of yesterday, but now with more of the new arrivals having traveled from sites more distant than San Francisco, such as Sonoma and San José.

[May 27th, 1848 • Saturday]

The initial excitement generated by Sam Brannan's extravagant announcement of the gold discovery had not abated during the past fortnight. If anything, it had grown only more intense, more infectious, and more overpowering with each passing day. Not even the deeply-rooted pessimism in the make-up of editor Edward Kemble, which had surfaced again in his rather sneeringly contemptuous words in the May 20th issue of the *California Star*, had diminished the heat of gold fever. The mercurially-minded Kemble had written:

> *Fleets of launches left this place on Sunday and Monday, closely stowed with human beings [heading for the gold sites]. ... Was there ever anything so superlatively silly?*

On that same day, though, ships at moor in San Francisco Bay that had been fully loaded and were on the verge of embarking to distant ports still lay at anchor, their crews having deserted to join the gold rush and their captains exasperated over their inability to set sail as scheduled. The enthusiasm Brannan recently had provoked flared more intensely a few mornings later when another of Sutter's launches from upstream arrived at the San Francisco port. The launch provided one more conveyance to be filled to capacity with gold-seekers on its return upriver, but equally important, a party of five Mormon miners were on board, fresh from Mormon Island, carrying pouches bulging with the gold they had recently found.

Besieged with questions, the miners answered them as best they could and then ignited even greater excitement when they exposed the contents of their large pouchs on the head of a freshly cloth-covered barrel — an almost mind-numbing array of glittering nuggets they and their partners had extracted from Mormon Island amounting to $20,000 [$576,000] worth. The men announced their intention quickly to purchase and replenish needed supplies and then to return immediately to the site of their newly discovered wealth.

Word of the Mormons' almost casual display of such enormous wealth had flashed through the town and its surroundings with the same lightning speed that Brannan's initial news of the discovery had precipitated earlier. More watercraft were launched to join those already dotting San Francisco Bay and the Sacramento River, heading upstream. Now, even more riders and walkers clogged the paths and roadways leading eventually toward Sutter's Fort, Mormon Island and Coloma.

Within a single week novice miners filled every available space for digging on the Mormon Island bar, and all the arroyos, gulches and little tributaries of the South Fork had been filled with novice miners, in many locations so closely clustered that they were prospecting virtually shoulder to shoulder. Serious disputes, moreover, were arising regarding digging rights on the Marshall-Sutter saw-mill properties that some of the newcomers felt strongly should be open to general prospecting.

To Henry Bigler, it seemed as if all at once the very portals of humanity had been opened to let loose this flood of people upon them. He was grateful that he had carefully staked his own claims, and he hoped he would be able to hold them without provoking violence from newcomers. Soon enough, he knew, he'd have to let them go, when he headed with the other Saints for Salt Lake City, but he wanted the release of his claims to be on his own terms, possibly through sales of individual small parcels, and not as a result of their being forcefully taken from him. Jim Brown, Bigler's burly fellow saint who shared his attitude, now kept his fully loaded rifle constantly close at hand.

Benjamin Hawkins, a former member of the Mormon Battalion's A Company, living in San Francisco when the news broke, apparently possessed his own share of Brannan's entrepreneurial strain. While others had rushed to pack their immediate needs and start off for the mines without delay, he had lingered long enough to buy, wherever he could locate them, all the remaining shallow baskets that had not yet been sold to Brannan. He had managed to purchase fifteen of them for an average of $3 [$86.40] apiece and only shrugged at the jeers and laughter of his fellows at his willingness to pay such an exorbitant a price for them — an outlay of $45 [$1,296] that he could really ill afford. The laughter diminished considerably, however, when he handily sold every one of them for $15 [$432] each before leaving for the mines — an easy profit of $180 [$5,184] beyond his initial investment.

Sutter was still hard pressed to keep up with the rush of people onto his settlement, the majority of whom were poorly prepared for the hardships ahead and who fully assumed that Sutter, always helpful in the past to travelers, would never fail to be hospitable. Sutter still tried courteously to provide for his visitors' needs, but both he and his patrons soon recognized the teeming crowds were overwhelming his hospitality. Everyone, it seemed to Sutter, wanted *something,* and fully expected him to provide it. When he could not, their anger and frustration increased, and the scene inside the fort slowly evolved into abject chaos. Once again, when he finally shut himself away from all that was occurring and wrote his diary entry for May 21st, it was with a hand made quite as shaky by nerves as by the amount of brandy he drank:

> *May 21st. Saml Kyburg [Kyburz] has erected or established the first Hotel in the fort, in the larger building, and makes a great deal of Money. A great Many traders [have] deposited a great deal of goods in my Store (an Indian was the Key Keeper and performed very well.)*
>
> *Afterwards every little Shanty became a Warehouse and Store; The fort [has become] a veritable Bazaar. As white people would not [actually, refused to] be employed at this Time I had a few good Indians attending to the Ferry boat, and tonight came up, and delivered the received Money, for ferryage, to me, after deduction for a few bottles of brandy, for the whole of them. Perhaps some white people would not have acted so honestly.*

When Benjamin Hawkins himself left San Francisco for the mines, he was accompanied by three of his former Battalion comrades — Lafayette Shepherd, Schuyler Hulett and Isaac Wriston, all of them, including Hawkins, formerly of Company A — plus another friend, Ashbel Haskell, who had come to California with Sam Brannan aboard the ship *Brooklyn*. They rode their horses and each led a trailing mule packed with supplies. When they arrived at the South Fork of the American River, a few miles below Mormon Island, they spied along the opposite shore an overturned rowboat wedged among some driftwood. With the aid of their horses, they managed to drag it ashore and plugged a leak with pitch from a nearby pine. They then lashed the boat between two of their horses and took it upriver with them a short distance.

Hawkins and his men were still a mile or more below Mormon Island when they crossed the stream to the north bank and set up camp, unobserved by anyone else, at the foot of a small bar. There they were hidden from the view of any passers-by on the south bank, all of whom were intent on reaching Mormon Island before stopping. As luck would have it, during their crossing they intercepted a rocker that had evidently escaped from someone well above and floated downstream. It was great good fortune for them, since they were aware, as many of the miners were by this time, of how the device was made to work. They set it firmly in place at the foot of the small bar and commenced using it the following morning, shoveling into it sands and gravels from the bar itself. Working in relays without pause through the daylight hours, by nightfall of that same day they had washed out $4,000 [$115,200] worth of nuggets — $800 [$23,040] apiece, at which Hawkins remarked, in classic understatement:

"Well, boys, looks like we've each of us earned a fair day's pay for our labors." He chuckled and then added, "Maybe we'll do better tomorrow."

They did.

Far to the east, in the coastal regions of the United States, not a whisper had yet arrived regarding the incredible California gold belt, and life continued in its routine pattern. G. N. Christy of The Christy Minstrels singing group had, on February 25, premiered a song, written by an essentially unknown 21-year-old composer, that had already become an instant sensation. The piece was called *Oh! Susanna!* and its young composer was named Stephen C. Foster.

In the world of literature, among the very popular books published during 1847, which many emigrants now moving westward on the Oregon Trail had packed in their trunks, were W. H. Prescott's remarkable two-volume work, *History of the Conquest of Peru,* Herman Melville's new work entitled *Omoo,* poet Henry Wadsworth Longfellow's brilliant *Evangeline,* and two new, rather intense, eyebrow-raising novels written by a pair of English sisters, *Jane Eyre* by Charlotte Bronte and *Wuthering Heights* by Emily Jane Bronte. And just this past February 4, a remarkable new form of almost instant communication over long distances had been installed in a wire line stretching from New York City to Chicago — a communication method being called *telegraph.* And just two months ago, on March 28th, with the news of the telegraph just now beginning to stretch into the West, the richest man in America had died — the man who had become noted as the great baron of the American fur industry, and who had also dabbled so extensively in real estate that he was called New York City's landlord — leaving behind an estate valued at more than $20 million [$576 million]. His name: John Jacob Astor.

Now, with virtually incredible fortunes being made by some in just a matter of days, Edward Kemble — unabashedly denying he had ever doubted that gold deposits existed in California or that he had denounced as fools those who had — wholeheartedly endorsed and proclaimed "the employment in which over two thirds of the white population of this country are engaged," but it was a bit too late to white-wash those initial rash words, and his reputation as a newsman was irreparably damaged. His abrupt change of heart did not, however, prevent him from continuing to publish letters from readers who still disbelieved, such as the old San Franciscan whose ranting letter remarked:

> *I doubt, sir, if ever the sun shone upon such a farce as is now being enacted in California, though I fear it may prove a tragedy before the curtain drops. I consider it your duty, Mr. Editor, as a conservator of the public morals and welfare, to raise your voice against the thing. It is to be hoped that General Mason will despatch [sic] the volunteers to the scene of the action, and send these unfortunate people to their homes, and prevent others from going thither.*

Kemble seemed to gloat in publishing such letters and was not at all hesitant to add, both in editorials and in news stories, his own strangely warped impression of what was occurring; some of it directly and honestly presented, but much of it a diatribe against whatever he disliked - and he heartily disliked the gold story. Now, in the final issue for this month — May 27th — the editor's remarks underlined the morose instability of his thinking. He wrote:

> *Stores are closed and places of business vacated, a large number of houses tenantless, various kinds of mechanical labor suspended or given up entirely, and nowhere the pleasant hum of dutiful industry salutes the ear as of late; but as if a curse has arrested our onward course of enterprise, everything wears a desolate and somber look, everywhere all is dull, monotonous, dead. ... Pay up before you go — everybody knows where. Papers can be forwarded to Sutter's Fort with all regularity. But pay the printer, if you please, all you in arrears. ...*

The amazing finds of gold that were continually being made as May progressed, however, soon compelled all the debunkers to pull in their horns and, in fact, many of these doubters themselves joined the rush as the great gold field continued to expand expanded. One of the earlier deposits, discovered at a considerable distance from the valley of the American River, was a large bar located to the north on Feather River, westward from Bidwell Bar. Even the men who initially pioneered the placer mining there were astounded by the fruits of their efforts. At first they called the site *Monterey Bar,* but before very long the name was changed to bear the name of one of the leading gold-seekers in their group. Job F. Dye described their findings in the Santa Cruz Sentinel newspaper:

> *I was a member of the party of seven men who took out $70,000 [$2,016,000] worth of gold after forty-two days of work at the rich diggings at Monterey Bar, later called Longs Bar, averaging $1,666 [$47,980] daily, which is $238 [$6,854.40] per man per day, every day for six weeks!*

Through all of this, when by all rights he should have been profiting enormously, John Sutter began caving in and making decisions that seldom benefited himself, but he was quick to blame everyone but himself for his myriad growing problems. He could have earned phenomenal wealth, but his every act seemed doomed to make things worse for himself. From the Sutter-Marshall Saw-mill, he did fairly well; he personally found gold downstream from Coloma, and he finally sold his half interest in it for $6,000 [$172,800], but it was in his poor management of the grist-mill at Brighton that his fortunes turned sour. Though he had spent some $30,000 [$864,000] in his attempt to complete it, the whole operation finally just fell into decay, for which he blamed the gold discovery first and thereafter everyone about him. Putting his complaints into words, which he proceeded to do almost constantly, he wrote:

> *My grist-mill never was finished. Everything was stolen, even the stones. There is a saying that men will steal everything but a mile-stone and a mill-stone. They stole my mill-stones. They stole the bells from the fort, and gate-weights; the hides they stole, and my salmon barrels. I had*

just had 200 barrels made as salmon containers. I was just beginning to cure salmon; I had put up some before, enough to try it, and to ascertain that it would be a good business. The tan-yards were flourishing and the vats were full of leather. All this dried up and rotted — all ruined — and so it was in all the shoe-shops, saddle-shops, boat and blacksmith shops — all were vacated and the work was left half completed. Some of the cannon at the fort were also stolen, and some I gave to neighbors that they might fire them on the 4th of July. My property was all left exposed, at the mercy of the elements and the rabble, when gold was discovered. My men all desert me, which is not strange. I cannot shut the gates of my Fort and keep out lawless men and rabble without spilling their blood. The many immigrants drive their stock into my yards, and trample my grain with impunity. They drive off my stock by the hundreds and care not of it. Expostulation does no good. I am alone. There is no law. If one feels one's self insulted, one might shoot the offender. One man shot another for a very slight provocation in the fort right under my very nose. Philosopher Pickett shot a very good man who differed with him on some question.

On and on the diatribes continued, growing increasingly more bitter . The hands in the fields, he complained, asked for raise after raise in their pay. When they finally demanded ten dollars [$288] per day, Sutter felt compelled to let them go, and he did so. Shortly after they left, so too did his clerk, and then his cook, and then his mechanics. He groused:

The Mormons didn't like to leave the mill unfinished, but they got the gold fever like everybody else, and now they are gone and the grinding of grain is ended. At the tannery, which is just now for the first time becoming profitable, leather is left to rot in the vats and an additional two thousand collected hides are rendered valueless. So it is, too, in all the manufacturies, the shoe-shop, the saddle shop, the hat and blacksmith shops; the men have deserted, leaving their work in a half-finished state. I was able to hold my Indian help long enough to get my wheat crop cut, but with no one left here to thresh it, an estimated forty thousand bushels is going to waste.

Finally, his long connection with the Mormons ended entirely, and in mid-May he wrote in his diary:

Paid off all the Mormons which has been employed by me, in building these Mills and other Mechanical trades, all of them made their pile, and some of them became rich & wealthy, but all of them was [sic] [off] to the great Salt Lake, and spent there, their fortunes to the honor and Glory of the Lord!

As for the Mormons, who once had lived in fear, or at least with deep respect, of his power, they now thought of him with contempt or a vague sense of pity. As Bigler put it:

Sunday, May 14th. Gold hunters arriving every day and the place is filled with people, as much or more than any other in California. It costs 25 or 50 cents [$7.20 or $14,40] to get a shirt washed, and everything is high in proportion. . . . This day I have made a claim to one square mile of land, and have laid the foundation of a house. In the afternoon I helped Brown lay the foundation of a cabin about a mile below. It is thought Sutter and Marshall cannot hold so much land as they have taken up.

Of all those who were recording in one way or another the California goings-on these days, none was more keenly observant, literate or astute than the man who was the consul of the King of France in Monterey. Formerly an officer under Napoleon Bonaparte, he had traded in South America and had previously been consul for the Netherlands in Valparaiso and for the United States in Tahiti. Smooth, suave, handsome, he had been a favorite courier of young Queen Pomar and the prime negotiator for France in her acquisition of the Society Islands. The book he had written on his voyages to the South Seas had earned worldwide respect from geographers and historians alike. Additionally, he was very nearly as skilled with a fine paintbrush as with a pen and enjoyed, as a pastime, the delicate painting of miniatures, which also brought him considerable acclaim. Despite such varied accomplishments, he was generally considered a very modest and unassuming individual.

His name was Jacques Antoine Moerenhout, and his letter written in San José to the French Minister of Foreign Affairs underlined the competence for which he was justifiably noted. He wrote:

> *Pueblo de San Jos de Guadaloupe*
> *Monsieur le Ministre: May 15, 1848*
> *I cannot yet tell Your Excellency of [all] the many discoveries of mines of precious metals which have been made in all parts of Upper California, but es-pecially in this district, where all other riches seem to be combined with those of agriculture; but the most important new discovery, and [the one] which just now is causing the most excitement, is that of a gold placer, which is found in the plain of the Sacramento near New Helvetia. Being unable to go there myself to examine it I have written to M. Sutter, the owner of New Helvetia, to ask him for some details of this discovery. The discovery of a platinum mine is also spoken of; but although this country may be rich in mines of precious metals, and the existence of the placer proven to me by the gold put in circulation, reports which are being passed around are certainly either false or exaggerated, and until I can myself go over the ground where the mines are, or until I receive reports from trustworthy persons, I believe that I should limit myself to informing Your Excellency that they have been claimed (dnounces) and that it is probable that they exist.*

At this same time Sutter recorded in his own personal *diary* that in the past week upwards of a thousand gold-seekers had passed through Sutter's Fort and that the throngs of such travelers was increasing daily. The reports of James H. Carson fully verified the numbers arriving and the level of excitement prevailing. He had finally reached the valley of Weber Creek, where much placer mining was occurring and the sight of what they were finding greatly stoked the fires of enthusiasm in his own heart. As Sgt. Carson put it himself on May 15th:

> *"... Kelsey's and the Old Dry Diggings had just been opened, and to them I next set out; a few hours' ride brought*

me to the Indian-trading camp of Captain Weber's famed company, where I saw sights of gold that revived the fever again. I saw Indians giving handsful of gold for a cotton handkerchief or a shirt — and so great was the income of the Captain's trading houses that he was daily sending out mules packed with gold, to the settlements. And no man in California was more deserving of this good fortune. . . . it was the centre of attraction for gold diggers. The population (exclusive of Indians) consisted of about three hundred — old pioneers, native Californians, deserters from the Army, Navy, and Colonel Stevenson's volunteers — all mingled together, the happiest set of men on earth. Every one had plenty of dust. From three ounces to five pounds was the income per day to those who would work. The gulches and ravines were opened about two feet wide and one foot in depth along their centres [sic], and the gold was picked out from amongst the dirt with knife. When they failed to realize two or three ounces per day by this method, the diggings were pronounced worked-out, and new ones were hunted up. Clothing was not to be had, for love or gold; and I have seen many an hombre with as much gold as he could carry, whose skin 'peeped out through many a rent'. The first reports of the immense quantities of gold found on every river, gulch, & ravine, was [sic] not believed by these good pioneers of 1846, & the continuing arrival of pounds, arrobas and fanegas of the precious metal, soon quiets all doubts on the subject, and a general stampede is taking place in the different settlements. The great many comic scenes that are enacted would fill a volume of humour. Men who were once content to labor years for a few hundred dollars, & many hard-working honest fellows who never had twenty dollars at one time in their lives, are now fully convinced that, they have but to procure a pick, pan, and knife, go to the gold region and their eternal fortunes are made.

The gold-seekers' exalted confidence which Carson mirthfully described was sometimes justified - but more often not! While a certain number quickly found fabulous fortunes that set them up for the rest of their lives, a far greater of them found nothing, gained nothing, lost everything.

Black men, who had never before on this continent known equality, found it now on the gold fields where skin color was clearly not a criterion. Thus, it was little wonder that whole crews of Blacks jumped ships lying at anchor in San Francisco and Monterey Bays and rushed to the gold field, seeking the opportunity to find gold, as well as the right to be accepted as no more nor less than just more human beings seeking their fortunes.

A good many of the prospectors were by this time turning their backs on the difficult labor of trying to recover gold dust and flakes and choosing instead to concentrate primarily on nuggets, their principal tools being no more than a long-bladed knife and, if they were lucky enough to have one, a straight crowbar with one end sharpened into a blade. These goldseekers were intent upon picking up the "easy stuff" — the nuggets that were clearly visible in clefts and cracks of the stream's rock base, or those that could be gathered quickly through turning over the surface materials of bars. For now it was paying off well for them, and they were gathering from ounces to actual pounds of gold in a single day.

Every hour of every day reports were exchanged of vast yields from richer and richer diggings, not only in the valley of the South Fork but on every hillside, in every valley, in each gulch or ditch, arroyo or ravine, in each pasture and woodland and in the beds of every stream, creek or rill for hundreds of miles. All such tales, true or false, provided wings to the feet of those en route to find their fortunes, filling their minds with wild dreams of riches beyond imagining. By now it was estimated that well over 800 miners were hard at work in the diggings at the Sutter-Marshall Saw-mill at Coloma and at Mormon Island alone, and many more than that were lining every creek and ravine within conceivable reach — and yet their numbers somehow continued to increase.

Sam Brannan was busier than he had ever before been in his entire life; his holdings were increasing; his properties were expanding; and his investments were rewarding him many times over. The same held true, however, for Brannan's few competitors, even though they operated on a much smaller scale than he did. Thomas Fallon, for example, also turned a large profit from the fact that the demand for suitable mining tools far exceeded the supply. On a visit to San José, Fallon had met Methodist minister Elihu Anthony, who had arrived here last year with his wife and infant daughter, and who had brought west with him just over fifty-five long-handled picks that he had hoped to sell for a dollar or so apiece. Now, in view of the gold discovery, his asking price had trebled to $3 [$86.40] apiece. Fallon, as quick to smell an opportunity as Brannan, purchased the entire lot from him for $165 [$4,752] and then almost immediately sold them all for 3 ounces of gold apiece — $48 [$1,382.40] each — netting himself the immediate phenomenal profit of $2,592 [$74,649]!

At Sutter's Fort and at the Brighton and Coloma mill-sites, it had not taken long at all for the prices of everything to escalate fantastically. The most difficult thing to buy was physical labor; no one wished to work for others when he could work for himself with the potential of earning a lifetime's wages in a few days or weeks. As James H. Carson wrote:

> *The discovery of has gold raised the price of stock in proportion with everything else. Horses and mules in the mines are worth from one to two hundred dollars [$2,880 to $5,760] per head. I have seen men give two and three hundred dollars [$5,760 and $8,640] for mules and horses — ride them from one digging to another — take the saddles off, and set the animals loose (never looking for them again), remarking that "it was easier to dig out the price of another, than to hunt up the one astray."*

As one miner put it. Hopelessly exasperated over the unbelievably high prices for everything vitally necessary for mining, "The whole damned world's gone crazy!"

At Sutter's Fort store, the S. Brannan Company was constantly filled with a milling throng of customers who groused bitterly about his exorbitant prices, but paid them, nonetheless; consequently, almost overnight his sales of equipment, tools, clothing, and supplies were averaging about $5,000 [$144,000] each day. Brannan's agents, still scouring the Territory for him, were continuing to collect every imaginable sort of container they could find — bottles, jars, tin cans, snuff boxes, tobacco tins, vials, even lengths of pipe or brass tubing, anything that could be used to hold or store raw gold; all of these diverse purchases quickly appeared on Brannan's shelves marked up to astronomically high prices, and, nevertheless, sold as rapidly as they appeared. The new store he was erecting to serve the miners at Coloma was already doing a brisk business even before it was more than half-built, and the same was true with the Natoma store serving the miners clustering at Mormon Island.

Apart from all this, Brannan's regular collection of tithes from the Saints was a money-maker far exceeding even his wildest expectations. The ties of the Mormon miners to the Church of Jesus Christ of Latter Day Saints were still strong, and all contributed their ten per cent of whatever gold they mined, which in most cases was substantial and in many cases prodigious. Most gave such tithes gladly, content in the belief the wealth was going into the coffers of the Church to benefit every member. Some gave reluctantly, silently fuming at having to contribute so heavily. None dreamed that what was being collected was going anywhere except to the Church itself.

All were wrong.

No written record was ever kept of the tens, scores, and hundreds of thousands of dollars worth of gold Brannan was collecting from the miners now in the name of the Church, but every cent of it went into his pockets alone. There was no doubt in his mind that one day, sooner or later, there would be an inquiry into where the funds had gone, but without any records to show they had ever been collected, who could prove otherwise? Even if charges of apostasy were made against him — and even if such charges were believed — what measures could the Church possibly take against him in addition to mere excommunication?

Brannan worked hard to conceal a basic truth from the central California area members of his Mormon flock: He had apostatized from the Church long, *long* ago.

Chapter 3

[June 1st, 1848 • Thursday]

Bits and pieces of information concerning the California gold discoveries began filtering to the East, but the few reports arriving there were generally word-of-mouth accounts, things "heard from others" which were generally dismissed as ridiculous, unbelievable rumors.

Governor Mason was somewhat convinced that gold had been found, and he had, in fact, mentioned it to others in some of his correspondence. As of yet, however, he was reasonably certain that what had been found amounted merely to several isolated pockets of the precious mineral which would quickly be depleted, and he cautiously conveyed these reservations in his letters. Yet there was now no denying it; the reports he'd been receiving, especially from Consul Thomas Larkin, confirmed the discovery of large quantities of gold spread over vast areas of central California. During a visit to San José less than a week ago, Larkin had written Mason about what effect the alleged gold discovery was having there:

> *[The month of] May had not wholly passed when at San José the merchant closed his store, or if the stock was perishable left open the doors that people might help themselves, and incontinently set out upon the pilgrimage. So the judge abandoned his bench and the doctor his patients; even the alcalde dropped the reins of government and went away with his subjects. Criminals slipped their fetters and hastened northward; their keepers followed in pursuit, if indeed they had not preceded, but they took care not to find them. Soldiers fled from their posts; others were sent for them, and none returned. Valuable land grants are surrendered, and*

> *farms left tenantless; waving fields of grain stand wholly abandoned, perchance opened to the roaming cattle, and gardens are left to run to waste. The country seems as if smitten by a plague. .... Last night several of the most respectable American residents of this town arrived home from a visit to the gold regions; next week they, with their families, and I think nine-tenths of the foreign store-keepers, mechanics, and day-laborers of this place, and perhaps of San Francisco, leave for the Sacramento. The town is full of people coming from and going to the gold mines.*

Larkin conveyed this same attitude in a letter he was presently writing in his Monterey office. He hoped that what he was reporting today to his headquarters in Washington would not be construed as a reaction too rash to be taken seriously; he could only rely on his own reputation as being steady and level-headed. Were that not enough, he reasoned to himself, surely his own present position here, in addition to being U.S. Consul, as U.S. Naval Agent and covert secret agent, would imbue endow his words with credibility. He was, after all, noted in high government circles as being, even in the most strained of unusual circumstances, a very unexcitable diplomat, and he sincerely hoped that this would add greater weight to what he desired to impart in this letter.

Now that he had journeyed to San José and San Francisco, had witnessed the large quantities of prospected gold which had been brought there, and had noted the populations of both cities' explosive reaction to these recently discovered riches, he was himself entirely convinced of the magnitude of this gold discovery, and he tried to fathom what effect the major impact of the further spreading news would have, not only among the Californians, but very soon in the East and, for that matter, throughout the world. San José was, for example, an eye-opener, since gold fever had struck hard and only two of its 500 male residents — Isaac Branham and Frank Lightston — remained at home. Monterey was a bit more conservative; some of the residents had gone off at once to Sutter's Fort, but the majority seemed content to await some form of more reliable confirmation of the remarkably good news. With such considerations in mind, Larkin had early this morning begun writing this detailed preliminary report to his immediate supervisor, the Honorable James Buchanan, U.S. Secretary of State. Now he paused in that writing to read over what he had already written, hopeful that his unbridled enthusiasm had not overstepped the bounds of decorum.

> *San Francisco (Upper California), June 1, 1848*
>
> *Sir: I here report to the State Department one of the most astonishing excitements and state of affairs now existing in this country, that, perhaps, has ever been brought to the notice of the Government. On the American fork of the Sacramento and Feather River, another branch of the same, and the adjoining lands, there has been discovered, within the present year, a placer — a vast tract of land containing gold, in small particles. This gold, thus far, has been taken on the bank of the river, from the surface to eighteen inches in depth, and is supposed deeper, and to extend over the country.*
>
> *On account of the inconvenience of washing, the people have, up to this time, only gathered the metal on the banks, which is done simply with a shovel, filling a shallow dish, bowl, basket, or tin pan, with a quantity of black sand, similar to the class used on paper, and washing out the sand by movement of the vessel. ...*

Larkin had paused at this point in his report, still wondering if he were perhaps being too extravagant in his description of what had thus far taken place in San Francisco. He briefly considered accompanying the letter with a copy of the *Californian* fly-sheet published last Monday, the 29th of May, in which its editor, James Buckelew, his previous skeptical, sarcastic attitude toward the gold-discovery rumors now totally vanquished, exuberantly made the following proclamation shortly before bolting for the gold fields, himself:

> *GOLD DISCOVERY IS REAL*
>
> *The whole country from San Francisco to Los Angeles, and from the seashore to the base of the Sierra Nevada, resounds to the sordid cry of gold! GOLD!! GOLD!! ! while the field is left half planted, the house half built, and everything neglected but the manufacture of shovels and pickaxes, and the means of some sort of transportation to the spot where one good man obtained $128 [$36,864] worth of the*

> *real stuff in one day's washing, and the average for all concerned is $20 [$576] per diem! This paper cannot be made by magic, and the labor of mechanism is quite as essential to its existence as to all other arts; and as neither men nor devils can be kept to service, the wheels of progress here must rest a while. Because the majority of our subscribers and many of our advertisers have closed their doors and places of business and left town and, in fact, our entire staff has followed them to the diggings, the Californian is compelled to suspend its publication until further notice.*

After some reflection, however, Larkin decided against including a copy of Buckelew's euphoric confirmation with his report; newspapers were all too notorious for playing loose with the facts in order to titillate reader excitement. The piece might undermine Larkin's credibility. It would be difficult, moreover, for the average person in the East making roughly $20 per month to grasp the reality of inexperienced prospectors here making far more than that much money in a single day!

Ironically, despite Larkin's fear of straining the credulity of his superiors by what he had written thus far, he had yet to mention that nearly three hundred men had already left the town and stampeded to the mines. The Consul was genuinely concerned that his words would already be taken as exaggerations and decided not to comment extensively on the departures thus far. He continued his report, still struggling to avoid what might be perceived as gross exaggerations. Larkin also decided against revealing that even most of the San Francisco shopkeepers had decided to try their luck at the diggings and had closed their shops entirely or had hung notes on their doors telling those who remained to take what they needed and put the money for payment in the provided container. Still deeply concerned that his superiors would not take him seriously, Larkin continued with his report:

> *It is now two or three weeks since the men employed in those washings have appeared in this town with gold, to exchange for merchandise and provisions.*

I presume nearly 20,000 dollars [$576,000] has yet been so exchanged. Some 200 or 300 men have remained up the river, or are gone to their homes, for purpose of returning to the Placer, and washing immediately with shovels, picks, and baskets; many of them, for the first few weeks, depending on borrowing from others. I have seen the written statement of the work of one man for sixteen days, which averaged 25 dollars [$720] per day; others have, with a shovel and pan, or wooden bowl, washed out 10 dollars [$288] to even 50 dollars [$1,440] in a day. There are now some men yet washing who have 500 dollars to 1,000 dollars [$14,400 to $28,800]. As they have to stand two feet deep in the river, they work but a few hours in the day, and not every day in the week.

A few men have been down in boats to this port, spending twenty to thirty ounces of gold each — about 300 dollars [$8,640]. I am confident that this town (San Francisco) has one-half of its tenements quite empty, locked up with the furniture. The owners — store-keepers, lawyers, mechanics, and laborers — all gone to the Sacramento with their families. Small parties, of five to fifteen men, have sent to this town and offered cooks ten to fifteen dollars [$288 to $432] per day for a few weeks. Mechanics and teamsters, earning the year past five to eight dollars [$144 to $230.40] per day, have struck and gone. Several U.S. volunteers have deserted. U.S. barque Anita, belonging to the Army, now at anchor here, has but six men. One Sandwich Islands vessel in port lost all her men; and was obliged to engage another crew at 50 dollars [$1,440] each for the run of fifteen days to the [Sandwich] Islands.

One American captain having his men shipped on this coast in such a manner that they could leave at any time, had them all on the eve of quitting, when he agreed to continue their pay and food; leaving one on board, and carried them to the gold regions — furnishing tools and giving his men one-third. They have been gone a week. Common spades and shovels, one month ago worth 1 dollar [$28.80], will now bring 10 dollars [$288], at the gold regions. I am informed 50 dollars [$1,440] has been offered for one. Should this gold continue as represented, this town and others would be depopulated. Clerks' wages have risen from 600 dollars to 1000 [$17,280 to $28,800] per annum, and board; cooks, 25 dollars to 30 dollars [$720 to $864] per month. This sum will not be any inducement a month longer, unless the fever and ague [cold and flu] appears among the washers.

Writing at the same time as Larkin did, Reverend Walter Colton, *alcalde* of Monterey, decried in his own *diary* for May 29th, the fact that so many of the men of his town had hurried off to the gold sites. As he put it:

Our town was startled out of its quiet dreams to-day, by announcement that gold had been discovered on the American Fork. The men wondered and talked, and the women, too: but neither believed. The sibyls were less skeptical; they said the moon had, for several nights, appeared not more than a cable's length from the earth; that a white raven had been seen playing with an infant; and that an owl rang the church bells. I have dispatched a messenger to the mines to determine for myself and for the good people of Monterey if the astounding reports are true.

There was, Larkin admitted to himself, such a strange aspect of unreality to everything about this remarkable gold discovery and everyone, including even the laconic *alcalde* of Monterey, could scarce believe the reports being bandied about. As for the Monterey and San Francisco newspapers, they continued to seem quite incapable of withstanding the impact of so incredible an event.

One of the accounts Larkin had received had come from a man he considered to be highly reliable. He was E. Gould Buffum, a San Franciscan of impeccable character, who was one of four prospectors who had tried their luck along the Middle Fork of the American River. They were prepared to set up a rocker system, but before they could do so, in a little hollow leading down to the Middle Fork but some fifty yards distant from it, they came to a large granite boulder partially embedded in the earth. Scratching around the base of it, they quickly came to gravel and clay, and in removing several inches of that coating, came to a level of black sand atop solid bedrock. Mingled with the black sand was a significant scattering of gold, ranging from pea-sized nuggets to some almost as fine as sand, all glittering brightly against the black. They concentrated first on picking up the larger nuggets with their fingers, and on that day they picked up a total of 26 ounces — $416 [$11,980.80]. As Buffum later wrote of it:

The next day, our machine being ready, we looked for a place to work it, and soon found a little bench which extends back some five or six yards before it reached the rocks. The upper soil was a light black sand, on the surface of which we could see the particles of gold shining, and could in fact *gather them up with our fingers. In digging below this we struck a red stony gravel that appeared perfectly alive with gold, shining and pure. We threw off the uppermost top earth, and commenced our washing with the gravel, which proved so rich that, excited by curiosity, we weighed the gold extracted from the first washing of 50 pansful of earth, and found $75 [$2,160], or nearly five ounces of gold to be the result. The full day's work amounted to 25 ounces — $400 [$11,520]! — A little lower on the river we struck the stony bottom of 'pocket,' which appeared to be of pure gold, but upon probing it, I found it to be only a thin covering which by its own weight and the pressure above it had spread and attached itself to the rock. Crossing the river I continued my search, and after digging some time struck upon a hard, reddish clay only a few feet from the surface. After two hours' work I succeeded in finding a pocket out of which I extracted three lumps of pure gold, and one small piece mixed with well-oxidized quartz — 29-1/4 ounces for the day; not much short of $500 [actually and accurately, $13,478.40!].*

Reflecting on Buffum's account, Consul Larkin sighed, dipped his pen, paused for a moment to consider what next to tell the Secretary of State, and then resumed writing his letter:

John Sinclair, at the junction of the North fork and the Middle Fork tributaries of the American River, displayed fully fourteen pounds of gold — $3,584 [$1,032,219.20] — as the result of one week's work, with fifty of his tame Indians using closely woven willow baskets. He had secured $16,000 [$460,800] in five weeks. Another party of eight miners made each $50 [$1,440] per day; their own calculation for their fortnight of washing was fully two pounds and four ounces of gold to each man" — $576 [$165,888].

Mr. Chester L. Lyman, prospector, a gentleman of education and worthy of every credit, said he had been engaged with four others, with a machine on the [South Fork] American fork, just below Sutter's [saw-]mill; that they worked eight days, and that his share was at the rate of $50 [$1,440] a day; but hearing that others were doing better at Weber's *place, they had removed there, and were on the point of resuming operations.*

What he had thus far seen with his own eyes, Larkin went on, corresponded very accurately with the stories that continued to filter in to his office. Many of them, however, seemed so outlandish and so exaggerated that he adamantly refused to add them to his own letter. Still, in every case thus far, including even the most seemingly incredible accounts, further checking had proven them to be quite true. A case in point was the miner named Antonio Francisco Coronel, who stated under oath that in three days of digging by his party of thirty Indians in a bar of the Stanislaus River, he recovered, *per day,* 45 ounces, 38 ounces and 59 ounces — an astounding "take" of close to nine pounds — 142 ounces of pure 23-karat gold that was valued at $2,272 [$654,984]. At the very same placer, a miner named Enriqué Valdés, of Santa Barbara, found beneath a large flat rock, "more gold than he could carry in a towel," and, upon selling the claim to another prospector, the latter found, in just eight days' time, 52 pounds of gold — 832 ounces valued at $13,112 [$377,625.60]! Despite all this, it was the Middle Fork American River that was consistently producing most staggering finds, including individual nuggets bigger than any as yet discovered anywhere else. As Larkin wonderingly related:

> *I have had in my own hands several pieces of gold, about 23 carats fine, each weighing from one to two pounds, and I have it from good authority that pieces have been found weighing 25 pounds! I might tell of hundreds of similar instances. There are [sic] a class of stories, such as those related by H. L. Simpson and the Rev. Colton, of an even wilder and more romantic nature, apparently as easy to tell as those by writers of proved veracity, and which, whether true or false, I will not trouble my reader with.*
>
> *The Californian, printed here, stopped this week. The Star newspaper office, where the new laws of Governor Mason, for this country, are printing, has but one man left. A merchant, lately from China, has even lost his China servants. Should the current excitement continue through the year, and the whale-ships visit San Francisco, I think they will lose most all their crews. How Col. Mason can retain*

his men, unless he puts a force on the spot, I know not.

I have seen several pounds of this gold, and consider it very pure, worth in New York 17 dollars [$489.60] to 18 dollars [$518.40] per ounce; 14 dollars [$403.20] to 16 dollars [$460.80], in merchandise, is paid for it here. What good or bad effect this gold mania will have on California, I cannot fore tell [sic]. It may end this year; but I am informed that surely it will continue many years. Mechanics now in this town are only waiting to finish some rude machinery, to enable them to obtain the gold more expeditiously, and free from working in the river. Up to this time, but few Californians [Mexican Californios] have gone to the mines, being afraid the Americans will soon have trouble among themselves, and cause disturbance to all around. I have seen some of the black sand, as taken from the bottom of the river (I should think in the States it would bring 25 to 50 cents [$7.20 to $14.40] per pound), containing many pieces of gold; they are from the size of the head of a pin to the weight of the eighth of an ounce. I have seen some weighing one-quarter of an ounce (4 dollars [$115.20]). Although my statements are almost incredible, I believe I am within the statements believed by every one here. Ten days back, the excitement had not reached Monterey. I shall, within a few days, visit this gold mine, and will make another report to you. In closed [enclosed] you will have a specimen.

I have the honour to be, very respectfully,
(signed) THOMAS O. LARKIN

Hon. James Buchanan
Sec'y of State, Washington
P.S. This placer, or gold region, is situated on public land.

Still beset by doubts over how what he had written might be taken in the nation's capital, Larkin took the letter to a friend, one of the principal merchants of San Francisco, for his opinion, as well as to Captain Joseph Folsom of the Quartermaster Department. Both read carefully what he had written, and both assured him that he had been very modest in his comments, considering what had been occurring since mid-May. Folsom added a comment of his own, which Larkin considered highly significant.

"You have made no mention," Folsom said, "of the total lack of crime at the mining sites. These men, a lot of them, are leaving their gold-filled pouches right in plain sight in their camps, and their tools — which are figuratively worth their weight in gold — are left in their holes unguarded, but nobody takes them. How long that'll last, I have no idea, but I think it's rather incredible, don't you?"

Larkin nodded. "Yes, it is, but I think I've already got enough incredibile material in the letter without adding more. I'll save that for another report, along with what they're doing with the gold they've recovered."

The Consul was referring obliquely to the fact that the posession of treasure worth so much was distorting the reasoning of many to the point where dollar values now seemed to matter little, and skyrocketing costs for the simplest of supplies were ceasing to trouble the newly rich miners. Some of the miners, relaxing in their tents after nightfall, would play a few hands of cards, actually using nuggets as chips and, hardly giving a second thought to gambling away veritable fortunes at merely the turn of a card; or, for that matter, to buying a pint of cheap liquor from merchants like Sam Brannan at a price fifty or more times its actual value. By the same token, there were those who were, indeed, hoarding every grain of the gold they found and were accumulating wealth that would easily last them the remainder of their lives.

Thanks apparently to the rapidly expanding abundance of gold deposits being found, most of the miners grew to know each other well, and there was remarkably little rivalry; disputes over claims were surprisingly rare, and when occasionally they did occur, they almost never resulted in serious trouble. With such an incredible plethora of gold available, one or the other of such disputing parties simply packed up and moved on to another area, where the gold was equally or perhaps even more abundant. The prospectors were very open in their activities and dealings. Most miners gave a hearty welcome to strangers and there was virtually no jealousy evident and little effort to conceal one's luck, whether good or bad.

These were all matters Larkin planned to explore in greater detail in his later reports. Nor did he mention that the first ship to leave San Francisco Bay with news of the gold strike had left port only yesterday — the schooner *Louisa*, en route to Honolulu, carrying with it two full pounds of gold nuggets, and Larkin shuddered at the reaction he expected this would create — almost surely a deluge of gold-seekers arriving at California's West Coast.

In the Eastern United States, life went on in its prosaic way, with no one yet aware of the discovery of gold in the far West. In the nation's capital, orders were drawn on May 30th awarding Colonel Richard B. Mason, military governor of California, the brevet rank of brigadier general "... *for meritorious service,"* though it would take the news a considerable while to reach him; and on the east side of the upper Mississippi River on that same day, Wisconsin was admitted to the Union as the 30th state - but news of the gold strike had not yet even reached the Mississippi Valley.

Thus far, 1848 was turning into a year far more memorable than any the West Coast had ever before experienced. There was, for the gold-seekers, a complete absence of any sort of governmental controls or regulations; everyone involved with the discovery was clearly enjoying it to the fullest, with seemingly no end in sight to the riches that could be earned with a modicum of hard labor. For practically everyone in California Territory, it was like some wildly wonderful, extravagantly happy dream come true.

For now, anyway.

[June 30th, 1848 • Friday]

The month of June had seen more changes occur throughout the Territory of California than at any time previously in its history. Men by the tens, scores, hundreds, even thousands, penetrated areas never before subjected to close scrutiny by non-natives, as the magic of discovering gold in its natural environment became an elixir intoxicating nearly the entire population. Every stream the prospectors followed and every bar that lined its inner bends, every little intersecting arroyo or ravine or rill, and every merging creek bore amazing treasures of the yellow metal that stirred men's souls.

No one yet knew the limitations of the deposits, and each calculated estimate of how ubiquitous and widespread mineral was throughout California — no matter how extravagant — had thus far grossly underestimated the abundance and the widespread regional presence of this precious metal. Typically, almost inevitably, an isolated bar bearing gold was soon discovered to be merely one of many similarly rich bars extending upstream and down from the initial discovery. Shorelines and hillsides, forest ravines and meadow brooks, tiny rills only a foot wide and even dry erosion beds, where gold deposits seemed extremely unlikely, often held bounties merely for those willing to look. The eddies behind every emergent boulder, or those alongside and beneath and behind every protruding log or branch or other obstruction seemed to have collected their shares of placer gold; from tiny grains of "dust" to minute pebbles to larger nuggets to impressive rocks to virtually incredible boulders comprised of solid gold.

A vast swath of California had rapidly become a wonderland of phenomenal riches — instant wealth that fired the imagination and fueled the greed of an entire population; the tendrils of its presence stretching ever farther and ever stronger, beckoning irresistibly to gold-seekers of both sexes and all ages, from doddering oldsters limping along with the aid of a makeshift crutch to children as young as seven-year-old Edwin Austin, who at five years of age had reached California aboard the *Brooklyn* under Sam Brannan, and who was now digging for gold with great energy and success at Mormon Island.

The rains of late winter and early spring had now ended, and the creeks were drying up, the mud becoming dust. Without running water, separating the gold became much more difficult; gold-bearing soils had to be carried much farther to find water in which to wash them, and the average gold recovery for the miners began to drop, dwindling from as much as ten to twenty ounces of gold per day for each miner, to now only four ounces, or two, or even less.

The rushing tide of humanity streamed into Sutter's Fort and then spread from there into the wilderness beyond where previously only wild animals and primitive men had roamed. John Sutter's dream of establishing a major city called Suttersville, downstream on the left bank of the Sacramento, several miles below the mouth of the American, had instead become a nightmare of wasted time and energy. Sutter's Fort, despite being plagued by serious potential hazards of flooding, was closer to the jumping-off point to where gold could be found. Further, those who had come without the necessary shovels and picks and pans and supplies for prospecting could purchase them in the greatly expanded quarters of Sam Brannan's new store, despite his astronomical prices. The fort and its surroundings, still called New Helvetia by Sutter himself — and Sutter's Fort by almost everyone else — was lately being referred to as Sacramento, though it was certainly not an official designation. Not yet. The excited crowds continued to overwhelm Sutter's dream, but ironically were driving the site's rapid evolution into the most important interior city in all of California.

This was the place where the tents of would-be prospectors were being pitched by the scores and, for those without canvas shelters, overnight quarters were available, if not already filled, providing the miners a brief respite during which to formulate their plans for where to go and what to do in the days ahead. There was no dearth of inspiration; miners were returning with tins and pouches brimming and bulging with veritable fortunes collected in only weeks or days or sometimes mere hours. They gladly showed onlookers their treasures, boasting not only of what they had found but, quite as much, of what they had left behind, which was still waiting for those possessing both the gumption — and the necessary tools — to go and dig it out, even where the visible surface treasures had already been collected.

The Coloma vicinity had changed remarkably over these past weeks. Coloma itself had become a substantial town, boasting a wood-frame hotel and, in addition to the already-established cabins, 300 new homes were under construction; the booming site's population had already swelled to 2,000.

The newest general movement of gold-seekers had been southward from the already famed sites at the Sutter-Marshall Saw-mill or at the great river bar called Mormon Island, where more than 300 men were still digging for, and sometimes finding, their fortunes. The prospectors were now moving in greater numbers into the valleys of Weber Creek and its little tributaries, and then even farther south into the valleys of the Cosumnes and Mokelumne Rivers, the Calaveras and the Stanislaus Rivers and even the far distant Tuolumne and Merced River systems, as well as into their many tributaries, fully a hundred miles and more southward. Distance, however, didn't seem to matter; amazingly, wherever the miners searched, they were still finding gold.

Everyone seemed aware of Charles M. Weber's phenomenal success in the French Camp rancho located in the valley of the creek now named after him and in its varied tributaries. Just lately Weber had been joined by a neophyte Mexican rancher-turned-miner named José Jesús from San José who, with his large crew of Indian ranch-hands, was eager to learn from one who obviously knew what he was doing. As soon as Jesús had grasped the fundamentals, he selected his twenty-five best Indian workers and gave them a quick but thorough course in the fundamentals of panning, using their native baskets, and sent them to their home area in the valley of the Stanislaus River.

"To you," he told them "these yellow stones mean little, but to some of us they are very important. Go to your home river and all its smaller streams and do as Mr. Weber and I have just taught you to do. In exchange for those stones you do find and bring to my store, I will supply you with abundant food, clothing, blankets, and other goods. You will be very happy with what you receive for them."

The natives left, and Jesús expected them to be gone for many weeks, but in less than a fortnight they returned, their pouches bulging with gold, almost all of it consisting of the larger nuggets called coarse gold. One of the solid gold lumps they found was enormous — a kidney-shaped nugget that weighed just over five pounds, 80.5 ounces, valued at $1,288 [$370,944]! Its significance was clear: this gold's larger size and its decided coarseness, definitely pointed the way to deposits where the gold had originally formed — to a mother lode, at last.

The news of these discoveries spread rapidly and ignited this most recent rush to the southern streams, where very quickly miners were finding significant gold in deposits they named after themselves — *Wood Creek, Sullivan Bar, Jamestown, Don Pedro Bar,* and others. At the first-named site, Wood Creek, Benjamin Wood, John Heffernan and Levi Savage, using only their picks and knife-blades, dug out $200 to $300 [$5,760 to $8,640] a day each for the first couple of weeks. Such spectacular finds motivated William Knight to quickly establish a trading post in the area at the point soon called *Knight's Ferry*.

The southern mines, hence, quickly validated themselves, but those prospecting further north of the original gold-strike sites were also enjoying success. Job Dye, determined to avoid the crowds by traveling further north in early April. Accompanied by some of his Indian workers, Dye worked his way up the Sacramento to the point where the river swung westward and the powerful Feather River entered from the north. Following the Feather upstream, he finally veered off on a much smaller waterway which he named *Antelope Creek* after a small herd of pronghorns the group had encountered. Like most of the area's running streams, it had bountiful bars, and almost immediately Dye found gold in abundance there. He had planned to push farther north, but he and his Indians began finding so much gold that they remained anchored to that single creek. Except for pauses to rest, sleep, and eat, they worked almost constantly, and by June 1st, with no more containers of any kind left to fill, he decided that he had more than enough. He paid off his Indians in foodstuffs and clothing, and returned to Sutter's Fort. In those seven weeks he had collected enough to retire for the rest of his life — fully 273 *pounds* of nuggets, flakes and dust — a total of 4,368 ounces of gold valued at $69,888 [$2,012,774.40]!

Another of those prospectors set off southward to pursue their fortunes was a seafaring cook named Hector Belknap, who had jumped ship on May 18th as it lay anchored in Monterey Harbor. He headed directly eastward toward the Sierra Nevada foothills and soon reached George Angel's Camp on the creek bearing the same name. There he spent all his money — just over $100 [$2,880] for nothing more than a pick, a pan, a blanket, and a supply of jerked beef. Belknap had no idea where to search, but having overheard several successful miners praising the area, he then simply walked upstream and made his own little camp on the untouched bar of a small feeder creek close by. There he found several wheat-kernel-sized gold nuggets, and then he started his own solitary digging and panning. On June 1st, nineteen days after having jumped ship, Belknap returned to Monterey. With his clothing all but shredded, his face barely recognizable beneath an untrimmed beard, his sea-bag slung over his shoulder, he surrendered himself to his ship's captain. The skipper, assuming Belknap had merely gone on a lark and spent his pay in area taverns on liquor and loose women, was pleased to have him back, but stern nonetheless. He lectured the cook at length, locked him in the brig for a week and docked him three months' pay for his unauthorized absence. Hector could not have cared less; when he left the Angels Camp area, he had sold his tools and blanket for more than he paid for them initially, and safely hidden in the bottom of his sea-bag was a container filled with gold amounting to $4,000 [$115,200] — far more than he would ever otherwise have earned in his entire lifetime.

At the *California Star* in San Francisco, Edward Kemble could o longer cling to his own narrow prejudices regarding the gold-seekers' widespread discoveries. In a piece he wrote for a special edition of the newspaper, appearing on June 10th, he reluctantly conceded as much and even admonished other die-hard skeptics. In his most complete and honest evaluation of the current gold situation in California, he wrote:

> ***The Excitement of Gold Washing Still Continues — Increases***
>
> *Many of our countrymen are not disposed to do us justice as regards the opinion we have at different times expressed of the employment in which over two thirds of the white population of the country are engaged. There appears to have gone abroad a belief that we should raise our voices against what some one has denominated an "infatuation."*

We are very far from it, and would invite a very calm recapitulation of our articles touching the matter, as in themselves amply satisfactory. We shall continue to report the progress of the work, to speak within bounds, and to approve, admonish, or openly censure whatever, in our opinion, may require it at our hands. It is quite unnecessary to remind our readers of the "prospects of California" at this time, as the effects of this gold washing enthusiasm, upon the entire country, through every branch of business are unmistakably apparent to every one. Suffice it that there is no abatement, and that active measures will probably be taken to prevent really serious and alarming consequences. Every seaport as far south as San Diego, and every interior town, and nearly every rancho from the base of the mountains in which he gold has been found, to the Mission of San Luis, south, has become suddenly drained of humans. Americans, Californians, Indians and Sandwich Islanders, men, women and children, indiscriminately. Should there be that success which has repaid the efforts of those employed for the last month, and next, as many are sanguine in their expectations, and we confess to unhesitatingly believe probably, not only will witness the depopulation of every town, the desertion of every rancho, and the desolation of the once promising crops of the country, but it will also draw largely upon adjacent territories — awake Sonora, and call down upon us, despite her Indian battles, a great many of the good people of Oregon. There are at this time over one thousand souls busied in washing gold, and the yield per diem may be safely estimated at from fifteen to twenty dollars [$432-$576], each individual. — We have by every launch from the embarcadero of New Helvetia, returns of enthusiastic gold-seekers — heads of families, to effect transportation of their households to the scene of their successful labors, or others, merely returned to more fully equip themselves for a protracted, or perhaps permanent stay. — Spades, shovels, picks, wooden bowls, Indians baskets (for washing), etc., find ready purchase, and are frequently disposed of at extortionate prices. The gold region, so called, thus far explored, is about one hundred miles in length and twenty in width. These imperfect explorations contribute to establish

> *the certainty of the placers extending much further south, probably three or four hundred miles, as we have before stated, which is believed to terminate about a league north of the point at which first discovered. The probable amount taken from these mountains since the first of May last, we are informed is $100,000 [$2,880,000], and which is at this time principally in the hands of mechanical, agricultural and laboring classes. There is an area explored, within which a body of 50,000 men can advantageously labor. Without maliciously interfering with each other, then, there need be no cause for contention and discord, where as yet, we are gratified to know, there is harmony and good feeling existing. We really hope no unpleasant occurrences will grow out of this enthusiasm, and that our apprehensions may be quieted by continued patience and good will among the washers.*
>
> *California Star — Saturday, June 10, 1848.*

Now even the earlier miners, whose claims were well marked, feared they might well lose the digging sites they had claimed due to the overwhelming influx of would-be miners from other areas. As Henry Bigler put it in his own *diary* this same day, he had been fearing, since June began, that his own claim would be wrested away from him. As he had written on those first June days:

> *June 1st. — I have done nothing on my house since the 15th of May. I have no idea that I can hold it. The miners pay no attention to Sutter and Marshall's claim. People have come in so fast that the banks of the river and the ravines are filled with mining camps. It seems as if everybody in California were here. Report says that all business at San Francisco has stopped.*
>
> *June 2nd. — Spent half of the day getting my oxen across the river. In the afternoon washed out nearly $20 [$576].*

Thus far Bigler's own claim had not been infringed upon, but it had been a constant worry to him, and consequently he was glad the time was soon approaching when he could just sell his claim — or, if necessary, abandon it. The Mormon Battalion veterans who had been poised to start their overland journey to Salt Lake City since the beginning of June had found it necessary to postpone their departure day after day due to the heavy accumulations of snow still smothering the higher peaks and passes. They were, however, ready to leave the moment the snow had cleared off sufficiently, and Henry Bigler was now quite ready to leave his claim and join them.

Virtually echoing Bigler's private comments, Jacques Moerenhout, in his own correspondence to the French foreign minister this same day, wrote to him from his office in Monterey, declaring that:

> *... all of the Americans previously in town, who have not been detained by important business, have already left for the mines.*

Nor was he the only official in town commenting about the mass exodus that had been occurring. In the nearby governor's office, Richard Mason wrote to Secretary of State Buchanan in Washington on the following Monday, June 12th, that he and his chief aide, Lt. William T. Sherman, were prepared to embark immediately on a tour through northern California in order to visit the mining districts and see for themselves what was occurring. As Mason observed:

> *... to visit the newly discovered 'gold placers' found through the valley of the Sacramento, but will hold myself in absolute readiness to return to my Office should you, or any other important business require it.*

At the same time, without even rising from his desk, he dashed off a note containing roughly the same information to Consul Larkin, who was lingering in San José, but added, at its close:

> *The golden-yellow fever has not yet, I believe, assumed its worst type, though the premonitory symptoms are beginning to exhibit themselves and doubtless the epidemic will pass over Monterey, leaving the marks of its ravages, as it has done at S.F. and elsewhere. Take care you don't become so charged with its malaria as to inoculate and infect us all when you return. ...*

It was a jovial warning given just a mite too late. Lt. Sherman had already fallen prey and was, in fact, the motivating factor in convincing his commander — if Mason actually needed any convincing, which was doubtful — that such a trip to the mining areas was a responsibility they needed to consider. Sherman had already written in his own private journal:

> *I of course could not escape the infection, and at last convinced Colonel Mason that it was our duty to go up and see with our own eyes, that we might report the truth to our Government. As yet we have no regular mail service to any part of the United States, but mails have come to us at long intervals, around Cape Horn, and one or two overland.*

What little residue of the white population currently remaining at Monterey was itself poised to vacate, as a letter written several days earlier to Consul Larkin by Monterey resident Jackson McDuffee made clear:

> *Monterey is very dull, nothing doing, the gold fever is beginning to take effect here. A large party will leave for the Sacramento the last of the week. Shovels, spades, picks and other articles wanted by these wild adventurers are in great demand.*

Governor Mason and Lt. Sherman finally left Monterey on horseback early on Saturday, June 18th, accompanied by a small detachment of mounted guards from the local barracks. Sherman had taken the time to dash off a brief notation in his journal:

> *... he gold-fever surely being at its height, by Colonel Mason's orders I made preparations for his trip to the newly-discovered gold-mine at Sutter's Fort. I selected four good soldiers, with Aaron, Colonel Mason's black servant, and a good out-fit of horses and pack-mules, we started by the usually traveled route for Yerba Buena [San Francisco].*

Almost at that very same moment the discharged Saints of the now defunct Mormon Battalion began assembling several miles distant from the Old Dry Diggings site in a reasonably level prairie valley. Parties of Saints began arriving in various groups throughout the day, some of them driving loose horses or cattle before them, others just swelling the camp with their wagons and effects gathered for the long journey. Among them was Henry Bigler, who had joined their rendezvous at the Brighton grist-mill the day before and helped guide them to this location. As he wrote of these events on June 18th:

> *The next day, the eighteenth, we found a spot we thought would do — a distance, as we thought, about forty-five miles from the flouring mill. ... We quickly gave the name of our little meadow valley, Pleasant Valley. Here we felled pine timber and very soon had built a large corral ... some of the boys arrived with our band of loose horses, and the twenty-two wagons began to roll in, mostly drawn by oxen, followed by our cows and calves.*

Two days later, on June 20th, the sparse male population remaining in Monterey gathered in the Central Plaza to listen as their *alcalde*, Walter Colton, greeted the messenger he had sent out to inspect and report on the situation in the valley of the upper American River. They were intensely eager to learn if the stories of abundant gold were actually true. As Colton himself recorded the scene:

> *He dismounted in a sea of upturned faces. As he drew forth the yellow lumps from his pockets, and passed them around among the eager crowd, the [remaining] doubts, which had lingered till now, fled. All admitted they were gold. ... The excitement produced was intense; and many were soon busy in their hasty preparations for a departure to the mines. The blacksmith dropped his hammer, the carpenter his plane, the mason his trowel, the farmer his sickle, the baker his loaf, and the tapster his bottle. All were off to the mines, some on horses, some on carts, and some on crutches, and one went in a litter.*

Just as southern gold deposits in the bars near the Mokelumne River had abruptly come into prominence in the tributaries of Angel Creek, so now, well to the north, the tributaries of Bear River were suddenly coming into their own, with heavily gold-laden bars and flats. Foremost among these was an area quickly named *Dutch Flat* and its surprisingly rich depression appropriately dubbed *Steep Hollow*, as well as the relatively adjacent site that was named *Alder Grove*, also called *Upper Corral*.

A bit farther north on the Yuba River, just east of a major cleft being called *Timbuctoo Ravine*, prospector Jonas Spect opened a very rich but limited bar which he named Spect Bar and then followed up with the discovery of another bar along the river's south shore. This was where San Franciscans Jacob Leese, Patrick McChristian and Jasper O'Farrell, along with William Leery and Samuel Norris, set up camp, struck it rich and quickly mined a most impressive number nuggets later valued at $75,000 [$2,160,000].

In the same stream system, the very rich *Long Bar* was established near the mouth of the Yuba and named, not for its size but after its initial miner, Dr. John Long. A young and quite literary Scot named John C. McPherson also mined in the area and, under the pseudonym of Juanita, which he used as a newspaper correspondent and as a composer, wrote a song in praise of the Yuba which became a favorite of the miners in the area. In this same area Peter Hardeman Burnett and his companions from Oregon first began their California mining. The population of the Long Bar area at that point was eighty men, three women and five children, and, though they had very poor digging tools, they made remarkable finds on the three principal bars — *Long, Parks,* and *Foster* — reaping from $60 to $100 [$1,728 to $2,880] daily from their digging and washing for many weeks.

The fact of the matter was, bigger and greater gold strikes were occurring every day, motivating the incoming goldseekers to pay attention to every creek, every tiny stream, every eroded cleft. For the most part, they weren't disappointed, as gold seemed to be present just about everywhere.

On June 20th, three days after leaving Monterey, Governor Mason and Lt. Sherman, with their small escort, arrived in San Francisco and found the town to be almost entirely vacant, a situation which they found understandable but strangely depressing. Ships in the harbor lay as a ghost fleet at anchor, without manpower to set sail, their crews having abandoned ship to seek golden fortunes. It was, to Governor Mason and Lt. Sherman, as if the once bustling town had simply rolled over and died. The two officials could not leave the place quickly enough, and they likely did not soon forget the desolation they had witnessed.

In one case, they were told, the skipper of the Flora out of New York, Captain Helve Potter of New London, had anchored in Whaleman's Harbor on the opposite side of the bay. When the gold discovery news reached his ship, he had tried to forestall his crew's desertion by weighing anchor and heading out to sea, but the sailors, discovering these plans, had refused to do duty until the ship turned and put to anchor in San Francisco Harbor. Then, during the night that crew mutinied, overpowered and gagged the watch, fled to the shore in a lowered whaleboat, and then made the long trek inland to the gold sites. The *Flora* was, at that time, 26 months out and contained in her hold some 750 barrels of whale oil. As Lt. Sherman wrote:

> *The whaling ship Euphrates, of New Bedford, left here a few weeks since for the United States, to touch on the coast of Chili [sic] to recruit. The Minerva, Captain Frederick Perry, of New Bedford, has abandoned the whaling business, and is now on her way to Valparaiso for a cargo of merchandise. Although two large ships, four barks, and eight or ten brigs and schooners have arrived in port here with large cargoes of merchandise, their entire invoices have been sold. Vessels are daily arriving from the islands and ports upon the coast, laden with goods and passengers, the latter destined for the gold washings.*

At this precise moment, fully a continent away to the east, the politicians in Washington, D.C. were girding themselves for the national election. Democratic Party administrative officials had already decided that there was no way they would tolerate James Knox Polk for another term; he had sealed his own political fate when he had secretly allocated $2 million for the reestablishment of General Santa Ana from exile, staking his presidency on the latter's promise to end the war at once. That hadn't happened, however, and while Polk had somehow managed to avoid impeachment for his gross blunder, he had thereby lost the support and the confidence of Americans everywhere. Instead, the War of 1812 hero, Lewis Cass, on June 21 became the choice of party regulars to carry the standard on a slavery compromise platform. The party split on that choice, and rebellious Democrats had turned instead to nomination of ex-President Martin Van Buren in a Free-Soil third party candidacy. The Whigs, on the other hand, chose to back the crusty war general, Zachary Taylor. At this point it was a toss-up as to who would emerge victorious, especially since it was quite possible, some saying even probable, that California and the new West might become aligned with the slave-holding South.

Eastern politics were extremely remote from the thoughts of the gold-seekers in California, however, as they continued spreading throughout the region. Despite his own ingrained stodginess, *Alcalde* John Sinclair was not immune to the extraordinary pull of the fever. With a crew of 50 of his Indian workers, he set up an operation on the bars of the North Fork of the American River, just above its junction with the South Fork, and in just one week, ending June 23rd, the party gleaned *pounds* of gold, for which he paid his workers about $60 [$1,728], but which netted him a very substantial and gratifying $3,484 [$100,339.20]. He named his site *Sinclairs Washings*, but good though it was, its yield was eclipsed this same day by the discovery made by a party of Californio Mexicans on the Middle Fork, some 12 miles northeast of Coloma. This turned out to be the most fabulously rich gold deposit of any site yet discovered in that entire region.

Impatience was growing among the Mormons gathered at Pleasant Valley; all were eager to be on their way to Salt Lake City, yet the memory of the Donner Party tragedy sobered the majority with an acute but justifiable sense of caution and, hence, most members of the party decided to remain in place until the mountain passes were no longer so choked with snow. This didn't sit well at all with a trio of the Saints — Captain Daniel Browett, Ezrah H. Allen and Henderson Cox — who were eager to leave at once and resolved to do so. The others thought it was too risky an undertaking, not only because of the snow but because of the recent increasing troubles with the Indians. The three scoffed at such an idea and on June 24th they set off by themselves, saying they would travel slowly, hunt out and mark the best way to cross the Sierra Nevada and would meet the others when they followed, somewhere in the mountains.

On that same day, June 24th, John Murphy of San José had been attracted by the excellent results of gold-seekers prospecting in the area where George Angel had such remarkable success in the stream now bearing his name. He outfitted himself well, though at considerable cost, at Sam Brannan's Emporium store in Sutter's Fort, then traveled some 60 miles south of Coloma to Angels Camp. Unwilling to compete with all the miners he found digging there, he made his way seven miles upstream, well beyond where others had prospected. Here he discovered not another bar but a quartz outcropping heavy with gold, which was definitely a mother lode. The fortnight Murphy and his hired Indians spent digging into the lode rewarded him by the evening of June 24th, with an incredible amount of gold, most of which he buried in secret locations nearby. It was soon rumored about that he had found — and buried — gold to the value of $2 million [$57.6 million]! Whether the rumor was true or not, it was clear that John Murphy had found gold enough to make him very wealthy for the remainder of his life.

Four days later, on June 28th, his tour of the mining areas completed, Consul Thomas Larkin finally returned to his office in Monterey. The California capital had been nearly empty of its male residents since mid-June. On June 14th, two miners, en route back to Los Angeles from Mormon Island, paused briefly and fired the hearts and minds of Monterey's residents when they proudly displayed their recent discoveries: Nuggets, flakes and dust totaling 92 ounces, which they had gathered in less than a month — $1,472 [$42,393.60]. This extremely convincing, astonishing exhibition galvanized the great majority of Monterey's male population into motion toward the gold fields.

Larkin was still in a virtual daze over all he'd seen and heard, and he longed to convey to his superior the exciting and influential events he had experienced in the course of his tour, yet without appearing to be quite as dazzled and exuberant as he actually was. Wasting no time, while events were still fresh in his mind, he immediately sat at his desk and began composing a detailed letter to Secretary of State James Buchanan in Washington, while struggling to repress somewhat his excitement over what he had witnessed. He wrote:

> *Monterey, California, June 28, 1848*
>
> *Sir: — My last dispatch to yourself at the State Department was written in San Francisco, the first of this month. In that I had the honor to give some information respecting the new placer, or gold region, lately discovered on the branches of the Sacramento River. Since the writing of that dispatch, I have visited a part of the gold region, and found it all I had heard and much more than I anticipated. The part that I visited was upon a fork of the American river, a branch of the Sacramento, joining the main river at Sutter's Fort. The place in which I found the people digging was about 25*

miles from the fort by land.

I have reason to believe that gold will be found on many branches of the Sacramento and [San] Joaquin rivers. People are already scattered over one hundred miles of land, and it is supposed that the placer extends from river to river. At present the workmen are employed within 10 or 20 yards of the river, that they may be convenient to water. Northward on Feather river there are several branches upon which the people are digging for gold. This is two or three days' ride from the place I visited.

At my camping place I found, on a surface of two or three miles on the banks of the river, some fifty tents, mostly owned by Americans. These had their families. There are no Californians who have taken their families as yet to the gold regions; but few or none will ever do it. Some from New Mexico may do so next year, but no Californians.

I was two nights at a tent occupied by eight Americans, viz.: two sailors, one clerk, one [actually, two] carpenters [sic], and three daily workmen. These men were in company — had two machines each made from 100 feet of boards (worth there $150 [$4,320]. In Monterey $15 [$432] — being one day's work), made similar to a child's cradle, 10 feet long, without the ends.

The two evenings I saw these eight men bring to their tents the labor of the day. I suppose they made each $50 [$1,440] per day: their own calculation was two pounds of gold a day — four ounces to a man -- $64 [$1,843.20]. I saw two brothers that worked together, and only worked by washing the dirt in a tin pan, weigh the gold they obtained in one day; the result was $7 [$201.60] to one, $82 [$2,361.60] to the other. There were two reasons for this difference: one man worked less hours than the other, and by chance had worked ground less impregnated with gold. I give this statement as an extreme case. During my visit, I was interpreter for a native of Monterey, who was purchasing a machine or canoe. I first tried to purchase boards and hire a carpenter for him. There were but a few hundred feet of boards to be had; for these the owner asked of me $50 [$1,440] per hundred ($500 [$14,400] per M.). and a carpenter washing gold dust de-

manded $50 [$1,440] per day for working. I at last purchased a long dug-out, with a riddle [riffle] and seive [sic] made of willow boughs on it, for $120 [$3,456], payable in gold dust at $14 [$403.20] per ounce. The owner excused himself for the price, by saying he was two days in making it, and even then demanded the use of it until sunset. My Californian has told me since, that himself, partner, and two Indians, obtained with this canoe eight ounces ($128 — [$3,686,400] the first and five ounces ($80 — [$2,304]) the second day.

I am of the opinion that on the American fork, Feather river, and Copimes river, there are nearly 2,000 people, nine-tenths of them foreigners. Perhaps there are 100 families, who have their teams, wagons, and tents. Many persons are waiting to see whether the months of July and August will be sickly, before they leave their present business to go to the Placer. The discovery of this gold was made by some Mormons, in January or February, who, for a time kept it a secret. The majority of those who are working there began in May. In almost every instance, the men, after digging a few days, have been compelled to leave for the purpose of returning home to see their families, arrange their business, and purchase provisions. I feel confident in saying there are fifty men in this Placer, who have, on an average, $1000 [$28,800] each, obtained in May and June. I have not met with any person at all who had not been fully employed in washing gold one month; most appear to have averaged an ounce ($16 [$460.80]) per day. I think there must, at this time, be over 1000 men at work upon the different branches of the Sacramento; putting their gains at $10,000 [$288,000] per day, for six days in the week, appears to me not overrated.

Should this news reach the emigration of California and Oregon now on the road, connected with the Indian wars now impoverishing the latter country, we should have a large addition to our population; and should the richness of the gold region continue, our emigration in 1849 will be many thousands, and in 1850 still more. If our countrymen in California, as clerks, mechanics, and workmen, will forsake employment at from $2 [$57.60] to $6 [$172.80] per day, how many more of the same class in the Atlantic states, earning *much less, will leave for this country under such prospects? It is the opinion of many who have visited the gold regions the past and present months, that the ground will afford gold for many years, perhaps for a century. From my own examination of the rivers and their banks, I am quite of opinion that, at least for a few years, the golden products will equal the present year. However, as neither men of science, nor the laborers now at work, have made any [or] give any opinion as to the extent and richness of this part of California. Every Mexican who has seen the place, says that throughout their Republic there has never been any "placer like this one."*

Could Mr. Polk and yourself see California as we now see it, you would think that a few thousand people, on 100 miles square of the Sacramento valley, would yearly turn out of this river the whole price our country pays for the acquired territory. When I finished my first letter, I doubted my own writing, and, to be better satisfied, showed it to one of the principal merchants of San Francisco, and to Capt. Fulsom [Folsom], of the Quartermaster's Department, who decided at once I was far below reality. You certainly will suppose, from my two letters, that I am, like others, led away by the excitement of the day. I think I am not. In my last I inclosed [sic] a small sample of the gold dust, and I find my only error was in putting a value to the sand. At that time I was not aware how the gold was found; I can now describe the mode of collecting it.

A person without a machine, after digging off one or two feet of the up-per ground, near the water (in some cases they take the top earth), throws into a tin pan or wooden bowl a shovel full of loose dirt and stones; then placing the basin an inch or two under water, continues to stir up the dirt with his hand, in such a manner that the running water will carry off the light earth — occasionally, with his hand, throwing out the stones. After an operation of this kind for twenty or thirty minutes, a spoonful of small, black sand remains; this is, on a handkerchief or cloth, dried in the sun — the emerge is blown off, leaving the pure gold. I have the pleasure on inclosing [sic] a paper of this sand and gold, which I, from a bucket of dirt and stones, in half and hour, at the edge of the water, washed out myself. The value of it may be $2 [$57.60] *or $3 [$86.40].*

The size of the gold depends in some measure upon the river from which it is taken, the banks of one river having larger grains of gold than another. I presume more than one half of the gold put into pans or machines is washed out and gone down the stream; this is of no consequence to the washers, who care only for the present time. Some have formed companies of four or five men, and have a rough-made machine put together in just a day, which works to much advantage; yet many prefer to work alone, with a wooden bowl or tin pan, worth fifteen or twenty cents [$4.32 or $5.76] in the States, but eight to sixteen dollars [$230.40 to 460.80] at the gold region. As the workmen continue, and materials can be obtained, improvements will take place in the mode of obtaining gold; at present it is obtained by standing in the water, and with much severe labor, or such as is called here severe labor.

How long this gathering of gold by the handfuls will continue here, or the future effect it will have on California, I cannot say. Three-fourths of the houses in the town on the Bay of San Francisco are deserted. Houses are sold at the price of the ground lots. The effects are this week showing themselves in Monterey. Almost every house I had hired out is given up. Every blacksmith, carpenter and lawyer are leaving; brick-yards, saw-mills and ranchos are left perfectly alone. A large number of the volunteers at San Francisco and Sonoma have deserted; some have been retaken and brought back; public and private vessels are losing their crews; my clerks have had 100 per cent advance offered them on their present wages to accept employment. A complete revolution in the ordinary state of affairs is taking place; both of our newspapers are discontinued from want of workmen and the loss of their agencies; the Alcaldes have left San Francisco, and I believe Sonoma likewise; the former place has not a Justice of the Peace left.

The second Alcalde of Monterey to-day joins the keepers of our principal Hotel, who have closed their office and house, and will leave to-morrow for the golden rivers. I saw on the ground a lawyer who was last year Attorney-general for the King of the Sandwich Islands, digging and washing out his ounce and a half per day; near him can be found almost all his brethren of the long robe, working in the same occupation.

To conclude: my letter is long, but I could not well describe what I have seen in less words, and I now can believe that my account may be doubted; if the affair proves a bubble, a mere excitement, I know not how we can be deceived, as we are situated. Gov. Mason and his staff have left Monterey to visit the place in question, and will, I suppose, soon forward to his department his views and opinions on this subject. Most of the land, where gold has been discovered, is public land; there are on different rivers some private grants. I have three such, purchased in 1846 and '47, but have not learned that any private lands have produced gold, though they may hereafter do so.

I have the honor, dear sir, to be, very respectfully,
Your ob't serv't, THOMAS O. LARKIN
Hon. James Buchanan, Sec'y of State, Wash'ton City.

Larkin was by no means the only public official who was gravely disturbed by the virtual abandonment of the coastal towns by most of their male and even many of their female inhabitants. Walter Colton echoed Larkin's concerns, wondering how such communities could survive when their inhabitants were rapidly abandoning them. Acutely aware of the futility and virtual impossibility of trying to prevent such widespread community abandonments, he tried to imagine how California's towns might, nevertheless, survive. After considerable thought, Colton offered only one solution: The gold being discovered must be kept in circulation, and the only reasonable way of doing that, he believed, was by turning it into coin, which would tend to bring a degree of balance back to the present unstable economy. Thus, on this final day of June, he busied himself writing a letter to a U.S. Congressman in Washington, D.C. How strange, he wrote:

... that this ore should have lain here, scattered about in all directions, peeping every where out of the earth, and sparkling in the sun, and been [sic] trod upon for ages by white men and savages, and by the various emissaries of every scientific association in the world, and never till now have been discovered! What an ass man is, with all his learn-

ing! He stupidly stumbles over hills of gold to reach a rare pepper-pod, or rifle a bird's nest!

The whole country is now moving on the mines. Monterey, San Francisco, Sonoma, San José, and Santa Cruz, are emptied of their male population. A stranger coming here would suppose he had arrived among a race of women, who, by some anomalous provision of nature, multiplied their images clearly without the presence of the other sex. But not a few of the women have gone too, especially those who had got out of tea — for what is a woman without her teapot — a pythoness without her shaking tripod — an angel that has lost his lyre. Every bowl, tray, warming-pan, and piggin, has gone to the mines — every thing, in short, that has a scoop in it that will hold sand and water. All the iron has been worked up into crowbars, pick-axes, and spades; and all these roll back upon us in the shape of gold. We have, therefore, plenty of gold, but little to eat, and still less to wear. Our supplies must come from Oregon, Chili [sic], and the United States. Our grain gold, in exchange for coin, sells for nine and ten dollars the ounce, though it is well known to be worth at the mint in Philadelphia eighteen dollars the ounce at least. Such is the scarcity of coin here.

We want a mint. Let Congress send us one at once over the Isthmus; else the grain gold goes to Mazatlan, to Chili [sic] and Peru — where it is lost to our national currency. Over a million of gold, at the lowest computation, is taken from these mines every month — and this quantity will be more than doubled when the emigration from the States, from Oregon, the Sandwich Islands, and the Southern republics arrives. Send us a mint! I could give you forty more illustrations of the extent and productiveness of these mines, but no one will believe what I have said without my name, and perhaps but few with it.

For most of the Mormons poised and waiting at Pleasant Valley for the snow to clear away at the upper elevations so they could set out in some degree of safety for Salt Lake City, the delay seemed interminable. For some of them, however — Henry Bigler among them, the delay was enjoyable, giving them a final opportunity to prospect a bit more before the trek eastward over the Sierra Nevadas began. Working mainly by himself, and aided by his now considerable experience at goldseeking, Bigler quickly located a productive ravine, and during these final two days of June he washed out a bonus of small nuggets and flakes to the value of $68 [$1,958.40].

"How is it, Brother Bigler," asked one of the Saints who was newly arrived from Los Angeles, "that you seem able to find gold where no one else can?"

"Three reasons," he replied. "For one thing, I do an awful lot of looking. Secondly, I also do quite a lot of digging and washing." He paused and then added with a chuckle, "Finally, if those first two aren't coming through very well, I also do a great deal of praying."

[July 6th, 1848 • Thursday]

Sam Brannan had been convinced from the beginning that sooner or later his tithe-collecting from the Saints under his dominion would come to an end.

The confrontation prompted by his longstanding fraudulent behavior finally took place almost immediately after Governor Mason and his entourage, at John Sutter's eager invitation, had stopped off for a day's rest here over the Fourth of July. The little official group had continued on tour yesterday to view the mining activities where they were actually underway, and Brannan did not have long to wait for the long expected reaction.

Brannan was busy in his new large store, overseeing his Indian employees who were busy restocking the somewhat depleted shelves, when Riley G. Clark, a former Mormon Battalion private from Company A, entered and approached him, trailed by several of his companions. The little group stopped and waited expectantly for the merchant to complete his inventory of what was being replaced on a specific shelf. After a few moments Brannan finished checking off items on his handwritten list and then looked at them and smiled.

"Good morning, Brethren," he said politely. "How may I help you today? Have you perhaps come to pay your tithes?"

Clark, a large, unsmiling individual, stepped a pace forward from the others, who were grinning as if anticipating what was coming. He shook his head. "We've come about the tithes, all right," he said, then added flatly, "but not to pay 'em. Not today and not ever again."

Brannan folded and pocketed the inventory sheet he had checked off before responding. He was still smiling, but all vestige of warmth had fled from the expression. "And may I ask why not?" he inquired, his voice level, betraying no emotion.

"We went to Cap'n Sutter's quarters last night. The governor's staying there and we talked with him."

"And?"

Clark fidgeted. "About the tithes you've been collecting."

Brannan's smile became even less friendly. "And?" he repeated. "What about them?"

The former private, now a prospector at Mormon Island, dipped his head and spoke more rapidly, in a somewhat sing-song manner, as if his comments had been rehearsed: "We asked him flat-out what business you had to collect the tithes here and whether or not it was legal for you to collect them from us."

"And he replied — ?" Brannan left the question hanging.

Clark flushed faintly but pressed on, speaking more rapidly now. "He asked if you were head of the Church of Jesus Christ of Latter Day Saints here in California and we told him you were and that you've been compelling us all to pay ten per cent of whatever gold we pan out or dig up. We asked him if you had the right to do that."

Brannan's smile remained frozen. "To which he responded how?"

"His exact words were, 'Mister Brannan has a perfect right to collect the tax, if you Mormons are fools enough to pay it.' That's exactly what he said and ... and ... well, we're not. Not any more. I, for one, won't pay it any longer, and neither will these boys, and we're going to spread the word to all the Saints, at all the gold camps."

"You certainly have every right to do so," Brannan said levelly, "but it remains your bounden duty, as members of our Church, to pay tithes from what you earn so the work of the Lord can continue and expand. If you choose not to do so, the consequences are entirely of your own doing and you run the grave risk of excommunication."

"Excommunication be damned!" Clark exploded. "I don't believe that for a minute, and we're going to let Brigham Young himself know what's been going on. He'll want to know where all that gold's gone you've been collecting from every Saint here. Hundreds of the brethren, and you're getting' ten per cent from every one of 'em? Of all the gold they've found? He'll sure as hell want to know, and we do, too!"

There seemed nothing more to say and, after a moment, he turned and he and his little troop surged outside. Brannan walked to the entry after them and watched for a moment as they moved away, then closed the door and turned back to what he had been doing. A small smile, more genuine now, played at his lip corners and he shook his head slightly, his usual aplomb settling in nicely. He'd known from the very beginning it wouldn't last forever. It would undoubtedly be a while before the news would spread to all the miners that they no longer had to pay tithes to Sam Brannan, but in the meanwhile, he'd continue to collect from them as long as he could find Mormon miners who were willing to pay. It had been a good ride for as long as it lasted; he'd made a fortune from it, and that was what really mattered. The tithe-gold collected thus far from all the gold-digging Saints had made him a very wealthy man — quite possible the wealthiest in all of California. If and when — almost surely when — Brigham Young came back at him, he was entirely ready.

Sam Brannan had no intention of giving up the smallest single grain of the gold he'd collected.

[July 9th, 1848 • Sunday]

It was quite unlikely that any other community in California's history before now had ever undergone so swift a metamorphosis as had occurred during the past few weeks at Sutter's Fort — or, as many were already calling it, Sacramento. From a relatively simple post with a very few small buildings, it had evolved into a thriving metropolis of sorts, with hundreds of people coming and going and new construction occurring everywhere. Inside and outside the high adobe walls, significant changes were occurring daily.

Long before the settlement had met the criteria for designation as a city, the riverfront community was experiencing phenomenal growing pains. Several relatively permanent camps had been established outside the walls, and tents had blossomed like blooming daisies in a meadow. Inside the fort walls, space had become a scarce, costly commodity for anyone desiring to the erect shanties, log huts, stores, hotels and saloons. No room, anywhere, ever stayed vacant for more than mere minutes before being snapped up by someone else at a significantly higher price than the previous owner had paid.

Whenever a demand developed, enterprising individuals quickly developed a supply to meet it: Merchants and saloon-keepers were providing not only their own specialized services, but several had now begun providing banking services to the miners. To satisfy the myriad miners' need for food, especially meat, local hunters from San José shot great numbers of waterfowl in the marshlands of Alviso, and grizzlies, deer and other wildlife in the Diablo Range and shipped the meat to Sutter's Fort for sale. Antonio Sunol closed his general store in San José and headed for the gold country to open a similar operation there, and Zachariah Jones did the same with his Half Moon Hotel in order to rush to the mining camps to build and open a similar establishment.

The air at Sutter's Fort was alive with the sound of rasping saws and banging hammers as new living quarters and store areas were erected, and the cacophonous construction noises were accompanied by the constant, overpowering din of the voices of hundreds of men assembling in ragtag groups within and without the fort's walls. The relative solitude this site had enjoyed for the past decade now seemed a remote, almost forgotten memory.

The Sacramento River itself was alive with every floatable craft imaginable, including several large schooners that had plied their way upstream and finally taken anchorage within a stone's throw of the rudely fashioned Sutter embarcadero. Sutter's own launches, five of them now, plied regularly up and down the river, all the way to San Francisco and back, and still they were not numerous enough to handle the human tide seeking to utilize them. The cross-river ferry system, which now included a barge, was running constantly, bringing across the broad Sacramento River the wagons and baggage and tools of those arriving gold-seekers who could afford the fare. The rudimentary roads leading to the fort were constantly choked with the traffic of mule-drawn wagons, ox-carts, a multitude of freight-movers, horsemen, and mule-riders. The crude roads also swelled with walkers burdened with bulging blanket-packs, knives and pistols. Virtually none of these men had any specific, planned destination in mind, other than Sutter's Fort itself, where one and all believed that somehow their destinations beyond would become clear. Above it all, the constant rattling din of pans and picks, shovels and spades in created a cacophony which nearly overwhelmed the endless drone of voices.

It was virtually a great circus-like parade of snorting horses and braying mules, of creaking wheels and scuffling feet tucked into floppy black boots or shapeless dust-cloaked footwear. It was a prolonged woebegone procession of weary, ragged, rough, bewhiskered men clad in largely unkempt clothing — drab homespun and checked woolen shirts and baggy, formless trousers — and from whose throats rolled a polyglot chorus of English and French, Mexican and German, and Indian voices, accompanied by hoarse cries, coarse laughter, shrill whistles, and sometimes even by singing.

Sutter's Fort had evolved in mere weeks from an isolated outpost in a vast wilderness — one that offered hope and haven to lost or weary travelers — to a staging ground for a self-centered multitude driven by an overpowering element of obsessive greed. Where the mines themselves were still models of harmony and togetherness, Sutter's Fort had become a seat of disruption and contention; the hoards occupying the site had witnessed two murders within the past week or so — one man shot and another stabbed — plus assorted incidents of whisky-inspired mayhem, robbery and horse theft - and there was every indication this was only the beginning of a contagion of moral disintegration.

They had come a long way, most of those who were arriving, and while their shoulders slumped with weariness and their bodies ached with unfamiliar pains, they were all possessed by the frenzied anticipation of finding gold.

[July 14th, 1848 • Friday]

The first credible news to touch Oregon Territory regarding the gold strike in California finally reached the mouth of the Willamette River by an extremely roundabout route. Had such tidings been able to travel up the Sacramento and over the mountains of northern California and southern Oregon into the Willamette's upper tributaries, they likely would have reached the Willamette Valley settlements much sooner, but at this point time there were very few emigrants in this vast area capable of spreading the good word. The higher passes had remained choked with deeply drifted snows this past spring, restricting land travel until well into summer.

The news had at first gone westward by ship to Honolulu and then spread from there aboard other ships bound for South America and Australia and the Orient. One such ship, the English brig *Mary Dare*, under Captain John Scarborough, plied its way from the Sandwich Islands far to the northeast, into the Strait of Juan de Fuca. From there it had sailed southward in Puget Sound to its southernmost navigable reaches at Nisqually, before making its way back up the sound and then down the West Coast before finally arriving at the mouth of the Columbia River. From there it sailed upstream past Astor's Fort and then another seventy-five miles on before finally reaching the mouth of the Willamette.

The white population in Oregon at this time was some ten thousand individuals, with many more approaching the region, now strung all along the Oregon Trail, but as the news from California flashed through the entire Willamette Valley, most of the male population seemed energized and intensely eager to move southward on a trek towards California and its gold fields. Indeed, by autumn virtually all of Oregon's male and many of its female settlers had abandoned the Willamette Valley for what they perceived to be much greener — or more golden — pastures.

[July 15th, 1848 • Saturday]

The *Californian* weekly newspaper made an effort to stay alive with the publication of an issue this day, but it was an effort largely wasted. There was no staff member left to produce the issue except the editor himself, and, equally important, there was no one left in the town to read it. The single-paged issue ccontained a feature story under the headline of *The Whole World at War,* dealing with the revolution occurring in France, but that was hardly a momentous concern here in California.

More pertinent, perhaps, was the smaller, boxed article near the bottom of the page, a copy of the proclamation just issued by Governor Mason, decrying the amount of desertion occurring in the Army and Navy alike, as soldiers and sailors abandoned their posts to join the gold rush. Mason sought the help of California citizens in apprehending the deserters, but the few who read it could not have cared less.

Finally, there was a notice, which came as no surprise, that due to students and teachers alike joining the rush to the gold sites, the public schools were being ordered closed indefinitely.

It was decidedly a humdrum issue of The *Californian* and the last for a long while.

[July 16, 1848 • Sunday]

The wildly fluctuating prices for everything in the California coastal region were sowing seeds of disruption and instability for its inhabitants. Within mere hours the value of goods or property could rise a hundredfold or drop as much; California's economy was in turmoil. The arrival yesterday in San Francisco Harbor of the stately brig *Belfast,* out of New York City prompted a development which epitomized the economic chaos: Her crew at once off-loaded the first real cargo of goods from the East since the gold discovery, stacking them at the Broadway Wharf. The price of such goods in town instantly dropped twenty-five percent, while at the same time the value of real estate jumped 50 to 100 percent higher.

On the day before yesterday, a downtown San Francisco lot at Washington and Montgomery Streets was offered at $5,000 [$136,000] and was entirely ignored. Then, yesterday, the *Belfast* arrived, and today that very same lot quickly sold for $10,000 [$272,000] and could very likely have garnered a higher price.

Charles Doler, a banker lately from Baltimore, shook his head and exclaimed in an utterly flabbergasted tone, "The whole damned country has gone utterly crazy!"

No one took issue with the comment.

[July 18th, 1848 ♦ Tuesday]

The Californios — native California Mexicans who, thus far, had resisted the temptation to prospect — were finally becoming much more active throughout the gold belt. Among them was a man who broke that previous mold of cautious indifference in fine style. Pierre "Don Pedro" Sansevain, had long been itching to do some serious gold prospecting of his own. He was a well-known, highly respected pioneer who had owned a small land grant near San José since 1839, and he had been one of the first, when news of the gold discovery began filtering through the Territory, to head for Sutter's Fort.

Learning all he could about where the gold was being found, he mined first for a short time in early May in the Sutter-Marshall Sawmill area and did well there, until Marshall made the site out of bounds to outsiders. He then drifted downstream along the South Fork until he reached Mormon Island, and there, too, enjoyed moderate success for a while, but became disenchanted when the big bar became so heavily crowded with miners.

Striking out on his own, determined to find gold where no one else had yet looked, Don Pedro Sansevain headed south and finally reached the Tuolumne River. He began moving upstream until he encountered some substantial gold in ravines emptying into the river. In a large bar rimming the river's southeastern shoreline, he encountered gold in quantities far beyond his expectations, consisting of navy-bean- sized nuggets considerably larger than he had recovered either at the saw-mill site or at Mormon Island. Staking out his claim, he settled in, digging entirely by himself with nothing more than a crowbar, pick, small shovel and a pie pan, and within one week, ending today, he had accumulated fourteen *pounds* of nuggets, valued at no less than $3,584 [$97,485]!

As such accounts filtered into the coastal communities, soon virtually every California male felt a strong compulsion to gravitate to the mines. At this time while Monterey's *alcalde*, Walter Colton, was residing with Governor Mason and Lt. Layman of the U.S. Navy, all of the office and household staff members suddenly disappeared. As Colton wrote of it in his *Journal* today:

> *Saturday, July 15. The gold fever has reached every servant in Monterey; none are to be trusted in their engagement beyond a week. Gen. Mason, Lieut. Layman, and myself, form a mess; we have a house, and all the table furniture and culinary apparatus requisite; but our servants have run. This morning, for the fortieth time, we had to take to the kitchen and cook our own breakfast. A General of the United States Army, the commander of a man-of-war, and the Alcalde of Monterey, in a smoking kitchen, grinding coffee, toasting a herring and peeling onions! These gold mines are going to upset all the domestic arrangements of society. I have resolved to go to these gold mines with some select friends, starting today, and see for myself the situation that exists.*

He did exactly that.

[July 19th, 1848 • Wednesday]

Henry Bigler stared with sorrowful eyes at the large stack of rocks before him; rocks that he and the other Saints in their company had formed into a square about eight feet to the side and then neatly piled others on top until a dense rock monument had been formed about three feet high. He hoped it would last for a very long time.

Like Bigler, his other forty-five fellow Mormons were silent, and sober, each one shrouded in his own bleak thoughts. They were on their way home at last, this group; oddly enough, to a *home* that none of them had ever seen, but which had become the Zion of the Church of Jesus Christ of Latter-day Saints — a home now called Salt Lake City. Simultaneously, they were turning their backs to a temporary existence that, for many, had grown surprisingly dear to their hearts. It had been an interval that none of them would ever forget, and all seemed to know that however long they might live, the memory of these past months would remain in their minds and hearts nearly as fresh and clear and memorable as it was this very day.

They were now a unit again, these forty-five men and one woman — she being Melissa Coray, wife of the former First Orderly Sergeant of Company B, William Coray. It was an unofficial but tightly-knit unit they had formed, moving together as one. They anticipated no trouble on their way to Salt Lake City, but just in case an unexpected conflict might develop, they had organized themselves into groups of tens, each such group with an appointed captain. They had also elected, as their over-all commander and captain, Samuel Thompson, former second lieutenant of Company C of the old Mormon Battalion. They had organized themselves in this manner sixteen days ago at the place they had named Pleasant Valley. That had been on July 3rd, and the discipline and perseverance they had learned during their former Battalion's grueling cross-country march last year, would now surely stand them in good stead for whatever might lie ahead.

They had begun their present trek by following the high-climbing divide between the American and the Cosumnes Rivers, following the blazed trail that the trio of their brethren — Daniel Browett, Ezrah H. Allen and Henderson Cox — had left for them to follow. The three men had done an exemplary job at selecting the best possible passage for those who would be following, though the work of cutting and clearing a passage for the seventeen wagons and their droves of 150 horses and the same number of cattle still required a prodigious effort. Often in steep ascents and declivities, passage could only be made by raising or lowering the wagons by means of ropes, with every hand working at the effort.

The Mormon party labored on, day after day and finally, yesterday, they paused to recover some cattle that had become lost, as well as to rest and regain their strength while a party of five of the men pushed ahead to see where the blazed trail was taking them and how much longer it would be before they were traversing the eastern downslope of the Sierra Nevadas. As Henry Bigler wrote of it in his *diary*:

> *July 18. Camp laid by to hunt some stock that was lost out of the herd yesterday. While myself and four others went to work on the road, which we did for about four miles, and*

> *as we were returning to camp we found the place where we supposed our three pioneers had camped by a large spring, running from the mountains into the Cosumnes. Near where they had their fire, was the appearance of a fresh grave. Some of us thought it might be an Indian grave, as near it was an old wickey up [wickiup], but the more we looked at it, the more we felt there lay the three men. When we got back to camp all the lost stock was found, and we made a report of the road, and the grave, etc. ... Tonight for the first time we put out camp guard. I believe every man had a musket.*

This morning the Mormons started their march by sunrise, but because the rough terrain slowed their progress significantly, it was afternoon before they had covered the five or six miles leading to the running spring Bigler and his companion had found yesterday. Here they decided to stop for the night, turned out the stock and then gathered around the spring to quench their thirst. Only moments later one of the men called out loudly:

"Hey, look here. An arrow!"

He stooped and retrieved the shaft and the others gather round to see. It was not a well-made shaft and its fletching was ragged, but, more important, it was liberally stained with dried blood. They began searching further and quickly found the cold remains of a small campfire and then more blood-stained arrows and a spot where two men had slept close together and another a small distance away. Bloodstains were now found on emergent rocks in the area, and then another of the Saints, fifteen or twenty feet away, issued a concerned cry:

"Look here! This is Brother Allen's gold pouch." He stooped and picked it up from where it lay almost hidden in some grasses. It was clearly the pouch that Ezra Allen had worn on a loop around his neck and inside his shirt. The gold nuggets it had contained were still inside.

Within a few minutes more they assembled at the grave near the dilapidated old wickiup and now there was no doubt what they had to do. They began digging at the low mound of recently turned earth about eight feet square. In only a few minutes more, buried less than two feet deep, they found the remains of their three brethren, Allen, Cox, and Browett. All three bodies had been stripped naked and were horribly mutilated. As Bigler wrote of the sobering discovery in his diary:

> *July 19. Rolled out from Leek Spring; had hard, heavy pulling, the road very rocky in places; broke our new axle tree, and in passing over a snowbank Mr. J. [Jonathan] Holmes' wagon broke down. Made only five or six miles and encamped at the spring near the fresh grave; determining to satisfy ourselves, it was soon opened. We were shocked at the sight. There lay the three murdered men robbed of every stitch of clothing, lying promiscuously in one hole about two feet deep. Two of them [Cox and Browett] were lying on their faces. Allen was lying on his back and had the appearance that an ax had been sunk into his face and that he had been shot in the eye. The blood seemed fresh still oozing from their wounds. When we came to examine round about, we found arrows plentifully on the ground, many of them bloody and broken. Examining still closer, the rocks were stained with blood, and Mr. Allen's purse of gold dust was lying about a rod from the grave. The gold was still in the sack. It was known by several of the boys who had seen him make it. He had attached a buckskin string of sufficient length so as to put it over his head and around his neck and letting the purse hang in his bosom inside of his clothes, We judged they were killed the second night out, which would make it the twenty-seventh of June. Some [of us] thought their guns and saddles might be in their grave with them, for they had set out leaving the camp having each a riding animal and a pack mule.*

Bigler's latter speculation was incorrect. The guns and saddles were not there, having been taken by the Indians along with their animals. The Saints had then spent a morose time digging a deeper grave on the spot, laying out their dead companions in blankets, and gently recovering them with the earth, then building the cairn over the gravesite to both mark the site and protect the bodies from being unearthed by wolves. On a large nearby pine, they cut away the bark and etched with the knives in the bare wood the names of the three, their ages and the manner of their death. In addition, they carved into the wood a final inscription:

To the Memory of
Daniel Browett, Ezrah H. Allen,
and Henderson Cox,
who were supposed murdered
and buried by Indians
the night of
27th June, A.D. 1848.

After nightfall, when all the chores were finished, and they had gathered about their campfires, their stock suddenly became alarmed and closed in towards the men and campfires, "... their eyes shining like balls of fire in the darkness," according to Bigler. As swiftly as it could be done, one of their small cannons was loaded and fired. The belching of the cannon fire in the darkness and the tremendous boom it made, echoing repeatedly throughout the surrounding hills, so terrified their animals that they scattered in every direction, and it was not until late into the following morning that all of them were recovered, some having run a considerable distance on their back-trail.

If, as the majority of the Saints were convinced was true, the Digger Indians were in the vicinity and had been creeping up upon them, the cannon report apparently frightened them into fleeing, since nothing thereafter was seen of them. The Indians were almost entirely unacquainted with the use of firearms, and the cannon roar itself, in the night's stillness, undoubtedly terrified them. In the morning light the men of the party would follow and round up the scattered stock and start on their way again. But tonight they held an impromptu prayer service for their fallen comrades and then, as a final measure, they named this melancholy site.

They called it *Tragedy Spring.*

[July 24th, 1848 • Monday]

Christopher "Kit" Carson rode into St. Louis this day, weary to his bones. He'd been in the saddle almost constantly since leaving the West Coast exactly eighty days ago, on May 5th. Since he was one of the better known — and recognizable — of the mountain men of the West, word of his arrival spread swiftly, and he was soon besieged by a horde of newspaper reporters seeking interviews. Their questions were fired at him in rapid pace: What was the news from the far West? Where did he start from? Which route had he taken to get here? Were any Indian tribes on the warpath? What was the situation in California?

Carson answered as best he could but, exhausted from his weeks of almost constant travel, he largely brushed aside the questions and said, "Boys, I been on the go a considerable while an' I'm right tired. California was quiet when I left and Colonel Mason was military governor. That's 'bout all I know, 'cept what I heard when I first got here, that the war 'tween us an' Mexico is over. I've come through Taos, Santa Fe and Fort Leavenworth an' all I want right now, soon as I deliver some messages, is a bath and to be let sleep for three days runnin'."

They let him go, disgruntled that there wasn't much of a story. He didn't mention the discovery of gold, simply because he hadn't heard about it before he left, but then neither had anyone else here along the Mississippi or eastward. That they soon would learn of it was certain. But not just yet.

[July 25th, 1848 • Tuesday]

The proclamation issued to the general citizenry by Governor Mason in Monterey today minced no words, and it was clear in its very brevity that he was highly irritated about the sharp rise in desertions from the armed forces — and not only angry, but serious about eliminating the problem. The strongly worded proclamation he issued was clearly meant not only to facilitate the apprehension of the many military deserters, but to effectively discourage those who had not yet defected from attempting to do so:

> *NOTICE AND APPEAL*
>
> *PERSONS EMPLOYED AT THE MINES ARE REMINDED THAT UP TO THIS TIME THEY HAVE ENJOYED THE HIGH PRIVILEGE OF DIGGING GOLD ON GOVERNMENT LAND WITHOUT CHARGE AND WITHOUT HINDRANCE. IN RETURN FOR THIS PRIVILEGE THEY ARE BOUND TO ASSIST IN APPREHENDING DESERTERS AND OF GIVING NOTICE TO THE NEAREST MILITARY OFFICER WHERE THEY ARE CONCEALED. A DRAGOON FORCE WILL SOON BE AT THE MINING DISTRICT AND WILL TRAVERSE IT IN EVERY DIRECTION, TO ARREST DESERTERS FROM THE ARMY AND NAVY AND TO APPREHEND SUCH CITIZENS AS EMPLOY THEM.*

[July 26th, 1848 • Wednesday]

Despite the unfortunate loss of his pick, James H. Carson was finally finding the gold he had hoped to locate.

Even the abundant deposits along Weber Creek had been partially abandoned as miners, hearing rumors of great finds being made to the south, especially in the valleys of the Mokelumne, Stanislaus and Tuolumne Rivers and their tributaries, loaded up their gear and headed that way, hoping to at last stumble upon the mother lode. The tributaries, large and small, that had previously been unnamed, were now becoming known by specific designations, very often the names of the miners who were first to tap their resources.

John Sutter had now transferred his large crew of Indians and Kanakas to a stream that they were calling Sutter Creek, which was producing well. John M. Murphy had established his Murphy's Camp; Dr. Henry P. Angel's location was being called Angels Camp, but it was often confused with the nearby Angel's Camp established by George Henry Angel. William Knight was doing well at Knight's Ferry and, of course, Don Pedro Sansevain was continuing with his remarkable success at Don Pedro Bar.

Sgt. Carson was doing far better than he had ever anticipated he would, and by following some Indians back to their diggings, found an excellent deposit on an unnamed tributary creek of the Stanislaus River, which he promptly named after himself. After he teamed up with prospector James Wood, the pair had located another excellent deposit on still another unnamed Stanislaus tributary, which they named *Wood Creek*. A few other prospectors in the area were also doing well, especially considering that they were working with only pick and knife, averaging between $200 and $300 [$5,440 and $8,160] daily per man. Over the past 10 days, teaming up with two other prospectors who wouldn't give their names, the four panned 11.25 pounds of gold — a total of 720 ounces (180 ounces each as they divided it) and worth $9,280 [$252,416].

Ever more gold-seekers were moving in, and a remarkable sort of camaraderie developed among them. Disputes over deposits were almost unheard of; there seemed to be more than enough gold for everyone, easily obtained by moving on farther up the bar or to the next bar along the shore. Carson, commenting on this rather unusual sense of fraternity, wrote in his journal:

No person here actually digs for gold on a Sunday, but

the Sabbath is often spent in prospecting in the area. Many others spend that day playing cards and using gold nuggets as their chips, careless about how much they win or lose. Others will often sit in small groups under trees, singing songs and reminiscing and telling tales that stretch one's credulity, or just sitting and sipping from a flask of whiskey. In all these activities, fun and harmonious good will toward one another are prominent factors. Anger for any cause is rarely displayed; yet, though there are ministers of the gospel among us, no one preaches. Religion, at least here, appears to have been forgotten, even by its Servants.

[August 7th, 1848 • Monday]

Acting on the information received yesterday by special courier from Lt. Col. Burton in La Paz, California's military governor, Colonel Richard B. Mason in Monterey, today issued a proclamation in both English and Spanish to the residents of his territory that was decidedly anticlimactic: The War with Mexico was now officially ended by the Treaty of Guadalupe Hidalgo. The treaty had been ratified by both Mexico and the United States: For the sum of $15 million, California had now been sold to the United States, and the governor's declaration informed the existing residents that those who wished it had the option to either become American citizens or to leave the new American territory.

Mason also dispatched an order that he was very relieved to make: Colonel Stevenson's regiment was to be mustered out of the U.S. military service at once and the only forces remaining were the U.S. Artillery company at Monterey and a single company of U.S. Dragoons at Los Angeles.

No one paid much attention and, so far as was recorded, no one left the territory under protest.

[August 10, 1848 • Thursday]

More than half a continent to the east, the 2,000 copies of the April 1st issue of the *California Star* that Samuel Brannan shipped so many weeks ago had finally reached St. Louis, Missouri, one week ago. Most of these copies were relayed onward, but a certain percentage were sent up the Illinois River, with a few copies eventually winding up in such Illinois towns as Springfield, Peoria, Ottawa, and Joliet, but the majority of them were shipped on to Chicago. Other similar bundles of the papers, taken farther east, were dropped off in Louisville, Cincinnati, Cleveland, and Detroit. The greater bulk of them, however, were shipped farther eastward, destined mainly for New York City.

One copy of the newspaper somehow found its way into the waiting room of a physician named Jonas Peale in Ottawa, Illinois. Although the doctor had placed it in his waiting room with other reading material there, few patients over the past several days had given the slim newspaper anything more than a cursory glance. The single exception, however, was a 32-year-old businessman named Alonzo Delano — who, while awaiting his turn as the doctor finished with an earlier patient, perused the *Star* issue carefully. Noting that, of all things, it was a California newspaper, he wondered with vague amusement how it happened to be here in Illinois.

Filling six full columns on the front page of that issue was an article, written by a physician named Dr. Victor Fourgeaud, entitled *The Prospects of California.* For his own part, Delano had only vaguely heard before now of that distant place called California, but the piece rather piqued his curiosity and he read with mounting interest about that far-off land at the western edge of the continent and what it offered. He was immediately and most intensely struck by one of its comments, to the effect that not only did California have a wonderfully healthful weather the year around, but that the climate was known to be especially beneficial for those suffering from asthma or other breathing disorders, as well as from what it termed as "heart trouble and consumption."

A bit further into the article, Delano was struck by a particular paragraph that cleverly snagged his interest. The learned Dr. Fourgeaud had written:

> *We saw, a few days ago, a beautiful specimen of gold from the mine newly discovered on the American fork. From all accounts the mine is immensely rich, and already we learn that gold from it, collected at random and without any trouble, has become an article of trade in the upper settlements. This precious [metal] abounds in this country. We have heard of several other newly discovered mines of gold, but as these reports are not yet authenticated, we shall pass over them.*

This newspaper article turned out to be the second of two incidents occurring today that had profoundly affected Delano. The first, not at all pleasant, had manifested itself in the severe chest pains he'd been suffering at intervals recently, which had brought him once again to the office of Dr. Peale, his friend and longtime family physician. Delano's was here today was to learn the results of the battery of tests Dr. Peale had lately performed on him, though he doubted they would be of any real consequence.

Contemplating further the article he'd just finished reading in the doctor's waiting room, Delano could not help being intrigued by the idea of someone just going out with a pick and shovel and digging up actual gold. This was something he'd fantasized about often as a boy. Once he had found a half-inch-square cube of brassy iron pyrite that he mistook for gold, and now he remembered the thrill he had experienced in the belief that it really was gold - until his error was pointed out. He still had that piece, after all these years, perched on a shelf of knick-knacks. Too bad, he thought, that this described place was clear across the continent; what a great thrill it would be to search for gold in a place where it actually existed.

"Why is it," he murmured to himself, "that really intriguing things like this always seem to happen in far-away places?"

Delano's own life here in Illinois had become, to his way of thinking, markedly humdrum. His marriage had long ago become stagnant, he and his wife, Mary, having grown somewhat apart in recent years and lately sharing almost no interests in common; his business, owning and operating the little enterprise in the town of Ottawa called *Delano's General Store,* which at first had been both fun and profitable, had, despite its financial success, become tiresome and no longer challenging for him. He was moderately successful socially and had become Grand Noble of the original Ottawa Lodge of the IOOF — Independent Order of Odd Fellows — but even that had grown stale, to his way of thinking, and he often found himself wishing he had done something *different* with his life. The only thing that had held his interest at all in recent years was the regular column he wrote for their local newspaper, the *Ottawa Standard*.

"Alonzo."

His name being called roused him from his reverie, and he set the newspaper aside and followed the beckoning Dr. Peale into the private office. He smiled at his old friend but felt a little tug of alarm when the physician's usual responsive grin was absent. Delano settled himself in the leather chair and waited with a growing sense of apprehension as the doctor closed the door, returned to his desk and sat down behind it with a barely audible sigh.

"Alonzo," he said again, adding without preamble, "you have a very serious problem. It's a condition that some people call consumption. Actually, it's TB — tuberculosis. Very little that can be done about it."

"How much —" Delano began, then paused.

" — time do you have left?" Peale finished for him. "Difficult to say for sure. A year or two, if you're lucky. Probably somewhat less. I'm sorry."

"Isn't there anything we can do about it?"

Dr. Peale shrugged. "Undoubtedly, our climate here certainly aggravates it. Getting into a drier climate is apt to slow it down, but there's no guarantee."

"Like out west, maybe?" Delano asked.

"Possibly. Some of my patients have done that; along with greater physical activity it sometimes helps. Not always, unfortunately, but occasionally. As I said, there's no guarantee."

They had talked more, but Delano had already made up his mind, and he was noted for sticking to a decision once he'd made it. He would make preparations immediately and head west, and, considering the article he'd just finished reading, California seemed just the place. He might not have much time left, but he was determined to enjoy what remained of his life. As he wrote in his *diary* this evening:

> *It seems my constitution has suffered sad inroads by disease incident to midwestern climate, and my physician frankly told me that a change of residence and more bodily exertion is absolutely necessary to effect a radical change in my system — in fact, that my life depends upon such a change, and I finally conclude to adopt his advice. ... the astonishing accounts of the vast deposits of gold newly discovered in California have reached us, and besides the fever of the body, I am suddenly seized with the fever of the mind for gold; and in hopes of receiving a speedy cure for the ills of both body and mind, I have turned my attention "westward ho!" and have already commenced making arrangements for my depar-ture. Mary [his wife] and the children [16-year-old Fred and 6-year old Harriet] will remain here and tend*

> *the store until I can get to California and get established somehow; and if I survive, which I am convinced will occur, I will then write to them to come join me. ...*

Despite what he had just written, Delano was not at all convinced he would survive. Though she didn't voice the thought, neither was his wife.

[August 12th, 1848 • Saturday]

No one in California or elsewhere had any truly accurate idea of what the current Indian population was in the territory, but the most credible estimates set the number at somewhere in the vicinity of 300,000. Of these, only a relatively small number had attached themselves to the whites and worked for them, more often than not simply in exchange for food and clothing. The several thousand that worked for Captain John Sutter, either as full-time employees or as part-time or seasonal help, were the exception. More often than not the natives — many of them derogatively called "Digger Indians" — avoided the whites where possible, or preyed upon them for foodstuffs, clothing and animals where they could do so without too much endangering themselves.

The numerous, greatly fragmented tribes that lived in the far west had little by little been pushed farther and farther into the more remote regions of the Sierra Nevada Mountains, and their resentment over such displacement had grown throughout the years. Still, they had managed to maintain a balance of sorts for many years, if they were not too greatly encroached upon in this final retreat.

The discovery of gold was changing all that.

This year, quite suddenly, there were whites roaming all over the land, far into areas they had never penetrated before. The Indians, by and large, had little interest in gold itself and harvested it only as a trading device with the whites who seemed so enraptured by it. But with ever more whites entering areas of Indian domain now, vast regions that had always before been Indian domain, conflicts and disaster were becoming far more commonplace.

The greatest problem for the tribes — especially the Maidu and Konkow tribes along the Feather River and the Miwok and Nisenan and other tribes in the valleys of the American and Merced, Mokelumne and Tuolumne Rivers and their tributaries — lay now in the fact that their final home lay in the midst of the gold regions. The whites, for the most part, did not look upon any of these Indians as human beings. Rather, they were, in their eyes, an unfortunate form of vermin that it was best to destroy wherever encountered. It had become quite commonplace for whites roaming through the mountains to simply shoot down, without second thought, any Indian they encountered. For some of the whites, in fact, it had taken on virtually the aspect of a sport. But now, for the first time, the Indians who had been pushed on and on through the years began to resolve among themselves that they would no longer allow this to occur; that they could and would push back just as fiercely.

It was a decision they should have made a long time ago, because now it was too little — and much too late.

[August 15th, 1848 • Tuesday • 1:00 p.m.]

Of all the individuals living in California at this time, none had greater opportunity to amass fortunes — and none squandered their opportunities quite so flagrantly — as did John Sutter and James Marshall.

Sutter, at least, capitalized to some degree in the rush that enveloped them. Greatly disheartened by the surge of gold-seekers flooding into his fort and the damage they were wreaking, Sutter for a time had not known what to do about it. The newcomers had trampled his crops, slaughtered his cattle and sheep, stolen his tools and supplies and so infected his workers with gold-fever that he lost a large majority of his Indian workers. He was, in essence, watching his little empire crumbling away and initially didn't really know what to do about it beyond mourning his losses.

At length, with a hundred of his Indian workers and fifty of the Kanakas, whom he loosely organized into what he called Sutter's Mining Company, he had started upstream on the American River from Mormon Island, appalled at the four thousand miners already on hand and making excellent finds there — totaling around $50,000 [$1,440,000] per day or more. Sutter and his men went upstream beyond them a few miles and there they struck gold. It was by no means a major strike, but certainly it was significant enough and, in the process of working it, from dawn until dusk each day, he accumulated enough gold to pay his workers, wipe out some of his current debts, and still retain a bit extra for himself. He might have made even more, but he and his group had been followed, and suddenly hordes of gold-seekers were moving in on him, overcrowding the area so badly that no one could work advantageously.

With well-founded rumors reaching him of major strikes being made south of Mormon Island in a stream now being called Weber Creek and its tributaries, and in locations even more distant, rumors accompanied by accounts that even those creeks were becoming lined with miners, Sutter was repelled by the thought of going there. Simultaneously, however, he remembered a stream he had once followed well south of there, a tributary of the South Fork Cosumnes River. It was an unnamed stream he recalled as having numerous bars, and so he headed there with his entourage on July 28th.

Sutter was gratified when his party arrived there to find that the little stream, still flowing but very low, gave no indication that any gold-seekers had yet been here. Quickly moving upstream, he encountered bars that showed great promise, and he promptly named the stream *Sutter Creek*. Once again, however, he and his group had been followed, and overcrowding became a problem here, too. Not only did Sutter despise the harsh living conditions, but gambling and drinking quickly became major problems, and Sutter became very suspicious of his own workers; he was convinced that they were cheating him by hiding nuggets in their boots, belts and pockets. Calling his men together, he addressed them angrily: "You boys have been cheating me. I know it, damn it, and I won't have it! Get moving, back to the fort, right now, by God! This company is dissolved as of now!"

Sullenly, his men moved off and he followed. The deposit they had been working was claimed by other prospectors before they were even out of sight, and Sutter, now certain that he was making a big mistake, concluded that it was too late now to rescind his order. When his party reached the fort again, Sutter conferred with Lansford Hastings, who had recently arrived, hoping to persuade Hastings to enter into a business partnership with him and to help him open a general merchandise store at Coloma. Hastings agreed and the store was quickly built, but their inventory was stolen before they could open the business. Sutter lost a great deal, and Hastings simply walked away, wanting nothing further to do with the enterprise.

Returning to the fort, Sutter continued to sell goods at a fine profit and quickly accumulated enough gold to pay off, with interest, the remainder of his creditors, including the Russians, who had initially underwritten his purchase of Fort Ross. Then, during the night of August 6th, Sutter was suddenly robbed at gunpoint in his quarters of all the funds and gold he had accumulated, and as the masked bandits rode off, they set fire to his clusters of wheat that had been stacked in sheaves. Though he still had the assets of his fort and the goods in storage there, as well as his interest in the gold-mining areas on his property, John Sutter was at this point very close to ruin. Deciding then to visit the mines, he rode off abruptly.

Meanwhile at the limber-mill site, James Marshall was not doing at all well. Prospectors had shown up in droves, and neither requests not threats could discourage them from trespassing on the mill property. All who came seemed aware that Marshall was the initial discoverer of California gold and were under the impression that he had some supernatural power, some secret store of knowledge about exactly where to prospect successfully for the precious metal. They implored him for this knowledge, and when he professed to have none, they cursed and berated him. When still he couldn't — *wouldn't*, they believed — tell them exactly where to look, the pleas turned to threats. They produced a rope and threatened to hang him from the saw-mill structure if he didn't tell them what they wanted to hear.

Marshall finally slipped away at night, bitterly disillusioned with all that had happened this year. He took the lynching threats of the sawmill intruders seriously and was afraid to return. But here he was, with neither a place to go, nor even any equipment to call his own. He finally returned to the ranch he had built on Butte Creek, which he had once envisioned as his future retirement retreat, but, instead, he was forced to sell it in order to pay off debts and to raise funds to sustain him. After that, he wandered off toward the south hoping there to come across a previously unclaimed deposit similar to that which he had lost at the saw-mill.

Hardly had Sutter, himself, departed from the fort than the *S. S. Sacramento* slipped into dockage at the Sutter embarcadero, disgorging its huge number of passengers en route to the gold fields. One such passenger, a young man of about 20 years walked directly to the fort. He was nearly overwhelmed by the frenetic activity and the hordes of people moving about. When he asked a bystander to see the man in charge, the man pointed to a youngish man wearing a derby hat and nattily clad in a vested black suit on the porch of a nearby large mercantile establishment. Seeming somewhat disappointed, the newcomer nevertheless approached the man, who looked at him inquiringly.

"May I help you?" he asked.

"Yes, please, if you will," he replied. "Can you tell me where I will find Captain Sutter?"

The man shook his head regretfully. "Afraid you're just a bit too late. He was here earlier, but he rode out for the mines about an hour ago. He'll most likely be gone for a week or so. My name's Sam Brannan and I own this store. Perhaps I can help you. May I ask where you've come from and who you are?"

"I've just come from Europe. I'm called Augustus, but my full name is Johann A. Sutter, Jr. I'm the Captain's son."

Brannan's uncanny ability to detect an opportunity for turning a profit prompted him to usher the young man into his private office within his store and to immediately send for his latest set of cohorts, which included Colonel William Stewart, Sheriff George McKinistry, John Bidwell, Major Samuel Hensley, and the clever lawyer, Peter Burnett. After meeting briefly with these associates, Brannan invited them into his office, where a circle of chairs had been positioned for them. After introductions were completed, Col. Stewart, at an almost imperceptible nod from Brannan, introduced himself and added in a cultured voice:

"I represent the Russian-American Fur Company in San Francisco. I've been selected to fill you in as briefly and completely as possible on the situation existing here. Your father, I'm afraid, has been plagued with numerous serious problems and peccadilloes. He has for some time been under a great deal of strain, as he has numerous creditors knocking at his door who threaten to take all he has if they are not paid what is due them. Foremost among such creditors is the Russian Foreign Minister, to whom your father owes the majority of his debt, presently $80,000 [$2,304,000]. He, your father, that is, also has a serious problem with the consumption of alcohol, which tends to cloud his thinking and cause him to make significant errors in judgment. Finally, he creates uproarious scandals, by frequently and sometimes flauntingly engaging in promiscuous behavior with young Indian women who work here or who live nearby with their husbands who work for him. The latter two matters — the drinking and the promiscuity — are personal problems that he must contend with himself. The debt, unfortunately, is not.

"The Russians," he went on smoothly, "are on the verge of attaching this entire fort for debt. We all live in grave fear of his losing everything here, including our own holdings, which are inextricably intermeshed with his. With your arrival, however, we see a ray of hope for escaping such a grim and sobering future. If we can, with your help, convince your father to transfer all his property holdings into your name, there is at least a reasonable expectation of paying off the debts from rentals of fort properties and from the profits of the various companies in which Captain Sutter holds interest. That is, of course, provided your father can be prevented from squandering the profits on liquor and squaws."

Big and bluff, George McKinistry spoke next, briefly but carefully explaining the promising possibility of selling off some of Sutter's land around the fort and at Suttersville, four miles down the Sacramento, which included valuable river frontage property. Young Sutter appeared to be inundated with all that needed to be done here, but when they finished, both Augustus and the big sheriff had committed themselves to making every possible effort to save Captain Sutter's ventures from collapse and, simultaneously, to preserve his properties with their enormous potential value to benefit his heirs.

Before they left, young Sutter had long talks with John Bidwell, Samuel Hensley and the elder Sutter's crafty lawyer, Peter Burnett. When the other men finally left, Brannan and Hastings lingered with him, and the three were soon joined by yet another of Brannan's Californio partners, Theodore Cordua. They discussed the plan to develop the town site closer to the fort, as well as abutting it with the Sacramento River at the point where the American River flowed into it; this proposed project actually amounted to an expansive enlargement of what was already being called Sacramento. Young Sutter agreed that the wisest course would be to sell town lots for from $250 to $500 [$7,200 to $14,400] each, with the more valuable riverfront lots to go for considerably more to miners very eager to spend their gold. It was obvious that as the lots rose in value, speculators would begin to make sizeable purchases, and the elder Sutter's debts could gradually be absolved.

Left on his own at last, young Sutter roomed in his father's quarters and rummaged about, trying to bring about some semblance of order to the mess that all the old papers and records were in. In doing so he found a large number of debts owed as well as a great many old IOU's Sutter had collected from others and never redeemed. More than ever, he was determined to make order out of all this chaos and try to save what remained of Sutter's assets, not only for himself but equally for his mother, sister and two brothers.

Abruptly, earlier than anticipated, Captain Sutter returned, reeling under the effects of whiskey. Confronted by the son he had not seen in decades, he was initially thunderstruck, but then grew furious as he learned what his son had committed his father and himself to accomplish. He drew his pistol and threatened to kill Augustus but was restrained by Burnett, Hastings and Cordua, who wrested the gun from him and finally were able to talk some reason into him. Sutter, finally realizing that with the transfer of his properties to his son, they would then be safe from attachment and all remaining debts could gradually be paid off, he at last agreed and the papers were drawn up and signed. Though he still bemoaned the idea of creating Sacramento in an area sure to be flooded, he gave in, and today, August 15th, 1848, the enterprise they had envisioned would become a major metropolis was officially begun.

[August 15th, 1848 • Tuesday • 7:30 p.m.]

Robert "Bob" Johnson, a miner at the Old Dry Diggings was this evening writing a *Letter to the Editor* of *The Californian* in San Francisco. He reasoned that whoever might still be in San Francisco really ought to have an opportunity to get a fair share of what was being found. Still, so no one would come down on him for letting the cat out of the bag, he decided he would just use his own initials, inverted, to sign his little account of what he had found here. He wrote:

> *At the lower mines the success of the day is counted in dollars, at the upper mines, near the mill, in ounces, but here at the Old Dry Diggings in pounds! The earth is taken out of the ravines which make out of the mountain, and is carried in wagons and packed on horses from one to three miles to the nearest water, where it is washed; $400 [$11,520] has been an average for a cart-load. In one instance five loads of earth which had been dug out in a day sold for 47 ounces ($752 [$21,657.60]), and yielded after washing $16,000 [$460,800]. Instances have occurred here where men have carried the earth on their backs, and collected from $800 to $1,500 [$23,040 to $43.200] in a day. Here one Davison Wilson took $2,000 [$57,600] from under his own door-step. Three Frenchmen discovered gold in removing a stump which obstructed the road from [Old] Dry Diggings to Coloma and within a week secured $5,000 [$144,000]. Robert Birnie, an employé of Consul Forbes, saw the 200*

miners here making from 50 to 100 ounces ($800 to $1,600 [$23,040 to $46,080]) daily! The actual fountain-head yet remains undiscovered, but with the proper machinery introduced and the hills cut down, huge pieces must be found. At this time tidings have just arrived of new placers on the Stanislaus, and many of the 200 miners here are accordingly preparing to leave ground worth $400 [$11,520] a load, in the hope of finding something better in the south. J.B.

[August 16th, 1848 • Wednesday]

This had been a most outstanding day and, in his Monterey quarters, the Reverend Walter Colton marveled at the accounts that had just provided proof — especially to any lingering disbelievers in Monterey — with regard to the gold deposits being tapped. If any here had been any lingering doubts about the existence of gold — or its abundance — in California, they had just been put completely to rest.

Only a bit over an hour ago, four citizens of Monterey, newly returned from their prospecting along the Feather River, not only reported that some remarkable fortunes were being made in that area, but brought with them tangible proof of their own finds. The four, who had been working with three others and employing some thirty Indians to find gold for them, had worked exactly 52 days before quitting and equally dividing their accumulation of gold. It had amounted to very nearly $11,000 [$316,800] apiece — a treasure which each man showed now to Colton. The seven men had come away with a staggering total of $76,844 [$2,213,197.20].

Hardly had this jubilant group left when one of Colton's old friends showed up, beaming with delight, having just now returned from his own solitary dig on a bar in the Yuba River which, in 64 days, had earned him $5,356 [$154,252.80]. Even as Colton examined the man's remarkable finds, another, and final, miner of the day, Jubal Rossiter, dropped by to proudly show off the results of his own 54 days of digging in a small ravine that emptied into the Mokelumne River. It was a fine assemblage of nuggets with a total value of $3,467 [$99,849.60], which was an exceptional find under the circumstances: He was only 14 years old.

[August 18th, 1848 • Friday • 9:00 a.m.]

Early this morning Governor Richard Barnes Mason, in his headquarters office at Monterey, completed briefing Lt. Lucien Loeser on his forthcoming mission as special courier to Washington, D.C.

"I cannot overstate to you the importance of this mission you will be undertaking," he said, "nor the value of this container you will carrying with you." He indicated, with a tilt of his head, the carefully sealed tea caddy perched at the corner of his desk. "It is not to leave your possession, or your view, under any circumstances, until you personally surrender it, along with this report you will be carrying, into the hands of Brigadier General Roger Jones himself. General Jones, as I'm sure you're aware, is Adjutant General of the United States, and I will also be including a special letter to be delivered into his hand alone.

"How you will travel," he continued after a moment, "will very much have to be up to you, dependent upon what means of transportation are most expeditiously available. It is highly imperative that you reach Washington as swiftly as possible. The only vessel presently at anchorage that will get you part way on your journey is the bark *Lambayecana*, out of Peru, which is scheduled to embark for there in twelve days, on August 30th," he grimaced, "assuming the skipper, Captain Henry Cooke, can keep his crew from jumping ship, which he has assured me he can. He'll be bound for the port of Payta in Peru, and from there you'll be entirely on your own."

"I'll be aboard her, Sir," Loeser said, "without fail, and the box and dispatches will not leave my immediate possession at any time until I turn them over to the Adjutant General."

Mason nodded, and for a moment studied the tall, angular Lt. Loeser. He was a steady officer here at headquarters, having recently been promoted from Second to First Lieutenant, but he had already proven himself well in his duties, and Mason was pleased with Lt. Sherman's recommendation of him as courier, aware that with Loeser the important job would be done as well as anyone could do it. It was not necessary to inform the officer that the box he was carrying contained just over fourteen and a third pounds of gold — valued at $36,608 [$1,054,310.40] — that had been donated by various miners. It might — Mason stifled a small smile — cause even an exemplary officer such as Loeser to consider disappearing, along with the box.

"All right, Lieutenant," he said at last, "get your affairs in order and prepare to leave on the thirtieth."

"Yes, Sir!" At the dismissal Loeser snapped a sharp salute, turned about and left the office.

Mason nodded again, returned his attention to reading the long, detailed letter composed in his name yesterday by Lt. Sherman of what they had encountered on their extensive tour of the mining regions. He read slowly and paused frequently to consider the words well and occasionally to jot his suggested revisions on a separate sheet of paper:

Head-quarters, 10th Military Department
Monterey, California, Aug. 17, 1848

Sir: — I have the honor to inform you that, accompanied by Lieut. W. T. Sherman, 3d Artillery, A.A.A. General, I started on the 12th of June last to make a tour through the Northern part of California. My principal purpose, however, was to visit the newly discovered "gold place," in the valley of the Sacramento. I had proceeded about forty miles when I was overtaken by an express bringing me intelligence of the arrival at Monterey of the United States ship Southampton, with important letters from Commodore Shubrick and Lieut. Col. Burton. I returned at once to Monterey and dispatched what business was most important, and on the 17th resumed my journey. We reached San Francisco on the 20th, and found that all, or nearly all, its male inhabitants had gone to the mines. The town, which a few months before was so busy and thriving, was then almost deserted. On the evening of the 24th, the horses of the escort were crossed to Sousoleto [Sausalito] in a launch and on the following day we resumed the journey by way of Bodega and Sonoma to Sutter's fort, where we arrived on the morning of the 2d of July. Along the whole route mills were lying idle, fields of wheat were open to cattle and horses, houses vacant, and farms going to waste. At Sutter's fort there was more life and business. Launches were discharging their cargoes at the river, and carts were hauling goods to the fort, where already were established several stores, a hotel, &c. Capt. Sutter had only two mechanics in his employ, (a wagon maker and a blacksmith,) whom he was then paying ten dollars [$288 each] a day. Merchants pay him a monthly rent of $100 [$2,880] per room; and while I was there, a two story house in the fort was rented as a hotel for $500 [$14,400] a month.

At the urgent solicitations of many gentlemen, I delayed

my stay here to participate in the first celebration of our national anniversary at the fort, but on the 5th resumed the journey, and proceeded twenty-five miles up the American fork to a point on it now known as the lower mines, or Mormon diggings [Mormon Island]. The hill sides were thickly strewn with canvass [sic] tents and bush arbors; a store was erected, and several boarding shanties in operation. The day was intensely hot, yet about two hundred men were at work in the full glare of the sun, washing for gold, some with tin pans, some with close woven Indian baskets, and the greater part had a rude machine known as the cradle. This is on rockers, six or eight feet long, open at the foot, and at its head has a coarse grate or sieve; the bottom is rounded, with small cleets [sic] nailed across. Four men are required to work this machine; one digs the ground in the bank close by the stream, another carries it to the cradle and empties it on the grate, a third gives a violent rocking motion to the machine, while a fourth dashes on water from the stream itself.

The sieve keeps the coarse stones from entering the cradle, the current of water washes off the earthy matter, and the gravel is gradually carried out at the foot of the machine, leaving the gold mixed with a very heavy fine black sand above the first cleets [sic]. The sand and gold mixed together are then drawn off through auger holes into a pan below, are dried entirely in the sun, and afterwards separated by blowing off the sand. A party of four men thus employed in the lower mines average $100 [$2,880] a day. The Indians, and those who have nothing but pans or willow baskets, gradually wash out the earth and separate the gravel by hand, leaving nothing but the gold mixed with sand, which is separated in the manner before described. The gold in the lower mines is in fine bright scales, of which I send several specimens.

As we ascended the South Branch of the American fork, the country became broken and mountainous, and at the saw mill, 25 miles above the lower washings, or 50 miles from Sutter's [Fort], the hills rise to about a thousand feet above the level of the Sacramento plain. Here a species of pine occurs, which led to the discovery of the gold. Capt. Sutter, feeling the great want of lumber, contracted in September last with a Mr. Marshall to build a saw-mill at that place. It was erected in the course of the last winter and spring, and a dam and race constructed; but when the water was let on the wheel, the tail-race was found to be too narrow to permit the flowing water to escape with sufficient rapidity. Mr. Marshall, to save labor, let the water directly into the race with strong current, so as to wash it wider and deeper. He effected his purpose, and a large bed of mud and gravel carried to the foot of the race. One day Mr. Marshall, as he was walking down the race to this deposit of mud, observed some glittering particles at its upper edge; he gathered a few, examined them, and became satisfied of their value. He then went to the fort, told Capt. Sutter of his discovery, and they agreed to keep it secret until a certain grist-mill of Sutter's was finished. It however got out, and spread like magic.

Remarkable success attended the labors of the first explorers, and in a few weeks, hundreds of men were drawn thither. At the time of my visit, but little more than three months after its first discovery, it was estimated that upwards of four thousand people were employed. At the mill there is a fine deposit or bank of gravel, which the people respect as the property of Capt. Sutter, although he pretends to no right to it, and would be perfectly satisfied with the simple promise of a pre-emption, on account of the mill which he has built there at considerable cost. Mr. Marshall was living near the mill, and informed me that many persons were employed above and below him; that they used the same machines as at the lower washings, and that their success was about the same — ranging from one to three ounces of gold per man daily. This gold, too, is in scales a little coarser than those of the lower mines. From the mill Mr. Marshall guided me up the mountains on the opposite or north bank of the south fork, where, in the bed of small streams or ravines, now dry, a great deal of coarse gold had been found. I there saw several parties at work, all of whom were doing very well; a great many specimens were shown me, some as heavy as four or five ounces in weight, and I send three pieces labeled No. 5, presented by a Mr. Spence. You will perceive that some of the specimens accompanying this hold mechan-

ically pieces of quartz; that the surface is rough and evidently moulded [sic] in the crevice of a rock.

This gold cannot be carried far by water, but must have remained near where it was first deposited from the rock that once bound it. I inquired of many people if they had encountered the metal in its matrix, but in every instance they said they had not; but that the gold was invariably mixed with washed gravel, or lodged in the crevices of other rocks. All bore testimony that they had found gold in greater or less quantities in the numerous small gullies or ravines that occur in that mountainous region. On the 7th of July I left the mill, and crossed to a small stream emptying into the American fork, three or four miles below the saw-mill. I struck this stream (now known as Weber's creek) at the washings of Sunol and Co. They had about thirty Indians employed, whom they pay in merchandise. They were getting gold of a character similar to that found in the main fork, and doubtless in sufficient quantities to satisfy them. I send you a small specimen, presented by this company, of their gold. From this point we proceeded up the slight stream about eight miles, where we found a great many people and Indians, some engaged in the bed of the stream, and others in the small side valleys that put into it. These latter are exceedingly rich, and two ounces were considered an ordinary yield for a day's work. A small gutter, not more than a hundred yards long by four feet wide and two or three feet deep, was pointed out to me as the one where two men — William Daly [Daylor] and Perry McCoon, had, a short time before, obtained $17,000 [$489,600] worth of gold.

Capt. Charles Weber informed me that he knew that these two men had employed four white men and about a hundred Indians, and that, at the end of one week's work, they paid off their party, and had left $10,000 [$288,000] worth of this gold. Another small ravine was shown me, from which had been taken upward of $12,000 [$345,600] worth of gold. Hundreds of similar ravines, to all appearances, are as yet untouched. I could not have credited these reports had I not seen, in the abundance of the precious metal, evidence of their truth. Mr. Robert B. Neligh, an agent of Commodore

Stockton, had been at work about three weeks in the neighborhood, and showed me in bags and bottles over $2000 [$57,600] worth of gold.

I might tell of hundreds of similar instances; but, to illustrate just how plentiful the gold was in the pockets of common laborers, I will mention a simple occurrence which took place in my presence when I was at Weber's store. This store was nothing but an arbor of bushes, under which he had exposed for sale goods and groceries suited to his customers. A man came in, picked up a box of Seidlitz powders, and asked its price. Capt. Weber told him it was not for sale. The man offered an ounce of gold, but Capt. Weber told him it only cost 50 cents [$14.40], and he did not wish to sell it. The man then offered an ounce and a half [$432], when Capt. Weber had to take it. The prices of all things are high, and yet Indians, who before hardly knew what a breech-cloth was, can now afford to buy the most gaudy dresses.

The country on either side of Weber's creek is much broken up by hills, and is intersected in every direction by small streams or ravines, which contain more or less gold. Those that have been worked are barely scratched; and although thousands of ounces have been carried away, I do not consider that a serious impression has been made upon the whole. Every day was developing new and richer deposits; and the only impression seemed to be, that the metal would be found in such abundance as seriously to depreciate in value.

On the 8th of July I returned to the lower mines, and on the following day to Sutter's, where on the 10th I was making preparations for a visit to the Feather, Yutah [Yuba] and Bear rivers, when I received a letter by messenger from Commander A. R. Long, United States Navy, who had just arrived at San Francisco from Mazatlan, with a crew for the sloop of war [U.S.S.] Warren, with orders to take the vessel to the squadron at La Paz. Capt. Long wrote to me that the Mexican Congress had adjourned without ratifying the treaty of peace; that he had letters for me from Commodore [T. Ap Catesby] Jones, and that his orders were to sail with the Warren on or before the 20th of July. In consequence of these, I determined to return to Monterey, and accordingly *arrived here on the 17th of July. Before leaving Sutter's, I satisfied myself that gold existed in the bed of the Feather river, in the Yutah [Yuba] and the Bear, and in many of the small streams that lie between the latter and the American fork; also, that it had been found in the Cosummes [Cosumnes] to the south of the American fork. In each of these streams the gold is found in small scales, whereas in the intervening mountains it occurs in coarser lumps. Mr. Sinclair, whose rancho is three miles above Sutter's on the north side of the American, employs about 50 Indians on the north fork, not far from its junction with the main stream. He had been engaged about five weeks when I saw him, and up to that time his Indians had used simply closely woven willow baskets. His nett [sic] proceeds (which I saw) were about $16,000 [$460,800] worth of gold. He showed me the proceeds of his last week's work — fourteen pounds avoirdupois of clean-washed gold. ... The principal store at Sutter's Fort, that of Brannan & Co., has received in payment for goods some $36,000 [$1,036,800] worth of this gold from the 1st of May to the 10th of July. Other merchants have also made extensive sales. Large quantities of goods are daily sent forward to the mines, as the Indians, heretofore so poor and degraded, have suddenly become consumers of the luxuries of life. I before mentioned that the greater part of the farmers and rancheros had abandoned their fields to go to the mines. This is not the case with Captain Sutter, who was carefully gathering his wheat, estimated at 40,000 bushels. Flour is already worth, at Sutter's, 36 dollars [$1,036.80] a barrel and will soon be 50 [$1,440]. Unless very large quantities of breadstuffs reach the country much suffering will occur; but as each man is now able to pay a large price, it is believed the merchants will bring from Chili [sic] and the Oregon Territory a plentiful supply for the coming winter.*

The most moderate estimate I could obtain from men acquainted with the subject was, that upwards of 4,000 men were working in the gold district, of whom more than one-half are Indians, and that from 30,000 to 50,000 dollars [$864,000 to $1,440,000] worth of gold, if not more, were daily obtained. The entire gold district, with very few ex-

ceptions of grants made some years ago by the Mexican authorities, is on land belonging to the United States. It was a matter of serious reflection to me, how I could secure to the Government certain rents or fees for the privilege of securing this gold; but upon further considering the large extent of country, the character of the people engaged, and the small scattered force at my command, I resolved not to interfere, but permit all to work freely, unless broils and crimes should call for interference. I was surprised to learn that crime of any kind was very unfrequent [sic], and that no thefts or robberies had been committed in the gold district. All live in tents, in bush arbors, or in the open air; and men have frequently about their persons thousands of dollars worth of this gold; and it was to me a matter of surprise that so peaceful and quiet a state of things should continue to exist. Conflicting claims to particular spots of ground may cause collisions, but they will be rare, as the extent of country is so great, and the gold so very abundant, that for the present there is room and enough for all. Still the government is entitled to rents for this land, and immediate steps should be devised to collect them, for the longer it is delayed the more difficult it will become. One plan I would suggest is, to send out from the United States surveyors with high salaries, bound to serve specified periods.

A superintendent to be appointed at Sutter's Fort, with power to license to work a spot of ground — say 100 yards square — for one year, at a rent of from 100 to 1,000 dollars [$2,880 to $28,800], at his discretion, the surveyors to measure the ground, and place the renter in possession. A better plan, however, will be to have the district surveyed and sold at public auction to the highest bidder, in small parcels — say from 20 to 40 acres. In either case there will be many intruders, whom for years it will be almost impossible to exclude.

The discovery of these vast deposits of gold has entirely changed the character of Upper California. Its people, before engaged in cultivating their small patches of ground, and guarding their herds of cattle and horses, have all gone to the mines, or are on their way thither. Laborers of every trade have left their work benches, and tradesmen their shops.

Sailors desert their ships as fast as they arrive on the coast, and several vessels have gone to sea with hardly enough hands to spread a sail. Two or three are now at anchor in San Francisco [Harbor] with no crew on board. Many desertions, too, have taken place from the garrisons within the influence of these mines; twenty-six soldiers have deserted from the post of Sonoma, twenty-four others from that of San Francisco, and twenty-four more from Monterey. For a few days the evil appeared so threatening that great danger existed that the garrisons would leave in a body; and I refer you to my orders of the 25th of July, to show the steps adopted to meet this contingency. I shall spare no exertions to apprehend and punish deserters, but I believe no time in the history of our country has presented such temptations to desert as now exist in California. The danger of apprehension is small, and the prospect of high wages certain; pay and bounties are trifles, as laboring men at the mines can now earn in one day more that double a soldier's pay and allowances for a month, and even the pay of a lieutenant or captain cannot hire a servant. A carpenter or mechanic would not listen to an offer of less than fifteen or twenty dollars [$432 or $576] a day.

Could any combination of affairs try a man's fidelity more than this? — and I really think some extraordinary mark of favor should soon be given to those soldiers who remain faithful to their flag throughout this tempting crisis. No officer can now live in California on his pay, money has so little value; the prices of necessary articles of clothing and subsistence are so exorbitant, and labor so high, that to hire a cook or servant has become an impossibility, save to those who are earning from thirty to fifty dollars [$864 to $1,440] a day. This state of things cannot last for ever. Yet from the geographical position of California, and the new character it has assumed as a mining country, prices of labor will always be high, and will hold out temptations to desert. I therefore have to repeat, if the Government wish to prevent desertions on the part of the men, and to secure zeal on the part of officers, their pay must be increased very materially. Soldiers, both of the volunteers and regular service, discharged in this country, should be permitted at once to locate their land war-

rants in the gold district.

Many private letters have gone to the United States giving accounts of the vast quantity of gold recently discovered, and it may be a matter of surprise why I have made no report on this at an earlier date. The reason is, that I could not bring myself to believe the reports that I heard of the wealth of the gold districts until I visited them myself. I have no hesitation now in saying that there is more gold in the country drained by the Sacramento and San Joaquin rivers that will pay the cost of the present war with Mexico a hundred times over. No capital is required to obtain this gold, as the ordinary laboring man wants nothing but his pick and shovel and tin pan, with which to dig and wash the gravel; and many frequently pick gold out of the crevices of rocks with their butcher knives, in pieces of from one to six ounces. Mr. Dye, a gentleman residing in Monterey, and worthy of every credit, has just returned from Feather river. He tells me that the company to which he belonged worked seven weeks and two days, with an average of fifty Indians (washers), and that their gross product was two hundred and seventy-three pounds of gold [$69,888/$20,127,744]. His share (one seventh), after paying all expenses, is about thirty-seven pounds [$9,472/$2,727,936], which he brought with him and exhibited in Monterey. I see no laboring man from the mines who does not show his two, three, or four pounds of gold. A soldier of the artillery company returned here a few days ago from the mines, having been absent on furlough twenty days. He made by trading and working during that time $1500 [$43,200]. During these twenty days he was traveling ten or eleven days, leaving but a week in which he made a sum greater than he receives in pay, clothes and rations during a whole enlistment of five years. These statements appear incredible, but they are true.

Gold is also believed to exist on the eastern slope of the Sierra Nevada, and, when at the mines, I was informed by an intelligent Mormon that it had been found near the Great Salt Lake by some of his fraternity. Nearly all the Mormons are leaving California to go to the Salt Lake; and this they surely would not do unless they were sure of finding gold there, in the same abundance as they now do on the Sacramento.

The gold "placer" near the mission of San Fernando has long been known, but has been little wrought, for want of water. This is in a spur that puts off from the Sierra Nevada (see Frémont's map), the same in which the present mines occur. There is, therefore, every reason to believe that in the intervening spaces of five hundred miles (entirely unexplored), there must be many hidden and rich deposits. The "placer" gold is now substituted as the currency of this country; in trade it passes freely at $16 [$460.80] per ounce; as an article of commerce its value is not yet fixed. The only purchase I have made was of the specimen No. 7, which I got of Mr. Neligh at $12 [$345.60] the ounce. That is about the present cash value in the country, although it has been sold for less. The great continuing demand made for goods and provisions made by this sudden development of wealth has increased the amount of commerce at San Francisco very much, and it will continue to increase.

I would recommend that a mint be established at some eligible point of the Bay of San Francisco, and that machinery and all the necessary apparatus and workmen be sent out by sea. These workmen must be bound by high wages, and even bonds, to secure their faithful services, else the whole plan may be frustrated by their going to the mines as soon as they arrive in California. If this course be not adopted, gold to the amount of many millions of dollars will pass yearly to other countries, to enrich their merchants and capitalists ...

I have the honor to be your most ob't serv't,
R. B. MASON Col., 1st Dragoons, Commanding
Brig. Gen. R. Jones, Adj't Gen. U.S.A., Wash'ton, D. C.

[August 19th 1848 • Saturday]

Positive news of the discovery of gold in California had finally reached New York City, and an article about it appeared today in the *New York Herald*. It was a matter of interest, indeed, and it even prompted a small number of adventurous New Yorkers to pack up their good and begin heading west. By far the greater number of readers, however, took the news with obvious intense skepticism, considering it at best a heavy-handed, hyperbolic exaggeration, and, at worst, an out-and-out hoax, and wisely refused to even consider emigrating to California.

What interested the public of the Eastern United States much more, at the moment, was the approaching Presidential election and the volatile crisis of the slavery issue in the United States, which was now becoming the primary concern driving future national elections. With President Polk still in widespread disfavor among the public and not even nominated for re-election, he was clearly out of the picture. Democratic Party regulars were still staunchly behind their candidate, Lewis Cass, who was running on a slavery compromise platform. The Democrats adhering to the more rebellious segment of the party, however, were just as strongly backing election of former President Martin Van Buren, who was running as the Free-Soil third party candidate. No one seemed to be giving much credence to the Whig candidate, General Zachary Taylor; after all, the Whigs had been suffering almost total exclusion from political offices for twenty years now, and so far as the *New York Herald* and other newspapers would have it, Taylor simply didn't stand a chance.

This, everyone seemed to know, was an election that would be decided on issues, not on personalities. The biggest issues of all were slavery and the West. The Democrats, led by Webster, were noisily denouncing the vast arid wasteland that Polk had secured to the United States — "... as if anybody ever even wanted it," many opposition newspapers cried. Whether that West would be free or slave-holding and become, therefore, allied with the South, remained yet to be determined.

The letter written months ago by Consul Oliver Larkin in Monterey to Secretary of State Buchanan in Washington had finally reached its destination seventeen days ago, on August 2. It carried not only Larkin's first reports about the gold discovery, but also a clipping of *The Californian's* first news story, brief though it was, about the same event. The missive had initially made it's way promptly to an in-box that had just been emptied and there, overlooked, it continued to lie, as numerous other incoming messages from various points in the world were placed atop it.

There it remained yet today, and there it would continue to repose for a very long time, wholly neglected.

[August 28th, 1848 • Monday]

The relative ease with which fortunes were being made — and

lost — had been thoroughly exemplified to newcomer Preston Stanley just yesterday when he visited a nearby trading camp along the Mokelumne River. Several merchants had set up their tents, calling them *Stores*, and Stanley was personally on hand to witness an incident that turned out to be one of the more bazaar occurrences he'd ever encountered — one that quite clearly delineated how blasé so many of the miners had become with respect to vast amounts of money.

Taking their cue from Sam Brannan, many of the merchants had jacked up prices for their goods dramatically, and Stanley, a 26-year-old native of Evansville, Indiana, had dropped by in an effort to attempt to replace a broken trowel. Astounded at the prices being demanded for any kind of digging tools, he absolutely refused to pay the asking price of $12 [$345.60] for a replacement. While he was there, however, a tall Irishman named Francis Frank, whom Stanley had previously met at the diggings, showed up.

Already tipsy from what he'd drunk previously, Frank made his way at once to the adjacent liquor tent where he quickly downed two quaffs of whiskey at an exorbitant cost, which he paid for with two tiny nuggets out of a bulging sack of gold he had withdrawn from his pocket. Another miner already having a drink, an Ohioan named Tom Brewster, with whom Stanley was only vaguely familiar, shook his head and clucked his tongue.

"Ought'a be more careful with all that there gold, Francis," he said, "or you're sure as hell apt t'lose it."

The tall Irishman stared at the man who had spoken with an expression that he might well have been holding in reserve for an annoying bug, and then he grinned rather unpleasantly. "Wal now, Tommy-boy," he snorted, "you think I should worry 'bout a little thing like that?" He grasped the bottom of his still widely open pouch and flung his arm out in such a manner that the entire contents were widely scattered in the surrounding ankle-deep grasses. "I sure as hell don't! I k'n always get plenty more where that come from!"

Later that evening, back in his own camp, Stanley wrote in his diary about the incident and concluded: "... He [Francis Frank] had three lbs. in the purse at the time, and it was nearly all lost."

[August 29th, 1848 • Tuesday]

Very nearly benumbed by the extravagant amounts of gold being recovered from various locations, in another of his continuing letters to U.S. Secretary of State, James Buchanan, Consul Thomas O. Larkin added today:

> *At present the people are running over the country and picking gold out of the earth here and there, just as a thousand hogs loosed in a forest would root up ground-nuts. Some get eight or 10 ounces a day, and the least active one or two. They make the most who employ the wild Indians to hunt it for them. There is one man who has sixty Indians in his employ; his profits are a dollar [$28.80] a minute. The wild Indians know nothing of its value, and wonder what the pale-faces want to do with it; they will give an ounce of it for the same weight of coined silver, or a thimbleful of glass beads, or a glass of grog. And white men themselves often give an ounce of it, which is worth at our mint 18 dollars [$518.40], or more, for a bottle of brandy, a bottle of soda-powders, or a plug of tobacco.*
>
> *As to the quantity which the diggers get, take a few facts as evidence. I know seven men who worked seven weeks and two days, Sundays excepted, on Feather River; they employed on an average fifty Indians, and got out in these same seven weeks and two days 275* pounds *— $70,400 [$2,027,520] — of pure gold. I know the men, and have seen the gold, and know what they state to be a fact — so stick a pin there. I know 10 other men who worked ten days in company, employed no Indians, and averaged in these ten days $1,500 [$43,200] each, so stick another pin there! Not one of these statements would I believe, did I not know the men personally, and know them to be plain, matter-of-fact men — men who open a vein of gold just as coolly as you would open a potato hill.*

Chapter 4

[September 9th, 1848 • Saturday]

For Californians, the Gold Rush continued to be the most dominant factor in their lives as summer progressed and then moved into September, accompanied by the first faint hints of autumn's arrival.

The occasional cooler days in the Sierra foothills seemed to divide the gold miners into two distinct tiers. The first sizeable group consised of those who had made their "bundles" quickly and had already crossed the Sierras heading eastward — as many among the Mormans were already in the process of doing — or those who had also made rich finds and had decided to return to San Francisco or San José or Monterey and spend the winter months and rainy season enjoying to the fullest the fruits of their summer and autumn labors. The second large group consised of those who were among the unfortunates; prospectors who had found little or nothing thus far and were determined to keep trying, rainy season or not, until they hit the "bonanza" that each and every one of them fully expected.

Only a relative few of those who had struck it rich fairly quickly in their searches elected to continue looking for more until the approaching winter would finally drive them out. Thousands of resident Californians — the Californios — had trooped toward the mines and spread themselves over a vast area; they had sought gold in various gullies, ravines and streambeds eastward to the heights of the Sierras, northward in the Sacramento River drainage towards the border of the Oregon Territory, and southward to the farthest reaches of the San Joaquin River's drainage — in all a vast area of hundreds of thousands of square acres of primitive wilderness. Many of the individual prospectors and miners, moreover, filled journals, diaries, letters, and reports with largely unembellished accuracy, of the rich and varied gold discoveries which they or their fellow miners had been making during the past months. Exaggerated accounts undoubtedly would occur much more frequently as recovering the gold became more difficult, but for now they were entirely unnecessary.

Another peculiar phenomenon was the absence of crime occurring in most areas. As Sgt. Carson stated it in his diary on August 6:

> *Honesty is the ruling passion amongst the miners here now. Old debts are paid up, heavy bags filled with gold dust are carelessly left lying in their brush homes, mining tools, though scarce, are left in their places of work for days at a time, and not one theft or robbery is committed.*

Still, the very impatience of the men drove them on; if gold wasn't being found easily enough and in great enough abundance, they simply picked up and moved elsewhere. The feeling was very nearly universal among the miners that, no matter how good the "pickings" were at the present site, especially if they were standing in the often icy cold water of the streams, something "much better" was always just over the next hill or up the next stream, and consequently the mining communities experienced an almost constant flux. Age and physical condition were rarely criteria for digging or washing the earth for gold; those too young to shave and those with long flowing white beards alike worked hard and were sometimes being compensated with wealth far beyond their wildest dreams. Finally, as the result of a public meeting of merchants in San Francisco, the value of the gold being mined in California was stabilized. Until this time the values had greatly varied, from as low as $4 [$115.20] per ounce to twice that amount, but almost never as much as the current $18 [$518.40] value of it in the Eastern States. Now, for the whole of California Territory, it was set at a flat $16 [$460.80] per ounce.

While many of the miners might have been accumulating personal fortunes far beyond their expectations, the prices of food, goods, and services were keeping pace only too well with their increasing incomes. Tools, for example, having already reached exotic levels, were still climbing. Picks, pans, shovels, spades, and crowbars all essential for prospecting, were priced anywhere from $50 to $200 [$1,440 to $5,760] *apiece,* depending on the whim of the seller. Ordinary, normally inexpensive butcher knives could rarely be found priced at less than

$10 to $25 [$288 to $720] each, and newcomers with carpentry skills were making and selling the rockers they had built for rarely less than $200 [$5,760] apiece; indeed, many often demanded as much as $800 [$23,040] for a single ten-foot unit.

By comparison foods were relatively inexpensive, but here, too, there were no bargains whatever to be found: Most items — potatoes, apples, cabbage, carrots, and peas — sold for a flat $2 [$57.60] per pound. Clothing was nearly as expensive as tools, with woolen work shirts priced at $50 [$1,440] each. Cheaply made boots and shoes sold for a minimum of $25 [$720] for a low-grade pair of shoes and upwards of $150 [$4,320] for a sturdy pair of boots. Miners, of course, having no choice, willingly paid these outrageous prices. And no merchant was more successful at price-scalping than Sam Brannan himself. He clearly drew a perverse pleasure from being considered "the richest merchant in California," and he made no secret of the fact that he intended to become "a whole helluva lot richer!"

The miners gradually developed a pronounced lackadaisical view towards the value of the gold they were finding. While there were a fair number of Negro miners, for the most part they were not often welcome at the various stores and accommodations set up to serve the whites. Such bigotry, however, disappeared at the gaming tables, where Blacks were nearly always welcome. Along the Tuolumne River where a number of deposits were being mined, one of the miners, a husky black fellow who had struck an especially good deposit, quickly took out a total of $100,000 [$2,880,000] from his claim. He lost it all in a single evening of gambling and was said to have merely shrugged and gone back to his claim to dig some more. This was fairly typical of how quickly values changed for most of the miners: To them the gold supply seemed virtually inexhaustible; it was there for them to continue harvesting indefinitely, and there was indeed some justification for reaching such a conclusion. Miners who would put their backs to the work easily earned, as Carson calculated:

> *... from $100 to $500 [$2,880 to $14,400] per day; and in confidence of this good fortune continuing, these heavy earnings were foolishly spent in drinking and gaming, purchasing fine horses, and dressing in the gaudy Indian style. [Yet,] honesty is the ruling passion of '48. If an hombre gets broke, he asks the first one he meets to loan him such amount as he*

> *wants, until he could "dig her out." The loans are always made, and always paid according to promise. I, on one occasion, was accosted by name at the Old Dry Diggings, by a rough-looking case (with whom I had no acquaintance) for the loan of some dust until a specified time. His rough hands and muscular arms proclaimed him a working man, which was all the security required. Without asking his name, the amount (fifty ounces — $800 [$23,040]) was handed to him. On the very day appointed it was duly returned, with an additional pound, and a bottle of brandy for, as he remarked, "old acquaintance sake," telling me at the same time that he considered me to be, "a damned fine feller!"*

The most northerly point being mined just now was well up the Trinity River only a few miles northeast of the peak that Pierson Reading had dubbed Middle Peak and where he and his large crew of Indian workers were mining a broad bar that he had named *Reading Bar* after himself. The Trinity had its source near the Sacramento and ran westward, passing through the coastal range of mountains and entering the Pacific just about 100 miles north of San Francisco. The bars, Reading found, were very rich and, the site was proving to have very rich placer washings, but his operations there were cut tragically short. His party was abruptly attacked on August 7th, 1848 by a large group of rough prospectors who appeared while on their way south to the gold fields. Fresh from the savage attacks being waged against their settlements by the Indians in southern Oregon Territory, they spied Reading's native workers and, embittered by what they had already endured and asking no questions, they immediately attacked. Several of Reading's Indians were killed, and he had no choice but to flee from the area with the survivors.

In the American River drainage, two different deposits identically named *Horseshoe Bar* had begun producing dust and flakes, but few nuggets. The lower one, just below the confluence of North and Middle Forks, produced reasonably well for a while but soon played out; the second, sometimes called *Horseshoe Number Two*, was on the Middle Fork where the river looped so severely that it almost doubled back on itself, and it was initially very good; one group of miners washed out forty ounces totaling $640 [$18,432] in a single day.

At the same time, not too many miles distant "in a ravine north of Coloma" on the South Fork, prospector David Hudson, working by himself, washed out over a period of six weeks, $2,000 [$57,600] in flakes and small nuggets, and a 17-year-old miner named George Davenport got 77 ounces one day and 90 ounces the next — a total of 167 ounces valued at $2,672 [$76,953.60].

As impressive as such finds were, it was clearly evident that the surface gold was rapidly disappearing from the earliest-discovered sites, and more difficult work was necessary to locate and retrieve whatever deposits were still there. The most effective measure for this was a new process called ground sluicing, though it involved much greater difficulties and required considerably more labor. Prospectors, upon discovering a small, dry gulch or ravine entering the river system, would resort to ground sluicing if they found even faint traces of gold there. It was a wasteful method that allowed smaller gold particles — dust and flakes — to be washed through, but it was far more effective in exposing larger nuggets than the gold pan or even the rocker, which typically was four times as effective as panning.

In the ground sluicing process, water from the nearest higher source would be diverted and channeled in through a series of ditches or wooden flumes or aqueducts to flow into the very top of the gulch or ravine. There it would be allowed to wash down the rift's entire length, eating away the banks and sides as it flowed, carrying away the dirt, clay, sand, and debris and leaving behind in the clefts of bare rock the heavier nuggets that had become exposed.

With the "easy" gold in the northern districts no longer so prevalent, it was now the more southerly sites that began yielding truly significant finds. The deposit called *Shaw's Flat*, after its initial claimant, Mandeville Shaw, began yielding spectacular results and thereby attracted widespread attention. According to widespread rumors, Shaw had been trying to establish an orchard on the spot and only discovered the gold as a result of his digging to plant the saplings he had brought from Oregon Territory. During the month of August, the rich diggings, some two miles in length, quickly produced a great amount of gold dust and flakes, plus one large, single, solid gold nugget weighing one pound, ten ounces, which was valued at $416 [$11,980.80].

Shaw's orchard endeavor was clearly an inspiration to a pair of the San José miners who had been singularly unsuccessful thus far in their search for gold. Louis Pellier and Gioachino Yocco quickly gave up as miners, but they took Shaw's orchard ideas back to the coastal city with them and today began establishing what they intended to become the largest and most productive orchard on California's coast.

Lured by rumors of even more fabulous gold discoveries being found in the south, many miners migrated in that direction, and Charles Weber took quick advantage of the movement. On his own French Camp Rancho he had, during the autumn of 1847, laid out a little town along the San Joaquin River which he named *Tulesburg*, and at that time he had established a store there. It had become, since then, a jumping-off place for anyone heading into the perilous southern areas where troubles with the Indians had quickly escalated. Now, however, Capt. Weber had returned from the mines and was taking active charge of the community; he had the town re-surveyed, and he changed its name to *Stockton* in honor of the American naval commander. Almost instantly it became a flourishing tent city and an important site linking the southern route to the Sacramento River flowage, serving the same role as Sacramento had been doing in the north. Weber, calling himself and his men the Stockton Mining and Trading Company, shrewdly envisioned the location's potential as a future center of trade, and swiftly erected a new store which became as dominant here as Brannan's business was at Sacramento.

Far to the south of Stockton, near white-capped Mount Ophir, a party of Mexicans had moved in on a newly discovered deposit that was producing prolifically. Their reports, which inspired hundreds of their fellow Californians to join them, were not mere exaggerations. With only a minimum of digging being employed, the party had, in just its first week of gold-seeking, taken out $217,000 [$6,249,600], almost exclusively in nuggets.

James H. Carson was still among the miners who, if not getting rich, was still holding his own. He was managing to put aside a little gold to eventually take home, despite the exorbitantly high cost of living here. As Carson became aware, moreover, gold-seekers were doing things solitarily rather than participating in groups or partnerships. Consequently, if a man these days was taken sick in the mines, for the most part he received little if any attention from others. What surprised Carson, however, was the unflagging concern the American sailor-miners' loyal concern for their fellows. If one of them was taken sick, his comrades were very solicitous and paid him every attention until he recovered — or died. Yet these were the same sailors who had jumped ship in San Francisco and were now fugitives of military justice. As Carson noted:

The sailor is generally happy and jovial anywhere, but particularly so in the gold mines. One or two days work in the mines gives him the means of a good spree; and if he has clothes to wear, all he seems to care for is his grub and rum, which he freely indulges in, and all his earnings generally go to the shops; yet his basic jollity and proverbial good heartedness never deserts him.

On September 1st the official planning and surveying of the town already being called Sacramento was commenced by Lt. William T. Sherman, who had been hired for the job by young John Sutter, Jr. Due to the large number of squatters already encamped in a broad area surrounding Sutter's Fort, it became almost instantly a flourishing little metropolis, though comprised at this stage of structures that were little more than makeshift hovels constructed from the reclaimed timbers and canvasses of about a score of derelict ships deliberately run aground along the Sacramento River's eastern shoreline. The configuration of the new town, as indicated by the multitude of stakes driven into the ground, was somewhat in the shape of an inverted letter "T", with the current east-west extremities stretching some two miles, from the Sacramento River eastward from what was designated as I Street at China Slough to O Street, and the north-south extending straight up J Street to Seventh Street. Lt. William H. Warren, of the U.S. Topographical Engineers, was on hand to assist in the fundamental work of surveying Sacramento into lots and blocks.

Less than a week later, Mountain Man Jim Clyman, recently returned from St. Louis to California, wrote in his *Journal*:

September 5. I arrived here in the Napa Valley without accident or interruption of any kind worthy of notice. Matters and things here are very strangely and curiously altered since I left this country.

Governor Mason and Lt. Sherman left Monterey this same day for yet another tour of the mines and, though they traveled through areas they had not previously visited, they found conditions and activities very much as they had found them initially. As Sherman noted:

> *Colonel Mason, Captain [William] Warren, and I, made another trip up to Sutter's Fort, going also to the newly-discovered mines on the Stanislaus, called "Sonora," named from the miners of Sonora, Mexico, who had first discovered them. We found there pretty much the same state of facts as before existed at Mormon Island and at Coloma, and we daily received just intelligence of the opening of still other mines north and south.*

What they did note in particular, however, was that by far the vast majority of those citizens who had left their West Coast homes and traveled to the gold regions had anticipated little more than a short stay in the mining areas — only long enough, in most of their imaginations, to pick up a pot filled to the brim with gold — and they were already finding themselves drastically short of supplies of almost every variety. They were completely unprepared to endure the rainy season without adequate equipment and shelter. Consequently a great many who were experiencing severe deprivation now understood clearly a fundamental rule of commerce: When intense and widespread demand far exceeds the supply and the means of transporting that supply, prices will soar accordingly. According to the reported costs of sale and services, the following price scale had become all but standard:

Flour, probably the most important item of consumption, was now valued at fully $800 [$23,040] a barrel; sugar, coffee and pork, at half that amount per barrel; any pick, shovel, tin pan, pair of boots, untorn (but not necessarily clean) blanket, a single gallon of whiskey, and, as Sherman put it, " ... plus about another 500 items not listed," $100 [$2,880] each. Eggs (not guaranteed fresh), $3 [$86.40] apiece. One flat can of sardines, $16 [$460.80]. One pound hard bread, $2 [$57,60]. A pound of butter or cheese, $6 [$172.80] each. One bottle of ale, $8 [$230.40]. Liquid medical drugs, $1 [$28.80] per drop, and pills of various types, mostly patent medicines, the same amount apiece. A doctor's visit might cost $100 [$2,880] or $50 [$1,440] or nothing at all, depending upon the benevolence (or exhaustion) of the doctor; a cook's wages, $25 [$720] daily, usually in advance. A wagon and team for hire, $50 [$1,440] per day; the rental of a gold rocker (unmanned), $150 [$4,320] daily. So warped, indeed, had the value of gold made the value of everything else that such staggering prices hardly generated a raised eyebrow. As one journal-keeper noted, quite seriously:

Extravagance is spending much when one has little. Gold is too plentiful, too easily obtained, to allow a little of it to stand in the way of what one wants. It is cheap. Perhaps there are mountains of it nearby, in which case six barrels of it might be easily given for one barrel of meal.

Prospecting in the vicinity of Log Cabin Ravine, newcomer John Schwan thought for a short time on September 6th, that he had stumbled into one of those amazing. monumental beds of gold rivaling the extravagant discoveries many of his fellow miners claimed to have made. As he wrote about it in his diary this evening:

Sept. 6th. This morning after breakfast I went up a short distance in one of the small ravines leading into Log Cabin Ravine and stopped at the foot of [a] little fall in it, about 2 feet, and there was a small pothole in it, which went down about 18 inches. I had my pan with me, though there was no water nearer than our camp. I had a very long sheath knife with me, and I could just get my hand and part of my arm into the hole, and I commenced scraping with the point of my knife. After scraping a while I began to see gold shine, and as I worked away at it I saw it was a small nugget, but it held fast in a crevice in the hole. But from what I saw of it, I thought I was bound to have a 5- or 6-ounce piece. At last it gave way, and instead of being a large nugget, it was only a small one worth $26 [$748,80]. A small knob had kept it jammed. I was quite disappointed, and though I spent this afternoon near the pothole and worked hard with pick and crow-bar, I only got about $5 [$144] more gold.

Today, September 9th, after going completely silent for eleven weeks, The *Californian* newspaper resumed publication as its editor, Edward Kemble, finally returned to San Francisco from his extended tour through the mining areas. He no longer doubted the myriad accounts of the discovery of an extremely rich gold resource in California. News of the discovery was also now beginning to reach far distant ports, as occurred today when a schooner bearing details of it docked at Canton in China. The story flashed through numerous communities and caused an immediate and important reaction. Kwangtung Province had long been torn by a variety of disasters, including typhoons, massive flooding, severe droughts and viciously destructive civil war. Even a vague promise of such riches as California was allegedly offering the "ordinary man" was all that was needed to ignite a fire of migration, and almost overnight thousands of Chinese had mortgaged all they owned in order to board junks quickly preparing to embark for what the Chinese press was calling Gum Shan — Gold Mountain.

A similar situation was occurring in Honolulu, where the initial skepticism of the *Sandwich Islands News* had given way to the enthusiasm being generated among the island's inhabitants as a result of letters received from California and rumors that had grown rampant. The store-ship *Matilda* had arrived, having left New York, with interim stops at Valparaiso, Callao, and Monterey, with important mail having been picked up at the latter port. One of the letters it bore was to John Damon, esteemed editor of the *Friend* monthly newspaper in Honolulu, from the Reverend Walter Colton. Damon, on the verge of going to press, immediately included the entire letter, accompanied by his own editorial comments which provoked a rising excitement.

Almost in the *Matilda's* wake had come the Spanish brig *Flecha* from Santa Barbara and San Francisco, under Captain Luis Vasquez, with additional letters and more news supportive of the gold discovery. That brig was quickly followed into port by two other ships, the Hawaiian brig *Euphemia*, under command of Captain Vioget and, several days later, the schooner *Mary*, under Captain Belcham, both of whom came down their gangplanks brimming with comments about the gold strike for the assembled reporters.

The *Polynesian* newspaper, now no longer scornful of the gold reports, spoke seriously in its July 8th issue of the growing enthusiasm of the Hawaiian populace and of the scores of passports being issued by the Minister of Foreign Relations to all who wished them, except debtors attempting to abscond, for the return passage to the Golden Gate. And today, September 9th, islander Samuel Varney wrote to Consul Larkin:

> *The gold fever rages here, and there is much preparation occurring for emigration to California. All berths were rapidly filled in those ships preparing to leave here for the return to California and now even deck space is being sold to pas-*

sengers, but the captains lament that such decks are not spacious enough to hold all who wish passage.

In the log of the *Polynesian* it was recorded today:

July 15th, one crowded vessel departed the 11th, and half a dozen others are making ready; 24 varied persons give notice of their intention to depart this kingdom; 200 will probably leave within two months, if passage can be procured. I have learned that 69 passports have been issued, and quite as many more have left without passports. Three vessels sailed within a week; one man set out in a whale-boat. Real estate has become a drug in the market. Business low; whole country changed. Books at an auction will not sell; but shovels fetch high prices. Common salutation, When are you off? On Oct. 7th the ship Lahaima will sail with 40 passengers; Honolulu to sail the 9th, and every berth engaged: heavy freight $40 [$1,152] per ton; cabin passage, $100 [$2,880]; and steerage $80 [$2,304]. Deck passage $40 [$1,152]. Set for forthcoming Oct. 21st, 27 vessels, aggregating a tonnage of 3,128, will leave Honolulu carrying some 300 passengers, be-sides [sic] a great many natives On Oct. 28th five more to sail with 15 to 40 passengers each. The islands suffer in consequence. Upward of 1,000 pickaxes have already been exported from here. More than one party of sailors has absconded from here in small craft.

Additional news of the gold discovery was just now beginning to reach the United States East Coast. There, however, of far greater interest at the moment was the heat building in the East politically. It had by now become quite apparent that despite early newspaper prognostications to the contrary, Zachary Taylor had surged into the lead as the most promising candidate, and the Whigs were excited over the possibility of a victory after so long a drought in the party's fortunes. Such stories created headlines and filled the front pages.

Still, occasional pieces *were* appearing in various newspapers alluding, usually very cautiously, to a supposed discovery of gold in California. Even the staid *New York Herald,* with an attitude regarding a gold strike that was virtually churlish at the onset, was mellowing a bit about such news. Though continuing to relegate these items to deep-inside pages, the paper was now carrying a new regular column called *Paisano's*, in which excerpts of letters from the West were printed that extolled, in one way or another, the gold mining efforts occurring there.

Public reactions in the East to such reports, however, were far more cautious than those occurring in the Orient. A few adventurous souls set off at once for the West, but for most part, there prevailed an air of "let's- wait-and-see" that rooted in place even those who were keenly interested. Their lifestyles may not have been perfect, but they were good enough to hold in abeyance any impulse to converge into a gold rush until some very definite sign of confirmation became apparent.

What such a sign might be was not clear in anyone's mind, yet the sense was there that when it came, it would be immediately recognized — and acted upon.

[September 10th, 1848 • Sunday]

Religion of any kind was thus far all but absent at the mining camps.

It was an odd but authentic phenomenon, becoming clearly apparent once the Mormons had pulled away on their journey to what they termed their "Zion" at Salt Lake City. Just as the remaining prospectors and miners had, for the most part, become free of the strictures and laws of society and simply lived in quiet harmony together, usually repressing such emotions as envy, jealousy, and hatred, so too the rigid tenets of organized religion had been put aside, and paradoxically they all somehow seemed the better for it.

For that reason alone, today was an unusual day on the American River South Fork, since today had been set aside for a religious service under the guidance of a fairly new miner to the area named Jacob Palmer — Parson Palmer, as some called him. A few of the miners who were most closely associated with him averred that he had "onct been a powerful revivalist preacher in Alabama or Georgia" but had lost his flock due to some sort of indiscretion on his part that had to do with someone else's wife, but that was merely gossip, and no one knew for sure. What they did know was that since having become a gold-seeker himself, the Parson had become far more carnal in public than he'd ever before revealed himself to be, and he would cheerfully guzzle the whiskey of anyone who would invite him to do so. He also boasted at length of the numerous young ladies in his flock whom he had "saved from the abysm of everlastin' Hell," and whose gratitude to him had been manifested in sexual favors which, he had suggested to them, were his due. Here at the mines, however, his religious fervor had all but deserted him, and he rarely brought it up anymore.

Today, however, was an exception, as one of Parson Palmer's fellows — a grizzled old miner named George Bishop, who was much liked by the others, was to be buried. Bishop had unexpectedly succumbed to "heart failure" early yesterday and now lay wrapped in his tattered blanket several hundred yards from camp, ready to be planted in the grave that had been prepared for him. A fairly sizeable group of men from the camp, including visitor James H. Carson, were on hand for the solemn ceremony, at which the Parson was determined to officiate "in order to provide as reasonable a funeral as circumstances will allow." As Carson wrote of it in his journal:

> *A goodly number [of miners] had collected, amongst whom tin cups passed swiftly around, and many a drink went down to the repose of the soul departed. The Parson never missed a 'round', and by the time we got the corpse into the grave, Parson Palmer had become somewhat muddled. ... With the miners gathered around, the Parson read a long chapter from the Bible, after which he declared it was necessary we sing a Psalm. No hymn-book could be found, however and no one on hand admitted to having committed a hymn to memory, with the exception of the Parson, who soon started one to the tune of Old Hundred.*

The Parson succeeded in remembering the first verse and got through it just fine, but as he began the second, he got stuck at the end of the first line. He made several more attempts but finally shook his head and said, "Boys, the Lord has obliterated from my memory the balance of that fine ol' Psalm, so we'll jus' go t' prayer." Some men remained standing, but a number of the miners knelt around the grave except, as Carson wrote of it in his *Journal*:

> *"... one old case who sat down, remarking, 'I know when the Parson's got his steam a little up, he's hell on a prayer, and I'm gonna to take it easy.' The Parson had been praying*

some ten minutes when some of those kneeling around the grave commenced examining the dirt that had been thrown up and found it to be (as they expressed it) 'Lousy with gold!' This discovery necessarily created an excitement in the assembly. The Parson had become 'warmed up' and his supplications for the soul of the departed could be heard 'echoing through mountain, hill, and dell, when he suddenly stopped — opened one eye — and looked down to see what was disturbing his hearers, and very coolly enquired, 'Boys, what's that?' and then continued, 'Gold, by God! An' the very richest kind o'diggin's! The very dirt we been a-lookin' for!' The truth flashed across his mind — and then he raised his hand and with a comic expression of countenance, informed us that 'the congregation are dismissed' and it was highly necessary that that dirt should be well tried before we proceeded any farther, and away he 'scud' for his pick and pan. Suffice to say that poor George B. was not buried there, but taken from his rich hole , and a grave made for him high up the mountain's side.

[September 16th, 1848 • Saturday]

Despite all of the successful mining that was occurring throughout the entire known gold range at this time, there were many miners who were just not all that successful in finding and exploiting rich deposits. Equally, there were others who, although they had found reasonably good deposits and made substantial profits from them, were just not all that keen about continuing to "grub around in the dirt" for gold. Sam Brannan was living proof that fortunes could be made in other ways, especially, in "mining the miners," as he put it. John Sutter's former clerk, John Bidwell, was one of those who, despite his successes with mining, chose to abandon the diggings in favor of "a cleaner form of enterprise."

Toward that end, Bidwell now set up a trading post in the Oroville area, where the Feather River was formed by its three principal tributaries, the North, Middle and South Forks. Investing virtually all of his gold mining earnings in the purchase of supplies, he filled its shelves with goods purchased in San Francisco, San José, Monterey, and Santa Cruz, supplies which he, as a former miner, knew would be most important to his clientele. While he did not jack up the prices for such goods nearly as high as Brannan had in his stores, he nevertheless charged enough to make a substantial profit, and he was soon earning as much or more from his sales as he ever had from his diggings.

William Knight of Indiana, who had come to California as an emigrant in 1841, had recently done the same thing farther to the south along the Stanislaus River, with his river-crossing establishment on the south side of the river he called Knight's Ferry, a store which rapidly became a stopping place favored by men traveling to and from the southern mines. The brothels which sprang up nearby, of course, accounted for much of the site's appeal. The prostitutes were from many classes — white girls from the United States and France being the most favored and the highest paid, but also large numbers of Chinese, Polynesian and Latin American "ladies of the night" were also highly popular. Most of these women made fabulous amounts of money for dispensing sexual favors to miners who, to their way of thinking, had been "deprived for much too long."

In most cases, the "Madam" of the House closely oversaw the duties of her charges and took a substantial "cut" from what the customers paid. If she, in fact, happened to be the one especially desired by a customer, she was often accommodating, but usually to the tune of twice as much as her "girls" charged. Admittedly, the girls with skin of a tawnier hue were paid less than those who were unmistakably white — French girls were especially favored — and the darker-skinned ladies were often poorly treated. Hundreds of "Latin ladies" recruited in San Blas and Mazatlan and other ports were indentured for their passage to the mines, housed in "fandangos" and "poor men's brothels," and only rarely ever became able to buy their way out of their indentured status. Chinese girls in particular were enslaved in certain of the houses, and disturbingly high numbers of them died very young through mistreatment, both by employers and by customers. Though early on the men treated white prostitutes with some measure of respect, that treatment, too, gradually changed over the weeks and months.

The Monterey *alcalde*, Walter Colton, having spent the past six weeks in the mines, "seeing for myself what all the furor is about," returned now, entirely convinced of the presence of gold and its extent. He had arrived, he told all who would listen, at the first site with his three companions, and he had, within mere minutes of starting to dig, found samples of gold. The remainder of his six weeks was filled with a recounting in his journal of the amazing amounts of gold others had been finding, or were continuing to find. What struck him very nearly as forcefully were the wholly outrageous prices being charged for virtually any kind of goods or equipment, where flour was selling at $400 [$11,520] a barrel, sugar at 4$ [$1,520] a pound, and whiskey at $20 [$576] per quart. Outrageous, yes, but as soon as such supplies came in, they were sold out. A letter Colton had written on July 2 had been published in the weekly *Philadelphia North American* newspaper provided a glowing account of the simplicity of the mining, the rush to the diggings, the grossly inflated prices, and the spectacular finds being made. He set the number of miners at 5,000, which was too many for July 2nd, and he estimated the mining area, at the same time, to be 50 miles by 100 miles, a tract simply too extensive for that date, but the remainder of the account was reasonably accurate, and it became highly popular. His final sentence was one which lodged in the mind of many a fascinated reader:

> *Your streams have minnows in them, and ours are paved with gold!*

Colton noted in passing that in the Coloma area, a long water-ditch, named the El Dorado, had been dug to bring in the necessary liquid to the placer fields, a distance of six miles — the first of what would undoubtedly become a network of similar waterways — and here was located the first ferry on the South Fork, as well as the first bridge.

By this time, mid-September, a bit of knavery began to develop in the mining areas, as those who were less successful in their gold-seeking efforts began to prey on the efforts of those more fortunate. A case in point occurred with a miner named Lewis Belcher who was working in the same area of Log Cabin Ravine where John Schwan and Bill Roberts were working their respective claims. Belcher was unwilling to put into his claim the work it would take to dig to the gold level. Knowing Roberts to be very religious and wholly opposed to working on the Sabbath, Belcher waited until the next Sunday, and then, under the pretense of going out to look for missing horses, went directly to Roberts's claim, and using the tools that were there, dug out during that single day, a total of 18 ounces of gold, amounting to $288 [$8,294.40]. As Schwan wrote of it in his journal:

> *If he had done this with some men, they would have shot*

him. Most of the miners thought this [what he did] was a dirty action, though have no doubt, Belcher thought he was doing a smart thing, for such tricks laid in his line, and he had no scruples on the subject.

[September 20th, 1848 • Wednesday]

For the first time since the discovery of gold occurred eight months ago, there were miners afield now who were beginning to realize that they could no longer afford the luxury of independence. As many miners as there were who had made — or were still making — fortunes in mere days or weeks, that number was easily doubled, trebled, even quadrupled by those who had not yet found one iota of the heavy yellow metal. While the air was frequently punctuated with the exultant cries of those who hit "pay-dirt," even more frequent and pervasive were the low groans of exasperation and despair from those who not only had found nothing, and whose reserves of food and clothing were severely depleted. These men were left with only one of two choices — either go home and once again and find conventional employment, or remain in the gold country as employees of those who had struck it rich and needed help to exploit their discoveries.

Another common but seldom considered problem was the emotional stress caused by desperately searching for gold with little success, save for negligible amounts - far too little net treasure, where prices for food and supplies were so astronomically high, to keep them afloat. Added to that was the physical toll taken on one's system by working very hard at an unaccustomed task of digging beneath a scorching sun or squatting for hours in icy, knee-deep water that seemed to suck away one's very reserves of energy; and then, when the day's fruitless labors were finished, to find rest only in a very rudimentary shelter, or even none at all, in order to sleep chilled and damp upon the bare ground, Little wonder, then, that sickness became widespread and that scurvy, from insufficient, vegetable-deprived diets, afflicted so many of the hopeful prospectors. Thus, growing numbers of solitary miners were being forced, in order to survive, to labor for others, for wages seldom exceeding more than scant shelter and food, a predicament which eliminated all remaining hope of finding the elusive deposits that might make the exhaustive efforts all worthwhile once again.

Far, far to the east, a population remained poised, awaiting the sign they ardently hoped would come — a decisive, unambiguous signal that would galvanize them with the determination to turn their backs on the life to which they had become so accustomed and head into a great unknown, in hot pursuit of the vague promise of a better existence, a more glowing future.

[September 23rd, 1848 • Saturday]

During the exactly eight months since gold was first discovered at the Sutter-Marshall Mill — its name now changed to Coloma — the news of it had remained fairly much confined to California Territory. Here and there murmurings of it had circulated beyond the territory's boundaries, but such rumors had been greeted with either healthy skepticism or scornful disbelief. Now, very slowly, very gradually, that was beginning to change.

Oddly enough, the stronger reactions began to occur not within United States locations, but from communities bordering the Pacific, in many cases far more distant from California than were the states east of the Mississippi River. First to react, despite the general skepticism of the newspapers which carried articles about it, were the citizens of the Sandwich Islands — Hawaiians who began booking passage to the California coastal cities, especially San Francisco and Monterey. The news then filtered from there into the basins of the Columbia and Willamette Rivers and stirred a degree of response from settlers in the Oregon Territory, but even this was limited, due to various problems, including severe Indian troubles, occurring there.

More enthusiastic reactions occurred as the word filtered southward into Mexico and then to coastal South America. Substantial numbers of Mexicans, especially from the Sonora and Baja regions, began the overland trek to the north or else embarked on voyages in a wide variety of craft from Mazatlan, across the mouth of the Gulf of California and then up the west coast, some stopping off at San Diego or Los Angeles, but by far the greater majority continuing northward to disembark at Monterey or, even, preferably, at San Francisco. Since these Sonoran adventurers included a considerable number who were experienced gold miners from the Mexican mines, these new immigrants assumed that their labors would bear fruit quickly and well. They did, and so it came as no surprise, that when they set up operations on a stream called Woods Creek, a southeastern tributary of the Mokelumne River, they named the camp *Sonora*.

At the same time a veritable flood of Peruvians joined the rush by sea from the ports of Payta and Chimbote as well as Callao and Lima, and soon thereafter from points much farther south, as Chileans from Antotagasta, La Serena and, especially, Valparaiso, also joined the rush. Equally great numbers were already en route from China — from Shanghai and farther up the Yangtze River to Nanking and then southward coastally to Macau, sailing mainly in their small, rickety-appearing junks crammed tightly with bunks and devoid of sufficient light or adequate ventilation. The cost of the voyage from Canton to San Francisco — which might be accomplished in as little as four weeks or as much as eight, depending on weather conditions — was $50 [$1,440], which in the majority of cases represented an entire family's lifetime savings. These same ships brought cargoes of dried fruits, candied ginger, lumber, brocaded silks, and even prefabricated houses in pieces that could easily be assembled.

The spreading news of the gold discovery caused a major stir in Tahiti and the Philippines, as well as in Papua, New Guinea, and even in the major coastal cities of Australia, especially Brisbane and Sydney.

Everywhere the news touched, wholly confirmed by shipments of gold of tremendous value, the California gold strike became the foremost topic of discussion, stirring into motion individuals and clusters and groups and hordes of people who had never in their lives had much of anything of value, touching them deeply with a hope they'd never before experienced; a hope of actually acquiring a greater wealth than they had ever even *conceived* as being possible. Each ship arriving from the American West Coast brought greater details of the fabulous fortunes being found: Accounts of individuals who, like themselves, had been very poor and who, in a few months or weeks or even mere days had suddenly, and with seemingly minimal effort or cost, had become phenomenally wealthy.

San Francisco, which had teetered on the brink of becoming a ghost town after a large portion of its population had departed for the gold regions, abruptly became the commercial epicenter of the American West Coast, busier as a port than ever before in its existence, as barks and brigs and schooners arrived through the Golden Gate from major ports of call everywhere within the entire reaches of the Pacific. These were vessels loaded not only with people in every available space, but virtually bulging with cargoes of provisions and clothing, tools, machinery, and lumber. Many residents who had failed at gold mining were now returning and finding great profit in sales, trade, and speculation. Failed or failing businesses were quite suddenly rejuvenated to far greater expansiveness than ever before, and scores of new businesses took root and thrived. The newspapers churned back into bustling daily activity with expanded content and wider circulation. Employment now thrived as never before, and all who were willing to work earned high wages — wages virtually unprecedented for any work force in previous history. Home and business real estate values rose phenomenally, and quite as fast as structures could be built, they were snapped up as the seemingly insatiable demand for them merely increased.

It was not until September 12th, however, that the first relatively serious news story appeared about California's gold strike in Louisiana. It was a brief but pertinent account in the *New Orleans Daily Picayune*, based on an interview given by Lieutenant Edward F. Beale in Mexico City while he was en route to Washington, D.C. with dispatches from Commodore Thomas Jones and Consul Oliver Larkin. Whether it was Beale or the story's reporter who was guilty of exaggeration was not clear, but the report cited Beal's claim that California prospectors, working with no tools other than spades, were earning $70 [$2,016] daily, that both San Francisco and Monterey had been all but abandoned, and that prices for all goods had been grossly inflated, magnified all out of proportion to actual value, all of which, the reporter insisted:

> *... matters not, where gold is so plentiful. There is simply no doubt existing that California is destined to become probably the richest and most important country on the continent.*

Three days later an *official* notice, so designated, appeared in the *New York Herald* of Friday, September 15th. Buried on an inside page amid tidbits of town gossip, it revealed virtually nothing about the California gold discoveries:

> *INTERESTING FROM CALIFORNIA*
>
> *We have received some late and interesting intelligence from California. It is to the 1st of July. Owing to the crowded state of our columns, we are obliged to omit our correspondence. It relates to the important discovery of a very valuable gold mine. We have received a specimen of the gold.*

A great many readers were deeply outraged at such a cavalier allusion. Here was a matter of such great potential interest as to significantly affect virtually every reader, and for the paper to repress any details about the issue was intolerable. So strong was public pressure brought to bear upon him that the paper's publisher, James Gordon Bennett, pressured by a cascade of his readers' criticism, had little recourse except to follow up with a more comprehensive piece two days later in the Sunday, September 17th issue. He did so by devoting the larger portion of an inside column to a letter from its fictitious California correspondent, Paisano, in which the correspondent admitted that Publisher Bennett:

> *... had better fill his paper with, at least, far more probable tales and stories and not such outrageous fictions as rivers flowing with gold. But, believed or not, this is the situation in California. The entire population has gone to the mines, many to return a few days later with hundreds of dollars in dust and nuggets. Spades and shovels sell for at least $10 [$288] each and blacksmiths are making at least $240 [$6,912] per week. Why, even a child can pick up three dollars [$86.40] worth of gold in a day from the treasure streams. Easily, in comparison with California, the famous El Dorado was but a sand bank, the Arabian Nights were tales of simplicity!*

There was no doubt whatever any longer in the minds of "the powers that be" at the *New York Herald* that the matter of the California gold discovery was vital news beside which the front-page items of Free-Soil Party meetings, and General Zachary Taylor's recent grand fancy ball paled into insignificance.

[September 30th, 1848 • Saturday]

The extreme reluctance of the American press to openly and honestly cover the news of the gold discovery in California now seemed mystifying. One could certainly understand — and sympathize with — the desire of American newspapers not to fall victim to a hoax, but for them to continue to largely ignore one of the most amazing, exciting stories in American history, and to do so despite being confronted with highly authoritative accounts and evidence, simply made no sense.

The September 18th issue of the *New York Herald*, for example, had included a front page devoted largely to news from across the Atlantic — an election in France involving considerable turbulence, and rioting; rebellion in Ireland; a war in Italy; an outbreak of cholera in London. Buried on page three, once again as part of the farcical coverage of the Paisano column, was a scant mention of the California gold discovery, presented in such a manner as to provoke disbelief or, at least, to undermine any sense of the real importance of what was occurring. Nor was such studious avoidance of the California news limited to the *New York Herald*. Other major newspapers in Boston, Baltimore, Philadelphia, and Washington D.C. followed essentially an essentially similar strategy where such news was concerned. Only one small newspaper with a limited circulation, the *New York Journal of Commerce*, took the matter seriously and tried to provide its readership with a balanced, newsworthy approach.

By this time, of course, letters from individuals in California to relatives, friends and acquaintances in the East had at last begun reaching their recipients, and a vague general excitement was beginning to stir and grow. Those who knew the writers well and trusted their honesty, believed without reservation, but others continued to vacillate and doubt the credulity of such reports. Clearly, the private letters urged the recipients in strong terms to sell out their eastern properties at almost any sacrifice and start their journey to California at once. Recipients compared their letters, all of which seemed to share a strong, urgent recommendation: Opportunity was knocking loudly, and the time to act was now, while the gold was still plentiful and while fortunes were still being made with ease.

In the face of all this, certain enterprising individuals in the East began making preparations to participate in what promised to become a great westward exodus A large and growing number of people were clearly transfixed by the prospect of a grand, extremely profitable adventure. Virtually everyone, it appeared, was talking about California and the opportunities it was offering. The recent Mexican War had developed in the nation a vast horde of young men inured to hardships and eager for adventure of some kind, and if such adventure could result in the accumulation of great wealth, who could be foolish enough to resist the call? In every state east of the Mississippi, great numbers of young men suddenly became eager to pursue a goal that promised an escape from low wages and limited opportunities, and these excited citizens were not intimidated by the prospects of hardships and dangers they might have to endure in their pursuit of these dreams.

Even the nation's capital was stirring with the contagious excitement — Washington was beginning to seethe with it. While partisan newspapers continued to play their political games and politicians continued to maneuver for platforms upon which to launch careers in government, the general population was turning its thoroughly aroused attention westward. As the *Washington Union* newspaper remarked bitingly:

> *There, Mr. Webster, is the country you declared was surely not worth having! Why, it is a solid mass of gold, which, if worked properly, would pay for all the expenses of the late war in less than a fortnight.*

If the tales of California gold were true, then it was clear that the benefit to the people of the entire nation would be manifold. It seemed clear that if the frequently defeated bill for a trans-continental railroad were reintroduced now, it would surely pass, and had not Congress been in recess, that might well have already occurred. Clearly, a mass emigration from East to West would ease the congestion of the crowded metropolitan locations in the East and help immeasurably in halting — or at least substantially easing — the current downward trend of wages there. Markets and industry would expand enormously to meet the demand and the tired and faltering old Bank of the United States could rise Phoenix-like from its own bed of ashes and issue new currency backed by a voluminous supply of gold that could stabilize the economy. As one reporter jubilantly put it:

> *Here's to our new territory! Here's to the United States, bounded on the north by the Aurora Borealis, on the south by the procession of the equinoxes, on the east by the rising sun, and on the west by the day of judgment!*

It was an infection, a contagion, a fever rising in the American public, stirring their souls and beginning to enflame their minds. It was a subject that was becoming the core of conversation from the busiest of street-corners to the most remote of rural arenas. It was a dream, a promise, a *future* beyond any that even the most imaginative of minds had previously envisioned.

It lacked but one thing: The trigger that could galvanize an entire nation into an enthusiastic grasp for a better tomorrow. The entire East remained in a state of delicate balance; poised, it seemed, for that critical moment when a certain "something" would occur, that "trigger" which somehow, in some way, would be pulled, which none could yet articulate, but which everyone when it came, would immediately and unmistakably recognize.

[October 30th, 1848 • Monday]

Though it attracted very little attention, a major event had occurred in New York City early this month that held the promise of becoming very significant for the West Coast. On October 2nd, the first of the three side-wheeler steamships built to establish a regular mail run from New York to San Francisco had been launched. She weighed 1,050 tons and had been christened the *California*. Her sister ships, the 1,099-ton *Oregon* and the 1,087-ton Panama were both nearing completion, as well, and both were scheduled for launching well before the year's end.

Four days later, under command of Captain Cleveland Forbes, with a crew of 36 men and carrying a full capacity of 500 tons of coal as fuel, the *California* slipped her lines and churned her way southeast out of New York Harbor, en route on her maiden voyage around the entire South American continent. On board were provisions enough to last a full year. She had aboard, as well, a complete set of spare machinery. As it turned out, her cabins and holds were all but empty of anything except the shipment of mail being transported; though she had room for 60 saloon passengers and 150 more in steerage, she was empty of passengers for California because recent rumors of the discovery of gold had just reached the East and were still being treated with cautious skepticism.

Across the continent in California, James H. Carson's visit with George H. Angel at the latter's camp had been very pleasant, but the number of miners who had congregated there along Angel Creek had made Carson and his companions feel confined, and now all three were ready to move on by themselves. So far as Carson could determine, no one had yet done any exploring south of the camp, and so they headed in that direction. Four miles to the south, along a creek which skirted the north base of a substantial hill, they discovered gold in rather large nuggets, and during the first day of searching there they collected 13 ounces of nuggets valued at $208 [$5,990.40]. Carson named the stream after himself, and during the next ten days the three men found a total of 180 ounces worth $2,880 [$82,944]. A cold rain set in the eleventh morning, raising the creek level and making further digging distinctly uncomfortable. Agreeing among themselves that it was time to head back to Monterey, they divided their findings equally, and by mid-morning were on their way home.

On the previous Sunday, Captain Joe Folsom, in his headquarters office in San Francisco, had spent much of the Sabbath day writing a letter he had been putting off for a considerable while: A long overdue report to his chief in Washington, D.C., the Quartermaster General of the United States Army. A small portion of what he wrote in his lengthy, redundancy-filled letter clearly extolled the great quantities of the precious metal being discovered and expressed the monumental excitement building in the normally staid character of Captain Folsom:

> *San Francisco, California, Oct. 8th, 1848*
>
> *My Dear Sir: — The prices of labor here will create surprise in the United States. Kannakas [sic], or Sandwich Islanders, the worst of laborers are now employed constantly about town in storing and landing merchandise at a dollar [$28.80] an hour each; and the most indifferent laborers are hired by the week together at six or eight dollars [$172.80 or $230.40] per day. Mechanics obtain, when employed by the day, eight or ten dollars [230.40 or $288] per day, and by the month about six [$172.80]. In a few days, as the sickly season is over, I presume wages will advance, for most of the laboring classes are returning to the mines.*

It was ten days ago, on October 20th, when one of the major eastern newspapers began taking serious notice of the gold discovery in California. This was the *Washington Union,* which reprinted the gold-confirming letters sent from Commodore Thomas Jones and Consul Thomas Larkin to the State Department, and then suggested editorially:

> *The danger in California is from want of food for the residents, still more from streams of immigrants. Would not*

> *some of our sage merchants find it profitable speculation to send cargoes of biscuit, flour, &c, 'round to the Pacific coast?*

The time of year, now late October, was far too late for overland travel across the continent to California;it was, after all, virtually the end of October, but many were making preparations for the following spring. Over the past couple of months the *New York Herald* had continued, and increased the frequency of its coverage of the California gold strikes, although most of its references occurred in the fraudulent Paisano column, while its front pages continued to emphasize campaign speeches by the leading Presidential candidates, along with the usual disquieting news from Europe.

Here and there, however, numerous newspapers' advertisements were appearing, emphasizing the parties which were being organized for the Spring journey to California, all of which were preparing to embark in April from western Missouri in extensive wagon trains. There were, as well, offerings from large distributors of camping gear and mining equipment for sale.

Hardly noticed amid the increasing hubbub, the Royal Mail steamship *Europa* had set off from New York City fully a month ago, on September 27th, for London, bearing with it ample news of the discovery of gold in California. The *Europa* reached its destination on October 10th at which time the editor of the *London Times* scanned the latest accounts from the United States. He found an account of the gold discoveries in California and promptly buried it on page four amidst Latin-American commercial notices. At the end of the article, an editorial comment stated:

> *The placera sand is said to be so rich, that if exported to England or the United States, it would be very valuable. Consequent upon this excitement, the price of provisions has increased enormously. We need hardly observe that it is necessary to view these statements with great caution.*

Much more emphasis in that newspaper was placed on the massive disruption in France, where revolt was everywhere in evidence. The monarchy of King Louis Philippe had been overthrown and a republic government instituted. A full civil war had resulted in June, and not until now had French leaders gained strength enough to hold a national election. The *London Times* editor, tersely commenting on the reports of gold, remarked that it reminded him of a pool that had been searched for some imaginary treasure:

> *The whole body of turbid water has been strained — but the stream held in its depths no lumps of California gold — a fine and even sand alone darkened the waters, and a worthless deposit is all they leave behind them.*

Little wonder, then, with such negative newspaper coverage, that no gold fever fire ignited in England. It undoubtedly would, in time, since already half a million Brits had been transplanted to Canada, and how long could they resist so intriguing a discovery at their virtual back door? Highly placed governmental figures were already asking themselves a crucial question: Might not California now present a new outlet to relieve the population pressure threatening British colonies worldwide? Yet, despite the presence of such thinking, London newspapers continued generally to scoff at reports of gold being found there.

Much closer to home, however, gold fever was spreading rapidly along the Pacific shores and many hundreds of hopefuls, especially in South American coastal cities, rapidly crowded the ports, trying to find passage on any ship, large or small, that could transport them to any port in California, but preferably San Francisco. The mail-ship *SS California,* which had been nearly empty of passengers when it left New York City on October 2nd — and remained so after docking at Rio de Janeiro — was quickly filled almost to capacity upon docking at Valparaiso in late December, as eager would-be Chilean miners flocked aboard. When the ship finally reached Callao, Peru on December 29th, literally hundreds of miners sought similar passage, but there was room for only 50 additional passengers before she set off for her final destination, San Francisco.

At the same time, Lt. Sherman and his fellow officers, once again on a tour of the mines and now on the fringe of the gold belt, camped together close to Mormon Island and, as Sherman wrote of it:

> *Warner [actually Warren], Ord, and I camped on the bank of the American River, abreast of the fort, at what was known as the 'Old Tan-Yard.' I was cook, Ord cleaned up the dishes, and Warner {Warren] looked after the horses; but*

> *Ord was deposed as scullion because he would only wipe the tin plates with a tuft of grass, according to the custom of the country, whereas Warner [Warren] insisted on having them washed, after each meal, with hot water. Warner [Warren] was, in consequence, promoted to scullion, and Ord became the hostler. We drew our rations in kind from the commissary at San Francisco, who sent them up to us by a boat, and we were thus enabled to dispense a generous hospitality to many a poor devil would have had nothing to eat.*

As the days of October passed their mid-point and dwindled away toward the month's end, greater numbers of early miners, who had spent most of the summer in the various digs or prospecting for new ones, began returning to San Francisco, San José, Monterey and other coastal communities. Many had accumulated far more wealth in gold than they had ever anticipated and were content with what they had found. A large number of these planned to return to the eastern United States as soon as the Sierra passes were negotiable in the spring, to settle in with riches that would allow them to establish businesses of their own and to live in relative luxury for the remainder of their lives.

Still, quite a substantial number of the withdrawing miners had every intention of returning to the digging as soon as possible when the rainy season ended and the warmer weather returned. Many, in fact, debilitated by their hard work and poor diets for weeks, even months, were aware that it would take as many weeks more just to recuperate somewhat from the illnesses they'd contracted and to regain their strength for another season of serious gold-seeking. Apart from these were those who elected — either from lack of funds or from the relentless drive of gold fever — to remain in the gold belt throughout the winter and to continue their prospecting and digging despite whatever inclement weather and discomforts they might encounter. At Dry Diggings alone some 800 decided to stay, and other principal deposit areas had wintering populations far beyond what most had anticipated, but they were rarely the happy camps that had so enjoyed the summer and early autumn.

Rigorous though it was for those who stayed, the rewards were often considerable. The deposits to the north, along the Yuba, remained relatively crowded, and numerous new camps had sprung up, either on or close to the most productive sites. Here the hardy miners, despite the rugged conditions, were averaging five ounces of gold — $1,280 [$36,864] per day for each group and the returns from other sites, both north and south, were similarly impressive. When soaked and shivering miners bolstered their own flagging spirits with such comments as, "By God, with what I'm digging here, I will die rich!" Many had no inkling of just how prophetic the words were or how very soon such prophecies would be fulfilled.

Those with some degree of sense took the time to temporarily shelve the lust for gold, and if they had no tent, to build log cabins or shanties that offered at least some degree of protection from the elements. All too often, however, the gold fever was so pronounced in them that they could not bear to stay away from the digs, and at night lay shivering beneath the meager shelter of well worn and tattered blankets that provided very little warmth and almost no protection. It was only too apparent that a fair number could not possibly survive until spring. Sicknesses prevailed in virtually every camp, and death was an all-too-common visitor.

As autumn progressed and the weather became consistently worse, even many of the several thousand who thought they could hang on were forced to give up and drag themselves, disappointed and sick, back to the towns, cursing their individual misfortunes and the miseries they had endured. Few who returned could present an appearance that even approached respectability. They were ragged, weather-burned, dirty, mud-smeared, often shoeless, and plagued by blistered and clumsily bandaged feet. Not surprisingly their untrimmed whiskers, long and scraggly hair and fever-bright eyes imparted a decidedly ghoulish appearance.

The face of San Francisco itself was changing dramatically as ever more miners returned and either reoccupied their former abodes or bought, with their abundance of gold, new homes that were rising as rapidly as they could be built. William S. Clark bought a large chunk of land at the bay's edge, which he named Clark's Point, and here, adjacent to where the extensive city wharf was being built, 40 inches wide and extending 250 feet out into the bay from the northeast corner of Battery and Broadway, he erected a large warehouse — the largest building yet in San Francisco. He anticipated that the structure would become a very busy place, since it would certainly become the favored landing place for the multitude of passengers arriving by sea. Even before being finished, it was nearly full of various cargoes that had arrived from all over the Pacific.

Saloons were being built in remarkable numbers, and many of them were staffed by quite comely barmaids who were often gold-widows of miners who had decided to spend the rainy season at the mines — so staffed at least before they were filled to overflowing, day and night, with returned miners eager to spend their nuggets and dust on liquor and card games — and ladies. Such establishments were almost always riotously busy at all times.

Now October was virtually at its end, and the rainy season was just commencing. Through all of the previous three months, the influx of gold-seekers had increased, and they were now well spread out over the gold belt, so far as its dimensions were presently known. By now a complex, extensive system of supply had been developed — haphazard though it was — to cater to the various needs of the miners, though universally at great cost, beginning with the high prices charged by freighters. It had cost E. Gould Buffum, for example, $300 [$8,640] to have three barrels of flour, one barrel of pork, and 200 pounds of small stores hauled a mere 50 miles.

The principal storekeepers — Sam Brannan at Sutter's Fort and Coloma, Charles Weber at French Camp, William Knight at Knights Ferry, and Abraham Syrec at Mokelumne Hill — were the masters of commerce within the golden frontier. For the most part these merchants operated out of flimsy tents or rudimentary shacks, and the supplies they had available were at first limited to the necessities, including picks, shovels, prybars, boots, shirts and trousers, plus the fundamental consumables such as jerky, salt pork, flour, ship's biscuit and, highly important, coffee, tea and whiskey. These goods were purchased from whatever became available at the Port of San Francisco, and from there, transported by sloop or schooner to the Sacramento embarcadero. They were transported from there by packhorse men or wagon freighters for delivery to the stores, such as they were, at the diggings.

General cargo shipments were reaching San Francisco Bay regularly now from the Sandwich Islands, while flour and lumber were being brought in from Oregon and beef was being supplied by the multitude of ranchos at or near the coast. Significantly, scores of launches and other small craft were now regularly plying the waters of San Francisco Bay, and packers and teamsters had penetrated the western Sierra foothills in large numbers. What all this boiled down to was simply that supplies of most kinds were now usually available to the gold-seekers, providing one had the good fortune to be able to pay the exorbitant prices demanded.

As for crime in the gold fields, it continued to remain almost nonexistent. Murder and other forms of violence were practically unknown. When, on rare occasions, serious crime did occur, the miners took swift, definitive action. As James Carson wrote of it:

> *I believe there has been but one case of high misdemeanors tried thus far in 1848. A Frenchman had become rather notorious for horse stealing in the neighborhood of the Dry Diggings — his propensity for horse and mule flesh became so great that it attracted the attention of the miners, and we determined to put a stop to it. He was quite soon caught in the very act of horse-stealing, brought in and tried, and two hours after he was taken he was dangling between heaven and earth at the end of a rope. This severe but just punishment put a stop to horse-thieving exploits. ...*

Only one other serious crime occurred during this autumn: A Spaniard named Revain Lamros on the American River Middle Fork was caught with a stolen bag of gold dust in his possession. Identical justice in this case was swiftly meted out.

By mid-October Sgt. Carson, still with ample leave-time remaining, was in San Francisco, where he applied at a public house for lodging and, getting settled in, wrote:

> *Oct. 16th — I got beef broiled, hard bread, and a cup of awful coffee, for which I paid the moderate sum of five dollars [$144]. By furnishing my own blankets and paying a dollar [$28.80], I received permission to sleep on a bowling alley, after the rolling had ceased, which was near two o'clock in the morning. Gambling seemed to be the ruling passion — there is no value set on money, as it does not procure the comforts of life, or bring lasting amusement or pleasure to the holders; millions of dollars are recklessly squandered at the gaming tables and drinking shops. ... The rains commence, which drives full two-thirds of the miners down to the coast. ... Those who remain in the mines ... make but little at mining, as the supplies for their subsistence are so high*

> *as to absorb all they make — but the traders amass fortunes. ... We live on beef & beans — beef dried, fried, roasted, boiled and broiled, morning, noon and night; as much as every man wants, without money or price; with a change, at times, to elk, venison and bear steak. The emigrants do not expect to find any luxuries in California, with the exception of a balmy atmosphere and rich soil — and they well know that industry will, hopefully, soon supply the rest.*

On this final day of October, Brigadier General Stephen Watts Kearny, the man who was as much responsible as anyone for the occupation and acquisition of California as a territory to the United States; the man who had directed a Battalion of 500 Mormon soldiers on foot across more than 2,000 miles of largely desert wasteland to occupy California; the man who had fended off attacking armies of Mexicans; the man who had briefly assumed the role of military governor, first of California and then of Mexico, was brought to his end this day by a tiny Mexican foe he didn't even see.

General Kearny died just before sunset today, victim of a bite by Aëdes — the host mosquito of yellow fever.

Also on this final day of October, Samuel Brannan was summoned to the door of his large San Francisco mansion by a deputation of his flock of Mormons whom he had shepherded aboard the ship Brooklyn from New York Harbor to San Francisco Bay. Their leader bore in his hand an official document that had arrived only an hour ago from no less a personage than the leader of the Church of Jesus Christ of Latter-day Saints.

"Brother Brannan," the spokesman said solemnly, "I have been directed by our esteemed President, Brigham Young, to hand you this summons." Brannan made no move to accept the document. The spokesman, decidedly flustered now, continued: "You, sir, are accused of collecting tithes amounting to great sums of money and retaining them for your own personal uses."

Still Brannan said nothing, and after a moment the Saint folded his arm back and pretended to read from the document, although it was clear that he was familiar with every word it contained. "By decree of Brigham Young," he continued, "you are ordered, to repair immediately to Salt Lake City, by the swiftest means possible, to explain to him and the Mormon High Council your collection of tithes from all the Saints here in California. Further, you are to turn over to them, for the Church, all the monies and all the gold, you have collected through tithing in the name of the Church. If you fail to follow these directives at once, you are in danger of excommunication."

A small, humorless smile touched Brannan's lips. He had been expecting something of this nature for a very long while, and he was quite prepared for it.

"There is no documentation existing," he said smoothly, "that I have ever collected tithes for my own personal use. I have no intention whatsoever of going to Salt Lake City to see Brigham Young or the Mormon High Council or anyone else, either now or later, and I have no intention of surrendering funds of any kind to anyone."

Ignoring the stunned look of the messenger, Sam Brannan stepped back inside his house and closed the door firmly. He reached up and clicked the lock, still wearing the same tight, humorless smile.

"Apostasy isn't all that bad after all," he murmured.

[November 1st, 1848 • Wednesday]

Within an hour after the arrival of Commodore T. Apt Catesby Jones at Monterey, he was conferring earnestly with Governor Richard Mason in the seclusion of the latter's private office. The subject of their discussion was nothing less momentous than the immediate future of California. It was becoming painfully clear that while crime rates were remarkably low in the mining areas, the same could not be said for the more heavily populated coastal communities.

Both men were keenly aware that the Territory could not continue to exist as it was now, essentially without government and without law. It had managed to do so thus far, almost from the beginning of the year, thanks to the fact that since gold had been discovered, criminal behavior had been virtually absent in the mining districts for all that while — an amazing phenomenon that could not possibly last, a situation which, if immediate steps were not taken to provide stability, must surely deteriorate into anarchy.

Governor Mason's stance in all this was doubtful at best, and he lamented in his private *Journal*, if to no one else, the problems of being chief authority, both civil and militarily, in a country where the forts were without soldiers, where ordnance was without sufficient troops to utilize and guard it, where towns were bereft of able-bodied men to defend them, and where communication with the home government was always extremely difficult, delayed by weeks and months. As Evander Smith of Monterey put it in a letter to his brother Roswell, in Baltimore:

> *The Army officers could have seized the large amount of funds in their hands, levied heavily on the country, and been living comfortably in New York for the last year, and not a soul at Washington be the wiser or worse for it. Indeed, such is the case with which power can go unchecked and crime unpunished in this region, that it will be hard for the officers to resist temptation; for a salary here is certain poverty and debt, unless one makes up by the big hauls [of gold].*

That the territory's citizens did not often yield to such temptation was, under the circumstances, simply remarkable. Governor Mason and Adjutant Sherman were clearly being driven by their inadequate salaries to take on supplemental, unofficial work to eke out a living, and such efforts provoked one Charles Pickett to levy charges against these two and a fellow officer, Captain Folsom. Sherman in his Memoirs (pp. 64-65, stated that Mason never speculated monitarily, even though urged to do so, but that:

> *... he did take a share in the store where [which] Warner [Warren], Bestor and I opened at Coloma, paid his share of the capital, $500 [$14,400], and received his share of the profits, $1,500 [$43,200]. I think he also took a share in a venture to China with Consul Larkin and others, but on leaving Calif. was glad to sell out without profit or loss.*

That California territorial military officers rarely yielded to potentially illegal temptations under such circumstances vindicates the honorable reputation of the disbursing officers and collectors of the special war tax, known afterward as the civil fund. This was a duty levied on imports by the U.S. authorities in California during the military oversight of custom-house laws throughout the entire country. In California the tax amounted to a significant total of $600,000 [$17,280,000]. Assistant Quartermaster Capt. Joe Folsom was custodian of the fund at this time, under no bond, accountable to no one except his commanding officer. Actually, he was collecting duties from American importers as if he were the servant of a foreign power, when, in reality, he was the servant of no official power at all, since no authorized government existed in California whatsoever after 30 May 1848.

Application had been made long ago for stable governmental controls to be established to terminate the supposedly temporary military governorship under which the Territory had been existing but, so far as either man knew, nothing had changed. As Governor General Mason had said to Commodore Jones then:

"I believe that should Congress adjourn without providing a government for California, we should assist the people here in California in organizing a temporary constitution for themselves, at which point I would, of course, turn over to the provisional government the civil service fund for operating expenditures."

Commodore Jones had been in full agreement with the plan, and so they had waited for a response from Washington. Now, having received no U.S. Government response and acutely aware at this late date that no such communication could reasonably be expected this year, the two commanders set about doing as they had planned. Unfortunately, however, their good intentions had been misconstrued as a bid by the military to more firmly establish its control over California, and now civilian leaders were openly declaring the military government was attempting to more firmly implant itself in the ruling seat for the Territory. These civilian critics were accusing the United States military forces of exercising unjustifiable power and thereby impeding the development of self-government for Californians. Neither group was aware that an agent from Washington was currently on his way here, having been commissioned to observe and report upon the character and disposition of the inhabitants, with a view to determine whether or not it was wise to encourage political movements in California, in the event the current struggle in Congress over the issue of slavery should be prolonged.

The agent in question was William V. Voorhies, who had been employed by the U.S. Postmaster General to make arrangements for the establishment of post offices, and for the receipt and conveyance of letters in both California and Oregon. Secretary of State James Buchanan had authorized Voorhies to make these arrangements as well as to negotiate more private matters. The letter of introduction furnished to Voorhies by Secretary Buchanan, however, contained no such specific authorizations. To the contrary, Buchanan, after expressing the regrets of President Polk that California had not yet received a territorial government, added:

> *The government left at the termination of the war still exists and is valid, when not in contradiction to the Constitution of the United States. I therefore urgently advise the people of California to live peaceably and quietly under the present military government, consoling themselves with the knowledge that such state of affairs will endure but for a few months, or until the next session of Congress. They are advised further to live peaceably and quietly under the government de facto, half Mexican and half military.*

Such a split form of government, however, was precisely what the representatives of the California people had already decided they would not tolerate. Even before Secretary Buchanan's message arrived, they had begun to act upon their own convictions, and it was highly unlikely they could be turned back. A case in point: Mrs. Hetty C. Brown of San Francisco, having been deserted by her husband, had applied to the governor for a divorce almost a year ago, in December, 1847. Governor Mason at that time had decided that neither he nor any *alcalde* possessed the authority to grant a divorce, but he declared that "... there being no law in California on the subject of divorce, and she being left without any support, she might view her husband as dead, so far as she is concerned."

Continual complaints, moreover, had been made concerning the *alcaldes*. Lt. Pickett of the Eighth Infantry wrote to General Kearny (not yet knowing that he had just died) that:

> *John H. Nash, the alcalde at Sonoma, is ignorant, conceited, and dogmatical, and governed by whims; [and] he is also clearly under the influence of a pettifogger named Green. The unrestricted powers assumed by these magistrates are laying the foundations for much litigation in the future, when their decisions will be appealed. ...*

Pickett's judgment was vigorously echoed in a letter received by Gov. Mason from J. S. Ruckel in regard to affairs at the pueblo of San

José. Ruckel wrote that:

> *... matters which were originally bad are daily growing worse and worse — large portions of the population, lazy and addicted to gambling, have no visible means of livelihood and of course must support themselves by stealing cattle or horses. ... Wanted, an alcalde who is not afraid to do his duty, and who knows what his duty is.*

Charles White, the *alcalde* at San Jose, however, expressed the opposite point of view in a late-March letter to Governor Mason, writing in an aggrieved manner:

> *I have received true information of 60 men organizing, and daily receiving recruits, who have constant communication with volunteers in the service, who have in view to soon attack the prison in Monterey and release the prisoners. They also have formed the distinct plan of establishing an independent government in California. They are well armed; [and] the good people of the country [are] standing in fear of exposing these people, lest they might be killed in revenge. Immigrants have taken possession of the missions of San José and Santa Clara, injured the buildings and destroyed the vineyards and orchards, having no respect to any part of them except the churches. At the same time wild Indians are making organized and successful raids on the stock belonging to Americans and immigrants, and are aided by the mission Indians.*

Months later a committee consisting of James C. Ward, W. D. M. Howard, and C. V. Gillespie met in San Francisco to consider the currency issue. After deliberating at length the committee presented the following resolution to Governor Mason:

> *1st. That the gov'r be petitioned to appoint one or more assayers to test the quality of the gold taken from the placers on the Sacramento.*
>
> *2d. That the gov'r be asked to extend the time presently allowed for the redemption of the gold-dust, deposited as col-*

lateral security for payment of duties, to 6 months, so as to allow time for the importation of coined money into the country for that purpose.

3d. That the gov'r be requested to at once appoint a competent person to superintend the conversion of gold into ingots of convenient weights, the same to be stamped with the name of the person furnishing the gold to be cast, the expense of casting to be defrayed by the person furnishing the raw material. Last resolution not carried.

4th. Appointment of a committee to petition congress to establish a mint in this town — the petition to be circulated both in the Sacramento Valley and elsewhere for signatures. The said committee to consist of C. V. Gillespie, James C. Ward, W. D. M. Howard, and Capt. Jos. L. Folson, U.S.A.

All of these matters and more came into focus in a meeting held at the *alcalde's* office in San José, chaired by Charles White. Among the resolutions recited: That Congress had not extended the laws of the United States over the country as recommended by President Polk, but had left it without protection; that the growing frequency of robberies and murders had deeply impressed the people with the necessity of having some regular form of government, with laws and with officers to enforce them; that the discovery of gold would attract immigration from all parts of the world, and add to the existing danger and confusion; therefore, trusting to the government and people of the United States for sanction, it is resolved that it is not only proper but necessary that the inhabitants of California should form a provisional government and administer the same; and while lamenting the inactivity of Congress in their behalf, they still desire to manifest their confidence in and loyalty to the United States.

The city officials in San Francisco and San José approved of these recommendations and urged the citizens of all communities throughout California to hold meetings and to elect delegates to represent them in a Convention to be held on March 6th, 1849 at San José for the purpose of drafting a form of government to be submitted to the people for their sanction. In San Francisco a meeting was scheduled on October 15th to elect five delegates from the district to the Convention at San José. Sam Brannan offered a resolution which specified that the city's elected delegates be instructed to "oppose slavery in every shape and form in the

Territory of California." James Buckelew proposed that because the United States Congress has not provided a government for the people of the Territory, the duties collected at all California ports since the disbandment of the extraordinary military force justly belong to the people of this Territory, and should be claimed for our benefit by the state government the city officials were seeking to create. After some discussion the convention officials adopted both of these resolutions.

For those unsure of the exact meaning of all the legalistic jargon, the essence was now clear enough: California, now independent of Mexico, but not yet fully organized as a United States territory, had finally begun to assert itself.

[November 11th, 1848 • Saturday]

San Francisco was once again swelling: Most of its own population had returned from the mines for the duration of the rainy season, and a continually growing influx of transients were arriving, mainly by ship from ports throughout the Pacific. The mushrooming city, consequently, seemed to have taken on a new life. More new housing was being erected as rapidly as possible at wages which labor contractors were much more able to pay than they had been earlier, and a great number of businesses — especially hotels and saloons — were appearing, and all of them were immediately crowded with customers, despite the exceptionally high prices still being demanded for foodstuffs, whiskey and lodging.

While there was a decided increase in the number of theaters and "pleasure parlors" — *whorehouses*, as the less genteel accurately referred to them — there was an upsurge of interest, as well, in both schooling and religion, as educational and moralistic values began reasserting themselves. On November 1st, for example, many of the upright citizens of San Francisco assembled in the newly reopened schoolhouse. There they approved the hiring of recently arrived Presbyterian minister Timothy Dwight Hunt as city chaplain in a nondenominational role at an annual salary of $2,500 [$72,000]. While he might have made that much in a few days of good digging at the mines, Hunt nevertheless felt the "call" and accepted the position. Since there was as yet no church, the schoolhouse facing on the plaza was selected for the site of his weekly services until an actual church could be built.

Far to the south of Sutter's Fort, the bustling of miners at Angel's Camp abruptly diminished to nearly nothing, as by far the greater majority packed up what they would need of their gear and slogged off through rain and mud on their return to Sacramento and San José until spring. Only a small handful of men remained, among them George Angel himself, who had elected to stay at the site throughout the winter to protect it from possible claim-jumping. Only some twenty miles northwest, not far from the Mokelumne River, the number of miners still hovering in the area near a large hill induced the trader Abraham Syrec to drive his wagon laden with provisions to the spot to possibly supply their needs. It proved to be so profitable a move that he opened a store right at the hill there as November began, and his earnings far exceeded his expectations. His operation quickly became a very important trade center for the entire mining region, and the hill itself turned out to be immensely rich with gold. Much farther to the north, at the Russ Diggings on the Middle Fork American River, father and son miners Emanuel and Adolph Gustav Russ, well-known pioneers of San Francisco, took out in a mere "few hours" 64 ounces of gold valued at $1,024 [$29,491.20].

Far across the Atlantic Ocean, in England, the *London Times* openly scoffed at the reports being received of California gold and denounced the entire reportage as "delusionary." In its staid editorial, the editor wrote:

> *The discovery of gold deposits in the Sacramento, like that of Communism in the Seine, has produced a confusion of rank and a startling degree of equality ... even politics have disappeared and republicanism ceased to be preached for the moment. ... We must hear more of this El Dorado before we bestow upon it our serious consideration. There are some textures which will not bear many weeks washing, and the gold mines of the Sacramento may be one of them.*

For James Marshall, matters had not gone well since he had been driven away from his own lumber mill at Coloma by the secret group who called themselves the "Hounds," and he had drifted about, prospecting here and there without any significantly tangible results for the past several weeks. Now, however, with the rainy season at hand, he had finally come to San Francisco "on business," as he described it in his *journal*, and was amazed at the increase in its population and the prodigious amount of construction of new houses occurring here. He had not encountered so bustling a community since being in St. Louis, and he was intrigued by all that was going on. He took a room on November 5th at one of the newer small hotels on Jackson Street, and while sitting in its reading room, he fell into conversation with an individual who identified himself as a professor of geology, a man newly arrived from the East who was decidedly imbued with his own importance and education, and who, despite the fact that he had not yet visited the mining areas, was entirely convinced he held the key to all the riches of California.

Marshall had encountered such men before, and he listened with feigned interest as the man expounded on matters of mineralogy and his conviction as to where the mother lodes of gold "simply *had* to be located," which Marshall, from his own experience, knew was entirely wrong. When the newcomer finally ran down on the subject of gold, he invited Marshall to join him and two others in a game of euchre, and the men sat down at a table to play. Other hotel guests drifted up and watched their game for a while and Marshall, tiring of it, gave his seat to one of them and took a chair apart from the crowd, beside another guest who had been eyeing him speculatively.

Though strangers to one another, they recognized each other as prospectors and began discussing their own personal efforts at locating gold. The stranger, who identified himself only as "Jake," had evidently thus far been even less fortunate than Marshall in his prospecting, and he was intensely interested when Marshall showed him the collection of small nuggets he still had with him in a buckskin pouch. Marshall was somewhat surprised when the man gestured with the Hounds' signature hand-signal. Knowing it well, Marshall returned the sign, and the two immediately began discussing the most recent activities in which the secret gang had been involved. Professing, accurately enough, to have been pretty much out of touch lately due to his own prospecting, Marshall listened as Jake filled him in on the most recent occurrences.

"I've just come here for the first time myself," Jake told him, and then added, assuming Marshall to be part of the Hounds' subversive local chapter, "so I'm not entirely familiar yet with everyone in our group. I've met with some of our members, though, and I am very excited about what's planned."

Gradually Marshall drew from Jake the information that the San Francisco Hounds had been organizing an ambitious operation which they intended to pull off within the next three or four months. As Marshall listened intently, Jake, related excitedly that the local Hounds had been preparing to burn and sack San Francisco itself in early spring. To prevent discovery of their plans, he said, the Hounds had formulated new hand signals and signs, hand-grips and passwords and countersigns to identify themselves to one another, and he seemed quite pleased with himself as he cheerfully explained them all to Marshall to bring him "up to date" on the latest.

When Marshall was finally able to break away, he was intensely uneasy about all he had learned and convinced that San Francisco was in imminent danger. Unsure of what else he could do, Marshall went directly to the shop facing on the Plaza that was owned by an old acquaintance from the mines, Michael Johnson.

"I've got something very important to share with you," he told Johnson, "but I don't want us to take the slightest chance of being overheard. Where can we go?"

Johnson suggested they mount his horses and take a quick ride out of town to open areas where they would truly be alone. They did so and in a quiet little copse far from any eavesdropping ears, Marshall told him all he had learned. To his credit, Johnson took what was said quite seriously. The Hounds were, he was well aware, a gravely serious threat, and their acts of murders and robberies had increased dramatically in recent months because no law-enforcement agencies of any kind were available to deter and punish the gang's crimes. When Marshall finished, Johnson shook his head and gripped his friend's shoulder.

"I don't wonder you're concerned about all this," he said, "as I am, too. The question is, what do you intend to do about it? Surely you don't mean to keep information about a terror organization such as this to yourself, do you? Aren't you going to tell the authorities about it?"

"What authorities?" Marshall countered. "Exactly who am I supposed to tell? The Hounds have infiltrated everywhere. Any saloonkeeper or grocer or blacksmith might be part of their group. If I start talking about it without being very sure of who I'm talking to, I will inevitably wind up dead. And even if I talked to people who aren't part of the organization, why would they believe me? I know almost no one here in town. I'll tell you, Mike, this is scary business. If anyone could guarantee me enough money to be able to leave California within twenty-four hours, I'd be willing to take the risk of telling all I know.

Marshall shook his head and clenched his fist in exasperation as he continued. "But who do I know to tell, apart from you? What authorities could I possibly go to who, first of all, would believe what I say, and, secondly, might not be secretly allied to the Hounds themselves? I've got only one life, Mike, and self-preservation's high on my list. I have no intention of committing suicide, which is what this would amount to. The risk is too big and the reward, if any, is way too small. But how 'bout you? That's why I came to you. You're well known and respected here. You'd be believed."

Johnson was shaking his head even before Marshall finished. "I'm no hero, James. This is your project, not mine. It's up to you to find and tell the proper authorities. I have a family, a wife and children. I can't do it. I *won't*."

Neither would James Marshall.

Only two days later, two miners referred to only as *"a Mr. Pomeroy and a companion,"* were murdered in the mining district for the gold dust they carried. The *Star and Californian* newspaper — the newly published merger of both the *Star* and the *Californian*, with the virtually omnipresent Edward Kemble as its editor — seized upon the occasion to ignite a flaming agitation for the establishment of civil government, but with little effect. Not just yet.

In San Francisco the next morning, Thursday, November 9th, the new Post Office opened at the corner of Clay and Pike Streets, and the following morning saw the arrival of James H. Carson, who wrote that he had:

> *... followed the miners to the towns on the coast, where about two-thirds had gone to winter. San Francisco, Monterey, and Los Angeles had received the greater portion of this heterogeneous mass; men ragged and filthy in the ex- treme, with thousands of dollars in their pockets, filled the houses and streets, drinking and gambling away their piles. No supplies or accommodations could be obtained. In San Francisco, in particular, every house and tent was nightly crowded with these beings, who were in many cases packed away in rooms like shad.*

Election Day — November 11th — found the eastern states enshrouded by a persistent dismal rain, but the weather did little to keep voters away from the polls when there was so much at stake. The most pressing issue, aside from election of a new President of the United States, was the question of slavery and whether it was to be extended or dissolved, especially in the vast regions of the West that the U.S. had acquired in its victory over Mexico earlier this year.

While the Free-Soil Party standard bearer, former President Martin Van Buren, explicitly opposed extension, neither he nor Lewis Cass, the new Democratic Party candidate, took a clear position on the issue. Because of his own former role in the Democratic Party, Van Buren split the Democratic vote in New York, which held a powerful, pivotal position in the election, and this splintered vote, consequently, undermined the strength of the Democratic Party and swept the Whig candidate to victory.

Zachary Taylor defeated Cass in the Electoral College by a vote of 163 to 127, and then the former U.S. Army commander went on to carry half the remaining states — seven in the North and eight in the South. Van Buren made a dismal showing of only 291,616 votes, as opposed to Cass, who garnered 1,222,674. But it was Taylor who swept the day with a vote in his favor totaling 1,362,101.

When inauguration day arrived, the new President of the United States would be Zachary Taylor.

In the far West it was now becoming quite clear that the dramatically inflated prices for everything could not be blamed entirely on the realities of shortages and transportation costs. Bearing a great burden of the blame for so distorted an economy was the absolutely reckless spending of miners who suddenly found themselves — often in extraordinarily short spans of time — wealthy far beyond their wildest expectations. The excess of so much unaccustomed wealth resulted in not only wildly excessive spending but inevitably brought about wildly excessive prices imposed by merchants taking crass advantage of such loosely held wealth. To a man who has, in a matter of a week, dug from the earth gold in the amount of thousands of dollars [tens or hundreds of thousands at present values], the expenditure of considerable amounts for items of inconsequential real value was virtually meaningless. So what, if eggs were selling for $12 [$345.60] per dozen, potatoes at $1.50 [$43.20] per pound, apples for $5 [$144] apiece and a single good shovel brought as much as $50 [$1,440]? Prices had elevated swiftly to what the miners would willingly pay for what they wanted, and, for a fair percentage of the miners who struck it rich, virtually no price was too high for something they even whimsically needed or desired.

[December 5th, 1848 • Tuesday]

The spark needed to ignite gold fever in the American people east of the Mississippi was finally struck at 10 o'clock this morning by none other than President of the United States James Knox Polk during his fourth annual address to Congress. With no possibility existing of his being re-elected, it was also the President's farewell address to Congress and the nation; an address considerably different from that which Knox had initially planned, due to the arrival of Lt. Lucien Loeser at War Department offices in the pre-dawn hours three days ago.

Loeser, with the bulky tea caddy containing more than 14 pounds of raw gold still padlocked to his wrist, had finally reached New Orleans on November 23rd. Bedraggled and exhausted, he was intensely thankful to be back in the United States and pleasantly surprised to discover that there was actually a new telegraph office in the city. Without delay he arrived there and kept the telegrapher busy for more than half an hour, tapping out a detailed message directed to the U.S. War Department in Washington, D.C. In it he briefly outlined his journey over the past twelve weeks from San Francisco by ship to Payta, Peru, and then by British steamer to Panama; his laborious crossing of the isthmus; and then his continuing voyage, first to Kingston, Jamaica and, finally, to New Orleans. In closing, he mentioned that the tea caddy entrusted to his care by Governor Mason had never been opened, and had not for one moment left his hands since his departure from San Francisco exactly twelve weeks before; its contents were perfectly intact. He requested that the Adjutant General, Brigadier General Roger Jones, and President Polk be notified at once that he would set out immediately by the earliest available and swiftest transportation he could find, either by stagecoach or by railroad car or a combination of both, for Washington, D.C.

Foregoing any further delay in New Orleans, Lt. Loeser had immediately set out on the final leg of his long journey. The trip consumed nine more days, and in a record ninety-five days since leaving San Francisco, he arrived in the nation's capital by train an hour before daybreak on December 2nd. To Lt. Loeser's credit he successfully masked the fact that he had completed the long odyssey in a personally unprecedented state of total exhaustion.

General Jones was roused by a special messenger at his quarters, and he hurriedly dressed and arrived at the War Department just after sunrise and found the special courier, barely able to keep awake, seated in the Adjutant General's outer office. The heavy tea caddy was finally unlocked from Lt. Loeser's wrist and extended personally to the Adjutant General, who studied its contents wonderingly and who twice read through the enclosed report from California's military governor. It was General Jones himself who then hand-carried the report to the White House and personally delivered it to President Polk. The President spent remainder of that day making extensive revisions in his already prepared address to Congress: The address he was now delivering to that august body on this very morning of December 5th.

President Polk expounded in detail to his attentive Congressional listeners on various domestic and foreign issues, but he focused on the potentially explosive currently preoccupying Congress: slavery in the United States and the compelling need to gradually abolish it permanently from the United States and to prohibit its spread into any U.S. territories, especially those of Oregon and California. At the same time, however, the President blunted the force of his assertions by confirming the right of Californians to decide the slavery question for themselves.

The President finally came to the topic of the discovery of gold in California, and suddenly the press gallery became much more lively. Pens furiously scratched as reporters recorded every word he spoke on the topic. After acknowledging the recent arrival of reports from California received by Secretary of State James Buchanan from Consul Larkin on June 1st and 28th and July 1st, as well as from Commodore Jones to the Secretary of the Navy on July 28th, President Polk continued: "The accounts of the abundance of gold in California Territory," he said, "are of such extraordinary character as would scarcely command belief were they not corroborated by authentic reports of officers in the public service, who have visited the mineral district, and derive the facts which they detail from personal observation."

More than fourteen pounds of this gold, the President told them — actually an accurate weight of 230 ounces, 15 hundredweights and 9 grains — had already been transported to Washington and was currently on guarded display at the War Department, its quality in raw form analyzed and verified at more than $18 [$518.40] per ounce; the full sampling presently on hand and on display, valued at no less than $3,680 [$105,984]; yet this sampling, cheerfully provided by miners, represented only the tiniest fraction of the amount of gold being found in

California within a region at least fifty miles wide by at least several hundred miles in length, an area still growing as further explorations were conducted; an area currently being prospected by some ten thousand miners who apparently had barely begun to scratch the surface of so amazing a resource. The President reported that the gold deposits were so incredibly abundant that they would overwhelm any attempt to estimate their total value; but surely that value exceed by hundreds of times the total cost for the United States of its War with Mexico. The California deposits, he insisted, comprised a reserve of gold so extensive it could not possible be exhausted for a hundred years, possibly a thousand; it was, indeed, a national treasure of awe-inspiring and entirely incalculable value.

Reporters from all the major newspapers of the East were on hand, as well as numerous foreign correspondents from major cities worldwide, and they reported not only what they President had said, but added their own provocative information, citing reports of immense gold nuggets and rich-paying claims and publishing letters received in the East by relatives of miners who were doing incredibly well in California and who told how easy it was to mine gold there.

Editor Horace Greeley of the *New York Tribune* editorialized:

> *[In California], Fortune lies upon the surface of the earth as plentiful as mud in our streets. We look for an addition within the next four years [to] equal to at least One Thousand Million dollars to the gold in circulation.*

The *National News* enthusiastically reported:

> *Gold is everywhere you look, sparkling in the sun and glittering in the streams. It lies on the open plain, in the shadows of deep ravines and it glows on the summit of the mountains.*

Acclamation by newspapers and individuals was by no means universal. There were many who instantly decried the reports and vigorously ridiculed the purported discoveries, but such arguments no longer bore significant weight, now that the President himself had attested to actually seeing the gold and receiving the official reports which could not be denied or dismissed. Newspapers everywhere in

America now began to fill with accounts from the mines, and throughout the entire country these stories became a compelling, dominant topic of discussion, one often evolving rapidly from an interest to an obsessive excitement, and ultimately for many thousands, to a fever to participate in the greatest treasure hunt in the history of the world.

New arrivals from the West brought even more glowing accounts and expanded on the reports of the vast dimensions of the gold field and the volume of the precious material being found by individuals with no previous prospecting experience whatsoever, reports emphasizing the fact that *anyone* with the desire, the determination, and the will to expend the necessary time and effort such a project would require, stood an excellent chance of reaping a fortune. The volume of letters received by families in the East from miners who had already ventured West seemed to mushroom within mere hours, bringing myriad accounts of even richer and more extensive discoveries — stories which created an elixir that virtually intoxicated an entire nation and set into motion those who had, until now, not taken such reports seriously. Almost instantly tens of thousands began making elaborate plans: Purchasing and assembling a multiplicity of tools, tents, wagons, and equipment of every description; curing and jerking meats, rounding up livestock, and planning farewell gatherings before setting off on a grand fortune-seeking endeavor which would transform their lives.

There was no longer any denying the impact of what was occurring. Although travel by sea couldn't begin until ships could be filled with people and goods, and although overland travel couldn't possibly get underway before the spring, the fact of the matter was now vividly clear: A great American gold rush was definitely beginning to take shape.

[December 31st, 1848 • Sunday]

During the weeks following President Polk's final address to Congress, the rapidly spreading news of his remarks riveted the attention of millions throughout the United States, indeed throughout the whole world, thereby creating a widespread storm of excited interest and bustling activity. The President had at last set mere rumors to rest by verifying and authenticating the gold discovery in California.

On December 8th, three days after the President's stirring announcement, the first shipment of gold was sent to the U.S. Mint in Philadelphia, carried in hand by David Carter of San Francisco, and turned over to National Mint Director R. M. Patterson. This first consignment consisted of just under 113 pounds of pure gold in the form of nuggets, flakes and dust. It was inspected and tested very closely by Director Patterson himself, who wrote of it three days later to Secretary of the Treasury Robert J. Walker:

> *Mint of the United States Philadelphia, Dec. 11, 1848*
>
> *Sir: — Early on the 8th inst. we received the first deposit of gold from California ... deposited by Mr. David Carter. ... It weighed 1804.59 ounces Troy. On the 9th inst. another deposit was sent by the Secretary of War, which weighed 228 ounces. The gold was melted in six parcels ... the average of the whole being 894 ... slightly below the standard fineness, which is 900. The average value of the bullion after melting is $18.50 [$532,80] [per ounce]. The whole value of the gold in the two deposits was $36,492 [$1,050,969.60], besides a few ounces reserved in the native state for the Secretary of War, at his request.*
>
> *Very respectfully, your faithful servant,*
> *R. M. PATTERSON, Director, U.S. Mint*

The second consignment, received today from the U.S. Secretary of War, weighed exactly 14-1/4 pounds. The total amount — exactly 2,032.59 ounces, valued by the director at just a few cents over $18 per ounce, made the entire parcel of gold worth $32,521.44 [$936,617.47]. The assays, which included those of specimens sent to select private persons, agreed that the gold's cumulative aggregate average quality was .894 fine, which brought it to a comparative level with the gold from the finest raw gold sources in the previously known world.

The results revealed in these government reports spread to newspapers all over the world, and most of them covered the story in considerable detail. Typical of these myriad accounts was one which appeared in an editorial of the *Washington Union* on December 6th, which commented:

> *We readily admit that the account so nearly approached the miraculous that we were relieved by the evidence of our own senses on the subject. The specimens have all the appearance of the native gold we have seen from the mines of North Carolina and Virginia; and we are informed that the*

> *secretary will send the small chest of gold to the mint, to be melted into coins and bars, and most of it to be subsequently fashion[ed] into medals commemorative of the heroism and valor of our officers. Several of the other specimens he will retain for the present in the war office as found in Cal., in the form of lumps, scales, and sand; the last named being of different hues, from bright yellow to black, without much appearance of gold. However sceptical [sic] any man may have been, we defy him to doubt that if the quality of such specimens as these be as great as has been represented, the value of the gold in Cal. must be greater than has been hitherto discovered in the old or new continent; and great as may be the emigration to this new El Dorado, the frugal and industrious will be amply repaid for their enterprise and toil.*

Such accounts stirred an unprecedented restlessness in a significant portion of the populace and created a gold-fever world-wide: A virtual human tide began preparations to flood into San Francisco Bay in both scores of ships and many hundreds of land caravans, irrespective of the hazards to be faced en route on stormy seas or through virtually unexplored and often very treacherous reaches of wilderness in plains, deserts and mountains. Ignited by the President's address to Congress, a significant number of the public's overwhelming eagerness to reach California as quickly as possible, was epitomized by the departure of the bark, *John Benson*, setting sail for the Panamanian Isthmus with sixty passengers on December 11th, only six days after President Polk's speech. Ironically, had these men, or those who followed them, had any clear notion of what they would encounter in attempting to cross the isthmus, they may well have given up at the outset.

The sea journey's first phase, down the Atlantic East Coast and through the Gulf of Mexico, was usually easily made and without incident, but good fortune ceased once the Gulf shore of the Isthmus was reached at Chagres, a tiny village located in the midst of a low, swampy area at the mouth of the Chagres River. The small harbor was secure and defended by a formidable castle built upon a high bluff, but the village itself was deplorable; its native population, numbering no more than 500, and its streets so mucky that logs were laid down the middle of them to allow walking without sinking knee-deep in mud. An American traveler, who identified himself only as Viator, wrote of the place in mid-December:

> *Its climate is, without doubt, the most pestiverous for whites in the entire world. The coast of Africa, which enjoys a dreaded reputation in this way, is not so deadly in its climate as is Chagres. The thermometer ranges from 79 to 85 degrees all the year and it rains every day. Many a traveler, who has incautiously remained here for a few days and nights, has had cause to remember Chagres; and many a gallant crew, who have entered the harbor in full health, have, ere many days, found their final resting-place on the dark and malarious banks of the river. Bilious, remittent, and congestive fevers, in their most malignant forms, seem to hover over Chagres, ever ready to pounce down on the stranger. Even the acclimated resident of the tropics runs a great risk in staying any time in Chagres; but the stranger, fresh from the North and its invigorating breezes, runs a most fearful one.*

Trade at this port, if such it could generously be called, was limited to merely the forwarding of goods across the Isthmus; only a small shop or two existed in the village to provide residents with scanty clothing. It was far more a transient depot than anything else, as its own limited produce consisted chiefly of hides, India rubber and sarsaparilla, with a smattering of gold dust, most of which would be sent down the river for transshipment to the United States and the West Indies. There were no accommodations whatsoever available for travelers, most of whom learned quickly to merely pass through the village as speedily as possible and head upriver without pause for even an hour.

The upriver journey, on that stream — dark, muddy, swift, sometimes extremely narrow and sometimes as broad as 1,500 feet — was performed in tiny, narrow dugout canoes propelled by two or more polers. There were only two points where the traveler could land with any degree of safety — first at the village of Gorgona, some 50 miles upstream, and then at Cruces, a similar distance beyond. The river travel always engendered a singular feeling of depression in the traveler, due to its dark and somber aspect and the fact that the traveler was himself forced to lie outstretched near the unstable dugout's stern, to prevent upsetting the craft. This section of the dugout was covered over with a palm-leaf thatching called *toldo*, which shut away most of the view, while baggage, stowed carefully amid ship, was covered over with oiled cloths called *encerrados*. The boatmen expertly propelled their craft upstream with many cries and strange exclamations and there were no signs of civilization along the swampy banks except for the two towns noted, only lush vegetation, including dense mangrove growths, extending down into the water, well out from its shore. Along these banks were vast populations of alligators and caimans, as well as monkeys, ocelots, jaguars, tapirs, and a variety of venomous snakes. A light canoe with two oarsmen and but one passenger could make the journey to Cruces in 12 hours or less; a heavier load required upwards of thirty-six hours in passage. As Viator commented:

> *The passenger must take his provisions with him, as none are to be had on the river, and a good water filter will be found of great convenience, as the river water is so muddy that it is apt to derange the bowels, unless filtered in some way before drinking it. ... In view of the great and sudden influx of passengers to Chagres at the present time, it is impossible to say how they will all be accom-modated with canoes and what the journey will cost. In former times the supply of canoes was limited, and the charge depended upon the celerity with which the journey was performed. A dubloon ($16 [$460,80]) was the lowest charge for a single passenger, and from that up to two or three or even four doubloons. As for taking out boats from here [the U.S.], and rowing them up the river, I should think it would be a hopeless attempt. Hardy boatmen from our south-western states, who are accustomed to much similar mode of travel on their rivers, would probably be able to accomplish it; but in that burning and unhealthy climate, for young men fresh from the North, unacquainted with the dangers of such navigation, and all unacclimated, to attempt such a feat would be madness indeed.*

Once the traveler reached Cruces, however, the worst part of the journey was behind, and he was then only 21 miles of land-travel away from the Pacific shore. From this point he traveled on horse or mule-back, with a pack mule for baggage and a muleteer who acts as guide.

The trail, due to the rains, was abundant with mud-holes which could be treacherous and often deep. The traveler had to carry provisions with him because, while there was wildlife abounding along the way — guinea-hens, wild pheasants, macaws and parrots abound — any hope of shooting such game along the way was futile, since the jungle here was just as dense as along the river, and only the native Indians could enter it with any prospect of success; others were likely to become lost within mere feet of the bridle-path.

After traveling along this narrow path for some eight or ten hours, the broad savannah of Panama was at last reached, and sight of the blue waters of the Pacific and the white towers of the Cathedral of Panama, visible at a distance of about four miles, brought the weary traveler assurance that his journey was nearly completed. In about four hours more he was able to reach the suburbs of Panama [City] itself, which was located on the shore of a beautiful bay and had a population of some 7,000. It was a trade city, with most trade consisting of importing dry-goods from Jamaica to supply the Isthmenians, as well as of forwarding produce goods from neighboring Veragua, the Pearl Islands and the towns of Chiriqui and David, and their vicinities, southward to the Pacific ports of Payta in Peru and Guayaquil in Ecuador and to Jamaica in the Gulf of Mexico.

The year-round temperature at the city of Panama rarely varied more than five degrees from about 82 degrees Fahrenheit, but the rainy season was long and severe. Accommodations and markets were very limited, and because of the overpowering and constant heat and humidity, fish caught in the morning spoied by afternoon. The same held true for beef, goat meat, and pork, which had to be consumed immediately after butchering to avoid spoilage. Chickens or fowl of any other kind were expensive, and such vegetables as yams and *yukars,* as well as various tropical fruits were scarce. Tea, coffee, and chocolate were very expensive, and wines and liquors, usually of inferior quality, were very high-priced due to the transportation costs across the Isthmus. Accommodations, except for one small and very poor hotel, were almost non-existant and travelers had to depend upon the hospitality of those to whom they carried letters of introduction. As Viator concluded in his account:

> *The healthiness of Panama is far greater than that of Chagres. With due care, avoiding all excesses and the night*

air, a person can preserve his health; still, the very heavy rains and continual damp atmosphere render it necessary to take every precaution; for though healthy when compared to Chagres, it is by no means a safe place for unacclimated passengers from the North.

And now, having taken the traveler for California across the Isthmus, let me conclude by giving a word of advice. If he has a passage engaged through to San Francisco, the Isthmus route is decidedly the quickest and, all things considered, the least weary. But — and I speak now more particularly to those who have but a limited amount of funds — just sufficient to carry them through to San Francisco without any stoppage — let these travelers beware how they try the Isthmus, if they have only engaged passage as far as Chagres: after their toilsome journey to Panama (if they escape delay and fever at Chagres,) they may have to wait weeks for a passage to San Francisco, and when at last the long wished-for opportunity occurs, they will find themselves unable to take it, as expenses in Panama will have exhausted their means. Thus situated in a strange, unhealthy country, moneyless and friendless, their spirits depressed by their situation, it requires no prophet to predict a most heart-rendering termination to their golden schemes. Trusting that many of this class of passengers will pause and reflect ere they place themselves in such an unfortunate position,

I am, sir, your most obedient servant, VIATOR
December, 1848

The prospects of a journey across the Panamanian Isthmus aside, clearly, part of what created such a compelling motivation for tens of thousands of Eastern U. S. citizens, apart from the gold itself, were the greatly unsettled conditions, both political and economic, existing literally in the current world's passing scene. In America this was manifested not only by the widespread relief with the resolution of the War with Mexico, and by a growing excitement over the consequent acquisition of immense, virtually vacant territories — an excitement prompted by the sobering reality that the majority of its citizens were struggling to make a living near the level of abject poverty.

For the remainder of the world, the prospect of mining California gold was compellingly alluring for great multitudes of peoples who, for far too long, had been buffeted and battered by brutal, virtually endless wars and stifling political oppression from the Mediterranean to the North Sea, and from the Atlantic Coast of Europe eastward to the Pacific. In essence, the gold dream ignited unlimited hope and direction, as well as dogged determination within the masses of human beings who had been — for a very long while, perhaps all of their lives — without even a semblance of either.

In the meanwhile, in California new mining sites were continually being found and exploited. One of the prime sites now, in December, was called Botilleas — so named because of its excellent spring and the great many water bottles left lying there — which was discovered between Sutter Creek South and the Mokelumne River, and mined by Col. Apollo Jackson, who subsequently gave his own name to the town of Jacksonville, which developed there and quickly supplanted Botilleas. Originally a favored site because of the very good spring located there, it quickly became noted for its amazing deposits of the precious yellow mineral, vast amounts of which were extracted.

The inestimable value of this California Territory to the United States was by December all too evident, and suddenly civic-minded territorial citizens were organizing widespread efforts to apply for admission into the Union as another of the United States. This agitation, which had been fermenting for more than a year, had escalated considerably in recent weeks, and meetings were held in both San Francisco and San José for establishment of a civil government. The participants in these meetings concluded that should the U.S. Congress fail to act on the matter before the close of its session in March, a Constitutional Convention would be organized in California in order to force the issue.

In the meanwhile, John Sutter finally found his way out of some of his suffocating debt by selling his half-interest in the Sutter-Marshall Saw-mill at Coloma to John Winters and Alden S. Bayley on December 18th for $6,000 [$172,800]. At the same time, they purchased from Marshall one-third of his interest in the mill for the sum of $2,000 [$57,600], with Marshall carefully reserving to himself the right of pre-emption, and only selling the right to cut timber for mill purposes, and the mill-operation privilege itself.

For Americans populating the eastern third of the nation, the gold discovery announcement by the President quickly focused their thinking, and provided them with a highly motivated sense of purpose; it fanned in tens of thousands the spark of imagination and adventure into an unquenchable thirst to fuse their own future with a prospect for great wealth far beyond what they had ever before been believed possible, much less actually attainable. From Maine to Florida and westward towards the Mississippi Basin, multitudes of citizens were gripped with a compelling intrigue. For these citizens California had become the core of virtually every conversation, every speech, every sermon, and they eagerly read and discussed all news from the far West. They put aside former wistful armchair preoccupations, and many began making vigorous preparations to head to the California gold fields.

By far the most in-demand reading material available now was a 40-page pamphlet by J. Ely Sherwood, just published, with the prodigious title of *California, and the Way to Get There; with the Official Documents Relating to the Gold Region*. Were that not enough, it's inside sub-title was the clincher: *California, her wealth and Resources; with Many Interesting Facts respecting the Climate and People*. This title was followed by a letter dated August 11th, 1848 from Sutter's Fort, providing the experiences of a successful digger, along with a few pages touching upon Mexican life in the Territory. If more impetus was necessary, these pages were followed by the full text of Consul Thomas Oliver Larkin's letters to Secretary of State James Buchanan and excerpts of Governor Richard Mason's official report which directly addressed California and its gold. A gold-enthusiastic letter from the Rev. Walter Colton came next, followed by a so-called description of the gold region that gave virtually no description of it whatsoever. Then came excerpted comments previously published by *The New York Journal of Commerce*, and *The New York Sun*, and further testimonials and descriptions by a variety of miners. On the inside of the back cover was the memorial to Congress by Stephens, Chauncey, and Aspinwall, proposing a railroad clear to the West Coast and, finally, on the outer back cover was the reprint of a brief treatise from the *New York Herald* entitled *Practical Suggestions to Persons about to Cross the Isthmus of Panama*. Even while this instantly popular publication was making its debut, a follow-up volume, far more elaborate in scope, was being prepared for publication a few months hence.

The second book was scheduled to bear the rather ponderous and pretentious title of *The Pocket-guide to California; A Sea and Land Route-Book, Containing a Full Description of the El Dorado, its Agricultural Resources, Commercial Advantages, and Mineral Wealth; including a Chapter on Gold Formations; with the Congressional Map and the Various Routes and*

Distances to the Gold Regions. To Which is Added Practical Advice to Voyagers. This work, also written by J. Ely Sherwood, included an initial 19 pages of geographical commentary, followed by copies of letters from Captain Joseph Folsom to Quartermaster General Jesup in Washington, D.C., originally published in the *Washington Globe*. Thirty-one pages of assorted advertisements followed these texts, graphically revealing what was available to the traveler of this time, including not only characteristic necessities, but a variety of superfluous goods the emigrant could find useful, enjoyable, and interesting during and after such a gargantuan trip. It was strongly — and rather ominously — recommended that those planning to emigrate, either temporarily or permanently, to insure their lives before leaving and also have daguerreotypes taken to leave with family members or friends as a memory token, in the event the subject should, for whatever reason, never return.

Among the many interesting advertisements were those by E. N. Kent, who provided tests for gold; Alfred Wheeler who prepared passports (which he intimated, but did not directly declare, were necessary); Haven & Livingston, promoting their express service called Thomas Kensett & Co.; Wells, Miller & Provost for their preserved foodstuff provisions; the Union India Rubber Co. for portable boats, wagon-floating devices, clothing of all kinds, blankets and tents; prefabricated "California Houses," with three-days' notice to the manufacturer and promoted as "sheet-iron cottages of the most substantial character, built in sections"; oil-cloth roofings, guaranteed water-proof, at thirty cents per square yard; a number of different types of gold washing devices; a wide variety of footwear, matches, bags, mess hampers, drugs, guns and ammunition, and waterproof boots.

Massive undertaking though it was, the sea route, at least for the present, was the most favored for reaching the gold fields. It had been thoroughly tested through innumerable voyages of piracy and discovery, and more recently it had become the standard passage and principal commercial link to California for ships of the China trade, for vessels of the fur trade, for craft of the United States Navy, for whalers, and for the regular carriers of hides and tallow. The multitude of ship passages made through the Straits of Magellan had provided a body of nautical knowledge for the passage and its requirements, removing much of the perceived risk from it. In essence, of the several possible ways of reaching the gold fields, it was quite probably the most predictable, and the only one for which both the difficulties and conveniences could be reckoned most accurately in advance.

With the sea route, always open and thought by many to be much safer than overland travel, and with less preparation required for outfitting, demand for cruises to California by sea increased dramatically. Much of the maritime travel planning assistance was offered by A. Zuruatuza and his agents — A. Patrullo in New York City, and John Bell at Vera Cruz — plus at least two-score or more additional travel services available for all who would wish to take advantage of them on a cruise around the Horn, and up the western coast. What the travel agents avoided mentioning, if at all possible, was that the sea voyage from New York City, down the Atlantic, around the southern tip of South America, and up the West Coast all the way to San Francisco amounted to a minimum of 17,000 nautical miles — and often 18,000 or more, depending upon currents and storms — and required at least four months, and sometimes up to eight months, to complete: An insufferably long sea voyage for landlubbers, who made up the bulk of gold-seekers.

There were, simultaneously, those prepared to take the short-cuts westward across coastal Mexico, Nicaragua and Panama. The movement of ships toward California, begun in November, a mere trickle at this point, had nevertheless, following President Polk's speech, expanded to the dimensions of a full-blown rush by mid-December, despite the continuing scorn of some of the world's largest and most powerful newspapers, exemplified by the *New York Times*, which, in an attack on President Polk, editorialized:

> *But to one topic he returns again and again. The mines or rather the fields of gold and quicksilver in California. ... . Paragraph after paragraph glitters with gold and groans with bullion. The 4,000 gold hunters wild scraping the sands ... the greedy haste with which whole crews desert their ships for this Lotus shore; and all other circumstances of a real El Dorado are fully described with gloating ecstasy. A mint is forthwith to be established on this western coast, which is to deluge Asia and Polynesia with glittering tokens of the fortunate Republic. There was need of many mines to gild the Mexican War, and to pay its expenses. These acquisitions have cost the Union twenty-five millions [$680 million] of our money. If in the course of twenty years, the principal and interest be repaid by the dust collected from the rivers of*

California, the Union may deem itself most fortunate.

A second early book on travel from the East to the West Coast, this one anonymous, was published in Boston during the late autumn, under yet another prodigious title: *California Gold Regions, With a Full Account of its Mineral Resources; How to Get there and What to Take; the Expense, the Time, and the Various Routes, etc.* Unfortunately it said almost nothing not already discussed in Sherwood's book. Furthermore, not to be overlooked in among the accounts for the year 1848 was the 80-page production entitled *The Gold Regions of California, etc.*, edited by G. G. Foster, including a good map, published by Dewitt & Davenport of New York City. It was, by far, the fullest and most valuable account published in the East this year.

There was no doubt whatever that virtually tens of thousands of inhabitants of the eastern portion of the United States were intensely interested in the prospect of gold-seeking their way to wealth. As editor Horace Greeley of the *New York Tribune* proclaimed:

> *Bakers keep their ovens hot night and day, turning out immense quantities of ship-bread without supplying the demand; the provision stores of all kinds are besieged by orders. Manufacturers of rubber goods, rifles, pistols, bowie-knives, etc., can scarcely supply the demand. It is coming — nay, at hand, there is no doubt of it. We are on the brink of the Age of Gold! We look for an addition, within the next four years, equal to at least one thousand millions of dollars to the general aggregate of gold in circulation and use throughout the world. This is almost inevitable.*

Anything being produced that might, even in the most far-fetched of ways, be useful in the recovery of gold from the soil was sold in an unprecedented wave of buying by the public; labor-saving devices of every imaginable kind to separate gold from earth, whether verified in real-world use or not, could not be kept on the shelves. All manner of patented machines, pumps, cranks, engines, attachments for overshot water wheels, dredges designed to suck up and spit out the bottoms of creeks down to bare rocks were fast sellers, as was any other kind of machine or tool the general public could be made to think was a gold-finder, and at rapidly rising prices.

With the national election now settled and political turbulence subsiding, the economy throughout the Eastern States was shifted into a sharp upswing. Every manner of ship — schooners, brigs, steamships, clippers — was taken from dry-dock storage, refurbished and set afloat, and wharves from Virginia to Maine, were suddenly alive with activity; passenger lists were rapidly filled with hopefuls and already ships were embarking for the Golden Shore as rapidly as possible. Slickers, waterproof boots and rain hats were prime items at Salem; clothing prices in Baltimore soared in wild speculation on old stocks bound for the Pacific Coast; Philadelphia was shipping off almost unbelievable amounts of flour aboard cargo vessels; large numbers crowded aboard ships at Charleston, and a veritable flood of New Orleans citizens met in the staid St. Charles Hotel to organize a California expedition; a meeting of 100 Bostonians put up $500 each for a ship and cargo and were relying on their ability to sell their goods in San Francisco to reimburse them many times over for the costs of their passage. Posted sailing schedules announced, for the month of February alone, 11 ships embarking from New Bedford, 70 each from Boston and Philadelphia, and 60 from New York City. As one anonymous New Yorker commented on matters in a late December editorial:

> *Any person strolling along our docks cannot help being struck with the quantity of specific and general merchandise of all kinds, which is marked for shipping to the new El Dorado. ... Nearly a million dollars [$28,800,000] worth of supplies have been shipped from this port alone, of which not less than $400,000 [$11,520,000] have been sent within the last thirty days.*

In a great many of the Eastern newspapers, letters from the mines were reprinted, in which so many miners told how very easy it was to find gold in California, and these letters alone encouraged many to simply "drop everything and go!" As the *Hartford Daily Courant* reported :

> *The California gold fever is approaching its crisis. ... By a sudden and accidental discovery, the ground is represented to be one vast gold mine. Gold is picked up in pure lumps, twenty-four carats fine. Soldiers are deserting their ranks, sailors their ships, and everybody their employment, to speed*

to the region of the gold mines.

With such incredible wealth in gold so readily found in California, and kept so very casually in a variety of jars, cans, pouches and pokes, often lying in open sight on blankets or in tents at the various campsites, it would seem that theft would be a great problem at the mining camps, yet, the phenomenon which had previously stirred such wonder continued to do so: Such crimes still occurred only rarely. Theft during this first year following the discovery of gold was almost totally absent. Fully two months ago, on October 24th, even Gov. Mason had written to Lansford Hastings:

> *Although some murders have been committed and horses stolen in the placer, I do not find that things are worse here, if indeed they are so bad, as they were in our own mineral regions some years ago, when I was stationed near them. On the other hand, I find complaints of outrages committed by disbanded volunteers at Monterey; of robbery and horse-thieving around the bay missions, by a gang from the Tulare Valley, said to be composed chiefly of deserters. Even Dr. Marsh's residence on the Pulpunes rancho being plundered.*

The earlier remarkable absence of racial discrimination in the mining areas, however, was evolving. So long as the white Americans were able to predominate in the very productive mining areas, they could afford to be generous. If, however, the Chileans or Chinese, Mexicans, Peruvians, and other racial groups congregated and dominated in a particular area, especially areas in which the deposits turned out to be very good, the Americans set up a howl that "foreigners" were taking over and should be heavily taxed. In many cases, such a tax became more a penalty than anything else: A penalty so harsh that it usually drove the foreign groups out, sometimes peacefully, but often accompanied by acts of brutality, including even murder.

English-speaking foreigners, such as the English, Irish and Australians, were accepted without much contention, and despite the language barrier, so, too, were Germans and Scandinavians. On the other hand, Spanish-speaking groups, Italians, French, Portuguese and Orientals were all too often given short shrift, and if they objected, violence could — and very often did — erupt. Much, of course, depended upon the individual miners themselves and their own inherent prejudices. In general there was an intuitive democratic willingness to accept individuals on the basis of their abilities and performance, as opposed to their race, religion or skin color. Such attitudes, however, were usually dependent upon the outlook of the individual American; and American perceptions of foreign outlandish cultural customs and practices could fluctuate from amusement to indifference, or to condescension or to visceral discrimination, including violence and cruelty.

The old-line Californios, having had years of experience with the Americans, probably fared best, and large numbers of them, after the first season of mining, were quite content to return to their farms and ranchos a considerable distance away from the gold belt and settle down, usually to agricultural pursuits. Frenchmen, on the other hand, tended to be very clannish, and Americans considered them too impractical, and too foppish to be ideally suited to the mining life. They referred to the Frenchmen as *Kesky-dees*, a term derived from the oft repeated French question, *Qu'est que se dit*?

While Americans respected Mexicans and Chileans because of their expertise in mining, it was a cool respect grudgingly given, often amounting to mere toleration. The Chileans, indeed, were so low on the social-class totem pole that when the well-known Pérez Rosales was mistakenly believed to be a Frenchman, he thought it wise not to let it be known that he was actually Chilean.

Probably no other race, however, suffered as much discrimination — or deserved less of it — than the Chinese, whom the other miners, especially the Americans, had difficulty accepting even as human beings. A large intensely bigoted California group calling itself The Hounds, harassed the Chinese even more than they did the Mexicans. The Orientals were called Celestials by all the other ethnic groups at the diggings, and the first of them to show up to engage in mining were regarded more with tolerant curiosity than anything else. Merchant Franklin Buck's reaction to them was favorable; he considered them good customers. He even engaged one to paint for him a sign in Chinese characters that he could hang out as an invitation for their trade. But as more and more of their Oriental compatriots came flooding into California until they ultimately constituted twenty percent of all the miners, they became victims of hostile resentment and often violent discrimination. Worse yet, they became the primary target of the Foreign Miners Tax, and even when the individual Chinese miner was able to pay such a tax, the Caucasian miners made sure that they opened no new claims, and only worked the left-over tailings the whites had discarded. The Agua Fria Mining District in the Mariposa area banned them entirely from mining there. As a result of this widespread bigoted intimidation, the Chinese who came to America to discover gold, did, indeed, find it, but in primarily in restaurants and laundry services, rather than in the mines.

Back across the country, in the wake of the widespread feverish excitement ignited by President Polk's late-December address to Congress, large groups of men immediately gathered together and began serious preparations to head for the mines as soon as the weather permitted. One of myriad such groups was a Massachusetts outfit with the top-heavy title of *The Boston and California Joint Stock Mining and Trading Company*, which had begun organizing in mid-December, and now at year's end had enlisted its agreed-upon membership goal of 150 men. The company had recruited its membership through the distribution of a twelve-page prospectus, produced by The Joint Stock Mutual Insurance Merchandizing [sic] Company. It was entitled *To Emigrants to the Gold Region: A Treatise, Showing the Best Way to California*, and was written by Sidney Roberts of New Haven, Connecticut, who had infused the document with the fervor of a religious tract. He raised serious objections to anyone going by sea, either around South America or through the Gulf of Mexico, and across the Isthmus of Panama and recommended, instead, going overland, cross-country, along the trail established by the Mormons. He gave nine reasons for doing so:

> *(1) oxen, horses, and wagons are available; (2) the climate is quite salubrious; (3) the Mormons have made a road and offer facilities for recruiting; (4) the Mormons are hospitable; (5) companies of Mormon travelers will assist in curbing Indian dangers; (6) a stop-over is quite feasible at Salt Lake [City]; (7) wagons and animals will be useful in all the diggings; (8) since California is notably highly productive, emigrants should take seeds; and (9) the eight preceding arguments are facts.*

Included in the *Joint Stock's* roll of members for the trip were eight whaling captains, two clergymen, four doctors and seventeen other professional men, seventy-six mechanics, and forty-three businessmen and farmers. The ship's crew added another twenty men, half of whom were former mates aboard sailing vessels. This company adopted a constitution and by-laws formulated to govern the group during its voyage, and afterward, during its mining and trading in California. Fines were to be imposed for gambling and swearing, and all declared themselves to be opposed to drinking, and to unnecessary work on Sundays. By popular vote, Henry Smith was elected president and captain. The group pooled its funds, bought outright the ship *Edward Everett,* and immediately set about stocking her with provisions for two years. They also loaded her with a carefully selected cargo of wheelbarrows, shovels, picks, wagons, building bricks, a steamboat, four steam engines and two quite large prefabricated houses, plus a pair of mounted cannon with which, if necessary, to repel pirates.

On the Sunday preceding departure, Harvard's President and the ship's namesake, Edward Everett, arrived with a present of a large number of books. The fully assembled company was then addressed by the father of two of its members. He distributed a Bible to each man and declared, "Take the Holy Word in one hand and your New England civilization in the other, and implant your principles on California soil."

There was keen community interest in this ambitious venture; its members included many of New England's finest young men who were poised to embark, filled with an almost exalted purpose, as one observer noted, "a missionary zeal that only the proper Bostonians could have thought to associate with a business so sordid as gold grubbing."

Far across the continent in California, the weather had suddenly become grim as the year drew to a close. Extraordinarily heavy rains began to fall in the Sierras, which quickly turned to snow, covering even the western foothills with three inches of white crystals, and dropping the temperature, as far west as San Francisco, to a penetrating and uncomfortable 37 degrees Fahrenheit. Drifting snow closed all mountain passes with the single exception of the Santa Fe Trail, which was farthest south. Even the coastal areas could not escape the wrath of uncommonly fierce winds and gigantic waves. In the Eastern United States, however, gold mania continued to spread among prospective miners eager to depart as soon as travel conditions made it possible, and this frenzied excitement had now begun stirring on a world-wide basis.

It was very clear to one and all that as soon as the weather permitted in 1849, California would most definitely become the target destination of a gold rush unprecedented in the world's history.

Chapter 5

[January 1st, 1849 • Monday]

In every major seaport of North America's East Coast, as well as in many of the interior cities, large groups of adventurers were forming, gathering the materials they would find necessary for the major undertaking ahead and booking passage, wherever available, to the now fabled western port of San Francisco. A great many were still torn by the decision that had to be made, whether to go by sea or, if space was not available in a ship, then by land, with all the evident hardships that would be entailed.

Among this latter group, amassing in the nation's capital, was a young writer who was determined to explore and experience exhaustively the current cultural hysteria in California in order to write the most accurate, literate, and definitive possible account of the gold rush. His name was J. Goldsborough Bruff, and he was quite prepared, at least mentally, for whatever lay ahead. In his bags were a dozen or more pads of paper, along with plenty of quills for pens and numerous bottles of imperishable India ink, all of which would be necessary for the detailed accounts he intended to write.

Since the weather clearly dictated that a departure time for any trek westward was still months away, Bruff and the others who had gathered in Washington were gradually forming themselves into companies and accumulating the varied gear vitally necessary in order to undertake such a significant journey. Some companies were adopting virtually a constitution to govern themselves, electing officers, meeting to discuss the problems that would surely face them on their prospective expeditions, and some were even adopting uniforms of sorts that would identify them as belonging to their specific companies.

While Bruff did not care to become quite that regimented, he was indeed aware that solid planning was an absolute requisite. He had already consulted the literature available, the sparse and varied books and reports already published by such men as Frémont, Palmer, Bryant, and Hastings, and, from what sparse governmental records were available, he had already traced maps he hoped would become very useful. The greatest problem seemed to be that virtually no individual among the gathering throngs of would-be travelers had any conception whatever of what such a journey would entail, or of the multitude of hazards that lay ahead.

Undoubtedly, everyone would find out soon enough what those grimly arduous hazards would be — many to their profound regret.

[March 5th, 1849 • Monday]

With James Knox Polk out of office as President and former General Zachary Taylor now the twelfth and newest President of the United States, the nation's capital was abuzz with the current significant developments. Foremost among these was the creation today, by an act of Congress, of the United States Department of the Interior, with the former Secretary of the Treasury, Thomas Ewing, as its director.

The Department was created as a sort of general *housekeeper* for the government and scheduled to become custodian of the nation's natural resources. Already two other important offices had been transferred into its realm: The U.S. Patent Office, which since its creation in 1790 had been an adjunct of the State Department, and the Bureau of Indian Affairs, which since its creation in 1834 had been a part of the War Department.

The new governmental office was already abuzz with life and plans.

[April 5, 1849 • Thursday]

Over the past year Samuel Brannan had become, several times over, the richest man in California, and he had done so without once wading in an icy cold stream or swinging a pick to accumulate the gold that now so abundantly filled his coffers.

Today, as he had been expecting since last summer when the California Saints had finally rebelled against his regular tithing collections, a letter had come from Brigham Young. Brannan had known with certainty that the wrath of the foremost figure in the Church of Jesus Christ of Latter-day Saints would be great, but that prospect no longer filled the dapper San Franciscan with fear. Brigham Young, as was all too well known, had a harsh temper, and this aspect of his personality was clearly recognized as having become even worse since he had led his flock on their perilous migration from Nauvoo in Illinois to the place where he had now established Salt Lake City.

Evidence of Young's anger was clearly manifest last fall when he loudly castigated various officers of the church for having engaged in a counterfeiting scheme that had widespread ramifications and that had even prompted charges that he, himself, had headed the counterfeiting operation. If these accusations were true, then Young had since covered his own tracks well; hard as the government agents had tried, they could prove nothing against him. Young and the Mormon Quorum of Twelve Apostles had, in fact, made their own positions all the more impervious by excommunicating several of their fellow church officials who had been proven to be clearly guilty.

Additional evidence of Brigham Young's fiery temper had come last fall and winter as groups of Saints from the disbanded Mormon Battalion had finally straggled in to the new Zion near the southeast shore of the Great Salt Lake to resume their places in Mormon society. Within mere weeks of their return, Young, highly indignant over their more worldly behavior, had thundered with great epithets and threats against them and once again brandished that powerful cudgel he always had close at hand, the dire promise of excommunication if they did not immediately change their ways.

"The Battalion Boys, since returning from the Army," he roared to the assembled congregation of his followers, "have become idle, lazy and indolent and, with very few exceptions, are dissipated, indulging in vice and wickedness without restraint. With an openness that has taken on the proportion of mockery of our high standards, they have corrupted the morals of young females in our flock and are undermining the very precepts of our faith!"

A few more excommunications had occurred then, more than enough to snap former Battalion members back to "the straight and narrow path of righteousness" from their former army life, located "much too close to the edge of perdition."

At one time such ire from their leader would have filled Sam Brannan with the same overwhelming fear as had affected those brother Saints who had repented of their ways and returned to the embrace of their faith and its leaders — but not so any longer. Having far more than merely tasted the rewards of dishonesty and obsessive materialism, Brannan had long since quietly ceased to take religion seriously, and he had been shrewd enough to cover his own transgressions so well that he was virtually impervious to any accusations backed by evidence that would hold up in court. This very fact had indeed been proven only recently when, as his personal wealth and property holdings had expanded enormously, his former California Saints actually sued him in an effort to have the court force him to distribute his prodigious wealth among them, according to the precepts of the Church. It hadn't worked; Brannan had not only denied all their allegations; he presented to the court the document they had signed, but which he very carefully had not, which bound them to give to the Church a full tithe of all their earnings.

"Since I am the official head representative of the Church in California," he explained glibly to the court, "such wealth and holdings and tithing were, by our own concordances, to come to me. My responsibility is only to the Church itself."

Brannan had obviously taken Young's example of self-protection quite to heart and had left no room for himself to be cornered.

The California court in San Francisco found itself with no choice but to rule in his favor, and since then, Brannan's entrepreneurism had continued to expand so rapidly that he now wielded great power and was held, especially by non-Momons, in enviable esteem throughout the entire Territory. His compulsive tendency to flagrantly flaunt his great wealth, indeed, made him exceptionally popular, especially to those currying his favor. As much as his investments had met with success in the past, they had become even more widespread and remunerative since the trial. There were those who claimed, "Sam Brannan's got his finger in every pie in the Territory," and there were none who could dispute it.

In addition to all the other multitude of properties he owned, Brannan had cleverly convinced young Augustus Sutter to deed over to him, free of charge, two hundred lots in the newly laid out Sacramento town limits under the implied threat that if he did not do so, Brannan would move his business enterprises out of the community to a different location. Since it was Brannan's stores and various other businesses of his at Sutter's Fort that were the drawing cards for so many of the gold-seekers converging in the area, young Sutter readily relinquished the lots to Brannan, and the powerful recipient's enterprises there and elsewhere continued to expand. He had just now completed another well-built and fully stocked frame store at the corner of J and Front Streets in Sacramento which, even before completion, was doing an enormous amount of business; the entrepreneur was, moreover, selling off, at high prices, many of the town lots that had been given to him.

Sacramento was still largely a tent community, and while the *Brannan Emporium* was not the first permanent structure within the town limits, as many thought it to be — the tiny log houses of settlers Edgar Gillespie and Charles V. Carpenter held that honor — it was by far the most prominent. In addition, Brannan quickly had another shop erected — a single story, sturdy adobe building some fifty yards east of the fort. Before winter's end, because he owned so much property in Sacramento, San Francisco, San José, and Monterey, some of the remaining loyal Saints in California had become even more deeply angered and resentful over the fact that he showed no inclination whatever to share his wealth with them in accordance with their original understanding. They were, however, in the minority, since others of the Saints were also prospering, even though not so grandly as Brannan himself. Great opportunities, coupled with obsessive greed, were now clearly apparent in the *Brannan & Company* empire.

The New Hope community of pioneer Saints had little choice at this point but to abandon their grandiosely founded project and to acquire farms of their own or else move back to San Francisco. It came as no surprise when all of New Hope's numerous improvements, including even the farm originally reserved for the Quorum of Twelve Apostles, were quickly appropriated by none other than Sam Brannan.

So today had come the long-anticipated letter from Brigham Young, which Brannan slit open neatly with his ornate letter-opener and read with something akin to amusement. It was, as Brannan had known it simply had to be, a special order for him to turn over to the Quorum of Twelve the tithing "unrighteously withheld from the Church." The letter continued, with an aura of frustrated, threatening anger that could not be veiled:

> *If you will deal justly with your fellows and deal out with liberal heart and open hands, making a righteous use of all your money, the Lord is willing you should accumulate the rich treasures of the earth and the good things of time in*

> *abundance; but should you withhold when the Lord says give, your hope and pleasing prospects will be blasted in an hour you think not of, and no arm can save. ...*

Still smiling faintly and vaguely wishing he also had the copy of this letter that he knew Brigham Young would have on file at Salt Lake City, Brannan carefully refolded it, replaced it inside its envelope, and then leaned forward and consigned it to the glowing embers in his fireplace.

[April 9th, 1849 • Monday]

Alonzo Delano had finally reached St. Louis, and he marveled at what a large and bustling city it was, far beyond whatever expectations he may have previously harbored. Its relative nearness to his native home in Ottawa, Illinois, only emphasized how little he had traveled in his thirty-two years and how bound he had become to the strictures of what had been his own small society. Now, having embarked on what was to him a gigantic enterprise, he was impressed by the scenes he was now witnessing.

St. Louis was by no means the largest city he had ever seen, since he had visited Chicago on several occasions, which was less than one hundred miles distant from Ottawa, but St. Louis was upwards of two hundred miles from home, and he'd never before had the opportunity to see it.

In the midst of his preparations to go west, Delano had received word that a group of men, calling themselves *The California Company* was forming at the little town of Dayton, only two miles northeast of Ottawa, and on that very day, December 14th, he had ridden there to learn more details. Several dozen men were already on hand in a vacant lot on the town's center square on the west bank of the Fox River, and Delano was immediately introduced to the small party's recently-elected commander, a burly, competent-appearing, 60-year-old man named Jesse Greene, who had been given the title of "Captain."

"We welcome any good men of responsible character and means," Captain Greene told Delano, "And since you are a businessman of obvious stability and substance, you are an excellent candidate." His voice took on a note of authority as he continued. "As with everyone else in our party, you will be expected to abide by the rules we have set up for the company and the party's captain — that's me, as you already know —

will choose the route we are to travel and will be the final authority in all matters of dispute. You will be responsible for your own wagon or wagons, your own weapons, goods, horses and livestock, if any, as well as anyone you bring along in your employ. And, of course, you will need suitable funds to provide for you and your party throughout the long trip with any special needs or transportation, and later you will need sufficient funds to establish yourself after our arrival at our destination in California."

"We plan to rendezvous," Greene continued, "to collect the final contingent of our party, at the city of Peru, which, as I'm sure you're aware, is sixteen miles west of Ottawa. That will bring our company's strength to about sixty men. We will probably, at that point, give the Company its final name, which, so far as I can see, since the name Peru is already taken, we may as well call ourselves *The Ottawa Company*. There we will board a steamer that will take us down the Illinois River to its mouth and then down the Mississippi a relatively short distance to St. Louis, where you will have an opportunity to buy whatever final items you may need for the journey. Agreed?"

"Agreed," Delano echoed, pleased the Company would hereafter be known by his own town's name. "When will *The Ottawa Company* leave?"

"You'll have plenty of time to prepare. Reservations have already been made. On April 6th we'll board the steamer at Peru and start downstream from there to St. Louis. We will board a different steamer there, and go upstream on the Missouri to the final western rendezvous point, which is at St. Joseph, on the northwestern edge of Missouri. Beyond that is Indian Country. From St. Joseph our final very long journey across plains, deserts and mountains begins, and I expect, barring misfortune, we will arrive at the gold region center in the California Territory — a place, I'm told, called Sutter's Fort — sometime in late August. I guarantee you, sir, it will be as rugged a journey as you, or any of us, for that matter, has ever undertaken."

"Understood," Delano said. "With other members of *The Ottawa Company*, I will meet the remainder of our Company at Peru on April 6, fully prepared, I trust, for any difficulty or emergency we might encounter."

The following weeks had been filled with Delano's preparation efforts. He purchased the cattle he intended to drive along with them, and he hired a small group of experienced men to herd them westward to St, Joseph, where they were to hold them in readiness for his arrival. His horses and wagon he would ship ahead to the same rendezvous via steamship. In addition, he recruited a couple of strong and adventurous young men of Ottawa who were burning to go hunt gold in California, to accompany him and assist him on the long journey. He would, he told them, take them into *The Ottawa Company*, pay their expenses, and provide them with horses for the long trip, with the understanding they were to repay him for their share of the supplies and expenses by agreeing to give him one-half of whatever profit from gold they would acquire during their first year at the mines. This was a relatively familiar contract these days, one to which the pair — Eben Smith, and Matthew Harris — eagerly agreed on their word. Before it was time for them to leave, a third Ottawan of Delano's acquaintance joined them under the same conditions, a happy-go-lucky 33-year-old man named Isaac "Fred" H. Fredenburg.

Finally, Delano was delighted to discover that he was not the only resident of Ottawa who had risen to the bait of the company's proposed adventure westward. A long-time family friend, four years his junior, 28-year-old Dr. M. B. Angle, had become a member of the party and would, Delano hoped, provide enjoyable company during the long journey.

Delano made it a point to meet with the Osman brothers, Moses and William, who were publishers of the local weekly newspaper, the *Ottawa Free Trader*, and who, when he suggested it, readily agreed to pay him in the form of one or more mail subscriptions to the newspaper in exchange for his writing a regular *California Correspondence*, both while en route to California and continuing after his arrival there, to be published in the paper under a title of his choice. Pleased, he told them the column would be called *Chips from the Old Block*. As important and relevant as he intended for this newspaper column to be, it was in his own private *Journal* that Delano fully intended to maintain an exhaustively comprehensive and accurate accounting of whatever lay ahead on the great adventure upon which he was embarking.

Shortly after dawn on a Thursday morning, April 5th, Delano bade goodbye to Mary and the children, all of them tearful and all wondering if they would ever see him again. He tried to present a cheery, confident demeanor, but silent tears flowed down Mary's cheeks, and little Harriet was sobbing audibly. Both Delano and his son, Fred, tried their best to maintain composure, but it was too much. When the porter pulled away with his employer beside him on the wagon seat, and the four hired hands seated together in the lightly loaded leading wagon bed, neither father nor son saw very much, their vision hampered by eyes swimming in tears.

Delano's traveling party reached the little city of Peru late in the afternoon and carefully pulled the wagons aboard the steamer *Revolution,* amid cattle horses and cows penned on the broad deck. Delano's porter was instructed to make his way back home afoot, and early the next morning the day's transit to St. Louis began. As Delano recorded it:

> *The day I left Ottawa was beautiful overhead, but the soft soil of our beautiful prairies, hub-deep to the wagon, together with the pleasing antics of a baulky [sic] horse and the frequent opportunity of having my boots blackened with some of Nature's best — no thanks to the porter — as we lightened our load by jumping out into the deep, deep mud, proved well that all was not gold that glittered. At evening, under command of Capt. Jesse Greene, we went on board the good steamer Revolution and the next morning left Peru on our golden voyage. We take considerable pride in being called The Ottawa Company.*
>
> *"Hung were the heavens in black," and ere long a revolution took place overhead. I have not the least doubt that the deluge was occasioned by the windows of heaven being opened. It appeared to me that the flood gates were open now, for it literally poured; and I should think that twenty days of such rain would be sufficient to drown all the rats — two-legged as well as four — in Ottawa. We had an agreeable company on board, however, a good captain and crew, and as it rained or poured only two days and nights of the four we were going down the river, I can't complain. I do not intend to give you a sketch of the scenery along the Illinois River, as it is too familiar to the most of your readers; but I was utterly astonished at the vast multitude and height of the Indian mounds from Beardstown quite to the mouth. I had often read of them but had never formed an adequate idea of their number. Every prominent bluff seemed covered and attest that a dense population of a race, now unknown, once covered this beautiful region, and whose history is written*

in these hillocks that crown the summits of the bluffs or are scattered over our rich prairies. ...

The remainder of *The Ottawa Company's* journey to St. Louis aboard the *Revolution* was without incident, as was their arrival at the big river town. Warned that this was the last place where supplies could be purchased relatively cheaply, it became a busy time as Delano tried to stock up carefully on whatever he imagined might be needed. As Delano recorded the events in his *Journal*:

Monday morning [April 9th] dawned upon St. Louis with a washing-day face, and we poor miserable bipeds, as usual, had to "stand from under" or take a ducking. The day was quite a busy one, however, for, as an excellent boat was advertised to leave for St. Joseph this evening, I was anxious to complete my outfit and ship my wagon on board of her. I therefore adopted the Sucker mode of tucking the ends of my nether garments into my boots, took an umbrella and, in company with Mr. Fredenburg and some others of our Ottawa friends, set out in search of rations. These we found advanced in price in consequence of so many calls for California; but by the hour of starting we were told that in consequence of the rain, the Embassy could not complete her lading until the following day.

There were large numbers of emigrants in the city, but not as many as I expected to find from previous accounts. Some of the boats went out with large loads, while others had more moderate ones; but there is no doubt but many thousands will attempt to cross the plains. I met acquaintance at every turn.

At St. Louis Delano and his companions were preyed upon by hucksters making false allegations as to the futility of their efforts to outfit themselves from shops in the city. One shop-keeper put it into words for them with seeming great earnestness.

"There's so many emigrants," he said, "that supplies enough just can't be obtained, scarcely at any price. Folks up the river — the Missouri, not the Mississippi — they're sending down the river to us for provisions. Why, board alone is seven bucks a week at the hotels."

Such comments made Delano and his friends very nervous about progressing any farther without getting whatever was available of what they needed, regardless of price. That, of course, was precisely what the merchants had in mind, knowing full well that prices for everything at those far western Missouri outposts were considerably less what they, themselves, were charging here at St. Louis. In the end, Delano and his friends stocked up on everything at St. Louis, which sorely depleted their funds. When they left in the morning for the long pull up the Missouri River aboard the side-wheeler *Embassy*, they were joined by a still another Ottawa native. As Delano wrote of him in his *Journal*:

> *We were joined in our trip up the river by a young man named Robert Brown, who was looking out for some opportunity of going to California, and who was proceeding to St. Joseph for this purpose.*
>
> *There was a great crowd of adventurers aboard the Embassy. Nearly every State in the Union was represented. Every berth was full and not only every settee and table occupied at night but the cabin floor was covered by the sleeping emigrants. The decks were covered with wagons, mules, oxen, and mining implements and the hold was filled with supplies. But this was the condition of every boat — for since the invasion of Rome by the Goths, such a deluge of mortals had not been witnessed, as was now pouring from the States to the various points of departure for the golden shores of California. We of The Ottawa Company are only one company of a great many embarking on this unparalleled adventure.*
>
> *Visions of sudden and immense wealth danced in the imaginations of these anxious seekers of fortunes, and I must confess that I was not entirely free from such dreams, and like our very sage statesmen, cogitating upon the condition of the National Treasury, with the extinguishment of the National Debt, I wondered what I should do with all the money which must necessarily come into my pocket!*
>
> *Our first day out was spent in these pleasing reflections, and the song and the jest went round with glee — [the following added later, marginally:]. ... while the toil, the dangers, and the hardships, which surely must come, were not thought of, for they were not yet understood.*

[April 12th, 1849 • Thursday]

The rapidity with which San Francisco was growing was stunning, and with the arrival of more ships bearing gold-seekers, the town was uncomfortably crowded and very busy. Construction was evident everywhere, with new houses, businesses and hotels rising every day, and property values — inevitably — increasing incrementally everywhere. Nor were the changes limited to San Francisco alone; the entire Territory was changing.

A major governmental change had evolved during the past seven weeks: Brigadier General Persifer F. Smith arrived, bearing the War Department's orders to replace Richard Mason in his command of the military in this territory. Smith had arrived aboard the steamship *California* on February 28th, the same ship that had disgorged into San Francisco the first wave of "outside" gold-seekers. Mason, who had been governor-general ever since the departure of General Kearny in early summer of 1847, was abruptly being recalled to Washington as soon as his gubernatorial replacement arrived shortly thereafter. Today, only seven weeks after Smith's arrival, the U.S. transport ship *Iowa* arrived, bearing Brigadier General Bennett Riley, who was Mason's successor in the Territory's top civil position.

For the first time since the discovery of gold there was now solid evidence that San Francisco was not merely going to survive; it was clearly destined to become one of California's major cities. Throughout last summer when the town's population had all but abandoned it to go to the gold mining areas, San Francisco seemed doomed to simply fade away. With the arrival of the rainy season in mid-October, however, the gold-seekers had returned in force, and in the interval since then the town had sprung back with a new vibrancy and gaudiness that made it clear this bayside community was going to become a vitally important center of commerce. As one of its prominent residents, Bayard Taylor wrote:

> *The very air is pregnant with the magnetism of bold, spirited, unwearied action, and he who but ventures into the outer circle of the whirlpool is spinning, ere he has time for thought, in its dizzy vortex.*

Scores of new house been erected throughout the winter months, and perhaps more important, the town had become the gambling, drinking, and entertainment center of the entire West Coast. At the new hotels — the Parker House and the El Dorado, for example — women were singing or dealing cards, bands were playing raucous music, and gold nuggets, now the principal medium of exchange, were piled high on the bars and gaming tables. The air, night and day, was filled with the continual rumble of voices, blaring music, hoarse yells from the gambling tables, and shrill laughter. Above all came the incessant sounds of hammering and sawing as the community stretched and grew with phenomenal speed. A community whose human numbers had only recently tumbled to a few hundred had sprung back with a far more vibrant population than ever before, numbering now in the thousands and still continuing steadily, day by day, to grow.

The returned miners were hungry for more than just good food. They wanted places where they could relax, where they could spend with abandon the gold they had acquired through weeks and months of panning and digging and separating. They wanted to shed their dirtied, muddy digging garb and to don fresh new corduroy trousers and new shoes or quality boots, fine flannel shirts, gaudy sashes and sombreros. They wanted to *spend* what they had earned, and an amazing upsurge in trades people were more than eager to help them toward achieving such aims. Even more importantly, the more thoughtful among them wanted good new houses and well-supplied markets, stores, and banks, and they had virtually no concern about the cost. As a result, the town proceeded to grow with greater speed and complexity and appeal than anyone had imagined possible.

During this period many of San Francisco's citizens attested to sensing personally an unprecedented atmosphere of comradeship and freedom. Daguerreotype shops, of which there were already several, were doing a booming business of preserving images of young gentlemen wearing flamboyant clothes and carefree grins. Most of the men were armed with holstered pistols, yet sounds of gunshots were rare, and when they did occur, usually denoted exuberance and celebration rather than anger. If and when quarrels did erupt, they were settled far more often with diplomacy and carefully considered words rather than by acts of bravado and anger. As a recent newcomer, J. D. B. Stillman, wrote of it in his *diary*:

There is more intelligence and generous good feeling than in any country I ever saw. Men are valued for what they are.

The town's rapidly increasing population of citizens, miners and newcomers over the winter months became most apparent on Sundays when the main streets in San Francisco thronged with men who had gathered for rest, relaxation and marketing. The ringing of church bells was significantly absent, and from the first light of dawn until well into the night, every saloon was packed with miners more than eager to gamble the gold they brought with them in their pokes. The more the miners drank, the more tipsy they became, and the more they bet in the card games. There was a sobering sense of loneliness among the majority of them, and they were quite willing to share their gold for the purchase of round after round of purchased drinks for newfound *friends,* who were always quite willing to hang around and share the good fortune until the gold was gone.

Most evident in the saloons, apart from the bartenders themselves, were the professional gamblers in their immaculate shirts and suits, with their easy, friendly and sober manner — since rarely did they themselves drink — encouraging the miners to bet ever more heavily, which they did, although they seldom prevailed against such professionals. Even when these men lost considerable sums of money, however, they were rarely overwhelmed with remorse., "Oh, well, there's always more where that came from," they stoically reasoned, and there nearly always was.

Nearly always, too, a bully was on hand who boasted loudly of his ability as a lifter of scalps, as a duelist if it became necessary, and as a pummeler of those weaker than himself; such men always seemed to be itching for a confrontation of some kind, until their days were finally neatly ended with a bullet hole in the middle of their foreheads or chests, and they were mourned by no one. The effeminate dandy, too, was usually on hand here or there, along with rollicking sailors, usually in small groups. The miners, however, were virtually ubiquitous in San Francisco, usually appearing with slouch hats and grubby clothing, wearing a happy grins as they treated their "friends" to whatever they wished to drink. And here and there on Sundays, preachers, too, were often proclaiming loud and long from beneath a shady tree or on a street corner about the sins sired by "the root of all evil"; they, too had come to partake, just a little, in what that gold could buy.

As bawdy and rough as the town had become, in many respects, it had also acquired a dignity, a palpable sense of permanence and pride as well as a strong but indefinable aura of creativity focused primarily upon the town's potential future. As if to keep pace with the changes that were so swiftly occurring, the *Star and Californian* newspaper enlarged both its physical size and circulation and then, with its edition of Thursday, January 4th, changed its name to the *Alta California,* therewith becoming San Francisco's — and California's — first daily newspaper. Less than a week later, the town's first bank — called The Exchange and Deposit Office — was founded by businessmen Richard H. Sinton and Henry M. Naglee; it was erected in the center of town on Kearny Street facing onto Portsmouth Plaza. Sinton, who had been paymaster aboard the U.S. Ohio, was one of the many who had come to San Francisco with Commodore Thomas Jones.

Just as so many good things were occurring in the new town, so too there were occasional disasters: On January 11th, for example, the town suffered its first major blaze as the Shades Hotel caught fire and burned to the ground. The flames then spread rapidly to flimsy nearby structures. Fortunately there was no loss of life, yet the conflagration was intense enough to cause an estimated at $5 million [$136 million] in damages. The serious blaze, however, did prompt a drive to establish a municipal fire department to combat any similar future disasters.

On the day immediately following the fire, a group of concerned citizens met at the Plaza and formed what they called the Legislative Assembly of the District of San Francisco, consisting of fifteen elected members. Such aggressive civic action prompted newspaper editor Robert Semple to editorialize on the following day, February 13th:

> *We have alcaldes all over the country, assuming the power of legislatures, issuing and promoting their bandos, laws and orders, and oppressing the people. The most nefarious scheming trickery and speculating have been practiced by some. Why should we endure this inefficient military rule? We need more laws of our own!*

Three thousand miles away, in Washington D.C., moreover, changes were occurring which would significantly affect San Francisco's development. On January 22nd, President Polk had appointed John White Geary as Postmaster, with the power — and explicit directions — to expand postal service to encompass the entire Territory. Less than a fortnight later, on February 2nd, the brig *Eagle* arrived from Hong Kong, bringing with it as passengers, Charles V. Gillespies, along with three Chinese citizens, two men and a woman, all determined to find gold. They brought California's total Chinese population at this point to a mere seven individuals.

By far the greater majority of miners who flocked to San Francisco, San José, or Monterey during the rainy season quickly became bored and yearned for the excitement of opening a new placer and reaping whatever treasures it might hold, riches which, in most cases, were never quite enough. Most of these men had no training whatever in geology, and the greater majority firmly believed that the gold in the streams and arroyos and gulches had been washed down from some as yet undiscovered source in the mountains, where the gold lay in solid beds, ready for the taking for men bold enough or farsighted enough to seek it out.

Large numbers of the miners staked their futures on such wild dreams and became dissatisfied with what they were finding, regardless of the amount, as they persistently envisioned bigger and better bonanzas somewhere ahead. *Someone,* they had no doubt, was going to find it, but they feared they would not be participants in this mind-boggling find. Thanks to this widespread, obsessive search for the elusive mother-lode, new ordinary deposits were discovered with amazing frequency, and the great California gold field expanded so much farther than anyone had ever dreamed. As rich as such digging might be, the obsessed miners were always ready to pull stakes and head for another reported find, one that might be that great mother-lode bonanza; and in their crazed, illusory wake came others, seemingly without end.

Overwhelmed by such reasoning, miners frequently abandoned claims that had been paying them $50 to $200 [$1,440 to $5,760] daily in order to rush off to fresh diggings that might be better, but all too often profoundly disappointed them and in many cases, turned out to be utterly worthless. Then, when the miner returned to his abandoned claim, he most often found it taken over by another miner, and thus he would be compelled, by absolute necessity, to continue his search for greener — or more golden — pastures.

"I've come here," was the usual commentary, "to find gold —

now, not next year, an' by God, not by the thimbleful, either! I aim t' find it by the bushel!"

With such an attitude, collecting $200 [$5,760] worth of gold a day, meant it would take ten days to secure $2,000 [$57,600], a hundred days to bring out $20,000 [$576,000] worth, and a *thousand* days to make $200,000 [$5.76 million] worth — and what he wanted was to make his $1 million [$28.8 *million*] *a whole lot faster* than that — in ten days or a couple of weeks or maybe even a month, but surely no longer than that! Incredibly, many believed precisely that, and most of those who did were destined to join the throng of haunted-eyed wanderers who, somehow, never quite found that gargantuan, incredibly illusive bonanza.

While many citizen-miners appreciated a momentary reprieve from the labors of mining, they were soon overwhelmed by a growing impatience and were soon awaiting the rainy season's end with a virtually agonizing anxiety; they desperately wanted to renew their search for gold. That attitude changed significantly, however, on February 26th with the arrival of the steamship *California* at Monterey, bearing not only the first contingent of gold-seekers from the East Coast but also California's new military commander, Brigadier General Persifer F. Smith, bearing orders from the War Department that had been dated November 15, 1848, in Washington, D.C.:

> *By direction of the prest [President], you are hereby assigned, under and by virtue of your rank of brev. Brig.-general of the army of the U.S., to the command of the third geographical or Pacific division, and will proceed by way of New Orleans, thence to Chagres, and across the isthmus of Panama to Cal., and assume command of the said division. You will establish your headquarters either in Cal. or Or., and change them from time to time, as the exigencies of the public service may require. Besides the general duties of defending the territories of Cal. and Or., and of preserving peace and protecting the inhabitants from Indian depredations, you will carry out the orders and instructions contained in the letter from the department to Col. R. B. Mason, a copy of which you are herewith furnished, and such other orders and instructions as you may receive from your govt.*

Because of the problems he'd had almost immediately upon his arrival at Panama City with the Peruvians aboard the *California*, General Smith had written from that location to the Secretary of War:

> *... I am partly inclined to think it would be right for me to prohibit foreigners from taking the gold, unless they intend to become citizens.*

He then wrote terse notes to the consuls in the major cities of the South American and Central American West Coast that the laws of the United States forbade trespassing on the public lands and that it was his intention to strictly enforce these laws against encroaching foreigners, though not against citizens of the United States. As he continued to the Secretary of War:

> *I shall consider every one [who is] not a citizen of the United States, who enters on public land and digs for gold, as a trespasser, and shall enforce that view of the matter if possible, depending upon the distinction made in favor of American citizens to engage the assistance of the latter in carrying out what I propose. All are undoubtedly trespassers; but as congress has hitherto made distinctions in favor of early settlers by granting preëmptions, the difficulties of present circumstances in California may justify forbearance with regard to citizens, to whom some favor may be hereafter granted.*

Soon after the arrival of the *California* at San Francisco, other vessels arrived, ship after ship, singly at first but very soon the broad Pacific beyond the Golden Gate was liberally dotted with approaching sails, and the expansive anchorage before San Francisco became very liberally studded with a wide variety of hulks that presented a veritable forest of masts bearing the flags of different countries, though with American ships predominating.

By March 1st, the combined populations of San Francisco and the Sacramento area had increased to nearly 50,000, and Suttersville had been overwhelmed by rampant growth. By mid-month San Francisco's growth was so dramatic that Peter Burnett made an apearance in order to meet the incoming flood of gold-seekers and direct them on, up the great river to its new namesake city. At the same time, Gen. Smith irritated many San Franciscans by declaring San Francisco's magnificent harbor to be " ... poor, because the seas are too rough and it is located on a peninsula with little water and few food supplies."

At very nearly the same time the first disturbing tendrils of racial prejudice began manifesting themselves, occurring at Ferry Bar on the North Fork Yuba River, between Bullards Bar and Fosters Bar. There, a large company of Chileans settled in. Their mining skills soon had them bringing in significant quantities of gold, far more, in fact, than Americans had gleaned from the site; indeed, both the bar and the streambed proved themselves to be very rich. The Americans at nearby Foster's Bar took great offense at this and thereafter denigrated the Chileans at every opportunity and declared loudly, "They ought'a be ejected!" So far this was just talk, but the general feeling prevailed that it could soon escalate into actual violence.

It was on Saturday, March 31st, when the steamship *Oregon* came to a mooring in San Francisco Harbor and some three hundred fifty excited passengers disembarked, including Postmaster John Geary, who brought with him the first regular mail delivery from the United States. Having learned of the problems the *California* had recently experienced with its crew deserting, the skipper of the *Oregon*, Capt. Robert H. Pearson proceeded with prudence: Instead of anchoring and giving his crew an opportunity to desert, he crossed the mouth of the bay to Sausalito and ran up to anchorage beside the line-of-battle ship, *Ohio*, from whom he asked for — and received — permission to leave his entire crew of eleven men as prisoners until he was once again ready to put to sea. Nevertheless, despite his precautions, several members of his crew managed to slip away in disguise.

On Monday, April 9th, the U.S. transport ship Rome arrived and anchored close by, bearing two full companies of U.S. Infantry under Major Heintzelman. Three days later another transport, the *U.S.S. Iowa,* arrived and took up anchorage in Monterey Harbor bringing the officer ordered to assume Gov. Mason's office — Brevet Brig. General Bennett Riley — along with his brigade, consisting of three more infantry companies. His orders from the Secretary of War were to assume the administration of civil affairs in California, "... not as a military governor, but as the executive of the existing civil government."

The 56-year-old Lt. Col. Riley, described as "a grim old fellow" and "a fine free swearer," had a slight defect in his speech but had little trouble making himself understood. He was not well acquainted with civil affairs, but he knew how to obey orders, and so he fully assumed, how to make subordinates obey *his* orders. His brigade of 600 men was well officered by Lt. Hayden, commanding officer of Co. H; Surgeon Turner; Adjutant Jones, commanding Companies C and G; Lt. Murray over Co. K; Lt. Schareman of Company A; Lt. Jarvis for Co. B; 2nd Lt. Hendershot for Co. F; 2nd Lt. Johnson for Co. E; and 2nd Lt. Sweeny for Co. D.

As for Capt. Pearson, he hastened away from San Francisco Bay today, April 12th, even though his remaining 70-ton supply of coal was only barely enough to enable the *Oregon* to carry him to Mexico's port of San Blas. From there, her coal-hold once again replete, the *Oregon* could then dutifully continue her return voyage to the United States, carrying with her the first government-authorized U.S. mail shipment west-to-east, the first private treasures shipped by sea from the mines, and the first United States-bound passengers from the Land of Golden Dreams.

[April 20th, 1849 • Friday]

Herman B. Scharmann was a big, bluff, generally good-natured German living in New York City. He was a good man — hard-working, quite intelligent, reasonably well read, and energetic. His greatest asset, however, seemed to be an unwavering determination to complete whatever challenge he set for himself to undertake. His greatest liability was his inability to take seriously any idea that varied with what he had already decided was the right course to follow. To put it bluntly, he was a very bullheaded man virtually incapable of finding fault of any kind within himself, who unfailingly considered his own ideas and opinions about anything and everything to be absolutely correct.

He could not actually have been described as a devoted husband to his wife, whom he had married seventeen years before when they both were twenty years old. Somehow he always seemed to view their marriage far more as a liability than an asset, as penance he was required to fulfill rather than as a particularly happy union. He was a vaguely caring, though strict, father to their three children, two sons aged 15 and 12, and a two-year-old daughter.

Like many others he was currently preoccupied with the prospect of growing wealthy by the apparently simple expedient of harvesting gold just about anywhere in California. Earlier he had been fascinated by early reports of the gold strikes in California. Later, when the President himself verified these discoveries, Scharmann's wanderlust and acquisitive fervor could not be denied. In mid-February he joined a collection of his acquaintances who had organized an emigration group they named the *German Company*, and were preparing to head for California. Sixty men had joined and, with their families, the group totaled well over one hundred. Scharmann was honored, as the group elected its officers, to be chosen as president. On March 20th they started westward and he wrote of it in his diary:

> *20 March 1849 — Tuesday — A German company strongly attracted to the new Eldorado by a spirit of Wanderlust and by a desire for gold, had chosen me as its president [on March 15th.] With preparations made, today we started from New York City for the gold regions of California, 4,750 miles away [actually, 2,482 miles.] Truly:*
>
> *"To Travel often gives much pleasure.*
> *But the gods, who are wise, stay home."*
>
> *Through Mr. [James] Gubert, the agent of Bingham's Transport Line in Philadelphia, an agreement was made for our transportation as far as St. Louis, — a distance of about 1600 miles [actually, 948 miles today by Interstate Route] — at $10.50 [$302.40] per person. The trip began at six o'-clock in the evening.*

Throughout the night, the group, including various dependents, had traveled, and at 7 a.m. they arrived in Philadelphia. Violent thunderstorms occurring at half-hour intervals throughout the day delayed them until 8 o'clock in the morning on Thursday, May 22nd, when they finally boarded the train. All that day and throughout much of the following night the train rumbled westward.. They arrived at Columbia in the pre-dawn darkness, and there, with their baggage, they were quickly herded into a canal boat. As Scharmann wrote in his rigid cursive:

> *... we were packed so tightly that I almost despaired of living through the night in such a condition. But where there is a will, there is a way.*

The group spent following four days cramped on that canal boat, all the while skirting the Susquehanna River until they finally reached the foot of the Alleghany Mountains. On March 28th the party again boarded a train which transported them up and down the mountain with machinery built for precisely that purpose. As evening approached, they were once again subjected to cramped quarters aboard another canal boat, which Scharmann discovered, to his dismay, was even smaller than the first one. As Scharmann wrote briefly in his *diary* that evening:

> *We felt that our spirit was put to a hard test.*

The journey continued throughout the ensuing days until at last, at 7 o'clock in the evening of April 1, what he termed "the city of smoke" — Pittsburgh — lay before them. As he wrote of it:

> *We had no time for a closer inspection of this active and quite flourishing factory town, for at ten o'clock, only three hours after our arrival, we boarded the steamer "Enterprise" which was to carry us down the Ohio to St. Louis. Pittsburg [sic] has a beautiful waterfront. As we passed by, I counted fifty-seven steamers.*

It was not until the evening of April 3 that Scharmann wrote in his *diary* again:

> *The excellent trip on the glorious Ohio recompensed us for all the earlier inconveniences. Its romantic banks bear witness to the capabilities of man, which develop when he is given unrestricted opportunity to achieve his happiness by means of his own labor. For, all along the river prosperous farms produce a strong and healthy type of man. Our steamer was filled to overflowing with emigrants who, like ourselves, were moving to California. On the deck, oxen and mules stood in quite close files, and many persons had to camp between or beneath them. Charming little villages, trim towns rolled past our eyes in this splendid panorama. Every emigrant ought to be advised to spend his money for a home on the Ohio rather than to chase after California gold.*

> *Cincinnati, the queen of the West, soon rose up before us. Her business and trade, her stores and her laborers leave a very pleasant impression upon the mind of the traveller [sic] and justify her claim to royalty.*
>
> *Wednesday — April 4th. In Louisville we stopped for several hours, which gave me an opportunity to inspect this pretty city. It shows a certain decided compactness and gives the impression that here any kind of labor that is, at fill, adapted to the country, is assured of a more than adequate compensation. Prices of all commodities ranged very low; thus a dozen eggs cost five cents. I bought three dozen, but while absorbed in the sights, I did not notice where I was going, and stumbled, breaking the eggs. I was lucky to get off with a slight limp.*

Again Scharmann broke off writing until, on April 8th, they reached the point where the Ohio River merged into, the powerful and exceptionally broad Mississippi. As he wrote at that point:

> *Sunday — April 8th — On the eighth of April we reached the junction of the Ohio and the Mississippi, and sailed up the "Father of Waters" toward St. Louis. The land on either side is level and is barely cultivated. Yet here the best soil is found both for settlement and agriculture, as is proved by the strong growth of the trees, especially the oak. Further up, as the land becomes more hilly and undulating, more settlements and brick farmhouses are seen.*

Three nights and four days later — on April 11 at 7 p.m. — the *Enterprise* finally neared St. Louis.

"Well, by golly, we've made it!" the steamboat's captain chortled with such high enthusiasm that it might have been his first time instead of his twentieth or more. Everyone aboard the steamer laughed, at which the captain doffed his cap and made an exaggerated bow, then added, "So! I think it would be very nice if you people would sing a happy folk song from the old country as we come in to dock — and I will fire our guns as a salute."

They did exactly that; the steamer moored amidst a somewhat jumbled and off-key but happy rendition of *Ach du Liber, Augustine,* during which they were joined by many of the laborers on the dock and the booming of the steamboat's little signal cannon. The Scharmanns bade their captain farewell and spent the next several days purchasing and laying in a store of provisions for the long journey still ahead. They found the large river steamer, *Isabella* in the process of being loaded for a journey upstream and, as Scharmann noted in his diary:

> *On the fifteenth of April I concluded an agreement with the master of a steamship to take us up the Missouri as far as Independence for $2.50 [$72] per person. The distance to Independence is 360 miles.*

Scharmann penned nothing about the upriver trip on the Missouri until after they reached their destination at Independence about two hours ago, at which time he wrote:

> *Friday, 20 April 1849 — We arrived here on the twentieth of April, pitched our tents, made other preparations, and then waited for the arrival of the committee which was to bring the cattle. The Missouri [Valley] region may be called a veritable paradise. The dark soil of unsurpassable quality has allured many German settlers, and at the first glance their farms give evidence of their prosperity. Here, in the sunshine of political and civic freedom, work becomes pleasure, and its proceeds, instead of enriching the princely drone, are the reward of the worker.*

Even though Herman Scharmann continually groused about trivial details of the overland journey westward thus far, he would not have elected to go any other way. In the planning stages he had considered both the 'Round-the-Cape voyage and the Panama Route, but had turned thumbs down on both, primarily because he disliked traveling by ship — his one experience, Europe to America, had rendered him grey-green with sea sickness for almost the entire voyage, and he had no desire to put himself through such torture yet again. Besides, he liked the ability to more or less see and calculate the distances traveled, which on land was easy enough, but very difficult when at sea. He also liked being able to see a variety of birds and mammals along the way, liked the feel of a good horse beneath him and the sense of accomplishment that came in driving a sizeable herd of cattle before oneself. More than anything else, though, his ultimate consideration was that land travel was infinitely cheaper than the ocean-bound routes.

The Scharmann family's basic travel provisions consisted of a suitable gun and ammunition, a good axe and hatchet, a supply of tools and, of course, provisions in the form of home-grown or home-produced staples such as bacon and flour, dried fruits and vegetables, seed vegetables of many kinds, parched corn and cornmeal. A farmer's work clothes, moreover, were ideal trail garments, and his canvas-covered farm wagon became, in essence, a home on wheels. Finally, Scharmann had been advised that when one reached his final mining-site destination, the wagon and everything in it could be converted to many good uses. In addition, two other essential overland travel advantages continued to influence his thinking: One just didn't get seasick walking or riding in a wagon or on horseback, and one made his own decisions instead of having to bow to the will or whim of a sea captain. For him, those factors counted for a great deal.

The multitudes of wagon trains being formed near St. Louis attested to the fact that tens of thousands of other emigrants shared Scharmann's perspective. So long as one could find decent grass for his stock and good water for both himself and his animals, he could gradually overcome the formidable barriers of mountains and deserts. Crossing major streams would be another matter entirely. River-fording places were limited, and at each the lines of those waiting would soon resemble the shape of a massive spearhead with the tip at the ford. Many days, it seemed, could be lost just awaiting one's turn for getting across. Even those without livestock save for the animals pulling their wagons would be forced to the use the ferries, and turn-taking would require many hours, often days, as tempers grew ever shorter. Fights breaking out over who had priority for crossing were certain to become frequent and some, they learned, might even result in gunfights and deaths.

An actual non-ferried crossing of a substantial stream, itself was always fraught with peril. Wagons might sometimes be floated and pulled across with ropes or even by teams, but doing so would always place the wagon, its animals, its contents, and sometimes even its humans, at great risk. If sawyers — floating but almost submerged trees — struck crossing wagons or animals, the resulting violent collisions could easily destroy goods, equipment, livestock, and human lives instantaneously. Few emigrants were foolhardy enough to consider such a risk worthwhile.

Getting to where the overland trails began was a relatively simple matter and required only a fraction of the cash outlay required in ship travel. What one had available on almost any farm provided virtually everything required for the long overland trip: A good supply of horses and mules and oxen, and, most importantly, a sturdy wagon with conestoga top — though it need not be as big and heavy as the true conestoga. Wagon size was a very critical factor, and this frequently became the source of inexperienced easterners' made most serious mistakes: They often procured excessively large wagons and loaded them so heavily that even the strongest draft animals could pull them for only short distances. The ideal wagon was no more than four feet wide, nor more than ten feet long. More often than not, a bucket of grease for the wheels was hung from the center of the rear axle.

Everyone loaded his wagon in his own particular way, and very often loads had to be unloaded and reloaded several times before they were properly balanced and convenient for man and beast alike. Certain fundamental supplies were crammed into virtually every wagon, not to mention numerous things that turned out to be not so fundamental after all: Usually a cook-stove made of sheet metal of some kind was included, as well as such foodstuffs as ham, bacon, jerky, rice, beans, dried peas, molasses, syrup, honey, barrel-packed butter and dried and salted fish, breads and biscuits and hardtack, coffee and tea in quantity, pots, pans, utensils, farming and mining tools, guns and ammunition, tools for any kind of emergency repairs, musical instruments and devices of various kinds, including even massive pianos, small organs, grandfather clocks, medicines and quilts and vegetable and flower seeds, plus a good supply of needles of varying size for various types of repairs, from darning socks to repairing wagon covers, bedding and robes, waterproof India-rubber sheeting to keep goods dry, locks and chains as wagon restraints on steep pitches, and collapsing telescopes for long-range viewing and route-planning.

Milk cows trudging with the emigrants on tethers would provide good milk, and a covered can of fresh milk hung from the inside hoops of the wagon would, in a few hours time, produce a ball of butter of a decent enough size to supply each day's needs. Chickens, if brought along, would produce eggs, which could be stored safely for travel in the flour barrels, so long as they weren't touching one another. Few women participated in this migration, but for those few who did — almost without exception women traveling with their husbands — it would be the first time in their lives they had ever worn trousers, and they reveled in the freedom such garments gave them as opposed to cumbersome, floor-length skirting.

By mid-April, the spacious prairies for three or four miles to the north, east and south of Independence, Missouri were tightly packed with emigrants impatient to be on the move and held back only by the very real fear of death awaiting those who would head westward too quickly: if the overland emigrants started too early in the spring, before grass was high enough to nurture their grazing animals, the train was doomed; if they waited too long, however, trains ahead of them would have eaten the better, more accessible grasses, and in searching for other patches, time would be lost and animals weakened; and if one was delayed too long in such pursuits, the better gold sites could be claimed by others before they could be reached or, even worse, trying to cross the Sierras could well become a death sentence, a fate the Donner Party had suffered in 1846, a tragic account which preyed heavily on the uneasy minds of this year's emigrants.

"Th' dam' "ifs" 'bout sech trekkin'," one Kentuckian remarked sourly, "are sure 'nuff apt to drive a feller plum' to perdition!"

Even the choice of what sort of animal to use to pull the wagons became profoundly important. Horses seemed the most logical, but they were a bad choice due to their inability to bear up under the constant strain as other livestock could and to subsist on poor graze which suited mules and oxen. Mules were good, but they weren't as strong as horses or oxen, and their obstinate temperaments and their inclination to run away worked against them. Ordinary cattle, even milk cows, could be used in a pinch, but they were never ideal. It was the ox that usually won in the matter choice. As Peter Burnett had said of it when he was himself emigrating:

> *The ox is the most noble animal, patient, thrifty, durable, gentle and does not run off. Those who come to this country will be in love with their oxen. The ox will plunge through mud, swim over streams, dive into thickets and he will eat almost anything.*

The biggest problem with oxen, of course, was the fact that they were slow movers, not often reaching a top speed on the trail of roughly two miles per hour. Most of the time wagon locomotion came down to a choice between mules or oxen. Mules were certainly faster and could forage on almost anything, just like the ox; but the animal's fundamental obstinately perverse nature and the fact that it simply didn't have the staying power of the ox were serious disadvantages. Many of the emigrants recorded in their diaries, early on, that the mule wagons passed them by — but along about halfway through the great trek, the oxen would steadily plod right on past the rapidly weakening mules. Emigrant Henry Cook seemed to sum it up very well when he wrote:

> *What perverse brutes these mules are. The beasts! How I hate 'em!*

Emigrant John Clark added to that:

> *We had to risk our lives in roping them. After being kicked across the pen some half-dozen times and run over as often, we at last succeeded in leading them out. It was laughable.*

Laughable, yes, at times, but also serious business and all too often the forerunner of very real tragedy. Little wonder, then, that the sturdy, dependable, gentle ox quickly became, and remained, the favorite wagon-pulling animal of all.

Bumpy trails were sure to make the hard wooden wagon seats too uncomfortable to sit upon for any length of time, and consequently, most of the travelers would wind up walking by far the greater part of the distance traveled. All too often the Easterner loaded his oversized wagon with a ton or even more of essentially useless furnishings, including large upright pianos and massive cabinetry. Even on level ground, the draft animals quickly exhausted themselves trying to pull such loads for very long. The trails early on were well littered with furnishings that had finally been abandoned by their owners, and the rougher and hillier the terrain became, the more the emigrants were compelled to discard heavy, non-essential items.

In the smaller wagon, which had much smaller wheels in front than in the rear, a complex under-carriage system centered around a central kingpin that allowed the front wheels to pivot easily for sharp turns when necessary. Emigrants learned, often too late, that wide wheels with broad tread were the most effective in soft, sandy soils, but narrow-rimmed wheels worked much better on hard surfaces. The cotton covers, rarely canvas, were usually drawn snugly shut and tied both front and aft to ward off as much dust as possible, and the emigrants partially water-proofed the material by rubbing it with linseed oil; this process was only temporarily effective, however, and hence, most covered wagons leaked badly.

Truly massive axles bore the brunt of the load and were most often hewn from oak for the strength the wood provided. If such axles broke, as occasionally they did, there was essentially no recourse but to abandon the wagon entirely or else cut it down to a much smaller two-wheeler with significantly limited carrying capacity. Sturdy, long toolboxes were absolutely essential to all overland wagons, attached to one or both sides, along with a water-barrel or two strapped tightly in place, usually close to the tailgate, and — highly important, especially in the mountains — well-turned hardwood brakes.

The staging area near Independence was so over-crowded that one emigrant who absolutely *knew* his friends were camped there, searched long and hard for four days before finally locating them. Rumor and gossip circulating through the masses of people ranged from amusing and harmless to deeply frightening and nerve-wracking. Before them, as all were by now aware, lay at least five or six full *months* of grueling daily travel, perhaps even more, depending on what degree of misfortune was encountered. With oxen, the draft animal of choice, covering ten to fifteen miles in a single day would be considered a very good trek, and covering twenty miles was rare indeed.

As the month's end neared it was clear that already more than 20,000 wagons and nearly five times that many people had gathered near Independence, clearly representing sizeable portions of the population in nearly every city, town and community in the Eastern states, and still more were showing up daily. In another week or two the new grasses would be high enough to support the animals, and the great trek could begin.

There was little doubt that colossal traffic jams would occur initially and at intervals along emigration route. A great many of the greenhorns from the East had little or no wagon-driving experience and had never yoked oxen or driven mule teams. Such drivers had very often already upended their wagons, bumped into trees or other wagons, run through campfires, broke through rope-corral-fences or had harnessed animals that simply refused to go in the direction the driver wanted. Frequently they already had become stuck and had to be partially or completely unloaded in order to be pulled out from the mud, only then to be reloaded, all at a great cost of effort and lost time. Accidents early on were frequent: Broken rims or axles, detached wheels upended entire wagonloads, as well as broken harnesses, tongues, wheel-ribs, causing great delays if spares were not lashed to the undercarriage. Small wonder that once most emigrants were finally within a few miles from the Independence trailhead, they were already aware that their wagons were badly overloaded and had already began the process of throwing out all sorts of furnishings, trunks and fundamentally useless equipment.

Within the first ten or twenty miles on the trail, a fair percentage of the wagons would be temporarily or permanently disabled. The majority, however, would plod on and for the travelers themselves, this memorable period would almost certainly come to rank as one of the most exciting times of their lives.

[April 22nd, 1849 • Sunday]

For Alonzo Delano, everything he was seeing or doing these days was very new to him, a total departure from the routine of the placid life he had been living for so long in the town of Ottawa. There was, in this enormous gathering of emigrants at St. Joseph, a vibrant undercurrent of excitement and anticipation that grew more pronounced every day. The emigrants' acute awareness that they were on the fringe of the great West and preparing to step off into the unknown at almost any moment was both highly stressful and exciting.

The sojourn in St. Louis had been relatively brief, but very expensive. Delano's purchase of equipment and provisions had cost him considerably more than he had anticipated, convinced as he had been by merchants there that *everything* in such jumping-off places as Independence and St. Joseph were much higher priced than anywhere else. Delano was simultaneously exasperated and amused by his discovery that he had been suckered by such comments, only to find on arrival here at St. Joe, that prices for goods, though definitely expensive, were a good bit cheaper than those in St. Louis.

The upriver trip from St. Louis to this point had by no means been devoid of excitement, nor of tragedy. With all his own personal goods marked, loaded and stowed in the steamship *Embassy's* hold, Delano had boarded and stood at the rail with the majority of the four hundred who had boarded here with him, including not only the handful of *The Ottawa Company* members, but considerably larger organized companies from the cities of Tecumseh, Michigan, Dayton, Ohio, Lynchburg, Virginia, and Louisville, Kentucky. As the *Embassy's* lines were slipped and the great side-wheels turned, thrusting them out into the broad, muddy stream under the skilled hands of her skipper, Captain Joshua Baker, Delano joined in with genuine enthusiasm the three cheers that erupted from all aboard; cheers immediately answered in kind by the hordes of lookers-on at the dock.

The throb of powerful engines driving the covered paddlewheels amidship was a deep rumble, at first very apparent but then gradually subsided to white-noise levels and hardly even noticed any longer. The wheels' powerful thrust, however, sent the gleaming black bow of the *Embassy* knifing through the turbid waters and created a substantial curling wave that fanned out on both sides of the craft in a great spreading V behind them.

Delano recalled with a small surge of amusement the conversation he'd had with the steamship's office clerk when he purchased passage on this craft. Feeling a bit aristocratic at the time, Delano had thought he would splurge and take cabin passage for himself. Standing at the counter with his wallet in hand, Delano had asked the clerk, "What is the fare to St. Joseph?"

"Eight dollars [$230.40], sir," the agent replied.

It was far more than Delano expected, but he was still game for it. "Can you show me a stateroom?"

"I'm sorry, sir, but they're all taken — not a berth left, but we can give you a good comfortable mattress on the floor. You will be very very comfortable, I assure you! In fact, it's just as pleasant as the berths."

"Hmmm, no doubt, but I think I'll try the deck. How much for deck passage?"

"Three dollars [$86.40]," the agent replied with a pained expression, "but it will be very unpleasant."

"No matter, it'll go to break-in and I might as well begin it now." So, he had taken the deck passage and used the money saved to insure his wagon and goods all the way to St. Joseph. It turned out to be a very wise choice. The cabins were so overcrowded that many who had been assigned to them could not even get a mattress to sleep upon, and the long dining tables had to be re-set five times in succession before all could eat. Finally, the air inside was so confined that several who had bought such passage left it and begged, instead, to sleep in the wagons secured on deck. Well ensconced in his own wagon, Delano wrote of it for his column:

> *The discomforts of the deck are pure air, a large roomy wagon with an excellent cover over it, plenty of buffalo skins and blankets to sleep on; in short, a little territory of our own which is respected by all, with a good chance to boil your own coffee at a public stove, and the privilege to eat when and how you may please. It was a most fortunate hit for me this time, and I am now writing in my own wagon with as much ease and comfort as I could in your own office. I have repeatedly had the offer made me to swap berths, but I have good, sufficient reasons to be content with what I have.*
>
> *This day of our leaving, one of The Dayton (Ohio) Company had his leg broken by a fall on the boat. The fracture was a bad one and he was left at St. Louis by his companions. And another quite serious accident occurred before starting, in The Virginia Company. A thoughtless greenhorn wishing to display his skill with a pistol, discharged it through the deck into the cook-room, where the ball lodged in the shoulder of one of the boys belonging to the boat. The ball was cut out by a surgeon, and the skillful marksman had his passage money returned and was set on shore to follow as best he could. It has perhaps served as a lesson to others, and the exhibition of pistols, bowie knives, and such innocent toys are not quite so common as before. We, of The Ottawa Company, intend to be very careful in our handling of weapons.*
>
> *We entered the Missouri, twenty-five miles above St. Louis, some time after dark.*

Delano closed his journal for the night and napped for a while in his wagon, but was up again and at the rail as the first light of day illuminated the river. He found the banks to be high, rocky, and quite often precipitous, even though the river valley was sometimes as much as two miles wide. In his *journal* he jotted a note to himself:

> *The water is constantly wearing away the soil of the bottoms, which are only a deposit of the stream at some former*

period. This makes the Missouri a muddy stream, resembling the water in a puddle after a shower; but after being allowed to settle a short time, the water is sweet and wholesome.

A sense of mirth had pervaded among the passengers ever since leaving St. Louis, but all levity quickly vanished, and even the very stoutest of hearts blanched as a voice loudly raised on deck shouted a bone-chilling warning:

"The cholera is on board!"

At once there came a hubbub of voices filled with hysteria-tinged fear: "The cholera?" "Good heavens, how?" "Who's got it?" "Where on the ship?"

From that moment on through the rest of the voyage, a great anxiety prevailed, and all minds were riveted on the same questions: Who was the person who had it and who had been in contact with him? As highly contagious as it was, who would be next to fall victim? At length the initial; excitement and fear abated somewhat. The one infected turned out to be a 23-year-old gentleman of *The Virginia Company* who, it was rumored, had indulged in some imprudence in his eating and drinking while in St. Louis and was now besieged with cramps and vomiting. The victim was quarantined in a cabin, and the ship's doctor attended him closely, but to little avail. His condition steadily worsened, and at ten o'clock in the morning, hardly twenty-four hours since the disease first manifested itself, the young man died. As Delano now wrote of it for his column:

Here was a melancholy beginning for the company. One of their number, a favorite, too, one of high hopes, with many friends behind, was suddenly stricken from their midst, though in the full enjoyment of health but a few hours before, and was to become food for worms in a strange land, far from those who loved and cherished him as their own. Yet he was not neglected. All was done that could be under the circumstances, and though he had no mother to smooth the pillow of his sufferings or weep over his distress, yet there was not a heart on that boat that did not yearn to do something for his comfort. A rough box was made, instead of a coffin, of the only material that could be had, and a little before night the boat lay up to the shore to give an opportunity to bury him.

> *It was in a gorge, between two lofty hills, and a place was selected about midway of that on the right hand, beneath a cluster of trees on a bright green sward. Many concerned and willing hands, including every man of The Ottawa Company lent their aid in digging his grave, after which, later on, a procession was formed from the boat and proceeded to his last resting place with all the respect and solemnity used in such occasions at home; and when the corpse was lowered into the grave, and, by the faint twilight, a friend read the Episcopal funeral service, although it was in the very middle of a drizzling rain, every hat was removed simultaneously, and every heart seemed softened with respect for the deceased and in reverence for God. How little can man foresee his own destiny? How thin is the thread of life! The first use made of the spade that was taken to turn up the golden sands of California, was to bury one of their own companions amid the rocky bluffs of the Missouri.*

As the steamship *Embassy* resumed its upstream journey, Delano became sadly convinced that their slow progress against heavy current, combined with very strong head-winds, would throw them far behind schedule, taking them perhaps twice as long as expected to finally reach the St. Joseph dockage. There was, however, no help for it, and Delano had long ago learned the wisdom of accepting philosophically that which could not be changed. Instead, he amused himself by looking on at the card games that had quickly become popular among the emigrants as they continued upriver. In a short while he was pleased with himself for not playing, since he spotted some sly knavery in evidence by the well-dressed "dealer." One of the group which Delano viewed privately as "victims" but which he termed aloud as "the sporting gentry," was fleeced of every cent of his money at such a game, and two of the cabin passengers were robbed by having their pockets cut open while wholly unaware of what was occurring.

Finding supplies of breadstuffs too limited for the long journey, several of the men decided to procure some on their own. Delano was one of these. They had passed several small towns with no success at buying baked goods at any of them, so when they reached the substantial community of Boonville, Delano was first to jump off and rush into town to the bake shop. Having there acquired "a good supply of eatables," he returned to the *Embassy*, arriving back just as Brown also returned from his own jaunt to find and buy baked goods which, he proclaimed, he had bought in plenty. Close behind came Ebenezer Smith with baked goods he had located in a different shop and, behind him, Fredenburg with the same. On taking inventory, Delano found *The Ottawa Company* now had 40 loaves of bread, 72 rusks, 15 cards of gingerbread, and sizeable quantities of apples, nuts, crackers and fresh milk — for once a more than ample supply for their immediate little Company.

By Monday evening, April 16th, the *Embassy* was only five miles below the landing place for Independence, and all were anxious to reach moorage and see something of the preparations being made there for the western push. It was not to be. A furious rainstorm arose quite suddenly, and when the steamer was heavily struck by floating trees twice in succession, Captain Baker refused to run any more of a risk. With considerable difficulty he had the steamship run alongside an island, in order to remain in its shelter for the night. On the following day Delano wrote:

> *Tuesd., April 17th, 1849 — We lay by the island until daylight, when we ran up to Independence landing. The town of Independence lays [sic] three miles from the river, and the landing is only a small cluster of log houses, with two or three poor warehouses. A high limestone bluff runs from the river and is ascended by a difficult road about a quarter of a mile in length. At St. Louis we had been told that an immense throng had congregated at Independence, some five or six thousand, and that the landing was lined with wagons for a mile, so that it was difficult to find a passage through them. I counted six wagons at the landing and forty on the bluff belonging to different companies; and I was told by a gentleman, who was collecting the names of all the emigrants, that he had visited all the encampments, that within a circle of 15 miles there were about 2,500 only at that time.*

After an abbreviated stop at Independence during the morning of April 18th, they moved on and in a short time passed the mouth of the Kansas River on the right bank. From that point on, Captain Baker pointed out, the lands to the west were all Indian territory and without visible habitation except for Fort Leavenworth, which they soon passed — the impressive fortification situated on the west bank less than 400 feet from the Missouri River and, as Delano noted in his *Journal*:

> *... like an oasis in the wilderness of prairie and cottonwood on the bottoms, with its neat barracks and surrounding brick buildings.*

In the later afternoon of the following day, they finally glimpsed ahead of them the welcome sight of St. Joseph, about which Delano remarked in his *Journal*:

> *Thursday, April 19th. Since leaving St. Louis the weather had been cold and a strong headwind has blown for eight days in succession, which has, perhaps, had a favorable effect on the health of our passengers; still, our long trip has made us anxious to be free from the imprisonment of a steamboat. The tedium ... was at length relieved by a view of the pretty and thrifty town of St. Joseph, about 4 o'clock p.m., after a ten-days' confinement, from St. Louis. It is situated upon a level plot, in a kind of amphitheatre, high ridges of broken prairie in the rear, with the river in front. It is the county seat of Buchanan County, has a fine spacious courthouse, two or three churches, a population of two thousand souls, twenty-one mercantile stores, mechanics in proportion, three steam flouring mills and a fourth under contract, three saw-mills, and I was informed that fifty-four brick and ninety frame houses were erected last season. Twelve thousand hogs were slaughtered here last fall, and large quantities of bacon, hemp, and tobacco are brought in from the surrounding country. It is only five years since the town was first surveyed and laid out, and it promises to be a place of much importance. It is already one of the prominent starting places for California and Oregon emigrants.*

Delano went on to discuss the prices of provisions and equipment in St. Joseph, noting with irony that most prices were equivalent to or considerably cheaper than those in St. Louis, and berating himself for being hoodwinked by St. Louis merchants. As he jotted in his *journal*:

> *Other supplies can be had on quite reasonable terms, and I should advise all who are coming not to buy in St. Louis but to complete their outfits here.*
>
> *We found on our arrival that Mr. [Jesse] Green's [Greene's] company had decided to move up the river to Fort Kearny, ninety-six miles. The season is backward, and it will probably be ten or fourteen days before the grass will allow the emigrants to start. By going to Fort Kearny they avoid crossing the Platte [River]. A good military road extends through the interior; the streams are all bridged, and they are forty-five miles advanced on their journey, having the advantage of settlements so far. We found the first South Bend, Indiana, company here, but on the point of moving to Fort Kearny; and I think many men will adopt the same course, This will make a division in the main body, so that a much wider range will be had for our cattle. My cattle, with those of Mr. Daniel Cutting, are thirty miles in the country awaiting our orders. Mr. Cutting arrived yesterday and we have dispatched Mr. Smith for our cattle, having determined to take the Fort Kearny route.*

Delano wrote nothing more in his *Journal* until Sunday, April 21st, when he penned:

> *We intend to leave here on Tuesday. We have to sadly make the melancholy record of the death of Mr. [Bruno] Zeluff, a member of Mr. Green[e]'s company. He was taken with diarrhea and suffered it to run without attention six days, when vom-iting and cramps set in and terminated his existence in a few hours. That company left here a few hours before our arrival and went out five miles, when Mr. Zeluff died, and yesterday they stopped to bury him.*
>
> *Messrs. Morrel [John Morill] and Thorn [Benjamin K. Thorne], who are attached to our mess, went on with Mr. Fredenburg's wagon in The Dayton (Green[e]'s) Company, and we expect to overtake them at the Fort [Kearny], and then we intend to unite with Captain [Charles M.] Tutt's*

company of South Bend, all old friends of mine.

There are here, and in this vicinity, from 2,000 to 2,400 men, but not over 3,000 at this time. Every steamboat brings its hundreds, and the next ten days may swell the number to five or six thousand. ... In the motley crowd assembled at this point, you see every variety of costume and arrangements for traveling according to the taste and ability of the emigrants. It seems to be a general disposition to set fashion at defiance, or rather it is fashionable to be unfashionable. ... Almost every boat reports one case of cholera, but in every instance it seems to have been brought on by imprudence or neglect; you may set this down as certain; and there is no case here among those who take proper care of themselves. We are advised that large numbers of foreigners are on their way to California, and I have heard but one determination expressed by our emigrants, and that is to assist our government to prevent foreigners of all nations from digging and carrying off the gold. They say, too, that if the government will do nothing, they will organize among themselves to prevent it. A militia formed from the emigrants will be an efficient force, for every man goes well armed and provided with ammunition, and will surely form no mean army of themselves with a proper organization. Added to this, they are almost entirely composed of energetic, well-informed, resolute law-and-order men, who have characters at home and who cannot at once depart from the habits and mental training from childhood of a civilized and moral community. I have scarcely seen a rowdy or intoxicated man among the emigrants — not one in five hundred. It is emphatically the case here that you cannot judge a man by his dress. The checked shirt, the broad-brimmed hat, the quaint coat or wrapper, and the everlasting boots, reduce all to a level in appearance — the man of science, the scholar, the merchant, the lawyer, the farmer, the laborer, or the dandy.

It remains to be seen how well we shall sustain the sentiments that we have been educated in. I shall endeavor to keep you advised of our movements from this place, and after we get off of all mail routes; we shall embrace every opportunity of sending an account of our doings, with, perhaps a sprinkle of some of our sayings.

Today, then, settled in at last for the time being in St. Joseph, Alonzo Delano jotted a brief notation in his journal that he had heard his cattle had arrived safely and were waiting, under the charge of Henderson — who bore the unlikely first name of Hazel — about a day's journey into the Indian country. He dispatched Smith to notify Henderson of the *Ottawa Company's* arrival and instructed him to bring the cattle in. The Delano party's goods and wagon were soon landed and, upon discovering that every public house in town was already overflowing with emigrants, Delano suggested they simply sleep and mess in their own wagon in one of the town's back streets, and as he wrote in conclusion for the day's events:

> *... and up to Sunday night we were all enjoying our usual health.*

Exactly how long that sense of good health Delano mentioned was a question no one could yet answer for certain. Considering the growing numbers that were daily contracting cholera, it seemed unlikely to last very much longer.

Not very long at all.

[April 26th, 1849 • Thursday]

The Atlantic coastal waters all the way to the southern reaches of South America, as well as the Gulf of Mexico and the Pacific coastal waters northward from the Strait of Magellan all along the west coasts of South and Central America, were more alive with ships now than had ever before been recorded. The Pacific, even more than the Atlantic was dotted with vessels, a great many carrying passengers from New Zealand and Australia, Indonesia and the Orient, all being drawn, as if by an overwhelmingly powerful magnetic force, toward the port most of them had barely heard of — San Francisco. The very name had a magical ring to those caught up in the ever-spreading spell of gold fever.

By the end of December at least a hundred ships filled with eight thousand men and their equipment were sailing in this roundabout course for the great natural bay on North America's West Coast, and week by week through the early months of this new year the number increased. No one knew for certain how many ships and men were en route now on this great journey, but it was a prodigious number. These were the vanguard of a polyglot horde of some ten thousand people already calling themselves Forty-niners, who were wholly convinced that what beckoned them so irresistibly was the promise of great fortune and a far better future than had ever before been even remotely possible.

The leader of all the vessels was the mail ship *S.S. California* which, having circumnavigated coastal South America and filled every berth and every available space with men accumulated at Valparaiso and Callao, Payta, and Panama, was now on the final leg of her voyage. She had touched at Rio de Janeiro on the first day of November, but had left there nearly as empty as when she arrived, the news of the gold strike not yet having reached this point. At Valparaiso, which she reached near the end of December, and at succeeding ports, where word of it had reached, she had taken aboard a great many, but with commitments made to pick up more at Panama, she left untold hundreds more still behind at the docks, clamoring for passage and forced to wait for whatever ships were coming behind. She reached Panama on January 17th, where a fortnight layover was scheduled.

It was there that the *California* filled her passenger berths to absolute capacity by taking aboard a final 280 waiting gold-seekers, most of whom had left New York City aboard the steamer Falcon for Chagres on December 1st. From there they had made the difficult passage across the Isthmus by dugout, donkey and afoot to reach Panama City in time to connect with the *California,* which ultimately had to leave 70 others behind at the dock. Among those who boarded the *California* here was General Persifer F. Smith, en route to Monterey to take command of the U.S. forces on the Pacific Coast and to relieve General Mason as California's governor. He made himself not at all popular to the 69 Peruvians who had come aboard at Callao, when he announced in blustery tones that none but American citizens were permitted to enter upon the gold-bearing public lands of the United States. The Peruvians did not believe him and refused to be intimidated, refused even to go ashore lest their return aboard be barred. After considerable discussion a compromise was met whereby the Peruvians vacated their staterooms and accepted improvised quarters aboard.

By a rather involved combination of ticket scalping, bribery, lottery, priority, and trickery, all such measures involving mass meetings and organized committees of protest, the Americans on shore were closely screened, and many among them were allowed to board — some admitting that they had paid bribes of up to $1,000 to be included just as steerage passengers.

The *California* had finally sailed on the last day of January with 401 persons aboard, including the crew of 36. The steamer made very brief mail stops at Acapulco on February 9th and at Mazatlan on February 13th, followed by similar stops at San Diego and Monterey; at this latter port Consul Thomas Larkin and Lt. William Sherman came out from shore in a small boat to officially greet General Persifer Smith, California's new military commander. Here, too, the Reverend Samuel H. Willey with three others, all missionaries, departed from the ship. The *California* immediately pulled away and arrived at last at San Francisco on February 28th, the complete voyage from moorage at New York City to moorage at San Francisco having consumed 144 days, only a few days shy of five months.

As she passed through the Golden Gate, the 1,050-ton *California* was greeted by a thunderous salute from Commodore Thomas Jones and his Pacific Naval Squadron anchored there. Soon after the mail ship and her crowded cargo of passengers came into dockage at San Francisco, she was met by a great crowd of wildly cheering residents and considerable fanfare. It was a very special day, not only for those aboard the *California,* but for all of San Francisco as well. Unfortunately the euphoria prompted by the gala occasion was dimmed considerably when by the end of the day, the entire crew of the *California,* except for her Captain and one engineer, abandoned ship to rush to the gold fields.

After the *California's* arrival, all San Francisco-bound ships, without exception, experienced their full share of difficulties, ranging from extended periods of calm, windless weather delays to outbreaks of rampant disease that swept through crews and passengers alike with fatal results. Shipboard funerals became commonplace, and scores, perhaps hundreds, of weighted bodies wrapped in sheets were consigned to the blue depths. There were occasional humorous episodes, as when three hens were blown off the deck of the *La Grange,* but were rescued when the captain turned about and scooped them back aboard. Far more often, however, it was tragedy that visited, usually in the form of disease: Outbreaks of measles and pox, mumps and whooping cough, each epidemic carrying off its share — multitudes — of victims before dissipating. The ship *Duxbury* fell victim to thirty cases of mumps and fifteen of measles, leaving very few passengers and seamen unscathed.

On virtually every ship baited hooks were trolled behind and fine catches were made of sailfish and marlin, dolphin and albacore and a variety of other fish. Crew members and passengers initially resorted to fishing to escape from ship-board tedium but thereby provided beneficial changes in the usual table fare that often produced scurvy. Such fishing lines as well, most notably as the ships skirted multitudes of islands near Cape Horn, caught a host of seabirds — albatrosses and goonies, gulls and murres — all of which provided a welcome change in diet. Unfortunately, many of the gold-seekers also practiced their marksmanship by firing pistols with reckless abandon at the porpoises that paced the ships at their bows and frequently leaped from the water in exuberant displays.

The *Edward Everett* out of Boston was exemplary of many ships that followed her: two ministers were aboard, who alternated in their Sunday preaching, though attendance at services was not compulsory. Smoking was permitted on deck, but not below, and passengers were invited to participate in such events as athletic contests of various kinds, amateur theatricals, readings — often from the *Bible* but frequently from more-favored story-tellers. Special on-board holiday celebrations of Christmas, New Year's Eve, and Easter were also organized, all accompanied by surprising pomp and ceremony, including elaborate repasts, appropriate oratory, and rounds of toasts with wines and liquors that brought a happy little buzz to many.

Some of the ships, including the *Edward Everett*, the *Gold Hunter's Log*, and the Barometer, actually printed a single copy of a ship's newspaper, which was read aloud and evoked many chuckles and guffaws at the expense of certain passengers and crew and, on occasion, even the ship's captain and other officers. Such issues included passenger gossip, verse, broad humor and personal notes. Those who had musical talent, either for singing or for playing such instruments as violins, clarinets, flutes, and guitars were always in demand and greatly appreciated, and those who could combine signing with the playing of an instrument, as could James A. Varney aboard the *General Worth*, were extremely popular. Singing groups, such as the self-styled Sacramento Minstrels, who featured fiddle, banjo and tambourine accompaniment as they often sang selected Stephen Foster songs, were in high demand; indeed, no melody seemed to inspire the Forty-niners quite so much as *Oh, Susannah*, for which entertainers concocted a hundred-odd different verses, but none so popular as the two-line ditty that fitted the newly-moving miners perfectly, whether emigrating by ship or cross-country:

> *"Oh, Susannah, oh don't you cry for me,*
> *For I'm off to California with my wash-bowl on my knee."*

The ships would not always hug the East Coast during the first half of the voyage, and many, taking advantage of favorable winds, sailed southeastward to almost within sight of Africa, before turning southwest and setting course for the South American port cities of Rio de Janeiro, Santos, or Santa Catarina. Such ports had offered a much welcomed relief to monotony and diet of the ship voyagers' routine, relief consisting of veritable feasts of fine steaks, roasted chickens, baked hams, green cheese and citron, watercress and crisp lettuce, tasty bananas and oranges and grapefruits, guava jellies and excellent claret and Madeira wines, the whole accompanied by the finest coffee many had ever before tasted.

The tedium of the Atlantic portion of the voyage always came to an abrupt end as the ships reached the eastern approach to the Strait of Magellan. Few less experienced captains chose this route, though it was so much shorter than sailing around Cape Horn, simply because the passage was narrow and difficult and studded with very real dangers in the form of severely strong currents, wholly inhospitable shorelines, very few available anchorages, most those very poor, and, almost always, heavily overcast skies, sharp headwinds and frequent blizzards for the better part of two full months. It was a passage which neither crew members nor passengers ever enjoyed, one they almost always regretted. Some ships navigated through it quite well: The pilot schooner *Anonyma* sailed through beautifully, and the brig *Saltillo* made it in exceptional time, a mere 52 days. The *Acadian* took 57, and the *Velasco* wallowed through in 70, but even that was better than the schooner *John A. Sutter*, driven ashore in the midst of a blizzard and lost, though the crew and passengers were saved. The bark *Hebe* had allowed some men to go ashore to trade, but harsh winds came up with an abetting tide and the ship could not hold, even with anchors dragging. The passengers, consequently, had to be saved by a later-arriving vessel.

In some areas the natives were decidedly unfriendly, and some of these seized the mate and a passenger of the *John Allyn* when they came ashore. The passenger was ransomed, but the mate was held until finally, on the 97th day of his captivity, he gambled his life by swimming in the bitterly cold water out to a British ship, which brought him aboard. From it the mate transferred to a whaler, and then, finally, to a California-bound ship. Nearly all accounts of ships voyaging around Cape Horn, rather than braving the Strait of Magellan, vigorously insisted that the dangers of taking the latter shortcut were too severe to justify any time that might be saved in the course of the always perilous voyage to California.

Circumnavigating Cape Horn — better known as just *The Horn* — while better than the Strait, was by no means a picnic for any sailor. Some made it in as short a time as a few weeks, though most required anywhere up to 40 days to reach the Pacific. A good many of the earlier sailing ships were held up for long periods, by severe headwinds. The *Golden Eagle*, for example, battled such weather for three full months before getting through. Many ships of the China trade simply gave up and chose to reach the Pacific by sailing eastward around the world. Adding to the difficulty of such passage was the bitter Arctic cold and severe pitching waves, the latter often so overwhelmingly powerful that men were always in danger of being swept overboard and lost. During such a passage, most who were not actually required to go on deck, constantly stayed below.

[April 28th, 1849 • Saturday]

Although San Francisco had become indisputably the fastest growing city on California's West Coast, it had a decided competitor inland — Sacramento. Both cities were growing prodigiously and, as a result, property values increased enormously.

Monterey, which had so long been the territorial capital, had become little better than a ghost town, kept alive primarily by the U.S. governmental offices still located there. By far the greater portion of its population was still at the mines, and there was little likelihood that things would change there in the near future.

San Francisco, on the other hand, having weathered its first abandonment by the populace in search of gold, had bounced back over the past winter with an enthusiastic burst of building construction and civic pride that was little short of amazing. Moreover, the hordes of people funneling into San Francisco by ship from Eastern United States ports, as well as from major ports throughout the entire span of the Pacific virtually guaranteed that the city would never again teeter on the verge of total abandonment.

Sacramento, though not developing so rapidly as San Francisco, exuded a greater feeling of stability and permanence. The fact that it was clearly the only significant municipality anywhere near the gold deposits and indisputably the jumping-off place for the great majority of miners made it vitally important as a staging area, and consequently, its population, too, was swelling. John Sutter's prognostications that late winter and early spring flooding of the Sacramento River would wash the city away had not occurred. True, the severe mid-January flood waters inflicted hundreds of thousands of dollars worth of damage, destroying buildings and stored merchandise, but the community had weathered it and was springing back with even greater determination. Town lots that could hardly be given away for $200 [$5,760] or less just months ago, had suddenly taken on much greater significance, and it was clear that by autumn's onset they would be priced at $30,000 [$864,000] or more. Larger and more permanent downtown buildings were being erected and given such names as *The Humboldt, The Mansion, The Gem, The Diana,* and *The Empire*; more streets were being laid out, and their facing lots were selling briskly. The town's permanent population, estimated now at 150, was projected to increase to at least 6,000 by October. The first sales of lots had been near the fort, but that quickly changed, and it was the lots close to the normal shoreline of the Sacramento River that now came into huge demand, the prices of which escalated accordingly.

John Sutter, who was seldom at his fort anymore, preferring the fine home he had built some twenty miles upstream on the Sacramento at the place he had named *Hock Farm,* complained to all who would listen about the losses he had been suffering, in lands and crops and most especially with his cattle: "When the floods came, as I clearly predicted they would, my cattle were obliged to take refuge on the knolls, where my vaqueros could not guard them at all. The butchers from surrounding camps and communities came in and caught and slaughtered them in great numbers. In addition there are squatters everywhere on my property who simply will not leave and who only laugh at my threats to have them ejected."

The squatters established their own association, which quickly gained in power, and no matter what Sutter threatened regarding their trespassing, they insisted that his land grants were fraudulent and would never be recognized when the new California Land Commission met. They scoffed and jeered at Sutter's argument that the grants stemmed from the original Mexican charters, and were granted under Mexican law, and that the American authorities surely would recognize such just claims. The squatters stridently insisted that the U.S. would win its land claims, that these lands belonged to the colonists who developed them, and that the mining claims, too, constituted development.

No sooner had the spring flooding subsided than once more the hordes of prospectors set out in all directions over the land, although significantly more people remained behind in San Francisco than had done so a year earlier, thereby eliminating the prospect that the town would founder. Now, with gold no longer so abundant on the surface as it had been in the past, the gold-seekers quickly developed new and better methods for harvesting their treasure. The answer was twofold: The miners would have to begin digging deeper than previously to locate additional, as-yet-untapped placer deposits, and, even more important, they had to find the mother lodes and then painstakingly follow their traces wherever they might lead.

This morning, April 28th, a new weekly newspaper was started in Sacramento, calling itself the *Placer Times*. It was published and edited by the ubiquitous Edward Kemble, and this first issue lauded the young city highly, proclaiming that it was already a major center for shops and services. The *embarcadero,* it pointed out, could boast 25 or 30 stores of various kinds — all housed in tents, of course — and near another dozen were located in the fort or in its near vicinity, including such businesses as hotels, a printing office, a good restaurant, blacksmith shops, a well-recommended bakery, a tin shop, a fine billiards room, an excellent bowling alley, numerous well-supplied saloons and gaming houses providing various card games for those who wished to gamble, as a great many did, dancing girls and — while it didn't come right out and say so, the inference was clearly there — prostitutes with such inventive alliterative names as *Sensational Sally, Clever Clara, Demure Diana,* and especially the ever popular duo, *Heavenly Hannah* and *Extraordinary Ella.*

Though Sacramento was already an exceedingly healthy place, the article argued, it should have a good hospital because serious accidents were not uncommon in mining communities and "quality medicines and medical care should be as good or better in Sacramento as those in any other community in the Territory."

Not surprisingly, however, the news that dominated the inaugural issue was gold — where and in what quantities it was being found, how it was being mined, and how certain individuals were rapidly becoming incredibly wealthy.

The newspaper estimated that on January 24th of this year — the first year anniversary of the discovery of gold at the Sutter-Marshall Lumber Mill — no less than $100 million [$2,880,000,000] in gold had been extracted throughout the gold field. The fact that new gold deposits were continually being found — and that even greater discoveries were being made from deposits that had already supposedly been worked out — ignited a whole new fire of enthusiasm among the gold-seekers returning to the deposits, as well as the great many who were arriving among them for the first time.

On January 18th, one of the miners who had elected to continue working through the rainy season, José Jesús Pico, ended four months of mining at the Arroyo Seco, paid off quite generously the ten men he'd had working for him, and still wound up with a profit for himself of $14,000 [$403,200].

One of the first Australians to arrive, a tradesman named Josh Higgins, set up a store a quarter mile below Salmon Falls, where "very rich diggings" first exploited by the Mormon miners, continued to produce well and there, at what he named *Higgins Point*, he very quickly made his own fortune by taking Sam Brannan's advice about "mining the miners."

To the south, where Diasa Amador had last summer done his mining in the location appropriately dubbed *Murderer's Gulch*, miners not more than a fortnight off the mail-ship California, were already accumulating impressive amounts of gold, and they all felt assured that much more treasure was still available at the site. Close by, at what had become known as *Drytown*, newly arrived New Yorkers were digging with obvious success close to where Seth Lee Beckwith had built the first log house last November. Beckwith was just now ending his three-month stint here; for the better part of two weeks of that period he had averaged $110 [$3,168] per day. Beckwith left on February 12th, vowing he would never again have to perform manual labor, and with over 96 pounds of nuggets in his packs totaling 1,540 ounces — valued at $24,640 [$709,632] — he was undoubtedly correct.

When William R. Gardner approached James H. Carson excitedly in late February concerning a new gold discovery, Carson took special note. Gardner was neither an excitable man nor a newcomer. He'd lived in Monterey for the past fifteen years, and some of his many Mission Indian friends near the San Miguel Mission had shown him large specimens of pure gold which they told him had come from the still largely unexplored Kings River area. Gardner said he was fitting out an expedition to go to the area and wanted Carson to go with him. Despite the fact that there were hostile Indians in that area, Carson was tempted to go, but when he saw the poorly defended manner in which Gardner was equipped, he decided against it. Gardner left without him, on March 1st, having a train of six ox wagons with Indian drivers and four Spaniards as companions.

Gardner and his party traveled through the Coastal Range at San Miguel Pass, crossed the lake slough adjacent to Tulare Lake, and then went up the north side of Kings River into the Sierra Nevada foothills. Here he was met by a significant number of Indians from the mountains who had large quantities of freshly removed gold. They were quite friendly, but refused to trade with him unless he would come to their settlements. Gardner was glad to do so and traveled with them into the mountains for two days. There they attacked and killed him and all in his party except one Sonoran, who was allowed to go back, taking with him some of Gardner's papers, including his journal, which was shown to Carson. In the last entry, Gardner had written:

> *We have travelled [sic] about twenty miles today, the number of Indians around us have increased every hour for the last three days, and now number over a thousand — most of them have gold, which is generally coarse, and to my inquiries of them where they obtained it, they pointed to the Eastward. There is a great stir among the Indians, and their squaws and children have left. I have now the greatest fears for my safety.*

Carson noted in his own Journal:

> *The Indians who murdered Gardner & party, were the Chowchillas, the Chowwochicimnies & the Kaweeahs — the most thieving, treacherous and blood-thirsty tribes of the Tulares.*

Daniel Woods, noted among the miners for being a very conservative and honest man, reliably reported that the brothers Edward and Robert Sherwood accidentally discovered gold in a small square of ground in the Mariposa region in mid-February and quickly extracted $30,000 [$864,000] worth of nuggets, which they took to Monterey to deposit. There, according to Woods, two sailors overheard them, took a seven-week furlough, and followed them back to their Mariposa claim. In digging close to the Sherwood claim over the next five weeks, the pair returned to their ship with nine pounds of gold — 144 ounces — valued at $2,304 [$663,552].

By mid-March the placers in the Stanislaus River drainage were decidedly coming into their own and producing significant amounts of gold, not only abundantly but in nuggets generally somewhat larger than the wheat-grain variety already so common. One of the more productive of such placer sites was *Sullivan's Diggings*, located on Sullivan's Creek. Miner Lewis C. Gunn was among the first to exploit it and, as he recorded in his journal:

Went to Sullivan's Diggings, five miles off [from Jamestown]. Found about $5 [$144] in about one hour; felt quite elated with my success. Others here are doing well, but the labor is immense and requires several to work in company. They sink holes thirty feet deep, and while one keeps pumping out the water all the while, another digs the dirt, and a third and a fourth wash it. In some holes they have two pumps constantly at work. The scenery at Sullivan's is truly sublime, high hills, in fact mountains, and very steep, so that we could scarcely ascend and descend them; in many places it was impossible.

James H. Carson was quite disturbed over how suddenly meaningless vast amounts of money had become to a sizeable majority of the miners, but he was quite encouraged with the knowledge that there were some who were making their mark and very cautiously avoiding the temptations to spend it meaninglessly. As he wrote of it in his Journal:

> *As soon as a miner becomes flat broke, he wends his way to the mines again, to replenish his pile, and then have another bust. Some few, as soon as they procure eight or ten thousand dollars [$230,400 or $288,000], avail them-selves of the first opportunity & leave for more quiet lands. I have*

> *seen men with from thirty to fifty thousand dollars [$864,000 to $1,440,000] worth of dust, shipping as sailors before the mast for ports in the Pacific, from which they could reach the United States.*

The swiftness with which deposits were prospected, camps formed, deposits mined, deposits exhausted and camps abandoned was little short of incredible. For most, a gold deposit was considered worthwhile for only so long as it was accessible and mineable with a relative minimum of effort and output. As soon as a deposit began to require more concerted effort to reach the gold level than the miner wanted to expend, he abandoned it, and many sites fell into disuse and were categorized as "played out" when, in fact, rich treasures still existed for just a bit more effort. At the *Volcano Diggings* not far from Amador's camp, one miner abandoned his claim as "too damned hard to dig the gold out," when, in fact, he had removed from it in just a few days, $8,000 [$230,400] worth of gold. In a similar case — a report which Carson viewed with some skepticism — hardly more than 100 yards distant, an unidentified Mexican miner, working by himself, removed from a single pocket, over a period of three weeks, 28 pounds of nuggets — 448 ounces — valued at $7,168 [$2,064,384].

One of the more productive of gold sites at this time was the one developed by a German named William Stoutenberg — or Wilhelm Stoutenburgh — who was a member of the West Coast Mining Company and who established a "dig" on Coyote Creek near Murphy's Camp early this spring. He evidently did so well there that by today, April 28th, a flood of other miners had moved in on him, and now the place was being described as "a town of about 50 tents and nearly as many 'bars', plus two or three blockhouses, a sturdy house built of good planking, three American and four French dining rooms, two doctors' or drug shops, a private post office and about twenty gaming tables." The place also had a duly elected *alcalde*, sheriff, and constable. The majority of the miners at the site at this time were French.

What this whole episode seemed to demonstrate, more than anything else, was that a tremendous amount of gold still remained to be excavated by those miners with the foresight and energy to dig *just a little farther and just a little deeper* than those who had preceded them. Oddly enough, having been "spoiled" by the earlier "extremely easy pickings," there were few miners around who were willing to expend that kind of effort.

One entrepreneur who refused to be seduced by complacency was the one who had not yet dirtied his hands with pick or shovel — Samuel Brannan — but whose investments had already clearly made him the richest individual in California. Today, having viewed with interest the build-up of miners that had already arrived in San Francisco by ship, and learning from them of the staggering number of companies and individuals poised to emigrate overland in this direction as soon as the weather allowed, Brannan quickly initiated a brand new ferry service from Sacramento to Mormon Island — a service that would undoubtedly net him tens of thousands of dollars more.

[April 30th, 1849 • Monday]

While he hadn't put the thought to words, either written or spoken, what had plagued Alonzo Delano more than anything else since leaving St. Louis was a persistent fear of cholera. Having witnessed only too closely, while aboard the *Embassy*, the speed with which the dreaded disease attacked and destroyed its victims, he was admittedly very fearful of it; and his fears had merely been resoundingly confirmed by his experiences on the trail since departing from Missouri.

It had been just a week ago today — April 23rd — at four o'clock in the morning when Delano and other members of the *Ottawa Company* were awakened by a series of fearful groans and cries of distress coming from outside the wagon. They were confused at first, questioning one another, and Delano's voice, groggy from awakening from a deep sleep, overrode the hubbub:

"Who is that? Who's in trouble? What's the matter? Who's sick?"

"It must be Mr. Harris," Brown responded, "he's not in here with us."

From outside the wagon came an agonizing response: "It is me! — Oh, I'm in such pain! I'm very sick!"

They leaped up and raced outside, and as they had feared, found Matthew Harris leaning against one of the wagon wheels, doubled over by intense spasms of pain. On learning from him that he had been up and outside several times throughout the night, they stretched him out on the ground, where he lay writhing and, as Delano wrote of it:

> *We became at once satisfied that the cholera had insinuated its poisonous fangs amongst us. I immediately gave*

him a large dose of laudanum, the only remedy or palliative at hand, and sent for a physician, who came within an hour and commenced an active course of medicine.

He grew worse, however, notwithstanding all our efforts. The vomiting, purging, cramping became excessive — with cold limbs and hands, and cold sweat pouring from his brow; still we worked over him till noon, when we found the symptoms had changed. The vomiting, purging and cramping ceased, his limbs became warm and the pain in the bowels was much less severe.

With his eyes brightening and becoming more focused, Harris became more coherent, and he was at that point quite sure, as they all were, that he had weathered the worst of it and would now gradually improve. Harris remained in that more alert condition, and during the next three hours his companions continued their exertions — rubbing him and applying the balm the physician had left. Soon everyone concluded that he was out of danger. They were actually congratulating one another over their "doctoring" skills when, at about 4 p.m., abruptly, without warning and while lying at apparent ease, Harris abruptly began gasping for breath.

In less than five minutes he was dead.

Delano and his men could scarcely credit their senses. As Delano wrote in his Journal:

He, who but the night before bid as fair to live as any one of us — he, who passed the good-natured jest with us, in the fullness of health and strength, now lay extended, an inanimate mass of clay, "one of the things that were." Alas! It was too true, and our friend had "gone to that bourn, from which no traveler returns."

They laid Harris out on the ground decently and as well as their own slender means would allow. Delano and Brown kept a melancholy watch near the remains of their companion and friend throughout the night by the light of the campfire. Delano wrote further in his *Journal*:

If an honest, well-meaning man ever lived, poor Harris was one, and his simple habits and virtuous inclinations had endeared him to us all. He was a man of singularly honest and upright intentions, of great moral worth, simple in his habits and sincere in his professions. A Christian, he lived as near to what he believed his duty as the weakness of human nature allowed him. We felt that one of our best men had been taken. This is the only case that I am cognizant of where cholera has been fatal to a temperate man. He never drank ardent spirits as a beverage and was temperate in all his habits. We dug his grave, ourselves, in the morning, and with no tolling bell to mark the sad requiem, we buried him in a cluster of trees, by the side of a beautiful rivulet.

My wagon-tip had received some injury when getting it on board at St. Louis, and while repairing it, after the sad duty of burying Mr. Harris, Mr. Henderson and Mr. Smith arrived with the entire complement of our cattle.

By late in the morning they were again prepared to continue their journey. Robert Brown was installed in Harris' place, and under Fredenburg's direction, the party started off to follow the track of *The Dayton Company,* while Delano remained behind at a house where he was able to obtain lodging, hopefully to receive any letters there that might have been forwarded to them from Ottawa. He was crestfallen to learn that no mail had arrived there.

Delano caught up with his company and participated with several others on wagon maintenance work while the vehicle moved along the trail. By evening, Delano, not at all accustomed to heavy labors, felt exhausted after his somewhat strenuous work during the past few days, and he decided to turn in early. Before falling asleep he began to feel very strange. He wondered if there had been some kind of subtle change in the weather, because no matter how he wrapped himself in blankets, he couldn't seem to get warm. He donned some of his extra clothes, but still it didn't help and he felt as if he were inside an ice house. Cold chills crept down his back, and he involuntarily drew up his knees and put his head under the covers, but still to no avail. He was freezing and very shivery and then, abruptly, terribly thirsty, desperately wishing that he had a stream of ice-water running down his throat. As he wrote of it later:

At length I began to grow warmer, warmer, then hot,

> *hotter, hottest! I felt like a mass of living fire — a perfect engine, without the steam and smoke. There seemed to be wood enough from some source, but I poured in water until I thought my boiler would surely burst, without allaying the raging thirst which consumed me. At last the fever ceased and them indeed, the steam burst in a condensed form through the pores of my burning skin, and my body was bathed in a copious perspiration, that left me as weak as any sucking dove. I had had a visit from my old friends, chill and fever.*

Delano was sustaining an attack of the dreaded cholera, and he was by no means comforted by his awareness that very few of those attacked could survive the ravages the disease imposed upon the system. Contemplating with intense anxiety Harris's recent fate, Delano was determined this was *not* what was going to happen to him. He continued to roll and toss through the night, at intervals shaking with chills or liberally bathed in the sweat of a raging fever.

Thursday's dawn finally came, but Delano felt too ill and too exhausted to even consider riding, and so he remained in bed throughout the day and the ensuing night. On Friday morning, when he thought the worst was past, he abruptly lapsed into another spasm of what he perceived to be "a baptism of fire and water," and, as he later wrote of it:

> *Determined to be with my friends if I was doomed to be sick, and as our medicines were in the wagon, I mounted the pony, Old Shabanay, which had been left for me, and although so weak I could hardly keep my seat, I started. I soon found my strength increase in the fine air, and when I reached Savannah, a pretty town fourteen miles above St. Joseph, I felt quite well, though weak.*
>
> *On Saturday morning, April 28th, I made the chief part of my breakfast from blue pill, and started off in pursuit of my wagon, which I overtook in a ride of ten miles. Suspecting my illness, The Ottawa Company had driven slowly, in order to let me overtake them.*

Continuing the ride at an easy pace, on Sunday the company

reached English Grove, a little community some 65 miles above St. Joseph and 38 miles below Fort Kearny, and here they learned that *The Dayton Company* had decided to cross the Missouri at a ferry just established, called Harney's Landing, and then to remain on the western bank until it was ascertained that there was sufficient grass to satisfy the needs of the cattle. If that worked out satisfactorily, they had decided to strike out westward on an obscure route over which only one train had passed previously — *four years earlier*! Delano's party joined them without hesitation.

By heading westward in this manner, they estimated that they would intercept the St. Joseph-Platte River Trail at a point which, they were told, would put them in advance of the *St Joseph* and *Independence* trains by at least ten days, and on a route which would provide fresh grass ahead of them each day. Delano, however, was still feeling very weak, and in his *Journal* he wrote:

> *Feeling that it was absolutely necessary for me to lay up and nurse myself, and as there was plenty of time [for me] to overtake the train, while the boys in our party went on with the wagon, I made acquaintance of Mr. Van Leuvin and family, to whom I am much indebted for the many kindness which a sick man requires, and went resolutely into "drugs and medicines."*

Throughout the day he wrote the entire text of his column for the *Free Trader* and was very pleased when Van Leuvin volunteered to mail it for him. He concluded the column by observing:

> *I have an opportunity to forward this to St. Joseph tomorrow and shall embrace it. I think I shall be able to write you again before we leave. It is twelve miles to the nearest post office.*

[May 2nd, 1849 • Wednesday]

While still largely "a community of masts, sails and tents," Sacramento was steadily growing and rapidly changing, evolving almost daily into an increasingly permanent, stable settlement. Indeed as many ships — even very large, deep drafted vessels — were sailing right through San Francisco Bay at this point as were stopping there, and its

"Bay of Masts", as some were calling it, was clearly manifested in the number of ships dropping anchor or deliberately running aground on the Sacramento shoreline.

A large number of these vessels, no longer sufficiently seaworthy or useful, were now forming a makeshift waterfront community at Sacramento; they were utilized as storage structures, saloons, hotels, gambling dens, even houses of prostitution, and dotting the waters nearby were a huge collection of smaller, privately owned trading vessels, as opposed to the big freighters and passenger ships. A veritable forest of masts rose from the river surface with the appearance of a burned-over forest, where only the blackened trunks had escaped the blaze.

There were still far more tents than structures in Sacramento, but this was rapidly changing as new houses were completed and occupied, either before or immediately after being put up for sale. None remained unsold for more than a few days. Sacramento continued to be overwhelmed by newly arriving people, residents and transients alike, nearly all prattling about gold, especially where to find it, how to dig it, and how best to spend it. Even more so than San Francisco, Sacramento was essentially a community of men, who outnumbered women by nearly 25 to one; and more often than not, those rare female creatures were not available for anything more than shy, yearning glances or outright desirous stares. Older men, too, were almost as scarce as women, although their absence didn't trouble the younger men nearly as much.

Where nationalities were concerned, by far the greater majority fell into one of six categories — Americans, first, followed in succession by Mexicans, Germans, Britons, Chileans and Frenchmen. Other continents contributed smaller percentages to increase the total: Africa represented by three principal groups — Negroes, Moors and Abyssinians; Asia and Australasia providing a wider variety, comprised of pig-tailed Chinese mainlanders, blue-garbed interior Mongols, and diminutive Nipons, generally lithe Malays and dark-skinned Hindus, Maoris and Kanakas from the Pacific Islands; and, finally, from the Middle East, stately turbaned Ottomans and, intermingled among all, and clearly noted at the time, "ubiquitous Hebrews, ever to be found in the wake of movements offering trade profits, but many of the latter group often trading under assumed names because of a general, almost inherent dislike of their race by so many others."

How these various races converging upon Western America were viewed by the resident settlers clearly underlined the inherent prejudices based largely upon color and creed. In this respect, the majority were fairly neatly categorized and regimented by those who described the populace of the times. The preponderance, by far, however, were those of North America — whites, urbane and picturesque Hispanics, and half-naked aborigines.

What was clearly and very distinctly apparent in marking nationalities were their dress and manner, which, not surprisingly, were clearly much more noticeable in the burgeoning population centers such as San Francisco and Sacramento, than in the mining areas themselves, where more standardized mining garb predominated: red-checked and blue-checked woolen shirts, open at the throat, tending to boast a sort of shaggy robustness, as did a loosely secured kerchief about the neck. Dress-up apparel for a heavy proportion of the miners, if they ever submitted to dressing up at all, consisted of pantaloons half-tucked into high and wrinkled boots, and belted at the waist, where bristled an arsenal of knives and pistols, the armament in most cases far more for show than for protection.

Gradually, certain distinctive manifestations of dress developed and easily categorized the wearer into the specific social, cultural or professional classification toward which he seemingly leaned: Traders and clerks in their carefully creased suits; gamblers in puffy white shirts with diamond studs and often accompanied by a breast-pin or heavy, looping chain of nugget specimens; dandies wearing broad-brimmed hats, often with perky feathers or fluffy squirrels' tails anchored at the band and frequently a scarlet sash or white silk cloth wound around the waist or tossed over a shoulder with a degree of insouciance; the British tending toward a tweed jacket with leather-rimmed pockets usually witha deep-bowled tobacco pipe; northeastern Yankees in their Sunday-go-to-meeting, unadorned black clothing, including the stovepipe hat; the French, especially Parisians, with their snugly-fitting tapering cuts, stiff, stand-up collars and derby hats. Then there were the nondescript miners, who were by far the least concerned with dandyism in any form, usually with nothing better to wear than the cleanest shirt and trousers from their pack, baggy, tacky and unfashionable, but more often than not with a bulging pouch of gold in dust or flakes or nuggets somewhere on their person, wealth crying to be spent; and finally, intermingled among all, garishly rouged and lipsticked dancers and prostitutes with upswept hair-dos and feathered boas and tiny pearl-handled single-shot or double-barreled, small-caliber pistols hidden in bosomed or gartered holsters.

The blistered and battered and horny hands of the miner were his badge of honor which he wore with pride, while the immaculate hands of the clerk or gambler or banker or preacher were an abomination to him, proclaiming as they did a softer, cleaner lifestyle dependent upon the labors of others, especially miners.

The miners, irrespective of race, were a class in and of themselves, most of them very rugged men, whether tall, muscular and broad-shouldered, or slight and gaunt and wiry; they wore their own pride as a uniform, and their moustaches and whiskers almost as if they had been ordained. For the most part, they seemed — with the exception of some of the Mormons still on hand — incapable of formulating a sentence without the benefit of profanity, though uttered far more often with casual joy than with serious direction, and almost always tempered with twinkling eye and frank good humor.

A typical miner's speech and behavior almost always reflected a dissolution of tired conventionalities and the adoption of new patterns that discarded old prejudices and encouraged liberality in the miner's thought and expression. He found a heretofore unknown freedom that set moderation aside and welcomed enthusiastic and energetic self-reliance and vigor in whatever task he encountered. His own inner spirit thereby bloomed with unhindered enthusiasm, unconfined by conventionality or false propriety. For the miner very day was an excitement, and every day freed latent strengths previously bound by sanctioned dictates of society; he often cast tradition aside and gave imagination free reign. A general, relatively sudden freedom from restrictions unfettered a virtual reckless and provocativemental attitude within multitudes of miners which provided them with a new and infectious perspective on life itself.

The miners' prevailing, undeviating mania was intensely acquisitive. They looked upon San Francisco and Sacramento, along with virtually all of the gold camps, not as new homes but as temporary, vitally important communities comprising the means to their obsessive ends: To acquire, as quickly as possible, as large a fortune as possible before heading for home, wherever home happened to be.

Wages for unskilled laborers rose to a dollar an hour here in California, as opposed to an average of considerably less than half that per day in the East, and for artisans of various skills, fully $20 [$576] per day, provided any artisans could be found who were willing to work at a job rather than to follow the exciting and often incredibly rewarding avocation of searching for gold. One of the peculiarly unforeseen consequences of the acquirement — *or hope for the acquirement* — of great wealth through gold, was the amazing leveling of rank that resulted — a democratic equalization never before even approached and one which easily shattered previously held notions of class and rank; where riches lay so accessible to all, the accumulation of them became equal for duke or drudge. It was he who displayed and maintained the greater aptitude for grasping opportunity who succeeded, not necessarily he who was born into a higher class.

For many of the previous "higher class" members who had never before been required to complete for anything to maintain their station, suddenly success became more a matter of inherent abilities and developing skills than privileged birth. As a result, it was not surprising that while titles and surnames had a tendency to disappear if good fortune did not prevail, epithetic nicknames very frequently came into use, quite often descriptive of a person's character, physical attributes, or nationality. This, then, was the reason for the sudden increase in the use of shortened baptismal names coupled with character traits, such as One-Eyed Charley, Dutch Fred, Long-Legged Jack, Happy George, Baker Jake, Honest George, and Lucky Lou.

As was becoming obvious, the blunt, unrestrained creation of such designations resulted in a much less formalized companionship throughout the gold camps — a blunt and unrestrained fellowship that virtually eliminated stiff and formal courtesy. Oddly enough, the fundamental honesty of the greater majority of miners prevailed everywhere, and instances of violence or theft were still virtually absent. In the few instances where crime did occur and it was necessary to try an individual, the breathtaking speed with which matters were carried out — the jury selection, the case presented, the verdict given and the punishment carried out — was remarkable.

For jury trials some of the gold camps preferred panels of six, while others insisted upon as many as ten or twelve or even twenty. Sometimes the decision was simply put to all who were present in court, and the majority decision prevailed. Such courts, while agreeable enough to listening to testimony, had very little patience for prolonged argument. Further, with a distinct lack of jails existing or personnel to stand guard, such juries specialized in swift punishments, including hanging, whipping, ear-cropping, branding, or absolute banishment — or even a combination of some of these, depending upon the offense committed.

Milus Gay, resident miner in the Dry Diggings area, described in his *Journal* a typical case of such nature:

> *I was called up last night 11 or 12 o'clock to assist in taking and trying a man for stealing money — George Gillin, late of Ioway — Took him up to Dry Town — went into the 'Southern House' — I was appointed Judge — selected 12 men for Jury — tryed [sic] him — found him guilty Sentenced him to 39 lashes on the bare back — blind folded [sic]. Tryal [sic] occupyed [sic] the night — Jury verdict rendered about sun up — took him out — tied him up and applyed [sic] the lash — required him to leave by 3 p.m.*

San Francisco miner Richard J. Oglesby was also on hand to witness one such trial and wrote of it:

> *I was present one afternoon and saw with painful satisfaction ... Charley Williams whack three of our fellow citizens over the bare back, twenty-one to forty strokes, for stealing a neighbor's money. The multitude of disinterested spectators had conducted the court ... I think I never have seen justice administered with so little loss of time or at less expense.*

Meanwhile on the east coast, so great was the increase of passenger traffic from New York City and Boston to the California coast that the Pacific Mail took advantage of the heavy demand for transportation to increase its rates to $300 [$8,640] for cabin passage and $150 [$4,320] for steerage. It also increased its capabilities by securing additional equipment, which included chartering the British steamship *Unicorn*, and buying outright for $200,000 [$5,760,000] the massive 1,275-ton steamer *Tennessee*, which had been built to ply only the waters between New York City and Savannah.

One of the more important needs in the gold mining country was becoming painfully clear: Public transportation of any kind in California remained virtually nonexistent until a newcomer showed up with a novel plan. Acquiring one of the shipboard rowable lifeboats often referred to as a whaleboat, Alexander Todd offered passage from San Francisco to Sacramento for one ounce of gold to those who would agree to pull one oar. So enthusiastic was the response that John Whistman acquired an old omnibus stagecoach and a mixed team of mules and mustangs and offered "an adventurous and exciting ride" from San Francisco to San José, in precisely nine hours exactly for a fare of two ounces $32 [$921.60]. From the very day of its inaugural run, Whistman never had an empty seat.

These successes encouraged other entrepreneurs for whom gold prospecting this far had been signally unsuccessful. At Sacramento, John Birch became the first stagecoach operator. He started out with a light emigrant wagon and a team of fractious mustangs, hauling passengers from a depot at Sutter's Fort to Mormon Island for two ounces of gold. He, too, never had an empty seat, at least not on the outbound trip.

From such modest beginnings began the development of a remarkable system of public transportation. San Francisco Bay and its principal tributaries were soon being well churned by the big paddlewheelers and smaller propeller-driven boats after numerous river boats were built for this specific purpose. Quite soon bay and river boats were providing essential linkage between San Francisco, Sacramento, Stockton, San José, Marysville, and the eastern and northern shoreline cities of San Francisco Bay. New ships were added to the Pacific Line Transportation Co., and such craft as the *Goliah, Oregon Run,* and *Seabird* quickly gave Los Angeles, Santa Barbara and San Diego their first regularly scheduled contact with the civilized world.

In New England and New York, craftsmen designed and built new and better ships, including such sleek and sturdy clippers as *The Sea Witch, Sovereign of the Seas,* and *The Flying Cloud,* all three of which immediately set new records for a day's run, outward passages and homeward passages. Not uncommonly, such clippers paid out their construction costs on the very first voyage.

[May 9th, 1849 • Wednesday]

That so many miners could have rushed into the gold district so swiftly was baffling to James Carson. It seemed hardly more than yesterday that what lay before him was wilderness and the only movement to be seen was a circling hawk or vulture, or a wandering coyote or shambling bear. Now the prairies and hills stretching out before him were liberally dotted with the straggling clusters of tents, and every stream, every arroyo, every little run-off seemed choked with miners virtually shoulder to shoulder.

In the middle of last month he'd been southward, in the Mariposa Creek area, finding a little gold here and there, but for the most part he had not been able to access the area he was certain would be the most rewarding because of the number of miners already at work at that site. So many, in fact, had crowded into the Mariposa Creek drainage that he had finally turned his back on it in disgust and traveled farther north again, reasonably sure he'd find some little creek or ravine somewhere that wasn't crowded. As he wrote in his *Journal* on May 1st:

> *Not being pleased with the discoveries South, I started back with a small party to the scenes of my former good fortunes; but when I arrived, 1st May 1849, a change had come over the scene since I had left it; Stockton, that I had last seen graced only by Joe Buzzel's log house with a tule roof, was now a vast linen city. The tall masts of barques brigs, and schooners were seen pointed in the blue vault above — while the merry "Yo ho!" of the sailors could be heard, as box, bale, and barrel were off-loaded onto the banks of the slough. A rush and whirl of noisy human beings was continually before the eye. The magic wand of gold had been shaken over the desolate place, and on it a vast city had arisen at the bidding.*

Dismayed with what they had found at Stockton, Carson and his companions departed immediately and angled southeastward. As they neared the area where he had previously mined, his party paused to rest, and Carson quickly dug out his *journal* and recorded what lay before him:

> *We continued on to the old diggings from Stockton. When we reached the top of the mountains overlooking Carson's and Angel's Creek, we had to stand and gaze on the scene before us — the hill-sides were dotted with tents, and the Creeks filled with human beings to such a degree that it seemed as if a day's work of the mass would not leave a stone unturned in them; here they were now measuring the ground off with tape measures, under the direction of the alcaldes,*

so as to prevent disputes arising from the division.

In the great emigration that had taken place, the City and State of New York had the majority against the balance of the states; although the greater part of them were gentlemen, and quite good-hearted fellows, yet there were also some of the smallest [-minded] specimens of the human family amongst them that I ever before saw in California. I have seen some of these arrive in the diggings, and in their settlements quarrel about the amount of four cents' difference. A man who would quarrel in the gold mines of California, in '49, about such an amount, must surely have had a soul so small that ten thousand of them would not make a shadow.

We did not stop, but proceeded on to Wood's Creek in hopes there to find more room to exercise our digging propensities. But here it was worse — on the long flat we found a vast canvas city, under the name of Jamestown, which, similar to a bed of mushrooms, had sprung up in a night. A hundred flags were flying from [tented] restaurants, taverns, rum mills and gaming houses. Those gambling tables had their crowds continually, and the whole presented a scene similar to that of San Francisco during the past winter. I have there seen Spaniards betting an arroba [25 pounds] of gold at a time, and win or lose it as coolly as if it had been a bag of clay. Gold dust has risen in value from what it was in 1848 — as high as $10 [$288] per ounce was given for gold dust at the monte banks. Woods Creek was filled up with miners, and I here, for the first time after the discovery of gold, learned what a miner's claim was.

Such a vast assemblage of miners required, quite obviously, a reliable food source, and those who turned their attention in this direction rather quickly made as much or more than would have been their fortune had they stuck with gold mining. Large hunting parties were continually going out after whatever deer and bear they could find and, though both species had been quite plentiful before the gold discovery, already deer were becoming scarce and, while black bears were still not at all unusual, grizzlies, once very abundant, were now rarely seen except in the most remote areas.

A new food source, however, was proving itself to be a gold mine of its own. This was the great sea-bird rookery known as the Farrallon Islands, located in the Pacific 27 miles almost due west of the Golden Gate. Wildlife on these barren rocks included a wide selection of sea birds and a huge population of fur seals and sea lions. Russian and Yankee sailors had been harvesting the sea mammals for their pelts, meat and blubber since the beginning of the century without making any substantial dent in their population, and they had only rarely harvested the birds. Now that was all changed.

Enterprising hunters had come in and harvested the marine mammals in enormous numbers, salting the meat down in barrels and shipping it to distribution points in both San Francisco and Sacramento, and from there — with greatly escalated prices — to prospectors and miners throughout the gold belt. The rocks and crannies of the Farrallons were absolutely alive with such sea birds as cormorants and auklets, murres and puffins and gulls, and every possible level spot had its eggs, the most favored of which were the murre eggs. Beautifully blotched with color, the murre eggs were very large — larger even than those of the Canada goose — and, when freshly laid, very tasty; so good, in fact, that single murre eggs were quickly selling at many of the mines for $5 [$136] apiece, and "egging" had suddenly become a big business.

One of the earliest of the newcomers to profit from such an egg source was "Doc" Robinson, a pharmacist from Maine. With at least half a million breeding pairs of murres on hand, so profitable was his gathering, shipping and selling of the eggs at the mines, that he quickly earned enough from the rookeries on the Farrallons to build and fully stock his own pharmacy in San Francisco — from which he subsequently made an even greater fortune.

Very far distant, on the southern shore of Australia at the international port of Adelaide, tidings of the California gold discovery were finally delivered by the sleek clipper-ship *Peregrine*, arriving from the northeast. Hardly had she docked than the exciting news from California began to spread into a veritable web of fascinating tales.

A great sense of friendliness and companionship sprang up almost at once among the passengers already eagerly seeking a ship to book themselves upon as soon as possible for the voyage from Adelaide to San Francisco. The unusual camaraderie that rapidly developed among three prospective passengers boded well for the journey ahead that would launch them all into the heady search for gold.

[May 14th, 1849 • Monday]

Today the Delano party averted its first potentially significant disaster since embarking on its odyssey into the unknown western prairies.

It all came about when Dr. Hall, in searching for his cattle which had strayed, returned to the group with word that he believed he had discovered a good fording place for the Great Nemaha River, about a mile upstream from where they were camped. Before breakfast this morning, he and their group's leader, Jesse Greene, after riding up to reconnoiter the site, found it to be highly suitable and named it *Hall's Ford* in the doctor's honor.

While crossing the ford, however, Greene's horse stepped into a hole and when his saddle's girth strap abruptly loosened, he slid forward and pitched into a full somersault clear over his horse's head and into the river. Snorting and sputtering, Green struggled back to his horse and re-cinched the girth strap.

"Cold baths," he said, his levity returning, "are recommended by physicians, so I guess I've just had the water-cure principle against future disease."

Everyone hooted with laughter at that, and none more genuinely than Greene himself. When the train was brought up and made ready to cross, Greene brought his horse in front and took the lead to show the way. As luck would have it, the saddle's cinch-buckle loosened again, pitched him forward exactly as before, and once again he flipped over his horse's head and into the current. When he surfaced, the laughter was even more boisterous than before, and Greene was shaking his head when he tightened up the girth and mounted into the saddle yet again.

"This makes me," he chuckled, "the best marksmen in the whole doggoned company; without firing a shot I've gotten a brace of ducks!"

Such a sense of good humor had prevailed within Delano's party members since early May, and this good-natured rapport contributed significantly to their confidence in their future perilous emigration efforts. Delano was recovering rapidly from his illness, and on Wednesday evening, May 2nd, he finished what he feared might possibly be the last column he could submit to the *Free Trader* for what could prove to be a good while. He wrote:

Dear Free Trader — I left my comfortable quarters,

> *where I had stopped to recruit [recover] and dose off the chills and came here to join our Ottawa Company. They have been encamped on the opposite side of the river in Indian Territory several days, but as the grass is good out at least fifteen miles, they have broken up their camp and have determined to move as far as grass will allow. I shall cross the river after dinner and overtake them. We shall then be beyond any regular public conveyance — shall have to depend entirely upon chance. I shall embrace any which may occur to continue my correspondence. I am happy to say that my health is re-established. I learn that all our company are well. We do not go to Fort Kearny, but strike for Grand Island on the Platte. And now commence our wanderings, and whether they will continue as long and be as varied as those of the Children of Israel, remains to be seen. I fear, however, that one of their evil deeds will be in some measure initiated by us; that is, the worship of the "Golden Calf." May we not forget, however, that there is a God in Israel. This is sixty miles above St. Joseph.*

Delano elaborated somewhat more in his own private Journal:

> *Wednesday, May 2 — ... again mounting old Shab, I rode to the ferry, where I learned that the company had started out that day, determined to go on as far as the grass would allow the cattle to be driven. After dinner, dropping a few words to my friends by the last regular mail, I crossed the river, which is, perhaps, a third of a mile in width, and stood, for the first time, in the Indian country.*

The *Ottawa Company's* camp, Delano discovered, had been set up about a mile and a half below the ferry, on the bottom, but he found it vacated when he reached the spot, though the trail of their wagons was plainly to be seen, leading up to the top of the high bluff, which was running parallel with the river. There he turned his pony's head toward the Platte.

Ascending a long hill, Delano found the land was only sparsely covered with timber and very broken as far as he could see among the trees. The road marked by his own party's train, however, was on an easy ridge, which led beyond the broken ground into the interior. The timber continued for another four or five miles and then abruptly ceased, and ahead lay a broad expanse of rolling prairie so extensive, it seemed to Delano that sky and plain had finally merged into one another in a vast green carpet. He scanned the scene ahead, searching for any sign of a farmhouse or road, a cultivated field or some grazing cattle, but no such sign of civilization met his eye. As he wrote of it:

> *All was still and lonely, and I had an overwhelming feeling of wonder and surprise at the vastness and silence of the panorama. It seemed as if the sight of an Indian would have given relief, but not one appeared, and on, on I rode, without seeing a sign of life, and with none but my own thoughts to commune with. A little before nightfall, on rising a hill, I came suddenly in sight of the encampment of our Company, consisting of seventeen wagons and fifty men, all of whom were from the neighborhood of Ottawa. They were encamped in a hollow, near a fine spring, and putting Old Shab to his best gait, in three minutes I stood among my friends, with a glorious appetite to partake of their savory supper of bacon, bread, and coffee. They had made about fifteen miles. Soon after my arrival, all hands were summoned by the blast of the bugle, for the purpose of adopting general rules for mutual safety in traveling and also to detail a guard for the night.*
>
> *My own mess was now composed of Messrs. I. H. Fredenburg, Benjamin K. Thorne, Robert Brown, Hazel Henderson, John Morrill, Eben Smith, and myself. It was the intention of our Company to keep the dividing ridge between the Great and Little Namaha [Nemeha], to a certain point, which had been marked out, and then strike off to the St. Joseph Road, which we had been assured we could reach in about eight days, and we relied much on following the trail of the train which had passed over the ground four years before, and which here was very plainly perceptible. Our guards being posted, we all turned into our tents, and fatigue and the novelty of our situation were soon forgotten in the arms of the god of sleep.*

Early on the following morning, the entire company assembled and, well arranged and provisioned for the great journey ahead, prepared to set off. Every wagon was carefully numbered, and Captain Greene, with the concurrence of the members, directed that each wagon should, in turn, take the lead for one day and then, falling in the rear, give place to the succeeding number, and so on, alternately, until all seventeen wagons had advanced in turn. Every mess was provided with a light, portable cooking stove which, though not absolutely necessary, was often found convenient due to the scarcity of fuel. Every man in the company was armed with rifle, pistol, knife, and abundant ammunition, and each mess had a good, substantial tent. Each wagon was drawn by anywhere from three to six yoke of good cattle, and it was agreed that they should be prudently driven; all accompanying members were acutely aware of how helpless they would be should the cattle be lost on the plains, where there could be no hope of stock replacement.

Fearing that the animals might stray or even be stolen by Indians during the night, the company established a watch while the cattle were feeding, and at nightfall they were driven in and tied to the wagons so as to be constantly under the supervision of the night guard, to prevent their being stolen by night-raiding Indians.

Shortly before sunrise each morning, the cattle were driven out to graze. By this time all hands had risen, and some were already preparing breakfast. The tents had been pitched outside of the circled wagons, creating a second barricade. Hence, if thieves were attracted, they would be compelled to penetrate this tent barrier to reach the valuables within the inner circle — and both barriers were heavily guarded. In this configuration, too, if the company members were attacked, they could be quickly maneuvered into the inner, tighter barricade.

Most of the densely-packed wagons included a good stash of firewood. Brown was installed as the company cook, and consequently, others assumed his night watch shifts. Henderson drove the Delano cattle and Smith made himself generally useful in collecting the fuel, pitching and striking the tent and similar chores. At about 9 a.m. the company broke camp, stowed the tents aboard the wagons, herded in and yoked the cattle, and commenced another day's trek on the plains.

The country was now decidedly rolling prairie. Four or five miles to the right was the Little Nemaha, vaguely marked by a line of trees or shrubbery which occurred nowhere else. Old Mr. Greene, father of The Dayton Company's captain, was well experienced in traversing the western prairies, and so to him fell the duties of chief guide. He was rarely at fault, although many of the others were frequently confused.

Although this was only their second full day in Indian country, they soon learned a hard lesson. About 10 a.m., Delano had walked about a mile ahead of the train and was just a little behind Greene and Fredenburg, when two strangers abruptly appeared in sight riding on a knoll ahead of them and leading three mules and three horses. The pair halted and gazed at *The Dayton Company* for a few minutes, and though everyone thought the pair would either wait or move to approach the company, the two began instead to angle away. Greene and Fredenburg, eager to make some inquiries, set off at speed to intercept them.

The two men reined in as Greene and Fredenburg galloped up to them. When they approached, the strangers told them they were part of a company of 100 wagons. "We started out from old Fort Kearny," the elder of the two told them, "an' got ourselves 'bout forty miles out on the plains when th' damn new grass jus' plum' give out. Our comp'ny hadn't no choice 'cept to camp a while, and we got sent to the settlements for some supplies, but me an' Slim here got turned 'round a bit. 'Sposed to be a li'l town called Savannah somewheres back thataway," he pointed in the direction from which Greene and Fredenburg had come. "Leastway, we *think* so. K'n you fellers mebbe point us in the right direction to get there?"

Glad to help, Greene gave them directions, and the pair thanked him and set off. A little later Delano caught up to his own comrades, and the three started back toward the train. In another half-hour of riding, they encountered three riders — two white men and an Indian — who told them they were in pursuit of the two men leading horses and mules. That pair, they said, belonged to no company, and the tale of a 100-wagon train was just a big lie; the two had stolen the animals they were leading from an Illinois Company stationed at Fort Kearny. The whites said they suspected the Indian who was with them was in cahoots with the pair, and so these two had forced the brave to come along with them in the pursuit. As Delano continued the little saga in his *Journal*:

> *Before night the two men with the Indian returned to our camp, saying they had overtaken the thieves who, on seeing they were being pursued, jumped from their animals and*

made their escape in the timber on the bank of the creek. At this point the Indian asked permission of his two white companions to ride one of their fine horses to intercept the rogues, which would prove he had not been in cahoots with them.

One of the pair dismounted from the recovered animal and the Indian mounted and instantly set off in a round gallop and quickly disappeared behind a hill. After waiting some time for his reappearance, they happened to look in another direction and saw the Indian making off with their horse, a new saddle and an overcoat that had been tied to the saddle. It was now too late for them to think of overtaking the red runaway and they had to submit to their loss with the best grace they could, cursing their own credulity, but giving the Indian credit for his ingenuity.

Delano, Greene and Fredenburg rode back to their own *Ottawa Company* together, fully convinced never to accept too readily a story told by strangers.

On the following morning — Saturday, May 5th — on driving the cattle up to the camp, they discovered that one of Greene's oxen had become too sore to be harnessed. He was turned loose and a cow hitched in his place and, according to Delano, she served the purpose exceedingly well. It had rained heavily during the night, and hence, the ground was soggy, the travel slow. As Delano remarked in his *Journal*:

... the wind, which blew a gale every day, retarded our progress with our high, canvas-covered wagons. It was found to be a fault in having the tops of our wagons too large, for the force of the wind against them made the labor much harder on our cattle, and we resolved to stop at the first convenient place and reduce their dimensions, as well as to overhaul provisions. We discovered that we had been imposed upon in St. Louis in the purchase of our bacon, for it began to exhibit more signs of life than we had bargained for. It became necessary to scrape and smoke it, in order to get rid of its tendency to walk in insect form.

We are now about forty-five miles from our starting point, and have approached by the windings of our course,

> *to within about a mile of the Great Nemaha, on our left. And now the course of both streams was plainly visible from the ridge. We drove to the bank of the Great Nemaha and spent most of the day in overhauling our meat, and in reducing our wagon covers to proper size, which was found to be a decided improvement. We had been in bed but a short time after the labors of the day were brought to a close, when some drops of rain pattering on our tents, admonished us that our preparations for a storm were incomplete, and one of the boys turned out and dug a trench around the tent, so that when the storm came upon us, we were prepared, and kept perfectly dry.*
>
> *Since leaving the Missouri, we had seen no game except a few plover, which were wild and shy, and though we had been traveling in the Ottoe country for five days, not a single Indian , save the one pursuing the horse thieves, had been seen. Grass was now scanty, and fuel scarce, and our practice was, when in the vicinity of streams, to gather wood enough to last two or three days, and carry it with us. Distance five miles.*

Virtually all members of the train believed that they had been wise to go farther up the Missouri before moving cross-country on the so-called Nemaha Cut-Off to intercept the regular trail many miles out, because this would give them good grass all the way. That assumption, unfortunately, had been a significant error. They lost their way in the trackless prairie where there were no distinguishing features whatever, simply unending expanses of dried grass stalks from the previous year. During their wandering they saw a single elk and one wolf, but precious little wildlife beyond that. The landscape was dreary and the cover offered little food benefit for the horses and cattle; instead of gaining eight or ten days on those who had stuck to the trail, they lost all they had gained plus a week or more besides. The weather grew significantly colder, and day after day of cold, rainy, windy weather benumbed and discouraged them as well as making the cattle herd fractious and extremely difficult to control.

Not until May 9th did the topography begin to change a bit, presenting much more agreeable scenery. As Delano wrote of it:

In the afternoon the country was less broken, and afforded us many very beautiful views. We were on a ridge, with a broad valley on each side and many little creeks making down into the Nemahas, and their courses were marked by timber sparsely growing on their banks. All around the grass was green and luxuriant, and it seemed, as we ascended one rise after another, that each view was still more charming than the other. I did not wonder that the aborigines were attached to their delightful country, and had it been mine, I should have defended my possessions against the encroachment of any lawless intruder. We had contrived up to this time to procure wood enough for cooking purposes, but now it disappeared and in place of it was an abundance of rosin weed, which was an excellent substitute. This contained a resinous gum, which exuded beneath the leaves, and it burned freely. It seemed as if when we were about to be deprived of one essential comfort, Providence had substituted another for our good, and an armful of these excellent stalks could be gathered in a few minutes.

Having gained sufficient strength, I reported myself accordingly, and for the first time was detailed as one of the night guard. At the appointed time I shouldered my rifle and commenced my two hours tour of duty. The night was dark, though clear, and there was not even a bush to magnify into an Indian. But I found it a glorious opportunity to think, and as I "Pac'd my lonely rounds," wonderful old reminiscences passed rapidly before me, so that my guard was by no means a work of labor. I reviewed the scenes of a somewhat eventful life, checkered with good and evil fortune, from boyhood, when, with my early and still loved friend, Ed Morgan, I got into a glorious scrape, in throwing fire balls to frighten the girls of a boarding school; the parental lecture which followed; then of the love scenes of later years, during which I fooled one good looking girl, and pulled the wool over her eyes in such a way as to make her believe I was a handsome young scamp, and she took me for better or worse, and is now the mother of my children; then other friends came up, as in Richmond's dream, not to frighten, but to enkindle old feelings of endearment; in short, I was in a most glorious train of thought, when the sergeant of the guard shouted, in the stillness of the night, "relief turn out," and soon my retrospections were buried, like my head, between two as good blankets as ever covered a nomad specimen of humanity. Alas! For poor nature, California was many days journey distant, and I had ample time to indulge in day dreams and retrospections, before I "dragged my weary length along" in the valley of the Sacramento. Distance 18 miles.

The following two days passed with nothing of consequence occurring except the bagging of a raccoon for a breakfast repast in Delano's mess on Friday, May 11th, of which he wrote:

We had a capital breakfast — a welcome change from our ordinary fare. Occasionally, men's appetites grow aristocratic on the Plains, and for once we felt disposed to indulge in this anti-plebeian taste. A raccoon had been killed on the previous day, and an ample share was divided with our mess. As the merit of fresh meat is not properly appreciated at home, where it is too common, owing no doubt to the ordinary way of preparing it, I beg leave to append a recipe for the best mode of preparing 'coons for the delicate taste of epicures. MEMO: First, catch your 'coon and kill him, skin him, and take out the entrails; cut off his head, which throw away; then, if you have water to spare, wash the carcass clean, but if you have not, omit the washing. Parboil an hour to take out the strong musk, then roast it before the fire on a stick. While it is roasting, walk ten miles, fasting, to get an appetite, then tear it to pieces with your fingers, and it will relish admirably with a little salt and pepper, if you happen to have them. A tin cup of boiled coffee without milk, taken with it, makes, under the circumstances, a feast fit for the gods.

During the day we saw antelopes [sic] for the first time, but they were extremely shy, and our hunters could not approach them near enough to get a shot. They played around at a distance, and frequently stopped to gaze at our train as it passed along, with evident wonder, as if to ask what strange race we were, and what the dickens we were doing on their stamping ground.

We crossed the Pawnee trails in the course of the day, but the lords of the soil still kept aloof. About noon we came to a little tributary of the Great Nemaha, which we crossed by building a bridge, and here we found the trail again, and the remains of a bridge which the emigrant train had built four years before. We were in momentary expectation of reaching the St. Joseph road, and every eye was strained in the distance to catch the first view of the throng, who, like ourselves, were bound upon a golden voyage, but still we saw it not. Distance 17 miles.

It rained during that night, and the next morning the train found the road heavy, but the day was cool and their course direct. At close to noon they reached the Little Nemaha and, again, faced the necessity of building a bridge in order to cross it. Shortly thereafter they found a beautiful camping place along the river's west bank, with an abundance of luxuriant grasses for the animals, which put the men into admirable spirits. At this point *The Ottawa Company* members supposed they were only a few hours' drive to the road, and they congratulated themselves over the prospect of soon meeting civilized men in the form of fellow travelers. They found antelope running about in all directions, and the river itself was liberally coated with ducks swimming about. The men went cheerfully about their construction task and by mid-afternoon had finished constructing a good bridge, having dug the steep banks to a better taper for the cattle, and having created a much-improved crossing place.

Delano and a companion, Peter Hoes, took their rifles and sauntered out into the prairie a couple of miles and, after crossing ditches, forcing their way through bushes and becoming very tired, returned to camp, to their chagrin, without having fired a shot. B. K. Thorne had much better luck, returning before dark with several ducks. During the night they all had a bit of a show, and as Delano wrote in his *Journal*:

... we had a grand illumination; the dry grass on the opposite bank was on fire for a long distance, and as occasionally a current of air swept along, the blaze in a huge semi-circle glared up through the darkness like a sea of fire, rolling along from place to place, as the dry grass became ignited, with a

most grand and pleasing effect.

May 13th, 14th and 15th passed, still with no evidence of the trail they had long been seeking before Dr. Hall finally found his fording place across the Little Nemaha. At that point old Mr. Maxwell Greene, father of *The Dayton Company's* leader, decided it was time for him to strike out on his own to try to locate the long-missing trail. He left with two other men but with neither guide nor compass, depending solely on his long experience traveling over prairies, and upon his rifle for safety. Still, when he had not returned by sunset, the entire Company became concerned for his welfare. His son took the flag and climbed up upon an eminence overlooking an extensive view of the prairie, hoping that it might serve as a beacon for his father.

Finally, much to Captain Greene's relief, the old gentleman was spotted about a half-mile distant — though not accompanied by the two men who had been with him — and exchanged signals with his son. Suddenly, however, the old man changed course and dashed off across the plain as fast as his mule could carry him and soon disappeared behind the low hills. The company grew tense with worry once again at nightfall when the old man had still not returned. No one could fathom the mystery. A group of the men climbed up to the top of one of the higher hills and there built a large fire. As it was burning fiercely as a beacon, they fired off their rifles in volleys for several minutes to further signal the old man, but to no avail. As Delano wrote briefly in his Journal:

> *... all was in vain. Time slowly wore on, the roll was called, the guard set, and no one lay down this night upon his hard bed, without an anxious feeling for the safety of our brave old pioneer.*

[May 26th, 1849 • Saturday]

By today, the final Saturday in May, virtually all those who hoped to be across the great Sierra Nevada Range before heavy snows of autumn closed the passes, were on their way. From Independence and St. Joseph the trains had funneled out into the great unknown prairies in an almost unbroken month-long string of animals, wagons and humans. Although the Oregon Trail had been in use for a good many years now, the heavy density of the traffic on it this year was unprecedented.

Day upon day, company after company left behind them the final elements of civilized society and spread themselves in a gradually merging line that slid westward, resembling the pace of a great lumbering snail with the gracelessness of a thin, long, arthritic snake. Along some early stretches of the trail, the stream of wagons creaked along in an unbroken line from daybreak until nightfall, bunching up at times where the crossing of dangerous streams required ferrying rather than fording.

At night, as far as the eye could scan ahead and behind, the individual campfires glowed and twinkled, forming a squiggly but uninterrupted line from horizon to horizon. Bayard Taylor, as one of the hundred thousand or more travelers in the great emigration, wrote in his diary:

> *The rich meadows of the Nebraska or Platte were settled for a time, and a single traveler could have journeyed for 1,000 miles, as certain of his lodging and regular means as if he were riding through the old agricultural districts of the middle states.*

The initial days and weeks of the journey were relatively easy, though most of the travelers had no experience-based standard for judging what was easy and what was not. To many the early portions seemed very difficult, indeed, until they reached progressively more frightening and nearly impassable trails yet to come, which more often than not would cause them to look back on these early days and miles with a wistful sense of nostalgia.

During those earliest days and weeks and miles, the travelers were happy trekkers, filled with anticipation for what lay ahead, viewing every rain gully, stream-crossing or muddy expanse as a new challenge to be overcome by an indomitable spirit. A spirit of camaraderie reigned among them, an almost eager willingness to help one another along, to free one another from difficulties, to plod onward into a future which might be uncertain, but they hoped was full of promise, and their high hopes stoked their enthusiasm. Only as the great marches continued day after interminable day and discomforts and accidents and delays accumulated rapidly did the geniality ebb and a surging sense of competitiveness take on a more important role among the myriad emigrants. But such a sobering evolution lay still in the future. Now in these beginning days and weeks, the travelers engaged in pleasant exchanges of chat and laughter and repartee and news, all accompanied by an almost constant medley of shoutings and whistlings, whip-snappings and whinneyings, bellowings of cattle and men alike, and by the ever-present creaking of the wagons and the discordant jangling of their varied contents.

When occasionally a specific group would pause to rest or eat or even, if possible, to bathe, those following would quickly, smoothly fill the gaps, and the long line would continue unbroken toward a great indeterminate but ever-present goal called simply, The West. Toward the end of each day, this long undulating line coalesced into smaller groups for the night. The wagons were ringed for safety against possible foes, as well as for later corralling after the livestock had grazed. The fires were built for the preparation of meals; the guards mounted for intervals of watch. The women cooked and talked; the children were given an interval of play. The men tended the animals and tinkered with equipment. They discussed the trail, the weather, and whatever problems were at hand or anticipated. Later voices were raised in song and humor and easy conversation; the beds were prepared within and without the wagons. Tents were unfolded and staked into positions, and the exhaustion of a day's travel gradually drained away in the blessed interval of sleep.

The prairies were aflame with the flowers of May, in streaks and patches and great swaths of color and aroma against a background of variegated greens, and there was a singular sense of "aliveness" to all that was occurring. And throughout each and every day a veritable stream of wagons, seemingly without beginning or end, passed by.

Finally, as the trains reached the Platte some ten or fifteen or twenty days after they had embarked on the long trek, a sense of established order began to prevail, and the routine of the march held sway until the vast prairies were left behind and the going became far more difficult: Passages through broiling deserts, over steep mountain passes at sometimes freezing elevations; passages past geysers and boiling, seething springs; passages through viscous mucks that sucked a wagon's wheels down to hub-level; and passages along roadless trails that the emigrants, themselves, had to construct through boulder-choked chasms and arroyos.

Some of the emigrants preferred not to think about what lay ahead, but to merely take things as they came, hoping for the good fortune to survive the journey. Others, far less confident in the vagaries of luck, figured what lay ahead "might be just a little more difficult" than what they had already encountered — a comment that was all too frequently uttered and that gradually revealed itself to be a mind-boggling understatement.

Chapter 6

[May 27th 1849 • Sunday]

For the first time since their journey across the plains began, T*he Ottawa Company*, to which Alonzo Delano was attached, encountered two successive days of splendid weather. With the shallow but broadly sprawling Platte River to their right and the Oregon Trail beneath their feet, spirits were high and the miles slid behind as smoothly as they had at any time since their westward trek had begun.

Nevertheless, the fear and uneasiness provoked by the inexplicable disappearance of old Mr. Greene, their guide and the father of *The Dayton Company's* leader, Jesse Green, had only increased when by daybreak on May 16th, he still had not returned. The sky, mirroring the mood that infected them all, was heavily overcast, and daylight came upon them slowly. Determined to find out one way or another what had happened to the older man, a group of six men volunteered to ride out and search for him while the remainder set to work on completing construction of the temporary bridge they'd begun yesterday to span the steeply banked stream barring their progress.

Perhaps influenced by the continuing gloomy weather, the entire camp became increasingly sober and nervous. In mid-morning a trio of men volunteered to take a position atop the nearest large hill and maintain a vigil there throughout the remainder of the day. They did so, but concern mounted even more when, an hour before noon, the missing man was still missing, as were those who had gone in search of him. Then, as Delano recorded the details in his Journal:

About eleven o'clock a shout arose from those on the look-out, and the old gentleman made his appearance over a knoll. The word was passed, "He's coming! He's coming!" All rushed from their labors to welcome him and a treble round fired as a *feu de joie* for his safe return.

They plied old Mr. Greene with questions, of course, and he filled them in on what had occurred. He had imediately the evening before, recognized his son, Capt. Greene, as he approached but, at almost the same moment he startled an antelope. Thinking this to be a fine opportunity to bring some fresh meat into camp, especially since he had himself had nothing to eat since early morning, he started to follow the animal. The pronghorn, however, kept ahead of its pursuer, just out of range of a shot. After several miles the antelope tired of the game and sprinted away and out of sight.

By this time, having lost his sense of direction, thanks to the animal's circuitous course, and with darkened skies obscuring the sun's location, old Mr. Greene felt lost. Maintaining perfect composure as evening closed in, he removed the saddle from his mule, and swaddling himself in the saddle blanket, he lay down to await the dawn. When light came, still darkened with clouds, he was able to get his bearings. Re-saddling his mule, he quickly found the proper direction and headed that way, and now he had safely returned.

Not so the rescue party, so another group mounted up and went in search of them, and it wasn't until evening that all were finally back in camp and able to chuckle about what had occurred. They talked well into the night about the genuine scare the whole affair had ignited among them.. Despite the relief they all felt, their anxiety persisted: They had, after all, not yet found the trail. With more than an hour of daylight remaining, Orderly Sergeant John Traverse decided to head out and explore the country to the southwest, the area where most of the emigrants felt the trail had to be. Morrill volunteered to accompany him, and off they went. After journeying about fourteen miles, they returned and, as Delano noted in his Journal:

> *... at night without making any discoveries as to our locality, and brought the unwelcome intelligence that after passing ridge after ridge and crossing several creeks, they had not found the road. Nevertheless, it was still resolved to continue our west-southwest course by the next day's light. Some of our men were successful in catching fish, and we were enabled to add another luxury to our meager fare.*

At dawn all the men were astir, and having yesterday completed the bridge, left their excellent campground, crossed the stream, and passed over what Delano described as

> *... a charming bottom of more than two miles in width before we reached the high table-land of the prairie on the south. Although our anxiety to reach the road was great, we were in good spirits and not daunted, for fifty able-bodied men, well armed and provided with the substantial comforts of life, were not to be easily discouraged. Wild onions grew in abundance on the bottom. They were about the size of a hickory-nut, and covered with a kind of close net-work, which is stripped off like a husk, leaving the onion clear and bright and equal in flavor to any I ever ate. Signs of buffalo began to appear, and we passed several skeletons which were bleaching on the plain, but we saw none alive. ...*

Delano and his companions were strongly impressed with the lushness of the country they were passing through and agreed it would have made ideal habitat for the mastodon and all sorts of mammoths to cavort in. That they considered this a distinct possibility was reflected in Delano's comment hastily penned into his *Journal*:

> *If we see signs of any before we reach the road, which is quite likely, I'll surely make note of it here in my journal."*

More than anything else at this stage of the movement west, Delano was struck with the lack of rocks since crossing the Missouri, some 200 miles behind. As he noted, occasionally, where a bluff was worn by water, a small amount of gravel appeared, and near the heads of both the Great and Little Nemaha Rivers there was some trace of limestone schist that became evident, but the ground consisted for the most part of simply deep, rich black soil, which Delano judged as being ideal for wheat, cereal grains, and hemp. The streams had no gravel beds, like the ones he and his fellow emigrants were accustomed to seeing in eastern brooks. Instead the bottoms were nothing but quick-sand or mud, and the water flowing in them was, to his delight, softer than rainwater and very palatable. Nevertheless, he thought the lack of timber and stone would be a distinct impediment to any rapid settlement of the country. In his Journal, Delano noted that:

We found the country during the day's drive very level, and a little after noon we reached a plain, where there was not a tree or shrub, nor a sign of life except our own train, as far as the eye could extend. The glare of the sun upon the distant plain resembled the waves of a sea, and there were appearances of islands and groves, from the effect of the mirage.

Once they were across the height of a tableland and almost imperceptibly descending into the drainage of what they believed to be the Big Blue River, the grass became dry and scanty, and all traces of even slightly marshy ground vanished. The soil was now thin and light and, as Delano noted:

... decidedly the poorest we had seen since leaving the Missouri. Badger holes were numerous, and occasionally our hunters brought in an animal of that species, which we found quite palatable. ... For the last few days the rosin-weed had disappeared and our fuel was dry weeds and buffalo excrement, which served us quite well to boil our coffee and fry our bacon. We had been able to keep a direct course through the day, from the nature of the country, and made a good drive of eighteen miles.

As he wrote in his *Journal* about their travel the next day, Delano's wry sense of humor returned in several of his notations:

May 19th. Saturday. The country quite resembles that of the previous day ... and as we looked over the broad expanse of prairie, till earth and sky seemed to blend, we could not repress a feeling of loneliness. We passed, during the day, a large town of prairie dogs, but its inhabitants, having notice of our approach, did not vouchsafe their presence to welcome us, and we gained no information with regard to their peculiar manners and customs. The little hillocks which marked their abodes stood arranged in regular order, with streets about twenty feet wide, crossing themselves at right angles. Notwithstanding we had no fuel but such as has been previously mentioned, and that scarce, our appetites were so keen that we could have devoured our bacon — ate, perhaps a young prairie-dog without the usual process of cooking; and had an elephant made his appearance, we might have been able to have masticated one of his tushes by way of dessert.

We observed a rich pink flower blooming from bunches of a bright green color, from which many of our men formed nosegays, for their fragrant odor. After a while some of them had the curiosity to taste this rare plant, and found it to be nothing more or less than wild cives [chives], of an excellent quality, when in a moment the nosegays were thrown aside, and a supply of this member of the onion family gathered for our evening meal. ... Upon halting at night, a foot-race excitement was got up, and many trials of speed were made among the younger portion of our company, but the long legs of [Benjamin] Kent Thorne ran off with the palm. Distance to-day, sixteen miles.

The following day — Sunday, May 20th — their travel was over a broad table-land on which they were able to maintain a direct west-southwest course. But they continued to question one another, " *... where the dickens is the St. Joseph road? Where are we? — and where have we been?"* They had now been out nineteen days upon the wilderness. Their object in taking this new route had been to save time and to move ahead of other trains. The question now began to deeply trouble them: Had they succeeded? Had they gained anything by their erratic course?

For the past three days they had been enabled by the nature of the country to make a direct line towards the road. When traveling between the Nemahas, they supposed that they were within five or six miles of the road, yet since then they'd covered more than fifty miles without reaching it; and so far as they could see — and their hunters were out four or five miles from the train — there was still no indication of it. Anxiously they drove on, with "hope deferred," wishing that the next knoll would bring the long anticipated object into view. Then at last, near four o'clock, their captain, who had ridden ahead four or five miles, was seen riding back toward them at full gallop, swinging his hat joyfully. As Delano swiftly scrawled in his *Journal*:

At once a shout was raised, "The road is found; the road

> *is found!" and our loud huzzas testified the joy of us poor Israelites, who had so long been lost on the prairie wilderness."*

The train encamped then on a fine bottom near a pretty creek, a mile from the road, and a camp of emigrants was reported to be below them. At this point Hazel Henderson relocated to this nearby camp, and after doing so, he learned from members of this company that a large number of wagons were ahead, and that St. Joseph was only 150 miles eastward. Upon learning these sobering facts, the members of the *The Dayton* and *The Ottawa* companies fully realized the magnitude of their error: During the past twenty-four days of their traveling, nineteen of which had been upon the prairie to reach this point, the trains that had come directly by the road had passed through this same location without difficulty in just eleven days!

The men of *The Ottawa Company* fervently hoped this would be the last such error they would make, but they were acutely aware that such mistakes would be difficult to avoid during the course of their long odyssey across this vast, virtually alien land. As Delano wrote in his *Journal* the next day:

> *May 21 — 1849 — Monday: Our desire to be upon the road induced us to be starting early, and we were moving as soon as our cattle had eaten their fill, when a drive of a mile placed us on the great thoroughfare of the goldseekers.*

What they saw on the nearby main trail at this point virtually stunned them. For as far as their eyes could see to the east and to the west, a varied, animated non-stop line of white-covered wagons moved slowly but steadily along, accompanied by multitudes of horsemen prancing about, and by legions of men tramping along on foot. Although the *Ottawa* emigrants would never have called this vast panorama attractive, nevertheless the display of banners from many wagons and the multitude of armed men gave the impression that a mighty army was on the march. Within moments The *Ottawa Company* found an opportunity to take its place in the long line of westward-migrating gold-seekers. As Delano continued to note:

> *To us it gave great relief, after being so long in uncer-*

tainty, and although we were strangers, yet there was a fellow-feeling in having one pursuit in common, and we drove merrily along, giving and receiving accounts of our various adventures since leaving Missouri.

At near mid-day they reached the point on the Little Blue where they intended to leave the river and to strike directly across the plain to the Platte River, which they estimated to be twenty-three miles away; hence, they took the precaution of filling their water barrels and reloading their wagons with what woody stems could be found along the river's course. They made this short trek without difficulty, and by the following morning were viewing the valley of the Platte River. As Delano wrote:

... as level as a floor, and the great artery of the Missouri, turbid, muddy waters, a mile in width, divided by Grand Island, came in sight.

Delano chuckled upon hearing a comment made by one of the easterners, who didn't think that this sprawling stream compared with the eastern rivers: "By grab," the man snorted, "that's just not the way a decent river should look. Now, if you just stood it on edge instead of all flattened out, it might make a pretty good river!" Delano was inclined to agree, and he was still chuckling as he jotted his own notation:

Here, too, was a scene of active life. Here the road from old Fort Kearny united with the St. Joseph road, and for the whole distance in view, up and down the river, before and behind us, long trains were in motion or encamped on the grassy bottom, and we could scarcely realize we were in an Indian country, from the scene of civilized life before us, and this was all caused by the magi talisman of gold. What will be the end? Who can foresee our future destiny?

As they approached the Platte, Delano abruptly sensed what he at first thought was a significant change in the atmosphere; the warm temperature seemed to drop so rapidly that he was compelled to don his overcoat. When no one else seemed to be similarly affected, Delano suddenly realized that he was experiencing the tell-tale symptoms of his cholera returning. Becoming too weak to walk any further, he awkwardly climbed into his wagon and fumbled for his medications. However quickly the symptoms had manifested themselves, they disappeared just as rapidly, and the chill passed. In a somewhat shaky hand Delano wrote:

> *When we arrived at the point of the hill above the valley, I observed a train coming in from the Kearny road, which I thought I recognized. Drawing nearer, I felt certain that it was a company from South Bend, Indiana, led by my friend, Captain C. M. Tutt, with whom I had parted company a month before at St. Joseph. Our own train stopping for a noon halt, I mounted the pony and rode over to them, when I found it really was that company, and that by a singular coincidence we had thus met at a distance of more than three hundred miles from where we had last parted. ... They had left St. Joseph and crossed the Missouri at old Fort Kearny ... and then had reached this point by a well-beaten road in eleven days, while we were boxing the compass, and wearying our legs on the prairie for nearly a month, in doubt and anxiety as to our position.*

From Captain Tutt, Delano learned the probable explanation for the fact that they had seen no Indians during their trek thus far. "The Pawnees and the Sioux," Tutt told him, "are at war and they've been keeping close to their villages and strongholds. Toward evening on the nineteenth, a band of eighty Sioux visited our camp, and I'll tell you, Alonzo, it was scary. They were all mounted and came up on us at full speed, every one of 'em armed: Bows and arrows, knives, tomahawks, clubs, spears, shields. I had no idea what their intentions were, but I went alone toward them and motioned 'em back. They'd been coming up abreast, and when they saw that, they just instantly dismounted and sat down on the ground in a line. The chief beckoned me to approach, and when I did, he got up and took me by the hand, and then every warrior there did the same, in succession, as a token of friendship."

Tutt chuckled and shook his head. "They told me that the Pawnees had been up over the winter into Sioux territory and had stolen several Sioux ponies. Now the Sioux were on the warpath against 'em, seeking vengeance and reprisals. 'Bout then they showed us, as proof of their word, five or six scalps already taken. They were worried about a Pawnee they'd wounded — four bullets passing through his lower body — but who had escaped, and they wondered if we white men had seen him. Actually, the Pawnee had come to our camp two days before, and we helped him every way we could, but told 'im he couldn't stay because the Sioux were too close behind him. So the Sioux left and we heard, after that, that the Pawnee had taken refuge in the wagon of another emigrant, who hid 'im till the Sioux passed, though they came right up to the wagon where he lay hidden and made inquiries about 'im." Tutt shook his head. "Would'a gone hard on our fella, an' maybe on all of us, too, if them Sioux had found that Pawnee in one of our wagons."

Feeling too ill to remain any longer, Delano bade his friend goodbye and returned to his own company, where he gratefully collapsed in his own wagon for the night. By morning of the 23rd, Delano was feeling much worse. The doctor was called in, and he immediately gave his patient a huge dose of calomel. Later when the company reached Fort Chiles near the Platte — the installation which had recently replaced Fort Kearny on the Missouri — Delano was too sick to stand, although well enough to write coherently in his *Journal*, and as he put it:

> *The Fort was nothing but a cluster of adobe, low, one-story buildings, sufficient for two companies of soldiers, who are stationed here as a check upon the Indians, but preparations are making to erect a horse-power saw-mill, as well as to enclose the barracks within a wall. It is situated on the right bank of the river, about a half-mile from the water, and not upon the island, as I had supposed. A day or two previous to our arrival, an emigrant was tried here for shooting one of his comrades. He was taking his whole family to California, when, a few miles beyond the fort, a man offered a gross insult to his wife. In a country where there is no law — where redress cannot be had by a legal process — he determined to protect his own honor, and raising his rifle, shot the scoundrel down. His companions took him back to the Fort, (with his consent,) where an investigation into the circumstances was made, and he was honorably acquitted.*
>
> *The banks of the Platte are high sand hills, scantily cov-*

ered with grass, and present many fanciful shaped cones and broken ridges, which I can compare with nothing else in form than huge drifted snow heaps. The valley through which the river flows is flat — four or five miles wide; and the scenery, though pretty, is neither grand nor imposing. There was no wood except on the island, which at this time was difficult of access, and our fuel was chiefly small willows and buffalo excrement — the latter being very plenty. We saw the bones of many buffaloes, but up to this time we saw none alive. Distance eighteen miles.

On Thursday, May 24th, Delano was still feeling cold and uncomfortable, but better able to cope with his ailments and even able to sit up a little. He hoped he would soon be out again. The morning rain ceased as they were starting, but the wind turned into a gale. By four o'clock they had encamped; their tents were erected again and deep ditches dug all around, enabling them to feel fairly secure. Then, however, the rain fell in absolute torrents, and the spray whipped into their tents as it had never done before. Throughout the evening the storm blew furiously, gaining strength by the hour.

During the violent storm, the men contrived to heat a poor supper by burning buffalo chips, and then they stretched out on their hard beds. Still feverish and weak, Delano was unable to sit upright for very long, and he realized that he certainly was not likely to improve soon. Less than thirty minutes before midnight, he momentarily dozed off, but awakened minutes later. Although he still had his boots on, his feet felt wet, and his efforts to draw them up into a dryer spot seemed merely to make things worse.

Smith was asleep in his own bedroll beside Delano's when the latter nudged him awake and said, "Smith, there's water coming into our beds!"

"Nothing new on that score, Delano," he mumbled. "My feet've been in water half an hour, at least! Keep dry if you can."

"You're not getting it," Delano replied. "The tent pins have pulled loose and it's going to blow down!"

"No, I guess not," he said, and almost instantly was snoring again.

The rain fell harder; the wind intensified, and now one corner of the tent was flapping. To make matters worse, the wind shifted direction and now blew in through the loosened front flap, soaking them all.

Still the tent's inhabitants all slept on, except for Delano, until finally Brown awakened, and finding his feet in water, sang out, "Boys, boys! Something's wrong!"

They didn't awaken and Brown redoubled his efforts. "Boys! Wake up! It's a fact, there's something wrong. John! Kent! Fred! Don't you hear?"

Kent finally opened his eyes and then leaped up to find the corner of the tent flapping in the wind, as more tent pegs had pulled free, His cries echoed Delano's, and finally Fred stirred; rubbing his eyes, he staggered to his feet and bellowed, "It's a fact, the tent's coming down! John! Hazel! Brown! Smith! Get up! The tent's coming down. Get up or you'll be drowned!"

Unable to find his boots, Hazel went out barefoot to try to refasten the tent pins. Morrill stood by, spouting expletives, and Smith hugged his blanket to his chin and burst into wild laughter. Outside Hazel shouted, "There went my hat! Now I'm really getting soaked!"

"Hammer down those pins!" Brown shouted. "But don't cut the cords with the ax blade."

"Ground's too soft to hold pins," Hazel yelled, as one pin after another popped free."

"To the wagons, boys!" someone yelled, and everyone but Delano and Hazel ran for it and ducked beneath the wagon covers. Delano just lay there, so miserably sick he didn't care whether he lived or died. Hazel shook his arm. "C'mon! Let's get to the wagon, the others are all gone!"

"Let me be," Delano groaned. "I'll stay here."

"What, in the rain? Are you crazy? The tent's almost down and will fall soon — you'll die here!"

"Just as well here as anywhere else," Delano moaned.

"Smith!" Hazel shouted. "Is the wagon open? Hold the cover open. Delano's coming!" Hazel then scooped up Delano as if he were a big doll and carried him to the wagon. Sick though he was, Delano couldn't keep from laughing at the big Norwegian's efforts, and he yielded with good grace. Together they struggled through the downpour and dove beneath the wagon cover, ensconcing themselves as best they could amid boxes and bales and covering themselves as best they could with their wet blankets.

Toward daybreak the rain finally ceased, but the temperature dropped dramatically. The men began shaking uncontrollably; their teeth were chattering. Near dawn they crawled from their soggy nests, still exhausted but glad to be able to stretch and breathe in the washed morning air. Fred, still exasperated with the discomfort and inconvenience, shouted, "I give up! I'm half dead already. I've seen enough of this danged world. California can't afford a better burying place than right here, right now. By God, here you can sink deep enough without even digging! Hey, Delano! What's your opinion?"

"Humph!" Delano snorted from his soggy roost. "*Non gustibus disputandum*!"

"And what the hell does that mean?" Fred growled.

Delano chuckled and broke out into a deep belly-laugh. "No argument with your taste." Later, after they were finally up and about again, Delano managed to write a brief entry in his *Journal*:

> *May 25th Friday. On crawling out from our sorry nests, we found a realizing sympathy from our wandering countrymen composing our train. There was scarcely a tent but what deviated from its upright character, and nearly the whole of the party, as our portion had done, had been forced to seek shelter in the wagons. The day opened cold, raw, and windy, and the drive was extremely disagreeable. I am shut up in my wagon, suffering intensely from pain, thirst, and feverish excitement. At evening the wind let down and the sun showed his glorious face once more, like an old but long-absent friend, above the blanket-clouds and promised a fair day on the morrow. Distance, fourteen miles.*

Yesterday, Saturday, Delano's *Journal* entry was brief, but acerbic enough to indicate he was feeling better and might actually live. He wrote:

> *May 26th. Saturday. The morrow has come, and although there is quite a heavy frost, the sun has come out according to promise. The day, for a wonder, was calm, and the genial atmosphere, together with the effect of the apothecary shop in my bowels made me feel that disease was subdued.*
>
> *During this day we passed a poor fellow who had fallen from his wagon, which passed over him, breaking his leg in two places. Doctor Gillespie, of Capt Tutt's company, kindly*

set it, and the unfortunate man once more turned his face homeward — a long and dubious journey for one in his condition. Distance, sixteen miles.

Today, May 27th, there had been a bit of excitement in the form of an encounter with Indians. This time it was a band of Pawnee warriors that created a problem the emigrating whites had never before encountered. Two men from one of the companies traveling in conjunction with Delano's were out hunting some four or five miles distant from the river. The men had deliberately separated themselves a bit in order to more likely startle some game into exposing itself. The pair were out of sight of each other when, with little warning, one of them found himself confronting eight Pawnees.

The Indian braves advanced on the hunter with smiles and gestures of friendship, including shaking hands with him, at which time they led him to understand he was among friends and he had no further need for his rifle, nor his knife and, for that matter, he could do very well without his clothes, too, which they removed from him garment by garment until he was entirely naked. Then, laughing among themselves, they filed off into the hills as quickly as they had appeared.

His companion, who had witnessed the whole episode from behind a small knoll, took to his heels to save his own clothes, and quite possibly his skin; while the bare and considerably chilled hunter, who finally made his way back to camp and, amid snickers and snorts, was given a collection of garments from others of the train who could spare them.

[June 3rd, 1849 • Sunday]

Alonzo Delano's latest recurrence of fever and illness had finally subsided, and he was feeling much better. Part of his improved morale, however, could be attributed to his realization, one shared by most members of the train, that they had simply taken too many heavy and unnecessary things with them and that the loads absolutely *had* to be lightened.

When they had stopped a week ago, the poor grasses of the area had not adequately nourished the livestock, and the river water was so muddy that the cattle refused to drink it. In the following morning's light they'd looked thin and hollow, and so the party decided to make the following day's march an easy one by stopping early, at a site where grass and water were plentiful. They had done so, and they cattle had taken full advantage of the much improved grazing conditions, amply regaining the vitality they had previously lost.

Delano's had a number of friends in *The South Bend Company,* which was now traveling near to his own outfit, and so he seized the opportunity to visit with them during the following several days. A severe thunderstorm struck again during the night of the 29th, but their tent had been pegged down tightly, so it didn't blow down, but the water beat in and there was little sleep for anyone. As Delano described the storm:

> *May 30th — Wednesday. Morning dawned gloomily enough. It seemed as if a water spout was discharging its floods upon us. Our rain storms at home were only gentle showers compared with this. The wind blew a hurricane, and our cattle, when grazing, kept moving off, apparently in hopes of getting away from the storm, and it was absolutely necessary to keep driving them back almost constantly to prevent them from straying off. Finding it impossible to keep them together, and as they could not eat, from the fury of the storm, we drove them in, where they stood all day under the lee of the wagons, tied to the wheels, — this being the only way we could keep them.*
>
> *In this dreadful storm hundreds of cattle were lost, and some trains were almost ruined; some lost half, while others had only one or two yoke left; and for several days after, we met many persons who were searching for their cattle, unable to proceed. No situation can be more deplorable than that of being left upon such a broad prairie, hundreds of miles from aid, without the means of locomotion. We found families, with women and helpless children, in this sad condition, and yet we were without means to give them relief.*
>
> *We had saved our own cattle by tying them up as we did, for it was impossible for oxen to stand still under such peltings. Many were found twenty-five or thirty miles off the road, while others were lost entirely, having strayed beyond the reach of the owners, or were stolen by the Indians. It took us till nearly noon to cook our breakfast. Our stoves were put into our tents, and the covers of boxes, or stray*

pieces of wood in the wagons, were used to start a fire, and then the buffalo chips were heaped upon the stoves until they got dry enough to burn, and in this way we contrived to do our cooking. The comforts of home crowded on our memories, and many a sigh was given for those we had left behind.

For *The Ottawa Company* members, in addition to other problems, they discovered that some of the cattle had become foot-sore and lame. While this train was able to attend to its ailing stock, some nearby trains had to leave behind cattle too lame to proceed further. In some trains, the men struggled to retain their ailing stock by forming rough boots of leather and fastening them over the sore hooves in such a way as to keep the dirt and sand from the ailing feet, which the men also smeared with tar and grease to ease pain and facilitate healing. McClasky, McNeil, and Rood, in Delano's train each had a lame ox, but managed to save the two beasts by taking them out of the yoke and wrapping up their feet in this way. The day continued to be a cheerless one, as the rain continued without pause, and the Delano's company, having attempted no march at all, retired in cold, damp blankets. Despite all this, however, the emigrants were not dispirited.

May 31st, was a heavily overcast, cold, wind-blown day resembling late November. *The Ottawa Company* members left their encampment about 8 a.m. and drove the animals slowly all day, frequently meeting groups of men looking for lost cattle and scanning the Delano party's herd to see if some of their cattle had become mixed in. Some had suffered severe losses; one company with a hundred head before the storm struck was left, when it ended, with only thirty; another lost nine of their eighteen cattle. They passed two family-filled wagons that had only three oxen tied to the wheels. As Delano commented in his *Journal*:

It was a kind of terra firma shipwreck, with the lamentable fact, that the numerous craft sailing by were unable to afford the sufferers any relief. We passed the forks of the Platte, and continued our route up the South Branch about ten miles to a ford, but hearing that there was a better ford still farther up, we continued on, leaving The South Bend Company, who concluded to cross here, which they did without difficulty.

> *We saw buffaloes for the first time in considerable numbers, on the opposite side of the fork, and were much amused in seeing the emigrants, who had crossed, dashing in upon them in gallant style. One was shot in our sight. Not only was the chase exciting, but witnessing it was extremely so; and as the herd dashed off, we could scarcely repress a desire to be after them, but this was impossible, for a broad and dangerous stream was between us.*
>
> *I had now regained strength enough to walk a little, and being a half-mile in advance of my train, I was overtaken by a mule wagon at the top of a hill, which contained Messrs. G. C. Merrifield, and A, M. Winn — old friends from Indiana — and whom I had not seen for some months. Meeting thus under peculiar circumstances afforded us much pleasure, and getting into their wagon, we passed an hour or two in that agreeable manner, which none but travelers in a wild region, far from home and friends, can appreciate.*

Delano recognized the fact that his group and others had been much too selfishly absorbed in foolish rivalry, in passing other companies or just keeping pace with them and, in the process, putting much too great a strain on the livestock. By doing so, these men were not only jeopardizing their cattle; they were creating a situation that could well leave them marooned and helpless in the vastness of these prairies, where no human aid could be obtained. Delano's thoughts in this regard underlined both his intelligence and his concern for men and beasts alike:

> *Men [are] placed in jeopardy of becoming helpless, by imprudence, even at this early stage of the great journey; and, were I to make the trip again, I would make it a point to stop every seventh day, wherever practicable, if from no scruples of conscience, certainly from dictates of humanity; and I do not hesitate to declare, that by doing so there would be a saving of time in the end, for both man and beast would more than make up the time so lost, by renewed vigor from rest. We daily saw many cattle giving out from want of rest, and imprudence in driving them beyond their strength, and it seemed clear that when they reached the barren plains be-*

> *yond the Rocky Mountains, many would be unable to drag their wagons, even after the loads had been reduced, by throwing away all but barely enough provisions to sustain life to the end of the journey. Distance 14 miles.*

Delano's company met many men during the day following — June 1st — who were searching for cattle lost during the great storm, and who were helpless until they had recoveredtheir livestock. Delano's group was pleased that they now had an abundance of buffalo meat, after having been so long confined to salted-down provisions. The fresh meat was a rare luxury, even though the emigrants found it to be more coarsely grained and inferior in flavor to domestic beef; nevertheless, they devoured it with gusto. Predictably, many soon paid the price for their over-indulgence: They were stricken severe bouts of diarrhea. Their drive on this first day of June was a moderate, comfortable 15 miles.

Yesterday, then, they had reached the spot where they were to ford the South Platte, even though the river here was fully half a mile wide with a rather swift current. The company quickly discovered that the wagons could ford the river successfully only if they were pulled by double-teams kept constantly in motion. Any hesitation in the process would give the wagons — especially the more heavily loaded ones — an opportunity to sink in the sand and gradually disappear. The men learned this lesson by bitter experience: One of the first wagons, being drawn by frightened, unruly oxen, began to sink and was belatedly drawn out of the quicksand only when the men hastily hitched on an additional yoke of well-trained animals.

The men found the deepest place in the crossing by riding a horse across the stream repeatedly, to determine the most suitable passage for fording . Once this was done, all the wagons could cross without getting into water deeper than the wagon beds. The north bank of the South Platte consisted of high, broken land, and the emigrants' course, after crossing, was almost straight north to the North Platte, about eight miles distant from this point. The unappealing land between the two forking rivers was broken and virtually barren.

After crossing the South Fork, Delano's contingent fell in with a company which included a young man named Harold Jenks, from Janesville, Wisconsin, who reported that his company had lost thirty head of cattle in the great storm. He was, Delano noted, fortunate enough to locate them all some twenty-five miles south of the trail. Jenks told him that during his search he had fallen in with another young man mounted on a fine horse, who also had been looking for lost cattle but, unsuccessful in his search, was on his way back to his own camp. When Jenks pointed to him, that he was going in the wrong direction in order to do so, the other man contended that he was correct and that Jenks was wrong. After arguing the point in vain, they separated and Jenks had reached the trail during the night. The other horseman was never heard of again, and it was believed that he either starved to death or was killed by Indians.

Delano noted that in a similar case, a man and boy belonging to a Missouri train became lost. The boy, after wandering three days without food, finally found the road again and, though weakened by virtual starvation, recovered well. The man was never seen again and was believed to have perished. These were only two examples of many similarly grim ones which compelled Delano to conclude that many an anxious heart at home would have occasion to remember and deplore the great storm the column had encountered on the Platte.

By this time buffalo had become numerous, and the novelty of seeing such herds had worn off. Toward nightfall Delano and his company descended into the bottomland of the North Platte, where they encountered luxuriant growths of new grasses and fine ponds of clear water, along with abundant dry willow branches for fuel, and so after a drive during the day of only eight miles, they resolved to lay over here for a full day of rest on Sunday.

So, today the company had taken advantage of their stop by airing out their clothing and some of the provisions that had become dampened in the river crossing, and they also made a few repairs to their harnesses, tie-downs, and other gear. Then, as many of the companies were now doing, they paused to reconsider the freight they were carrying: Heavy goods which, in many cases, were weighing the wagons down too much and clearly fatiguing the oxen. The emigrants, now fully aware of the problem, felt compelled to abandon some of the heavier belongings stowed in their wagons as well as to reposition other possessions in order to shorten wagon dimensions and thereby make them easier for the teams to pull. The superfluous baggage was virtually impossible to sell, and consequently, after successfully bartering his container filled with 50 excess pounds of coffee beans, Delano felt very fortunate indeed.

Like Delano, all the emigrants were abundantly supplied, and their wagons virtually groaned under the weight of their goods. They had no real choice now except to discard everything that was not absolutely essential: House furnishings, quantities of iron and steel in bars, coils of wire, trunks and valises, superfluous clothing and footwear, and whatever else had been brought along that had been desirable, but proved now not to be vitally necessary.

Thanks to this massive sizing-down process, the trail was soon littered with piles of bacon, flour, wagon parts, dressers, groceries and a diverse, chaotic variety of other items. After the emigrants departed, Indians, who had been tracking them at a distance, soon visited and pillaged their numerous rubbish heaps.

As Delano noted at the time they left home, virtually all of the emigrants had assumed that cornmeal would not keep on the plains without first being kiln-dried; that butter-crackers and flour would not keep well, and that bread-stuffs must necessarily preserved in the form of hard-bread. As he noted now:

> *This, we found, was a false impression and that a little care in airing out on occasion would preserve meal, flour, hams, bacon, sugar, and, indeed, almost anything just as well as in a store room at home. This overhauling was necessary only in the humid atmosphere of the Platte, and in crossing the South Pass of the Rocky Mountains. Even this care was not absolutely required — and under this mistaken impression, we had deprived ourselves of many comforts. Instead of suffering on the plains, the trip can be made, by taking the proper precautions, with comparative comfort and safety.*

Upon leaving home Delano had taken what he estimated would be enough clean clothing to last him for a good while. Now, however, rather than letting soiled clothing continue to accumulate, he decided to try his hand at washing. He joined a number of male emigrants who were taking their accumulated soiled laundry to a nearby pond; their ensuing struggle to wash these myriad filthy items constituted for many of them their first such effort in their entire lives. As Delano described the scene:

> *It was no trouble at all to throw our clothes into the pond, and rubbing in soap was not much, but when it came to standing bent over half a day, rubbing the clothes in our hands, trying to get out all the stains — higho!, a change came over the spirit of our dreams, and we thought of our wives and sweethearts at home, and wondered that we were ever dissatisfied with their impatience on a washing day. Had they been present, we should heartily have asked their pardon, and allowed them to scold to their heart's content. I verily believe that our clothes looked worse for the washing than they did even before we began, and my poor knuckles — oh!, they will be sore for a month afterwards!*

These emigrants finally concluded that sixteen hundred pounds of freight on a light wagon would require three yoke of strong cattle to start with from home. Delano wryly observed that, as far as he was concerned, this estimate was not conservative enough.

That evening other trains from Illinois encamped near *The Ottawa Company*, and while visiting one of them Delano recognized Frank Lindley and his family, from La Salle, with whom originally, before leaving home, he had expected to be traveling. He was delighted to see his friends and to spend an agreeable hour with them before finally returning to his own camp and turning in for the night.

[June 12th, 1849 • Tuesday]

California Governor Bennett Riley was working quietly but persistently in his efforts to establish a strong civil government in California which he hoped would soon convince the U.S. Government to reward the territory with statehood.. No other territory had ever acquired this status so swiftly, but that did not deter Riley from his mission; as he saw it, no other territories' statehood applications or petitions had ever been buttressed by California's remarkably extensive mineral deposits — resources which amounted to extremely valuable assets not just for myriads of individuals but for the nation, itself.

The steamer *Edith*, which he had sent earlier to Mazatlan to intercept and deliver more quickly to him any orders from Washington, had returned with the discouraging news that apparently the U.S. Congress had made little effort even to establish a suitably strong territorial government, much less to consider seriously California's formal bid for statehood. Riley was decidedly a military man, but having been placed in charge of California, he had lost no time in acquainting himself with the details of civil law and civil affairs. On June 3rd he had issued a proclamation in an attempt to reduce national congressional prejudice against military government by replacing the current one with a temporary civil government which, while small and unstable, might prompt the national government to take California's official actions more seriously.

Riley first proclaimed that the laws of the Territory of California, which were not in conflict with the laws, treaties and constitution of the United States, had the weight of national law until they were replaced or revised by national authority. The situation in California differed from that in Oregon, which was entirely without laws until a provisional government could be formed. What California had was more closely akin to Louisiana's government, the laws of which were recognized as valid until constitutionally repealed. Riley intended to fully enforce the laws established by California's provisional government, but he insisted upon making the administrators of these laws elective rather than appointive. At the same time he called for a convention of delegates from every part of the territory to form a territorial organization or state government to be ratified by the people themselves and then to be submitted to the United State Congress for approval.

The election of such officers was set for the first day of August, at which time, as well, delegates to the convention were to be elected, with those officers chosen given terms that would last until January 1st, 1850. The convention itself was to meet September 1st. A regular annual election would be held in November to choose members of the territorial assembly and to fill the offices temporarily supplied by the election of August 1st. To accomplish this, Riley divided the territory into ten distinct districts for the election of thirty-seven delegates, apportioned as follows: Two delegates each for San Diego, Santa Barbara, and San Luis Obispo, four each for Los Angeles, Sonoma, Sacramento, and San Joaquin, and five each for San José, Monterey, and San Francisco.

Riley's proposals did provoke skepticism. His critics asked, by what constitutional power could the President govern a territory by appointing a military governor during a time of peace? How could any government at all be established before the Mexican laws were repealed? By what right and authority did the United States Secretary of

War order General Riley to act as California Territorial Governor? Was not such skeptical reasoning as sound as General Riley's, when he declared that the people of California had no right to legislate for themselves without the sanction of Congress? This was not a new question; it had been argued at some length in the *Alta California* by Peter H. Burnett, who had come down from Oregon with gold-hunters in 1848, and whose experience with the provisional government there in the American community on the Columbia River had endowed him with a kind of umpire's credibility.

A day after Governor Riley issued his controversial proclamation , he issued another, this one directed specifically to the residents of San Francisco, who had taken it upon themselves to elect a "general assembly of San Francisco." Riley's new proclamation bluntly declared that "the body of men styling themselves the legislative assembly of San Francisco has usurped powers which are vested only in the Congress of the United States." Printed in both Spanish and English, the proclamation was posted throughout California and produced considerable excitement; and this controversy was aggravated by the return of the mail steamer with news, both of the failure of Congress to provide a government, as well as of the Congressional extension of the revenue laws over California, which included the appointment of a tax collector. This amounted taxation without representation, and for the people of California, it was not to be borne.

Peter Burnett responded to these developments by calling a meeting of the members of the legislative assembly committee and by delivering an address protesting against Governor Riley's proclamations. As Burnett asserted:

> *The legislative assembly of the district of San Francisco have believed it to be their duty to earnestly recommend to their fellow-citizens the propriety of electing twelve delegates from each district to attend a general convention to be held at the Pueblo de San José on the third Monday or August next, for the purpose of organizing a government for the whole territory of California. We would recommend that the delegates be intrusted [sic] with large and full discretion to deliberate upon the best measures to be taken; and to form, if they upon mature consideration should deem it advisable, a state constitution, to be submitted to the people for their*

> *ratification or rejection by a direct vote at the polls. ... From the best information, both parties in congress are anxious that this should be done; and there can exist no doubt of the fact that the present perplexing state of the question at Washington would insure the admission of California at once. We have the question to settle for ourselves; and the sooner we do it, the better.*

Responding to this political furor, 59 citizens signed an invitation, published it on leaflets, and distributed them throughout the town. Their invitation respectfully urged their fellow citizens to attend a public meeting, in front of the Customs House, Portsmouth Square, on Tuesday, June 12th, at 3 p.m., to address the necessity of electing delegates to a state Constitutional Convention.

The meeting was held today, Tuesday, June 12th, as planned; it was presided over by William M. Steuart and well attended by the citizenry. The majority of those San Franciscans in attendance agreed that delegates must be elected in order to convene and organize Upper California's own government. Those in attendance also passed resolutions declaring the right of the people of the territory, the U.S. Congress having failed them, not only to organize for their own protection, but also to to elect delegates to a convention to form a state government, "that the great and growing interests of California may be represented in the next Congress of the United States."

A committee consisting of of Peter H. Burnett, W. D. M. Howard, M. Norton, E. Gould Buffum, and E. Gilbert was appointed to correspond with other California districts in order to fix an early day for the election of delegates to attend the convention and also to determine the appropriate number of delegates to be selected. Several prominent leaders addressed the meeting: Burnett, Thomas Butler King, who was both a Congressman from Georgia and a confidential agent of the government, and William M. Gwin, a former Mississippi Congressman, as well as others. King had been sent out to organize the state movement, which he was doing in conjunction with the governor, and Gwinn had arrived on the same steamer, intending to become a senator from California.

The mass meeting of citizens that occurred at 3 p.m. today in San Francisco's Portsmouth Square was, if anything, anticlimactic, with everything transpiring exactly as planned; California, it seemed, had now taken its first official — and highly significant — step toward statehood.

[June 13th, 1849 • Wednesday]

Alonzo Delano was very glad that they had given the oxen and cattle a full day of rest on good pasturage. They had seemed to have fully rejuvenated during this interval, and the animals and men alike seemed considerably more eager than usual to begin the following day's march.

Their route on June 4th, along the North Platte's southwestern bank, had led through a bottom flanked by precipitous hills of oolite on their left a landscape devoid of trees and shrubs — a barren area as far as the eye could see. After traveling for two hours they began encountering a few stunted ash and cedar trees and occasional clusters of brush struggling to grow amid jumbles of rock.

Delano was well ahead of *The Ottawa Company* that day when, before noon, he came to an encampment of Missourians who had stopped to rest as well as to air out their clothing and provisions. Among them, Delano found several rather intelligent and accomplished gentlemen, with whom he had a brief but pleasant visit. One of them related to him details of an incident which had occurred the previous night. It had thrown their entire camp into an uproar, and had more or less precipitated this unusual mid-day stop. After the guard had been set for the night, a youngster who was about fourteen years old decided he would play a joke on the sentry. During the night, unperceived, he stole out of his wagon, draped a white blanket over himself and, in a manner he imagined as ghostlike, approached the sentry.

"The guard hailed him repeatedly," the man related, "but, getting no response, the guard decided he was an Indian creeping in to plunder, and so he raised his rifle and shot. He got a definite response then! The ball passed through the boy's arm and part of his side and he screamed inn painful despair, awakening the entire camp. It was a pretty bad wound, though not terribly dangerous, and he, as well as others in the camp, learned a grim lesson. "It's very unlikely," the men concluded, "he'll ever again tease a sentry who's on guard duty."

Delano continued on his way, and at about noon was obliged to leave the level along the river's edge when a high bluff imposed itself in his path, extending well out into the stream and forcing him to make a four-mile detour to get past it. The wind had come up fairly severely by this time, and as Delano recorded in his *Journal*:

> *... on reaching the top of the hill a multitude of hats were flying faster than the legs of their owners, and the pastime of running after them was not much enjoyed by the tired pedestrians. We descended into a deep and narrow ravine [which we] named Ash Hollow, so called from being covered with a stunted growth of ash trees. The rocks on each side were high and perpendicular, with a sandy bottom, through which a little brooklet meandered, made from springs — the first that we had met with since reaching the Platte, and which now entered the river below the ravine perhaps half a mile. Sheltered from the wind by the high banks, the ravine was warmed by the sun, and the cool shade of the trees, as well as the clear water, was delightfully refreshing.*

As they approached the river bottom at the mouth of the ravine, Delano and the others, to their alarmed surprise, encountered a village of Sioux Indians. Their conical lodges were constructed of tanned buffalo hides well inter-layered to resist the ravages of the weather. Delano quickly determined that both the men and women of the tribe were very handsome in stature and dress and, as he wrote:

> *... better formed than any Indians I had ever seen. The men were tall, and graceful in their movements, and some of the squaws were quite pretty, and dressed in tanned buffalo skins, many highly ornamented with beads, while many of the men wore barely a blanket around their waists, and one or two of them were quite naked.*
>
> *On our approach, one of the Indians, who was armed with an old sword, made us some kind of speech, and invited us into a lodge, where he motioned us to be seated. Several squaws were engaged in making moccasins, for which they found ready purchasers among the emigrants. Almost the first request made to us was for whiskey, for which I verily believe they would have sold their children — showing conclusively that temperance societies were not yet well organized on the Platte. Of course we had no fire-water whatever for them, and we left them lamentably sober, and encamped*

about a mile above them, where several came out to beg bread, whiskey, and shirts.

During the evening two young men came to our camp on mules, who had turned their faces homeward without supplies. They said that they were from Indianapolis, Indiana; that their mules had given out, and that they had determined to return, depending on the charity of the emigrants for their subsistence, which no doubt was fully and freely accorded to them. We availed ourselves of the opportunity to send letters to our friends, to be mailed at St. Joseph.

On the following day, June 5th, the weather became excessively warm. Because the trail they were following was quite sandy, footing was difficult and the cattle labored hard. At the same time, the river bluffs began to assume more interesting shapes, and the precipitous oolite cliffs, formed of clay, were now beginning to solidify into masses of rock, with deep, winding ravines often breaking the regularity of the layering. The emigrants studied the cliffs with grave interest, often assigning them names when they took the form of something familiar. Delano walked a considerable distance this day, but his overwhelming exhaustion by nightfall convinced him that he had not yet quite regained the strength that the fever had sapped from him. Because the night's campsite offered inadequate grazing for the livestock, the cattle looked somewhat sickly during the early morning's march on June 6th; near 10 a.m.; however, the men came to some good grass, and promptly unyoked the oxen and let them graze for a couple of hours. It was in the early afternoon, not long after they started again, when they came to a Sioux burial platform. Delano commented:

In a hackberry tree, elevated about twenty feet above the ground, a kind of rack was made of broken tent poles, and the body (for there was but one) was placed upon it, wrapped in his blanket and a tanned buffalo skin, with his tin cup, moccasins, and various things which he had used in life, were placed upon his body, for his use in the land of spirits. We gazed upon these sad remains of humanity without disturbing any of the arrangements.

A short distance from our place of encampment for the

night, I observed a newly made grave upon a green knoll, and in examining the wooden head-board, I found it to be the last resting place of one George W. Tindal, a young man from Tecumseh, Michigan, who had died of consumption. I became acquainted with him on our passage from St. Louis to St. Joseph, and was much pleased with his intelligence and amiable manners. Poor fellow, it was hard to die so far from home, and friends; and a sick bed on the plains is a desolate place, even when every attention is bestowed that the slender means of the traveler can afford.

Our hunters were very successful, and our camp was abundantly supplied with fresh meat, though it quickly produced diarrhea in many instances. Distance, fifteen miles.

On Thursday, June 7th, *The Ottawa Company* passed numerous low places saturated with alkaline particles. In the holes and wells dug by previous passing emigrants, the water, in taste and color resembling the lye of ashes, was totally unfit for use. Although even the thirsty cattle would not drink it, there had been several recent good showers, and the rain had reduced the strength of the alkali in the soil, thereby preventing its deleterious effect upon the feet of the already foot-sore cattle. During the day the company approached Court-house Rock, which extended over a broad bottom perhaps fifteen miles wide. They also encountered a stream dubbed Smith's Creek, which was by far the most beautiful stream they had found since leaving the Missouri. The stream flowed from the hills over a clear sandy bed and was cool and delicious to their parched mouths, especially after they had long tolerated the water of sloughs, or that of the muddy, insipid Platte. Delano noted:

The atmosphere in this region is of remarkable clearness, for which cause we were unable to estimate distances with any precision. Court-house Rock appeared only about two miles off, when in reality it was ten or twelve. Some of our men set out to walk to it, but as they approached, it appeared to recede, and after walking a couple of hours, some few returned, while those who finally reached it did not return till nearly nine o'clock at night, having walked steadily for about ten hours. It stood upon a little ridge above the bottom — was of circular form — with an elevation on the top much like a flattened dome, and at the distance at which we stood, it resembled a huge building. It was really about two hundred feet high, although from the road it appeared only about fifty. Near it, on the east end, was another blunt pointed rock, not quite as high, which was not particularly remarkable, but which is embraced in the same view. Both of these stand isolated on the plain, although a few miles west are bare bluff ridges of the same kind of rock — a soft sand and clay, intermixed with lime, easily cut with a knife — all probably of volcanic origin, and this is the general character of the rock in this region.

When within a few miles of this Court-house Rock, we came to a ledge called the Post-office, over which we passed. It was full of water-worn fissures, and in one cavity we saw a number of letters deposited, for individuals who were behind, and in the rock was cut in capitals, "POST-OFFICE." The usual mode of giving intelligence to friends behind, is to write on a bleached buffalo skull, or broad shoulder blade. Thousands of these novel communications lay upon the plain, and we frequently got intelligence in this way from acquaintances who preceded us.

About noon we came in sight of Chimney Rock, looming up in the distance like a lofty tower in some town, and we did not tire in gazing at it. It was about twenty-five miles west from us and continued in sight until we reached it on the following day. We encamped where there was good grass and water, after a drive of eighteen miles.

On the following day, June 8th, Delano's company traveled westward all day, yet never lost sight of Chimney Rock. The earth was so alkaline in this area that in many places the ground surface was coated with a whitened glaze much like frost. By evening they had reached their closest proximity to the monumental rock — about three miles distant — unless, of course, they chose to veer off the trail for a closer look. A number of the emigrants did just that, but Delano was still a bit too weak to make the effort, though he regretted not being able to do so. At this closest point on the trail to the rock, Delano wrote in his *Journal*:

The rock much resembles the chimney of a glass-house

furnace; a large, cone-like base, perhaps an hundred and fifty feet in diameter, occupies two-thirds of its height, and from thence the chimney runs up, gradually growing smaller, to the top. The height of the whole is said to be two hundred fifty feet above the level of the river, from which it is between three and four miles distant. It is a great curiosity and I much regret that I have not strength enough to visit it. I think it is decaying from the action of the elements, and it is quite likely that the chimney will be broken off in time, leaving nothing but its cone to gratify the curiosity of the future traveler. The hills in the vicinity present a fanciful appearance — sometimes like giant walls of massive gray rock, and again like antiquated buildings of olden time. During the day we met many old acquaintances, among whom I was gratified to meet Dr. M. B. Angle, from Michigan. The meeting was as agreeable as unexpected, for neither of us knew the other was a California adventurer until we met, far from kindred and friends.

Delano became intrigued with the wide range of names and comments fellow emigrants had painted on the wagon sides, and on the fabric of the conestoga tops. A procession of such ear-marked wagons bumped along before and after their train, with names easily seen from a considerable distance such as *The Enterprise, Live Hoosier, Iron Lady, The Dowdle Family, Gold Hunter, Rough and Ready, Lone Star, Wild Yankee, Buffaloes, Lucky Dig, Elephants,* as well as many other amusing designations and illustrations.

Evening camps were now being made a little earlier than previously, to allow for the proper picketing of the animals, for an extra bit of rest and diversion after the grind of the day's travel, and for the opportunity to visit with friends in other wagons. The earlier stops also enabled the emigrants to participate in the community amusements, such as group singing; talent shows, readings from the scriptures or from other books; dancing to concerts of individually played musical instruments — bugles, harps, violins, oboes, French horns, banjos, drums, tambourines, or ensembles of several types; recitations of poetry or anything else that might amuse or appeal and thereby ease the strain that the day's travel before weariness finally drove the emigrants to their bedrolls, inside wagon beds or often on the ground beneath them.

In morning's light, however, things changed. As Delano put it in his *Journal*:

> *... when morning came, and the day's work commenced, too frequently ill-humor began; and the vilest oaths, the most profane language, and frequent quarrels and feuds, took the place of good humor, which not unfrequently [sic] required all the patience that a patient man is possessed of to endure.*

On the following morning, June 9th, a cold, unpleasant wind was blowing as the company broke camp and the column began moving again, heading toward Scotts Bluff, which still lay several miles ahead. Delano became preoccupied with the fantastic shapes into which the winds had carved the hills and bluffs through which they were passing: Scenes such as he had never before seen or had ever expected to see. As he recorded the experience in his *Journal* for this day:

> *June 9th. 1849. Saturday. The bare hills and water-worn rocks on our left began to assume many fantastic shapes, and after raising a gentle elevation, a most extraordinary sight presented itself to our view. A basin-shaped valley, bounded by high rocky hills, lay before us, perhaps twelve miles in length, by six or eight broad. The perpendicular sides of the nearby mountains presented the appearance of castles, forts, towers, verandas, and chimneys, with a blending of Asiatic and European architecture, and it required an effort to believe that we were not in the vicinity of some ancient and deserted town.*
>
> *It seemed as if the wand of a magician had passed over a city, and like that in the Arabian Nights, had converted all living things into stone. Here you have the minarets of a castle; there the loop-holes of bastions of a fort; again, the frescoes of a huge temple; then the doors, windows, chimneys, and columns of immense buildings appeared in view, with all the solemn grandeur of an ancient yet deserted city, while at other points Chinese temples, dilapidated by time, with broken chimney rocks in miniature, made it appear distinctly as if by some supernatural cause we had been dropped in the suburbs of a mighty city. For miles around the basin this*

view extended, and we looked across the barren plain at the display of Almighty power, with wonder and astonishment.

The sites the emigrants were beholding, however, seemed to lose their identity the nearer they were approached; instead of fabled castles and minarets and towers, they evolved into bare, shapeless, wind-and-water-worn rocks. Delano felt that days could have been spent examining such curiosities, and he regretted that the column's lack of time — as well as his own enfeebled health — prevented him from inspecting them much more thoroughly. He did note that they were comprised, to some extent, of volcanic matter, similar to what he had seen at Court House and Chimney Rocks, formed of an odd admixture of marl, gravel, sand, and clay, combined into a sort of volcanic conglomerate for which he had no title. These were rocks and formations that had, over decades and centuries, yielded to the vagaries of wind and weather erosion. Every year, he was sure, wore them down more, slowly transforming their shapes into the other-worldly images that flanked them.

A violent rainstorm overtook the column as it reached the western extremity of the broad basin, and as it was by then late in the afternoon, the men hastily pitched their tents for the night. A large number of dead cedars nearby provided them with ample fuel, but the dead hulks also raised unanswerable questions: Where did they come from, since there were no other trees of similar size or type in the vicinity? Delano could only assume that somehow they had been washed to this spot by some gigantic flood of some long-past era: A mighty inundation that had caused the Platte itself to overflow beyond all bounds and inundate its entire broad valley.

Their camp for the night was, otherwise, not a good one; grass and water were poor, and the evening itself was wet, cold, and thoroughly unpleasant. The men ate their suppers in moody silence and subsequently turned in on their blanket-covered, hard-earthed beds in a dark, ill humor which nothing could dispel.

Close to dawn on June 10th, the wind died away, the overcast broke, and a bright morning sun restored nearly everyone's good humor. Delano observed that they had enjoyed no good water since leaving Smith's Run three days previously; the little they had encountered since was muddy, murky, foul-smelling, and bad-tasting. Delano's *Journal* comment for the evening seemed to sum up the feelings of the entire column:

We encamped at night by the side of a muddy pond hole, and were compelled to drink it, or have none.

On the next day the column continued, passing through tedious, uninteresting country. The day's march was enlivened only once when a buffalo they startled ran toward them and passed only a short distance away from the front of the column; before the hunters could retrieve their rifles, however, the big animal was out of range. Nevertheless, they settled into a good camp after a drive of sixteen miles.

Yesterday, June 12th, the emigrants continued their march through flat but similarly tedious, non-descript terrain which reminded them of how deeply weary they were of their traveling routine. After being so long confined to their meager prairie diet, they longed to gorge themselves on some good old-fashioned home cooking. Nevertheless, they plugged on, resolute in their determination to see this journey through to its end. Delano wrote:

Thus far we have gone without accident, and if our clothes are soiled and our beards unshaven, we have the consolation of thinking that no one could boast over another on account of good looks. About ten o'clock in the morning we were upon a ridge, when suddenly we got a view of the snow-capped head of Laramie Peak, fifty or sixty miles distant, and became aware that we were approaching a spur of the Rocky Mountains.

A drive of seven miles from our encampment brought us to Laramie River, where we found a multitude of teams, waiting their turn to cross a swift and not safe current. It became necessary to raise our wagon boxes about six inches, in order to prevent the water flowing in and wetting our provisions. We here found Capt. Tutt's Company and the Dowdle family, who had got ahead of us, waiting their turn to cross. The passage was made in safety, although I lost two pails which were hooked to my wagon.

Delano discovered that Fort Laramie was simply a trading post standing in a valley along the Laramie River, about a mile above the fording place — a square enclosure of neatly white-washed adobe walls. The entry into the courtyard was through a gate he felt was strong enough to resist Indian attack but which would have been of little account to an attacking army. As rough-hewn as the place was, it provided a welcome sight to the travelers who had been for so long away from anything that even suggested a civilized building. Scattered around was a motley crowd of wagons, cattle, horses, mules and men, which provided a pleasant impression of life and activity. All around, the place was surrounded by high, broken land, several distant spurs of which Delano believed must be the Black Hills barely visible on the remote horizon. (According to contemporary rumors, the Black Hills were spurs of the Rocky Mountains.)

Scattered about outside the fort walls were numerous wagons that had been sold or abandoned by emigrants, and here a sturdy, heavy wagon could be purchased for from $5 to $15 [$144 to $432]. Inside the trading post, the shelves were essentially bare, and the clerk claimed that although there usually were all kinds of small supplies available, the rush this year had exhausted the post's exorbitantly-priced inventory.

There was a large postal box here, a deposit for the large number of letters accumulated to be sent to the States, along with thousands more of "left letters" for friends, with postage paid of 25 cents [$7.20] each, which were to be deposited by some messenger in a postal box somewhere east of the Missouri River.

A mile below the fording place, the Laramie emptied into the Platte, and at this point the road that originated from Council Bluffs in the Iowa country united with those from both St. Joseph and Independence, making this an important junction which also marked the near half-way point to their ultimate goal at the gold fields. As Delano logged in his *Journal*:

> *We made but a short stay at the fort, and drove about a mile, when we overtook The Dowdle and The South Bend companies, at their noon halt by the road side, and after weeks of weary traveling, it was extremely pleasant to meet so many old friends and acquaintances so far from home, in a wild Indian country. In The South Bend [Company] they were a well-dressed, clean-shaved and good looking set of men, with civilized notions of good order and propriety, but*

now they belonged to the great unwashed, unshaved family of mankind, who spurned Day Martin's blacking, and rose soap as of "no account," while their uncombed locks, their ragged unmentionables, their sun-burnt faces, made them look as if a party of loafers had congregated together, to exhibit their contempt of civilized fashions. And, alas!, my old, greasy, buckskin coat and outre [sic] appearance proclaimed that I was an animal of the same species. Yet, as rough and weather-beaten as we were, our meeting was of the most cordial kind, and hilarity and good feeling animated us all.

On joining them, I was offered a piece of pie and cheese. Ye gods! Pie — veritable dried apple pie, which Charlie Lewis made with his own hands! — and although his own mother might have turned up her nose at it, to us, who had literally fed on the "salt" of the pork barrel for weeks, with pilot bread for a dessert, it was a perfect luxury.

My stay with them was brief, for our train went on, and I was compelled to follow, though with the hope of often traveling in their company. We took a road over a hill on the west, and about ten miles west of Fort Laramie we saw the first outcrops of sandstone and limestone which we had observed since leaving the Missouri. There we encamped, without water. To get this liquid for cooking purposes, Henderson took a pail and went a mile and a half to a luke-warm spring. Showers were falling on the hills all around us, and the night closed in, wet and uncomfortable, and we retired to our couches ill at ease and very dispirited. Drive, sixteen miles.

Today, Wednesday, June 13th, the day had begun somewhat more propitiously than previously with calm and clear atmosphere. Delano was concerned when Fredenburg exhibited symptoms of ague and fever. Several days prior to their reaching Fort Laramie, he had lain on damp ground beneath a hot sun during a noon halt, and perhaps for this reason one of his legs had become infected and badly swollen. It had become so painful that he suffered a great deal, could not walk and was forced to ride in one of the wagons, thus increasing the weight of its load by one hundred fifty pounds, which was hard on the oxen. Fortunately, by this time Delano was able to walk most of the day, though he did ride occasionally when the ground was favorable, and he exerted himself considerably to give Fredenburg a chance to ride.

The emigrants had traveled about a mile and a half from their encampment and were about a half-mile northeast of their road when they came to a warm spring gushing forth from a limestone hill, and though most of their cattle would not touch it as it spurted from its source, they didn't hesitate to indulge. Fortunately, this sort of dilemma quickly passed as, toward noon, they emerged from a narrow gorge and beheld a beautiful little creek of pure, cold water. They followed it several miles up a wooded bottom, fording it twice. Delano considered it "a perfect God-send" for the livestock and the company alike. By nightfall, however, after having traveled several miles beyond the creek, they were and forced to camp where there was little wood and no water at all; now, with no water left in their canteens, they resigned themselves to the prospect of eating their evening bread dry and hard and forcing it down as best they could. As Delano wrote of it in his *Journal*:

> *While we were gloomily submitting to our fate, with tongues already parched for want of moisture, a cry was head on the hill above, "Water! Water is found!" Captain Greene had gone over the hill about a quarter of a mile, and made the discovery of a small spring, and the announcement completely changed the complexion of things in our camp. In a moment, stoves were taken down, fires lighted, and men with buckets on their arms were seen going swiftly over the hill; there was a rattling of dishes and active preparations for cooking going on, and instead of going supperless and tealess to bed, our evening meal passed off as usual. After supper a consultation was held, at which it was resolved to divide our company, on account of procuring forage more readily, for we often found places where a small number of cattle could be supplied, while there was scarcely enough for so many together. This proposition was generally acceded to; however, among so many men it would be strange if any course should not be opposed by some. The wisdom of the measure, however, was proved, for we got along with less difficulty. Captain Greene continued in command of eleven wagons and twenty-nine men, and Mr. Fredenburg was elected to direct the movements of the remaining six wagons and twenty-one men. I fell in with the lot of the latter, and though I submitted*

with the best grace I could, I parted from Captain Greene with regret, for his modest, unassuming manner, and his sterling good sense had made me much attached to him. John Traverse was selected for our wagon-master, and as everything disorderly was at the moment voted a bore, the rest of us resolved ourselves into a company of orderly privates. Drive, fifteen miles.

[June 15th, 1849 • Friday]

Today, only three months after vacating his office as President of the United States, James Knox Polk, who did far more for his country than he would ever be given credit for having done, and who launched hundreds of thousands of people world-wide on a wild, unrestrained hunt for gold in the very territory he had wrested from the Mexicans for the United States, died in his own bed in Nashville, Tennessee, a victim of cholera.

[June 24th, 1849 • Sunday]

After being encamped for a solid month at Independence, Missouri, while they completed their outfitting with what could be purchased at the trading posts there, the Herman Scharmann Party today set off at last on their great journey to the far west to seek the gold that had now become such a powerful lure throughout the world. Afflicted with a life-long, incurably gloomy temperament, Scharmann persistently, compulsively groused about every matter in which he became involved, complaining to his family, his fellow travelers, and, most particularly, in his diary. At their departure from Independence on May 20th, he had written:

After a four weeks' stay we struck our tents, harnessed the horses to our four wagons, each of which was loaded with a minimum of three hundred pounds, and on May twentieth, with forty cows and four to five yoked oxen we started toward the prairie.

This overland journey westward is beyond doubt one of the most unfortunate undertak ings to which man may allow himself to be lured, because he cannot possibly have any conception before starting of this kind of travelling [sic]. To be sure, there is a beaten path which you see clearly before you but there are no stopping-places with even the slightest signs of civilization. Everyone is going and no one is coming back. You leave your camp in the hope of finding water, and a grazing place for the cattle, a few miles further on, but sometimes it happens that you are forced to halt in a place where neither grass nor water can be found. This means intense suffering for the cattle and often an irretrievable loss. In our case, some very serious blunders had been made in securing the wagons, the oxen, and the mules. An ox suitable for the journey over the prairies must not be under four nor over six years old, and must be well accustomed to the yoke. Every yoke must be of the same strength and quality, so that one ox does not pull ahead of, or pull down the other. The mules must also be young and well broken; whoever intends to break them in on the trip will surely not make any headway and will only ruin the animals. Horses are entirely useless.

The wagons deserve special attention. They should be made of dry and firm wood, and tongue and axle should be so strong that it would be almost impossible to break them. The wagon must be able to carry 6,000 pounds on a level road, and yet it must not be massive, and must run very easily. Four yokes of well-trained oxen or six mules should form the equipment for such a wagon, and it should not be loaded with more than 2,000 pounds. If you fall into holes, as is the case a dozen times a day when a wagon crosses a swamp, the oxen in front which have reached firm ground must help the others by giving them room to turn.

On some occasions I have seen the axles break in two, as though they were mere twigs. This happened with a wagon which was made for me by Mr. Ringelmann, a blacksmith and wheelwright in New York [City]. Fortunately, I had the especially good luck to be able to choose the best one of ten or twelve wagons which had been abandoned near the spot by other travellers. [sic] To this I harnessed seven oxen, and was thus able to ride over hedge and ditch without any danger.

From Independence to the Kansas River, a distance of 130 miles, there is only a boundless extent of prairie of the best grass land, but this landscape is so novel that you never tire looking at it.

The Scharmann journey continued with little of particular interest to note until they reached the point where they had to cross the Kansas at the mouth of the Big Blue, and then to follow that major tributary northward into the Nebraska country. As Scharmann wrote of it on June 4th:

> *Along the Kansas River I saw Indians [Potawatomies] for the first time in their primitive condition. Men and women ride; they wrap themselves in woolen blankets, wear beads on hands and feet, and put them around their horses' necks; they paint their faces red and blue. But notwithstanding all their odd and barbarous customs, they act in a fairly decent way. These Indians live mainly on the money which the United States pays them for their ceded territory.*
>
> *The Kansas River at the crossing is too deep for a wagon to ford it, so a boat has been placed on which they may be taken over. The cattle have to swim. My eldest son, Frederic, mounted Bill, the trusty leader of the oxen, and started across. Immediately the whole herd followed him. From the Kansas [River] to Fort Kearney [sic], a distance of 180 miles [we are told], the land is one large meadow with gently undulating hills and valleys.*

It was not until Friday, June 22nd, that Herman Scharmann began completing his diary entries in a more regular manner. At that point he wrote:

> *June 22-23 ... we reached Fort Kearney [Kearny] on Tuesday, June 19th, where we rested for two days [June 20th and 21st]. The fort, like all the other buildings around here, is built of dried bricks [adobe]. It is garrisoned by three companies of soldiers and guarded by several guns, in order to keep a check on the numerous Indians of this neighborhood. The site is on an immense plateau thickly covered with grass which could serve as a dwelling-place for an almost unlimited number of human beings, since the cultivation of this land and the raising of cattle Would amply recompense them all within a few years.*
>
> *I went to the commander of the fort and asked him for*

> *some fresh bread to satisfy my wife's longing. In the most accommodating and courteous way he supplied me with an order on the quartermaster's department, where I obtained fifteen pounds of fresh bread very cheaply.*
>
> *June 24th — Sunday. From Fort Kearney [Kearny] we set out once more, this time toward Fort Laramie, which is situated at the foot of the Rockies, about 340 miles from Kearney. In a short time we had reached the Platte River, which has a breadth of a quarter of a mile and whose water is always muddy because its bed consists of a very fine quicksand, constantly stirred up by the strong current.*

[June 28th, 1849 ◆ Thursday]

With the resurgence of good health, Alonzo Delano was taking a decidedly renewed interest in his surroundings and in the progress of the journey westward. The terrain, which had varied little for weeks on end, was now gradually becoming increasingly arid and offering far fewer active streams. Delano's company had crossed the last two significant streams on June 15th when they had waded across both Cross Horse Creek and the Rio la Bonta, which were, as Delano noted in his *Journal*:

> *... two beautiful streams of clear water, with pebbly bottoms. We had been in advance of the South Bend Company trains, but they passed us to-day. We came upon a tract of red ochre earth, which extended several miles, and it was so highly colored that it stained our clothes, while the road in the distance appeared like a stripe of red paint from the high points.*
>
> *At about eleven o'clock, after a gradual ascent nearly all the morning, we came to the ridge of the Black Hills, which we were to cross, and follow on the west side for several days. From this height we commanded an extensive view of the country, which was much broken and nearly destitute of timber; and the earth, particularly the broken bluffs, were highly colored with red ocherish earth.*

These hills, Delano discovered, consisted of a lofty mountain ridge bristling with a gray rock and sharply pointed fir trees which served as a virtual elevated wall, a high boundary between hostile countries. To the east of this imaginary line, the area through which they had long been passing, lay the territory of the statuesque Sioux, and now, ahead, lay the territory of the fierce, considerably less attractive Crow Indians. For Delano the marked differences between those two peoples were amplified as his company encountered various subtribes and villages: The Crows were much darker complexioned and significantly shorter in stature than the Souix. Nor were the Crows' costumes so well made and colorfully-appointed as those worn by the Sioux. To Delano, the Crows seemed to be a sort of connecting link between the Asiatic and Atlantic tribes.

As the emigrants' column passed over this spur of the Black Hills and descended on its western side, they entered into a valley through which flowed a fairly substantial creek of very clear water. A short distance before reaching it, however, they encountered a broad area of white pumice stone which, to Delano, offered proof that the terrain was of volcanic origin. The pumice was easily broken, Delano learned, by a sharp blow from another stone. He could clearly picture it, in his mind's eye, seething and bubbling in a great caldron — a manifestation of the earth's vast internal fires. Stunted, but nevertheless attractive, little trees along the stream's margin beautified the view, but away from the river's edge, the vista was barren and desolate. In conversations with others in the column, Delano discovered that a fair number of them thought that this entire area was the crater and residue of some very ancient, now-dorment volcano. After giving this theory considerable thought, Delano concluded that the area was, indeed, likely the scene of a great fire eruption in the primordial past.

Smith's swollen leg continued to be very painful; obviously he was suffering immensely from every little jolt the wagon took, and worse yet, the emigrants simply could not provide him with any degree of comfort. Captain Greene's *Dayton Company* passed them in mid-afternoon and was out of sight when *The Ottawa Company* members called a halt for the night and camped on a grassy plain, surrounded by high hills, but without water. They made do without, having secured enough early in the morning in their kegs to provide for the night's cooking needs. They had driven sixteen miles this day, and, as Delano noted in the beginning of his *diary* entry the next day:

> *Saturday, June 16th. How many beautiful creeks, and limpid streams of pure, cold water have I passed at home with*

scarcely a notice, while the deep shade of some pretty grove has often passed unheeded. How men change with circumstances! In passing through this desert country, over the barren hills, a clear, running stream is hailed with delight, and long remembered for the relief it gives the thirsty traveler, while a small cluster of stunted ash and willow bushes, charily scattered about on the banks of a brook, is a perfect oasis, for its cooling shade in the glaring summer sun. We found one such during this sultry day, and it made an impression on our memories never to be forgotten.

Our road was not as hilly as that of yesterday, but the scenery of the Black Hills, at whose base we are traveling, is peculiar and romantic. A very tall, narrow, rocky ridge is in our left, many hundred feet high, which stands like some nondescript monster, bristling at our approach; while peculiar lesser hills in various forms, attest the force of volcanic action.

Near their campsite, a near perfect cone of fine-grained sandstone had been thrown up some sixty to eighty feet high, which looked to the men as if it had been formed by the hand of man, so regular and perfect was its shape. Much of its attractive stone resembled Missouri oil-stone. Since it was perfect as whetstone, especially for fine-edging their pocket-knives, the men picked up quantities of it to take along for later use.

As evening approached the emigrants established their camp near the unusual cone, only to discover that the surrounding ochre-colored soil provided poor water and little grass. Because the cattle were obviously weary, they had little choice but to lay over for a day to give the animals a rest and the benefit of what little forage they could find. Knowing they were at this point only about six miles from the North Platte, they anticipated that on the morrow the river's level bottoms would provide them with plenty of grass, wood, and good water — a prospect they found particularly pleasing to anticipate.

For all of the men in the column, the following day turned out to be an object lesson in not counting one's chickens before the eggs were hatched. They had been toiling for the past five days over rugged roads, pushing a herd scantily supplied with either water or good grass, fully convinced that the area ahead would provide a beautiful stream and extensive flats of lush grasses. They pushed on at speed, pausing only briefly to refresh themselves at the lovely but limited little creek called Fourche Boise, and then rushed on into the valley of the North Platte several miles beyond. When they reached the bottom, however, they were astonished to behold bare, dry soil from which sprouted only a few unpalatable weeds the animals could not eat, an almost absence of drinkable water, and a sandy road leading over new hills ahead to whatever unknown fate awaited them. The company's only possibly remedy for their overwhelming sense of disappointment was to slog onward and hope for better very soon. As Delano expressed it in his *Journal* this night:

> *We were compelled to go on, with the naked Black Hills peering down upon us, like goblins, laughing at our way-worn wretchedness, and apparently deriding our search for gold, in the language of Macbeth's witches:*
>
> *"Double, double, toil and trouble,*
> *Fire burn and caldron bubble."*
>
> *Pshaw! If our caldron is full, we'll upset it, and begin anew, so drive on, Hazel. Ho! for California!"*

On again reaching the bottoms of the North Platte, they came to another concentration of alkali even more concentrated and pervasive than they had previously encountered. The alkali virtually choked the soil, compelling the men to conclude that the entire country must be barren and worthless for any agricultural purposes. At this point, Delano wrote in his *Journal*:

> *It is difficult to judge of the character of men on the road, by external appearances. A Mexican hat, a beard of twenty days' growth, an outer covering soiled with dirt and dust, a shirt which may have seen water in its youth, will disguise anyone so that he may look like a ferocious brigand, while at the same time his heart may be overflowing with the "milk of human kindness."*

This comment was prompted by an incident which occurred on Delano's morning walk near the North Platte. He had overtaken an elderly man who appeared to be a veteran of the plains, a man looking more like a well-digger than a gentleman or a scholar. With the ease with which travelers on the plains become acquainted, they began conversing with little ceremony, and, as Delano put it:

> *... instead of his being a plain country bumpkin that I had at first set him down for, I found him to be a scientific man, a gentleman of much education and research, and assuredly a most agreeable traveling companion, despite his California costume.*

The stranger turned out to be Colonel Joseph S. Watkins, presently from Missouri, but lately from Memphis, Tennessee. He had been a large contractor in the Norfolk Navy Yard at Norfolk, Virginia, and prior to his removal to Tennessee, he had been a member of the Virginia Legislature for twenty-one years; indeed at one period during his public career, he had wielded a great influence in the politics of his native state. He had also been actively engaged in business during his eventful life, and his connection with some of the most distinguished men of America gave him a substantial fund of anecdotal material. As Delano described the man:

> *... I scarcely knew which most to admire, his decided talents, or his prominent philanthropic goodness of heart, which he exhibited throughout our pleasant conversation. He gave me an amusing account of his setting out from Missouri, with a company from Tennessee. They were seventy strong, having a republican and military form of government, a constitution and by-laws, a president and vice-president, a legislature, three judges, and court of appeals, nine sergeants as well as other officers who, by their laws, were to be exempted from the performance of camp duty by virtue of their dignified stations — leaving it for the plebeians and common soldiers to do the drudgery of camp duty, and of standing guard at night. All this read very well on paper, and quite to the satisfaction of those who were to be exempt from labor, but, reduced to practice, it was not strange that it produced murmuring, which ripened into actual rebellion.*
>
> *Thinking it smacked too much of favoritism and aristocracy, the Colonel petitioned the legislature for an amend-*

ment of the constitution, which, after much discussion, was decided to be out of order, as it was not presented in due form by an honorable member of that august body, and no member was found willing to present a petition which compromised his own privilege. This led to an open rupture, and the Colonel withdrew, after holding up the folly of their course to view, followed by thirteen wagons, and which finally ended in the dissolution of the government of the traveling republic, whose legitimate business it was to guard against thieving Indians. Thus, this sublime government fell to pieces by the weight of its own machinery and exclusive privileges. I laughed till my eyes run over [sic] at the Colonel's ludicrous description.

The day finished poorly indeed for the men of the Ottawa Company. They soon learned that there was a ferry across the North Platte River — which they had to cross, about twelve miles distant from their encampment. Far worse, they were informed, the ferry was overwhelmed by at least 250 wagons and teams awaiting their turns. The traffic jam would delay the Ottawa Company's journey across the continent for at least several days. To make matters even worse, the men were informed that the grass in the vicinity was totally exhausted, and cattle were dying for the want of food. It was indeed a sobering dilemma and, for the moment at least, one for which there seemed to be no solution whatever.

There were no fording places on the North Platte in this entire region, and crossings had to be effected by means of such ferries as were available — extremely crude, primitive ferries. After convening a formal council and discussing the crisis at length, the *Ottawa Company* decided that Fredenburg and Delano should ride ahead in the morning and discover how — and when — the crossing was to be made.

Accordingly, the next morning — Monday, June 18th — after gulping down cups of coffee, Fredenburgh on Old Shab and Delano on McNeil's mule, set out at sunrise for the ferry. The road was similar to that of the previous day, although a bit more broken and difficult, and the North Platte Valley had become considerably more undulating. A few miles away from their encampment, as they were descending a hill to some low meadow-land near the margin of the river, the pair spied an ominous notice posted on a board by the road-side. It read:

NOTICE: Look at this! LOOK AT THIS!
The water here is poison, and we have lost
six of our cattle. Do not let your cattle
drink on this bottom!

Inspecting the water closely, the two men concluded that the water was so abundantly charged with carbonate of soda that cattle soon would soon die after drinking it. Neither the men of *The Ottawa Company* nor *The Dayton Company* had ever before had occasion to check cattle-watering places, but they vowed to do so hereafter until they reached their goal, since the loss of any of their animals could well presage disaster.

Within about three miles of the ferry, Delano and Fredenburgh observed a company of men building a raft on the river bank, half a mile from the road. Riding down to the men, the pair ascertained that they could have use of the raft, once the raft-builders' own train, plus two or three others, were ferried across. Since this could detain them for at least a day, the two decided that Delano should ride forward to the ferry, to see what chance there would be of gaining time there. Fredenburg remained behind to halt their train, when it should appear, until Delano returned.

At the ferry, Delano found some two hundred fifty wagons waiting to cross, among which were those of Captain Tutt's and the Dowdle families, from South Bend. The number of wagons arriving at the ferry site were increasing virtually by the moment. Delano learned that another ferry, one established by the Mormons, was also running four miles up-river, but that one, too, was overwhelmed by waiting wagons. Here at the main ferry, some forty head of cattle lay dead from having drunk the carbonated water and so, on discovering that it would be at least several days before they could cross, possibly much longer, Delano concluded that their best chance seemed to be to try the raft below. Fredenburg agreed.

After arriving back at the lower crossing and examining the raft-ferry more closely, they discovered the rig to be hopelessly primitive. The mode of crossing consisted of three small canoes lashed together which apparently proved sufficiently buoyant to sustain the weight of an empty wagon. A rope long enough to reach across the river was fastened to each end of the attached canoes; this was a slow and exhausting process thanks to the strong current. Each company, Delano and Fredenburg learned, had to furnish its own ropes and provide the labor. For the use of the lashed-together canoes, they would have to pay five dollars for each wagon. Delano remarked in his *Journal*:

While I was there, a man was drowned by falling out of the canoe and being swept down by the swift current. The cattle, horses and mules were swum over to the opposite bank, and very few accidents occurred to them, though occasionally one was drowned by being carried to where the bank was too steep to get out.

I rode back to the raft, and found our train just arrived, and all hands making preparations for crossing. A rope was attached to each end of the raft, in the same manner as to the canoes, and it was found capable of sustaining the weight of a loaded wagon, while thirty or forty men on each side pulled it back and forth quite expeditiously, and with perfect safety. The work went briskly on for awhile [sic]. By some mismanagement, however, one of the ropes was broken before our turn came, after crossing thirteen wagons; and all attempts to get the line across again before night proved abortive. Our train was thus compelled to remain on the south bank till morning. The detention was scarcely a loss; for notwithstanding the labor of ferrying was severe to us, our cattle had the benefit of rest, although the grass was poor and scanty. Distance, nine miles.

The following day, Tuesday, June 19th, proved to be considerably more productive. Word had swiftly spread that a new ferry was in operation and that even though primitive, it was getting men and their wagons across. As a result, the whole landing area quickly became choked with arriving trains vying for positions to cross. Because the ferry consisted of just one jerry-built raft and because the broken line had not yet been repaired, the slow-moving traffic line was stopped in its tracks and grew significantly longer. Several hardy men swam across the strong current and struggled to re-establish the rope. Everyone now realized that the previous day's relative success owed more to good luck than to anything else. Finally, after all other efforts to reestablish the rope had failed, Brown of Delano's company, mounted a strong horse and at length succeeded, by great effort, in carrying the rope to the opposite shore. By noon it was ready once again for operation. This time instead of being stretched completely across the river, as before, the rope was stretched to an island. The stream from the island to the opposite shore proved to be surprisingly navigable — a virtual fording place. Consequently, the crossings for a time proceeded very well; shortly after noon, however, the wind increased to virtual gale velocity, causing the wagon covers to act almost as sails.

The raft itself, being confined by the rope, frequently dipped beneath the surface of the water, and hence, the wagons were in danger of sliding off into the stream. Observing this problem building, Delano wisely removed the cover from his wagon, as did many of the others, and they were, consequently, ferried over in perfect safety. One New Jersey man, however, considered the cautionary effort unnecessary and refused to comply, despite the urgings of his friends. In the midst of the crossing, the wind blowing into the wagon cover acted like a lever, ballooning the fabric out and thereby raising one side of the raft until the wagon slid off into the river. It floated downstream about half a mile, when a sharp turn in the river brought it to the bank. The New Jersey man was able to secure two of the wheels, out of which he ultimately rigged a two-wheel cart; he was aso able to salvage part of his damaged provisions. He deplored his own carelessness, but his recent stupidity generated little sympathy from those around him. It was a hard lesson to learn, as was an additional one which Delano and others of *The Ottawa Company* learned a little later. As Delano recorded it:

> *Our men worked very hard in helping two mule trains across the river, on their assurance that they would reciprocate by assisting us. No sooner were they across, however, than they hitched up their teams and drove off, leaving us chagrined at their faithlessness, and vexed at our own credulity. Instead of following their example, our men toiled on to aid those who assisted us, and it was not until nightfall that we all met on the main shore, where our tents were pitched. Our cattle swam across safely to the island, and on the main shore we found a plat of grass that was better than we had seen for many days.*
>
> *Another company, who had been unable to cross, got their few cattle over, and among them, two fine cows, which they desired to have milked; when our wagon master, John Traverse, volunteered to perform the agreeable duty. Stripping off his clothes he prepared to wade to the island, where the cows were feeding, observing, "We'll go it to-night, boys! Let us have a rousing dish of mush and milk, and a feast fit*

> *for the gods for once in our lives!" Our men had not yet all come in, and we determined to give them an agreeable surprise.*
>
> *While Traverse was gone, I put a large kettle of water over the fire, and made mush enough for half of the company. There was plenty of dry wood, and as the evening was chilly, we built a roaring fire, and when the boys came in wet and hungry, we sat down with tin cups, pail covers, basins, and everything that would hold milk; and a more luscious feast I never enjoyed. The pail was full of milk — the kettle full of mush — the boys full of fun, notwithstanding their hard labor — and, with full stomachs, we closed the labors of the day.*

All of the country surrounding the emigrants bore evidence of volcanic action — trap rock in the dark mountain frowning down over them on the south; cones of burnt sand-stone scattered about — some as they appeared to have been originally formed, others worn into fantastic shapes by rain and the action of the elements — and knolls covered with burnt black gravel. There were several particularly immense cones, which appeared as if their tops had been smoothly and evenly cut off, or had been built as watch-towers by ante-diluvian giants; indeed, two ridges ran from the Black Hills to the skirt of the river bottom, resembling immense, even embankments, for railroads or canals, so perfectly were they formed. The soil was barren, with scarcely any grass. The vegetation consisted of wild sage bushes and prickly pear cactus — the latter virtuallu inedible, on account of its thorns, for man or beast. The sage is a scraggly shrub, generally from two to four feet high, with a stem from one to three or four inches in diameter, though in a few instances it may grow to a height of ten feet, with its trunk fully a foot in diameter. It has a leaf which resembles in smell and taste, that of the cultivated sage plant, but stronger and more bitter. It grows in barren, sandy ground, and burns easily, and for many hundreds of miles it comprises almost the only fuel a traveler can find.

The country the men were traveling through continued to surprise them in many ways. On the following day, Wednesday, June 20th, the trail they were following wound close to the river for four miles until finally they were compelled to diverge to the right on account of a mountain that approached near the river a little beyond the ferry above them. While the train stayed on the detouring road in the valley, Delano rode out to the hills and kept pace in a line reasonably parallel to the road. It was difficult terrain to cross, and he frequently found deep chasms of vitrified rock and, in the end, except for startling a little herd of antelope into a swift run, and disturbing a small pack of desert wolves which ran off at his approach, he found nothing to repay him for his taxing exertion.

A short distance before reaching the road, Delano encountered a dry pond several acres in area that was white with inches-thick carbonate of soda encrustations that everyone in the train was now referring to as salaratus, which, of course it was. Salaratus was used a good bit in cooking, especially in the making of bread, and Delano thought that here, for an enterprising individual, was a ready-made business; since it was every bit as fine and pure as the salaratus sold in the east, an enterprising individual need merely scoop it up and package it for sale. He estimated that here at this one pond alone, there had to be more than a thousand wagon-loads available, and they had passed hundreds of sites just like this.

Water had become ever more scarce, a problem which aroused the company's concern, considering their vital need for good fresh water for drinking, cooking and bathing. At the moment it was being found only in springs scattered here and there, which lately were as much as a dozen miles apart. In leaving the river and ascending a long hill, they found the country parched, barren and worthless, with even the hardy wild sage being short and scrubby, barely able to maintain itself in the dry soil. The Black Hills were still in view several miles distant to the south, covered with pine and occasionally with white spots of snow showing in the hollows. It was well past noon before they reached the North Platte again, after slogging through deep sand beneath a burning sun for some eight miles.

They passed the Mormon ferry at about 4 o'clock in the afternoon and found the valley liberally speckled with the white of covered emigrant wagons; this was the point, they had been told, where they would leave the North Platte for good and strike out due westward for the upper reaches of the Sweetwater River after crossing a gradually rising divide several miles in length. Somewhat later, having covered sixteen miles during the day's march, they camped for the night near a couple of ponds in which the water was poisonous, and except for what little remained in their canteens, they had nothing to drink.

The trek resumed shortly after daybreak on Thursday, June 21, and they found the country slightly undulating and both bleak and barren. Close to noon they reached the Red Buttes and found a small stream flowing through a narrow valley, but whatever good grass might have been there had been cropped long before by the herds ahead of them. They estimated at this point that there were easily a thousand wagons ahead of them and quite probably five thousand or more behind. As Delano wrote of it in his *Journal*:

> *The Red Buttes are three isolated mountains, south of us, between the road and the [North] Platte, large portions of which are of bare rock of a bright red color, showing the effect of volcanic fires in producing an ochre tint. They are singular and interesting in their appearance. The country around is a desert, with water only at long intervals, without grass, and not a tree to afford shade from the burning rays of the sun on the sandy soil, and not only ourselves, but our cattle, suffered much from thirst during the day.*
>
> *About four o'clock, we came to a singular outcrop of sand rock, standing up in perpendicular strata like a huge wall of more than a mile in length, and so perfect in its arrangement, that it seemed to be the work of art rather than an accidental formation. Under one portion of this, as well as in the bank of a little run of brackish water, I discovered bituminous coal of an excellent quality.*
>
> *We were compelled to drive between twenty-five and thirty miles, in order to get grass and water; and it was after dark before we reached a little, narrow brook where we could slake our thirst. It being three miles farther to Willow Springs before we could find grass and, our fatigue great, we concluded to unyoke our cattle here for the night. Several trains, like ourselves, had been hurrying over this desert; and although we were first to arrive, within fifteen minutes there were fifty tents or more around us, and their campfires of sage bushes glared up in the darkness, and made it look like the encampment of an army. All were anxious to reach the Sweetwater, where, we were informed, travelers' comforts existed in profusion; and we longed to taste an element which we felt must be refreshing, after drinking the nause-*

ating waters of the muddy Platte. Wearied from our long march, we slept soundly, after a drive of at least twenty-five miles.

At dawn the men yoked the hungry cattle, and after following a narrow, descending valley for about three miles, arrived at a beautiful spring, from which flowed a pretty little brook fringed with willows. This was the long anticipated Willow Springs. The soil, irrigated by the water, bore excellent grass, and, consequently, they halted to allow the cattle to graze and to prepare their own breakfast.

After a two-hour rest in the delightful spot, the company drove on perhaps another two miles to the top of the ascent, from which they had a good view of the charming mountain scenery. Viewed across an undulating plain, the Sweet River Mountains appeared to be only six or eight miles distant; in reality, however, they were still more than twelve hours ahead and probably thirty miles distant. Far ahead the men could see an alluring but illusionary scene — a large pond more than a mile in circumference. They would later arrive at the pond's edge only to find the water to be highly alkaline and totally unfit for their use.

Marching on for another fifteen miles, the column came at last to a creek. Though its waters were not ideal, they were drinkable and they stopped here for their noon break. Assuming the train would shortly be moving forward, Delano set out ahead of them after eating a hard biscuit covered with a slice of raw bacon. The day was intensely hot and Delano slogged on through burning sand, eager to reach the river to obtain a draught of good water. Not until he was upon a slight elevation some three miles distant did he discover the column had not moved and was evidently planning to remain in place for the remainder of the day. As fatiguing as the trail had been, Delano refused to even returning to the company. About Delano encountered a Mr. Marks, a young gentleman who was part of a company from Hennepin, Illinois, under command of Captain Ham, and, he accepted Marks' invitation to share the company's accommodations for the night, he accepted.

It was near sunset when the two reached the camp situated close to the Sweetwater River and, as Delano noted in his *Journal*:

There was not a tree or shrub to mark the river's course, and, although it flowed through a plain, the inequalities of the ground prevented our seeing it until we were almost upon its bank. It is perhaps eighty feet broad, fordable at this season at almost any point, and its waters, though not entirely clear, were so much purer and sweeter than those of the turbid, muddy, and insipid Platte, that it richly deserves its name. My first impulse was to take a long, deep draught of its refreshing water, and then to bathe my aching feet.

The train encamped in a depression on its bank, and in a short time the tents were pitched, camp-fires were burning brightly, supper was prepared and, with a glorious appetite, I sat down to a rich feast of antelope steak, and enjoyed, with a double zest, a very good meal, through their kind hospitality ... if you are an Epicure, for heaven's sake, walk to California across the plains, and you will learn to enjoy with a zest you know not, the luxury of a good meal.

Near our encampment and immediately at the ford stood Independence Rock, a huge boulder of naked granite, forty or fifty rods long, and perhaps eighty feet high. It stands isolated upon the plain, about six miles from the mountains on the right, and three from those on the left. It is not difficult of access on its southern point, and may be ascended in many places on the east. In a deep crevice on the south is a spring of ice-cold water — a perfect luxury to the thirsty emigrant. Hundreds of names are painted on its south wall, and among them I observed some dated 1836.

Fatigued as I was, a hyena might have tugged at my toes without awakening me, for I had paddled through the sun and sand twenty-two miles.

The following morning, Saturday, June 23rd, Delano parted from his Hennepin friends with regret and, as they moved on, he waited for his own *Ottawa Company* to come up. Since they had a good ten miles to drive to reach this point, he made a brief excursion to the closer mountain range. An hour's rapid walk brought him to the base, but instead of finding it level, as it appeared to be when viewed from Independence Rock, it was deeply gullied and broken. From the principal range, a spur extended in a point toward Independence Rock and gradually wore down to little more than an elevated point on the plain. Here he ascended the base of the mountain, which here was about two hundred feet high and little more than a jumble of rocks, with deep chasms and crevices, and reaching the top, he found it so difficult to navigate through the scraggly rocks and chasms that he returned to the level ground at the base. His own train came up just as he had arrived at this point, and here they halted for noon.

After their lunch of hard bread and raw bacon, they continued some five miles to a gap in the mountains over a deep sandy road. The gap was a narrow pass separating the Sweetwater Mountains and the Platte Range. As Delano described it:

> *Passing through the gap, as through a huge gateway, a very fine valley is opened to the view, with the Sweet Water meandering through, with bright green grass bordering its banks. On the right, as far as the eye could extend, a wall of gray granite rock, nearly perpendicular, ranged along, and on the south the rugged peaks of the Platte glittered with snow, and made us cause many a wishful glance at it, bringing forcibly to mind the deliciousness of an ice lemonade on the scorching sun which was pouring down upon us, the rays of which were rendered more intense by the reflection of the hot sand.*
>
> *About fifty rods below the mouth of the gap, a curiosity indeed presented itself. The river had apparently quite broken through the mountain, and passes through a chasm of perpendicular rock, probably over three hundred feet high. It was evidently done by volcanic force, for the blackened, burnt rocks which lay around, and a dyke of black trap rock which had been forced up in the granite on the right wall showed that it had been subjected to intense heat. The river flowed through this singular chasm nearly a quarter of a mile, quite through the mountain, when it again entered the valley which we had just left. At the base of the wall we found the remains of a mountain sheep, or ibex, which had prob-ably been driven off from the top by wolves; but his strong horns and stiff neck were not staunch enough to protect his life against such a force.*
>
> *There were large quantities of yellow mica in the stream, and as it was determined to turn everything into gold that was possible, some of our boys insisted that this was ore, but*

an application of nitric acid instantly dispelled the pleasing hallucination, and proved the Sweet Water Valley was not the valley of the Sacramento. Large masses of saluratus, several inches thick, and very pure, were found on the plain around, and it is not necessary for the emigrant to lay in a supply of this useful article any farther than to this point.

The singular chasm through which the Sweet Water runs, has not inaptly acquired the soubriquet of Devil's Gate, and it did truly seem as if his Satanic majesty had been cutting queer antics in this wild region. We encamped about a mile above this entrance, where we found excellent grass, and quite all the varied concomitants of a good camp. Distance seven miles.

On June 24th *The Ottawa Company* remained in camp until noon before moving onward another eight miles. At that point they found it would be necessary to leave the river for ten miles before getting back to it again; with neither grass nor water available in the interval, they deemed it advisable to lay over until morning. Where the trail turned from the river bottom toward the more elevated plain, they encountered sage once again, as well as vast hordes of crickets, many of which were crushed by the wagon wheels in passing.

On June 25th, following the trail, the emigrants shifted away from the Sweet Water River bottom lands for ten miles and encountered deep sand and penetrating dust which made the traveling difficult for men and beasts alike. For the men, the journey began now to exacerbate tempers, and as Delano observed in his *Journal*:

It is not, on the whole, surprising that the ill tempers of men should be called forth, and be exhibited in their worst features, in a journey of this kind. It almost daily happened, that when the day's journey was performed, we were tired enough to sink to rest without attempting to do more; but the moment the place of encampment was reached, much labor remained to be done. Our tents were to be pitched, our cattle driven out to graze, and a guard set to prevent their straying, or drinking poison water — wood and water must be procured, for which we are often obliged to go a mile or more; and then a fire to be built of buffalo excrement, or sage, or both; our suppers to cook, the dishes to wash; and then, a portion of our mess, in regular turn, to spend part of the night watching around the camp, to prevent the inroads of Indians, — all this added to our weariness, it was impossible that words or actions should always flow in the same even and smooth tenor. The bickerings and ill-humor would frequently break out in all trains, and sometimes lead to unhappy consequences. Still, I may safely say that there was perhaps as little among our men, with two or three exceptions, as in any train; and on the whole we got along passably well, with the thousand and one petty annoyances to which we were subjected.

During our drive in the early part of the day, on gaining a slight elevation we obtained a view of the lofty Wind River Mountains, covered with snow, at an apparent distance of thirty or forty miles. They are much higher than those of the Sweet Water, and present a magnificent appearance. On the north side of the road stood a bare, isolated rock of granite, sloping like a roof, which, though not as large as Independence Rock, was something of a curiosity, from its immense size.

In the bare granite range on the right was a mountain rock many miles distant, which resembled a castle with a dome, and it looked like the strong-hold of some feudal baron of olden time; but as we passed on, it soon changed its appearance to a shapeless, broken mass of granite. At night we again reached the river, where a new road had been made through a singularly gloomy gorge in the northern mountains, through which the river flowed. It was reported to be the best road, although it was necessary to ford the river four times, but it was said by this route we should avoid a heavy sand road, and we therefore thought we would take it. The grass, though not abundant, was passably good. Distance, fifteen miles.

The *Ottawa* column crossed the first ford on June 26th and entered the rocky gorge through which the river flowed, then proceeded another mile to the second fording place. Here a narrow pathway had been cut into the bank, capable of admitting only one wagon at a time.

The fording place was so deep that all wagon boxes had to be raised from their beds by about six inches to keep them from being flooded. The ford turned out to be very crooked and difficult to cross; moreover, with a large number of teams ahead of them impatiently awaiting their turns, it appeared very likely that they would have to be waiting here until at least noon or later before they could get through.

Considering the options available, *The Ottawa Company* men held a quick meeting and decided that their best alternative was to take the old road, despite its sandiness and difficulty. Consequently, they turned about, and on reaching the road and leaving the river, they encountered about four miles of the expected sand-covered road, but the rest of the way was relatively clear, and the distance did not exceed that of the one they had recently abandoned. Actually, they gained time, because upon reaching the point where the two roads united, at a distance of eight miles, they found themselves meeting trains that had been a full day ahead of them, and those men with them reported the road by the gorge had been poor, requiring the trains to cross the river four different times at inadequate, difficult fords, which had delayed them considerably.

The day grew excessively warm; the clouds of dust raised by the passing trains was almost choking in its density, and there was no water whatsoever for the next eight miles. The men's awareness that rain was obviously falling heavily on the mountains to the south, moreover, filled them with concern. It didn't help at all to note the rain falling heavily on mountains to the south. One peak, some four miles distant, was white with snow, although some of the boys in the column, in their ignorance insisted it was a ledge of white rock. When they halted for their customary noon break, Delano, on a whim, volunteered to go and bring some of the snow back to camp.

Young Thorne, who had an interest in the horse Old Shab, requested that Delano to ride this horse on his mission, and Delano gratefully accepted and started off. He had hardly gone a few paces, however, when Morrill confronted him. As Delano wrote of it:

> *Morrill, who also claimed an interest in the pony, ordered me to dismount. This proceeded only from ill-feeling towards me, from an imaginary insult which he asserted I had given him at home, long before I even knew him, and for which he vented his spite in a continued series of insulting acts and bitter language, better becoming a Billingsgate felon*

> *than a man of sense, when I was sick and helpless on the plains. I refused to obey, having the consent of an actual owner and worthy man, when he seized his rifle, and with the impulse of a maniac, began to approach me, raving like a madman. I was armed with a revolver and a double-barreled gun, and had he made an assault, I should have most surely have shot him down, unless he had been beforehand, for his abuse had been so glaring that he had rendered himself disgusting to every one, and all wondered that my patience had held out so long. But he stopped in his mad career, returned to his wagon, and I slowly and deliberately rode off, thankful that, notwithstanding his constant provocation, I had not shed his blood.*

Some two miles from the road, Delano found the plain becoming broken, and on reaching the mountain he followed a gulf which was thickly lined with dwarf fir trees and coarse underbrush, through which a little brook ran. In endeavoring to follow it, Delano was suddenly brought to a halt by a high, perpendicular wall of rock, with the snow still many hundreds of feet above him. He managed to get off a shot at a small herd of antelope but evidently missed, as they all ran off. Unable to surmount the wall, Delano started back, but had hardly begun when he was overtaken by a heavy hail storm, which pelted and drenched him considerably. Drenched to the skin and shivering with the cold, Delano continued toward the road in the direction of the train. He soon encountered a brook with enough water surging through it to turn a mill, and he followed it downstream until it sank into the earth and disappeared in the sand. At this point he realized that he was within a mile of the emigration trail.

Following the trail of the train, Delano overtook it about four o'clock in the afternoon, on the border of a morass, approximately a mile long by a half-mile broad. Some of the boys, believing water might be easily obtained, had taken a spade and, going well out on the dense wild grass, had commenced digging. About a foot beneath the surface, they struck not water but instead a layer of ice some five or six inches thick. Many trains were passing at the time and they all stopped and availed themselves of the newly discovered clear, cooling curiosity; the *Ottawa* train men filled their spare buckets with chipped ice As Delano wrote of it:

This natural icehouse is not only a great curiosity in itself, but from its peculiar situation, in this dry, barren, sandy plain, is justly entitled to be called the diamond of the desert. To the unsophisticated this may seem a traveler's tale, but it is easily explained upon natural principles. We were now at an elevation of about six thousand feet, the morass was clearly either a pond or a combination of springs, covered with turf or swamp grass, and at this high altitude the temperature of winter is very severe, converting the water of the morass to solid ice. Although the sun of summer is intensely hot in these mountain valleys, the turf and grass intercept the intensity of its rays, and prevent the dissolution of the ice, on the principle of our domestic ice-houses; thus a kind Providence affords a necessary and indispensable comfort to the exhausted traveler in these dry and barren regions.

We were now on a plain, sixteen miles distance to water. The sage here attained a great growth, being as high as my head, and the trunk frequently six inches in diameter. I observed a new species of prairie dog, or it may well be, a connecting link between the prairie dog and the ground squirrel. They are about the size of the latter, with much the shape of the former, and burrow under the sage bushes, to which they fly on the least alarm. We found them so numerous at some of our encampments, that we could knock them over with sticks, and the boys amused themselves in killing them with pistols. They were very fat and oily, but, on being parboiled and roasted, were quite good. Antelope were plenty, and droves of mountain sheep, or ibex, were upon the hills.

We made about six miles on the sixteen-mile stretch, when we encamped, with none but alkaline water, and scarcely any grass, and it required all our care to keep our cattle from straying in search of food, and to prevent them from drinking the fatal water.

Yesterday, June 27th, with their cattle suffering from want of forage and their own supply of ice-water exhausted, *The Ottawa Company* left their encampment at daybreak, in an effort to reach the river as early as possible. In passing over the sandy plain, which had varied little from that of the preceding day, they finally reached the river again at about 10 a.m., and there they found the conditions for a good camp. Their wagon-master, Traverse, was acclaimed as one of the best marksmen in the entire company, and during their morning transit he had drifted out onto the plains with his rifle and, had bagged two fine young antelopes.. While the cattle were turned loose to forage for their own rations in the lush near-river grasses, the men regaled themselves with antelope steaks.

Following their three-hour halt, the men resumed their march, traveling up the valley and over the ridge of a long hill, crossing the river three times in the process. This time they crossed the fords with ease; the river was now little more than a narrow, running creek. The road for the remainder of this day was excellent; the mountain wall was less marked, and yesterday evening, for the first time in many days, they found an encampment site which provided an abundance of fuel, water, and grass. An intrepid entrepreneur had established a temporary trading post nearby, consisting of a cluster of a half-dozen cloth and buffalo-skin tents, plus two or three loaded wagons. The emigrants decided they would take the time in the morning to visit the tents and see what was available.

This morning, then, Thursday, June 28th, the *Ottawa* train men crowded into the tented area, and the owner immediately invited them into what he called the Grand Lodge. Inside, Delano was surprised to discover a fine large carpet spread upon the ground, along with a comfortable camp bed, several reasonably comfortable chairs — including even a fine old, nicely cushioned rocking chair — along with several volumes of standard books and, to the men's great wonderment, a rather pretty and well-dressed American woman, with an easy, pleasant address, who was the proprietor's companion. Delano abruptly feeling keenly embarrassed, wrote of it in his *Journal*:

> *Of course my old, soiled buckskin coat and weather-beaten hat had to bow before the majesty of female influence, and I felt a blush of shame mantling my cheeks as I thought of my squalid appearance. Also in the company were several Spanish women, of mixed breeds, and attaches, with most villainous looks, and it seemed strange that a woman of her [American woman's] apparent character, could be content to pass her life in such a wild country, and among such an un-*

couth set of companions. But, as there is "no accounting for taste," I am not disposed to moralize on the subject, and simply let it pass.

A sign stood near the road labeled "Post-Office," along with a notice that one of the company was about leaving for the States, and would carry letters, "price, half a dollar [$13.60]." Many a half-dollar was left, but those letters which our company left for their friends never reached them, and it was only a pleasant ruse to gull travelers and "raise the wind."

Upon ascending a hill of nearly two miles in length, a fine view presented itself to our vision. On our right, twenty or thirty miles distant, the Wind River Mountains, extending from beyond the South Pass into Oregon, were mingling their snow-white crests with a rich drapery of clouds. On our left and partly behind us, as the road momentarily changed our direction, lay the granite cliffs of the Sweet Water, fading away in the dim distance, while east of north, a broad undulating plain spread out for many miles, with occasional bold buttes or solitary hills, rising from its surface.

Before us lay the hills which still marked the course of the valley of the Sweet Water, while on elevated plains were piles of rocks and stones, thrown up by volcanic force, which looked, at a distance, as if they had been gathered by the hand of man. Occasionally, in the hollows, heaps of snow glittered in the sunlight, and as we gathered it we found it delightfully and refreshingly cool, while perspiring in the sultry heat of the day.

The ascent to the South Pass of the Rocky Mountains is so gradual that we perceive no difference in the road, and had we not been assured by careful mathematical demonstration that such was the fact, we could scarcely have believed that we had been ascending since leaving the Missouri. The rarification of the air, which now began to be apparent in our short breathings, on going over hills, was often attributed by those unacquainted with the true cause, to some unaccountable failure of strength.

The face of the whole country from the Black Hills to

South Pass is very peculiar and interesting. High table elevations, with flat surfaces; solitary conical mountains with flattened tops, spurs similar to huge embankments for railroads or canals, running at angles from the main ranges, may here be seen. Red earth-column buttes seem to rise from the plain — the granite hills often assuming fantastic shapes which cannot be described, with here and there barren sage plains, and ponds of carbonate of soda. These are the general characteristics which mark this strange portion of the world. Antelope and buffalo are very numerous, and lizards and crickets, crawling in vast numbers over the burning sands, are the principal varieties of insect life which the traveler sees. The Indians are warlike and treacherous, and the solitary traveler may think himself well-off, if, after being robbed, he escapes with his life.

We passed many dead cattle during the last ten days. Their death was generally attributed to weariness and bad water, but my impression is that there existed another cause, which was generally overlooked, and that was possibly the rarification of the air. On driving up long and steep hills, we became almost breathless. The cause was suggested to our company, and we often stopped to give our cattle a chance to breathe. Many did not use this precaution, and cattle and mules sometimes dropped down in the harness, exhausted. We saw more dead cattle the first day after crossing the Pass than at any other time. This, with hard labor and scanty food, must have been the cause.

An express rider passed to-day, who told us that there was an immense throng behind, and that at least a thousand wagons were detained at the South Platte, on account of a sudden rise in the river, which prevented fording. He informed us that there was a vast amount of sickness and suffering among them; the grass was consumed and many of the cattle had perished for want of food. To us, their prospect seemed cheerless enough, for a great part of the way along the North Fork, and up to our present advance, the grass barely afforded sustenance to the trains already passed, and we were sometimes compelled to pass two miles out of the road to find forage. None would be left when they came

> *along. We crossed two or three ledges of rocks, cropping out from the top of high and steep hills, which made the labor for our cattle exceedingly hard.*
>
> *A singular accident of a serious nature occurred today in a Pittsburgh Company, at their noon halt. A young man belonging to their train was standing by a wagon, tieing [sic] his horse to a wheel. A loaded musket lay on a knoll at a little distance, and a horse was feeding near it. The horse passed over it, when his halter caught in the lock, and discharged the musket, the whole charge taking effect in the young man's knee, inflicting a dangerous wound, and it was found necessary to amputate the limb to save his life.*
>
> *Passing three fine creeks during the afternoon, we encamped on the river bottom for the last time, about two miles from the road, and then drove the cattle a mile below, where they found good grazing. Our encampment was in a large community of the species of prairie dogs I have mentioned, and they were running about like rats, and many were killed by the men, while endeavoring to escape to their holes. Distance, twenty miles.*

At this point in their long, arduous trek to California, Delano and several others in the train were sobered by their memories of an incident that had occurred months ago, near the outset of their journey in their camp near St. Joseph. They had been joined on one evening by Charles Dawson, a tall man who was rumored to have made three round trips from the Mississippi to the Pacific coast and back. After saying little as he supped with the men, he later made a random remark as they hovered near the dying campfire which now seemed full of foreboding:

"The first half of your wandrin' West is gonna' be th' easy part. Things don't start t'gittin' really rough 'till you git past th' Continental Dee-vide. Up to then its passable difficult. After that, though," he shook his head sorrowfully and spat to one side, "after that, it's jus' plain damn' god-awful hell!"

Chapter 7

[June 29th, 1849 • Friday]

This was the third time James Marshall had returned to the Coloma lumber-mill site. Twice previously on returns he had been driven out by threats of violence if he didn't reveal where all the gold was — as if he knew. They couldn't seem to get it through their heads that the only place he actually collected any substantial amount of gold was right here where they were looking. These people who had poured into this old mill-site were looking for "easy gold," and they couldn't seem to understand that simply going out and picking up gold off the ground surface was a thing of the past; it just didn't happen anymore. Yet, they persisted with their childish, reality-defying hopes, much to the irritation of their much more experienced gold-seeking bretheren.

Now, returning once again to the old mill-site, Marshall found his possessions scattered, the mill itself virtually torn apart for the lumber it possessed, and pitiful souls wandering aimlessly about, hopeful of picking up an overlooked nugget or two. Everyone still here seemed entirely convinced that James Marshall knew precisely where the gold was located, but that he was determined not to share his secrets with anyone. The *fools*! If he knew where it was, did they really think he'd keep coming back here to scratch for it? At least now he might be able to search in peace for a while. Hardly anyone remaining here would have recognized him in the first place, now that he had grown a full beard, wore tattered, dirty buckskins, and had adopted the stooped-over stance of the old-time miner.

Had Marshall been any kind of businessman when the gold was first discovered, he likely could have struck some kind of deal with the men who came rushing in from all directions, but he simply lacked the acumen necessary to broker some sort of settlement with them — a weakness the gold-seekers had instantly recognized. Though his frontier experience had certainly enabled him to survive and thrive in the wilds, he simply was poorly prepared to deal with the ways of worldly men and their unscrupulous nature; men who were only too eager to take advantage of situations where there was no law to thwart them and a court system dominated by corrupt, venal, and easily bribed officials. Marshall, moreover, was by nature generous and open-handed to a fault in all his dealings, slow to suspect anything nefarious, and frequently inclined to naively reveal matters much better kept in confidence. Perhaps worst of all, he did not belong to any of the "rings" of miners that had formed, rings whose power had grown dramatically in the course of the previous year.

Marshall had recently returned with the idea of perhaps reviving his lumber business and, simultaneously, doing some profitable prospecting on the side. Unfortunately, this time he was no better prepared to cope with competing prospectors than he had been before. He approached one group busily digging and washing dirt in flumes and sluice-boxes, and asked a big man who seemed to be in charge, if he might prospect "over there," and he pointed toward a small ravine where no one was working. The man he addressed only briefly raised his head to look, then shrugged and said he could. When Marshall asked if he could borrow a sluice-box, this was provided, too, as well as access to a limited supply of water from their diversion running through, for which he would pay them if and when he began finding gold.

It was only a week ago, on June 22nd, when Marshall, leaning against a pile of the lumber he had long ago sawn, was approached by a man who said his name was Hargraves, from Austrialia, and who wanted "advice from an old, seasoned miner" about where to dig. Marshall shook his head in evident exasperation.

"You say you're from Australia, Mr. Hargraves, so let me ask you a question. Why is it you don't go dig in your own mountains for gold? I'm told the conditions and terrain there are virtually identical to what we have here, and from what I have heard of your country, I have no doubt you would find plenty of gold there."

"Do you really think so?" Hargraves asked, intrigued by the idea.

"I do," Marshall replied.

Hargraves, taking the conversation seriously, terminated his own prospecting here and found passage on a ship returning from San Francisco to Australia.

Marshall's anonymity, however, didn't last. He worked by himself but had only been at it a few hours when someone stopped by, looked at him closely, and then exclaimed loudly, "By God, that there's Jim Marshall again, an' he's struck it for sure this time!"

The man rushed off, but quickly came back with his own equipment and with a score or more of other hopefuls following him, all of whom began digging close to Marshall without even asking a "by-your-leave." Marshall had no choice but to flee, and was peppered with curses and threats as he did so. He retreated, fully aware that he could never return again without being overwhelmed by a flood of angry, unjust harassment.

[June 30th, 1849 • 405 p.m. • Saturday]

Both San Francisco's and Sacramento's phenomenal growth continued apace, and consequently, the demand for accommodations far exceeded the availability. The din of perpetual construction filled the air day and night.

In Sacramento a banner over a huge tent was labeled *Eagle Theater*, and within its lofty expanse, every evening a production of some kind was performed. The repertoire, which changed nightly and played to full-house audiences, included staged dramas with such intriguing titles as *Charles II, Bachelor Buttons, The Wife, Othello, Dead Shot, Rent Day, William Tell, The Bandit Chief*, and *The Forest Spectre*, often with a shorter afterpiece added as a reward to enthusiastic audiences.

Sacramento, too, was changing daily: Over one hundred new homes were under construction, as were numerous businesses, especially in the downtown area, including the new City Hotel, located on Front Street between I and J Streets, its dimensions 35 feet by 55 feet and three stories in height. Its cost was $100,000 [$2,880,000] and, though not yet completed, had already been rented to Fowler & Fry for $5,000 [$144,000] per month. Some said the new U.S. Hotel, or the Sutter House Hotel, on Front Street between K and L were even better; others favored McKnight's American Hotel on K Street between Second and Third.

Another of the major businesses just now being founded in Sacramento was *Huntington & Hopkins*, a firm offering clothing, equipment, and food. This enterprise was founded by 28-year-old Collis Potter Huntington, a former Oneonta, NY, storekeeper, who gave up prospecting after working only one day at it, and his partner, Mark Hopkins,

36, who previously founded the *New England Trading and Mining Company,* and who came around Cape Horn with 26 men (each of whom contributed $500 to capitalize the venture) and a year's supply of stores and equipment. The two partners were also were planning to open a major iron and hardware store within the near future. Besides these large improvements, the Sacramento embarcadero was already home to eleven new major wholesale houses, including *Priest, Lee, & Co.,* with P. B. Cornwell as partner; *Hensley, Reading, & Co.; Brannan, Whitlock & Gibson;* and other firms established by such individuals as Samuel Norris, Edgar Gillespie, James Ingersoll, Everett Jones, Fayette Robinson, Dr. John Robinson, Douglas Hanna, Robert Gelston, and Frank Taber, as well as an additional fourteen smaller stores. In addition, James McClatchy, a newly-arrived 24-year-old Irishman, was already making plans to establish a new daily newspaper which he planned on calling the *Sacramento Bee.*

As busy as Sacramento was, San Francisco was surpassing Sacramento in all sorts of activities. Not surprisingly, Sam Brannan was among the leading businessmen there, as well. He had been investing heavily in, of all things, carpet tacks, which were suddenly in great demand in this era of canvas and muslin housing as well as in other current prevailing industries. Brannan continued relentlessly to amass one of the greatest fiscal fortunes along the entire Pacific coast.

The city of San Francisco had grown so swiftly and extravagantly that, in addition to hundreds of private homes, it now boasted no less than sixty-eight hotels, some little more than tents, and others of more substantial construction, even with multitudes of private rooms and dormitory-type accommodations. In addition, thirteen restaurants already dotted the city, along with five major gambling establishments, a number of government offices, and a similar number of large storage warehouses at city's wharf, which itself extended far out into San Francisco Bay.

The large San Francisco hill known as Sydney Town (later Telegraph Hill) had itself become a hotbed of shabby, mostly temporary residences of disreputable Australians, from which it took its name. It was currently home to a large number of prostitutes, thieves, former convicts, and assorted ruffians who populated numerous low-grade saloons and drinking houses bearing such names as *Tam O'Shanter, Magpie, White Stag,* and *Boar's Head.* This was a perilous area where unsuspecting guests or strollers risked being knocked into a daze by a vicious sand-bag blow to the head, then robbed and sometimes dumped into San Francisco Bay while still unconscious.

Collis P. Huntington, among the more enterprising of the area businessmen, early in the gold rush went after shovels, which he bought for as cheaply as $2.50 [$72] per dozen, and then stockpiled. Then, when demand overwhelmed the shovel supply and drove prices sharply upward to $125 [$3,600] per dozen, he peddled his entire stock at roughly $10.50 [$302.40] *apiece*! Huntington was only one of many who successfully milked the market for all it was worth. Nor was money-lending far behind. As gold production persisted and mounted, California came to have more money per capita, both in hand and in circulation, than any other location throughout the world; and paradoxically, although such fiscal abundance should have depressed interest rates, that didn't happen in California. The rate stood firm at three per cent to five per cent *per month*, sometimes even higher.

San Francisco's theatrical scene was no less ambitious than that at Sacramento; with more theaters available, a greater number of productions were always in evidence, and the city's hotels were crowded with acting troupes that rented entire wings or floors of the more prominent hotels. Among the more famed of entertainers, early on, was a chubby little Englishman named Stephen C. Massett, who billed himself as Jeems Pipes of Pipesville; with great versatility, his one-man-show, first at the city's *Old Police Court* on the southwest corner of Portsmouth Square, and then at the *Plaza Schoolhouse*, virtually captivating the entertainment-hungry population. In a strong rich baritone voice, he sang several of his own compositions, on the heels of which he imitated in clear falsetto tones an operatic diva, all the while accompanying himself on a small upright piano. This he followed with a series of hilarious monologues in imitation of Yankee characters, and then ended his presentation with a clever seven-part reproduction of a New England town meeting. He had shrewdly put together an entertaining variety show with a bit of sentiment, a bold dash of broad humor, an even greater dose of burlesque, and a masterful demonstration of stage versatility. Stephen Massett was extremely popular, and the high demand for his performances enabled him to charge $3 [$86.40] per seat, at each of show. Grossing a total of more than $500 [$14,400] per performance, he quickly became exceedingly wealthy.

Other entertainment productions in San Francisco included a popular minstrel show, and on Kearny Street near Clay, Joe Rowe erected a huge tent, within which he staged *The San Francisco Circus,* consisting of nine acrobats, assorted equestrians and an astonishing trained horse that seemed capable of doing just about anything, including reading the daily newspaper.

San Francisco's second major fire occurred before month's end when the ship *Philadelphia* caught fire at 5 a.m. and burned completely just as it was preparing to sail for the Sandwich Islands. The highly flammable material of which San Francisco was largely built, and the prevailing winds, made many of the more thoughtful citizens at this time uncomfortably aware that if a fire ever got started in the city, nothing would stop it. Aside from issuing grave warnings , however, the city officials took no steps at this time to protect itself from such an eventuality.

The first of a rapidly growing procession of gold-seeker bearing ships from the Atlantic seaboard had finally begun arriving at San Francisco Harbor, heralding the near-future arrivals of myriad vessels which would quickly exceed San Francisco's docking capacity and thereby force the later-arriving vessels to continue upstream to Sacramento, seeking to find anchorage and in order to discharge their passengers.

Indeed even by sunset today eleven such ships had arrived and taken up anchorage in San Francisco Harbor, representing merely a tiny vanguard of the great horde soon to appear.

[July 10th, 1849 • Tuesday]

For the first time since the California gold rush began, a year and a half ago, a swelling sense of pride had begun asserting itself among the permanent residents of both San Francisco and Sacramento.

By far the greater majority of people in those municipalities were temporaries — individuals who had been drawn here solely for the acquisition of gold. Once the precious element was acquired in satisfactory quantity, those individuals had no other goal than to return to the cities and towns and country-sides where they had been raised, the locations they called home. There, with the golden wealth they had acquired, they could establish businesses or make investments or do whatever it was they wished to do in their efforts to fulfill the dreams which they before had neither the opportunity nor the wherewithal to attempt.

Yet, in addition to the great numbers of short-term residents with short-term goals, a gradually growing number of determined individuals planned to remain in San Francisco or other parts of California. This group consisted of immigrants, even of foreign birth, who gradually began to view the territory as a new permanent home; as a place that needed strong laws, a cautiously structured government, and a carefully cultivated sense of community pride and achievement — a place that needed the political structure and credibility of statehood as rapidly as such could be achieved.

One of the newly arrived foreigners determined to make San Francisco his permanent home was an Italian tent-maker who had quickly established himself in the community, and was now producing quality canvas tents in abundance. His name was Domenico Ghiradelli, and having previously lived in Guatemala where he had closely observed the growing of cacao and having since his arrival here become keenly aware of chocolate's immense popularity among miners, he quickly established a factory in San Francisco for the production of chocolate, both as a condiment for cooking and for the making of fine candy in bar form.

For some time the gold rush had been attracting a number of physicians — or at least those who claimed to be trained medical professionals. How authentic such claimed credentials were in actuality was a matter of conjecture; some professed physicians were mere quacks whose level of ability went no farther than what was written upon a bogus certificate of graduation and whose only goal was to see as many "patients" as possible, to the tune of an ounce of gold per brief visit; there were others, however, who were skilled physicians with an ingrained sense of responsibility, for whom the workload was prodigious. Dr. John Frederick Morse was one such doctor, and he was the driving force in establishing Sacramento's first hospital, where the greater portion of ministrations to the ailing were of a charitable nature. Contagious diseases were rampant in the mining areas, as were a great variety of accidental injuries ranging from very simple to extremely serious. Mortality rates were high, and funerals simple, often with merely a ragged blanket as a shroud or a simple pine box as a coffin. Just as Dr. Morse was considered by many to be the "medical hope" of Sacramento, Dr. James L. Tyson filled the same niche at his large hospital tent near Emigrant Gap, which was heavily frequented by miners from Bear River and the North Fork American River. Other physicians, whose luck had been less than good at the mines, were returning to San Francisco to pursue their fortunes by caring for patients who had great accumulations of gold, some of which they were willing to spend on restoring and maintaining good health.

Independence Day had been celebrated in both Sacramento and San Francisco with limited displays of fireworks and some gunfire, but with the mid-afternoon temperature soaring to 114 degrees and the mercury never dropping below 85 degrees at night, the crowded celebrations afforded little pleasure. At Fowler's Hotel in Sacramento a crowd of concerned citizens held a meeting and passed a resolution to cooperate with San Francisco and other districts in forming a civil government. At a similar meeting held at Mormon Island under the chairmanship of C. E. Bigelow, with James Queen as secretary, resolutions were adopted declaring:

> *... in consequence of the failure of Congress to provide California with a government, that despite separation of this country from the mother county having been loudly talked of, we nevertheless pledge ourselves to discountenance every effort at separation, or any similar movement that may tend to counteract the action of the general government in regard to California. Also, that believing slavery to be injurious, we will do everything in our power to prevent its extension to this country.*

Just as such larger communities as these were beginning to sense the need to organize and establish rules by which to govern themselves, and thereby to eliminate or at least to more effectively control the chaos that lawlessness inveitably bred, so too were the mining communities beginning to establish rules and regulations for their own protection. Thus, in various meetings of miners occurring throughout the gold country, improvised rules were adopted to govern the size and title to claims, and to regulate the settlement of disputes. Usually, one of the first steps was to elect a recorder who would register all claims and then watch over the observance of the adopted resolutions.

Invariably, the size of claims was predicated upon the richness of the deposit, as well as its extent, always with due regard for the number of participants in the area, the availability of water, and the difficulty or ease of working the ground. In some districts where digging was easy and gold abundant, claims were limited to a mere ten feet square. In others, where the gold was less abundant and the ground harder to work, such claims might stretch 50 or even 100 feet along a stream, especially if the gold recovery involved deep digging or tunnels. Equally, much was dependent upon whether the claim was over ground that had never been worked before or, by contrast, ground that had been heavily worked.

It was the discoverer who most often had first choice for the claim; as the discoverer, he would be allowed a double-lot, a tract size allowed to no one else. Ten feet square — as the lowest recognized claim size, except for heavily trafficked Mormon Island where claims were generally four feet square — was the area that prevailed in many of the richer sites, and these claims were registered by the recorder for a fee of $1 [$28.80], and then usually marked immediately with stakes, ditches and notices. The stakes and notices were, in some camps, required to be in prescribed form, as to owner's name, size limits of the claim, and other such matters, with such notices placed in conspicuous boxes — tobacco tins were especially favored — or sometimes painted on stakes or cut into wooden plaques. Notices sometimes took a macabre or humorous bent, such as one at the Jamestown area which stated, clearly but ungrammatically:

"Clame Notise. Jumpers will be shot."

Once a claim was registered, moreover, the owner was then required to perform a certain minimal amount of work on it in order to maintain his ownership. In some areas, one full day's work out of three was required, unless the owner could verify that an illness made such frequent work impossible. In many cases, any absence of five days during washing times automatically resulted in the forfeiture of the claim. In some areas the owner was given three days in which to dig a ditch a foot wide and a foot deep around the claim, and on the island thus created he could leave his tools — and woe betide anyone who disturbed them in any way. River claims could be left untouched during winter without forfeiture occurring, and the same held true for dry ravine claims during the summertime. Very often the growing complexity of mining regulations, as well as their variations for different areas, left individual miners totally confused as to both their rights and their obligations.

One of the old-timers — meaning one of those who was among the first to search for gold deposits here, only a year ago — commented sourly:

"Certainly isn't like it was in the good ol' days, when the gold was just lyin' about wherever you looked and was simply waiting there to be picked up."

He was right; those good ol' days of easy gold-picking were indeed gone; but the gold was still there — in abundance — for anyone willing to expend the effort to dig it out.

[July 17th, 1849 • Tuesday]

Samuel Brannan had never considered himself a community-minded individual, and so it came as no little shock to him when today he was highly praised, both in Sacramento and San Francisco for his alleged "humanitarian" works and for taking so strenuous and courageous a stand against the "Hounds," who had now clearly become the scourge of civilized society in California and had recently brutally raided San Francisco's *Little Chile* near Jackson and Dupont Streets at the foot of Telegraph Hill

Last night, after a day when the temperature reached a strength-sapping 114 degrees, Brannan had spoken publicly from the roof of the *alcade's* office on the Plaza, addressing a great throng of sweaty listeners and demanding that all members of the Hounds, who were now changing their name to the more dignified title of The Regulators, be arrested and driven away. To effect this, 230 volunteer policemen were deputized by the newly-formed Law-and-Order Party, and placed on patrol throughout the city. In this role they descended upon the headquarters of The Regulators on Kearny Street at Montgomery — a huge tent dubbed Tammany Hall after the New York City hotbed of agitation with the same name — and before the night was over, the self-proclaimed leader of the Hounds, Lt. Sam Roberts, and eighteen of his henchmen were arrested. At the same time a fund had been established to aid the San Franciscan Chileans who had been severely victimized, and Sam Brannan had himself been involuntarily elevated to the role of hero.

That Brannan had taken such a stand for purely selfish motives — to protect his own investments and enterprises — seemed to make no difference at all. The two most rapidly growing cities in California were positively ripe for a hero figure, and now, whether he liked it or not, they had found just such a personage in Brannan. Presenting an ostentatious image had long been a way of life with Brannan, and his elevation to the role of "humanitarian" amused him considerably.

Brannan's own ostentatious residence was in the richest residential section of San Francisco, snuggled between the very fancy homes of financier Howard Mellus and Quartermaster Joseph Folsom on Mission Street between Second and Third Streets at the southern suburban outskirts of the city. All three of these residences were "cottages" that had been imported in sections from the eastern seaboard aboard the ship *Onward*, and had quickly become the pride of San Francisco.

Brannan had his fingers in so many different business operations that even he had difficulty in keeping them all straight, but his principal office was in his real estate business located on San Francisco's Market Street just north of California Street, and it was here or in his home that he entertained lavishly whenever anyone of importance arrived in the city. It was said, only half-jokingly, that "if you haven't dined at Sam Brannan's table, you haven't yet arrived in San Francisco society."

For the first time, too, San Francisco itself had begun encroaching into the waterfront of San Francisco Bay, first with the construction of a pair of short wharves at Clay and Broadway Streets, on land recently purchased by the city. Close on their heels came Central Wharf, also called Long Wharf, established along Commercial Street, and already extending far out into the bay, but projected to grow much larger. The previously-favored landing site had been on some rocks at Pacific and Sansome Streets, but these had no wharves, and now they had been supplanted by the Central Wharf enterprise. The original 800-foot wharf, which had been seriously damaged by fire, had now been rebuilt, and, while not yet completed, it stretched out 2,000 feet into San Francisco Bay and provided sufficient deep-water moorage for all three of the Pacific Mail steamers to tie up alongside. This new wharf had quickly attracted an extremely busy and noisy crowd of peddlers, and what were referred to as *Cheap John* shops, where virtually anything could be bought *for a price*. The wharf itself was owned by a joint-stock company, prominent among whose members were such enterprises as *Cross, Hobson & Co., DeWitt & Harrison*, and major individual businessmen of considerable wealth, such as James C. Ward, Joe Folsom, Sam Brannan, and Theo Shillaber. Already river steamers and sea-going vessels had begun unloading at the wharf, and new buildings, including several large warehouses sprang up rapidly along the swiftly developing concourse. The overnight success of the enterprise triggered the development of a rash of rival enterprises on every street touching or adjacent to the waterfront; from Market and California Streets to Broadway and beyond, these businesses added some two miles of roadway to the city, financed by an investment exceeding a million dollars, an amount quickly recovered by the business the enterprise generated. A few of the more choice city-owned properties were then developed into new streets and into an entire network of new wharves, both public and private.

What concerned the permanent residents of San Francisco most was the temporal façade it presented; more and more Europeans, Chinese, Australians, South Americans and Pacific Islanders flocked in and quickly transformed the area into the greatest cosmopolitan crossroad of the West Coast. In a mere eighteen months since the discovery of gold, California's non-Indian population had skyrocketed from 12,000 to well over 300,000, and it was reliably reported at one point this summer that San Francisco's population was doubling every ten days.

No less than 95 per cent of all newcomers were men, the majority of whom had never before left their home towns or had any substantial knowledge about wilderness living or mining. Free of the watchful eyes and oversight of wives and mothers and clergy, they had turned the extensive mining areas, and both Sacramento and San Francisco as well, into what could be conservatively described as wide-open towns where gambling was rampant, brawling was common, and both gun-fighting and prostitution were a way of life: A world in which the only effective means of maintaining a modicum of social order and individual protection was harsh vigilante justice.

Hundreds who had flocked to California to seek gold but who had failed to find enough of it to even minimally support themselves on a day-by-day basis, turned to hiring themselves out as workers of all kinds in the cities, providing the services that any metropolitan area requires for survival. Because of its location close to the coast and directly upon one of the entire continent's greatest and most protected anchorages, San Francisco rapidly became one of the more cosmopolitan cities in the world. Yet, in many respects, it was still rustic and crude and only beginning to find its own way. Even among the neediest of its population there was a certain self-assured insouciance that could not tolerate the haughtiness of those that had never known privation.

Many members of this more privileged group were becoming engaged in the service trades that keep a large city vital; they worked for the more successful miners and businessmen. Some accepted positions as porters, greeting newly arriving ship passengers and helping them transfer their luggage to places of lodging, but they deeply resented any who would look down at them for accepting such employment.

When a newly arrived passenger would hail a porter with, "You there, boy, here's a quarter; carry my bags," he was more likely than not to get the response, "Here's a dollar, jackass, carry them yourself!"

Virtually the only fuel in the city, both for cooking and for warmth, was wood, and so a great many of those who had thus far failed in mining now maintained themselves by chopping firewood and delivering it to the city. Others hired themselves out as hunters, supplying hotels and restaurants and wealthier individuals with a variety of game meats, including ducks, geese, quail, rabbits, deer and black bear, or whatever other game was available, or, if they were skilled mariners, with a selection of fish, shrimp, lobsters, clams, oysters, and other shellfish.

Many, with more specialized service-talents, hired out as proprietors or clerks or waiters or cooks in the many hotels and lodging-places springing up everywhere to meet the heavy demand. Even such lodgings as were noted as "the very best available" still left much to be desired in so rudimentary a city. The *Montgomery House*, for example, at this time one of the foremost lodging places in all of San Francisco, was little short of crude. It was a wood-frame structure covered with a hodge-podge of boards and canvasses almost haphazardly nailed into place and patched here and there with sheet zinc. It offered no heat whatever except for the kitchen stoves and ovens and a pot-bellied stove in the bar. All interior partitions consisted of cloth nailed to crude wooden frames, and most of the sleeping quarters were dormitory style with double-decker bunk beds and barely enough space between them for dressing or undressing, and primitive, odorous, portable toilet facilities. The accommodations at other hotels were considerably worse but, with nothing else available, such hopelessly inadequate lodgings were accepted with reasonably good grace.

The restaurants, generally speaking, were significantly more pleasant and accommodating than the hotels or boarding houses thanks to the fact that French, Italian, Spanish, Latin American, and Chinese cooks were in close competition and constantly sought to outshine one another; moreover, such efforts were aided by the fish, game, fruits and vegetables abundantly available in California.

Most appreciated and most frequented — as well as most deplored in many instances — were the drinking and gambling establishments, which were almost always crowded at any hour of day or night. These emporia most often occupied the largest tents or best buildings in the community, and they offered a number of attractions difficult to resist — bright lights, cheery atmospheres, abundant drinks, varieties of gambling tables, free lunches, bands or orchestras, singers, dancers, and performers of all kinds, large, unusual and lavish works of art, with a predilection toward sumptuous nudes, and wherever possible, comely young women to act as dealers or croupiers at the tables.

Such gambling and drinking establishments inevitably became the most popular places of common resort — the most likely places to hear the latest news, to find one's friends, to discuss business deals, and to temporarily forget one's personal troubles. Sometimes the gamblers had a streak of luck and made out well, though far more often they lost enormous amounts of the gold they had dug. Gambling away recently mined wealth with almost shocking abandon was common, as was accepting sometimes staggering losses with a simple shrug of the shoulders before returning to one's "digs" to accumulate more.

While the San Francisco citizens had rallied effectively to suppress the power of the Hounds, or Regulators, their efforts in the newly established City Council to outlaw, or at least stringently control, the gambling in San Francisco went down to stinging defeat when the gambling interests joined forces and voted that there be no formal government for the city. Such control would inevitably one day be enacted, but not yet. For the time being, San Francisco would remain California's most concentrated center of gambling.

[July 18th, 1849 • Wednesday]

It was exactly 9 a.m. today when *The Ottawa Company* first caught sight of the British trading post known as Fort Hall in the Idaho country. Not far from here, as Alonzo Delano understood it, the Oregon Trail and the California Trail would diverge and soon after, he had been told repeatedly, where the going would become far more difficult and perilous.

Exactly nineteen days ago, on June 29th, their company, under the leadership of John Traverse, had crossed the Continental Divide at South Pass, marveling at the ease with which it had been surmounted and hoping not to encounter more difficult terrain on their westward trek, yet knowing full well that they would. Still, as difficult as the march had been since then, the Company had traveled well and suffered no major mishaps. They had reached the fording place of the Sweetwater just two miles from their starting point, arriving with a sense of grim satisfaction that the waters of every flowing stream they would henceforth encounter would eventually empty into the great Pacific Ocean.

A few miles before crossing the Continental Divide, Delano unexpectedly encountered a cluster of Indian lodges, one of which was the abode of a white man. Delano first mistook him for an Indian, not only because of his simple elk-skin moccasins and garments, but also due to his long, black hair and swarthy, weather-beaten complexion. Doubting that he could communicate with this brave, Delano was shocked when the man — who appeared to be about 40 years old — addressed him in refined English. As the two neared each and shook hands in friendly fashion, Delano was reassured not only by the man's pleasant countenance and command of English, but by his mild blue eyes. Though Delano introduced himself, the stranger balked at doing the same.

"You will, I hope," he said, "forgive me for not revealing my name. My Indian name would be meaningless to you and my English name I prefer keeping to myself."

Delano thought that strange, but was respectful of the man's wishes. They had only been speaking together a few moments when several young women and a half dozen or more children emerged from the lodge. He found the man to be:

> *... well educated — far above the humble sphere of life to which he clearly had consigned himself. [Soon] He was surrounded by three or four squaws and a number of children, who seemed to look upon him as the grand head of the family, in the relative position of husband and father. He readily entered into conversation. ...*

"I have lived this Indian life," he said, "for eighteen years, without once having been back to the States, largely depending upon chance and hunting for supplies."

"And do you never think of returning?" Delano asked. "Don't old thoughts of home and friends intrude in your memory and awaken some feelings of endearment?"

The man thought about this for a moment, and when he replied there was an element of muted wistfulness in his response. "Oh, yes, very often. Once — it was about five years ago — I made up my mind to return, and even made my arrangements, but, after all, I just couldn't make myself leave, and when I think of it now and become almost determined to go once more, I look at my responsibilities — " he reached out and hugged one of the children to his side, a boy of about ten, who grinned and then broke away," — and I give up. You see, I have cares, but then I am so accustomed to this mode of life that I am unfitted for social intercourse in refined society. True, I think I actually will go at some time, but, then again, I may never do it. Who would protect my wives and my children in danger, if I was absent?"

Nature clings to its offspring, Delano thought. "Sir, my train is passing along and I must catch up. It has been a pleasure and an honor meeting you, and I wish you farewell and the best of luck."

They shook hands once more, and then Delano was again on his way. He quickly caught up with *The Ottawa Company,* and together they ascended a relatively steep hill from the bottom land. Near the summit they found a good and almost level trail leading directly to the South Pass, now only about eight miles ahead. A herd of about thirty buffalo, frightened by the distant procession of men, animals and wagons, thundered away over the plain at their approach.

So far as Delano could determine, there were no particular landmarks to differentiate the scenery of the east side of the Pass from that of the west, and the ascent was so gradual that the culminating point was a matter of doubt. Half a mile before they reached the highest knoll, which Delano decided was the summit, they spied two almost identical conical hills some seven hundred feet apart, between which their trail passed. This, Delano noted, was where both Edwin Bryant and John Charles Frémont fixed the culminating point, but in studying the area closely, he could not agree with them because from this point they passed over a crest, into a small declivity and then ascended yet another rise every bit as high as the one preceding it.

From the second little summit, the descent was regular and certain, and Delano found that on commencing this decline, the hills were not large on either side, but crowded so near to one another that, the wagon path between them resembled a small, water-worn gully. The descent on the west was more rapid than the assent on the east, but not really difficult, and the narrow trail continued for another mile and a half before they observed the first water flowing toward the Pacific. This water sprang from the earth in what they dubbed *Pacific Spring,* which was in boggy ground on their right, where there were also several small sulfur springs. The water burbling out of Pacific Spring was perfectly clear and icy cold, and it flowed away to the west.

As they descended further the valley expanded, and the hills to their left, bordering the pass, became several hundred feet high; no worse, Delano thought, than those on which roads were laid out on hills in the East. To the north they looked across a broken mountain plain to the snow-capped Wind River Range some thirty miles distant. The Company concluded that the South Pass proper was about two miles long, and led into a large basin some four miles in diameter, rimmed by peculiar table hills and ridges easy enough to ascend; indeed, this basin was the first of a series of similar basins, often interrupted by streams and hills, continuing clear to the far-distant Sierra Nevada. These basins seemed unique to the men, unlike anything they had encountered east of the South Pass. As Delano then described it:

> *From the culminating point the view is not as grand as at many places along the Sweet Water Mountains, for these mountains, though here they are much diminished in size, hinder any extended view in that direction, The point has an altitude of between seven and eight thousand feet, and the rarification of the air is so great that it is necessary to stop frequently to get breath on ascending the hills in the vicinity.*
>
> *We arrived at Pacific Spring a little after noon. Being told that our next day's drive would be twenty miles, without water, we stopped where there were tolerable grass and good water. The Hennepin Company had arrived just before us, and The Dayton Company were encamped just a short distance below, and we made and received visits to our mutual satisfaction.*
>
> *We were now in Oregon [Territory] — the ridge of the Rocky Mountains being its eastern boundary — and fifteen hundred miles from our homes. We had toiled steadily in our wearied journey for two months, and were but little more than half way to our point of destination; and although thus far no serious mishap had befallen us, no one could tell what trials awaited us.*
>
> *My own health had vastly improved, and I endured the labors of our daily routine, and the absence of comforts, much*

better than I could possibly have apprehended. One object of my journey was successfully accomplished, and I was in better health than I had been for years. Would the other grand desideratum be also accomplished and my labor meet its reward? Time alone could tell.

In a musing mood, I ascended a high hill opposite our camp, to take a final parting look at the Atlantic waters, which flowed toward all I held most dear on earth. Old and dearly cherished reminiscences were crowding on my memory. As I turned my eye eastward, home, wife, and children, rushed to my mind with uncontrolled feeling, and in the full yearnings of my heart, I involuntarily stretched out my arms as if I would clasp them to my bosom; but no answering look of affection, no fond embrace met me in return, as I was wont to see at home, but in its place there lay extended before me barren reaches of table land, the bare hills, and desert plains of the Sweet Water, while long trains of wagons, with their white covers, were turning the last curve of the dividing ridge, their way–worn occupants bidding a long, perhaps a last adieu to eastern associations, to mingle in new scenes on the Pacific coast.

Sad, but not dispirited, I descended the hill, and sought the dubious comfort of our weather-beaten tent, where memory kept busy till fatigue closed my eyes in slumber.

On leaving the Missouri, every train had been an organized company, with general regulations for mutual safety. Now, however, most had either divided or broken up entirely, making independent and helter-skelter marches, owing to the great difficulty of procuring grass for so many cattle. Others, disgusted by the frequent, indeed constant, foul language of some of their fellow company members, finally refused to endure it any longer. Still others separated simply from mutual ill feelings that generated disagreements among themselves. Delano concluded that small parties of about twenty men decidedly got along together best; with three men to a mess or wagon being sufficient for both safety and harmony.

The final day of June saw *The Ottawa Company* complete a 20-mile toilsome trek wholly without forage to the Little Sandy River, a tributary of the Green River. On their emergence from the narrows of South

Pass, they had observed for the first time, at a great distance southwestward, the Rocky Mountains towering into the skies in lofty grandeur, their snow white peaks stark against the intense blue sky. To their right lay the bleak, broken hills leading to the Wind River chain, and ahead, in cheerless, bleak and broken array, basins and tables stretching beyond vision. Delano ascended one of the basin rims and found at the top a conglomeration of pebbles and scoria with the appearance of having been scorched by raw fire.

Fourteen miles into the day's trek brought them to the bed of the Dry Sandy River, appropriately named because the bed was obviously dry, although by digging down some six or eight inches, one could find unpleasant, smelly water beneath the sand. Moving along the trail Delano's company encountered about once in every mile the remains of an ox that had given up, the carcass of which now hosted angrily croaking ravens devouring what remains the scavenging wolves had left behind.

The men persisted on the march and were rewarded for the day's total trek of 20 miles, by encountering the Little Sandy, a fine stream of pure, clear, sweet, cool water, although the surrounding area was virtually devoid grass and wood. Men and livestock alike rushed to the stream and gulped down the liquid. With the boon of good water, however, came the bane of vanished game, which heretofore had been reasonably abundant. Now, it seemed, they had entered a whole new realm where game was entirely absent.

In the morning — Sunday, July 1st — Delano discovered one of the best of his oxen was very ill and concluded that it was not the result of bad water and poor feed so much as mere exhaustion from the rarified air. He purchased Wilson's half-interest in a sturdy cow, the other half owned by Dr. Hall, and with the physician's consent, put her in the yoke and drove his own ox ahead unfettered. A mile and a half later they reached an important junction in the trail. By bearing left they would go southward to Fort Bridger, followed by the treacherous westward crossing of the Wasatch Mountains and, even more deadly, the 90-mile crossing of the Great Salt Lake Desert before finally reaching the valley of the westward-flowing Humboldt River, the route the ill-fated Donner Party had taken; bearing right would shunt them onto the directly westward-headed Cut-off known as Sublette's or Greenwood's, which would tie them into the Oregon Trail leading northward to Fort Hall in the Idaho country, then westward and southward over the uppermost regions of Great Salt Lake and southwestward down its west side to the Humboldt River Valley. This latter route, while deemed safer, was judged to be upwards of 150 miles longer.

Neither prospect was appealing, but nearly every west-bound emigrant was acutely aware of the Donner Party's nightmarish tragedy two years earlier, one fraught with cannibalism; hence, the *Ottawa Company*, along with virtually every other train, decided to take the longer, safer route and drove over an arid plain to the Big Sandy River. As this area would provide the last water and grass for a great many miles — no one was quite sure exactly how many — they let the livestock graze while they filled every available container with fresh water. Delano had a large India-rubber bag which he took to the stream to fill, but just as he was pouring in the final bucketful, the bag burst, rendering it totally useless. Finally, with all available containers filled and secured to the wagons, they started out.

The desert confronting them was an arid plain covered with a thick coating of white dust that stirred into clouds behind them, coating their faces and any other exposed skin with white and gagging them to the point that they feared they might suffocate. Though the area had not seen rain for what was apparently years, today, fortunately for them, a rainfall occurred which settled the dust for thirty miles, though in some places creating a very sticky mud. They set out at 4 p.m. and found that the rain had significantly cooled the sultry atmosphere and that the night air was comfortable. Delano had walked six miles during the day, and now he walked throughout the night, along with the others, slowly but steadily, their hundreds of wagons, horsemen and pedestrians forming a long, ghostly, single-file procession of great length. All walked who could possibly do so, to make the wagon loads as light as possible and to set an easy pace for the cattle. All talk, even profanity, ceased, and the only sounds heard were the creaking of wheels and howling of wolves.

As the night progressed an overwhelming weariness settled over Delano, and he had great difficulty keeping awake. He trudged along with the others in a half-slumber, occasionally tripping and sprawling headlong in the dust, struggling to rise and then staggering on beside his lead ox, Brown, who was as weary as he, perhaps even more so.

Eban Smith, unable to walk due to his painful, swollen leg, rode in the wagon and attempted to lighten the load by gradually emptying a complete 100-pound sack of cornmeal as they drove; a dangerous measure should their provisions fail. At daybreak, with this first desert half-crossed, the procession stopped for an hour to give men and livestock alike a break. Each of the animals was given a swallow of water from the canteens, and the brief rest seemed to revive everyone to a certain extent. They started again, and now the country became broken and difficult to traverse. There had been no rain in this area, and the dust was ankle-deep and gagging. Every man and beast was liberally coated with white dust; indeed, they looked like a procession of wraiths. All had difficulty breathing. When within five miles of the river, Delano, totally exhausted, could walk no more, and he crawled into the wagon and lay in its bed, helpless as an infant. It was now July 2nd, and it occurred to Delano that this was his birthday, the most difficult of his life; without sleep, to this point he had walked fifty-five miles.

At 5 p.m. they reached a creek, only to find it a dry and dusty bed without even sub-surface moisture. Without water or grass, everyone, man and beast alike, was suffering intensely. The only growing thing was a dry plant offering no moisture or food value whatever, and the cattle would not touch it. They had no choice but to un-harness the draft animals and let them and the cattle herds simply wander and find whatever they could that was palatable. The men, totally exhausted, raised a few tents and collapsed inside them or beneath the wagons and virtually became unconscious for the entire night.

At dawn on July 3rd the men estimated that they were within a couple of miles of the river, and so they rounded up the livestock and drove them over the hills to where a few company members had found some grass for them; then, after a while, the march resumed. After discovering that a ferry crossing of the river was only two miles ahead, the men delegated Delano to go ahead and make inquiries. The entire plain here was covered with tents and wagons of the trains that had congregated, along with a large detachment of troops en route to coastal Oregon Territory under command of a Major Simonton. The various trains were awaiting their turns to be ferried across the river.

Delano discovered that the ferryman kept a register so that each party could be ferried in its turn, which was fair, but it also meant at least a two or three day delay before their company could be taken across. With no other choice, Delano signed them up and then inspected the operation. The ferry was a small but effective scow, capable of ferrying two wagons at once. The craft was equipped with long oars to aid in breasting the heavy current, and when it reached shore, well downstream, it was towed back to a point opposite its starting place. The river itself, an icy-cold run-off from the Wind River Range, was deliciously sweet to the taste. Only a few cottonwood trees and willow bushes grew along the margins of the stream, and the remainder of the bottoms was sand, containing only meager growths of sage, greasewood and coarse weeds.

As he looked about, Delano discovered Capt. Tutt and some of his South Bend friends, who had arrived somewhat earlier. He was glad to learn they had gotten along well, without any serious accidents having befallen them. He wrote in his *Journal*:

> *Among others, I met for the second time on the plains, my old friend, Dr. M. B. Angel, formerly from Niles, Michigan — a generous, open-hearted and benevolent gentleman. With the enterprising spirit for which he is remarkable, he, in company with two other men, was building a ferry-boat, with the intention of remaining here a couple of weeks and then go down the river to the Salt Lake Road, and visit the Mormon [Salt Lake] city.*
>
> *Soon after my arrival, the whole encampment was thrown into great excitement by a cruel and fiendish murder, which was committed on the west bank. A reckless villain, named Brown, requested a young man who acted as cook in his mess, to get him a piece of soap. The young man was, at the moment, bending over the fire, engaged in preparing the meal, and replied by telling him to get it himself, as he was busy. Without further provocation, as it appeared, the wretch raised his knife and stabbed him in the back, killing the young man almost instantly. The murderer fled. A meeting of the emigrants was called and General Allen, from Lewis County, Missouri, was called to the chair, when the details of the atrocious deed were set forth, and it was determined by a series of resolutions to arrest the villain, give him a fair trail, and if found guilty, to execute him on the spot. Major Simonton seconded the views of the emigrants, in order to protect them against similar assassinations. In addition to a dozen athletic volunteers, who stood forth at the call, he detailed a file of soldiers to assist in the capture of the murderer.*

Several murders had been committed on the road, and all felt the necessity of doing something to protect themselves, where there was no other law but brute force.

On the following day, July 5th, little of moment occurred except that Delano was bilked of ten dollars [$288] when he bought an old ox, which he hoped would fill the place in his yoke of the cow he had temporarily installed there, but apparently Hendershot, who sold the old ox to him, failed to deliver it and would not return the money. Such unscrupulous incidents as this usually took on great importance and often resulted in someone being killed. Delano, however, merely accepted the loss with what grace he could muster, but vowed never again to trust neither Hendershot nor the man's partner, John Morrill.

The ferrying had continued night and day without pause, and finally, a bit before daylight on July 6th, it was *The Ottawa Company's* turn, and the passage was safely completed in about an hour. Although the water was very cold, the cattle swam across without difficulty and were ready to resume their westward march about noon. As Delano recorded what occurred next:

We had to drive through a broad slough before we reached terra firma, when, in the hands of Brown, my cattle became a little unruly, and suddenly drew the wagon to a deep place. The water came into the box and wet all my clothes, unstarching all my fine shirts, playing the deuce with my wardrobe, and doing considerable damage to sundry articles. For the next two days I was improving every moment of our noon halt to dry my goods and chattels. The nights were very cold, the ice forming in our buckets half an inch thick. This was generally succeeded by a sultry and oppressive heat during the day. Smith was relieved of his sufferings by having his leg lanced, and from this time he rapidly recovered. Leaving the river we drove down a sandy bottom, and then ascended a narrow ridge on the right, just wide enough for a good road, from which we had a view of the bottom and river which we had just left, and the broad bottom of a beautiful creek on the left, along which the road ran. To attain this by following the ridge, we made a half-retrograde movement of three miles to get the distance of one in a straight line. On reaching the creek bottom we found good grass, and for two days we had the comforts of forage, water and wood, and a level road.

On July 7th the company members left the creek, and for the next two days they passed over a broken country with difficult, barren hills. In the hollows they usually found good grass, but virtually no game except for mountain goats, which were numerous on the hills. In a few places they found ripe strawberries, but they were sour and unpleasant, and there was an abundance of wild flax and some patches of wild oats. When the company passed near an isolated log cabin belonging to an old mountaineer, Delano stopped and talked with him, gaining much useful information regarding the route to Fort Hall. He told Delano that the valleys were usually well filled with snow and that his home, where his wife and children were located, was east of the mountains where there was no snow and the grass was green all winter long. He had a good drove of horses and had accumulated a sizeable cattle herd from the sickly animals abandoned by emigrants, which initially had been in bad shape but had now recuperated and were excellent stock. As Delano wrote of the grass on this route:

We found it good and abundant, and were it not for the 54-mile desert of Sublette's Cut-off, I should recommend this route to future travelers. The mountaineer told us, however, that the season was unusual, and that there were more and later rains than he had ever known, and more grass than usually was there, but very little grass on the hillsides which were now well covered with it. The road leads through valleys, wherever practicable, in the general direction, but sometimes we found long and steep hills to ascend and descend, and during the afternoon we made the long ascent from a valley, the worst I ever saw a wagon driven over. It was up a narrow ridge with almost perpendicular sides, and had a wagon broke [sic] loose, it would have been dashed to atoms in a moment. We got over safely, however, and on the top we found a mountain plain, gradually descending, and an encampment. Over a bank on the left was a morass covered with cotton-woods, and where there was good grass and pure water.

On July 8th, a bright Sunday morning, they left that camp in excellent spirits along a fairly decent trail, and four miles later, near the top of this easily accessible mountain, they came to what Delano considered to be a singular novelty. As he described it:

> *This was nothing less than a truly beautiful grove of fir trees, standing thickly together — a kind of wooded island in the desert, say about half a mile in extent. The road passed directly through it, and our emotions were of the most pleasing kind, in once more getting beneath its cooling shade. It was the first grove of timber which we had passed through since leaving the Missouri, having seen none but the scattered trees which grew immediately on the banks of streams.*
>
> *For more than two months we had been traveling, exposed to the fervid heat of the sun, or the cold and stormy blasts along the Platte, without a leaf to offer protection; and none of the deep green foliage, the stillness which reigned unbroken, except the hollow sound of a woodpecker upon some decayed trunk, the dead trees which lay prostrate on the ground, brought forcibly to mind the wood-covered land which we had left; and thought and tongues were busy in reviewing the comforts and pleasures of that happy and favored land. Leaving with reluctance this mountain paradise, we drove on against a very cold wind, which afterwards increased to a gale, and found an encampment among the sage bushes — a long day's drive from the valley of the Bear.*

On the following day about noon, July 9th, the company reached the top of the final high hill of the broken country through which they had been passing and looked down gratefully at the rolling bottomland below, through which the Bear River wound its wavering course. Accustomed to eastern distances and often fooled by expansive and much longer views here in the West, Delano decided he would walk ahead of the train to the river, which he presumed to be no more than three or four miles away. The trail led him through a kind of rolling, lateral valley virtually devoid of vegetation, and it was not until nearly sundown before he finally reached the bottom, still a mile distant from the river. It was full dark before the train reached him, after a very fatiguing day's drive. At least the grass they found here was excellent and the water free of poisons. Soon after stationing their night watch, the entire group was fast asleep. In the morning, July 10th, they discovered the site they had chosen was not so innocuous after all, as Delano recorded in his *Journal*:

> *On driving up the cattle this morning, the beasts exhibited quite the appearance of having drunk alkaline water, and those who drove them reported the ground white in places with the efflorescence. The usual remedy was applied at once, after which we drove on till noon. As they appeared weak, we resolved to lay over.*

About a mile below their overnight camp on the mountain, after they had crossed a fine stream of fresh water, they came upon an encampment of several lodges of Snake Indians. As Delano noted:

> *They were very friendly, particularly the females, who showed no sign of fear, laughing and chattering with us as if we were old acquaintances. One of the best-looking women took quite a fancy to Brown, and made him propositions which rendered him the laughing stock of the Company for the hour, but he modestly declined the honor. These Snakes are of small stature, the men ill-looking and diminutive, who, in speaking to us, scarcely raised their eyes from the ground; in this particular they exhibited a strong contrast to their women, bringing forcibly to mind the adage of "the old gray mare is the better horse." We saw a marked difference between these Indians and those east of the Rocky Mountains. The Ottoes, the Pawnees and Sioux are a fine-looking race of people, often handsome and well-formed, warlike and bold. The Crows are not so well formed, are nearly as dark-skinned as the lighter shade of Negroes, broad-shouldered, and rather stout built, yet possessing courage and, it is said, much honor. The Asiatic features begin now to appear, which seem to become more apparent in the tribes as we approach closer to the Pacific, till they resemble the islanders of the South Sea, though generally of a darker skin. I speak of those I saw.*
>
> *We passed through a beautiful valley about five miles*

> *beyond, when, coming to a good encampment ground, we gave our cattle another dose of bacon, and, turning them out, took a substantial dose ourselves, but for quite another purpose. Distance six miles.*

Early on Wednesday, July 11th, they found their cattle perfectly recovered from their unfortunate potations of soda, and they pursued their journey at a lively pace along the valley of the Bear. Henderson set off on his own with his rifle, early in the morning, to do some hunting and quickly had the good fortune to down a fine mountain sheep. It was too heavy for him to carry, so he turned it over to a pair of men belonging to a passing mule train, who promised to bring it in for the reward of one-half the carcass. When Henderson reported in, the members of the party congratulated themselves at the prospect of having an excellent meal of wild mutton at their noon halt. Noon came, but the mule train did not, and *The Ottawa Company* was finally compelled to resort to their bacon, grumbling all the while at the bad faith of their neighbors and sincerely hoping that every mouthful they ate of the stolen mutton would choke them.

Ten miles later, having driven over a delightful grassy plain, they reached a branch of the Bear River called Thomases Fork, which was about fifty feet wide and which they crossed without much trouble. The bank was steep and one wagon was upset as it was being drawn up, but without any significant damage, The Bear River at this point was narrowly walled-in for about ten miles by mountains, and they had to cross one spur of it, which they found picturesque and interesting, but rather hard on their cattle. After traversing one long, steep descent and winding through a narrow ravine at the bottom for a mile or more, they encountered a beautiful valley through which flowed an attractive clear mountain brook. Immediately ascending another long hill — an ascent of about three miles — they passed through a crooked, rocky gorge and then once more gained an excellent view of the river and its valley more than a thousand feet below them. The beautiful view served to revive their spirits, and though the descent was steep and difficult, they drove on and down with the satisfaction of knowing that a good encampment awaited them. Again they found wild strawberries, although none were sweeter or tastier than those previously tried, and they again found occasional clumps flax and wild oats. They set up camp for the night near a village of Snake Indians of very friendly disposition.

In the morning, July 12th, they visited the village and discovered there were some white traders there as well, who had established a temporary post. The Indians had a large number of ponies, and Delano and his companions tried to work a trade with them, but the white traders interfered and nothing was accomplished. Delano was told that during hard winters the Indians ate their horses, just as the whites did their cattle and that they esteemed the steak from a lean horse quite as much as that from a fat ox. These Indians, they discovered, were very expert in catching the horses by tossing the noose of a lasso over their heads.

The following day, July 13th, Delano and his good friend, McNeil, set off together to hunt, making another excursion into the mountains. Viewed in the clear air, the distance to the base of the hills seemed hardly more than half a mile, but they walked steadily and at a good clip for an hour before they reached that point. As they followed a gorge thickly lined with bushes, they were suddenly assailed by such a cloud of mosquitoes that they were obliged to cover their faces with handkerchiefs, which the insects covered so completely the men could not see without brushing them off. As Delano described the scene:

> *The moment we stopped, the blood-thirsty insects covered us worse than the flies did the fox in the fable; and had we not fought with bushes and hands, a coroner's jury might have rendered a verdict on our bodies — "bled to death by mosquitoes." At length we came to a point which we could ascend, when we resolved to climb to the summit and take a view of the country. The ascent was a toilsome one, for we could not go more than ten rods without stopping to breathe. After clambering over rocks and threading narrow ledges, we finally sat down, exhausted, on the top, fifteen hundred feet above the valley, and the scenery richly rewarded us for our trouble.*
>
> *Along this green valley the river wound its serpentine course like a thread. At the south, a lake several miles in circumference laved the foot of the high mountains like a gem, (as it was,) in these solitudes, while behind us, as far as we could see, were unbroken ridges, valleys, and ravines, sparsely covered with fir and cedars. As we sat upon the bank of snow, the four seasons lay before us. Winter, with its snow, was under us; a few feet farther down, the mountain plants*

were just starting from the ground; and next the flowers and straw-berries were in bloom, while at the foot the growth of summer was parched to autumn dryness and withered under the fervid sun. ... After admiring the charming view till satisfied, we descended to the valley through another wooded ravine, committing then a second slaughter of thousands when we reached mosquitodom below, and overtook the train after noon, with a glorious appetite.

At night we reached the first Beer Springs, two conical mounds, twenty feet high, with a base of more than a hundred feet in diameter formed by the deposit of lime from the water. These are rather more than half a mile north of the road, and near them is a fine brook, lined with cedars, which runs into the river a mile or two below. These springs are one of the greatest luxuries on the whole route. They are highly charged with carbonic acid gas, and are as delicious as they are refreshing. They are equal to any soda water in the world, and though good without any additional concomitants, with lemon-syrup or sugar, they are delicious. Two miles below are a dozen more, near the brink of the river, some of which are even stronger than the upper ones. On the opposite bank of the river are numerous cones, formed by the deposit from springs, but the incrustation has completely prevented the water from flowing. A spring is in the right bank, near the Soda Springs, through which volumes of gas are discharged with a loud noise, resembling the ejection of steam from a boiler, and is, in consequence, called Steamboat Springs.

The surrounding country is barren mountains, romantic and peculiar, abounding with evidences of volcanic action. With the abundance of traveler's comforts which existed, and the way-worn and weary condition in which we were, we felt a strong desire to linger a week amid the curiosities of this place, but our great anxiety to reach the end of our journey induced us to spend only the night, after a drive of sixteen miles.

On the following morning after leaving Soda Springs — Saturday, July 14th — they found that the river made a sharp, short turn to the south, around a high, perpendicular cliff of black trap-rock. Here they took leave of Bear River and its attractive valley, in which they had found so many long deprived comforts. Bear River Valley disappeared among the mountains to the south, and hence, at this point *The Ottawa Company* followed a lateral, stream-less valley northward towards Fort Hall. Delano, now traveling ahead with Dr. Hall, wrote:

> *Nearly two miles on the plain west, we observed the craters of two extinguished volcanoes, and in company with my friend, Dr. Hall, I walked out to the southernmost one. Its form was conical, about eighty feet high, the crater being oval-shaped, and probably two hundred feet in its greatest diameter, and about forty feet deep. Around its base are black, burnt rocks and cinders, fallen off in places, leaving only a portion of its glazed, perpendicular walls standing, while a thin crust of soil at the bottom afforded a foothold for a small growth of sage. The crater on the north is about a half-mile from this one, and is covered with grass, within and without. The length is about the same, but it appears much older and near it are three or four tumuli, which looked as if they were thrown out when the volcano was in active operation. They all stand isolated on the plain, with high mountains all around in the distance. The direct approach from the road to these craters was somewhat difficult.*
>
> *There were lines of rocky ledges of basalt, miles in length, having wide continuous cracks in them, and occasionally funnel-shaped holes, sometimes quite small, and of which we could not determine the depth; although we descended fifty feet into one of the chasms, we could not see the bottom. This main chasm ran parallel with the road about two miles, and then turned towards the mountain, the road crossing it on a natural bridge of basaltic rock.*
>
> *Six miles from the Soda Springs we found another with a natural basic, formed by its gradual deposits of lime, and though its waters were sparkling, it was warmer and not so pleasant as those we had just left. Night brought us to the banks of a little mountain brook, which ran across the valley, but we could see no outlet, and it was probably lost in the volcanic chasms of the valley.* Distance eighteen miles.

It was close to noon on the next day — Sunday, July 15th — that *The Ottawa Company* reached the end of the valley and then passed through an ascending defile toward the top of the dividing ridge, between the waters of the Bear and the Columbia Rivers. For a few miles they had found the road to be very uneven, with several sharp hills, and in some parts of the defile they encountered remarkable growths of cottonwood and shrubby trees. When at last they attained the highest point, they found the descent precipitous, though not terribly difficult for them, and at nightfall they encamped in the Pass near a fine stream which broke out of the mountain and was, Delano believed, of sufficient capacity and force to turn a mill.

On the following day, July 16th the men made only moderate progress, and it was nearly nightfall before they got through the lengthy defile. As they passed through a grove of young poplars, they saw the names of some acquaintances and many strangers written, along with dates, on the white bark as testament to their passage. Among them were those which had been inscribed by *The Dayton Company*, which was now well ahead of them. On emerging from this narrow road onto the barren plain, surrounded by high mountains, they encamped on the bank of the Neuf River which, they had been told, was about a day's journey from Fort Hall.

The company members had by this time become extremely weary of the tedious daily routine of their continuous travel. They intensely disliked, for example, the evening task, of spreading out to gather — sometimes from as far as several miles distant — whatever wood or buffalo chips could be found for their camp's cooking fires. Even just the matter of getting water with which to brew coffee often entailed a hike of a mile or more to fill up a bucket and carry it back to their newly established camp. Confronted with such frequent time-consuming responsibilities after a long day of travel, the men often lost their tempers and squabbled angrily with one another. More than anything else, every individual in the train was infinitely weary.

Yesterday, July 17th, within only one more day's march away from Fort Hall, the Company decided to linger at the fort for a full day to rest themselves and their livestock and to replenish whatever they could of their depleted supplies, especially the more perishable foodstuffs that were virtually gone. With the planned rest in mind, and eagerly anticipating their arrival at the trading post that had long been a prominent landmark on the Oregon Trail, they started the day's march at the crack of dawn and traveled over a four-mile stretch of heavy sand. Beyond that the trail continued through a low plain filled with large springs of deliciously cool water, many of them forming little streams that flowed directly into the Neuf.

Near noon the column reached a barren bayou which led into the principal tributary of the Columbia River, here called the Snake River or, by some, the American River. Here the men confronted both extensive meadows of excellent grass, and enormous clouds of ravenous mosquitoes. Having heard that Fort Hall, too, offered plenty of mosquitoes but no grass, they decided to halt for the day and quickly set up their camp. Unaccustomed to having a "free day" to do as they wished, the men engaged themselves in a variety of endeavors — some, with yearning hearts, writing to friends or families or sweethearts at home, some washing or mending clothing, some airing provisions or making wagon repairs, and quite a few fishing, for trout and salmon, which were plentiful in the stream.

The men of *The Ottawa Company* turned in early and got a good night's rest and were up and on the move at daybreak this morning. They reached Fort Hall at about 9 a.m. and, as Delano wrote of it in his *Journal*:

> *Its form resembled that of Fort Laramie, although it is much smaller. It belongs to the Hudson Bay Company, who, by treaty at the cession of Oregon [Territory] to the United States by England, was allowed to retain possession nineteen years, in order to close its affairs, five of which have expired. We had hoped to obtain some supplies here, but were disappointed. The company were even purchasing bacon and flour from the emigrants who were overloaded. The fort stands on the left bank of the American Fork of the Columbia, sometimes called the Snake, and formerly Lewis and Clark's River, which is here perhaps five hundred feet broad. On the west nothing is seen but a vast barren plain as far as the eye can extend. On the north, at an apparent distance of thirty or forty miles, high buttes and mountains rise to the clouds, with nothing in the view to cheer the traveler; and this we felt more keenly after having passed through the fine valley of the Bear River.*
>
> *On applying at the fort, we were courteously told we*

could leave our letters, and they would be forwarded by way of Oregon the first opportunity, but there was no certain communication with the States, and that our surest way was to take them ourselves to California. While thanking them for their frankness, we felt disappointed at not being able to send our remembrances to our friends.

Around the fort were several lodges of Snake Indians, and a shirt was their only dress. The honesty of these Indians was so proverbial, that in our traveling through their country we had relaxed in our discipline, and did not consider it necessary to keep night guard — a confidence which was not misplaced. We were informed that it was eight hundred miles farther to the settlements in Oregon [Territory], and seven hundred to Sutter's Fort in California.

About six miles below Fort Hall, we crossed the Panack [the Bannock] River, a little above its junction with the American. It was here an hundred and fifty feet broad, and so deep that it was quite necessary to raise our wagon boxes to prevent our provisions from getting wet.

Ascending a steep hill after crossing the Panack, we found ourselves upon a barren, sandy plain, where nothing at all but the interminable sage and grease-wood grew. In the sultry sun, and through suffocating clouds of dust, we drove on till night. Our cattle found good grass below a steep hill on the bottoms of the American, after a drive of seventeen miles

Chapter 8

[August 1st, 1849 ◆ 9 p.m. ◆ Wednesday]

Alonzo Delano was delighted today when Charles Fisher, an old acquaintance from Ottawa, Illinois, rode into their camp on horseback. There was a great deal of laughter and happy talk at the reunion, and the men of each company were eager to learn what the other group had experienced thus far. Delano was first to go into any detail, and he quickly filled Fisher in on what had occurred between Fort Kearny and the point where they had encountered the Snake River.

Upon leaving Fort Hall — utterly dismayed with the trading post's crippling inability to re-provision them with much needed supplies — *The Ottawa Company* had continued down the Snake River on Thursday, July 19th. The stream was at first rather sluggish but, at about 20 miles below Fort Hall, its appearance and character changed considerably. Here it was about an eighth of a mile wide and bounded by high cliffs of black trap rock nearly perpendicular to the water on both sides. Here, too, they encountered the horse-shoe shaped American Falls, which dropped down for what several hundred feet. Nearby the ground was littered with black rock which, at first glance, appeared to be anthracite coal, but turned out to be nothing more than heavily burned volcanic rock that had been thrown to the surface.

Beyond the falls the trail became broken and difficult, often with steep pitches. However, the company traversed that portion safely and finally camped just at sundown, about a mile distant from a poorly-grassed hillside about a mile to the left. As Delano wrote:

> *After supper I went to the river and, descending an almost perpendicular rocky bank, I found, growing from a little beach, some of the finest red currants I ever saw. The were*

very like the English currant, nearly as large as a cherry, and grew on bushes at least ten feet high. Their flavor was excellent and I enjoyed a feast. While busily engaged in discussing their merits, I was startled by a strange puffing noise, and looking to the river, I saw several Indians swimming and pushing a frame-work of willows before them. On their landing a little below me, I found they had fish and came over for the purpose of trade. I tried my hand at making a bargain on reaching the wagons. They wanted a shirt for one small string and one fine salmon trout. I exhibited my stock, but they were unfortunately too small. I next offered them money — and quite as much as they were worth — but that they considered worthless. Some bright buttons were no better, but they offered to take a blanket worth five dollars [$144]. This was too hard a bargain for me, and I gave it up for a bad job, but finally I bought the whole lot for six fish hooks, both parties being equally well satisfied with their bargain. On their return, Hittle, Humpstead and Morrill swam over to their village with them and were received in the most friendly manner. Distance, eighteen miles.

Although the Indians had promised to come over the next morning and trade a pony for the blanket they wanted, they didn't show up, and so Delano had to walk, as usual. They crossed what was being called Fall Creek, a fine, clear little stream having a succession of low falls which were said to be — erroneously, Delano thought, and he was correct — petrified beaver-dams. Commenting about what occurred then, Delano wrote in his *Journal*:

Although there were some steep ravines, the road was far better than we expected, and we found it unnecessary to use ropes in letting our wagons down hill. We met a train of five hundred mules, from Oregon, loaded with supplies for the fort. There were both men and women in the train. The half-breed squaws with sun-burnt faces, soiled buckskin clothes, and wild, half-savage looks, made a very strange appearance. A long drive brought us to Raft River, or creek, for it is only two rods wide, flowing through a valley three or four miles wide, with good grass near the stream. Here the

> *road forks, one leading to California, the other to Oregon. Distance, eighteen miles.*

Upon reaching this point, the party turned southward and followed the creek upstream on a high-banked route which forced them to ford the creek three times during the day. Delano fought back anger upon discovering that a couple of horses had been stolen during the night. His first blamed Indians for the theft, but later, he and others concluded that the thieves were whites, whose own horses had perished due to their careless neglect. Indeed, they were encountering a growing number of emigrants who were afoot and begging for subsistence. While *The Ottawa Company* felt sorry for these unfortunates, they could spare little from their own meager supplies, which were barely adequate for their own needs.

As the men progressed, they found that the Raft River Valley was little different than others they'd encountered. High hills rose abruptly on both sides, with black trap rocks protruding from the surface and the earth itself, except for coarse bunch grass scattered on the very summits and in the immediate bottoms, wholly barren of vegetation. Wearied, the men traveled only sixteen miles during the day and camped after nightfall near a small spring discovered about a mile from their path.

Delano was pleased that since leaving the Green River they had heard of virtually no accident involving firearms. Previously he had been both bemused and concerned about the proliferation of firearms on the trail ever since they had crossed the Missouri and, subsequently, into the Indian Territory of Nebraska. Every man, it seemed, was displaying his firearms — pistols and rifles alike — in hand and usually with a spare pistol tucked inside the belt in front. No one even thought of leaving the wagons without his guns. By degrees, however, the firearms had been laid aside, and by the time they reached Fort Laramie, all firearms had been abandoned except for a knife, and sometimes a pistol, which might be seen peeping from a pocket.

Their train soon left the Raft Creek Valley, and they then turned up a small branch running between high hills. They ascended beside it throughout the remainder of the day and still had not reached the summit when night overtook them. They finally found a good spring about a mile to the right of their trail and camped near it. There were, by this time, a number of the trains traveling together again, which gave them the opportunity to see familiar old faces and sometimes make new acquaintances among the men. Far too often, however, the traveling was, day in and day out, very much the same, a mind-numbing routine often luring the men into a complacency that could become dangerous — a peril which gravely concerned Delano when he wrote:

> *The course of long travel, however, like true love, "does not always run smooth," and so I found during the day to my cost. On reaching the top of the ridge, which we did after proceeding about a mile, we saw a large basin, surrounded by high mountains, the road apparently running around at their base ... At a point nearly opposite, we judged the distance to be about twelve miles, it was the intention of the train to reach that place about noon and halt. I thought I could save six miles travel by walking straight across, which I concluded to do. When going out alone I usually put a luncheon in my pocket to guard against contingencies, but with the straight forward prospect before me, I deemed it unnecessary at this time, and accordingly started off across the plain alone, unarmed, and without provisions. I trudged along leisurely, stopping to eat red and yellow currants, which grew in great abundance, when, as I jumped over a little gully, my ears were suddenly saluted with a terrible, hissing noise. Looking forward about six feet, I saw a monstrous hissing snake, with its head elevated from the ground at least two feet high, its eyes flashing with anger, and quite apparently in the act of springing upon me. The temptation of Eve must have been from a different kind of serpent from this, for as it ran out its forked tongue, and issued its loud hiss, there was more of defiance than of persuasion in its tones and manner. On seeing the infernal reptile, I did just what anybody else would do on glancing at such play-things — I jumped aside about six feet, and then, ashamed of my own cowardice, I sprang toward him as he was elevating his head still higher, either for fight or flight (I could not tell which), and brought him a blow with my trusty cane, which set the monster to groveling in the dust; a few more strokes put him in a condition not to disturb the walks of future travelers. He was over six feet long. When the deed was done,*

I found my heart was palpitating somewhat faster than a lover's on confession, and with an eye out for anything like snakes, I plodded on.

Instead of saving himself time and distance, Delano became lost and suffered severely from thirst until he encountered a train on the path from Salt Lake City, the members of which generously shared their dinner with him and provided space in a wagon for a night's lodging. At dawn the following day he started off again and, after a dozen miles or more, finally found his party's train again, much to his relief. Still, his predilection for going ahead made him the butt of jokes on the following day, now that he had returned and relieved the fear they had been harboring for his safety. All during Tuesday, July 24th, he grimly suffered the teasing of the others.

"You'd better wear a guideboard on your back hereafter, Delano," chortled Henderson, "or you'll get lost altogether."

"If you don't stray away," someone else hooted, "you'll surely be stolen!"

"I suspect," called out a third, "you'd better never go out again without carrying along a full sack of bread and a side of bacon!"

Delano bore the jokes with reasonably good grace, realizing he deserved them and that he had been fortunate, indeed, not to have wandered in circles until he simply fell and perished. Fully recognizing the rarity of emigrants surviving major mistakes in the wilderness, he vowed to himself that he would never again allow himself to go out so entirely unprepared.

Through the remainder of that day, *The Ottawa Company* ascended a narrow ravine to the rim of the basin, traveling through difficult terrain with steep and sliding passes, while seeing at every step increasing evidence of high volcanic action. They encountered cones and colored hills, huge rocks split in half by immense forces, plus deep, rocky gulches which defied passage. Yet, the trail itself led over the most accessible ground, and they proceeded without accident.

At noon they descended to a little tributary of Goose Creek; the descent was so precipitous that many of their wagons had to be let down gradually with the use of ropes, and it was here, as well, that they encountered another train whose mules were so worn down that they were useless for pulling the wagons any farther. When *The Ottawa Company* men reached them, many had already wholly abandoned their wagons and much of their valuable property, and some men were attempting to use the wagon mules instead as pack-mules, hoping desperately merely to survive their ordeal. The Ottawa men were eager to help these unfortunates, but could not; their own weary mules had barely enough strength to get the party's own wagons through the difficult areas. They drove on, down through the wild and strange valley of Goose Creek, through an area where it appeared as if the world itself had tried to break up. The men were confronted with a vast panorama of numerous chaotic, bewildering conical up-thrusts, tables, jagged ravines, and seemingly countless hills white with lime. Delano took the lime coloring to be deposits of melted quartz in combinations of sandstone and volcanic grit which was often bisected with colored lines of demarcation — pink, red, brown, white, yellow and green — clearly laid out in zones or strata, almost as if planned. Delano, in commenting about these startling phenomena in his *Journal,* wrote:

> *It is an extremely interesting field for the geologist, as well as for the lover of the works of nature. We were told that men were digging for gold on Goose Creek, but this was untrue; yet it is far from improbable that gold, or [other] valuable minerals exist in these seared and scarified hills. On reaching the valley of the Creek, B. R. Thorne and myself, tired as we were, climbed to the top of a high table mountain which stood on the right of the road and found the surface flat, and covered with melted debris, such as I have seen among the cinders of a blast furnace. The road up the valley was excellent, and nightfall brought us to good quarters on the bank of the Creek. Smith, with a view of having extras for supper, collected a quantity of fresh-water clams and crabs. The latter were very palatable when boiled, but even with a hungry stomach and long confinement on salt bacon, I could not relish the clams.*

Their route on the following day — Wednesday, July 25th — proceeded through a passage that Delano identified as Hot Springs Valley, which occasionally opened into basins with high, bare and rocky mountains round-about, as well as into hills splashed white with a coating of lime or studded black with projecting trap-rock boulders. They passed many springs where the water was so internally heated that it was too hot for one's hand to be held in it for more than a few seconds; yet another spring only mere feet away would bubble with icy-cold water, clear and sweet to the taste. Good grass was frequently abundant in these areas, and the mules recovered their strength quickly with such a fine diet. In the afternoon they reached the extremity of the valley at the point where the road reached a rocky pass, and then they promptly camped after a returning emigrant told them that there was neither grass nor water near the next fifteen miles trail miles. *The Hennepin Company*, camping nearby, had lost three of their oxen since leaving the Green River but were otherwise doing well; they did not, however, wish to be passed, and so they surged on through the pass and to the canyon beyond.

Late in the day as Delano sat reading in the shade of his wagon, he was surprised to see an old acquaintance from Indiana, Mr. I. Schaffer, ride into camp on horseback with a companion, Seth Lee Beckwith from Rock Island, Illinois.

"We started," Schaffer explained, "with three yoke of oxen and ample supplies. Pretty soon, though, we found ourselves in the midst of a great crowd of emigrants and the grass was so scanty it could barely support the animals. Rather than run the risk of losing everything, we disposed of the cattle and the wagon and purchased these horses and took only what we could carry on them, which wasn't much, but it'll see us through. On the way, though, we've seen some terrible sickness in the camps along the Platte and witnessed the sad condition of lots of the emigrants, who couldn't bear to give up their wagons and goods and, instead, are having to give up their lives. We saw one family of eight, the whole lot of 'em except for one little girl, carried off by the cholera. She was taken in by strangers who said they'd see her through. Maybe. Maybe not. No matter what, it's *very bad* back that way."

Delano, commiserating with them, invited them to stay for the night with *The Ottawa Company* and to share the train's meager fare. Schaffer and Beckwith gratefully accepted the offer. The pair had already risen by the time Delano himself got up just at dawn on Thursday, July 26th, to the cry of "All hands, ahoy! Up and away!"

Everyone prepared quickly, and as soon as the oxen had finished grazing on the lush, green grasses, the men were again on their way, almost immediately entering the narrow cleft. As they traveled up the gorge, Delano attempted to jump across a stream but missed his mark and fell backward full-length into the water, to the amusement of all observers, except for Delano himself. As he put it in his *Journal*:

> *Squash — squash ... I had my boots full of water and should have drunk it with pleasure while on the Mormon Road, but here my want of taste — and a recurrence of more refined ideas — would not permit, so I emptied my boots on the ground and trudged on ahead of the train. About ten miles in our progress, I saw, a little off the road, a natural circular wall of rock, shaded by a single tree. The strange sight of a cooling shade led me up to it, and I found it to be an emigrants' post-office. Several newspapers lay on the natural stone seats within the walls, with a written request to "Read and leave them for others."*

Scrupulously complying with this request, Delano looked them over, carefully folded and replaced them, and continued on his way. It was a long, difficult walk in the hot sand without water, but after crossing the hills he found himself on the rim of another basin, and observing many wagons halted together on the plain below, he concluded that water was near. A mile more brought him to the wagons, where he found a small stream of lukewarm water, flowing in a trifling brook under the point of a rock. He drank freely, and then walked on about half a mile and lay down under the shade of a large sage bush, which screened his head from the sun. Very soon he began feeling stupefied and exhausted, and very sick to his stomach. He wasn't sure whether it was caused by the water he had just drunk, or by a bilious attack, but it came upon him in a rush, and he was considerably sickened. When at last his wagon came up, he crawled inside, unable to do anything more for the day.

That night a man who identified himself as Tom Clarkson of Toledo, Ohio, came into their camp afoot — armed only with a knife and pistol in his belt and his entire possessions in a small knapsack on his back, along with a couple of rolled blankets. He said that he had taken a passage in St. Louis in a spring wagon of the *Pioneer* line, at which point he shook his head sorrowfully as he continued:

"They were advertised to go through in sixty days, an' I believed 'em. Stupid of me. At Willow Springs our mules gave out, and there was a general distribution of property, only a small proportion of the party retaining mules and the remainder obliged to go on ahead for a thousand miles without additional supplies and told to 'Trust in luck and on other emigrants for provisions.' The passengers had each paid two hundred dollars [$5,760] for their passage, but now they were obliged to work it out. I'm one of the last remaining and, by God, I am damned well determined to get there!"

Of the incident, Delano wrote in his *Journal*:

> *No emigrant would see Mr. Clarkson suffer under such circumstances, and we cheerfully shared our poor fare with him. At the first water, however, we parted from Schaffer and Beckwith, who pressed forward on their very long and dubious journey. On leaving the brook, we journeyed on over a plain, where there was grass but no water and when night at length compelled us to stop, we found water by digging shallow wells in a moist place, but there was no grass at this point, and our cattle fared badly. The wind blew cold and our condition was cheerless enough. Our very excessive weariness soon drowned all our troubles in sleep, after a hard drive of twenty miles.*

First light in the morning on Friday, July 27th, had them all astir, and within five miles they again found decent grass, but no water. Nevertheless, they halted here four hours to let the oxen and cattle graze before proceeding across a plain a few miles to where they were able to find some brackish water in small, stagnant pools in the bed of a dry creek. The ground in many places here was distinctly white with the effervescence of salts. Fortunately, once again, nightfall found them in a broad valley with an abundance of grass and a good spring fully ten feet deep and bubbling with pure, ice cold water. Delano wrote of it:

> *No one can fully appreciate the luxury of a good spring, without crossing a desert plain, destitute of this essential comfort for the wants of man.*

Saturday, July 28th, dawned as a beautiful day, but it turned out not to be so grand for Delano, who again fell prey to bad water. As he wrote of it in his *Journal* soon after, he was much less garrulous than usual:

I felt extremely well this morning and, starting off well in advance of the company, I walked about four miles, when I came to a pretty brook fringed with willows. I took the tin cup, which hung from a string in my button-hole, and drank a hearty draught, and then lay down in the thick shade of bushes. Very soon I began to feel cold chills creeping along my back, and became satisfied that a day within the wagon was my fate. I felt almost discouraged when I reflected that the fell disease was gnawing at my heart; but there was no help for it, and when my wagon came up, I turned in, once again under the influence of chill and fever.

During the day we left this valley, passing some hot springs, and then by a gentle ascent, came as usual into another basin. The scenery was but little varied and I was too ill to take notes. There was but little grass, and the water was poor and brackish. The days are excessively warm, and the nights cold — ice frequently found in our buckets half an inch thick. Drive, twenty miles.

Sunday. July 29th. I was under the operation of cathartics, and spent a most disagreeable day. It is indeed hard to be sick in a wagon, while traveling under a burning sun, with the feelings of those around you so blunted through weariness that they will not take the trouble to administer to your comfort. At our noon halt we found good water, and a cup of tea revived me so much that I was able to walk some during the afternoon. Near our halting place we saw a party of Digger Indians, and I went over to them. As I approached, they advanced to meet me, offering their hands, and pronounced in good English, "How de do," followed by "Whoa haw!" They had picked up these few words from the emigrants, and pronounced words after us with surprising correctness. They were entirely naked, except a breech-cloth — of a dark complexion, nearly as dark as a Negro, and showed considerable obesity. Their stature was about five feet six to five feet eight inches, with well-formed limbs. Each was armed with a bow and a quiver of arrows, neatly made, tipped with iron. They saluted everyone who came up in the same way, laughing immoderately, and seemed a merry set of mountain rovers.

An amusing story was told of Hudspeth's company, when crossing the mountain from Bear River. His guide took them by the shorter route from Bear River, avoiding Fort Hall. The Indians had mostly retired to the hills, but they had learned quite a few English words from the teamster's vocabulary. On Hudspeth's approach, they met him in the most cordial manner with "How de do — whoa haw! God damn you!" It was, in fact, the most common language of the drivers. In short, the most profane swearing was the common dialect of a great majority of the emigrants, and the poor Indians only used it as a welcome to the whites. On another occasion a party were inquiring for a good camping ground, There were assured that there was "plenty of grass for the whoa-haws, but no water for the God-damn!"

At their usual camping hour the men reached a beautiful valley of good grass, and a good spring of water, and quickly turned off the trail to take advantage of these assets. After unyoking several of the teams the men discovered a thick coating of carbonate of soda on the bright green grasses. After a lengthy discussion, some of the men concluded that the coating consisted merely of salt. Delano, not believing that, took a handful of the white powder, mixed it with water in his cup, and then applied a little tartaric acid. The water quickly effervesced, revealing its high-soda content. Within ten minutes the emigrants re-yoked the cattle and moved out of this poisonous valley. That night the company paid a high price for their imprudence: Six of their cattle, having grazed on the alkali-encrusted grass, died.

The Ottawa Company men drove on another four miles and finally had to stop where there was grass, but no water, and they had no choice but to do exactly as they had done previously — leave by the earliest light. They did so at dawn on Monday, July 30th.

The men now desperately hoped to soon reach the substantial stream called the Humboldt River. As Delano wrote of this now-storied river:

It had long been our desire to reach this great River of the Mysterious Basin. Our guide books assured us that for three hundred miles we should find good roads, with an abundance of grass and water. We therefore felt a strong cu-

riosity to see a river flowing that distance, which had no outlet. We were now in the Great Basin, spoken of by Frémont. Since initially coming through South Pass of the Rocky Mountains, it had been a continued series of broad basins, or valleys, surrounded by a rough, broken, and sterile country; and although there was varied scenery in the route, yet here there was nothing significant to distinguish it particularly from what we had already passed over. There was no line of demarcation other than the Rocky Mountain Range, and this is, in fact, the eastern boundary of the Great Basin.

By sunrise we had driven two miles, when, in sight of hundreds of wagons, we reached the celebrated Humboldt, or Mary's River, where we made a long halt for breakfast and forage. Here we again overtook The Hennepin Company, on whom we had gained a day and a half since leaving Green River.

The Humboldt is a small stream, perhaps thirty feet broad at this point, having good current and pure water. It flows generally through a valley, several miles wide, with high and barren mountains on each side, which occasionally coming near to each other, the valley is contracted to very rocky caverns which cannot be traveled. At such points the road leads over spurs of high hills, several miles across. Generally, on the margin of the stream and its immediate bottom, good grass is found, but sometimes the deep sand extends quite to the river, and forms its banks.

Delano noted that game was again finally beginning to appear. Sage hens, ducks, wild geese, and cranes were abundant and very easily killed. A few fish were in the streams, but the emigrants were not able to catch any with a hook. Although Delano was still very much weakened from his illness, he was nonetheless able to walk slowly for most of the day and kept up with the train without too much difficulty. As he noted during the afternoon in his *Journal*:

It was a strange thing for us to have as many comforts as we found here, such as wood, water, grass and game; and the sage hens and ducks provided a delicious repast. To-day our sugar was used up, and from this time we were obliged to drink our tea and coffee without sweetening. It is astonishing what appetites we have, and how much the stomach could digest. It seems almost insatiable. I have quite frequently ate four slices of bacon and drank a quart of coffee at a meal, and still felt a desire for more; and I have seen one of my mess drink half a gallon of coffee at a sitting. This inordinate appetite, with the quantity of salt meat used, is probably one principal cause of frequent cases of scurvy on the road. Fortunately, we had a large supply of vinegar and acid, which, together with our getting out of bacon sometime before our arrival in California, prevented any such disease in our company. When laying in my supplies I bought one hundred pounds of sugar for four men, and it lasted only ninety days. Distance, eighteen miles.

Yesterday, the final day of July, was a day of rest for *The Ottawa Company* men, at least from their perpetual marching. There was no relief from the myriad other chores needing to be done, however, and the men were busy the entire day with equipment maintenance and repair tasks involving sundry goods, wares, merchandise and wagons, clothing, "... together with all such interesting occupations," as Delano sarcastically put it.

For a full day, as Delano drove his wagon for a change, he was accompanied by fellow company member Charles Fisher, who turned out to be a gloomy companion. Fisher shook his head sadly as he commented, "What have we come to, I ask you? What has the uncertain lure of gold done to the hearts and minds of *everyone*?"

Delano nodded, saddened that all who were engaged in this overpowering drive for gold — and he did not excuse himself from inclusion in the number — seemed to have lost an elemental sense of humanity they had all once possessed. Fisher soon rode on, and Delano, being assigned this night to guard duty over the cattle — a practice *The Ottawa Company*, now in Digger Indian territory, had resumed — shouldered his rifle and waded across the river to commence his three hours of rounds, which would last until midnight.

[August 12th, 1849 • 610 p.m. • Sunday]

The company with which Herman Scharmann was traveling to the gold fields had been, from the beginning, a very good choice. Undeniably, there was greater safety in traveling with a group, a sense of security that the lone traveler could never have. Yet now Scharmann, president of those comprising the train, was on the point of ending his association with them. It hadn't been an easy decision for him to make, yet one he found absolutely necessary if he were to retain his individuality and make his own claims when and wherever he saw fit in the future.

If he left his company, Scharmann had long since concluded, he would have to share with no one. Having the freedom to prospect and mine wherever and whenever he felt like it was terribly important to him; equally important was the right to retain for himself all the gold that he found. The thought of perhaps making an astounding find and then having to share it with someone else, or perhaps even an entire group, seemed to him self-defeating; when he found his gold treasure, it was going to be his alone — shared with his family, of course — but certainly not with some outsider eager to claim a share of it.

In the beginning travelling with a company made compelling sense; just *getting* to where the gold was would take every bit of strength and planning a man could muster; and there were so many pitfalls along the way that it only made good sense to band together for protection. That's what Scharmann had done from the beginning, and it was, he believed, a good choice — at least early on.

The journey westward thus far been relatively easy and interesting. Of course, Scharmann had certainly encountered inconveniences on the long odyssey, but he felt that he has handled them well. He had been less conscientious, however, in maintaining his diary, once the overland portion of it had begun; there would be plenty of time for maintaining a daily log, he felt, once he was finding gold on a daily basis. Until then a log was more or less a nuisance and served well only when there was something of significance to say. In his entry for July 2nd, for example, he had written:

> *Thus the journey goes on, always through the midst of the buffalo herds. One stray herd came running right into the midst of our cattle, so that our huntsmen took aim and brought down one of them, but unhappily they also killed one of our best cows. That certainly was an expensive buffalo!*
>
> *Horses and buffaloes are truly the mainstay of the*

prairies Indians. The buffalo meat serves as their nourishment; the skins they use for utensils or give them to the traders, who pass through the prairie every summer, in exchange for woolen blankets, carmosine red and indigo blue, and fine pearls which the squaws use for their artistic embroidery on dresses and shoes. Buffalo skins and rare deer skins are dyed most delicately and used to make dresses and shoes.

About 115 miles to Fort Laramie we met a fine band of Indians which — counting women and children — numbered 230 persons. The chief handed us a document, signed by the commander of the fort, which stated that the Indians of this branch of the Sioux were not hostile, but most friendly, and that there-fore every traveller [sic] should avoid insulting them. We soon learned that they had come in order to get some of our provisions, but our company was not very abundantly provided and could give them very little. I camped about 50 yards away from the general camp, with my wagon of provisions. Soon I counted some thirty-six Indians around my wagon. Among them was the chief, with his squaw and three children. Naturally, I was most curious to learn something of their customs. So I gave orders that the wash-kettle should be filled with tea and all other available vessels with coffee; also I had three large pancakes baked. My cows still gave quite a bit of milk, and so a supper was prepared for the Indians. The chief thought that he had more rights than the others, so he and his family sat close to the wagon. The others lay around the fire in a circle. When the other Indians saw that these were being feasted, they all came running up. I indicated to the chief that this was a very unwelcome thing to me, whereupon he immediately arose, held up his hand and cried aloud: "Womeski!" As though struck by lightning bolts, the approaching Indians stopped short and then turned back.

After the meal my guests left with many loud expressions of gratitude; only the chief and his family remained. I was very much drawn to this man, because of his unusual physiognomy and behavior. We sat together some time and smoked. Our conversation consisted of silence and signs.

Meanwhile his wife brought my wife a pair of deerskin shoes, finely embroidered in pearls. I made them a few presents in return.

For the next several days after that, Scharmann wrote nothing in his diary, but this changed shortly after his train passed the confluence of the North Platte and South Platte to form the principal Platte River. As he wrote on July 5th:

Eighty miles from Fort Kearney [sic], the Platte divides into two branches, the southernmost of which we had to cross. The many various parties of emigrants helped each other, and furnished the relays of horses in turn, so after great labor we safely reached the other side. The water came up to the body of the wagon and quite threatened to soak our provisions.

[July 10th, 1849] As we left the river and passed on toward the west, we came into the region of wild buffaloes. We were almost 50 miles from [beyond] the South [Platte] Fork when we suddenly noticed some figures on a nearby hill. It was a herd of thousands of buffaloes. It is a most difficult and usually a futile undertaking to chase after these animals on foot. Huge and heavily built, they are nevertheless swift runners, and it is just barely possible that a fast Indian horse may overtake them in a long run. One day I saw three buffaloes and a calf behind a bluff not more than three hundred feet away from me, so that I could inspect them at short range. As soon as they caught sight of me they stared at me with their fiery eyes so that even the devil, if I still believed in one, could scarcely have frighted [sic] me at that moment. I took to flight, but the animals also started to run. When I saw that we had a mutual dislike for each other's society, I stopped and watched them gallop off. The buffalo has a very broad chest, its front legs are slightly longer than the hinds legs, its head is broad and long, with crisp dark brown locks circling over the forehead. Its flesh is similar to that of an ox.

In my company there were several good marksmen, who crept up stealthily upon the herd in due form and carried off some booty. The air is so clear here that a slice of meat will

> *dry in twenty-four hours, only the traveller [sic] has not the time to wait for it. Other hunting is not to be thought of. I have not seen a single stag or deer, and there are no fish in the streams. Wolves [actually, coyotes], smaller than the European ones and quite harmless, come in hordes and in the evening. They deafen your ears with their howling roundabout the camp. There are mosquitoes here, especially near the streams, and they are so plentiful that man and beast are continually harassed by them.*

Scharmann then neglected his *diary* for an entire fortnight, but then he entered an account of his encounter with a party of Indians on the prairie and his brief visit with them. During the evening of Wedenesday, August 1st, he wrote in his *diary*:

> *The following morning, before we then resumed our journey, I visited their camp. My youngest son, Herman [Jr.], who just turned thirteen, drove the wagon and my oldest son, Frederic, accompanied me. Here I verified the truth that all good deeds are rewarded, for these savages strive earnestly to repay everything that they had received at my hands. Their huts are round, narrowing toward the top and covered with large skins; the camp is circular and in the midst of it is the chief's dwelling.*
>
> *As soon as the chief caught sight of me he shook hands and then took me into his tent and presented to me some dried buffalo meat. All the women that I saw there were busily making shoes and embroidering dresses with pearls. The chief's daughter, who was about nineteen years old, threw a rope of pearls around my son's neck while I gazed at her long and admiringly. My son was fifteen years old, of a strong, manly stature, yet he did not seem to guess at the thoughts which one might surmise were running through the girl's head. I experienced real regret at having to leave these savages who appeared to me to be more civilized than many so-called civilized men.*

Scharmann wrote nothing further of consequence in his diary until today, Sunday, August 12th, at Fort Laramie, when he briefly noted his dissatisfaction with the party with which he and his family had been traveling. He wrote:

> *At Fort Laramie we remained for three days, caring for the cattle and repairing our wagons. As I wished to hurry ahead as much as possible, I felt that it was advisable for me to leave the company, which was making far too slow a progress.*

Confident of his own abilities and those of his young sons, this was exactly what Herman Scharmann did today; carelessly turning his back on the leadership role he had accepted from the members of his party, he stole away with his family at dawn this morning when the others were barely stirring.

[*August 15th, 1849, 3:32 p.m.* • *Wednesday*]

After *The Ottawa Company* had arrived at the banks of the Humboldt River, Alonzo Delano marvelled at how strange the stream was. Unlike all other western streams they had encountered thus far, which were typically rimmed with stands of cottonwoods and willows, aspens, or ashes, the Humboldt was almost completely barren of trees except for a few growths of low willow scrub. The stream itself, flowing rapidly with clear, deep water, was rarely more than thirty feet wide and often squeezed down to as narrow as a dozen feet. That such a substantial flow of water would, somewhere ahead of them as they'd been informed, simply slow down and then vanish beneath the desert floor, seemed impossible.

The lack of trees meant, inevitably, a lack of firewood and, moreover, because the train encountered far fewer buffalo now, the animals' dried dung, so useful as fuel was virtually absent. What fires they were able to kindle for cooking, or at least for brewing tea or coffee, were fed primarily by sage and greasewood. Nevertheless, the men loved having a supply of fresh water close at hand for drinking and for the rare luxury of bathing.

Along the river waterfowl became the most plentiful form of game. Large numbers of ducks and geese, along with flocks of sandhill cranes and lesser numbers of avocets and plovers, frequented the river as well as the often extensive marshy areas adjacent to it. Fredenburg, the most skilled of the waterfowl hunters among them, hunted nearly every day, often with notable success.

Because the Humboldt was a winding stream, the train followed a trail that simply flanked it at a distance in a straighter line and on higher ground that was less marshy than the area closer to the river's edge. However, while the men were now not troubled by geographical line-of-march difficulties, they were encountering significant problems with the Digger Indians, who frequently followed them and, whenever possible, preyed upon their cattle. The Indians themselves went mostly unclothed and, their only weapons were pointed sticks and crudely made bows and arrows. The latter weapons, with rare exceptions, were normally not powerful enough to kill a steer or ox, but could puncture the animals painfully and weaken them to the point that they would eventually fall behind and could then be easily killed. The men of the trains became so outraged with the Digger Indian stalkers that they began shooting them on sight, prompting the Diggers to stay well beyond effective range of the emigrants' shots, at least during the daylight hours.

The line of wagons was still almost constant, snaking along near the river bottom and stretching out of sight before and behind, made up of numerous emigrant groups which now only drew together for their nighttime camps. As usual, Delano found great enjoyment in setting off afoot by himself, and then joining with his party later in the day when it was near time to set up camp. Then, after sharing dinner with them, he would write by lantern light of his day's experiences before settling in for his night's rest. Occasionally he would review what he had written in his *Journal* over the past week or so, sometimes adding to it, but most often merely refreshing his own memory in regard to what he had covered and what, perhaps, he might have neglected. On this particular evening he paged back almost two weeks and began reading what he had written since the evening of Friday, August 15th. At that point he had walked on in advance of his companions and encountered a wagon train that had originated in Columbia, Lancaster County, Pennsylvania. He received from Colonel John Halderman an invitation to dinner

> *... which was cheerfully given, and I found Colonel Halderman to be a well educated gentleman, to whose hospitality I was indebted. It seemed our train discovered the canyon road, and preferred it, thereby saving many hard hills and*

having good water all the way. Finding a good encampment, they halted for noon three miles below, and did not come up in three hours. There was a good deal of vexation among the emigrants who took the mountain road, on learning of the character of the lower one. Our afternoon drive was on a good road along which the valley resumed its breadth and character. Mr. [Edwin] Bryant speaks of cottonwood trees and willows, which fringed the banks of the Humboldt. The place at which I dined was the only point where I observed anything that might be called a tree in the whole length of the river, all the rest being shrubs of a few varieties, and willows.

Manifestations of Indian hostility began to appear. We saw an ox that had been shot during the night with arrows, which were found sticking in him in the morning. The same company lost several head of oxen the same night, and taking their trail into the mountains, found the remains of two, which the Indians had slaughtered and eaten. Drive, eighteen miles.

The next day's drive, August 4th, was little more than a continuation of the slogging along westward and of the growing sense of yearning among the men for the appearance of the Sierra Nevada Range, which must ultimately appear before them. Even near the river they now followed, the choking dust still remained a problem and, as Delano wrote of it this day:

One of the most disagreeable things in traveling through this country is the smothering clouds of dust. The soil is parched by the sun, and so the earth is reduced to an impalpable powder by the long trains of wagons, while the sage bushes prevent the making of new tracks. Generally, we had a strong wind blowing from the west, and there was no getting rid of the dust; we literally had to eat, drink, and breathe it. Two miles below our encampment the mountains again reduced the valley to a canyon, which was impassable for wagons, and we were obliged to cross a spur eighteen miles in extent, before we reached the river again.

I was taken with dysentery during the night, and being

> *too weak to walk, I had to take up uncomfortable quarters in my "moving lodge." On arriving at the river, after passing the rough mountain, I felt much better, and spreading my buffalo skin in the open air, I slept well. From this time forward I discarded the tent altogether, and, from choice, slept in the open air without experiencing any inconvenience. Distance, twenty miles.*

The emigrants continued to find the weather excessively hot during the daylight hours, but the nights very cool. This convinced them to change the order of their traveling, and instead, to lay-by during the hot daylight hours and travel in the cool of the night. To test out how this would work, they made only a short drive of six miles this day, starting off a little before sunset. There were broken clouds but enough moonlight for them to see their way and keep to the trail, and in the cool night air they made excellent progress. As Delano commented on Sunday, August 5th:

> *There were no trains moving but our own, and it was decidedly more pleasant than traveling in the hot sun.*

Delano walked ahead some miles, with his rolled blanket on his back, and upon coming to a crossing in the river, he lay down and slept until the train came up. After crossing the stream with his train, he again resumed his solitary walk. The road at one point lay right along the bank of the river, and Henderson, who was driving the cattle, but struggling in vain to stay awake, walked an eight-foot-high bank and found himself knee deep in the river and skinning his nose against the willow brush. He scrambled out at once with no hurt except for his dignity, and was soon plowing through ankle-deep dust again.

The men spent the daylight hours of August 6th resting or sleeping among the willows or in the shade of their wagons. Towards evening Delano and a companion, Charley Traverse, set out together on their night's walk. Their road led down to a level valley where the river meandered through a serpentine course. They advanced for several hours until coming to a point where they had to navigate around a poor, stony road. After they had proceeded for a mile on this route, their laborious progress was further impeded by a widespread, ankle-deep layer of dust.

Worse yet, depredations by the Digger Indians were becoming increasingly bold and troublesome, and consequently, it had become necessary for the men to maintain the utmost vigilance where their stock and mules were concerned in order to protect them. Delano and Traverse called off their excursion and momentarily joined a Missouri train from which, on the previous night, five head of cattle had been stolen. The Indians had accomplished a nearly incredible feat by running the rustled animals up an extremely steep slope. The company members had doggedly trailed the Diggers until they finally found them camped; the Indians had already slaughtered the stolen cattle, however, and were preparing for a grand feast. They heard the wagon-train members coming, though, and fled before the Missourians could wreak vengeance upon them. Unfortunately, many similar accounts were making the rounds; as the trains traveled over a 300-mile stretch, scarcely a single night passed when the Diggers did not make a raid on some company's cattle. As Delano wrote of it:

> *During the night it became common practice for those on guard duty to discharge their firearms frequently, to show all the Digger banditti that they were on the alert, but this precaution was not always effectual, and as we advanced the tribes became more bold. They cannot be seen in the daytime, but at night they prowl about like vicious beasts, and pounce upon their prey with comparative safety. The Hennepin Company lost five head of cattle and two horses during the night [of August 7th] and as soon as the grave loss was discovered, sixteen men set off to the mountains in pursuit. After going up a gorge something like six miles they recovered four head. The Diggers had killed one ox and succeeded in getting off with the horses. Another company lost ten head, and yet another lost four, in spite of all their vigilance. Not a day passed without hearing of similar depredations, and the emigrants resolved to pursue and chastise the robbers, if at all possible, in every instance. In some such cases this led to severe combats, and it was found that instead of being frightened at the sound of a gun, they would often stand and fight man to man with the most desperate courage, though they were usually well defeated on account of the superior weapons the emigrants used. If, under any circum-*

stances, the Indians came into camp, they were hospitably treated , and provisions given them, but war was declared to the knife when they made an inroad.

Captain Fredenburg was Delano's companion during the night of August 7th, and after a walk of fourteen miles over a reasonably smooth road, the pair spread out their blankets alongside the road among the sage bushes; they were then introduced to another peril: The night was "made hideous" by the incessant howling of wolves, which often advanced to within a few rods of them:

> *... keeping up an infernal serenade; but as the animals did not otherwise molest us, we returned the compliment by letting them alone. At the dawn of day, we roused up and left the river. Passing around the point of a small hill we again came upon the broad valley. Beyond this there was nothing for many miles but sage, except the willows which marked the course of the river. The ashy dust was very deep, and when we turned aside to find better walking, the parched and dry alkaline crust broke under our feet like frozen snow, thus making it excessively fatiguing to walk. A walk of six miles brought us to camp. The boys were enjoying a quiet snooze and we cooked our own good breakfasts, which we relished much. The valley was about fifteen miles wide, with grass growing only along the borders of the river. We began to observe a difference in the volume of water in the river at intervals. Occasionally it decreased materially, then again it was full and deep. The water began to be warm and slightly brackish, but still it answered all purposes for use, without deleterious consequences. Distance, twenty miles.*

Meanwhile problems with the Digger Indians continued unabated, and Delano was convinced that the principal reason for *The Ottawa Company's* good fortune in not losing a significant number of cattle owed much to their traveling at night and thereby having the cattle continually under their charge during the hours when they were most likely to be stolen. When time came the next evening, August 8th, for the company to set off again, once more Delano and Traverse headed off on their walk, which they pursued for fifteen miles before halting.

Scarcely had they spread their blankets and lain down, however, when the wolves' chorus began again, so nearby that sleep was out of the question. Several times the animals pressed to within about seventy feet of them, and the pair cocked their pistols and rose to give them a salute, but the wolves quickly withdrew beyond pistol range. They could see fires being kept burning brightly in camps not far distant and heard occasional gunshots, all of which, along with the continuous howling, prevented sleep despite their weariness. At daybreak they set out and followed the train to where it had encamped six miles beyond them, on the way finding a sort of "den" in the rocks which they judged could as likely be the residence of a Digger Indian chief as that of a grizzly bear.

On the following night, Thursday, August 9th, Delano could find no one to accompany him, so he set out on his walk alone. As he wrote of it when he stopped:

> *The scenery during the last two days has been growing more interesting. The hills are higher and much more broken, showing the upheavings [sic] to have been much greater, and the dislocation of black trap-rock more prominent than at most points higher up the valley. Sometimes valleys seemed to cross each other at right angles, these affording extended views in opposite directions, while the mountains seemed jumbled into a confused mass of sharp points, cones, and nebul [sic].*
>
> *The river, from being fifty or sixty feet broad, is now about twenty, and instead of its original purity, its water had become very discolored like the Platte. Its bends are often circuitous, and as grass is found only along its moist banks, we accordingly followed its course, increasing the distance much beyond the amount actually gained. The soil continued much the same. A quarter mile from the river it was a sand, or ashy plain, bearing nothing but sage or grease-wood bushes, without water of any kind.*
>
> *As no one seemed disposed to accompany me this evening, I set out alone, having first put my pistol in good shooting order. For ten miles the road was passing over deep quick-sand. Thinking that to walk barefoot would be easier, I pulled off my boots and stockings, but the dry sand grind-*

ing between my toes soon made them so sore that I was glad to resume their covering.

We now found that other trains had adopted our new course of traveling at night. This day and night the road was thronged with moving emigrants. I had gone only twelve miles, when, being worn out by the labor of walking in the sand, I scooped out a bed with my hands, and laid down and slept so soundly that I did not know when the train passed me. Towards daylight it became so cold that I could not keep warm, and when the morning star showed itself, I rolled up my blankets and set forward. A little after sunrise, on coming to a lateral valley, which extended many miles on the right, I discovered two objects lying in the road nearly in the wagon tract, and coming up, found they turned out to be Brown and Charley Traverse, quietly enjoying a sleep, where they could be conveniently run over by some passing wagon. Rousing them up, we followed the main valley about two miles, where we found our company encamped nearly a mile from the road, on the bank of the river. Distance, eighteen miles.

On Friday, August 10th, reports from other companies began reaching *The Ottawa Company* men that very hard roads were ahead, and there was no grass at all available at the Humboldt Sink, their name for the location where the Humboldt River simply disappeared into the sands of the desert. Ahead, so they were told, was a stretch of forty-five miles they had to cross with no trace whatsoever of water. Given their exhausted condition, they were appalled by this news and dreaded the grim prospect of what lay before them. Simultaneously, however, an "indefinite" rumor was suddenly being circulated among the emigrants that a new road had been discovered, by which Sacramento could be reached in a much shorter distance, altogether avoiding the dreaded desert, and that there was plenty of grass and water on the route. It was said, as well, that on this "new" route the Sierra Nevada Mountains could be crossed with but little difficulty, while on the old path it was "a work of great labor and some risk." At this point, Delano wrote in his *Journal*:

Near us was encamped Lieutenant Thompson, of the

Navy, who had been in California, and who had once made a trip overland to the States. As it was an object to avoid the desert spoken of, we thought it worthwhile to gain all the intelligence possible on the matter; so therefore, Colonel Kinkead, of Missouri, who was emigrating with his family, Mr. Fredenburg and myself visited Lieut. Thompson, for the purpose of making inquiries. The Lieut. was on his return to California with his family, having leave of absence, and was now on his way to join his ship at San Francisco. His information was simply the report of others — that there was a good road leading into the upper part of the valley somewhere; that the desert would be avoided, and that grass and water were plenty, but that the Indians were very bad, On the whole, this prepossessed us with a favorable opinion of the route, but we did not make up our minds on the subject at the time. On leaving the camp, alone, I walked ten miles. Becoming tired, I scooped a hole in the sand, and slept till the cold morning air awoke me, when I walked with stiffening limbs into camp. Distance, fifteen miles.

In consequence of the reported "hard route" that lay before them from the Humboldt Sink to the Sierra Nevada, the men of *The Ottawa Company* again, on Saturday, August 11th, shortened the running-gear of the wagons to eight feet, to make them run easier, but after some discussion, they concluded that their actual loads were already light enough.

The terrain they were encountering now continued much as before, except now there was no stream at all to follow, and the air became smoky, making progress more difficult. Many men moving now began wearing down, physically and emotionally, some to the point of abandoning their mules, their cattle, and even their wagons in their addled but extremely determined efforts to get through however they might. Their woebegone appearance and lack of equipment and goods stunned and dismayed the men of *The Ottawa Company* but, though they sympathized deeply with desperate stragglers' plights, they had absolutely nothing of their own that could be spared to give them; their own cattle had been prudently driven and were in good condition for what remained of the journey, but provisions were perilously low. Nevertheless, *The Ottawa Company* men remained confident that they could get through; they were, indeed, gravely anxious, but certainly not hopelessly discouraged.

On Sunday, August 12th, Delano's party held a meeting and decided that now they should resume their old practice of daytime travel; hence, on the following day they started out early in the morning, but soon halted and camped early in order to take advantage of a high plain with a good grassy bottom below, an ideal site for preparing themselves and their animals for the next fifteen-mile stretch of waterless desert ahead.

Yesterday, Tuesday, August 14th, Delano wrote in his *Journal*:

Among the pleasant acquaintances which I made on this journey, was that of Colonel Kinkead and family. He said he was originally from Kentucky, but had removed to Platte County, Missouri, where he had a fine plantation and was well established. The information which he received from California, of its climate, soil, and various advantages, gave him a desire to make it a permanent residence, and having an opportunity of selling out to advantage, he embraced it, and with his family and several Negroes [slaves] belonging to him, then joined the grand emigration of 1849. He was decidedly a fine gentleman of education and much urbanity, and was fully imbued with that hospitality which is characteristic of his native State, and which times of scarcity and trial cannot change. He had, with ourselves, a favorable impression with regard to the new route, and more especially as his cattle were much worn down, and it was somewhat problematical if they could pass the desert.

As our camps were contiguous at our noon halt, I stepped over to confer with him relative to some new information, or rather rumors, respecting the northern road. His eldest son proved he was a tolerable performer on the violin; while sitting in camp he gave us a few tunes to while away the time. When I was about returning, he invited me in such a hearty, cordial manner to stay and dine, that I could not refuse. Had it been at his home, I should have felt no delicacy in accepting the invitation; but here, three or four hundred miles from any supplies, where but few have more than they actually required for themselves, I felt like an intruder; but the Colonel would accept of no apology.

In addition to our usual traveling fare, with an excellent cup of coffee we had a delicious pie, made of a nameless (to me) fruit, which grows abundantly along the river in this part of the valley. It is about the size of a currant, growing in clusters on shrubs from four to ten feet high, and its flavor partakes of both the currant and cherry. It is as agreeable as either, and made into pies or stewed, is delicious.

Miss Eva Kinkead presided at our table (which was a buffalo skin spread on the ground,) and certainly with as much ease and grace as if it had been in a drawing room, at a fine mahogany table with brass castors. If you ever travel across the plain, by the time you reach the Humboldt you will well know how to appreciate a good dinner, even if devoid of manners approaching to anything like elegance. Ah! Pork and bread and long travel are sad levelers of refinement.

We made a long noon halt for the benefit of our cattle, in order to keep them in good order to cross the desert, provided we should conclude to do so. We now heard what proved to be true, that very great numbers of cattle had perished there; that the road was lined with their carcasses, and the effluvia arising from their dead bodies was insufferable, and that there was much sickness among the emigrants.

While Colonel Kinkead and Mr. Traverse rode well ahead to find an encampment, Mr. Fredenburg and I went on foot about five miles, and at dusk came to the spot selected by our pioneer for camping. It was near several trains — one from Lexington, Missouri, Captain English; another from Bloomington, Illinois. Soon after our arrival there, a Mr. Hammer, belonging to the latter company, brought out a banjo and gave quite an amusing concert of Negro songs, and we had a merry time by the light of the fire. While Hammer was playing, one of Colonel Kinkead's Negroes came in, and notwithstanding he had been walking all day, he found the music irresistible. He "jumped Jim Crow" in a perfect break-down style, amid shouts of laughter and cheering from the whole crowd.

From here to the Sink it was said there was but little grass, it having been consumed by the train in advance. Distance, sixteen miles.

A few miles distant from the "Sink" where the Humboldt River disappears, the parties began preparing to cross the daunting forty miles of desert that now faced them before they could reach the foothills of the Sierra Nevada. This desert they were approaching was an especially difficult one, not because it was worse than several stretches the men had already crossed, but because the men and beasts facing it were now totally worn down after months of previous traveling; they were in no condition to make any kind of arduous passage; yet that was precisely what they now had to do.

There was a choice available, but hardly a beneficial one, since the evils of each choice were about equal. One route was to take the trail straight ahead across the forty-mile desert to the Truckee River; the other was to take a southwesterly route, virtually the same distance, until the Carson River was reached. On the Truckee route, a notorious area called Boiling Springs at about the trek's half-way point did indeed spew bitter, boiling water which even when cooled, remained virtually too bitter to be consumed. The Carson River alternative route, however, did not even have this. Most of the trains would have chosen the Truckee River route without hesitation, were it not for the horrible reputation it had acquired after the details of the Donner Party tragedy on this trail began circulating nearly two years earlier. So, as it stood, the trains were about equally divided in their choice of these routes. Clearly, they were approaching one of the most difficult ordeals of the entire journey to California: An area through which few, if any, teams managed to pass unscathed. As animals and humans played out, others plodded ahead to get water and bring it back to those who remained stretched out beneath the dubious shade of wagon beds. How many of the trains now approaching this perilous stretch would make it through remained yet to be seen.

Now, fully aware of what lay ahead, and no longer so filled with confidence in themselves, *The Ottawa Company* paused to discuss their perilous situation. As Delano now wrote of this in his *Journal*:

> *August the 15th 1849 Wednesday. Learning that the faint northern road we had been following turned off about three miles below, we moved down, and turning our cattle out, held a consultation with regard to our course. A man on horseback reported that he had rode [sic] thirty miles out on the route; that in ten miles there was grass, in twelve grass and water, and in twenty, grass and water in abundance; and on reaching Rabbit Springs, a distance of thirty-five miles, there was neither grass nor water; that the road did not go to California at all, but to Oregon, and that the Indians were troublesome and bad. Some said that only half a dozen trains had gone that way; that they were led by McGee, a man who had lived in California and was well acquainted with the country and who expected to find a route*

over the mountains.

Colonel Kinkead was anxious to take this route, but his family becoming alarmed on hearing of the hostility of the Indians, and the various doubts and perplexities of going through an unknown, mountainous country, finally induced him to abandon the idea, and keep on the old beaten track — a measure which was most happy for him, and proved that at least sometimes a women's fears are well-grounded.

It was decided, finally, that we would go the northern route, although some of our company had misgivings. The younger portion, being rather fond of adventure, were loud in favor of the road. As we had been assured that there was grass and water on the way, we did not think it necessary to provide against these contingencies, any further than filling a small vinegar keg with water, for the purpose of getting over the first thirty miles, which, as it appeared a little doubtful in the way of essentials, we concluded to drive at night.

Yoking up the cattle a little before sunset, and bidding adieu to Colonel Kinkead and family, we then started off, Mr. Fredenburg and myself walking ahead. We left the Humboldt sixty-five miles above, where it disappears in the sands, continuing down its valley for two hundred and thirty-five miles. A lateral valley led quite far to the north, and in the very middle, towards the northern boundary, tall, irregular buttes arose, while high mountains were on either side. Our course was in a north-west direction, across the plain, towards a gorge, through which the road ran. The soil had the appearance of fine, dry ashes, or clay, without its tenacity — rendering the walking hard. At the distance of ten miles we entered the gorge, but instead of grass there was only the wild sage on a discolored soil. As we slowly wound up the gorge, scarcely able to crawl from fatigue, we strongly felt the dubiousness of our experiment. The thought of our Nemaha wanderings came upon us, and we did not altogether relish the idea of becoming Israelite-ish again.

It was eleven o'clock before Mr. Fredenburg and I reached the springs, which were a mile off the road; and suffering from thirst we took our cups and quaffed the first draught of pure, cold water which we had drunk for many days. We found a mule train camped around it, and, spreading our blankets, we soon forgot our weariness in sleep. Distance, twelve miles.

[August 31st, 1849, 5 p.m. • Friday]

For Alonzo Delano, it seemed that at long last his many weeks of difficult travel would soon be coming to an end. Although he had never openly admitted it, Delano left home convinced that he would never again see his beloved Mary, nor their children, Fred and Harriet. Yet, rigorous though this great overland journey had been, it had worked absolute wonders on his health. Considering that he had begun this trip with a medical death sentence hanging over him, he now felt better and more vigorous than he had at any time during the past decade or more, and he regarded the resurgence of such vigorous health as nothing less than miraculous. Now he could hardly wait to establish a home in California and then to send for his family.

Delano was acutely aware that his revived aspirations still dwelled in a cloudy future. His resurgent health might just be an illusion, a temporary respite before death would overtake him. Now, however, he no longer dwelled on the threat of imminent death; he was, in fact, virtually giddy with wonder over his revitalized health. While the past two weeks had been the most difficult phase of the entire journey for him, they had ignited within him a long semi-dormant determination to live.

Delano and Fredenburg had set out ahead of their train during the night and by the morning's first light on Thursday, August 16th, they could see nothing ahead but rugged, barren mountains and not a blade of the grass they had been assured they would find ahead. They found one spot, adjacent to three tiny springs, where grass had previously grown, but the herds of the trains ahead had consumed all that was available, and even the water from the springs sank into the ground and disappeared a half-mile away. As Delano wrote of the situation:

It was now twenty miles or more to Rabbit Springs, the next water. Our wagons had passed during the night, and were quite far in advance, so that we had the prospect of a late breakfast before us. Taking a parting drink from the pure fountain, we pursued our way in a north-west direction up the gorge to the ridge, and then following down another ravine.

At the distance of five miles from the spring we were upon the north-eastern rim of another barren sand-basin, in view of a broken country far beyond. About the centre of this basin, we overtook a wagon, standing by the road-side, when we begged for a drop of water; but, alas!, they had none for themselves, and we were obliged to go on without.

The pair crossed the arid basin, and just after topping another high hill, they overtook *The Ottawa Company* train just beginning to enter another defile to the northwest. There they paused long enough to refresh themselves from the acidic water in their vinegar keg, and this bitter repast revived them enough to push on, determined to reach the anticipated spring, as men and cattle alike were sorely in need of water. As Delano wrote of it:

The day was excessively warm, yet we hurried on and, descending a couple of miles through a defile, we passed the most beautiful hills of colored earth I ever saw, with shades of pink, white, yellow, and green brightly blended. Volcanic mountains were around us and, under ordinary circumstances, we could have enjoyed the strange and peculiar scenery. Turning westerly, we pressed on past a small basin beyond the defile, when, after ascending a little elevation, the glad shout was raised, "I see where the spring is!"

Delano and Fredenburg noted that several wagons had stopped in the road ahead and that a cluster of men were gathered around the spot where they assumed the spring was located, but the site was profoundly disappointing. Three or four wells had been sunk into the ground from which a tiny trickle of water percolated that was no larger than a stem of prairie grass. Each hole was occupied by a man lying on his belly and dipping it up in a small tin cup as it slowly filled the bottom of the little cavity. Each man was taking his turn to acquire and drink a cupful of the muddy fluid. Accumulating enough for one animal, much less a whole herd, was entirely out of the question. Beyond them lay a wholly barren desert waste very likely without a drop of moisture available for at least the next thirty miles. As Delano glumly scribbled into his *Journal*:

> *Instead of avoiding the desert, instead of the promised water, grass, and a better road, we were in fact upon a more dreary and wider waste, without either grass or water, and with a harder road before us. We had been inveigled there by false reports and misrepresentation, without preparing for such a contingency, as we might have done, in some measure, by cutting grass on the river. Our train then came up, followed by others. What was to be done? It was thirty-five miles to the river and about the same distance to the spring ahead, assuming it truly existed. Should we go back? Our cattle had already gone without food or water nearly thirty hours. Could they stand to go back? Could they possibly go forward?*
>
> *While we were deliberating, four wagons came in from the west on their return. They had driven ten miles more on the plain and, seeing no probability of reaching water, they commenced a retrograde movement for the river. A few of our older men hesitated, and they were of the opinion that prudence dictated we should return to the river, where we were sure of the means of going forward, rather than launch out into the uncertainties before us. But the great majority, without knowing anything of the geography of the country, decided they might as well go forward as back — trusting to luck far more than to judgment — a measure which reduced us to weeks of continued toil and increased hardships. We came to the determination that we would wait till near sunset, as the cattle could travel better without water at night than by daylight.*

As they remained in place at the insufficient springs awaiting nightfall, another emigrant from Illinois came into view with his wagon and joined them. His name was Robert Gard, and they had met him briefly at Goose Creek. He was traveling with his family, including small children and had pushed on ahead about six miles, when his cattle became exhausted, making it impossible for him to go either forward or backward with them. As they paused at the little well, Delano recognized Colonel [Joseph S.] Watkins:

... who had fallen into the same trap with us. He had driven over the desert about four miles when the cattle of his train gave out. Two of them he had got back to the spring, and got a little water for them, which, with a small quantity of flour, revived them so they got through. One dropped down in the road, when the Colonel took two pails and returned to Rabbit Springs twice in a day, for two consecutive days, and carried water, which he dipped up with a pint cup, and gave the exhausted animal, thus saving his life. The other cattle were unyoked and driven through to Black Rock Spring where, after recruiting a day, they were brought back, and hauled the wagon in.

While laying by during the day at Rabbit Springs, I had a visit from my old enemy, chill and fever, but luckily it was very slight, and though it weakened me I was able to walk after it. We started about 6 o'clock, with anxious hearts and sad forebodings, on our perilous journey. We were on a level plain of ashy earth, where nothing grew but a few stunted sage and greasewood bushes, with barren mountains shading the horizon in the distance on north and south. Our cattle traveled well, for they had thus far been prudently driven, and were in good heart, and we began to think it possible for us to get through without leaving our wagons.

About midnight, becoming worn out, I turned aside from the road and, spreading my blankets, was lost to the world and to myself in sleep, till the morning sun was shining on my eyelids. Even the wolves did not awaken me. Distance from first spring, forty miles.

The need for water became much worse and, too late, *The Ottawa Company* members realized that they, and others, were likely making a serious mistake in trying to find a better route for reaching and crossing the Sierra Nevadas by following a faint trail northwestward from the point where the Humboldt River suddenly angled southwestward. Delano, upon awakening from his exhausted sleep, found that the his company had passed him by and was now somewhere ahead, and so he rushed to follow on their trail. He became depressed by what he observed along the way. As he wrote later in his *Journal*:

> *As I walked on slowly and with effort, I encountered a great many animals, perishing for want of food and water, on the desert plain. Some would be just gasping for breath, others unable to stand, would issue low moans as I came up, in a most distressing manner, showing intense agony; and still others, unable to walk, seemed to brace themselves up on their legs to prevent falling, while here and there a poor ox, or horse, just able to drag himself along, would stagger towards me with a low sound, as if begging for a drop of water. My sympathies were excited at their sufferings, yet, instead of affording them aid, I was a subject for relief myself.*

Far in the distance, high above the plain in the direction the trail was heading, Delano could see a black, bare mountain, which he estimated to be some fifteen miles distant. Ahead he could see at least ten miles of flat, baked earth with no sign whatever of vegetation and which was, in many places, encrusted with a heavy white coating of salt. Near the trail he found pits in the soil dug by emigrants, some of which had partially filled not with water, but with a salty brine entirely useless for appeasing thirst.

Before leaving Rabbit Springs, Delano had managed to secure about a quart of water in an India-rubber flask, which he had husbanded with great care. Yet now, as he moved along, he came to a wagon straddling the trail, the harnesses empty. On the seat was a woman holding a little boy about three years old, who was crying for water. The mother, with tear streaks down her dusty cheeks, was trying in vain to pacify him. Delano walked up beside the wagon and stopped. He tried to smile, but it was a poor effort.

"Where is your husband?" he asked her.

"He has gone on with the cattle," she replied, "and to try to get some water for us, but I think we shall die before he comes back. We cannot endure it much longer."

Delano shook his head. "Keep up a stout heart," he told her. "A few more miles will bring us to a water source, and then we'll be safe. I have a little water left. I am strong and can walk in; you are welcome to it."

He extended toward her the rubber bag in which no more than a cupful of water remained, and she grasped it eagerly. "God bless you, sir," she gasped. "God bless you. Here, my son, here is water!" She let him drink nearly all of it, retaining only a mere swallow for herself, and Delano was moved by her concern for the boy and he later wrote about her:

> *Even in distress and misery, a mother's love is for her children, rather than for herself.*

Delano departed from her, reassuring her that her husband would soon be back with water, though he had no idea whether or not that was true. There was nothing more he could do to help, however, beyond what he had already done. He moved on, still following the trail laid down by *The Ottawa Company*. He did not catch sight of the woman's husband, but within another two hours — at about 10 a.m. — he overtook his main party just as they had finally reached the long-sought-after spring; the cattle were still moving sluggishly along after traveling some forty hours without food or water. Delano wrote in an unsteady hand:

> *If ever a cup of coffee and slice of bacon was relished by man, it was by me this morning, on arriving at the encampment a little after ten. We found this to be an oasis in the desert. A large hot spring — nearly three rods in diameter and very deep — irrigated about twenty acres of ground, the water cooling as it ran off. But we found the grass to be nearly consumed, and our cattle could barely pick enough to sustain life. The water in the spring was too hot for the hand, but around it there was formed a natural basin, with the water sufficiently cool to bathe in, and I, with many others, availed myself of this wonderfully grand opportunity to take a thorough renovation, which we found exceedingly refreshing.*
>
> *Everything around bore the marks of intense volcanic action. A little way above the spring was the mountain which we had seen from the plain, a bare pile of rock, that looked like a mass of black cinders, while at its base there were fragments of lava and cinders which resembled those of a blacksmith's forge. Desolation reigned around in the very*

> *fullest extent. The desert and the mountains were all the eye could view beyond the little patch of grass, and the naked salt plain which we had crossed, proved to be the dry bed of Mud Lake. After the snows melt on the mountains, and the spring rains come on, the plain is a reservoir for the waters, making an extensive lake, which the hot sun of a long summer evaporates, leaving its bed dry and bare.*

Far to the south of *The Ottawa Company*, the men could see another gorge, bounded on the east by a light gray granite mountain, leading to Pyramid Lake and to a trail which, as Delano knew, was the route taken by Frémont to California on his return from Oregon. Beyond the Black Rock Mountain were numerous other peaks uniting with a chain of mountains to the north of them and along the base of which they had decided to travel in a westerly direction. Learning, from a rapidly traveling mountain man passing by, that there was another, even larger oasis ahead, the men resolved to reach it promptly. Before they started in that direction, however, Delano, giving in to his innate sense of exploration and adventure, climbed alone to the top of Black Rock Hill. The air grew cooler as he ascended, and when he reached the top he was met by a storm of combined rain and hail, which chilled him to the bone. He was very glad to hurry down to a warmer climate — where he discovered it hadn't rained at all — and to hasten along in the wake of his wagon train.

When, near nightfall, they reached the second oasis, they found much better grass, but there was also a greater danger in leaving their cattle unattended there. In one spring they discovered the hide and horns of an ox that had evidently fallen in while trying to drink and had boiled to death. In some places, where the grass was deep, they had to step carefully lest they, too, should fall into a boiling pool hidden by the foliage. A traveler passing eastward told them of another fine oasis just five miles beyond this, where every requisite for a good camp was on hand, and so they drove on with the intention of giving their cattle and themselves a thorough rest at the first good stopping place, which they were able to do. They arrived at their destination with an acute sense of relief.

In the next morning's bright sunlight — Saturday, August 18th — the men of *The Ottawa Company* looked around the area more closely and discovered, not far distant, a beautiful hundred-acre plat of bright green grass, which was irrigated by the water from several hot springs. The men estimated that two of springs were large enough to turn a mill; but fifty yards below the spring the brook was still too hot even for hand-washing; indeed, the clear and deep spring-water was easily hot enough at the surface to boil bacon. The men brewed their coffee simply by setting the coffee-pot in the water. Oddly enough, near the boiling springs was another with merely lukewarm water, and still another one heavy with magnesia, as well an additional one so cold it was like liquid ice — and all of these springs co-existed within a quarter-acre area.

In this oasis the company encountered about fifty other wagon teams lying over to relieve and retrieve their cattle, after having lost a good many head during the difficult transit to Black Rock Spring. McGee had parked his three wagonloads of goods there and had gone on ahead to explore the road; the others were confident that he would lead them through if at all possible. Still, there were many members of the various trains who felt profoundly uneasy about trusting their lives to so unproven a route.

During the day, while Delano's company rested, most of the parties that had been camped there moved on; at the same time, a few others arrived from behind, having followed *The Ottawa Company's* trail from Black Rock Spring. One of these was Colonel Watkins' group. Watkins possessed all of the latest maps of California and Oregon, as well as a copy of Frémont's narrative, and as a large number of the men gathered around, they noted that it appeared they could follow Frémont's old trail to the south through the Granite Gorge near Pyramid Lake, and then from there join the old trail along Truckee River without losing anything in the process, perhaps not even time.

The *Ottawa* members were invited to come along on this route, but they backed away from the opportunity, doubting the supposedly prudential motives of those who acceded to it. So far as the Company members could determine, every account of a good trail having been opened from Oregon to California was dubious at best, and rumors of this or that good passage amounted to mere speculation. They did not ascribe to the prevailing chant which was "Drive ahead; if McGee can go it, we can," and so they declined and bore stoically the condescending remarks of other groups who suggested their reluctance was based more on cowardice than prudence.

From Colonel Watkins, Delano learned that emigrant Robert Gard had managed to find a little grass and more water in a ravine several miles from Rabbit Springs. After laying over for one day there, he had abandoned one wagon and put seven yoke of oxen to the other and had succeeded in reaching Black Rock Spring just before the Colonel left. The Company reasoned that they still had at least another twenty miles or more of deep-sand desert to cross, without water available in that stretch, and so, as Delano put it in his *Journal*:

> *... having it now in our power to do so, we provided ourselves against the trials already encountered, by cutting a good supply of grass with our knives, and filling our kegs with water. The latter was hot, but it cooled rapidly in the chilly night air, and was very sweet and good. Our cattle being recruited, we left about sunset, and soon were plowing our way ankle-deep in the yielding sand. Quite a number of men walked well ahead; and, finding the traveling so difficult, we occasionally turned from the beaten track to find more firm footing, but without effect. It being all alike, we finally returned and doggedly stuck to the proven path. When we arrived where we thought our morning walk would be easy, we lay down in the sand to rest, but the cold night air and the howling of hungry wolves, who would have made us bosom friends if they could, prevented sleep.*

Before the Dog Star glimmered in the east, Delano and Fredenburg were again on their way, and as Delano wrote of it in his *Journal* entry:

> *August 19th. 1849 Sunday ... although the train had passed us more than two hours, we overtook it and reached a place for halting two hours before it, with keen appetites for breakfast. This paradise was in the sage bushes by the road side. A little water and grass having been found a mile off the road, we stopped for breakfast and to let our cattle graze, and then hurried on. Our course from Black Rock [Spring] west of north, and parallel with the chain of mountains we wished to cross. Many actually supposed we were within fifty miles of the headwaters of Feather River, and some talked of shouldering a pack and striking across the mountains to it, ... so little did they understand the vast dis-*

> *tance, or appreciate the difficulties of mountain traveling. The measure would have been perfectly suicidal and I have no doubt that had the attempt been made, situated as we were, certain death must have been the result.*

After breakfast the company continued westward, and near noon they arrived at a somewhat wet valley containing several hundred acres of excellent grass and plenty of good water, a discovery which delighted everyone. The men realized they were now, at this point, across the desert proper. They were, nevertheless, acutely aware that they would encounter more long stretches of deep sand and barren highlands. Looking back, they could now ruefully understand and regret their own foolhardiness in having left the proven trail along the Humboldt River in an effort to avoid a forty-five-mile sand plain ahead of them. In doing so they had instead crossed the desert where it was a hundred miles broad, a route which by comparison had been far more arduous than the old Donner Party's passage.

The company men observed that nearly all of the trains that had preceded them were now encamped at the beautiful oasis, resuscitating their worn-down animals and roundly cursing their stupidity in leaving the old trail. As they joined the groups already camped, they learned immediately that the Digger Indians here were extremely bold and troublesome, having succeeded the night before in killing a horse and a mule in the camp, and in driving off several head of cattle. The remains of the horse lay near the trail and, as Delano put it:

> *... the gentlemen Digger epicures had cut off his head and had taken a large steak from a hind quarter, so very generously leaving the remainder of the poor, raw-boned carcass for the maws of the white devils who had brought it so far to grace an Indian board. I know well that the pungent air of the salt plain over which we had just passed is rather peculiar in producing good appetites, and I should hardly have had much choice between turtle soup and a horse-head stew; but never mind: the bacon was not all gone yet, though it was fast disappearing. Distance from Hot Springs, twenty miles.*

Responding to news of depredations by the Digger Indians, *The Ottawa Company* had once again, beginning on Monday, August 20th, established a strict guard during the night hours, and the other companies, too, were on the alert. Despite all their caution, however, the Indians came down from the hills, and with virtual impunity, had driven off a cow and a horse, while seriously wounding two other horses in the process — all of these animals belonging to a Mr. Watson from Independence, MO, who was emigrating with his family, and who had considered such precautions as wasted energy. One of the horses, shot in the side, died during the day; in the other, an obsidian-pointed arrow had passed completely through the spine and protruded six inches beyond; a testament to the impressive power with which the Diggers' short bows could deliver an arrow.

As was now customary, a volunteer party was formed to pursue the thieving Digger Indians; the party followed their tracks several miles along a lateral valley and into a gorge. They ascended the gorge for several miles, gradually finding themselves enclosed by steep cliff walls. They then were abruptly halted by a loud noise from above and, looking up, they spied the marauders on a high rock a thousand feet above, directing derisive gestures and sounds toward them. The emigrants concluded that it was pointless to pursue the miscreants further, and they turned back.

The Ottawa Company having at this point decided to rest for a day, moved about a mile down the valley to where the grass was much better and where the majority of other wagons had congregated. Additional wagons arrived at this location throughout the day, and by evening several hundred men had congregated at this spot. The Ottawa men, however, were surprised to learn from some arriving mule-train members that no less than 150 other wagons behind them had, on learning the dangers of crossing the desert, turned back to the first spring west of the Humboldt River's southward bend and took the older, proven trail again.

This profound change in route plans did not last long, as the rear trains, comprising a large portion of the emigrants, took the same route the company trying to reverse its direction, and the trains bound in both directions were overhwlemed by severe traffic congestion. After learning of these chaotic wagon-train traffic problems, the men of the assembled companies sharing the Ottawa men's location finally decided, in a mass meeting, that several trains should always travel within supporting distance of one another in order to be appraised of one or more company's changes of plans, and to better protect themselves, their herds, and their wagons from an Indian attack. Heeding this prudent mass-meeting decision, *The Ottawa Company* united with two Missouri trains led by Watson and Bacham.

Accounts again reached the trains, reporting significant losses of cattle in the desert beyond the Humboldt Sink and specifying that the trail was so filled with dead animals that the resultant effluvia from them was producing much illness in the passing trains. Hearing these grim reports, *The Ottawa Company* and the numerous trains now accompanying it rejoiced in having turned away and taken the Black Rock Desert route. Their relief, however, was short-lived, as their own portion of the desert — much more extensive — began producing the same sort of catastrophes, and soon the trail was littered with the dead bodies of the worn-out and starved animals, which in many cases, compelled their greatly weakened owners to abandon their wagons and goods and to struggle along on foot in a desperate exertion to get through.

On the following day, Tuesday, August 21st, Delano's wagon became part of a contingent of twenty-five wagons that left the encampment early in the morning and moved on within supporting distance of one another. Almost immediately the trail turned due west through a hilly plain abundant with sage. As Delano then wrote in his *Journal*:

> *... after traveling four miles, we came to the entrance of one of the most remarkable curiosities among the mountains. It was a cañon, or narrow, rocky pass through the mountains, just wide enough for a smooth, level road, with intervals of ample space occasionally, to afford grass and water. On each side were walls of perpendicular rock four or five hundred feet high, or mountains so steep that the ascent was either impossible, or extremely difficult. From this main avenue, lateral cañons frequently diverged and, upon ascending a mountain with much labor, the traveler reached a desert mountain plain above, where his progress was likely to be suddenly impeded by finding him self on the brink of a narrow chasm one hundred or more feet deep, having its own branches and ramifications, sometimes extending quite through the hill to a basin or open space among the high hills. Without this singular avenue, a passage through the mountains in this vicinity would have been impossible; it seemed as if Providence, foreseeing the wants of his creatures, had*

in mercy opened this very strange path, by which they could extricate themselves from destruction and death.

Delano, again itching to explore, diverged from the train soon after crossing the oasis where they had camped, and went through a small lateral valley on the left. He soon spied an opening in the rocks which, at first, looked as if it might be a cave or chasm. Boldly entering, he found it to be a narrow pass leading in the general direction the wagons were traveling, and so he followed it. The passage varied in width from ten to twenty feet, with perpendicular walls of trap-rock towering to a height of eighty feet and sometimes very nearly forming an arch overhead. As he moved along, his progress was occasionally impeded by drops of six or eight feet, which he clambered down with little difficulty. He fired his pistol in the singular chasm, and its report was louder than that of a musket in the open air. As he had resolved to take the passage to its end, he followed it no less than another mile and a half, when he became concerned that the train would get too far ahead of him. Taking advantage of a small open space, he climbed out by clinging with some difficulty to jutting rock fragments.

On emerging at the top, Delano found himself fairly near the road and in a place where an Indian snare had been set for catching rabbits or other small game. While continuing on the trail of the wagons, within a half-mile he came to where the wagons had been let down by ropes into a canyon, and Delano was very surprised, on descending, to find himself at the mouth of the very chasm he had been following. It was, he determined, the outlet of the great canyon to the valley of the oasis from which they had just departed. Had he continued only a little farther, he would have gone quite through the hill and into what he was now calling High Rock Cañon, and through which their trail now lay. As he wrote of it:

Between the high, rough walls of rock, we sped onward, perhaps four miles, when we came to an opening of probably some two miles in circumference, enclosed by rocky ledges, when it closed again with higher rocks than before. Threading our way onward, about twelve miles from our last encampment beyond the cañon, we now came to an opening of forty of fifty acres, covered with clover and wild oats that were taller than my head, when, with most of the other

> *trains, we laid up for the day.*
>
> *A short distance before we reached this our halting place, we observed a cave on the right, at the foot of the wall. It was twenty-five feet long by ten or twelve wide, with an arching roof fifteen feet high, and the remains of fires, grass beds, and burnt bones, showed it to be the habitation of this miserable race of beings who dwell in these mountains. In rocks around our encampment were other similar clefts and, from their number, we named it Digger Town. From the meadow there were lateral chasms leading out, one of which some of the men followed a mile without finding the end. The evening before our arrival, the Indians made an attempt to steal cattle from a small train encamped at this place, and several shots were exchanged between the Indians and guard. The Indians were finally driven off, having some of their number wounded, and no further damage was done. Posting a strong guard, the companies retired to rest. Distance, twelve miles.*

The next day — Wednesday, August 22nd — *The Ottawa Company* started early in the morning and continued through the canyon, finding good grass and water at convenient distances. As they neared their noon halt, they encountered a lower mass of rocks on their left, where an eight hundred foot hill was broken by a chasm which had the peculiar appearance of having been melted; its whole surface was glazed and had run together as if it had been earthenware in a furnace. With considerable difficulty, Delano climbed to the top of this odd, glassy flow, which was probably more than three hundred feet high, and found the same glossy formations continuing for half a mile, formations through which no blade of grass or anything else could grow. To Delano, the flow seemed virtually still molten, and he thought that even the most skeptical observers could not have doubted that it had at some period been subjected to extreme heat, though by what process he could not imagine, as there was no evidence of ancient volcanic activity in the area.

As the train continued without pause, Fredenburg, McNeil, and Delano followed a lateral canyon for a short distance, and upon encountering a place where they could scale to the top, they scrambled up to take a view of the country, pausing briefly on the way up to kill a large rattlesnake. Reaching the top, they found themselves standing upon a mountain plain bare of any vegetation except for decidedly stunted sage. Limiting their view some five or six miles ahead were some towering mountains, and the plain below was a maze of chasms and gulches, which they knew would make it very difficult to travel in a straight course. They were, however, able to trace the course of the principal canyon to a large opening some miles beyond, and well past that, to a distant vista of desolate red mountains.

On Thursday, August 23rd, The Ottawa Company drove on to the western extremity of the little valley, the grass and water getting progressively better the farther they went, and here, for three hours, the men let the cattle graze while they prepared their own breakfasts. Here a fine spring brook coursed through the basin and flowed down a lateral valley to the north, its course clearly marked for some miles by the willows growing along its shoreline. Resuming travel after their rest period, they again entered the canyon, which quickly became very rocky, requiring multiple crossings of the creek and thereby making impeding their progression. As Delano wrote of it:

> *This last cañon was about two miles long, and just as we were coming out, we were greeted with the sight of a drove of fat cattle and a party of men and wagons going to the east. It was a strange sight to meet travelers going in an opposite direction, and we mutually halted to make inquiries. We found this procession to be a relief party from Oregon, going to meet the troops on the Humboldt with supplies; and it was with much satisfaction that we learned that there was a good and feasible wagon road, leading from Goose Lake, beyond the Sierra Nevada, to California, which was opened last season; that the passage of the great mountain was not difficult, and that now there was grass and water all the way. This effectively ended all our doubts and perplexity on the subject, and lightened many a heavy heart.*
>
> *The best news was, that we should reach the gold diggings on Feather River in traveling a little over a hundred miles. On our emerging from the cañon, an open sage plain greeted our view, with occasional strips of grass in the depressions of the country. A drive of eight miles brought us to a small ravine; where we found tolerable grass, and good*

water in the bed of a creek, nearly dry. Colonel Joe Watkins had arrived a short time previous. Distance, fifteen miles.

On the next day, Friday, August 24th, *The Ottawa Company* found that the air was smoky and visibility limited and indistinct. Still, in the hazy atmosphere, they could clearly make out ahead the bold line of the Sierra Nevada Range, which separated them from their ultimate goal.

As Delano and Colonel Watkins walked on together in the morning, their attention was attracted by a large billowing of steam issuing from several hot springs just off to the right from their trail. The vapor clouds were by this time nothing new to them, and finding them unremarkable, they pressed onward. As the day progressed, however, the weather became quite sultry, which concerned them, since they had an estimated fifteen miles yet to go to reach good flowing water. Delano observed:

> *We had gone on a desert plain about twelve miles when, before us, we saw a pond of clear blue water, that was perhaps five miles in circumference, and when we all hurried to the muddy beach to quench our thirst, and eagerly dipped our cups full ...*
>
> *"Salt!" roared one of the emigrants.*
>
> *"Brine!" echoed another.*
>
> *"Pickle for pork!" added a third.*
>
> *... and so, with thirst unslackened, we resumed our very toilsome march. Turning an angle at the salt lake, from northwest to north, we continued on; entering a gorge, we began to ascend over a ridge about two miles long, when, coming to good grazing and water, we encamped.*

The Ottawa Company, taking stock of their present surroundings, noted that the mountains had begun assuming a more elevated outline on their left, with cedars and fir trees growing on their sides, a pleasant, highly welcome site to the emigrants who had been traveling across a virtually treeless world for what seemed like months. At this point their supplies were dangerously low; their bacon, flour, cornmeal, sugar, and vinegar were all gone, and they had to content themselves with what Delano referred to as "felon's fare" — hard bread and water — which, despite its meagerness, they considered to be much better than nothing at all. As Delano pointedly noted:

> *We were much better off with what we had than were many others on the road. Mr. Watson had an old cow that the crows had been quarreling over for a long time; and thinking a little fresh beef (save the mark!) might be acceptable, he slaughtered her. There could not be more rejoicing around the carcass of a camel by the Arabs on the desert, than we evinced around the poor, worn out, "knocked-down" brute, and we looked upon it as a sort of God-send, and like to have surfeited ourselves. Being out of meat, it seemed as if our stomachs only craved it the more, and our appetites grew much sharper at every halt. Distance, eighteen miles.*

The Ottawa Company's road continued through the defile for another five or six miles during the morning of Saturday, August 25th, until they finally came upon what Delano described as a "broad track, barren as usual," and over which they proceeded ten miles before at last finding water — an oasis formed by a warm spring.

They now could see that much snow still lingered on the higher peaks of the Sierra Nevada, and to them, the air felt much more like autumn than late summer. As they approached the base of the great mountain over which they were to pass, they noted the basins, or valleys, began to be more contracted and irregular, being broken by ravines, and points of land extending from the hills. At this point a sudden exhilarating deduction occurred to virtually one and all simultaneously: They would soon be among the greatest peaks in the California mountains and, at last, nearing the end of their incredibly arduous journey. On arriving at a fine spring, surrounded by good grass and plenty of fine sage for firewood, they laid over for the remainder of the day and night, having traveled fifteen miles.

The Sierra Nevada presented a mixed blessing for *The Ottawa Company*; it had been, for months, viewed as the beginning of their long-sought-after goal and now, simultaneously, it had become an obstacle quite as great as any yet encountered. As Delano recorded in his *Journal* on Sunday, August 26th:

> *In a day or two we were to leave the barren sands of the*

desert for a region of mountains and hills, where perhaps the actual means of sustaining life might not be found; where our wagons might be dashed mto atoms by falling from precipices. A thousand vague and undefined difficulties were present to our imaginations; yet all felt strong for the work, feeling that it was our last. ...

A drive of four miles brought us to the baked, dry bed of a lake, which I estimated to be twenty miles in circumference, surrounded on three sides by the mountains. Towards the upper end of this lake the Sierra Nevada seemed to decrease much in hight [sic]. And we could see even beyond the plain over which our road lay, that it seemed to blend with other hills on our right, and a low depression appeared, as if an easy passage might be made in that direction. ...

About a mile from the base of the mountain, and on the bottom land of the lake, were many acres of fine grass, with a fine mountain brook running through it, which sank as it reached the bed of the lake; and some little way from our place of halting there were perhaps an hundred hot springs, which induced us to call this place Hot Springs Lake.

It was now only eight miles to the pass, and the grass being excellent, the company halted for noon, with the intention of driving on in the afternoon to the crossing. I therefore availed myself of the opportunity to make an excursion to the mountains, not only with a view of gratifying my curiosity, but hoping that a chance shot might add something worthwhile in the way of flesh to our larder. At the foot of the mountain I was joined by two young men from a Missouri train, and we commenced the ascent. On the sides of the mountain we saw a species of nectarine growing on dwarf bushes not more than twelve or eighteen inches high; but they were sour and acid, not yet fully ripe. In the ravines were an abundance of wild black cherries, but those were not very good. Pines grew to a considerable height and we were refreshed by their cooling shade.

I had preceded my companions along the border of a very deep ravine and was about fifty rods in advance, when the ravine abruptly terminated in a perpendicular wall of rock several hundreds of feet high, around which there appeared to be a craggy opening or passage. While I was gazing on the towering rock before me, I momentarily changed my position, when the front part of my coat was grazed by something passing like a flash before me. Glancing at the base of the rock, I saw two naked Indians spring around a jutting ledge, and I comprehended the matter at once. I had been a mark, and they had sent an arrow, which grazed my coat, but without striking me. I then instantly raised my rifle and discharged it at the flying Indians, and sprang behind a tree. The noise of my piece quite soon brought my companions to my side, and going cautiously to the rock, a few stains of blood showed that my aim had not been decidedly bad; but we saw nothing more of the Indians.

Crossing a deep ravine, we climbed clear to the top of a rocky out-crop, from whence we ascended in a diagonal direction towards the road, which we reached in an hour of sliding, rolling, and tumbling along the ravine. We found we were about four miles from my train in the direction of the pass; and under the impression that the train would come up, I continued with my companions to their camp at the foot of the pass.

The day finally closed, and our train did not come, and I was indebted to the hospitality of strangers for a blanket, supper and breakfast. Distance, fourteen miles.

On the day that followed — Monday, August 27th — Delano, with rifle in hand, turned his course up the defile of the mountain he had long seen from a distance. The ascent was relatively easy, but occasionally there were benches he had to traverse. He was pleased, however, that the ascent was less strenuous than that of many of the hills he had already climbed.

Grass, he found, was growing clear to the summit, and pure, ice-cold water flowed in a rivulet along the path. About halfway to the summit, near a little stream that flowed into a grassy basin a short distance to the right, was what Delano considered to be a most beautiful cluster of dark pines, which shut out the rays of a hot sun. Beyond this, the trail led him to another bench and then to another basin; and a bit farther on, it rose to what Delano termed "the backbone of the father of hills." For a quarter-mile the ascent was steep, yet not steep enough to require that the teams be doubled in order to pull the wagons over.

On each side of the road at the summit the ground rose higher and the path they were following passed over a depression in the ridge. Delano was impressed with what he found at the top, and as he observed in his *Journal*:

> *Once arrived at the summit, the view of mountain scenery is grand and beautiful. Below, on the west, at a distance of a mile, is a broad green and grassy valley, abounding in fine springs. The valley is enclosed by high, pine-covered mountains which seem to kiss the clouds, and at the distance of ten miles, at the very extremity of the valley, is seen the broad, beautiful water of Goose Lake, adding a very charming variety to the scene. Turning to the east and looking at the pines already passed, the dry basin of the lake, with its dull gray bed, seems to lay [sic] at our feet, surrounded by the barren hills, which extend in a broken and irregular manner as far as the eye can see, and on each side these rocks and cliffs stand out in bold relief, the portals of the huge gate by which we enter the golden region of California.*

His curiosity gratified, Delano returned to the bottom of the hill and rejoined the train as it came up. They had found the forage so good at Hot Springs Lake that they had decided to remain there all the previous day, to give all the cattle an opportunity to recover a bit. It was about two miles to the summit, and this morning they drove about halfway up before halting for their noon break in the deep shade of the pine grove, which they found to be a perfect luxury after having been deprived of trees for so such a long time.

After lunch came the final pull, and at the steepest portion some of the wagons were double-teamed for the effort, although the majority didn't require this measure, and the company reached the summit without incident. As Delano described the passage in his *Journal*:

> *The time that was actually spent in traveling from the base of the summit was not over one hour and a quarter, and the dread we had so long indulged of crossing the great mountain, died away at once at seeing the few difficulties of the passage. The descent on the west is rather precipitous,*

but not dangerous, and the hill is probably near a mile long. My impression is that a little farther north, a still better passage might be found.

A little before sunset we were encamped on the green valley, about a mile and a half from the base of the mountain, near a fine brook, and beyond arrow-shot from the pines skirting the base of the hill to the left. Distance, twelve miles.

In the morning, the trail, as *The Ottawa Company* followed it, lay through a valley for three miles before turning into the pine forest. At a low point, to avoid an outcrop of trap-rock, the men rose to a higher plane and continued at that level until they reached Goose Lake. Several of the trains on this trail had intended to lay over for a day at the lake, hoping to bathe, fish, and rest. Unfortunately, they were in for a disappointment, and, as Delano recorded it:

August 28th. Tuesday. On reaching the lake, our anticipations were blown to the winds, for the whole shore was white with carbonate of soda, and the beach a perfect quagmire, so that it was impossible to reach the water except by throwing down sticks to walk on. The water was salt and soda combined, and was very nauseous to the taste. At the bottom of the hill were springs of pure, fresh water, and there was grass enough for our cattle at a noon halt.

The Ottawa Company men discovered that their route now led south along a broad valley near the lake shore, with broken, discolored hills to the left. Delano's spirits, high enough, became even more elevated when, as he recorded it:

A mile below where we descended to the lake, I observed the first out-crop of slate, which, in California, we have been told, clearly indicates gold. The character of the country began to change — the soil of the valleys a rich mould [sic], pines and fir covering the hills , and the sage at last giving way to other shrubs, and appearing only occasionally. About five miles below where we descended to the lake, a ledge of rocks bounded the valley near us on the left and, on going to it, I found it to be a strata of serpentine, the neat green and

> *gray stripes beautifully blended, and the lines as delicately drawn as if done by the pencil of the artist. Along the base of the ledge the driftwood and water-washed weeds showed that during the flood season this ground was overflowed. The lake extended many miles south and I estimated it to be twenty miles long by eight or ten broad. Night brought us to the end of the lake, yet the valley still continued, and but little above the water level, and we laid up on a mountain brook where the road forked — one branch going to California, the other to Oregon. Distance, fifteen miles.*

The Ottawa Company men remained in their camp until noon on Wednesday, August 29th, and then took a course directly down the smooth valley, during which they crossed two fine creeks and then finally halted for the night in a cluster of willow growth along the margin of yet another creek. There were paths leading through the willows to the brook, and in following one of these, a group of the men found a basket hanging to a tree in which were perhaps two bushels of small fish that had been dried in the sun, which they deduced was a portion of what the Indians there had caught and prepared as winter stores. In the absence of meat for their evening meal, the men brought some of the fish into camp, and after roasting them on the coals, found the fare to be very palatable. A mile from this camp, farther down the mountainside, they found half a dozen dwellings of the Indians that had been hastily vacated shortly before the emigrant trains approached. Delano wandered out to the shelters and found them to be conical structures of willow branches, each dwelling about ten feet in diameter at the base, covered over with grasses, and surprisingly insubstantial. The whites anticipated no trouble but, nevertheless, organized an alert guard force for the night.

It was on the following day — yesterday, August 30th — toward evening when *The Ottawa Company* men, looking ahead to the west side of the plain, discovered a number of fires glowing, some six or eight miles distant, and several of the men claimed to have seen wagons and cattle moving along in that direction. The men concluded that the road leading from Oregon to California came in near the location of the fires, and that they had merely observed the campfires of trains arriving from Oregon. Delano, anxious to stock up on some fresh supplies if possible, set out alone to approach these assembled trains.

His rapid, six-mile hike took him to the Pit River which, the men had learned, arose some five miles eastward in the mountains and was one of the principal branches of the Sacramento. Here it was hardly more than a little brook, and Delano leaped across it with ease. In only a few miles, however, its many tributaries turned it into a considerable stream. Still, Delano walked on, and soon came to a high, rocky canyon through which the river flowed, while the road he was following led over a hill on the left and then to the valley below. As he descended to the other side, Delano spied a train of six wagons, which he hoped were from Oregon, and from whom he could procure fresh supplies. He was, however, disappointed, and, as he wrote of it in his *Journal*:

> *... in approaching them I found they were from Davis County, Missouri — a company with whom we had previously traveled. Instead of a road from Oregon coming in here, I became convinced that the camp fires seen by our men was the grass set on fire by the Indians; the wagons merely clusters of bushes, and the clouds of dust, which had been remarked, was taken up by the whirlwinds from naked spots of soil, a circumstance very common on the dry and dusty plains.*
>
> *My hope of supplies was blasted, and not even one ounce of food could be procured; we were therefore compelled to stick to our hard bread. Some of the men of the Missouri train reported that there were plenty of fish in the stream, and a proposition was made to make a seine and drag the river. This party I joined with pleasure, and taking an old wagon cover, we proceeded to a beaver dam, and while a party went above to drive the fish down, we waded in the deep water with the primitive net. In three hauls we caught fifty-five fine trout, and going with them to their camp, we had a delicious feast, made quite the more acceptable by a sharpened appetite.*
>
> *While there, three footmen came up, begging to buy from the train a little flour. They had belonged to a small pack train, and their horses and mules had all been stolen by the Indians at the little salt lake between the High Rock Cañon and the Sierra Nevada Mountain, and they were getting through in the only way which was left. They had pur-*

sued the Indians twenty-five miles into the country, north, where they came to a large lake of fresh water in the mountains, but here they lost all traces of the marauders, and were finally compelled to relinquish the pursuit.

Being supplied with a small quantity of flour, they hurried on. Near the place of our halt were several singular outcrops of volcanic sandstone. There were between forty and fifty of these, standing isolated from each other, in the form of cones, being ten to fifteen feet high, and some of them were filled with yellow mica, which glitters in the sun like gold.

Our general course from Goose Lake was a little west of south, up to the close of this day, and we again found excellent quarters in the broad valley on the banks of the river.

About a half-mile from *The Ottawa Company's* encampment, Delano observed a hill that was bright white in color and which was washed at its base by the river. Intrigued, he strolled down to it and was quite surprised to find it a hill, over a hundred feet high, of magnesia as white as he had ever seen in a drug store. With some difficulty he climbed nearly to the top, where he detached large blocks and rolled them down the slope and into the water, where they floated off, as light and buoyant as corks until they became saturated. It seemed to Delano that there was enough there for the whole world. A little below this area he discovered more banks of the material, partially discolored with ochre and thus more impure.

Today the trail led the Company to a plain as level as a table, well above the Magnesia Hill, from which they turned west into the valley again for about a mile. As Delano made his *Journal* entry for this final day of the month:

August 31st. 1849 Friday. From the brow of this high hill we had a very charming prospect. The great valley extended many miles before us and, at the limit of vision, perhaps eighty miles distant, a high and apparently isolated snowy peak lifted its head to the clouds, like a beacon to travelers on their very arduous journey, and the clear water of the Pitt [sic] was quite sparkling in the morning sun, as it wound its way, fringed with willows, through the grassy plain.

The high, snow-capped butte was Mount Shasta, and though it appeared to us to be on a plain at the extremity of the valley, it was in fact surrounded by a broken and mountainous country, far from the course of the river. We crossed the river twice during the day by easy and safe fords, and found the volume of the water increasing every hour.

We were overtaken at our noon halt by three packers, who told us that the emigration had again turned upon this road, in consequence of the failure of grass on the old road, that there was much suffering on the desert, and that the Indians were becoming excessively bold and troublesome. If there was much selfishness shown on the road, there were occasional cases of genuine benevolence. They told us of one family in which there were several small children, whose cattle had all become exhausted, and had given out entirely. They were thus left destitute and helpless on the desert plain, without possibility of moving. A company of young men came along, who were touched with compassion at their deplorable condition, and immediately gave up their own team to the greatly distressed family, and traveled on foot themselves. I regret that I could not learn the names of these true philanthropists.

After crossing the river the second time, the plain was very sandy and rolling, but we found a beautiful encampment on the bank of the river. A mile from our camp we passed a most singular rock, of perhaps a quarter of an acre in extent, lying near a small pond, or marshy ground, that quite resembled a powder magazine. Its roof was regular, and the western end appeared like the gable end of a building. The roof seemed to project over the sides, while the earth below was apparently banked up around it. From its uniquely singular form we named it Magazine Rock. Distance, nineteen miles.

Chapter 9

[September 8th, 1849 • Saturday]

The incredibly swift and massive influx of people into both San Francisco and Sacramento now defied belief. A veritable parade of ships slid into San Francisco Bay, and an almost constant processions of horsemen, wagon-drivers, and pedestrians surged into Sacramento after having crossed vast prairies and deserts. The gold-crazed masses came not just by the scores or hundreds or even thousands, but quite literally by the tens of thousands, some arriving from all over the world, although the majority hailed primarily from the United States.

Irrespective of the mode of travel, these men, now universally referred to as "forty-niners," faced daunting, arduous hardships. For such men, so sorely afflicted with gold fever, braving prodigious difficulties was well worth the opportunities to become rich beyond their wildest dreams in a matter of mere months, or weeks, or even *days*. For those who set off with practically nothing but what they wore and carried, as well as for those who traveled in aristocratic style with an abundance of everything, the prairies, deserts, forests and mountains were obstacles that hampered them severely, but by no means stopped them, driven as they were by their compulsive obsessions. Probably no other person described the social turmoil of the contemporary California scene better than James H. Carson, who wrote on the first day of September:

> *Life in California at the present day marks well the great change that a permanent community has over a floating one. The change in affairs with us has been so great within the last twelve months that those who were acquainted with California as she was would scarcely know*

> *her as she is. Where we used to build a canvas city in a day, we have lately taken a whole week, and put them up of wood, stone, and brick. The miner, who a few months ago had to pack his kit along almost imperceptible paths, can now easily find in their place wide, well-beaten roads on which he can be hurried along in splendid coaches, at a rate such as is here required to keep up with the times. Where a short time ago it took from two to ten days to make a voyage in a launch up the broad rivers, to Sacramento and Stockton, [it] is now done in as many hours by fine, comfortable steamers, and the fare and freight charges are also a shade less by these fine conveyances.*

For Robert Shaw, his first nine days in California had been an uncommonly exciting experience, far more so than he had anticipated. San Francisco, he confided in his ragged *Journal*, was a city unbelievably garish, obscene, wicked, and exciting. On his first day here he had booked passage aboard a steamer for Stockton but the ship was so overcrowded that he was required to wait all these nine days before his passage could be honored. At this point he'd had his fill of San Francisco and wanted nothing more than to reach Stockton, outfit himself, and head at once into the interior in pursuit of what had brought him here all the way from Australia to begin with — gold.

He had arrived here aboard the clipper *Mazeppa* on August 30th, but with the great multitude of ships already at anchorage in San Francisco Bay or moored along the great Broadway Wharf, the anchoring of the sleek little clipper had scarcely been noted except by the Customs House officials, whose launch, the *El Dorado*, had soon come alongside. Crew, cargo and passengers had been thoroughly checked out and duties barely paid before the officials were on their way elsewhere to screen other new arrivals.

By then it was growing dark and so, along with the other passengers, he stayed aboard for this last night. Plans to go ashore early the following morning, however, were unexpectedly delayed. The *Mazeppa's* gig was found to be missing, putting the skipper, Cap'n Jason Mallo, in a towering rage, which was not quelled even when the clipper's rowboat was spotted, pulled up high and dry upon the near beach. Mallo, who prided himself upon the awe in which the crew held him, immediately went ashore, pulled by four of his men, saying he would return as soon as he paid his respects to the authorities, and that he would bring back the deserters in irons for punishment. It hadn't happened that way at all. When he reached the beach his anger only increased when he discovered the gig's crew had vanished. By the time he returned to the *Mazeppa's* deck he was even angrier, vowing severe punishment when and if the deserted seamen were apprehended.

By evening of that day, Friday, the two smaller craft had been lifted back aboard the Mazeppa and a guard stationed over them throughout the night, but this precaution had been futile. The remainder of the ship's crew had simply gone overboard under cover of darkness, determined to make it ashore by swimming or clinging to floating planks and kicking their way in. Apparently some of them made it, but several were believed to have perished in the attempt, not having counted on the water being so cold or on a tide that was running six knots. As Shaw wrote in his *Journal*:

> *Saturday, September the 1st — Our last evening on board was a thoughtful one. Our brilliant anticipations had been sobered down by the description given us by the Customs officials on the El Dorado, and the aspect of things damped, if it did not dismay us. But the time for exertion had arrived, and we all felt the necessity of unity. Knowing the mutability of some men's minds as well as the helplessness of many, it was with great misgivings that I listened to a number of the various projects propounded: I resolved to decide on none, but simply await the course of events and it was well that I did so.*
>
> *The next day — Sunday — we landed in [San] Francisco, at Miller's Point. Numerous tents and boxes and large quantities of baggage and merchandize were strewed about the beach above the high water mark. Near the principal landing place was a locality, called in American phrase, "a point," that is to say, a rendezvous for workmen; where about three hundred of the lower orders were here assembled, just waiting to be employed. Most of them had knives stuck in their belts, and their strange attire, unkempt hair, and unshorn visage, were anything but recommendatory.*

As Shaw could see, high hills rose far off to their right, and he was convinced that the town had been established on a regular succession of elevations; it became clear, however, that the structures of which it was comprised were at best only temporary, including a very large number of tents and rudely constructed lean-tos and sheds that were, for the time being, passing as domiciles and perched wherever there was available space. It was at least vaguely comforting for him to note that, at least in the central part of the town, where it was most densely populated, the greater majority of buildings were wooden structures constructed of nailed-together, unpainted planking.

Deeper into the town proper there was a plaza or central square, and rimming its vicinity, a remarkable number of wooden edifices and tents, including hotels, taverns, gambling houses and a few stores. Shortly after Shaw viewed with wonder the hodge-podge of structures, and noted on posted placards the prices being demanded for these thrown-together, shoddily constructed buildings, he tried to preserve his incredulous reaction by pausing to swiftly jot in his *Journal*:

> *The rent paid for some of little these houses is almost incredible: from sixty to eighty thousand dollars [$1,728,000 to $2,304,000] is the rent of some tavern-houses of timber, iron, zinc, or canvass [sic]. All lumber prices are unbelievably high, selling for $500 [$14,400] per thousand feet; and it mostly comes from China, Oregon, and the States; twenty millions of feet is said to be shipped yearly for the Californian market. ... hammers sound constantly, and work of every other description goes on actively and without pause.*

Shaw found that skirting the beach was an unbelievable chaos of tents, an unsightly rat's nest which had been dubbed Happy Valley, but he felt it should have been labeled Sickly Valley, since filth of every description and stagnant, smelly pools confronted one at every stride. He quickly discovered that congregated in these tents were a living refuse of all nations crowded together; a tent made for only two was rarely occupied by fewer than eight, all with their total worldly belongings — meaning rarely more than blankets, firearms and cooking utensils. Worse yet, scenes of absolute wretchedness, illness, and depravity shocked his moral sensibilities as much as the effluvia and filth gnawed at his nerves and sickened his stomach. So utterly insecure were one and all that it was rare, indeed, to see any sleeping individual whose hand was not firmly clasping his loaded revolver or rifle, cocked and awaiting a finger's pressure.

The ubiquitous presence of firearms — understandable considering the circumstances and the lack of legal protection — nevertheless, added great peril to the impossibly depraved scene. Lethal weapons borne by such a disorderly set of men, among whom fierce quarrels were frequent, sparked numerous altercations which sometimes resulted in serious injury or death. The unsettled state of the country and the large number of so many desperate characters prowling about, nevertheless, made it virtually mandatory for those who were physically weaker to "equalize" the odds by bearing arms and being quite prepared, if the necessity arose, to use them quickly and efficiently. Rarely did any bystander "step in" during such confrontations in order to see justice done or to protect the weaker or oppressed party. Oddly enough, armed robbery seldom occurred; murders resulting from disputes over trivial matters, however, were all too common, and law officers almost never investigated such incidents. The homicide victims who were relatively friendless were simply buried unidentified, a procedure motivated not by a sense of propriety or justice but by a concern about possible health hazards.

Robert Shaw had never before in his life shot at anyone and was not entirely sure he could do so now, but he was a reasonably good marksman, and he felt that if the circumstance arose and he were threatened, he would be able to handle himself and his weapon calmly and accurately. He owned no holster, but he kept the fully loaded six-shooter — its front sight filed off so it wouldn't snag on clothing if a fast-draw became necessary — tucked into the front of his belt at all times, making certain it was clearly visible and pleased with how frequently its presence prevented confrontation.

The virtual chaos everywhere evident kept the individual in a state of constant alertness, and as Shaw noted in his *Journal* on the evening of September 2nd:

> *It would be difficult to describe my sensations after the first day's ramble in [San] Francisco. I had witnessed so many startling sights that, had I not been well assured of their reality, I might have imagined them phantasies [sic] of the brain: Buildings were springing up "as at the stroke of an enchanter's wand;" valuable merchandize [sic] was*

> *strewed about in every direction; men of every costume and colour — Down-Easters with sharp-set faces, sallow Southerners, gaunt Western Squatters, vivacious Frenchmen, sedate Germans, plus sturdy English Colonists, Californians and Chileans, Mexicans, Kanakas and Celestials — hurried to and fro, pursuing their various avocations; and business, to an incalculable amount, seemed daily to be transacted. Looking at the rude sign-boards inscribed in various languages, glancing at the chaos of articles exposed for sale, and listening to the various dialects spoken, the city seemed a complete Babel.*

Gold was, of course, the powerful mainspring of all this incredible activity, and throughout San Francisco raw gold in dust, flakes and nuggets could be seen in many of the tents, both for exhibit and for sale. Often music was being played by skilled and unskilled musicians, who strummed at guitars and banjos and harps, blew vigorously on various horns and pipes, beat upon drums and shook tambourines, and even, on occasion, played on pianos brought from the East Coast by ship or wagon. The result was a raucous, cacophonous clamor that was simultaneously irritating and exciting. At the same time, in tents, speakers were making the most exaggerated statements, to all who would listen, in regard to where gold was to be found and in what amounts, and did the interested party wish to purchase a map that would take him to the spot that would quickly make him rich? Did he wish to buy nuggets at the present price at the mines, which was probably only half of what the specimens were actually worth? Did he wish to share his tools and goods with "less fortunate" miners who were temporarily down-and-out, but who would share their gains "fifty-fifty" with anyone who would stake them for another try where they were absolutely positive a previously untapped deposit lay?

Despite the excitement and the energy, the enthusiasm and the extravagance, despite the profusion of gold and the extravagant claimsof how it could be had, and of what it could buy, there was little of levity or openness in evidence, few signs of order or comfort perceptible, little representation of true happiness; instead, it was as if everyone, no matter how much he had, wanted more and ever more. On every side, as Shaw quickly became baware, the expressions of the men were wan and anxious, and his own gaze was returned by restless, eager-but-cautious eyes that appeared to be looking into him for the sole purpose of finding some weakness that could somehow be exploited. The surging crowds and the frequent by-standers seemed consumed with an obsessive avarice which was little short of frightening in its intensity.

The majority of the milling mass of men also seemed preoccupied with a sense of despairing hopelessness, likely resulting from personal neglect and discomfort. It seemed as if filth, rags and squalor had sired a voracious compulsive recklessness in bearing and manner — an all-absorbing sense of profound, enveloping selfishness, as if each man were seeking any means whatever by which he could take advantage of anyone and everyone with whom he came into contact. As Shaw described this in his *Journal*, he added, with a sense of sadness and fatalism:

> *These, as I saw them, were the strong characteristics of gold-fever, at once pitiable and repulsive; and for the first time, notwithstanding the gold I saw wherever I looked, a decided feeling of despondency and repugnancy swept insensibly over me and I briefly wished I were just anywhere on earth but here.*
>
> *Having landed our baggage on the beach, finding we could not obtain safe stowage, and that it was not the custom of the country, nor indeed practicable, to retain a superfluity of clothing, four of us agreed to erect an awning of sheets, and dispose therein our stock of wearing apparel to the best advantage to passers-by. So, constructing shelves and a counter of stray planks, we emptied our trunks of their contents, and exposed the articles to view. As it came about, I realized from the sale of my personal effects, $70 [$2,016].*
>
> *The beach around was covered with cast-off clothing; varnished French boots, satin and silk waistcoats, and similar luxurious but unfit articles of apparel, being discarded for others of more serviceable and durable materials. Boxes and baggage were perched on the ledges of the cliff, as safe from being pillaged as if they had been close-guarded; severe and summary laws against felony deterring the most knavish from stealing.*
>
> *One of my shipmates, Heath Durrell, having in his possession a few barrels of spirits, proposed retailing them, in*

conjunction with myself. Being wholly unable to procure a tent for our temporary grog store, we run [ran] a few posts in the ground, nailing quilts around and above for covering. On the first night of sleeping under our shelter, my companion, Heath, who had been drinking in company with some Mexicans during the day, fell asleep with a pipe in his mouth.

Late during this very day, the *S. S. Panama* arrived and discharged a great crowd of golds-seekers into the city, among whom, though Shaw did not know him at the time, was Hall McAllister, whom Governor Riley was expecting and whom he was prepared to appoint as district attorney of San Francisco. It was, in fact, well after nightfall this evening that Shaw finally closed their "shop's" makeshift door and rolled up in his own blanket to try to sleep. He managed to do so, but it was a frustrated effort, as he was jerked awake by suffocating smoke that was filling their little space. This was occasioned by his sleeping companion's clothing having caught fire as the result of his inadvertently spilling his still-living pipe ashes upon them.

In endeavoring to put out the flames, which had reached the quilt, Shaw inadvertently brought down the entire framework of their "store" upon them. Even this did not awaken Heath who, wholly drunk, lay on the ground entirely insensible of any danger. Shaw managed to grasp one of his legs and pulled him out from beneath the burning canopy. Of this he wrote in his *Journal*:

I then extinguished the fire, after which I wandered about till daylight, inwardly resolving never again to associate myself in any undertaking with an associate given to habits of intoxication. The next morning [Thursday, September 6th] was bitterly cold, and when I returned, my shipmate lay just as I left him. The dew and cold had somewhat sobered him, however, and after sundry admonitions, I left him. Thus passed my first night in California — and the remainder of this one was an education of itself.

The numerous lodging houses in [San] Francisco are very long, barn-like tenements, but owing to a deficiency of adequate sleeping places, sheds, stabling, and skittle grounds, are called into requisition. The one I subsequently resorted to is about sixty feet long, by twenty in width; it has no windows, and the walls, roof, and floor are formed of planks, through the seams of which the rain dripped through [sic]. Along the sides were two rows of "bunks", or wooden shelving, and at the end was some boarding that was serving well as a bar for liquors; here the proprietor slept.

From about ten, till twelve at night, men flocked in with blankets 'round them — for no mattress or bedding was furnished by this establishment — and a dollar [$28.80] being paid, your sleeping place was pointed out to you. If early, you had a chance of securing six feet of the top shelf; otherwise you stretched yourself on the floor. The bunks were decidedly preferable; for sometimes, of a wet night, upwards of eighty people would be packed together. Yankees, Africans, Chinamen, Chileans, all huddled together on the ground. As it was customary to sleep in one's clothes and boots, abominable odours [sic] arose, and creeping things abounded. When coiled up in your blanket, the smoking, chewing, and (as a necessary consequence) random expectoration, often prevented repose.

Towards morning the heat and effluvia became intolerable; on some few occasions, of a wet night, I have become oppressed with a vomiting sensation, and crept out in a profuse perspiration to inhale fresh air; sometimes I found a greasy cap close under my nose, or awoke sucking a boot. Restless sleepers, or unpleasant dreamers were not desirable neighbours [sic]; for a kick in the ribs, or on the head, in such a case, was an unavoidable occurrence.

Loaded pistols and other deadly weapons being numerous also, an accidental discharge would have lodged an ounce of lead in the body of those next. On fine nights, therefore, I always preferred the open air to such indiscriminate companionship. But although such sleeping accommodation — if such a term may be used — was wretched in St. [sic] Francisco, there was no lack of places of refreshment.

There were, in fact, eating houses to suit the tastes and purses of people of all varieties of means, and of all nations. The *table d'hote* at the best taverns was about three dollars [$86.40], at others a dollar [$28.80].

Inevitably situated at the corners of the Plaza and principal streets were stalls where coffee, cakes, pies, and a variety of other edibles were vended to those unable to pay the costs of tavern fare. Some of the eating places resembled English chop-houses, which many found to be decidedly preferable, with each person sitting at a side-table, ordering whatever he cared to choose from a hand-printed bill of fare; and if he was at all voracious, or choosy in his selection of the available foods, it was easy enough to spend, for a single meal, $10 [$288].

The majority of the eating houses were decidedly Californian in character. They were long, plank buildings in the shape of a booth, having two rows of tables placed parallel to one another and extending the entire length of the room. The sides and ceiling were covered with cheerful calico, as a substitute for wall-paper, and had prints stuck all over them as a form of decoration. The bar, for the sale of wine and spirits, was located at the far end of the room, and was almost always very crowded. The kitchen was located directly beneath it. The menu offered a heterogeneous mix of dishes that were all placed on the table at the same time, which included roasted and boiled meats, potted salt and fresh meats, various curries and stews, fried fish, rice, cheeses, molasses and frijoles, all of which were served up in smaller dishes and arranged indiscriminately on the table. Green vegetables or salads, however, were totally absent.

Such foods were not available on whim; indeed, quite the contrary. At intervals during the day, the beating of gongs and the ringing of bells from virtually all quarters announced feeding time at the various refectories, and such signals precipitated a crowded, chaotic rush to the tables. It was not at all uncommon to see the man who seated himself beside you, remove from his mouth a dripping quid of chewing tobacco and place it, for the time being, in his vest pocket, in his hat, or sometimes just beside his plate, and then commence vigorously attacking the available eatables. The contents of the large serving dishes disappeared very rapidly, and he who did not snatch and grab what he wanted was apt to get nothing, and meal refunds were never given. Considered very lucky was the man with a quick eye and a long arm, since everyone helped himself as quickly and as indiscriminately as possible, and he who had the manners to ask for something to be passed his way generally left the table hungry.

Regardless of what foods were placed on the tables for consumption, diners learned to move rapidly to get what they wanted, and once they grabbed such a bowl, it was next to impossible to get it away from them until they'd filled their plate or satisfied their appetite with its contents. The molasses bowl held a highly favored "fixing" that was eaten with just about everything.

Many of the less refined diners ate only with their knives, foregoing the use of forks or spoons; the knives delivering to their mouths whatever was available as food, and with remarkable speed and accuracy. Almost all meals were entirely finished in ten minutes or less. The American custom of rising from the table together was quickly emulated by those of other nations, except for the Germans, who somehow were almost always slower and very easily vexed.

After dinner was over and the diners had departed, the table was replenished for the next wave of hungry men, who descended upon the food just as ravenously as the first, while the greasy silverware was wiped somewhat clean before being restored beside the quickly swabbed plates. It was not unusual to see one of those who had already finished eating, picking his teeth with the fork, after which he replaced the tobacco quid his mouth lighted his pipe, and thereby released his smoke to mingle with the steam of the food in the fresh dishes.

Virtually all agreed that the very best eating-houses in San Francisco were those owned and operated by the Celestials, and conducted in Chinese fashion: The entrees were usually curries, hashes, or fricasees, served up in small dishes. The patrons expressed their delight with this fare by nearly always mopping their dishes clean with their bread, and no one was ever known to inquire about the specific ingredients which were responsible for such delectable eating experiences.

Aside from dining, gambling, too, seemed to be a virtually universal activity in San Francisco. Every block within the town had at least one gaming house and often several more, especially on the streets near the downtown area, and these concessions were always densely crowded. Some of the wooden hotels, especially those with several stories, had entire floors devoted to gambling. San Francisco's most popular gaming houses included the *El Dorado*, the *Parker House, Denison's Exchange Verandah*, the *St. Charles, Aguila D'Oro*, and the most prestigious of all, the *Belle Union*, all of which were crowded near the Plaza area. Called "hell-halls" by a minority of men who opposed their presence, the many gaming houses not located in hotels were usually either established in tents or in frame houses imported from the States, their interiors well hung with bright calico, mirrors and paintings — the latter very often featuring nudes, at which the women-starved population stared longingly and at length. Rarely did a gambling establishment not include a bar, one usually located unobtrusively near the far corner of the room. Square card-tables were located at regular intervals along the walls and scattered throughout the more open spaces, each with its complement of chairs for players. Spectators had to stand.

Merely entering such an establishment stirred in its arriving patrons a sense of excitement; they were usually greeted by loud music, vocal and instrumental, performed by professionals as well as by the sounds of clinking money and the rattle of nuggets. The air was always heavily redolent with wines and liquors and tobacco smoke. Such places understandably were extremely popular among those who sought shelter from the dust or the foul weather. The gambling halls were in operation day and night and imposed no entry restrictions, racial or otherwise. The proprietors enthusiastically welcomed anyone who had money or gold to risk in games of chance, and they mercilessly exploited every device likely to lure the men with wealth to the gaming tables.

The entertainment factor was, indeed, very important in luring prospective customers to the establishments and, once inside, to the tables. The *Aguila D'Oro* had a band called *The Ethiopian Serenaders* who sang, rattled their "bones," and played guitars or banjos. It hadn't taken long, however, for the gambling establishments to learn that employing women as dealers or roulette wheel spinners provided the most effective attraction for potential gamers — especially attractive women, often theatrically clad.

As for the games themselves, they included monte, *rouge et noir*, roulette, and faro, along with a new card game, not yet particularly popular, called poker. At each table sat two dealers, called bankers, and the center of the table was often piled with doubloons, gold eagles, silver dollars and gold nuggets. The bankers played to each other, presenting two cards, upon either of which the player staked his bet, and the result depended upon the next card drawn from the deck. Because the game was so straightforward and simple, there was little opportunity for deception of any kind, but the odds were always in the favor of the dealers. A player might have a "winning streak" for a while, but chances were if he continued to play, he would eventually lose it all back again. Only rarely was the bank ever broken, although it did happen on occasion.

Most of the players, of course, gambled as recreation, not for a living, and, hence, their gambling skills varied. Few among them knew even the barest and most elemental fundamentals of when to play and when not. When luck ran their way the excitement it caused was addictive, and few had either the courage or the ability to stop once the run of luck changed from very good to very bad.

In the gambling halls, everything was conducted in a most orderly manner; rarely was there any conversation, and the most skilled gamblers won or lost with little change of expression or demeanor, even when such transactions involved large amounts, such as whole bags of gold dust or flakes. It was the novice gamblers who reacted vocally when they won or lost, and they were rarely able to bear their losses with *sang froid*. Their expressions would become distorted, with compressed lips, clenched teeth, deep scowls, and blood-shot eyes. Not all that infrequently, when a novice gambler lost his entire stake, he simply walked outside and blew out his own brains.

It was far more common for the losers to drown their sorrows in drink, if they still had enough funds left to buy the wine or liquor, which numbed their sensibilities and made the losses easier to bear. Usually liquor was dispensed freely and on demand to those who were actively gambling. Robert Shaw, at this point very close to wishing that he had never left Australia, wrote of such activities in his *Journal*:

> *In some [gambling] rooms, loaded revolvers garnish the table on each side of the banker; he generally, however, secretes a very small weapon — a derringer — in a breast pocket. On the slightest disturbance, his rigid countenance becomes very agitated and often, without even enquiring into the cause of the tumult, [employs the weapon, knowing that] the ring of a pistol ball quite commonly suppresses confusion. At night, it is by no means safe for a winner to leave to return home or to his room, for outrages have been committed in the very heart of town. I have also seen a winner, at some tables, peremptorily called back, the banker insisting on his continuing to play. ...*
>
> *The streets of [San] Francisco are piled with merchandize [sic] of every description; high tiers of goods form barricades before so many houses, as ware-house room for stowage adequate to the shipping discharge simply cannot*

be had but the pathways abreast of the houses have been partially cleared of goods by a government proclamation.

Fronting the harbour [sic], is a large space of ground allotted for Customs House purposes; where cases, casks and bales, often to the amount of thousands of pounds value, lie in bond, exposed to the weather. With the duties being extortionately high, and these odd exports mostly unfit for consumption, the most costly productions, adapted only for a high state of civilization, perished when the rainy weather set in, for want of redemption.

In the roadways of the principal streets, the mud is in some places four feet deep; they are full of holes, and to form a footing, empty cases and casks are sunk in the slough; but it taxes the agility of pedestrians in leaping from one to the other. Incredible as it may seem, I have found a foot-hold across streets and pathways on Mexican beef, bags of flour, and bales of other damaged goods, devoted to that purpose. The roads having been worn and loosened during the summer, continual rains from the hills make them a flood of mire, and at some crossings, the soundings vary from two to five feet in depth. In one street a boat floated down the torrent of mud, much to the amusement of spectators; mules and carts frequently founder, and are with great difficulty dragged out.

It is quite reliably reported that a man's hat having been seen floating above a notorious quagmire on Pacific Street, on raising it, the head of the wearer was seen underneath; when extricated from this "Serbonian bog," he begged that the horse, which was underneath him, might likewise be rescued, but his very unfortunate steed was simply much too deep down to be got at. I cannot vouch for the veracity of this story.

[September 9th, 1842 • Sunday]

For the men of *The Ottawa Company*, the character of the country they were traveling changed little as the miles flowed behind them. Because the area into which they had entered on September 1st was so abundant with evidence of Digger Indian presence, they felt compelled to organize a new guard system which henceforth worked very well. On that day, after having traveled westward until mid-afternoon through familiar looking terrain, they then encountered a southward turn of the trail at about 3 p.m. Shortly thereafter their progress became significantly more difficult as they followed a canyon that took them through several hard passes in succession. At sixteen miles into the day's march they entered a small valley, which they followed for another three miles before finding a good, level site on which to camp, where there was both water and grass.

The next day brought a bit of excitement. *The Davis County Company* had camped about a mile below them, and Delano set off at dawn and joined their sentinel as he started their small herd moving toward his company's encampment. Even though it was now broad daylight and they had reached the fringe of the camp, a Digger Indian suddenly rose from concealment in the bushes and sent an arrow into a cow, which bellowed in pain. Delano and the sentinel rushed into the camp with the news, and a group of men pursued the Indian. They pressed him so hard that he was finally forced to discard some of his baggage, including his bow, a quiver-full of arrows, two hatchets and a heavy pair of bullet molds before finally escaping. The men turned back and reached the camp only to discover the wounded cow was too severely wounded to survive, so she had to be butchered, and the men were regaled with an unexpected repast of desert beef.

Delano had remarked at that point in his *Journal*:

> *We still continued in the cañon for eight miles, though at one point passing over a hard hill to avoid a towering cliff five hundred feet high; and had we not seen High Rock Canyon, this would have been a curiosity of itself. We crossed and recrosssed the river at least a dozen times. Three miles from our noon halt, after passing over the point of a hill, the valley again expanded, and here we came next to the junction of the Oregon and California trails. From the appearance of the Oregon fork, no teams had passed since spring, and all hope of any further supplies was at once cut off; but we now felt very sure we were within two or three days' travel of the valley of the Sacramento. So strong was this opinion among the emigrants, that afterward, when we had encamped in a fine place on the river, an emigrant came along on horseback and, on being invited to stop, he replied: "We're within ten miles of the diggings and I'll be god-*

> *damned if I'll get off my horse one more time until we get there!"*

The Ottawa Company camped then and on the next day — Monday, September 3rd — only three miles from where they had spent the night, they entered a fine valley that Delano estimated was at least twenty miles broad - a place with very rich soil and which, he was convinced, required only some good irrigation to be very productive. Shortly before that, McNeil, Pope and Delano, seeing that the road crossed the river there and fully expecting it would cross back over again quite soon, elected to continue under the mountain, along the bank, rather than wade the river frequently as they'd had to do the day before. As it turned out they had made an erroneous decision. On their right was a high ridge of trap-rock and, between it and the river, a narrow bottom that was quite rocky and well covered with a chaparral of willow, wild cherry and plum bushes. After a very laborious walk of a mile or more through brush that tore their clothes and scratched their faces, McNeil and Pope gave it up and waded across the river.

Unwilling to admit he'd been wrong, Delano stayed on the right side of the river and climbed up the crags clear to the top of the ridge, where he found himself on a desert plain devoid of vegetation. A little distance below, he could see a valley spreading out to the right a considerable distance. For about a mile he continued walking near the edge of the cliff, and in the process he found several circular walls of stone which he surmised had probably been winter dwellings of the Digger Indians.

As he descended from the ridge to the valley, Delano lost his revolver when, unseen, it dropped from his pocket while he was clambering over rocks, and he didn't discover the loss until it was too late to try to go back and look for it. As he reached the bottom and was pushing his way through tall weeds near the river, he spied Dr. Hall beckoning to him from the opposite side. Glad for the excuse to go over, he waded across.

"We just met a small mule train returning from California to Oregon," Hall told Delano, "and they told us we're still two hundred fifty miles from the mines and at least two hundred from the nearest settlement."

It was devastating news, considering they had been convinced they were only another day's journey away from the first tiny California settlement they'd reach, which they'd been told was called Lawson's Claim. They were also informed, Dr. Hall continued, that they were not following a tributary of the Feather River as they supposed but were, in fact, on the upper reaches of the Pit River, which was one of the farthest tributaries of the Sacramento. Having learned from the packers that within another ten miles they'd encounter some very difficult mountainous country, they decided to travel to the edge of the mountains and then to embark on the mountainous trail in the morning. Hence they halted for the night at a point a little above where the river entered a very rocky canyon. The morale in the encampment was not high this evening.

Their mood was hardly improved in the morning when some horsemen came through with further gloomy news, relating that just behind them, only a few days before, a small party of emigrants had engaged in fierce combat with several Digger Indians.

"Them damn Injens are getting' feistier all the time," one of the riders complained. "Ust'a be we could run 'em off easy enough. Not no more lately, though. They been gettin' very bold an' troublesome, not only along the Humboldt but on the plains an' on this side o' the mountains. Feller who, with his family, was part of one group, tol' us they'd had a good herd, but that the Diggers had driven off all the cattle belonging to him. They got a party formed to go after 'em and followed 'em for miles, but only found five head slaughtered an' all the meat taken from 'em. Damn Injens," he repeated, "jus' getting' feistier all the time."

At that point, the riders revealed that members of their own party had parted ways. One of their top men, Captain King, along with his brother and two others named Moore and Elliot had set off by themselves. They hadn't gone far when, as they traveled around a big rock, they'd encountered a party of four Indians who had immediately drawn their bows and precipitated a fight. Each of the whites selected an Indian to concentrate on, and right away Elliot seriously wounded his man, but the Indian was still able to flee. Moore had also wounded his, but only slightly, and the Indian kept shooting arrows at him as he tried to reload, managing to wound Moore severely in the neck. Captain King also wounded his man, then advanced on him with pistol in hand and shot and wounded him again, and then finally grappled with him in a knife fight and killed him. Captain King's brother took an arrow in his hand while trying to reload his rifle after a misfire, but the wound was slight, and he finished the reloading and shot the Indian dead. Elliot rushed to assist Moore who, though badly wounded, was still fighting desperately. The Digger tried to flee but Elliot raced after him, knife in hand, overtook him and wounded him severely in the neck. The wounded Indian instantly turned and tried to clinch with Elliot, but the latter sidestepped him and slit open the Digger's stomach with such force that his bowels fell out. The Indian fell to his knees but continued slashing wildly with his knife until he finally collapsed in death.

The riders related numerous other, similar stories: Grisly accounts of deaths and injuries suffered by emigrants at the hands of the Digger Indians who were now, it seemed, willing to engage any party of whites that were less numerous than themselves. These grim accounts were forcing many of the wagon trains to be more cautious and vigilant during the days, and to double or even triple the number of overnight encampment herd guards lest their cattle be run off before morning.

On Wednesday morning, September 5th, *The Ottawa Company*, no longer wishing to follow the Pit River on its generally westward course, turned away from it and struck out overland directly southwest, crossing almost immediately a long, rocky hill and traveling twelve difficult miles before reaching the first creek and two more streams more after that before they finally found adequate grazing grass. As Delano wrote of it this evening:

> *The day was too smoky to obtain an extended view, but what we saw showed us a very rough, mountainous country all around. For the first time, however, we found on the hillsides some oak shrubs and, as we descended at one point into a gulch, they were large enough to be called trees. We had been assured by the Oregon packers that, on reaching the mountains we should be among a tribe of honest Indians, who were neither hostile, nor would they steal our cattle; yet the first thing that met our gaze on arriving at our camp ground, were the remains of five head of cattle, which they had killed the night before. Of course our vigilance was not relaxed, and this same night an attempt was made to drive off our cattle but, happily for us, it proved to be unsuccessful. We found a good encampment for the night in a valley in which a fine mountain stream arose. Distance, fourteen miles.*

On the following day after they had driven only six miles over a very rough and hilly trail and then paused for noon break, a passing horseman warned them that it was fully fifteen miles to the next water, so they decided to camp at this location for the night. The next morning, which was the day before yesterday — Friday, September 7th — they discovered that the horseman's information had been incorrect; within six miles they discovered an excellent spring within several hundred feet of the trail they were following. As Delano wrote in his *Journal* this evening:

> *The days were now very hot, while the nights were so cold that ice formed in our buckets a half-inch thick. The road during the day was quite good and, before night, we arrived at a wide opening or valley in the mountains where there were lateral valleys opening into it, with high mountains on the sides, which gave us an extended view. One of the accompanying trains slaughtered an ox, and the science of cooking was never displayed to better advantage than in the camps around us, as well as in our own.*
>
> *About sunset, the general conversation turned upon Indians; and the course which each man would pursue in case of an attack was being discussed. Watson had, a moment before, come over to inquire about some arrangement respecting the night guard, when a cry was raised — "Indians! Indians! They are coming towards us!" Looking down the valley, we distinctly saw three coming up and, as they approached, we saw they were squaws.*
>
> *"Get the guns, boys! Shoot the Diggers!" was echoed, and several jumped for their rifles.*
>
> *"No, no," was the reply, "don't shoot the squaws. Let them come up; perhaps they're friendly."*
>
> *Every man was on his feet, and generally prepared for any exigency, while every eye was strained on the direction of the coming savages, endeavoring to ascertain their disposition, whether friendly or not. As they approached within a little distance, we were at once attracted by a loud guffatory "Haw, haw, haw!" from Watson and, looking again, we saw that the hostile squaws were just none else than his own wife*

> *and daughter-in-law, in company with another woman belonging to his train.*
>
> *A variety of interjections escaped the mouths of our valiant men, as they recognized their neighbors, who had only strolled down the valley, earlier and were now returning, but whose sun-burnt faces, soiled and dilapidated garments had made them look much more like mountain wanderers than civilized beings. No harm being done, a hearty laugh ended what could well have been a horrible catastrophe. Drive, eighteen miles.*

By noon the following day — yesterday, September 8th — *The Ottawa Company* found themselves some eight miles from where they'd spent the night along a fine creek which arose in the mountains a short distance away, but just as quickly disappeared into the sands of the valley before running more than a few miles. The road this day was excellent, although the temperature excessively warm. After their noon halt, Delano and Colonel Joe Watkins walked forward together, and, after about five miles, came to a broad valley adorned with a lake. The water, however, was so full of insect life that any cup dipped from it contained a multitude of "creatures" swimming about in it. The men could get water for their own use relatively free of insect life only by digging holes near the lake's margin and letting the water filter through the ground and fill the holes, water which was, in fact, cool, clear, and sweetly delicious. Last evening, Delano wrote in his Journal:

> *We passed, during the day, some of the most magnificent pines I ever beheld, some of them being over two hundred feet high, and at least six feet in diameter. Mr. Gard and his family came up with us here, entirely destitute of provisions; but the emigrants freely shared with him, although he had no money; thus enabling him to get safely through. He had lost eight head of cattle, but the others had recruited, so that he got along with one wagon. We found a beautiful place to encamp, under a grove of tall pines, and our cattle fared sumptuously. Distance, fifteen miles.*

Today — Thursday, September 9th –responding to rumors that the next water was fully twenty miles distant, *The Ottawa Company* commenced its day's march at first light. They found the trail to be reasonably good, and at fourteen miles, they encountered some decent grass for the cattle. Delano and Colonel Watkins, understanding that their train would drive twenty miles before stopping and that this ought to bring them into the valley of a tributary of the Feather River, had moved on well ahead of the company. When, however, after waiting a bit, the two detected no sign of the approaching train, Watkins was not inclined to walk farther; Delano, however, continued alone to whatever branch of the Feather River he might encounter. The whole distance, thus far, had been well wooded with magnificent pines. Occasionally he passed areas where volcanic rock protruded above the ground and the soil was discolored by yellow ochre.

It was close to sunset when Delano finally descended a steep pitch into a small valley, and it was here he found what he called Feather Creek. Here he paused to rest near a camp and then later wrote in his *Journal*:

> *While I sat near a camp, patiently awaiting the arrival of the rest of The Ottawa Company, and experiencing an anxious longing for a crust of hard bread, the shades of nightfall began to darken, and no train appeared. The prospect of no supper, and a bed without blankets, were rising before me, producing no very pleasant feelings at all, when a gentleman approached, and stopping before me a moment, observed, "You are alone."*
>
> *"Yes," I responded. "I am in advance of my train, which was to come to this place, but I fear something has detained them."*
>
> *"No matter," he replied. "I want you to come with me and spend the night at our camp."*
>
> *I admit I hesitated at first, wholly aware that no travelers in these mountains was so well supplied with provisions that he could just give such goods away, but the stranger, noting my hesitation, would have none of it.*
>
> *"Come," he said. "You must come and share what we have. No excuse, no ceremony."*
>
> *I nodded and followed him, and such as they had I freely shared, and the evening was whiled away in such pleasant conversation as well-bred and well-educated gentlemen*

know how to introduce. If there is any mystery in all this, it may be explained by saying they were Odd-Fellows; yet in all my journey, when circumstances have taken me from my own train, I have never, in a single instance, been denied the rites of hospitality; and although at this time, when our own route had been lengthened nearly three weeks — when every individual had scarcely supplies enough for himself, and when a single meal was distinctly an item of consideration, the courtesy of a civilized land was extended, and the very weary and hungered were not denied the enjoyment of hospitality, such as Messrs. Abel Cox and C. C. Lane, of Flemingsburgh, Kentucky, extended to me.

The train did not come up. It appeared that as they came to the fourteen-mile halt, a beautiful lake had just been discovered a mile and a half east of the road, and that they had driven to it, where, finding luxurious grass, they had concluded to lay up all day.

[September 14th, 1849 — Friday • 8:30 p.m.]

Considering he was quite literate and a reasonably close observer of all that occurred within his scope, the degree of Herman Scharmann's self-absorption was little short of remarkable. As he had since their odyssey commenced last spring, he continued the sporadic writing in his diary in a strangely singular vein, as if he were traveling all alone; as if no one but he was suffering the effects of obstacles that nature had quite deliberately put into his path; as if no one else, before or after, had ever taken such a journey as this, or had suffered such deprivation and discomfort. That his wife and sons and daughter were also suffering every bit as much as he, never for a moment seemed to occur to him; nor, as he wallowed in his own self-pitying misery and proclaimed loudly and persistently about it, did he care to hear about anyone else's difficulties. The very manner in which he wrote in his diary more than emphasized the "I ... me ... myself" train of his thoughts. His diary entry today — the first in many weeks — clearly illustrated the self-absorbed state of mind that so thoroughly possessed him:

I had to drive along the right bank of the Platte River for about 150 miles before I came to a place where the Mormons had constructed a ferry which carried me across the river. From Fort Laramie to South Pass the largely barren land is only very sparsely covered with grass, in altogether insufficient quantity for the countless crowds of emigrants that must pass over it. In addition to this, the road is rough and rocky, although it passes between the mountains instead of over them. Finally, without any climbing, the South Pass is reached. There a brook splashes merrily over the rocks and quite a good-sized grassy expanse greets the traveller's [sic] weary eyes. The brook is called Pacific Creek. On my arrival I found fully five thousand oxen and numerous mules and wagons, besides their human owners. These separated here, some to go to the Mormon [Salt Lake] City, others to join the California travellers [sic]. I attached myself to this latter division and so had plenty of company.

At the Big Santee [Sandy] River we rested for a day. Then we went over a forty-mile desert to the Green River. Here many pieces of shattered wagons were scattered all around, but several in good condition were among them, so we had a good chance to replenish our stock. After this I drove on over steep mountains and through deep valleys, continually wondering whether it would be possible to climb over them.

The mountains in this region are called Peak Basement and form a dome in a circle of about one hundred square miles. All are covered by low brushwood and grass, and present a very pleasant aspect. The most curious thing in this region is the fact that flax grows everywhere in among the grass. I examined a stalk and discovered that it was very like the European flax in quality. Thus the soil here proclaimed its own fertility. The only drawback is that it does not rain here during the Indian summer.

This is the only region during this part of the voyage that seems worthy of a farmer's notice. The land for all the rest of the way from Fort Laramie to California is not worth a cent. I think it consists of nothing but desert-land and bare mountains covered with boulders and red soil which make them resemble volcanoes. The very best thing the traveller [sic] can do is hurry on as fast as possible from one river to the other.

At the Bear River, in a valley from three to four miles wide, we gave our cattle a two days' rest. Here there was no lack of grass, but such grazing places are quickly traversed, and it is not possible for us to remain near them for any length of time. In a beautiful valley along the Snake River I met Snake Indians, who are closely related to the Sioux Tribe. Their chief occupations are hunting and fishing. They came on up to us and begged, but we discovered if you give something to one of them all the others come running to you. Their intellectual faculties are quite probably of the very lowest, as their language consists of an extremely limited vocabulary. They wore feathers behind their ears and many also used them to decorate their heads. We did not bother very much with them, simply gave them something and then going on.

All of us most earnestly desired to reach the Humboldt River as soon as possible and then follow its course for about three hundred miles. Truly, many of our longings were now satisfied; for in some parts this valley is very beautiful. On the north and south it is enclosed by mountains, and for the most part it is overgrown by a wild, useless mass of brushwood that looks and smells very much like the wormwood plant. The mountains here are apparently volcanic, reddish in color, bare and covered with boulders and rocks which have been burned by the heat of the sun. This gives the region a desolate, uncanny appearance. The winds hereabout form such extraordinary clouds of dust on an already dusty road that the wayfarer is soon as black as a Negro.

The poor oxen suffered intensely on this journey as we plodded on and on. We were still some five hundred miles from California, two hundred and forty of these were to take us along the Humboldt River. Until we reached the spot where the road turns off toward Oregon our slogan was "Fifteen miles a day!" At the crossroads many signs told us to take a new road, because it was one hundred and fifty miles nearer. For the sake of a handful of gold one man will oft cause another man's misfortune. That was the case here.

Captain [Jim] Palmer, who was accompanying a government supply train from Oregon to Fort Hall, advised us to follow the Oregon road, saying that it would take us well over the Sierra Nevada, a California mountain range, just as the South Pass of the Rocky Mountains would take us there, but that it was much nearer. He deceived us. From the spot where the road turns off we had two hundred and sixty miles to go by the Kansas River Road. By this new road it was a distance of five hundred miles, although he had assured us that it was only seventy-five miles. In the hopes of speedily ending the journey many thousands of emigrants followed this road.

As soon as we left the Humboldt River we came into a new desert, seventy miles wide, although it had been clearly represented to us as only thirty. Many wells had been dug in the midst of this desert, but nowhere was there any grass for the cattle. During the day we rested and at night, when it became a little cooler, we drove on. Even though we exerted all our strength, we took a day and two nights to cross the first part of the desert, where nothing but volcanic mountains on all sides could be seen. We had to travel thirty-three miles more before we could regard our cattle as saved. The heat was truly oppressive and clouds of alkaline dust enveloped us. I examined the soil and found it to consist of a mixture of salt, chalk, and ashes. Both in front and in back of us was a long train of wagons, so that at least I had company in my misery.

Now we came to a place where we saw a neatly arranged row of wagons. All of them were empty and abandoned. In order to save as much as possible, the owners had unharnessed the cattle and had driven them on rapidly. Those who had no families with them took their bundles on their shoulders and proceeded on foot. The families were all the more to be pitied.

I covered seventeen miles from eleven in the morning until eight in the evening, then I rested. My whole water supply barely sufficed to make a cup of tea or coffee for my wife. This was our whole supper. On the arid road over which I had travelled [sic] during the day I had counted eighty-one shattered and abandoned wagons, and 1,663 oxen either dead or dying, but no mules.

[September 17th, 1849 • Monday]

Alonzo Delano had begun writing a long letter to his wife, Mary, four days ago, on September 13th, and now, finally, after numerous interruptions, he had an opportunity to finish it. There was so much to say, so much ground to cover, so many experiences to summarize that he had hardly known where to begin. He had never expected to be writing such a letter, simply because when he had left them back in Illinois, he had been virtually certain he would never see her or their children again, that he would have died long before now. Yet, here he was, not only still alive, but having actually reached California and apparently in better health than he'd experienced for many years.

He wished desperately that Mary was with him now; he wanted to tell her in person how very much she meant to him and how very much he missed her. He now no longer doubted that they would one day be together again, but exactly how that would come about — or when — were questions that neither he nor she could answer just yet. The certainty in his own mind that they would eventually be reunited, however, seemed enough to him for now.

Before resuming the writing, Delano reviewed quickly what was in the letter, so he would not be repeating things already said. He had written in great detail about all he had experienced, right up to the present date — a letter that already filled a dozen pages in his tiny, neat handwriting. Having come to the end of that portion, he continued writing:

> *September 17th — Monday (Cont. from Sept. 13th) — At length I am in the settlements. We had arrived to within a little over fifty miles of Lawson's [Lassen's Settlement], and the road lay over barren mountains, and it was necessary for our train to lay over for a day or two at the last grass, and I concluded to walk on alone. Taking a shirt and tying the ends together to make a knapsack, I then shouldered it, together with my blanket, water-bottle, and tin cup, and set out confidently at about two o'clock p.m. The road was rocky and bad all the way, with long hills to go up and down, and water only at long intervals, and then in deep cañons (ravines) a mile from the road.*
>
> *I walked twelve miles and then came up with a Missouri*

camp with whom I was acquainted, and they invited me to spend the night with them. This was the last water for twenty-two miles. In the morning I started on, and at noon kindled a fire among the tall pines of a dense forest and made a cup of coffee with some of the water in my flask.

I was now on an elevated ridge one hundred feet high and in many places only wide enough for a road. This continued for sixteen miles, and at four o'clock I reached a watering place and went a mile down a precipice to fill my bottle — a very laborious task — and then went on two miles. Here I met Colonel Watkins, of whom I have spoken in my journal and with whom I have traveled a great deal. He insisted on my taking up quarters with him for the night, but his train had not one drop of water. From that in my flask we made a cup of tea and we were soon sleeping soundly on the ground. I preferred sleeping near a camp, for this forest swarms with grizzly bears and large wolves and panthers, their tracks being very frequent in the road.

In the morning we had a very little tea from the water left, though two of his men walked four miles after night and got a pailful. I then walked eight miles, where I went down a still more steep precipice to a creek, kindled a fire and made another good cup of coffee, which revived me very much.

About two o'clock I finally reached the Sacramento Valley, and at five I came in sight of the first house, belonging to Colonel [Peter L.] Davis of [Nashville] Tennessee. It seemed strange to see habits of civilization again, and I hardly knew what to say or do when I reached it. Only a mile below was Lawson's [Lassen's] and the plain was dotted with tents, wagons, and cattle of the emigrants and those going to the gold mines from below.

The wave of pure, raw emotion that had washed through Alonzo Delano at this moment of realization that they had indeed and in fact finally reached their goal was overwhelming. It weakened his knees and forced him to sink to the ground and gasp with wonder in the knowledge that the great western trek was at last all but completed. Unbidden tears flooded his eyes and slid down his cheeks, and for a long moment his shoulders heaved with the violence of his sobbing. At last he wiped his eyes and stared with enchantment at the surroundings. After so many hardships, after such a length of time, actually being here was a dream come true. This was the Sacramento Valley he was viewing, and once again his eyes flooded and his vision swam. The thought occurred to him that he might be dreaming and so he mentally — and then physically — pinched himself until it hurt in order to convince himself of the reality of the moment. He was not dreaming. Though he had never truly been a religious man. He murmured three words most fervently:

Thank you, God!

Now he continued to write in his very long letter to Mary about what was occurring right now:

> *My first thought was for something to eat. At Lawson's [Lassen's] I bought a pound of the best beef I ever saw, a pound of sugar, a quarter-pound of cheese, four biscuits, and a little salt, then went to cooking and fared sumptuously. Flour is selling here at $50 [$1,440] per 100 [lbs.]; beef, 35 cents [$10.08] per lb.; sugar, at 50 cents [$14.40], cheese, $1.50 [$43.20] per lb. I paid 10 cents [$2.88] for two table-spoons full of salt. These things are much cheaper to buy, I have been told, at Sutter's, which is now called Sacramento City; but here they sell at any price, as emigrants come in hungry and destitute of provisions.*
>
> *As for the prospects or the cost of mining, all agree that it ranges from eight dollars [$230.40] to a thousand dollars [$28,800] per day. If you get a good place, a few hours will yield hundreds, perhaps even thousands, but after getting the hang of the barn you are sure of eight dollars [$230.40]. This is the lowest that I have heard. Of course at this time I can say but little about it, but in the course of three or four weeks shall know more. There are various ways of making money, and my team will be worth a great deal to me either to haul loads or for beef. The latter is said to be worth a dollar [$28.80] per pound in the mines. If I go to the city I shall definitely write to you from there. You will direct all letters to me to Sacramento City, where, I am told, there is a post office. ... God bless you. I am Affectionately yours, A. DELANO*

[September 22nd, 1849 • Saturday]

It was on this day that several events relating to the California gold discovery occurred to underline the fact that despite the many difficulties and outright hazards faced by prospective gold miners, somehow they managed to retain a sense of humor.

In England, this was publication day of a tongue-in-cheek book illustrated by the noted London cartoonist A. H. Forrester, who cleverly portrayed the foibles and fancies of a fictional character named Mivins under the title of *A Good-Natured Hint About California*. At the same time, also in London, a far more detailed work by J. Tyrwhitt Brooks, M.D. entitled *Four Months among the Gold-Finders in Alta California, Being the Diary of an Expedition from San Francisco to the Gold Districts* appeared in print. The earlier readers of the book thought it to be so well written and so authoritative that it was propelled overnight to best-seller status and caused perhaps the foremost chronicler of the gold rush, Hubert Howe Bancroft, to state, "The book is well-written, and the author's observations are such as command respect." Other historians also joined in acclaiming the work, recognizing it as "surely one of the best descriptions of the northern diggings in 1848" and recommending it highly.

[September 25th, 1849 • Tuesday]

Abruptly, it seemed, many of the initial gold mining areas were becoming distinctly overcrowded, the "good deposits" all claimed, the best grounds all staked out, and consequently, the "easy gold" now began being perceived more as a legend than as an actuality. In reality, there remained yet an abundance of "good spots" being worked out, and a great many others were still being discovered in areas more remote, more difficult to reach, and much more difficult to work.

For many, it was far easier to go to the gold deposits already proven and largely claimed and then to complain loudly when they could not find gold in such abundance as had once been the case, and to be envious of those who had good claims. The "Americans," especially began to rail against the "foreigners" who were industriously working such claims with better results. Their envy-provoked anger and senseless discrimination were focused primarily upon the dedicated Chinese miners — Celestials, as they were called — who more thoroughly "cleaned" a deposit than any other groups or individuals.

When the easy gold had been plentiful for all to find with minimal effort, no one cared very much exactly who was finding it. Now, however, it was becoming the "lately-arrived" Americans, in particular, who initiated, developed and assiduously nurtured a fomenting prejudicial hatred against the Chinese, for whom the more established miners had previously nothing but praise. Among other disparaging terms, they dubbed these Oriental miners with such designations as "Chinks" and "pig-tailers," "yellow-boys" and "squint-eyes," inciting and fueling their own resentment by asking themselves by what right did these Chinese *dare* to come in and work the gold-deposits that were "rightfully" American? This ground-swell of jealousy-fueled anger and overt resentment against those whose racial characteristics were so clearly obvious — the Chinese and Negroes in particular — now threatened to manifest itself in vengeful violence.

Australian Robert Shaw — now grubbing for gold in the more southerly districts and, having staked a claim in an unnamed little tributary of the Stanislaus River — noted in his assiduously maintained *Journal*:

> *Lower down the river a great disturbance has occurred: a company of some 80 black men had been occupied in digging a fresh channel to get at an old bed of the river, which they conjectured contained the deposit of centuries. Having dammed one end, they diverted its course into the new channel, causing quite an over-flow of the banks and flooding the diggings of some others downstream, especially a noisy crowd of very unruly newcomers from Missouri. Indemnification was asked, but rejected; so then the inundated Missouri diggers, becoming angered, they commenced digging in the old river-bed, which had been exclusively properly staked out by those who belonged to what the Missouri boys disparagingly called the Nigger Band — a large body of former slaves only recently freed. A murderous attempt by the unsuccessful Missouri newcomers to eject them ensued, whereupon knives and picks, rifles and pistols, were all too freely used. For once the blacks, now freed men, did not back down as before. The Missouri Company men, being most numerous and by far the better armed, triumphed; however, not before deadly wounds had been inflicted on both sides.*

I viewed the whole terribly barbarous encounter from an eminence. At its termination, when I dared to visited the scene of battle, I was horror-struck at the sanguinary atrocities which had been committed: some men lay with their entrails hanging out, others had their skulls smashed with the pickaxe, and bodies lopt [lopped] with the axe, while a few lay breathing their very last, seemingly unscathed, but shot to death with bullets. I, in my little tributary, managed to stay clear of it all and continued to work quietly.

Some rather short time afterwards, this antagonistic feeling against the coloured [sic] races rose to a pitch of exasperation. At several other nearby diggings, capitalists had hired numbers of Chinese and Kanakas to work for them; and this system of monopoly was even carried on by the Americans of property and position, who employed Delawares and other Indians in their pay, to work the creeks far inland. This gang-system being very obnoxious to the native Californians, several parties of that description were voluntarily abolished; the obligations and agreements entered into being cancelled and annulled by the fiat of the vox populi.

The degree of cooperation between races was slight, however, and the existing situation was not improving. Today, September 25th, Shaw made an effort to sum up the deplorable situation in his *Journal*:

On the bars of various of these rivers — notably the Cosumnes, the Calaveras and the Stanislaus and their feeder streams — are collected various large bodies of people of separate nations. At the Chinese camp, called "Angel Camp" are numerous Celestials; while at the Calaveras and in the other parts of the Valley of the Monkelume [Mokelumne], there are numerous bands of Sonorians, Chilians [sic], and Kanakas, working on claims of their own account. The mines of late becoming more thickly populated by Americans, they — the Missouri Company miners — relying on their numerical strength, commenced acts of hostility and aggression on any "placer" that was inhabited by coloured [sic] people, if it were worth appropriating or which excited their cupidity. Ejectments [sic] constantly occurred, and the Chinese

> *and Negroes being driven from their claimed "placers," thousands have left the country; while others have penetrated farther out of reach into the hill ranges. These conflicts are very often extremely serious in their results; retaliations are often made, and where might makes right, retributions upon unoffending individuals frequently take place, which are nigh producing a war of race against race.*

Robert Shaw was fully convinced that this race-related animosity and violence, as serious and frequent as such incidents had already become, were only going to get much worse, and he had no idea where or how it would all end.

[September 30th, 1849 • 11:45 a.m. • Sunday]

Ramon Garcia had always wanted to find a large gold nugget.

As a small boy in Mexico City, he had dreamed one night that he had found just such a piece that was, as he described it, bigger than his head. He had prospected for gold all through his youth and early manhood for that great nugget he had dreamed of so long ago. For years in his middle and late twenties, he had lived and worked in the gold mines in the area of Pachuca, northeast of Mexico City in the mountain range called the Sierra Madre Oriental, and while he had found his share of gold over the years, it had always been in the form of dust or flakes or tiny nuggets. Once, while working at the Maria Mine a few miles north of Pachuca, he had found a seven-ounce nugget a little smaller than the shape and size of his little finger.

Now that he was 35 years old, his search had brought him to California. Although he had found a little gold here and there, however, his discoveries had amounted to barely enough to purchase the provisions he needed to keep himself going. Lately he had been prospecting along an unnamed little creek southwest of what had become known as Poverty Hill, at a bar that had first been prospected by David York, who had since drifted southward from Weber Creek in late August of 1848. Because York had established a camp there that attracted other miners, the place was soon being called Yorkville, and in the nearby bars York had, indeed, made some fairly decent finds — enough, in fact, that he was now prepared to retire and live off the proceeds of his mining.

In digging this morning at that same bar, Garcia encountered, only a foot below the surface, a lump of quartz, and after several hours of hard work, he managed to extract the lump shortly before noon.The lump weighed just a bit over 50 pounds. What was more important, it was liberally riddled with veins and pockets of pure gold — the gold alone totaling 19 pounds avoirdupois — 304 ounces!

Ramon Garcia's dream had finally come true. This single nugget contained gold to the value of $4,864 [$140,083.20]!

[September 30th, 1849 • 6:00 p.m. • Sunday]

Alonzo Delano finally completed his long overland journey from Ottawa, Illinois to Sacramento in the California Territory today. For Delano, it had been by far both the most grueling and the most exciting experience of his life. He was now most eager to prospect for gold, although he first had to deal with somewhat more mundane tasks.

Finding a place of lodging was an immediate concern but so too was bringing his *Journal* up to date without delay. Also, with postal facilities now available to him, it was important that he complete and send his account for the *Ottawa Free Trader*, as well as to compose various letters to his family and friends to let them know of his safe arrival and to provide them with the address at which they could contact him.

The first project to which he set his mind was his *Journal*, and he tackled this matter at once inside the tent he and an old acquaintance, F. C. Pomeroy, were sharing beneath a large old oak tree on a knoll within the current limits of Sacramento. There was a good deal to record, but he had made up his mind to abbreviate the events as much as possible, in order to complete the chore relatively quickly.

On September 17th, he had left Col. Watkins behind in camp and set off overland southward. Before his departure, the two had used what little was left of Delano's water to brew enough coffee for each to indulge in a swallow or two, but underway soon after, Delano regretted squandering the liquid; he quickly became thirsty, and he had to walk a full six miles before he encountered any water at all. He was still very stiff and sore from the exertion of the previous days. At the foot of an especially steep hill — a hill comprised of a succession of perpendicular ledges of rock which he descended with considerable difficulty — he finally found a spring bubbling with fresh water, from which he drank until he could hold no more, and then filled his flask.

Upon reaching the edge of a fine mountain stream — Cow Creek — he kindled a fire and prepared for himself a refreshing draught of coffee. Eager though he was to be on his way, the stream was so delightful with its flanking shade trees that he lingered for two full hours. Refilling his flask yet again, he climbed the hill to where he encountered a trail and then followed it to the top of its ascent; from there he could gaze rapturously at the long sought, long desired, and greatly welcome Sacramento Valley some five or six miles ahead to the south. As he now wrote of it:

> *How my heart bounded at the view! How every nerve thrilled at the sight! It looked like a grateful haven to the tempest-tossed mariner; with long strides, regardless of the weariness of my limbs, I plodded on, anxious to set foot upon level ground beyond the barren mountain desert. I could discern green trees, marking the course of the great river, and a broad, level valley, but the day was too smoky for a very extended view. There was the resting place, at least for a few days, where the very dangerous and weary night-watch over cattle herds no longer was needed, where the habitations of civilized men existed, security from the stealthy tread of the treacherous savage; where our debilitated frames now could be renewed and where our wandering would cease.*
>
> *Perspiring and fainting from exertion, I reached the foot of the last hill, and stood upon the plain. Yet, here I was disappointed, for instead of the high grass and rich soil I expected to find, for four or five miles after reaching the valley the earth was dry and baked by the sun; the scanty vegetation was dried and crisp, and the ground was strewn with round stones which seemed to have been thrown there by volcanic force, or washed by the floods from the hills. But onward I pressed, till I reached the first trees, which I had seen from the mountains, and found that they grew along the margin of Deer Creek, which I followed a mile, when the sight of a chimney attracted my attention. It was the house of Colonel Davis, eight miles from the foot hills. My sensations were singular on approaching the house. Although it was a simple abode, standing within a rough paling, it was indeed the very first peaceful dwelling of civilized man which I had seen for many months. While I hurried to it, I felt an almost irresistible repugnance to approach, and when at*

> *length I sat down on the porch, I felt extremely lost and bewildered with a degree of astonishment at actually seeing many men and women moving about at their usual avocations. I could only give short replies to the interrogatories which were made, and after sitting near an hour in a kind of half-stupidity, I found resolution enough to inquire where the trains were encamped.*
>
> *"About a mile below," was the reply, and I simply got up and walked off, leaving, probably, no very favorable impression as to my conversational powers.*

Delano had continued writing about how, upon reaching the encampment below and seeing hundreds of white tents and wagons, with multitudes of cattle cropping the grass, he felt once more at home. All his uneasy sensations had by then subsided, and he wondered why he had acted so perfectly foolish at the Davis house. In moving about among the assemblage, he met many former acquaintances, and numerous old friends enthusiastically greeted him. Two old trail acquaintances, Dr. Evard Hall and Tom Rood, promptly invited him to spend the night with them, and he gladly accepted their hospitality. They even accompanied him on a visit Lassen's settlement on the opposite side of the creek. There they found two or three small adobe buildings, one of which was generously termed a "store," which offered for sale such items as a small quantity of flour, as well as whisky and a few groceries. As Delano wrote of it:

> *Around the trading post were lounging gangs of naked Indians of both sexes, drunken Mexicans, and weary emigrants, enjoying their respite from excessive fatigue in the flowing bowl; and taking it all in all, it did not give me a very flattering impression of the morals of the citizens of the first settlement. My first act was to provide for the creature comfort needed; and, quickly purchasing a little beef, bread, sugar, and cheese, I returned to the camp to enjoy a feast to which I had long been a stranger.*

As much as Delano delighted in having connected with civilization once again, he was stunned by the prices being charged at Lassen's and noted several of them in his *Journal*. Flour was priced at $50 [$1,440] per 100-pound sack, and, by the pound, fresh beef at $35 [$1,008], pork at $75 [$2,160], sugar at $50 [$1,440], and cheese at $1.50 [$43.20].

It was clearly apparent to Delano that the emigrants were all keenly eager to discover where the best gold mines were but that their ardent efforts to seek out such intelligence were virtually futile; their inquiries met with a great diversity of opinions, all offering so little certainty that the bewildered gold-seekers simply scattered in all directions, as their own guesswork or fancy dictated. Some headed directly for the mines, while others moved onward downstream toward Sacramento to stock up on whatever supplies they felt were needed, necessities which they did not already have or which had been discarded as they slogged through the great desert. The city, Delano was told, not only carried on an immense trade but now boasted a population of several thousand which was increasing daily.

Delano sensed that a more limited population explosion was occurring even here at Lassen's trading post. Even while he and his tentmates stood watching, there was a steady flow of emigrants; some arriving, some leaving, while the camp and its trading center more closely resembled a large army depot just prior to an expedition being launched rather than a first halting-place for trail-and-toil-worn travelers who had just completed a march clear across a continent. He could not resist the temptation to repeat a brief line he'd already entered in his *Journal*:

Any man who makes a trip by land to California deserves to find a fortune!

Delano, now joined by Tom Rood and Dr. Hall, continued on the route to Sacramento, and on the 21st day of September, the three forded the Yuba River near its mouth, near another small settlement called Nye's Ranch, which consisted of nothing more than two low adobe houses and a crudely fenced corral.

Delano and his companions now took their time, enjoying the increasing lushness of the Sacramento Valley and marveling at how many trees and plants they were encountering that to them were nameless and exotic. They arrived within three miles of Sacramento late in the evening of September 26th; the lateness of the day and their numbing fatigue convinced them to postpone any attempt to cross the American River until the next morning. They retired for the evening.

The following three days were very busy ones for Delano and his companions, and for once, three nights in succession, he neglected writing in his *Journal*. So now, on this Sunday afternoon, September 30th, he bent to the task of combining his entry for all three days — four, actually, including today. Well rested and with his hand no longer so shaky as it had been while on the rugged cross-country march, he wrote:

> *1849 — September 27th to the last — Thursday/Sunday: — We had driven half of the previous night to reach our resting place; and we now learned that we were within three miles of Sacramento City and Sutter's Fort. After a frugal dinner of hard bread and water, Dr Hall, Mr. Rood and myself doffed our soiled garments, and after assuming habiliments more in accordance with civilized life, we set out at once for town, leaving our cattle and wagon in the care of Mr. [Wilfred] Pope.*
>
> *Taking off our clothes on reaching the ford, we waded across the American, a clear and beautiful stream, about four hundred feet wide, and reached the city of tents about four o'clock in the afternoon. And here I found myself more than two thousand miles from home, in a city which had risen wholly as if by enchantment since I had crossed the Missouri, a stranger, way-worn and jaded by a long journey, half famished for want of even the necessaries of life, practicing domestic economy to the fullest extent, with every prospect before me of continuing in the practice of that useful science; for on closely examining the state of my treasury, I found myself the wealthy owner of the full sum of four dollars! [$115.20] — enough to board me one day at a low-priced hotel. And I had come in the pleasant anticipation of raising a full supply of provisions, which would surely cost me not less than two hundred dollars [$5,760]. This afforded me an opportunity of enlarging my views of political economy, by studying "ways and means." How the thing was to be done I could not conceive. Could you, under these circumstances?*
>
> *While I was cogitating on the strange course of human events, as exhibited in my own particular case, and wishfully eying a piece of fat pork, which was temptingly exhibited for sale on a barrel head in a previous store, I met my old Captain, Jesse Greene, who, by keeping the old route and avoid-*

ing the Greenhorn [Greenwoods] Cut-off, had got in four weeks before, and made something in the mines.

A short time after, I met Dr. M. B. Angel [Angle], who had been equally successful, and they, understanding by intuition the very sad state of an emigrant's treasury, generously offered to supply me with the quid pro quo, verifying the old proverb that "friends in need are friends indeed;" and I think that under the circumstances, I was quite more rejoiced to see them than they could possibly have been to see me. Thus, through their kindness an arrangement was made, by which I could obtain a load of provisions, and which I designed to take to the mines, either to sell, or live upon, till McNeil and myself could make something by mining. It was with reluctance, however, that I accepted their proffered kindness, from the very uncertainty of California operations; but necessity compelled me to do so, or die, and I did not relish the idea of dying there, so far from home.

While strolling through the streets during the evening, I chanced to go into a hotel, where I met a fine old acquaintance, F. C. Pomeroy, who had been notably unsuccessful in the mines, and was looking for [a] business. As it was necessary for me to have assistance, I immediately made an arrangement with him to go with me to the mines.

Fortune seemed to be smiling on me, from a very small corner of her vacillating mouth. During the two days that I remained in town, Pomeroy and myself took up our quarters under a large oak tree near J Street, where we luxuriated on the fat things of a bacon cask, with a bountiful supply of bread and butter; in short, we fared sumptuously by cooking for ourselves.

One night, feeling a little aristocratic, we spread our blankets on the ground in an unoccupied tent, but the owner came in the morning before we were up, and charged us fifty cents [$14.40] for sleeping under the canvass [sic] roof. We thought it smacked of inhospitality, but we got used to it in time, and discovered that in California it was custom and not extortion.

Sacramento City contains a decidedly floating population of about five thousand people. It was first laid out in the *spring of 1849, on the east bank of the Sacramento River, here less than one-eighth of a mile wide, and is about a mile and a half west of Sutter's Fort. Lots were originally sold for $200 [$5,760] each, but within this year sales were made high as $30,000 [$864,000]. There were not a dozen wood or frame buildings in the whole city, but they were chiefly made of canvass [sic] stretched over light supporters; or were simply tents, arranged along the streets. The stores, like the dwellings, were of cloth, and property and merchandise of all kinds, lay exposed, night and day, by the way-side, and such a thing as robbery was scarcely known. This, in fact, was the case throughout the country, and is worthy of notice on account of the great and extraordinary change which occurred.*

There were a vast number of taverns and eating houses, and the only public building was a theatre. All these were made of canvass [sic]. At virtually all of the hotels and groceries, gambling was carried on to a remarkable extent, and men seemed to be perfectly reckless of money. Indeed, it seemed to have lost its value, and piles of coin and [gold] dust covered every table, and were constantly changing hands at the turn of a card.

At high water the river overflows its banks. . . . For a mile along the river lay ships, barges, and various water craft, laden with merchandise and provisions. Trade was brisk, and prices exorbitantly high.

On the north side of the city is a very large and deep slough, in which cattle frequently mire and perish, and at this time the effluvia arising from their putrid carcasses was almost insufferable. A little distance beyond the slough the American River empties into the Sacramento. This river is not navigable for vessels. The Sacramento River, though affected by the tide, is pure and sweet, and generally is much better to drink than the water of the wells, some of which are found to be slightly brackish.

Having brought his *Journal* up to date, Delano moved to another priority — the preparation of a long overdue column for the *Ottawa Free Trader*. Taking advantage of some additional spare time this evening, he proceeded to write his first newspaper column from California:

> *Sacramento City, Two Miles from*
> *Sutter's Fort September 30th, 1849*
>
> *MESSRS. EDITORS — I have been here four days and am on the point of leaving for the Upper Sacramento. I have much information to write you at my first leisure. It has been with much difficulty that I have written at all, our labors have been so severe, and it has been done chiefly at our noon halts under the shade of our wagon.*
>
> *The Sacramento Valley has been much misrepresented by writers with regard to beauty and fertility. I would not exchange a good farm on one of our rich prairies for the whole of it; and instead of the very beautiful Italian sky, it is smoky and unserene. The grass is dry and parched, with nothing green but the leaves of the oaks. But now there is gold in the mountains and opportunities for making money quite beyond anything I ever saw. The mines for some six hundred miles are yielding well, though it is a kind of lottery in finding rich leads. Many are discouraged at not finding it plenty enough to scrape up, and are disgusted and leaving for home; many have been sick, made so by very imprudent exposure and living. New mines are being discovered even up in the Cascade Mountains. I do not for a moment regret coming, and shall remain, for I can make something; so can anybody who will work.*
>
> *I hope you have received the other portions of my journal which have all been duly sent. Letters and papers I wish directed to me at Sacramento City, as there is a post office here. One word to all: Let no man come here who will not be willing to work steadily. As near as I can learn, a kind of average is about one ounce per day, though I have seen many who have not made more than five to ten dollars [$144 to $288], while many have made and are making hundreds — thousands — in a few hours. You may dig a week and do little or nothing, and this discourages many, and they leave disgusted; but all say the wheel will turn, keep digging. I shall be gone above about a month and in the time will try to give you a very true and impartial statement of things as they are*

without any poetry.

I am pleased to say that the South Bend and Hennepin Companies are all in safe, and I have lately met several fine old friends who had emigrated to Oregon some years before. Our company has now finally separated; most of them gone to the Yuba [Valley] mines, and some few to the Sacramento, and so on.

Truly yours,
A. DELANO

Other books in the
Winning of the West Series

The JSF has approximately 500 signed First Editions of this book for sale @ $35, plus $5 shipping. *Dark Journey* is also available as an ebook from Kindle, Nook, and iTunes.

The JSF has approximately 200 First Editions for sale @ $35, plus $5 shipping.